Media/Impact

an introduction to
mass media

NINTH EDITION

General Mass Communications

Anokwa, Lin and Salwen, *International Communication: Concepts and Cases*, First Edition

Biagi, *Media/Impact: An Introduction to Mass Media*, Ninth Edition

Bucy, *Living in the Information Age: A New Media Reader*, Second Edition

Craft, Leigh and Godfrey, *Electronic Media*, First Edition

Day, *Ethics in Media Communications: Cases and Controversies*, Fifth Edition

Dennis and Merrill, *Media Debates: Great Issues for the Digital Age*, Fourth Edition

Fellow, *American Media History*, Second Edition

Gillmor, Barron, Simon and Terry, *Fundamental Mass Comm Law*, First Edition

Hilmes, *Connections: A Broadcast History*

Hilmes, *Only Connect: A Cultural History of Broadcasting in the United States*, Second Edition

Jamieson and Campbell, *The Interplay of Influence: News, Advertising, Politics, and the Internet*, Sixth Edition

Kamalipour, *Global Communication*, Second Edition

Lester, *Visual Communication: Images with Messages*, Fourth Edition

Overbeck, *Major Principles of Media Law*, 2009 Edition

Straubhaar, LaRose and Davenport, *Media Now*, Sixth Edition

Zelezny, *Cases in Communications Law*, Fifth Edition

Zelezny, *Communications Law: Liberties, Restraints, and the Modern Media*, Fifth Edition

Journalism

Bowles and Border, *Creative Editing*, Fifth Edition

Chance and McKeen, *Literary Journalism: A Reader*

Craig, *Online Journalism: Reporting, Writing, and Editing for New Media*, First Edition

Hilliard, *Writing for Television, Radio, and New Media*, Ninth Edition

Kessler and McDonald, *When Words Collide: A Media Writer's Guide to Grammar and Style*, Sixth Edition

Poulter and Tidwell, *News Scene: Interactive Writing Exercises*

Rich, *Writing & Reporting News: A Coaching Method*, Sixth Edition

Stephens, *Broadcast News*, Fourth Edition

Wilber and Miller, *Modern Media Writing*, First Edition

Photojournalism and Photography

Parrish, *Photojournalism: An Introduction*

Public Relations and Advertising

Diggs-Brown, *The PR Styleguide: Formats for Public Relations Practice*, Second Edition

Drewniany and Jewler, *Creative Strategy in Advertising*, Ninth Edition

Hendrix and Hayes, *Public Relations Cases*, Seventh Edition

Meeske, *Copywriting for the Electronic Media: A Practical Guide*, Fifth Edition

Newsom and Haynes, *Public Relations Writing: Form & Style*, Eighth Edition

Newsom, Turk and Kruckeberg, *Cengage Advantage Books: This is PR: The Realities of Public Relations*, Ninth Edition

Research and Theory

Baran and Davis, *Mass Communication Theory: Foundations, Ferment, and Future*, Fifth Edition

Littlejohn, *Theories of Human Communications*, Seventh Edition

Rubin, Rubin and Piele, *Communication Research: Strategies and Sources*, Sixth Edition

Sparks, *Media Effects Research: A Basic Overview*, Third Edition

Wimmer and Dominick, *Mass Media Research: An Introduction*, Eighth Edition

Media/Impact

an introduction to mass media

NINTH EDITION

SHIRLEY BIAGI

California State University, Sacramento

WADSWORTH
CENGAGE Learning™

Australia • Brazil • Japan • Korea • Mexico • Singapore • Spain • United Kingdom • United States

WADSWORTH
CENGAGE Learning™

Media/Impact: An Introduction to Mass Media, Ninth Edition

Shirley Biagi

Senior Publisher: Lyn Uhl

Publisher in Humanities: Michael Rosenberg

Development Editor: Michell Phifer

Associate Development Editor: Megan Garvey

Assistant Editor: Rebekah Matthews

Editorial Assistant: Erin Pass

Media Editor: Jessica Badiner

Marketing Manager: Erin Mitchell

Marketing Coordinator: Darlene Macanan

Marketing Communications Manager: Christine Dobberpuhl

Content Project Manager: Tiffany Kayes

Art Director: Linda Helcher

Print Buyer: Susan Carroll

Permissions Editor: Margaret Chamberlain-Gaston

Text Researcher: Sarah D'Stair

Production Service/Compositor: Lachina Publishing Services

Text Designer: Riezebos Holzbaur Design Group

Photo Manager: Dean Dauphinais

Photo Researcher: Pre-Press PMG

Cover Images: Cover Images: iPhone image: Acclaim Images—Jim Goldstein; Front cover, row 1, left to right: Ray Tamarra/Getty Images; Douglas Mason/Getty Images; © Shirley Biagi 2007. Used with permission./Shirley Biagi; Getty Images; R. Gates/Hulton Archive/Getty Images; row 2, left to right: AFP/Getty Images; Michael Buckner/Getty Images; Michael Tullberg/Getty Images; Ethan Miller/Getty Images; row 3, left to right: Todd Williamson/WireImage/Getty Images; Joanne Ciccarello/The Christian Science Monitor/Getty Images; AFP/Getty Images; Mario Tama/Getty Images; Back cover, left to right: Chris Hondros/Getty Images; Justin Sullivan/Getty Images; China Photos/Getty Images; Noel Vasquez/Getty Images

Library of Congress Control Number: 2009920485

ISBN-13: 978-0-495-57146-9

ISBN-10: 0-495-57146-6

Wadsworth Cengage Learning
20 Channel Center
Boston, MA 02210
USA

Cengage Learning products are represented in Canada by Nelson Education, Ltd.

For your course and learning solutions, visit **www.cengage.com**.

Purchase any of our products at your local college store or at our preferred online store **www.ichapters.com**.

Printed in the United States of America
1 2 3 4 5 6 7 12 11 10 09

Brief Contents

Table of Contents

PART ONE   The Mass Media Industries

CHAPTER 1
Mass Media and Everyday Life

CHAPTER 2
Books: Rearranging the Page

CHAPTER 3
Newspapers: Expanding Delivery

CHAPTER 4

Magazines: Targeting the Audience

CHAPTER 5

Recordings: Demanding Choices

CHAPTER 6

Radio: Riding the Wave

CHAPTER 7
Movies: Picturing the Future

CHAPTER 8

Television: Changing Channels

CHAPTER 9
Digital Media: Widening the Web

PART TWO   Selling the Message
CHAPTER 10
Advertising: Motivating Customers

CHAPTER 11

Public Relations: Promoting Ideas

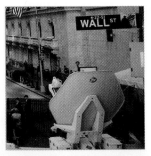

PART THREE Changing Messages

CHAPTER 12

News and Information: Getting Personal

CHAPTER 13
Society, Culture and Politics: Shaping the Issues

CHAPTER 14

Law and Regulation: Rewriting the Rules

CHAPTER 15
Ethics: Placing Responsibility

Impact Boxes

Preface

Your *Media/Impact* Journey Begins Here

While I was writing the 9th edition of *Media/Impact*, I received an email from one of my students, SheRee, which included a picture of her standing next to a plaque to commemorate the contributions of journalism pioneer Ida B. Wells. "Hey professor!" she wrote, "I was on vacation in Memphis and I saw this sign and thought about my assignment in your class." Nothing could have made me happier, and that's one of the reasons I'm so excited about the 9th edition of *Media/Impact*. (To learn more about Ida B. Wells, see page 58.)

To help a 21st century college student like SheRee connect with a 19th century journalism heroine like Ida B. Wells has always been a fundamental goal of this book. That's why, for me, the most important addition to this edition of *Media/Impact* are nine new TimeFrame features that emphasize crucial milestones in the history of each media industry. Students can see at a glance how one person, one invention or one event shaped today's media businesses—books, newspapers, magazines, recordings, radio, movies, TV and the Internet.

Since I wrote the first edition of *Media/Impact* more than 20 years ago, *Media/Impact* has developed a reputation as the most current introductory mass media textbook available. In that tradition, the 9th edition of *Media/Impact* has been updated throughout to offer students the latest information and the best possible background perspective to help them learn how American mass media industries operate today and what to expect in the future.

What's New in the 9th Edition?

Every day mass media businesses are in the news—buying, selling and merging companies; changing corporate leadership; cutting costs; introducing new technologies, services and products; challenging regulatory rulings; creating ethical scandals; and responding to the ever-increasing influence of the Internet and globalization. So this edition continues to include six different types of Impact boxes throughout the chapters to focus on industry experts, writing about current

developments. Here's just a sample of Impact boxes that are new to this edition:

IMPACT/ETHICS: "Just So You Know, No One Paid for This Article"

IMPACT/BUSINESS: "The Newspaper Death Watch"

IMPACT/CULTURE: "Finding Political News Online, the Young Pass It On"

IMPACT/PEOPLE: "101 Secrets (and 9 Lives) of a Magazine Star"

IMPACT/AUDIENCE: "Top 10 Countries with Free and Pay Wireless Locations"

IMPACT/WORLD: "Hundreds of Web Sites Censored at Beijing Olympics"

Additional *Media/Impact* features track the latest changes in mass communication, including:

- **Impact/Culture** boxes featuring an analysis of media coverage of the 2008 presidential campaign, the Google Digital Book Project and the use of skinny models in advertising messages to women.

- **Impact/Audience** boxes exploring the Nielsen Company's attempt to track the viewing habits of TV viewers in bars, gyms and on mobile devices; parents and children exploring social networking sites like Facebook together; and food companies limiting advertising to children.

- **Impact/Business** boxes showing how the business of media evolves and responds to current events, such as ESPN's addition of virtual reality for sports reporting and a list of average salaries of people who work in the broadcast industry.

- Coverage of the explosion of blogs and social networking sites and how they have transformed American politics.

- Discussion of the economic and cultural consequences of the Federal Communications Commission's new requirement for universal high definition television.

- Expanded treatment of the increasing importance of mobile media, which has turned cell phones into the fastest-growing media marketplace.

- Analysis of the migration of U.S. advertising dollars away from traditional media to the Internet and to global markets.

Proven Features That Continue in This Edition

- **Comprehensive Coverage of the latest in Digital Media.** *Media/Impact* details the latest innovations and controversies surrounding the Internet, mobile media, intellectual property rights, government regulation, convergence and social networking sites such as MySpace.

- **Analysis of Changing Delivery Systems for News and Information.** Chapter 12 particularly chronicles the declining popularity of television news as consumers personalize their information choices and use the Internet to stay current, as well as the ongoing controversy about journalists' use of confidential sources. This chapter, first introduced in the 6th edition when few people understood how consumers' changing news habits would affect the news business, has proven extremely popular with faculty and students.

- **Discussion of Current Media Issues.** Beginning on the first page of Chapter 1 ("Mass Media and Everyday Life") and continuing throughout the text, *Media/Impact* presents a broad and realistic picture of today's media, highlighting the latest controversies such as the Supreme Court's decision to order file-sharing Web sites to shut down (Chapter 5); the news media's use of all-platform journalists (Chapter 12); attempts to rescind the Patriot Act; and the jailing of former *New York Times* reporter Judith Miller for refusing to reveal her sources (Chapter 14).

- **Careers Information.** The media industries chapters include coverage of the organizational structure and jobs within each industry, giving students a handy introduction to media careers.

- **Graphically Illustrated Statistics.** Illustrations present statistics in a new, easy-to-understand graphical format with detailed captions to help students make sense of the numbers and see what critical media industry data mean. Where possible, the statistics include projections to give students a look at how the experts see the media's future.

- **Margin Definitions.** Designed to help students build a media vocabulary while they read, key terms are listed and defined in the margins of each chapter, giving students concise definitions right where they need them.

- **Comprehensive End-of-Chapter Review.** Each chapter's concluding materials include these useful resources:

  - **Chapter Summary.** Organized by headings that correspond to the chapter's major topics, the Chapter Review uses bullet points to summarize major concepts from each chapter.

  - **Key Terms.** A list of important terms with corresponding page numbers appears at the end of each chapter and in the comprehensive **Glossary** at the end of the book.

  - **Critical Questions.** Following the Key Terms, five questions enhance students' analysis of the chapter to help deepen their understanding and engage their critical thinking skills.

  - **Annotated Web Lists.** A list of ten Web sites includes a brief annotation that describes each site and notes its value for mass media students.

- **Media Information Resource Guide.** This invaluable student reference tool at the end of the book provides hundreds of resources to help students research media topics, including an alphabetical listing of nearly 200 Web sites referenced throughout the text.

Acknowledging Professional Support

Especially important to note for this very complex, completely redesigned 9th edition are the people who helped me at critical times in *Media/Impact*'s creation and production. The concept for the 9th edition began with the supportive, can-do attitude of Michael Rosenberg and Michell Phifer. Megan Lessard proved to be a tiger as a photo permissions assistant, relentlessly pursuing the best and most current photographs for the book until the very last deadline. I'm also convinced there is no better publications management company than Lachina Publishing Services, which gave me the intelligent assistance of the wonderfully patient and gifted Nikki Petel.

As a former student of mine and now as an invaluable teaching colleague, Professor Jan Haag of Sacramento City College, as always, contributed great ideas and major insights for this edition. Lisa Biondi provided detailed, timely research for the Web site listings and the Media Information Resource Guide.

I also owe many thanks to Professor Chris Burnett of California State, Long Beach, for thoroughly updating the *Instructor's Resource Manual* and the book's Companion Web site for *Media/Impact*. Chris also has created a wonderful series of podcasts to accompany *Media/Impact*. Each podcast is an interview that Chris held with a different professional in a mass communication career. Geared at sharing advice with newcomers to the Mass Communication world, Chris talked with everyone from PR professional Cathy Lawhon about her transition from 30 years in newspaper journalism to public relations, to 26 year old Francisco Rivera, who is an up-and-coming Spanish-language broadcaster in Southern California. These podcasts can be downloaded by accessing the Resource Center for Mass Communication. Access is available for free bundled with orders of the textbook. Please contact your Wadsworth sales representative if you're interested.

The 9th edition of *Media/Impact* reflects the suggestions, contributions and ideas of hundreds of students and colleagues who have written, e-mailed, telephoned and even confronted me in the hallway at school with ideas and changes for the text.

In addition, faculty reviewers who provided formal feedback that guided revision of the 9th edition are: David Baird, Anderson University; Christopher Burnett, California State University, Long Beach; William Burns, Brookdale Community College; Bonnie Edwards, Mesabi Range College; Camilla Gant, University of West Georgia; Tom Grier, Winona State University; Nigel Henry, National American University; Patricia Holmes, University of Louisiana, Lafayette; Rebecca Kamm, Northeast Iowa Community College; Rick Kenny, University of Central Florida; Allen Levy, Chapman University; Carole McNall, St. Bonaventure University; Steven Miller, Rutgers University; Jenny Nelson, Ohio University; Robert Ogles, Purdue University; Peter Parisi, Hunter College; Pamela Parry, Belmont University; Stephen Perry, Illinois State University; Brian Rose, Fordham University; and Don Stacks, University of Miami.

Acknowledging People Who Are Personally Important

My students, of course, have kept me honest through more than 30 years of college teaching by facing me in every class I teach using *Media/Impact*, offering candid opinions and challenging ideas. Students and teachers also regularly e-mail me from around the world, and their comments add an international perspective. *Media/Impact* now is published in Korean, Spanish, Greek and Canadian editions.

A special, personal thank you also goes to my closest media adviser and superb, unparalleled photo researcher, Vic Biondi.

I hope you have a chance to explore all of *Media/Impact*'s valuable features and I'm always interested to know what you think. My e-mail address is sbiagi@csus.edu.

Shirley Biagi
Sacramento, California

Accompanying Resources: An Exclusive Teaching and Learning Package

Media/Impact, 9th edition, offers a comprehensive array of print and electronic resources to assist in making the introduction to mass communication course as meaningful and enjoyable as possible for both students and instructors, and to help students succeed.

Resources for Students

Your students can access a wide array of interactive multimedia resources when you choose to package these options with every new copy of the text.* Students may also purchase access to many of these resources individually.

- *Media Impact* **Companion Web site:** Available to your students at no extra charge. This Web site includes quizzing and chapter-specific resources such as glossaries, tutorial questions and interactive flash cards. The site also includes a media careers guide and links to a wide variety of communication and journalism associations.

- **Resource Center for Mass Communication:** Offers a variety of rich learning resources designed to enhance your learning experience. These resources include self assessments, blogs (online journals), images, video, Web resources, podcasts and animations. All resources are mapped to key discipline learning concepts so students can browse for study tools on the topics they need. More than just a collection of ancillary learning materials, the Resource Center for Mass Communication also features important community tools that extend the education experience beyond a particular class or course semester.

- **InfoTrac® College Edition with InfoMarks™:** With their four-month subscription to this online library's more than 18 million reliable, full-length articles, students are able to use keyword searches to retrieve almost instant results from over 5,000 academic and popular periodicals in the InfoTrac College Edition database, including *Broadcasting & Cable*, *Columbia Journalism Review*, *New Media Age*, *Wireless Week*, *Time*, *Newsweek* and *USA Today*. Students also have access to

If you would like your students to have access to these resources, at no additional charge, please contact your Cengage sales representative.

InfoMarks—stable URLs that can be linked to articles, journals and searches to save valuable time when doing research—*and* to the InfoWrite online resource center, where students can find grammar help, critical thinking guidelines, guides to writing research papers and much more. For more information about InfoTrac College Edition and the InfoMarks linking tool, visit http://www.infotrac-college.com and click on "User Demo."

Resources for Instructors

Media/Impact also features a full suite of resources for instructors. The following class preparation, classroom presentation, assessment and course management resources are available:

- **Instructor's Edition (IE):** The instructor's edition of *Media/Impact*, 9th edition, is a student edition of the text that provides additional information specifically of interest to instructors. Examination and desk copies are available upon request.

- **Instructor's Web site:** The password-protected instructor's Web site includes electronic access to the Instructor's Resource Manual, downloadable versions of the book's PowerPoint slides and a link to the Opposing Viewpoints Resource Center. To gain access to the Web site, simply request a course key by opening the site's home page.

- **Instructor's Resource Manual:** *Media/Impact*'s Instructor's Resource Manual provides a comprehensive teaching guide featuring course outlines and sample syllabi, as well as the following for every text chapter: chapter goals and an outline, suggestions for integrating print supplements and online resources, supplementary research notes, suggested discussion questions and activities, InfoTrac College Edition exercises, and a comprehensive test bank with answer key that includes multiple choice, true-false, short answer, essay and fill-in-the-blank test questions. This manual is available on the password-protected instructor Web site and the Power Lecture CD-ROM, which includes ExamView Computerized Testing. You'll find more information about these teaching tools below.

- **Power Lecture CD-ROM:** This disc contains an electronic version of the Instructor's Resource Manual, ExamView computerized testing and ready-to-use Microsoft® PowerPoint® presentations, corresponding with the text and JoinIn on Turning Point. This all-in-one lecture tool makes it easy for you to assemble, edit, publish and present custom lectures for your course. More information about ExamView and JoinIn follows.

- **ExamView® Computerized Testing:** Enables you to create, deliver and customize tests and study guides (both print and online) in minutes using the test bank questions from the Instructor's Resource Manual. ExamView offers both a *Quick Test Wizard* and an *Online Test Wizard* that guide you step-by-step through the process of creating tests, while its "what you see is what you get" interface allows you to see the test you are creating on-screen exactly as it will print or display online. You can build tests of up to 250 questions, using up to 12 question types. Using the complete word processing capabilities of ExamView, you can even enter an unlimited number of new questions or edit existing ones.

- **JoinIn™ on TurningPoint®:** Transform your classroom and assess your students' progress with instant in-class quizzes and polls. TurningPoint® software lets you pose book-specific questions and display students' answers seamlessly within the Microsoft® PowerPoint® slides of your own lecture, in conjunction with the "clicker" hardware of your choice. Enhance how your students interact with you, your lecture and each other.

- **Turn-It-In:** This proven online plagiarism-prevention software promotes fairness in the classroom by helping students learn to correctly cite sources and allowing instructors to check for originality before reading and grading papers. Turn-It-In quickly checks student papers against billions of pages of Internet content and millions of published works, as well as millions of student papers, and within seconds generates a comprehensive originality report.

- **Resource Center for Mass Communication:** Offers a variety of rich learning resources designed to enhance the student experience. These resources include self assessments, blogs (online journals), images, video, Web resources and animations. All resources are mapped to key discipline learning concepts and users can browse or search for content in a variety of ways. More than just a collection of ancillary learning materials, the Resource Center for Mass Communication also features important content and community tools that extend the education experience beyond a particular class or course semester.

- **Resource Center on WebTutor for WebCT and Blackboard:** With the pre-formatted content and total flexibility of WebTutor, you can easily create and manage your own custom course Web site. This course management tool gives you the ability to provide virtual office hours, post syllabi, set up threaded discussions, track student progress with the quizzing material and much more. In addition, you can access password-protected Instructor Resources for lectures and class preparation. WebTutor also provides robust communication tools, such as a course calendar, asynchronous discussion, real-time chat, a whiteboard and an integrated e-mail system. For students, it offers real-time access to a full array of study tools, including animations and videos that bring the book's topics to life, plus chapter outlines, summaries, learning objectives, glossary flash cards (with audio), practice quizzes, Web links and InfoTrac College Edition exercises.

These resources are available to qualified adopters, and ordering options for the student text and supplements are flexible. Please consult your local Cengage sales representative for more information, to evaluate examination copies of any of these instructor or student resources, or product demonstrations. You may also contact the Cengage Learning Academic Resource Center at 800-423-0563, or visit us at http://www.cengage.com/.

About the Author

Photo by Jan Haag/Dick Schmidt

Shirley Biagi is a Professor in the Department of Communication Studies at California State University, Sacramento. Her bestselling text, *Media/Impact*, is also published in Canadian, Greek, Spanish and Korean editions. Biagi has authored several other Wadsworth communications texts, including *Media/Reader: Perspectives on Mass Media Industries, Effects and Issues* and *Interviews That Work: A Practical Guide for Journalists*. She is co-author, with Marilyn Kern-Foxworth, of *Facing Difference: Race, Gender and Mass Media*.

From 1998–2000, she was editor of *American Journalism*, the national media history quarterly published by the American Journalism Historians Association.

She has served as guest faculty for the University of Hawaii, the Center for Digital Government, the Poynter Institute, the American Press Institute, the National Writers Workshop and the Hearst Fellowship Program at the *Houston Chronicle*, and as an Internet and publications consultant to the California State Chamber of Commerce.

She also was one of eight project interviewers for the award-winning Washington (D.C.) Press Club Foundation's Women in Journalism Oral History Project, sponsored by the National Press Club. Interviewers completed 57 oral histories of female pioneers in journalism, available free on the Press Club's Web site at http://npc.press.org/wpforal.

In 2007, Biagi was nominated and served as a delegate to the Oxford Round Table's conference on Ethical Sentiments in Government at Pembroke College in Oxford, England. Biagi's other international experience includes currently serving on the board of the Arab–United States Association of Communication Educators (AUSACE) and guest lectureships at Al Ahram Press Institute in Cairo, Egypt, and Queensland University in Brisbane, Australia.

Media/Impact

an introduction to mass media

NINTH EDITION

1

Mass Media and Everyday Life

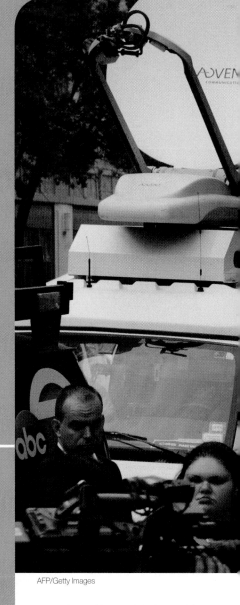

AFP/Getty Images

People wait outside to get into a June 2008 election night event for Democratic presidential hopeful Hillary Rodham Clinton at Baruch College in New York City.

What's Ahead?

> **"** What we're seeing, we've never seen in human history before. It's just the extraordinary availability and magnetism of electronic communication devices, whether it's cell phones or Blackberries or the Internet. People tend to—without knowing it or meaning to—spend a lot of time doing what I call screen sucking."
>
> Dr. Edward Hallowell, former Harvard Medical School faculty member and the author of the book *CrazyBusy*

You are *connected.*

In today's world mass media are waiting to bombard you every waking hour. When was the last time you spent 24 hours without the media? From the moment you get up in the morning until the time you go to bed at night, mass media are available to keep you informed, make sure you're entertained, and—most importantly—sell you products.

TimeFrame
3500 B.C. – Today

Three Information Communications Revolutions Form the Basis for Today's Digital Media

3500 B.C. The first known pictographs are carved in stone.

2500 B.C. **The Egyptians invent papyrus.**

Hulton Archive/Getty Images

1000 B.C. **The First Information Communications Revolution: Phonetic Writing**

200 B.C. The Greeks perfect parchment

100 A.D. The Chinese invent paper.

1300 Europeans start to use paper.

1445 The Chinese invent the copper press.

1455 **The Second Information Communications Revolution: Movable Type**

Popperfoto/Getty Images

1640 The first American book is published.

1690 The first American newspaper is published.

1741 The first American magazine is published.

1877 Thomas Edison first demonstrates the phonograph.

1899 **Guglielmo Marconi first uses his wireless radio.**

Hulton Archive/Getty Images

1927 *The Jazz Singer*, the first feature-length motion picture with sound, premieres in New York City.

1939 **NBC debuts TV at the New York World's Fair. On display were 5-inch and 9-inch sets priced from $199.50 to $600.**

MPI/Hulton Archive/Getty Images

1951 **The Third Information Communications Revolution: digital computers that can process, store and retrieve information.**

1980 The Federal Communications Commission begins to deregulate the broadcast media.

1989 Tim Berners-Lee develops the first Internet Web browser.

2008 Internet advertising income reaches $23 billion annually, more than twice what it was in the year 2000.

Today **Wireless digital technology is the standard for all mass media. Mass media is becoming personalized and mobile.**

Gareth Cattermole/Getty Images

Mass Media Are Everywhere You Are

Radio news gives you headlines in the shower and traffic reports on the freeway. Newspapers offer national and local news and help you follow the latest high school football standings, while online editions constantly update breaking news stories. Magazines describe new video games, show you the latest fashion trends and even help plan your wedding.

Should you do your homework or grab the newest paperback romance novel or watch the DVD that just arrived from Netflix or maybe use your iPhone to download the latest episode of last night's sitcom that you missed? Or maybe you should do your homework on your laptop, taking time out to answer e-mail from your overseas college friends, while downloading some new songs. All of that media certainly is more compelling than your homework.

According to industry estimates, today's adults spend more than half their waking lives with the media—more time than they spend sleeping. (See **Illustration 1.1**.) During the day, the average person spends more time with the media than without them. Some form of mass media touches you every day—economically, socially and culturally. The mass media can affect the way you vote and the way you spend your money. Sometimes the mass media influence the way you eat, talk, work, study and relax. This is the impact of mass media on American society.

The media's wide-ranging presence in America today means mass media capture more time and attention than ever. The media affect almost all aspects of the way people live, and the media collect unprecedented amounts of money for delivering information and entertainment. The American media industries earn about $436 billion a year. (See **Illustration 1.2**.)

Today's American society has inherited the wisdom and mistakes of the people who work in the mass media

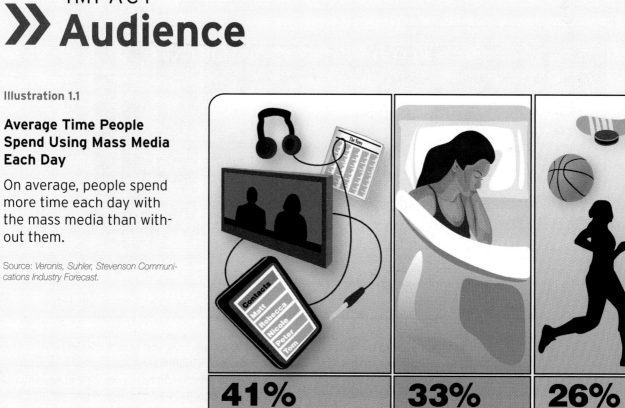

IMPACT
≫ Audience

Illustration 1.1

Average Time People Spend Using Mass Media Each Day

On average, people spend more time each day with the mass media than without them.

Source: Veronis, Suhler, Stevenson Communications Industry Forecast.

41%
Using media
590 minutes

33%
Sleeping
475 minutes

26%
Not using media
375 minutes

Total minutes in a day = 1,440

IMPACT
Business

Illustration 1.2

U.S. Media Industries Annual Income

The U.S. media industries collect $436 billion a year in income. Television and entertainment media are the top moneymakers. Television collects 42% of total media revenue, while book publishing and the radio industry collect only 5% each.

Source: VSS MediaResearchNet 2.0.

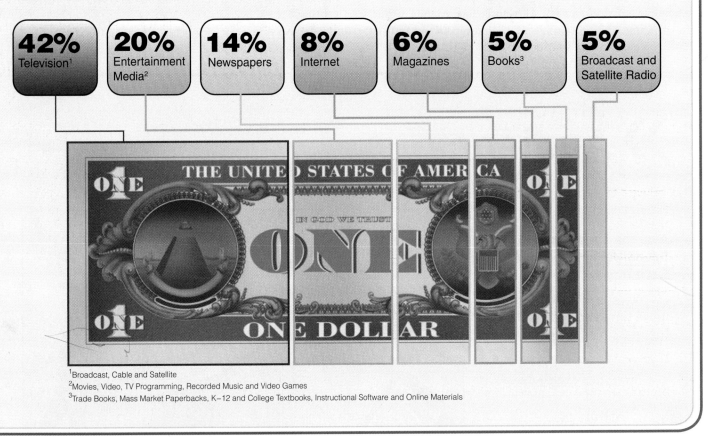

42%
Television[1]

20%
Entertainment Media[2]

14%
Newspapers

8%
Internet

6%
Magazines

5%
Books[3]

5%
Broadcast and Satellite Radio

[1] Broadcast, Cable and Satellite
[2] Movies, Video, TV Programming, Recorded Music and Video Games
[3] Trade Books, Mass Market Paperbacks, K–12 and College Textbooks, Instructional Software and Online Materials

industries and the society that regulates and consumes what the mass media produce. Consider these situations:

- You are shopping online at Amazon.com, trying to decide between Stephen King's latest novel and a travel guide to Peru. What are the economic consequences of these decisions by book buyers for the book publishing industry? (See **Chapter 2**.)

- You are an entrepreneur with $500,000 to invest, and you have decided that starting a new magazine must be relatively easy. Because you spend a lot of time outdoors, you think a rock-climbing magazine would be an instant success. What are the chances your new magazine will succeed? (See **Chapter 4**.)

- On the Internet, a friend e-mails you songs from the latest album of your favorite recording artist, which you download and publish on your personal Web site. You get the music you want, but the artist's music company sues you because you haven't paid for the songs. Will you be prosecuted? (See **Chapter 5**.)

- You are a reporter for a major newspaper and a judge orders you to give the court information you obtained from an anonymous source, yet you promised the source you would protect his identity. To whom do you owe allegiance—the court, your employer or your source? (See **Chapter 14.**)

People who work in the media industries, people who own media businesses, people who consume media and people who regulate what the media offer face decisions like these every day. The choices they make continue to shape the future of the American mass media.

Mass Communication Becomes Wireless

In the 1930s, to listen to the radio, your house had to have electricity throughout. You put your radio near an electrical outlet, with the furniture positioned so the family could listen to the programs. In the 1950s, you put an antenna on the roof so you could watch your new TV set, which was connected at the wall to an electrical outlet and the antenna. To be wired was to be connected. In the 1990s, you still needed an electrical outlet at home and at work to be connected to your computer, and the furniture in your family room still was arranged to accommodate the cable, satellite and/or telephone lines for your television set.

Today's technology makes mass media wireless (often called **Wi-Fi**, an abbreviation for *Wireless Fi*delity). New technologies give you access to any mass media in almost any location without wires. You can sit on your front porch and watch movies on your laptop, listen to radio by satellite and download music, books and newspapers to the cell phone you carry in your pocket. Today, you and your mass media are totally mobile.

The new mass media are as convenient as your cell phone or your iPod, complete with graphics and sound, offering massive choices of information, entertainment and services whenever and wherever you want them. You can

- Watch your favorite program whenever you want to see it.

- Download a first-run movie, your favorite TV sitcom or 100 new or classic books to a hand-held device you carry with you.

- Play the newest video game on your cell phone with three people you've never met.

- Drink coffee in a Wi-Fi café while you check your family ancestry to create an online family tree, leading

WireImage/Getty Images

If a friend e-mails you a copy of the latest song by your favorite recording artist, rapper Lil Wayne, and you use the song on your Web site without permission, can you be prosecuted for copyright violation?

you to connect with overseas relatives you didn't know existed.

- Stop on the street corner in a new town and, using a cell phone, retrieve directions to the closest Italian restaurant, complete with the latest recommendations about the best pizza to order there.

Wi-Fi An abbreviation for *Wireless Fi*delity.

Getty Images

Wireless technology means you can carry your media with you and freely send and receive messages any-time, just about anywhere you want. In Melbourne, Australia, Ian Bell of England uses his mobile phone during a fishing trip.

Today's digital environment is an intricate, webbed network of many different types of communications systems that eventually will connect every home, school, library and business in the United States. Most of the systems in this digital environment are invisible. Electronic signals have replaced wires, freeing people up to stay connected no matter where or when they want to communicate.

This global communications system uses broadcast, telephone, satellite, cable and computer technologies to connect everyone in the world to a variety of services. Eventually, this communications system will be accessible and affordable everywhere in the world. As futurist George Gilder phrased it, the issue is: "Who will ride the next avalanche of bits on the information superhighway—and who will be buried under it?"

Mass Communication Communication from one person or group of persons through a transmitting device (a medium) to large audiences or markets.

Medium The means by which a message reaches the audience. The singular form of the word *media*.

Media Plural of the word *medium*.

How the Communication Process Works

To understand mass communication in the digital age, first it is important to understand the process of communication. Communication is the act of sending messages, ideas and opinions from one person to another. Writing and talking to each other are only two ways human beings communicate. We also communicate when we gesture, move our bodies or roll our eyes.

Three ways to describe how people communicate are

- *Intrapersonal communication*
- *Interpersonal communication*
- *Mass communication*

Each form of communication involves different numbers of people in specific ways. If you are in a grocery store and you silently debate with yourself whether to buy an apple or a package of double-chunk chocolate chip cookies, you are using what scholars call *intra*personal communication—communication within one person. To communicate with each other, people rely on their five senses—sight, hearing, touch, smell and taste. This direct sharing of experience between two people is called *inter*personal communication. **Mass communication** is communication from one person or group of persons through a transmitting device (a medium) to large audiences or markets. In *Media/Impact* you will study *mass communication*.

To describe the process of mass communication, scholars use a communications model. This includes six key terms: *sender*, *message*, *receiver*, *channel*, *feedback* and *noise*. (See **Illustration 1.3**.)

Pretend you're standing directly in front of someone and you say, "I like your Red Sox hat." In this simple communication, you are the sender; the message is "I like your Red Sox hat," and the person in front of you is the receiver (or audience). This example of interpersonal communication involves the sender, the message and the receiver.

In mass communication, the *sender* (or *source*) puts the *message* on what is called a *channel*. The sender (source) could be your local cable or satellite company, for example. The channel (or **medium**) delivers the message (the signal). The channel could be the cable or satellite line that hooks into the back of your TV set. A medium is the means by which a message reaches an audience. (The plural of the word *medium* is *media*; the term **media** is used to refer to more than one medium.) Your television set is the medium that delivers the message simultaneously to you (and many other people).

The *receiver* is the place where the message arrives, such as your TV set. **Noise** is any distortion (such as static or a briefly interrupted signal) that interferes with clear communication. **Feedback** occurs when the receiver processes the message and sends a response back to the sender (source).

Using a very simple example, say your cable company (sender/source) sends an advertisement for a movie-on-demand (the message) through the signal (channel) into your TV set (medium). If you (the receiver) use the controls on your TV remote to order a pay-per-view movie, the order you place (feedback) ultimately will bring you a movie to watch. This entire loop between sender and receiver, and the resulting response (feedback) of the receiver to the sender, describes the process of mass communication.

Using a very general definition, mass communication today shares three characteristics:

1. A message is sent out on some form of mass communication system (such as the Internet, print or broadcast).

2. The message is delivered rapidly.

3. The message reaches large groups of different kinds of people simultaneously or within a short period of time.

Thus, a telephone conversation between two people does *not* qualify as mass communication, but a message from the President of the United States, broadcast simultaneously by all of the television networks, would qualify because mass media deliver messages to large numbers of people at once.

What Are the Mass Media Industries?

The term **mass media industries** describes eight types of mass media businesses. The word *industries*, when used to describe the media business, emphasizes the primary goal of mass media in America—to generate money. The eight media industries are

- Books
- Newspapers
- Magazines
- Recordings

Movies such as *Wall-E*, available to large groups of different types of people simultaneously, represent one form of mass communication.

DISNEY/PIXAR/THE KOBAL COLLECTION/PICTURE DESK

- Radio
- Movies
- Television
- The Internet

Books, newspapers and magazines were America's only mass media for 250 years after the first American book

Noise Distortion (such as static) that interferes with clear communication.

Feedback A response sent back to the sender from the person who receives the communication.

Mass Media Industries Eight types of media businesses: books, newspapers, magazines, recordings, radio, movies, television and the Internet.

IMPACT
>> Culture

Illustration 1.3

Elements of Mass Communication

The process of mass communication works like this: A *sender* (source) puts a message on a channel (medium) that delivers the message to the *receiver*. *Feedback* occurs when the receiver responds, and that response changes subsequent messages from the source. *Noise* (such as static or a dropped connection) can interrupt or change the message during transmission.

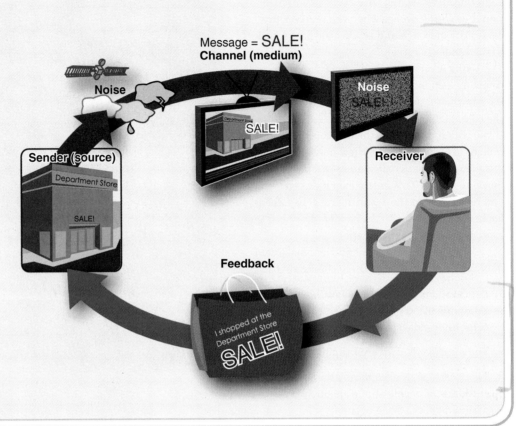

was published in 1640. The first half of the 20th century brought four new types of media—recordings, radio, movies and TV—in less than 50 years. The late-20th-century addition to the media mix, of course, is the Internet. To understand where each medium fits in the mass media industries today, it is important to examine the individual characteristics of each media business.

Books

Publishers issue about 40,000 titles a year in the United States, although some of these are reprints and new editions of old titles. Retail bookstores in the United States account for one-third of all money earned from book sales. The rest of book publishing income comes from books that are sold online, in college stores, through book clubs, to libraries and to school districts for use in elementary and high schools. Book publishing, the oldest media industry, is a static industry, with very little growth potential, although

book publishers are trying to expand their sales by selling e-books (downloaded copies of books) as an alternative to printed books.

Newspapers

There are about 1,500 daily newspapers in the United States. Newspapers are evenly divided between morning and afternoon delivery, but the number of afternoon papers is declining. Papers that come out in the morning are growing in circulation, and papers that come out in the afternoon are shrinking. The number of weekly newspapers also is declining.

Advertising makes up more than two-thirds of the printed space in daily newspapers. Most newspapers have launched online editions to try to expand their reach, but overall newspaper industry income is shrinking, and many major newspaper organizations have had to cut staff and sell off some of their newspapers to try to stay profitable.

Magazines

According to the Magazine Publishers of America, about 15,000 magazines are published in the United States, but this number is declining. More magazines are going out of business than new magazines are being launched. To maintain and increase profits, magazines are raising their subscription and single-copy prices and fighting to maintain their advertising income. Some magazines have launched Internet online editions, and a few magazines (such as *Slate*) are published exclusively online. Magazine subscriptions and newsstand sales are down. Magazine income is expected to decline over the next decade.

Recordings

People over age 25 are the most common buyers of recordings today because people under 25 are downloading music from the Internet, both legally and illegally, so people under 25 don't buy many CDs. CDs and online downloads account for almost all recording industry income, with a small amount of money coming from music videos. Industry income has been declining sharply because new technologies allow consumers to share music over the Internet rather than pay for their music. The only growing revenue source for the recording companies among people under 25 is individual music downloads, sold through online sites such as iTunes. In 2008, Apple announced that iTunes had become the largest music retailer in the United States.

Radio

About 13,000 radio stations broadcast programming in the United States, evenly divided between AM and FM stations. About 2,100 radio stations are public stations, most of them FM. Satellite radio, such as Sirius and XM, generates revenue through subscriptions, offering an almost unlimited variety of music and program choices without commercials. As a result, over-the-air broadcast radio revenue from commercials is declining because the price of a commercial is based on the size of the audience, which is getting smaller. In 2008, Sirius and XM asked for approval to merge the two services because neither service was profitable. The FCC approved the merger, and the combined company is now known as Sirius XM Radio.

Movies

About 30,000 theater screens exist in the United States. The major and independent studios combined make about 400 pictures a year. The industry is collecting more money because of higher ticket prices, but more people watch movies at home than in a theater, so the number of movie the-

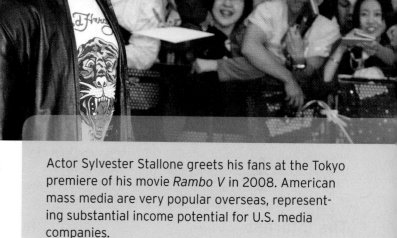

Junko Kimura/Getty Images

Actor Sylvester Stallone greets his fans at the Tokyo premiere of his movie *Rambo V* in 2008. American mass media are very popular overseas, representing substantial income potential for U.S. media companies.

aters is declining. The latest development in movie theaters is the introduction of stadium seating, which offers everyone in the theater an uninterrupted view of the screen. The major increase in income to the U.S. movie industry recently has been from DVDs, overseas movie sales and movie downloads. For the first time in a decade, overall movie industry income in 2005 was less than the year before, and that trend continues, indicating that the industry is continuing to suffer losses.

Television

About 1,600 television stations operate in the United States. One out of four stations is a public station. Many stations are affiliated with a network—NBC, CBS, ABC or Fox—although a few stations, called *independents*, are not affiliated with any network. More than 90 percent of the homes in the United States are wired for cable or satellite delivery. To differentiate cable and satellite TV from network television, cable and satellite television services are now lumped together in one category, called **subscription television**.

Subscription Television A new term used to describe consumer services delivered by cable and satellite television.

'You don't really know someone until you give them the remote.'

TV network income is declining while income to cable operators and satellite companies for subscription services is increasing quickly, so all the television networks also have invested heavily in subscription TV programming. Only one network, Fox, also owns a satellite delivery system, DirecTV. In 2008, AT&T began offering subscription television services using fiberoptic cable. Total television industry revenue is expected to grow steadily in the next decade.

The Internet

The newest media industry also is growing the fastest. About 73 percent of all consumers are online, and the amount of money spent for Internet advertising increased from $8 billion in the year 2000 to $23 billion in 2008. Internet media have become a new mass medium as well as an integrated delivery system for traditional print, audio and video media.

✳Three Key Concepts to Remember

The mass media are key institutions in our society. They affect our culture, our buying habits and our politics. They are affected in turn by changes in our beliefs, tastes, interests and behavior. Three important concepts about the mass media can help organize your thinking about mass media and their impact on American society:

1. The mass media are profit-centered businesses.

Concentration of Ownership The current trend of large companies buying smaller companies so that fewer companies own more types of media businesses.

2. Technological developments change the way mass media are delivered and consumed.

3. Mass media both reflect and affect politics, society and culture.

Mass Media Are Profit-Centered Businesses

What you see, read and hear in the mass media may tease, entertain, inform, persuade, provoke and even perplex you. But to understand the American mass media, the first concept to grasp is that the central force driving the media business in America is the desire to make money. American media are businesses, vast businesses.

The products of these businesses are information and entertainment that depend on attracting an audience of media consumers to generate income. Of course, other motives shape the media in America: the desire to fulfill the public's need for information, to influence the country's governance, to disseminate the country's culture, to offer entertainment and to provide an outlet for artistic expression. But American media are, above all, profit-centered.

To understand the mass media industries, it is essential to understand who owns these important channels of communication. In the United States, all media are privately owned except the Public Broadcasting Service (PBS) and National Public Radio (NPR), which survive on government support, private donations and minimal corporate sponsorship. The annual budget for all of public broadcasting (PBS and NPR combined) is less than 2 percent of the amount advertisers pay every year to support America's commercial media.

In some media industries, the same number of companies control ownership today as in the 1950s. There are five major movie studios today, for example, compared to the same number of major studios in the 1940s. The number of broadcast stations and the number of magazines has increased since the 1940s, but the number of newspapers and the number of recording companies has declined.

Overall, however, American media ownership has been contracting rather than expanding. This is because large companies are buying small companies. The trend is for media companies to cluster together into big groups so that fewer companies own more types of media businesses. A small number of companies now control more aspects of the media business. This trend, called ***concentration of ownership***, takes four different forms: chains, broadcast networks, conglomerates and vertical integration.

CHAINS. Benjamin Franklin established America's first newspaper chain in the 1700s, when he was publishing his own newspaper, the *Pennsylvania Gazette*, as well as sponsoring one-third of the cost of publishing the *South Carolina Gazette*. (He also collected one-third of the *South Carolina Gazette*'s profits.) William Randolph Hearst expanded this tradition in the 1930s. At their peak, Hearst newspapers accounted for nearly 14 percent of total national daily newspaper sales and 25 percent of Sunday sales. Today's U.S. newspaper chain giant is Gannett, with 91 daily newspapers, including *USA Today*. The word *chain* is used to describe a company that owns a number of newspapers.

BROADCAST NETWORKS. A broadcast network is a collection of radio or television stations that offers programs during designated program times. Unlike newspaper ownership (which is not regulated by the government), the Federal Communications Commission (**FCC**) regulates broadcast station ownership and operations. The FCC is a government regulatory body whose members are appointed by the president.

The four major networks are ABC (American Broadcasting Company), NBC (National Broadcasting Company), CBS (Columbia Broadcasting System) and Fox Broadcasting. NBC, the oldest network, was founded in the 1920s. This network and the two other original networks (CBS and ABC) were established to deliver radio programming across the country, and continued the network concept when television was invented. Fox is the youngest major network, founded in 1986, and serves only television.

Time Warner and Viacom each launched a TV network in 1996—WB (Warner Bros.) and UPN (United Paramount Network)—but neither of the new networks ever found an audience.

Networks can have as many **affiliates** as they want. Affiliates are stations that use network programming but are owned by companies other than the networks. No network, however, can have two affiliates in the same geographic broadcast area, due to government regulation of network affiliation.

In 2006, the TV networks announced they would offer shows on demand for downloading. Apple Computer and Disney agreed to make series programming available on video iPods. One month later, CBS and NBC announced

Getty Images

NBC's Chet Huntley (left) and David Brinkley were the first national TV network newscast team, presenting the news every weekday night on the Huntley-Brinkley Report. In 1968, Huntley-Brinkley reported the final results of the presidential election, won by Richard Nixon (note the vote percentages displayed behind the news desk).

they planned to offer series programs on demand for 99 cents an episode through Comcast and DirecTV. Looking for new ways to generate revenue, the networks are taking the programming to their viewers instead of waiting for viewers to come to them.

CONGLOMERATES. When you go to the movies to watch a Universal picture, you might not realize that General Electric owns NBC Universal, which owns the film company Universal. General Electric is a **conglomerate**—a company that owns media companies as well as other businesses that are unrelated to the media business, such as financial

FCC Federal Communications Commission.

Affiliates Stations that use network programming but are owned by companies other than the networks.

Conglomerates Companies that own media companies as well as businesses that are unrelated to the media business.

Wirelmage/Getty Images

Time Warner is an example of a business that is vertically integrated, a company that controls several related aspects of the media business at once. Time Warner owns AOL, CNN, TNT and TBS, as well as *Sports Illustrated,* the Cartoon Network and SI.com. In 2008, CNN, TNT and TBS covered the 14th Annual Screen Actors Guild Awards on-site from the Shrine Auditorium in Los Angeles.

services and appliance manufacturing. Media properties are attractive investments, but some conglomerate owners are unfamiliar with the idiosyncrasies of the media industries and struggle to make the media companies profitable after acquiring them.

VERTICAL INTEGRATION. The most noticeable trend among today's media companies is *vertical integration*—an attempt by one company to control several related aspects of the media business at once, with each part of the company

Media Monopoly

Vertical Integration An attempt by one company to simultaneously control several related aspects of the media business.

Convergence The melding of the communications, computer and electronics industries. Also used to describe the economic alignment of the various media companies with each other to take advantage of technological advancements.

helping the others. Many media companies own more than one type of media property: newspapers, magazines, radio and TV stations, for example.

Gannett, which owns the largest chain of newspapers, also owns television and radio stations, so Gannett is a chain that is also vertically integrated. The media company Viacom owns CBS, MTV, the radio group Infinity Broadcasting and Black Entertainment Television (BET). Rupert Murdoch's News Corporation owns newspapers, TV stations, magazines, 20th Century Fox Film and Fox Broadcasting. Time Warner owns Warner Brothers studios, HBO, Turner Broadcasting, CNN, TNT, TBS, *Sports Illustrated*, SI.com and the Cartoon Network. In 2008, Time Warner launched an HBO channel on YouTube.

Competition and Convergence Dominate

To describe the financial status of today's media industries is to talk about intense competition. Media companies are buying and selling each other in unprecedented numbers and forming media groups to position themselves in the marketplace to maintain and increase their profits. Since 1986, all three original TV networks (NBC, CBS and ABC) have been sold to new owners—sometimes more than once—making each of the three original networks smaller parts of giant media companies. Today's media companies face heavy pressure to deliver hefty profits to their shareholders.

Media companies today also are driven by the media *convergence*. The word *convergence* actually describes two developments taking place simultaneously. First, convergence means the melding of the communications, computer and electronics industries because of advances in digital technology. Second, convergence also means the economic alignment of different types of media companies with each other to make sure they can offer the variety of services that technical advancements demand.

The people who manage U.S. media companies today want to make money. As in all industries, there are people who want to make money quickly and people who take the long-term view about profits, but certainly none of them wants to lose money. One way to expand a company to take advantage of technological and economic convergence is to acquire an already established company that's successful. Such media acquisitions have skyrocketed for two reasons—public ownership and deregulation.

PUBLIC OWNERSHIP. Most media companies today are publicly traded, which means their stock is sold on one of the nation's stock exchanges. This makes acquisitions relatively easy. A media company that wants to buy another publicly owned company can buy that company's stock when the stock becomes available.

The open availability of stock in these public companies means any company or individual with enough money can invest in the American media industries, which is exactly how Rupert Murdoch, owner of Fox Broadcasting, joined the U.S. media business and was able to accumulate so many media companies in such a short time.

DEREGULATION. Beginning in 1980, the Federal Communications Commission gradually deregulated the broadcast media. ***Deregulation*** means the FCC withdrew many regulatory restrictions on broadcast media ownership. Before 1980, for example, the FCC allowed a broadcast company to own only five TV stations, five AM radio stations and five FM radio stations. Companies also were required to hold onto a station for three years before the owners could sell the station.

The post-1980 FCC eliminated the three-year rule and raised the number of broadcast holdings allowed for one owner. Today, there are very few FCC restrictions on broadcast media ownership.

Why Media Properties Converge

Ownership turnover is highest in the newspaper and broadcast industries. Six factors have affected the economic alignment of these properties:

1. Newspaper and broadcast properties are attractive investments. Many broadcast companies report profits of 10 percent a year, which is about double the average profit for a U.S. manufacturing company.

2. Newspapers and broadcast stations are scarce commodities. Because the number of newspapers has been declining and the government regulates the number of broadcast stations that are allowed to operate, a limited number of stations are available. As with all limited commodities, this makes them attractive investments.

3. Newspapers and broadcast stations have gone through a cycle of family ownership. If the heirs to the founders of

the business are not interested in joining the company, the only way for them to collect their inheritance is to sell the newspaper, and the only companies with enough money to buy individual media businesses are large corporations.

4. Newspapers and broadcast stations are easier businesses to buy than to create. Because these businesses require huge investments in equipment and people, they are expensive to start up. In broadcasting, the major factor that encouraged ownership changes in the 1980s was deregulation. This allowed people who had never been in the broadcast business before to enter the industry, using bank loans to pay for most of their investment. Some new owners of broadcast media companies see these companies the way they would look at any business—hoping to invest the minimum amount necessary. They hold onto the property until the market is favorable, hoping to sell at a huge profit.

5. In the 1990s, the introduction of new technologies, especially the Internet, changed the economics of all the media industries. Each industry had to adapt to the Internet quickly, and the fastest way to gain Internet expertise was to buy a company or to invest in a company that already had created an Internet presence or a successful Internet product.

6. The economic downturn that began in 2007 affected newspapers especially hard. Heavily dependent on real estate advertising and classifieds, and challenged by the dynamics of the Internet, many publicly owned newspaper companies began losing money at an unprecedented rate. This fall in profits drove down their stock prices to new lows, which made them vulnerable to takeovers and buyouts as the companies struggled to survive.

Supporters of concentrated ownership and convergence say a large company can offer advantages that a small company could never afford—training for the employees, higher wages and better working conditions.

The major arguments against the concentration and convergence of group ownership are that concentration of so much power limits the diversity of opinion and the quality of ideas available to the public and reduces what scholars call ***message pluralism***. Ben H. Bagdikian, Dean Emeritus,

Deregulation Government action that ends government control of an industry.

Message Pluralism The availability to an audience of a variety of information and entertainment sources.

Graduate School of Journalism at the University of California, Berkeley, describes how the loss of message pluralism can affect every aspect of communication:

> It has always been assumed that a newspaper article might be expanded to a magazine article which could become the basis for a hardcover book, which, in turn, could be a paperback, and then, perhaps a TV series and finally, a movie. At each step of change an author and other enterprises could compete for entry into the array of channels for reaching the public mind and pocketbook. But today several media giants own these arrays, not only closing off entry points for competition in different media, but influencing the choice of entry at the start.

Advertisers and Consumers Pay the Bills

Most of the $436 billion a year in income the American mass media industries collect comes from advertising. Advertising directly supports newspapers, radio and television. Subscribers actually pay only a small part of the cost of producing a newspaper. Advertisers pay the biggest portion. Magazines receive more than half their income from advertising and the other portion from subscriptions. Income for movies, recordings and books, of course, comes primarily from direct purchases and ticket sales.

This means that most of the information and entertainment you receive from the Internet, TV, radio, newspapers and magazines in America is paid for by people who want to sell you products. You support the media industries *indirectly* by buying the products that advertisers sell. General Motors spends $1 billion a year on network TV advertising. Sears spends $300 million a year just on newspaper advertising. Multiply the spending for all this advertising for all media, and you can understand how easily American media industries accumulate $436 billion a year.

You also pay for the media *directly* when you buy a book or a DVD or go to a movie. This money buys equipment, underwrites company research and expansion, and pays stock dividends. Advertisers and consumers are the financial foundation for American media industries because different audiences provide a variety of markets for consumer products.

Pictograph A symbol of an object that is used to convey an idea.

Phonetic Writing The use of symbols to represent sounds.

Technology Changes Mass Media Delivery and Consumption

The channels of communication have changed dramatically over the centuries, but the idea that a society will pay to stay informed and entertained is not new. In Imperial Rome, people who wanted to find out what was going on paid professional speakers a coin (a *gazet*) for the privilege of listening to the speaker announce the day's events. Many early newspapers were called *gazettes* to reflect this heritage.

The history of mass communication technology involves three information communications revolutions: phonetic writing, printing and computer technology.

Phonetic Writing: The First Information Communications Revolution

Early attempts at written communication began modestly with **pictographs**. A pictograph is a symbol of an object that is used to convey an idea. If you have ever drawn a heart with an arrow through it, you understand what a pictograph is. The Sumerians of Mesopotamia carved the first known pictographs in stone in about 3500 B.C.

The stone in which these early pictographic messages were carved served as a medium—a device to transmit messages. Eventually, people imprinted messages in clay and then they stored these clay tablets in a primitive version of today's library. These messages weren't very portable, however. Heavy clay tablets don't slip easily into someone's pocket.

In about 2500 B.C., the Egyptians invented papyrus, a type of paper made from a grass-like plant called sedge, which was easier to write on, but people still communicated using pictographs.

Pictographs as a method of communication developed into **phonetic writing** in about 1000 B.C. when people began to use symbols to represent sounds. Instead of drawing a picture of a dog to convey the idea of a dog, scholars represented the sounds d-o-g with phonetic writing. The invention of phonetic writing has been called *the first information communications revolution*. "After being stored in written form, *information could now reach a new kind of audience, remote from the source and uncontrolled by it*," writes media scholar Anthony Smith. "Writing transformed knowledge into information."

About 500 years later, the Greek philosopher Socrates anticipated the changes that widespread literacy would bring. He argued that knowledge should remain among the privileged classes. Writing threatened the exclusive use of information, he said. "Once a thing is put in writing, the composition, whatever it may be, drifts all over the place, getting into the hands not only of those who understand it, but equally of those who have no business with it."

In about 200 B.C., the Greeks perfected parchment, made from goat and sheepskins. Parchment was an even better medium on which to write. By about A.D. 100, before the use of parchment spread throughout Europe, the Chinese had invented paper, which was much cheaper to produce than parchment. Europeans didn't start to use paper until more than a thousand years later, in about A.D. 1300. The discovery of parchment and then paper meant that storing information became cheaper and easier.

As Socrates predicted, when more people learned to write, wider communication became possible because people in many different societies could share information among themselves and with people in other parts of the world. But scholars still had to painstakingly copy the information they wanted to keep or pay a scribe to copy for them. In the 14th century, for example, the library of the Italian poet Petrarch contained more than 100 manuscripts that he himself had copied individually.

In Petrarch's day, literate people were either monks or members of the privileged classes. Wealthy people could afford tutoring, and they also could afford to buy the handwritten manuscripts copied by the monks. Knowledge—and the power it brings—belonged to an elite group of people.

Printing: The Second Information Communications Revolution

As societies grew more literate, the demand for manuscripts flourished, but a scribe could produce only one copy at a time. What has been called *the second information communications revolution* began in Germany in 1455, when Johannes Gutenberg printed a Bible on a press that used movable type.

More than 200 years before Gutenberg, the Chinese had invented a printing press that used wood type, and the Chinese also are credited with perfecting a copper press in 1445. But Gutenberg's innovation was to line up individual metal letters that he could ink and then press onto paper to produce copies. Unlike the wood or copper presses, the metal letters could be reused to produce new pages of text, which made the process much cheaper.

The Gutenberg Bible, a duplicate of the Latin original, is considered the first book printed by movable type (47 cop-

The Gutenberg Bible, published by Johannes Gutenberg in Germany in 1455, was the first book printed using movable type. Printing is the second communications revolution.

ies still survive today, 555 years later). As other countries adopted Gutenberg's press, the price for Bibles plummeted. In 1470, the cost of a French, mechanically printed Bible was one-fifth the cost of a hand-printed Bible.

The second information communications revolution—printing—meant that *knowledge, which had belonged to the privileged few, would one day be available to everyone.* The key development of printing was one of the essential conditions for the rise of modern governments, as well as an important element of scientific and technological progress.

Before the Gutenberg press, a scholar who wanted special information had to travel to the place where it was kept. But once information could be duplicated easily, it could travel to people beyond the society that created it. The use of paper instead of the scribes' bulky parchment also meant that books could be stacked end to end. *For the first time, knowledge was portable and storable.*

Libraries now could store vast amounts of information in a small space. And because people could easily carry these smaller, lighter books, all different kinds of people in many different cities could read classical works simultaneously. Another benefit of the development of printing was that societies could more easily keep information to share with

vast amounts of information that previously relied on the written word.

Computer technology, which processes and transmits information much more efficiently than mechanical devices, is driving the majority of changes affecting today's media. This has become possible with the development of digital computers, beginning around 1950. Digital delivery means that changes in today's media industries happen much faster than in the past. Satellite broadcasts, digital recordings and the international computer network called the Internet are just three examples of the third information communications revolution.

Although each medium has its own history and economic structure, today all of the media industries compete for consumers' attention. Satellite and electronic technology is transforming the media business more than we can foresee—enabling faster transmission of more information to more people than ever before.

Computers, shown here being used by Chicago Bulls mascot Benny the Bull and a Cook Elementary School student, represent the third information communications revolution. The foundation of today's rapidly changing technology, digital delivery affects all aspects of today's politics, society and culture. In 2008, the Bulls basketball team helped sponsor the opening of the new Chicago Bulls Reading and Learning Center at Cook Elementary.

future generations. *Knowledge now was accessible to many; knowledge no longer belonged to just the chosen few.*

This effort to communicate—first through spoken messages, then through pictographs, then through the written word and finally through printed words—demonstrates people's innate desire to share information with one another. *Storability, portability and accessibility* of information are essential to today's concept of mass communication. By definition, *mass communication is information that is available to a large audience quickly.*

Computer Technology: The Third Information Communications Revolution

Today's age of communication has been called the *third information communications revolution* because computers have become the electronic storehouses and transmitters of

Media Take Advantage of Digital Delivery

The economics of the communications industries makes digital delivery very important. All the industries involved in building and maintaining this interconnected network—broadcast, cable, telephone, computer, software, satellite and the consumer electronics industries—want a piece of the estimated $1 trillion in income that digital delivery represents.

Leaders of the media industries in the United States can be the central driving force in this network because many Americans already have most of the tools that such a system needs and many of the companies that are developing digital products are based in the United States.

Because the United States already contributes so many of the digital environment's necessary elements, it has become logical—and very profitable—for the media industries in this country to drive the convergence technology to package and deliver information worldwide.

One-Way Versus Two-Way Communication

The classic model of mass communication (see **Illustration 1.3** on page 10) describes a process that begins with a *sender* (or source), who puts a *message* on a *channel* (a medium). The channel then delivers the message to the *receiver*. This is the equivalent of a one-way road—sender to receiver.

Digital delivery begins in the same way. The *channel* carries information and entertainment (*messages*) from many different sources (*senders*) to many different people (*receivers*). The messages that return from the receiver to the sender are called *feedback*. In the digital environment, messages and feedback can occur instantaneously because the sender and the receiver can communicate with each other almost simultaneously. This makes digital systems **interactive**.

To take advantage of this interactivity, today's delivery system is transforming from a communications system that works like an ordinary television (sending messages and programming one way from the sender to the receiver) into a two-way digital system that can send and receive messages simultaneously and that works more like a combination television, telephone and computer.

Dumb Versus *Smart* Communication

The television set is a "dumb" appliance; it only can deliver programming. You can change the channel to receive different programs, but you can't talk back to the people who send the programming to your television set to tell them when you'd like to see a particular program. You can't watch something when you want to watch it, unless you remember beforehand to record the program. You also can't add anything to the programs on your TV, such as your personal commentary about a football game or a bad movie. This type of mass communication—in which the programs are sent to you on an established schedule and you are a passive receiver (a couch potato) for the program—is *one-way*.

As communications devices, however, telephones are smarter. When you talk on the telephone, the person on the other end of the conversation can listen to you and talk back right away (and, in the case of a teleconference, this can involve several people at the same time). This makes telephone communication interactive, giving you the ability to talk back—to receive as well as to transmit messages. Telephone communications are *two-way*. (See **Impact/ Audience**, "Calling a Technology Timeout," page 20.)

To communicate rapidly, telephone communication uses a system of digitized information. When you talk, the telephone system uses electronic signals to transform your voice into a series of digits—ones and zeroes—and then reassembles these digits into an exact reproduction of your voice on the other end of the line. This method of storing and transmitting data is called **digital communication**.

Like telephone communications, computers also operate using digitized information and are interactive. Written words, audio and video are translated and stored as *bits*. These bits can easily be transmitted, using two-way communication. This is the reason that someone can, for instance, connect to the Internet on a computer and receive and send information. To communicate via the Internet, a computer uses a *modem* to connect to a telephone line or a cellular signal, making two-way communication possible.

And, unlike television and telephones, computers can store digital information for future use. This ability to store information makes the computer different from broadcast, cable, telephone and satellite communications. "In the information economy, the best opportunities stem from the exponential rise in the power of computers and computer networks," according to futurist George Gilder.

How Today's Communications Network Operates

Today's communications network combines many different elements from existing media industries. The broadcast industry produces content and delivers one-way communication by antenna and satellite; the cable industry delivers one-way communication and two-way communication by underground (or overhead) cable; the telephone companies deliver digital two-way communication using fiber optics and cellular technology; and the computer industry offers digital storage capability.

A digital communications network combines all these elements: content, two-way digital communication and digital storage. **Illustration 1.5** on page 22 shows how this communications network operates.

The Receiver (You, the Subscriber)

A digital network begins with you, the receiver/subscriber. For example, you go online to check your **e-mail**, then look around to decide which other services you want, such as

- First-run movie and music download services

- TV soap opera and sitcom downloads, available and priced per episode

- Worldwide video news services, including access to overseas news channels in a variety of languages

- Newspaper database research service, with a list of today's stories from newspapers around the globe on topics you've pre-selected

Interactive A message system that allows senders and receivers to communicate simultaneously.

Digital Communication Data in a form that can be transmitted and received electronically.

E-mail Electronic mail delivered over the Internet.

» IMPACT
» Audience

Calling a Technology Timeout

by Keith O'Brien

NEEDHAM, Mass.—With cell phones strapped to their hips and the Internet in their pocket, they hustle down suburban streets, always racing off to somewhere. One child's swim lessons, another's choir practice. There's Hebrew school to attend, and science projects to finish, and, finally, from many suburban families, there is screaming. People want to be unplugged, be unscheduled.

And so, in recent years, town officials have started giving people that opportunity. Month-long calendars have been created in Needham, Newton, Belmont, and Bedford suggesting daily activities that don't include watching television or instant messaging. Nights have been set aside in these towns—as well as in Northborough and Southborough—where meetings and school homework are forbidden, freeing families up to spend a quiet evening together. And in Needham—where the local "unplugged" or "unscheduled" movement began—a few brave souls decided to do something radical last Friday.

No e-mail. All day.

"When you combine the number of hours devoted to television and being online, it could be up to 10 hours a day or more," said Jon Mattleman, director of the Needham Youth Commission, who planned "Needham Unplugged." "So I really want people to think about it. If you're doing anything for 10 hours a day, what does that mean for your life?"

Researchers studying the impact of technology on our lives say it's a valid question, given the ways that digital gadgetry divide us as well as connect us. But in a world gone wired, calls for technological temperance often fall on unwilling ears—even when people say they want to go unplugged. And carving out family time for board games on the living room floor?

"That's great," said Ann Reynolds, a Belmont mother of three children, ages 13, 12 and 7. "But I've got hockey practice. I've got to be somewhere at seven o'clock. You have all these other things."

Many people, like Reynolds, say they are looking forward to their one night of no homework and no town meetings this month. But between other obligations, many families hardly have time to change much else. Some folks in Northborough were apparently too busy to even learn about their town's "unscheduled" night last week; there were four town meetings that evening. And Mattleman's "no e-mail" day didn't exactly excite Needham residents—or even Mattleman's own employees.

"They were bewildered," Mattleman said. "Seriously, I think they thought, 'That's a great idea. But how are we going to survive here?' "

What concerns Mattleman and others is the way that technology—and specifically the Internet—has infiltrated our lives. And recent studies by the Stanford Institute for the Quantitative Study of Society indicate that there is reason to worry. (See **Illustration 1.4.**)

The Stanford research showed that people who didn't use the Internet during a random six-hour window on a given day were likely to spend, on average, almost twice as much time with family during those hours than those who spent an hour or more online.

Kristen Backor, the institute's head research assistant, said this shows that while people may be connecting with others on the Internet they are disconnecting with loved ones to do so. That, Backor said, is changing how people relate within the home.

And this is not a trivial change, said Dr. Edward Hallowell, a Sudbury psychiatrist, former Harvard Medical School faculty member and the author of the book *CrazyBusy*.

"What we're seeing, we've never seen in human history before," Hallowell said. "It's just the extraordinary availability and magnetism of electronic communication devices, whether it's cell phones or Blackberries or the Internet. People tend to—without knowing it or meaning to—spend a lot of time doing what I call screen sucking."

Illustration 1.4

How People Spend Their Time on the Internet

People spend the majority of their time on the Internet communicating with other people.

Source: Stanford Institute for the Quantitative Study of Society. www.stanford.edu/group/siqss.

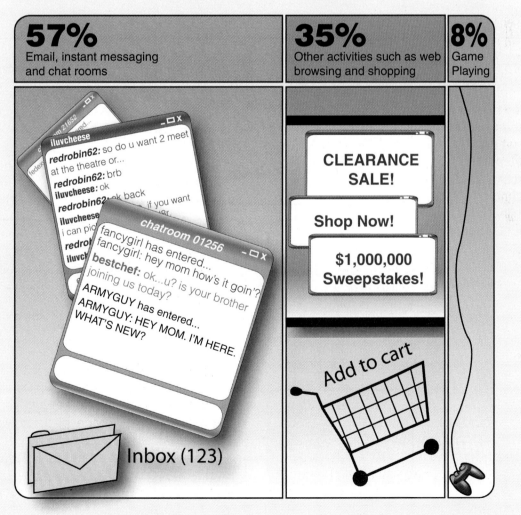

- Sports, family, travel, shopping and music video service

- Online video games and gambling sites

- Bulletin board discussion groups, chat rooms, blogs and video clips indexed by topic

You glance through the offerings of each service and make your choices. Your screen shows several windows simultaneously so you can use various services simultaneously, each on a different screen. For example, you check your bank balance while you play poker online and check your e-mail messages while you watch overseas news headlines.

All these services, which you take for granted today, weren't available even five years ago. The Internet's digital communications network is what makes all these services possible.

The Channel (Cable, Telephone, Satellite and Cellular Companies)

Cable, telephone, satellite and cellular companies provide Internet communications delivery, acting as a conduit—gathering all the services from national and international networks. Some companies offer only specific services, or they package services together (local, national and interna-

IMPACT
≫ Business

Illustration 1.5

How the Communications Network Works

Today's communications network combines different elements of broadcast, cable, telephone, satellite, cellular and computer technology to create an international digital communications service.

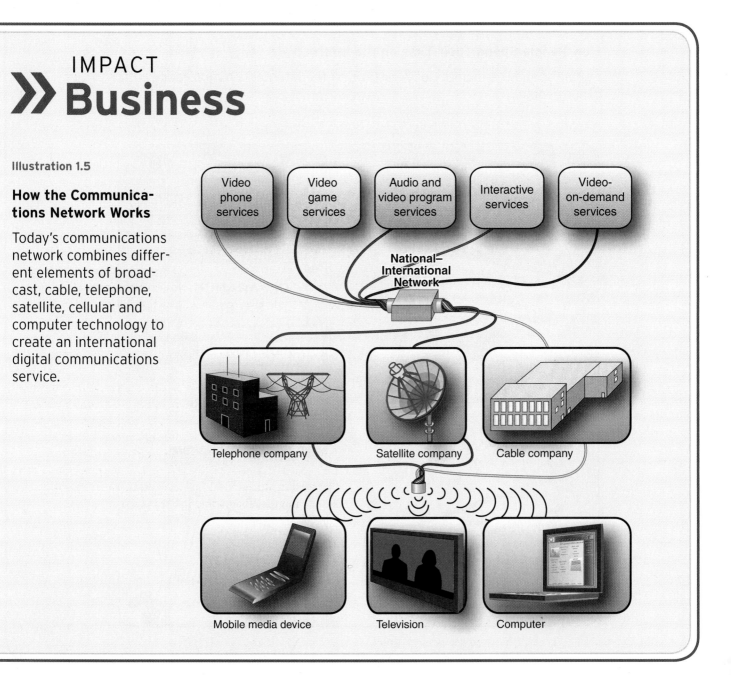

tional news services, for example); or they offer an unlimited menu of all the services that are available and let you choose what you want. Cable, telephone, satellite and cellular companies are competing today for consumers' Internet business.

You can choose the type of service you want based on each company's offerings and pricing. Some services are billed as pay-per-use (a $5 charge to view a first-run movie, for example) or per minute (to use a newspaper's archive for research, for example, billed to a credit card).

This international communications network and the satellite system to support it already are in place—long-distance carrier networks such as AT&T and satellite services such as DirecTV and Dish Network. The ***Internet***, as an international web of computer networks, forms the backbone of this communications network, available to anyone with a screen and a cable, satellite, cellular or telephone connection to the system.

"I'm going back to my room, where the media is a little less mainstream."

The Sender (Internet Service Providers)

Internet service providers (***ISP***s), such as America Online (AOL) and MSN, provide a way of organizing the information so it's easier to find what you want. Today's broadcast networks and cable and satellite channels already have become video program services, offering a group of programs for a specific subscription fee.

These program services are moving toward a different model, however, which will make it possible for you to choose programs from NBC and ABC and not CBS, for example, or pick 10 channels from a list of available channels, rather than having to accept a large number of channels—many that you don't necessarily want to watch—packaged together as they are now. When the complete communications network is in place, the ISP will offer program ***bundles***, and you will be able to select the specific bundle you want.

The Message (Content)

All text, audio and video that are digitized into bits are potential content for a digitized communications system. In a world of networked, rapid, digitized communications, *any* digitized textbook, novel, movie, magazine article, recording, video segment or news story, for example, qualifies as content.

Information and entertainment that already have been produced, stored and digitized form the basic content for this communications network. Companies that hold the copyrights on information and entertainment can quickly and easily market the content they already own as products, along with the ongoing information/entertainment they are producing, because they own the rights to their content and don't have to buy the rights from someone else.

Today, media companies that traditionally have produced content, such as newspaper publishers, book publishers, TV program producers and movie producers, are busy creating and buying more "inventory" for the online world. "Movie companies have been increasing production," says *The Wall Street Journal*, "because there is a general feeling that as 'content providers' they will be big winners."

Once information and entertainment products are digitized, they are available in many different formats. This is the reason a music video of Disney songs is available online as soon as—even before—Disney releases a new movie; a profile of a well-known musician, complete with video and sound, can be made available on the musician's Internet site during the musician's worldwide concert tour; and a publisher can assemble excerpts and photos from a new book, along with a video interview with the author, and make them available on the Internet to promote the book before it hits the bookstores. With convergence, the availability of digital content means all the mass media industries have become interdependent and interconnected.

Internet An international web of computer networks.

ISP Internet service provider.

Bundles A collection of programs and/or media services offered together for a set fee.

AFP/Getty Images

Satellite companies compete with cable, telephone and cellular companies to deliver all types of media to consumers worldwide. In June 2008, fans of the German national football team living in Berlin's Sozialpalast apartments who wanted to watch live coverage of their team competing in the Euro 2008 Championship needed individual satellite dishes for each apartment.

Selective Perception The concept that each person processes messages differently.

Mass Media Both Reflect and Affect Politics, Society and Culture

The media industries provide information and entertainment, but media also can affect political, social and cultural institutions. Although the media actively influence society, they also mirror it, and scholars constantly strive to delineate the differences.

For example, when the advertising industry suddenly started using patriotic themes to market products after the U.S. military moved into Iraq in 2003, was the industry pandering to the public, or were advertisers proudly reflecting genuine American sentiment, or both? Did the spread of patriotic advertising themes silence those who disagreed with the government? What role did the mass media play in setting the political agenda? If you were a scholar studying the mass media, how would you view these developments?

This is an example of the difficulty scholars face when analyzing the media's political, social and cultural effects. Early media studies analyzed each message in the belief that once a message was sent, everyone would receive and react to the message in the same way. Then studies proved that different people process messages differently—a phenomenon described as *selective perception*. This occurs because everyone brings many variables—family background, interests and education, for example—to each message.

Complicating the study of the media's political, social and cultural effects is the recent proliferation of media outlets. The multiplying sources for information and entertainment today mean that very few people share identical mass media environments. This makes it much more difficult for scholars to determine the specific or cumulative effects of mass media on the general population.

Still, scholars' attempts to describe media's political, social and cultural roles in society are important because, once identified, the effects can be observed. The questions should be posed so we do not become complacent about media in our lives, so we do not become immune to the possibility that our society may be cumulatively affected by media in ways we cannot yet identify.

"Marketers used to try their hardest to reach people at home, when they were watching TV or reading newspapers or magazines. But consumers' viewing and reading habits are so scattershot now that many advertisers say the best way to reach time-pressed consumers is to try to catch their eye at literally every turn," reports *The New York Times*.

According to the market research firm Yankelovich, a person living in a city 30 years ago saw up to 2,000 ad messages a day, compared with up to 5,000 today. According to *The New York Times*, "about half the 4,110 people surveyed . . . by Yankelovich said they thought marketing and advertising today was out of control."

Why You Should Understand Mass Media and Everyday Life

In the United States and other countries such as Japan and China that have encouraged technological advancements, communication changes are moving faster than ever before. For the media industries, this means increasing costs to replace old equipment. For consumers, this means a confusing array of products that need to be replaced soon after you buy them—DVD players replacing VCRs, HDTV replacing conventional TVs and iPods replacing CD players, for example.

The development of communications technology directly affects the speed with which a society and culture evolve. A town with only one telephone or one radio may be impossible for people in the United States to imagine, but there still are many countries in which 10 families share a single telephone and people consider a television set to be a luxury.

By today's standards, the earliest communications obstacles seem unbelievably simple: how to transmit a single message to several people at the same time and how to share information inexpensively. Yet it has taken nearly 5,500 years to achieve the capability for instant communication that we enjoy today.

After you understand how each type of media business works, you can examine why people who work in the media make the business decisions they do and the effects these decisions have on the U.S. and the world economy. Once you have traced the history of mass media development, you can consider their present-day effects on you and on society as a whole.

With a better grasp of technology's role in the evolving mass media landscape, you can see how technological change affects the media business. Only then can you truly begin to analyze the *impact* of mass media on your everyday life.

Review, Analyze, Investigate
REVIEWING CHAPTER 1

Mass Media Are Everywhere You Are

✓ Adults spend more than half of their waking lives with the media.

✓ Some form of media touches your life every day—economically, socially and culturally.

Mass Communication Becomes Wireless

✓ Historically, to be connected to media meant that you had to be near an electrical outlet.

✓ Because of the development of digital communication, most of today's mass media is wireless.

✓ Electronic signals have replaced wires, freeing people up to stay connected no matter where or when they want to communicate.

How the Communication Process Works

✓ Communication is the act of sending ideas and attitudes from one person to another.

✓ *Intra*personal communication means communication within one person.

✓ *Inter*personal communication means communication between two people.

✓ Mass communication is communication from one person or group of persons through a transmitting device (a medium) to large audiences or markets.

✓ By definition, mass communication is information that is made available to a large audience quickly.

What Are the Mass Media Industries?

✓ There are eight mass media businesses: books, newspapers, magazines, recordings, radio, movies, television and the Internet.

✓ Books were the first mass medium.

✓ The Internet is the newest mass medium.

Three Key Concepts to Remember

✓ Mass media are profit-centered businesses.

✓ Technological developments change the way mass media are delivered and consumed.

✓ Mass media both reflect and affect politics, society and culture.

Mass Media Are Profit-Centered Businesses

✓ All U.S. media are privately owned except the Public Broadcasting Service and National Public Radio, which survive on government support and private donations.

✓ Overall, American mass media ownership has been contracting rather than expanding, with fewer companies owning more aspects of the media business. This trend is called *concentration of ownership*.

✓ Concentration of ownership takes four forms: chains, broadcast networks, conglomerates and vertical integration.

✓ The mass media industries—books, newspapers, magazines, recordings, radio, movies, television and the Internet—earn about $436 billion a year.

✓ Above all, the major goal of the American mass media is to make money. Except for National Public Radio and the Public Broadcasting Service, all U.S. media operate primarily as profit-centered businesses.

Competition and Convergence Dominate

✓ Media acquisitions in the United States have skyrocketed because most conglomerates today are publicly traded companies and because, beginning in 1980, the federal government deregulated the broadcast industry.

✓ The economic downturn that began in 2007 made publicly owned newspapers especially vulnerable to takeovers and acquisitions.

✓ The trend of mergers and acquisitions is expected to continue as changing technology expands the global market for media products.

Why Media Properties Converge

✓ U.S. media industries continue to prosper, but the share of profits is shifting among the different types of media industries.

✓ Supporters of concentrated ownership and convergence say a large company offers advantages that a small company can never afford; critics say concentrated ownership and convergence interfere with message pluralism.

Advertisers and Consumers Pay the Bills

✓ Most of the income the mass media industries collect comes from advertising.

✓ People who want to sell you products pay for most of the information and entertainment you receive through the American mass media.

✓ Consumers support the media indirectly by buying the products that advertisers sell.

Technology Changes Mass Media Delivery and Consumption

✓ The invention of phonetic writing in 1000 B.C. was considered the *first information communications revolution*.

✓ The invention of movable type in 1455 marked the *second information communications revolution*.

✓ The invention of digital computers in 1951 ushered in the *third information communications revolution*.

✓ The new world of mass media uses wireless communications technology, an intricate webbed network of many different types of communications systems.

✓ The development of communications technology directly affects the speed with which a society evolves.

✓ Storability, portability and accessibility of information are essential to today's concept of mass communication.

Media Take Advantage of Digital Delivery

✓ Today's information network uses broadcast, telephone, cable, satellite and computer technology.

✓ The traditional delivery system for information and entertainment is primarily a one-way system.

✓ The ability to talk back—to receive as well as transmit messages—makes the telephone interactive.

✓ Today's communications network is a two-way, interactive system.

How Today's Communications Network Operates

✓ The communications network needs content, two-way digital communication and digital storage.

✓ Cable companies, satellite services, telephone and cellular companies deliver services on the new communications network.

✓ Many Americans already have all the tools that such a digital communications system needs—television, telephone, cellular, cable and satellite services and computers.

✓ Information and entertainment that already have been produced, stored and digitized have become the first content on the communications network.

✓ Many motives shape the American media, including the desire to fulfill the public's need for information, to influence the country's governance, to disseminate the country's culture, to offer entertainment and to provide an outlet for creative expression.

✓ Different media expand and contract in the marketplace to respond to the audience.

Mass Media Both Reflect and Affect Politics, Society and Culture

✓ The media are political, social and cultural institutions that both reflect and affect the society in which they operate.

✓ Multiplying sources of information and entertainment mean that, today, very few people share identical mass media environments.

Why You Should Understand Mass Media and Everyday Life

✓ In the United States and other countries such as Japan and China that have encouraged technological advancements, communication changes are moving faster than ever before.

✓ For the media industries, this means increasing costs to replace old equipment. For consumers, this means a confusing array of products that need to be replaced soon after you buy them.

✓ The development of communications technology directly affects the speed with which a society and culture evolve.

✓ It has taken nearly 5,500 years to achieve the capability for instant communication that we enjoy today.

KEY TERMS

These terms are defined in the margins throughout this chapter and appear in alphabetical order with definitions in the Glossary, which begins on page 372.

Affiliates 13

Bundles 23

Concentration of
  Ownership 12

Conglomerates 13

Convergence 14

Deregulation 15

Digital Communication 19

E-mail 19

FCC 13

Feedback 9

Interactive 19

Internet 23

ISP 23

Mass Communication 8

Mass Media Industries 9

Media 8

Medium 8

Message Pluralism 15

Noise 9

Phonetic Writing 16

Pictograph 16

Selective Perception 24

Subscription Television 11

Vertical Integration 14

Wi-Fi 7

CRITICAL QUESTIONS

1. Explain the differences between one-way and two-way communication, and explain why two-way communication is important for the new communications network.

2. Give three examples of how consumers pay both directly and indirectly for mass media in America.

3. Identify the three communications revolutions and discuss how each one drastically changed the world's mass media.

4. Summarize the advantages and disadvantages of the concentration of ownership in today's mass media business.

5. In traditional media, advertising aimed at consumers pays for delivery of entertainment and information. How has advertising's role changed on the digital communications network?

WORKING THE WEB

This list includes both sites mentioned in the chapter and others to give you greater insight into mass media and everyday life.

CBS Corporation
http://www.cbscorporation.com

Formed in 2005 from the separation of Viacom, CBS Corporation has operations in virtually every field of media and entertainment. The company consists of mass media brands including CBS Television Network, CBS Radio, Showtime, Simon & Schuster publishers, The CW (a joint venture with Warner Bros. Entertainment) and CBS Outdoor (out-of-home advertising). CBS Corp. also owns CBS Outernet (in-store media networks to grocery retailers) and CBS Interactive (its digital division).

Gannett Company, Inc. (owners of *USA Today*)
http://www.gannett.com

The United States' largest newspaper chain, Gannett publishes 85 daily newspapers, including *USA Today*, with a circulation of approximately 2.3 million. Usatoday.com is one of the most popular news sites on the Web. The company operates 23 U.S. television stations and has made strategic investments and partnerships in online advertising and marketing. Gannett's broadcasting group also delivers news and advertising to specific audiences through video screens in office building elevators and select hotels in North America.

General Electric (major owner of NBC Universal)
http://www.ge.com

This conglomerate has many businesses that include financial, industrial and health care operations in addition to its media and entertainment division. GE began in the 19th century with Thomas Edison's invention of the light bulb and continues to innovate by developing more energy-efficient products and services worldwide.

News Corporation
http://www.newscorp.com

News Corporation is Rupert Murdoch's diversified media empire and home of the various Fox media. Its operations include filmed entertainment, television, cable, satellite TV, magazines, newspapers and books. The company began in Australia and has many media outlets there and in Europe and Asia, as well as in the United States. News Corporation owns MySpace, the world's premier lifestyle and social-networking site, as part of Fox Interactive Media, and in 2007 bought *The Wall Street Journal*.

Sony Corporation of America
http://www.sony.com

This U.S. subsidiary of Sony Corporation is based in New York City. Its parent company, based in Tokyo, Japan, is a leading manufacturer of audio, video, communications and information technology. In the United States, Sony's principal businesses include Sony Electronics, Sony Pictures and a 50 percent interest in Sony BMG Music Entertainment (50 percent is owned by Bertelsmann AG).

Time Warner
http://www.timewarner.com

A leading media and entertainment company, Time Warner Inc.'s businesses include cable and broadcast television; interactive services; filmed entertainment; and publishing. In addition to entertainment companies (HBO, CNN and Warner Bros.), Time Warner also owns AOL and investment and global media groups.

Tribune Company
http://www.tribune.com

America's largest employee-owned media company, Tribune operates businesses in publishing, interactive and broadcast media. The company's leading daily newspapers include the *Los Angeles Times*, the *Chicago Tribune* and the *Baltimore Sun*. Its broadcasting group operates 23 television stations, WGN cable and the Chicago Cubs baseball team. News and information Web sites complement Tribune's print and broadcast properties.

U.S. Census Bureau Statistical Abstract: Information and Communications
http://www.census.gov/compendia/statab/cats/information_communications.html

This source presents statistics on the various information and communications media: publishing, motion pictures, recordings, broadcasting, telecommunications and information services such as libraries. Internet-use statistics also are included.

Viacom, Inc. (owners of MTV, BET and Paramount Pictures)
http://viacom.com

This spun-off publicly traded company was formerly known as the Viacom Corporation before it split from CBS in 2005. Its well-known cable networks and entertainment brands include Nickelodeon, Nick at Nite, Comedy Central and CMT: Country Music Television. Viacom, Inc. also owns Rhapsody, a membership-based music service, and Shockwave, a library of Web-based and mobile games.

Walt Disney Company (owners of ABC)
http://corporate.disney.go.com

This vertically integrated entertainment pioneer began as an animated cartoon studio in 1923. Today, Disney is divided into four major business segments: Studio Entertainment (Walt Disney Pictures, Touchstone Pictures and Miramax Films); Parks and Resorts; Consumer Products (including Disney Interactive Studios); and Media Networks (which includes the Disney-ABC Television Group, ESPN, Inc. and The Walt Disney Internet Group).

2

Books:
Rearranging the Page

Today, public libraries offer Internet access to vast collections of electronic resources as well as traditional printed books. At Boston's City Hall Plaza in June 2008, people line up at the Digital BookMobile to register for digital library cards, which allow customers to download books, music and films from the Boston Public Library.

What's Ahead?

"I'm not sure I can explain how to

write a book," said essayist and author E. B. White, who wrote 19 of them, including Charlotte's Web. "First you have to want to write one very much. Then, you have to know of something that you want to write about. Then, you have to begin. And, once you have started, you have to keep going. That's really all I know about how to write a book." The process of writing a book is

TimeFrame
1620 – Today

Book Publishing Becomes Big Business

1620 Imported books arrive in the colonies on the Mayflower.

1640 America's first book, *The Bay Psalm Book*, is printed at Cambridge, Massachusetts.

1731 Benjamin Franklin creates the first lending library.

1776 **Thomas Paine publishes the revolutionary pamphlet *Common Sense*.**

MPI/Stringer/Hulton Archive/Getty Images

1891 Congress passes the International Copyright Law of 1891, which requires publishing houses to pay royalties to foreign authors as well as American authors.

1900 **Elementary education becomes compulsory, which means increased literacy and more demand for textbooks.**

Margaret Bourke-White/Time & Life Pictures/Getty Images

1926 Book-of-the-Month Club is founded, increasing the audience for books.

1939 **Robert de Graff introduces Pocket Books, America's first series of paperback books.**

Transcendental Graphics/Getty Images

1948 New American Library begins publishing serious fiction by African American authors, including Richard Wright, Lillian Smith and Ralph Ellison.

1960 **Publishing houses begin to consolidate, concentrating power in a few large corporations, and decreasing the role of small presses and independent booksellers.**

Robert Holmes/CORBIS

1970s The most significant changes in book marketing begin with the growth of retail bookstore chains.

1980s Publishers begin producing audiobooks of popular titles.

1990s **Amazon.com begins doing business as an Internet retailer for books.**

Justin Sullivan/Getty Images

2000 Publishers launch e-books, electronic versions of paper books, which can be downloaded.

2004 Google announces the Google Book Project to scan the books of major research libraries and make their contents searchable.

Today Most books are sold through book chains and Internet retailers. Audiobooks are the only growing category of book sales, although publishers are trying to promote e-books, especially e-textbooks, as a cheaper, convenient alternative to traditional printed books.

a little more complex than White suggests, and every year in the United States publishers produce about 40,000 individual book titles. This number includes revised editions of previously published books, but most of the books are new.

Publishers Nurture Ideas and Try to Make Money

The publishing industry always has been tugged by what publishing scholars Lewis A. Coser, Charles Kadushin and Walter W. Powell call "the culture and commerce of publishing"—the desire to preserve the country's intellectual ideas versus the desire to make money. But a publisher who doesn't make a profit cannot continue to publish books.

Coser and his colleagues describe the four characteristics of book publishing in America today:

1. The industry sells its products—like any commodity—in a market that, in contrast to that for many other products, is fickle and often uncertain.

2. The industry is decentralized among a number of sectors whose operations bear little resemblance to each other.

3. A mixture of modern mass media production methods and craft-like procedures characterizes these operations.

4. The industry remains perilously poised between the requirements and restraints of commerce and the responsibilities and obligations that it must bear as a prime guardian of the symbolic culture of the nation.

Many new owners of publishing houses try to bring some predictability to the market. Says Coser, "Publishers attempt to reduce . . . uncertainty . . . through concentrating on 'surefire' blockbusters, through large-scale promotion campaigns or through control over distribution, as in the marketing of paperbacks. In the end, however, publishers rely on sales estimates that may be as unreliable as weather forecasts in Maine."

How American Book Publishing Grew

Today, the book publishing industry divides responsibilities among many people. But when Americans first started publishing books, one person often did all the work. Aboard the *Mayflower* in 1620, there were two dogs and 70 adults and only a few books. The pilgrims were very practical. They brought a map of Virginia and John Smith's *Description of New England*, but the main books they carried were their Bibles.

The first books in the United States were imports, brought by the new settlers or ordered from England after the settlers arrived. In 1638, the colonists set up a press at Cambridge, Massachusetts, and in 1640 they printed America's first book: *The Bay Psalm Book*. As the only book, it became an instant bestseller. There were only about 3,500 families in the colonies at the time, and the book's first printing of 1,750 sold out.

By 1680, Boston had 17 booksellers, but most of the books still came from England. Between 1682 and 1685, Boston's leading bookseller, John Usher, bought 3,421 books to sell. Among the books he ordered were 162 romance novels.

In 1731, Benjamin Franklin decided that Philadelphia needed a library. So he asked 50 subscribers to pay 40 shillings each to a Library Company. The company imported 84 books, which circulated among the subscribers. This circulating library was America's first.

The year after he established the circulating library, Franklin published *Poor Richard's Almanack*. Unlike most printers, who waited for someone to come to them with a manuscript, Franklin wrote his own books. The typical author sought a patron to pay for the book's printing and then sold the book at the print shop where it was published.

To expand readership, early publishers sold political pamphlets, novels, poetry and humor. In addition, three events of the 19th century ensured that the book publishing industry would prosper in the 20th century: the International Copyright Law, the creation of publishing houses and the establishment of compulsory education.

Political Pamphlets

The big seller of the 1700s was Thomas Paine's revolutionary pamphlet *Common Sense*, which argued for

WireImage/Getty Images

Novels with women as central characters have a long history of popularity with American readers, starting with the novel *Pamela*, first published in the United States in 1744. Women also are central characters in the contemporary novels of Nora Roberts, a bestselling author who often has two titles on *The New York Times'* bestseller list simultaneously.

United States' independence from Great Britain. From January to March 1776, colonial presses published 100,000 copies of Paine's persuasive political argument—one copy for every 25 people in the colonies—a true bestseller. Throughout the Revolutionary War, Paine was America's best-read author.

Novels and Poetry

Political pamphlets became much less important once the new nation was established, and printers turned their attention to other popular reading, especially fiction. Historians credit Benjamin Franklin with selling *Pamela* by Samuel Richardson in 1744, the first novel published in the United States, although it was a British import that first appeared in England in 1740.

Because there was no international copyright law, colonial printers freely reprinted British novels like *Pamela* and sold them. It was cheaper than publishing American authors, who could demand royalties. (See International Copyright Law of 1891.)

Like other media industries, book publishing has always faced moral criticism. Novels, for example, didn't start out with a good reputation. One critic said the novel "pollutes the imaginations." Women wrote one-third of all the early American novels, and women also bought most of them.

Especially popular after the Civil War and before the turn of the century were dime novels, America's earliest paperbacks. Dime novels often featured serial characters, like many of today's mystery novels. The stories and characters continued from one novel to the next. Eventually most of them cost only a nickel, but some early paperbacks were as expensive as 20 cents.

Poetry generally has been difficult to sell, and it is correspondingly difficult for poets to get published. Literary scholar James D. Hart says that although poetry was never as popular as prose, the mid-1800s was "the great era of poetry. . . . It was more widely read in those years than it has been since."

Humor

Humor has been a durable category in book publishing since the days of humorist Mark Twain. Made famous by his *Celebrated Jumping Frog of Calaveras County*, Twain became a one-man publishing enterprise. One reason his books sold well was that he was the first American author to recognize the importance of advance publicity. Like most books, Twain's novels were sold door-to-door. Sales agents took advance orders before the books were published so the publisher could estimate how many to print. Before 1900, more than three-fourths of the popular books people bought were sold door-to-door.

International Copyright Law of 1891

Before 1891, publishers were legally required to pay royalties to American authors, but not to foreign authors. This hurt American authors because books by American authors cost more to publish.

After the International Copyright Law of 1891, all authors—foreign and American—had to give permission to publish their works. For the first time, American authors cost publishing houses the same amount as foreign authors. This motivated publishers to look for more American writers. In fact, after 1894, American writers published more novels in the United States than foreign writers did.

Publishing Houses

Many publishing houses that began in the late 18th century or at some time during the 19th century continued into the 20th century. Nineteenth-century book publishing houses were just that—book publishing houses. They were nothing like today's multimedia corporations.

These pioneering companies housed all aspects of publishing under one roof: They sought out authors, reviewed and edited copy, printed and then sold the books.

Compulsory Education

By 1900, 31 states had passed compulsory education laws. This was important to book publishing because schools buy textbooks, and education creates more people who can read. Widespread public education meant that schools broadened their choices, and textbook publishing flourished (see **Impact/Business**, "A Textbook Ending? College Students Lured to Lower Costs of E-Texts," page 35). Expanded public support for education also meant more money for libraries—more good news for the publishing industry.

IMPACT
» Business

A Textbook Ending? College Students Lured to Lower Cost of E-Texts

by Bruce Mohl

The paper version of *Psychology*, a popular college textbook by David G. Myers, weighs nearly 5 pounds and costs roughly $90 new and $70 used. The digital version is easy on a backpack and costs $55.

Which would you choose?

CourseSmart LLC, a new company backed by the nation's biggest textbook publishers, is betting that many tech-savvy students looking to save some money will select the e-textbook.

The Belmont, Calif., company . . . offers about 2,000 e-textbooks now and hopes to have far more by next fall. But already Course-Smart is attracting considerable attention, particularly from college bookstores, which earn most of their revenue selling new and used textbooks and fear the publishers will sell directly to students and elbow them aside.

The National Association of College Book-stores issued a statement to its members last month saying it had directed its general counsel to review the antitrust implications of CourseSmart and the potential for the publishers to exercise "unreasonable control over the release and pricing of digital assets to the higher education marketplace."

Frank Lyman, executive vice president for marketing and business development at CourseSmart, said bookstores will continue to play a vital role in the textbook market, but he acknowledged the relationship between publishers and bookstores is changing.

Publishers are "not looking to cut out the bookstores, but certainly there's some shaking out of their relationship that's going to happen as we migrate to digital," he said.

That migration is still in its infancy, but there is a growing belief in publishing circles that electronic textbooks have a real change of catching on because of the savings, the convenience, and the features they have to offer.

Amanda L. Hyatt, a student at Viterbo University in La Cross, Wis., said she is accustomed to reading off a computer screen. But

Peter Hvizdak/Image Works

Publishers are beginning to offer e-textbooks directly to students, in competition with college bookstores that sell only paper texts. Although not widely available yet, the main advantage of e-textbooks, password-protected and downloaded through the Internet, is that they cost about half as much as traditional paper texts.

(continued)

IMPACT

>> **Business**

A Textbook Ending? College Students Lured to Lower Cost of E-Texts *(continued)*

she said it was still a "bit of an adjustment" studying an e-textbook.

"It's nice to have that solid book in our hands," she said. "With an e-textbook, you almost feel like you're not able to pull that information close to you."

Still, Hyatt said, she would probably buy another e-textbook and thinks students increasingly will go digital because that's the direction society in general is moving. . . .

The format of e-textbooks is still evolving. CourseSmart's product allows the user to highlight passages, type notes in the margins, and even search the text for a specific word or phrase. Users access CourseSmart books at the company's password-protected Web site, so Web access is essential. Lyman said CourseSmart will eventually sell downloadable books and possibly even downloadable chapters. . . .

Price is perhaps the biggest selling point for electronic textbooks. Textbooks currently cost students on average about $940 a year, or nearly $4,000 over four years. Course-Smart typically sells e-textbooks at half the price of a new paper textbook . . .

Jerry Murphy, president of the Harvard Cooperative Society, which sells textbooks to many students in Greater Boston, said the concept of e-textbooks hasn't been proven yet. He said few titles are available electronically and relatively few students are asking for them.

"A lot of people, for whatever reason, like to have touchy-feely paper," he said.

Cheaper Books Create a Mass Market

The first quarter of the 20th century enabled still more publishing houses, such as Simon & Schuster and McGraw-Hill, to meet the public's needs. Publishers that specialized in paperbacks started in the 1930s and 1940s: Pocket Books (1939), Bantam Books (1946) and New American Library (1948). If you drop a product's price drastically, sales can explode. That's exactly what happened to book publishing with the introduction of book clubs and paperbacks, beginning in the 1920s.

Book Clubs

Book clubs replaced door-to-door sales agents as a way to reach people who otherwise wouldn't buy books. Book-of-the-Month Club was founded in 1926, and Literary Guild in 1927. By 1946, there were 50 book clubs in America, and the Book-of-the-Month Club was selling nearly 12 million copies a year.

Paperbacks

In 1939, Robert de Graff introduced America's first series of paperback bestsellers, called Pocket Books, which issued titles that had already succeeded as hardbound books. They were inexpensive (25 cents), and they fit in a pocket or a purse. Suddenly, a book could reach millions of people who had never owned a book before. Paperbacks democratized reading in America.

The books were so small, however, that people at first thought paperback books were shortened versions of the original. So publishers printed messages to readers on the cover to assure them that the paperbacks were the "complete novel, as originally published."

More publishers joined Pocket Books to produce paperbacks: New American Library (NAL), Avon, Popular Library, Signet and Dell. NAL distinguished itself by being the first mass market publisher willing to issue serious books by African American writers—Richard Wright's *Native Son*, Lillian Smith's *Strange Fruit* and Ralph Ellison's *Invisible Man*. Signet's unexpected hit in the 1950s was J. D. Salinger's novel *Catcher in the Rye*, still popular today.

Grove Press Tests Censorship

Book publishers have always resisted any attempts by the government to limit freedom of expression. One of the first publishers to test those limits was Grove Press. In 1959, Grove published the sexually explicit *Lady Chatterley's Lover* by D. H. Lawrence (originally published in Italy in 1928); in 1961, the company published *Tropic of Cancer* by Henry Miller (originally published in Paris in 1934). Both books had been banned from the United States as obscene. The legal fees to defend Miller's book against charges of pornography cost Grove more than $250,000, but eventually the U.S. Supreme Court cleared the book in 1964.

The publisher again challenged conventional publishing in 1965, when it issued in hardback the controversial *The Autobiography of Malcolm X*, the story of the leader of the African American nationalist movement, by Alex Haley, as told by Malcolm X. The book became a bestseller.

Investors Buy Up Publishing Companies

Forecasts for growing profits in book publishing in the 1960s made the industry attractive to corporations looking for new places to invest. Before the 1960s, the book publishing industry was composed mainly of independent companies whose only business was books. Then, rising school and college attendance from the post–World War II baby boom made some areas of publishing, especially textbooks, lucrative investments for media companies that had not published books before.

Beginning in the 1960s, publishing companies began to consolidate. Publishing expert John P. Dessauer says, "Publishing stocks, particularly those of educational companies, became glamour holdings. And conglomerates began to woo every independent publisher whose future promised to throw off even a modest share of the forecast earnings." Dessauer acknowledges that the new owners often brought a businesslike approach to an industry that was known for its lack of attention to making a profit.

But, according to Dessauer, another consequence of these large scale acquisitions was that "in many cases they also placed the power of ultimate decision and policymaking in the hands of people unfamiliar with books, their peculiarities and the markets." The same pace of acquisitions continued through the end of the 20th century, and today large media corporations own many of the book publishing companies.

Book Publishing at Work

When authors get together, often they tell stories about mistakes publishers have made—about manuscripts that 20 or 30 publishers turned down but that some bright-eyed editor eventually discovered and published. The books, of course, then become bestsellers. Some of the stories are true. But the best publishing decisions are made deliberately, to deliver an awaited book to an eager market. Successful publishing companies must consistently anticipate both their competitors and the market.

Not only must books be written, but they also must be printed, they must be promoted and they must be sold. This whole process usually takes at least 18 months from the time a project is signed by an editor until the book is published, so publishers are always working ahead. The classic publisher's question is, "Will someone pay $25 (or whatever the projected price of the book is) for this book 18 months after I sign the author?"

Authors and Agents: Where Books Begin

Publishers acquire books in many ways. Some authors submit manuscripts "over the transom," which means they send an unsolicited manuscript to a publishing house, hoping the publisher will be interested. However, many of the nation's larger publishers refuse to read unsolicited manuscripts and accept only books that agents submit.

Publishers pay authors a ***royalty*** for their work. A royalty amount is based on an established percentage of the book's price and may run anywhere from 6 to 15 percent of the cover price of the book. Some authors receive an ***advance***, which is an amount the publisher pays the author before the book is published. Royalties the book earns once it is in print then are charged against the advance payment, so the book first must sell enough copies to pay off the advance

Royalty An amount the publisher pays an author, based on an established percentage of the book's price; royalties run anywhere from 6 to 15 percent.

Advance An amount the publisher pays the author before the book is published.

Book designers use digital technology to help them create the way a book looks inside and outside.

before the author gets additional money once the book is published.

Agents who represent authors collect fees from the authors they represent. Typically, an agent's fee is 10 to 15 percent of the author's royalty. If a publisher priced a book at $20, for example, the author would receive from $2 to $3 per book, depending on the author's agreement with the publisher; the agent would then receive 20 to 45 cents of the author's $2 to $3, depending on the agent's agreement with the author.

How Do Books Get Published?

In most cases, books start with the *author*, who proposes a book to an acquisitions editor, usually with an outline and some sample chapters. Sometimes an agent negotiates the contract for the book, but many authors negotiate their own contracts. Today the author is only one part of publishing a book. Departments at the publishing house called *acquisi-*

Subsidiary Rights The rights to market a book for other uses—to make a movie or to print a character from the book on T-shirts, for example.

tions, *production*, *design*, *manufacturing*, *marketing* and *fulfillment* all participate in the process. At a small publishing house, these jobs are divided among editors who are responsible for all the steps.

The *acquisitions editor* looks for potential authors and projects and works out an agreement with the author. The acquisitions editor's most important role is to be a liaison among the author, the publishing company and the book's audience. Acquisitions editors also may represent the company at book auctions and negotiate sales of **subsidiary rights**, which are the rights to market a book for other uses—to make a movie, for example, or to print a character from the book on T-shirts.

The *production editor* manages all the steps that turn a double-spaced typewritten manuscript into a book. After the manuscript comes in, the production editor sets up a schedule and makes sure that all of the work gets done on time.

The *designer* decides what a book will look like, inside and out. The designer chooses the typefaces for the book and determines how the pictures, boxes, heads and subheads will look and where to use color. The designer also creates a concept—sometimes more than one—for the book's cover.

The *manufacturing supervisor* buys the typesetting, paper and printing for the book. The book usually is sent outside the company to be manufactured.

Marketing, often the most expensive part of creating a book, is handled by several different departments. *Advertising* designs ads for the book. *Promotion* sends the book to reviewers. Sales representatives visit bookstores and college campuses to tell book buyers and potential adopters about the book.

Fulfillment makes sure that the books get to the bookstores on time. This department watches inventory so that if the publisher's stock gets low, more books can be printed.

Twenty thousand American companies call themselves book publishers today, but only about 2,000 publishing houses produce more than four titles a year. Most publishing houses are small: 80 percent of all book publishers have fewer than 20 employees.

Today, adult and juvenile trade books account for almost half of the books people buy, and textbooks make up about a third of all books sold. The rest are religious books and mass market paperbacks. The number of new books and new editions has stabilized, but publishers are charging more for each book. Today, paperbacks and hardbacks cost nearly three times what they cost 30 years ago.

Book Industry Has Five Major Markets

Books fall into five major categories. These classifications once described the publishing houses that produced different types of books. A company that was called a textbook publisher produced only textbooks, for example. Today, one publishing house often publishes several different kinds of books, although they may have separate divisions for different types of books and markets. (See **Illustration 2.1**.)

Trade Books

Usually sold through bookstores and to libraries, trade books are designed for the general public. These books include hardbound books and trade (or "quality") paperbound books for adults and children. Typical trade books include hardcover fiction, current nonfiction, biography,

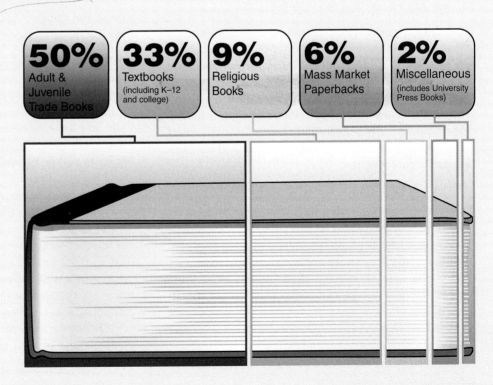

IMPACT
≫ Business

Illustration 2.1

How Do Book Publishers Make Their Money?

Most of the books people buy are adult and juvenile trade books, but textbooks (kindergarten through 12th grade and college) account for a substantial percentage of the book market.

Source: Book Industry Study Group, *Publishers Weekly,* June 2, 2008.

50% Adult & Juvenile Trade Books

33% Textbooks (including K–12 and college)

9% Religious Books

6% Mass Market Paperbacks

2% Miscellaneous (includes University Press Books)

literary classics, cookbooks, travel books, art books and books on sports, music, poetry and drama. Many college classes use trade books as well as textbooks. Juvenile trade books can be anything from picture books for children who can't read yet to novels for young adults.

Textbooks

Textbooks are published for elementary and secondary school students (called the "el-hi" market) as well as for college students. Most college texts are paid for by the students but are chosen by their professors.

Very little difference exists between some college texts and some trade books. The only real difference between many textbooks and trade books is that texts include what publishers call *apparatus*—for example, test questions, chapter summaries and CDs with extra assignments. The difference may be difficult to discern, so the Association of American Publishers classifies these two types of books (that is, trade books and textbooks) according to where they are sold the most. A book that is sold mainly through college bookstores, for example, is called a textbook.

Religious Books

Hymnals, Bibles and prayer books fall into the category of religious books. Recently, religious publishers have begun to issue books about social issues from a religious point of view, but these books are considered trade books, not religious books.

Mass Market Paperbacks

Here, definitions get tricky. These books are defined not by their subjects but by where they are sold. Although you also can find them in bookstores, *mass market books* are mainly distributed through "mass" channels—newsstands, chain stores, drugstores and supermarkets—and usually are "rack-sized." Many are reprints of hardcover trade books; others are originally published as mass market paperbacks. Generally, they're made from cheaper paper and cost less than trade paperbacks.

University Press Books and Book Clubs

University presses publish a small number of books every year and are defined solely by who publishes them: A university press book is one that a university press publishes. Most university presses are nonprofit and are connected to a university, museum or research institution. These presses produce mainly scholarly materials in hardcover and soft-

Mass Market Books Books distributed through "mass" channels—newsstands, chain stores, drugstores and supermarkets.

Blockbuster A book that achieves enormous financial success.

cover. Most university press books are sold through direct mail and in college bookstores.

Book clubs publish and sell books directly to a select audience. Although they were once very popular, book clubs today represent a very small portion of the book market.

Corporations Demand Higher Profits

Consolidation in the book business means the giants in today's publishing industry are demanding increasingly higher profits. The companies look for extra income in three ways: subsidiary and international rights, blockbuster books and chain and Internet bookstore marketing.

Subsidiary and International Rights

Trade and mass market publishers are especially interested in, and will pay more for, books with the potential for subsidiary and international rights sales. The rights to make a CD version of a book, for example, are subsidiary rights.

In the 19th century, the number of copies of books that individual readers bought determined a book's profit. Today, profits come from the sale of subsidiary rights to movie companies, book clubs, foreign publishers and paperback reprint houses. The same rights govern whether a character in a book becomes a star on the front of a T-shirt or a video game. For some publishing houses, subsidiary-rights sales and international-rights sales make the difference between making a profit and going out of business.

Blockbusters

Selling a lot of copies of one book is easier and cheaper than selling a few copies of many books. This is the concept behind publishers' eager search for *blockbuster* books. Publishers are attracted to best-selling authors because usually they are easy to market. A "brand loyalty" among many readers draws these loyal readers to buy every book by a favorite author, so publishers try to capitalize on an author's popularity in the same way movie producers seek out stars who have made successful films.

Judith Krantz, who received $3.2 million for paperback rights to her sex-filled *Princess Daisy*, explains the benefits of being a blockbuster author: "I'm no Joan Didion—there are no intelligent, unhappy people in my books. I want to be known as a writer of good, entertaining narrative. I'm not trying to be taken seriously by the East Coast literary establishment. But I'm taken very seriously by the bankers."

Following are some amounts that publishers and moviemakers have paid for blockbusters:

- In 2007, Carnegie Mellon Professor Randy Pausch reportedly received a $7 million advance for his book, *The Last Lecture*. (See **Impact/People**, "Dying of Cancer, but Full of Life Lessons: Author Randy Pausch," page 41.)

IMPACT
» People

Note: In September 2007, Professor Randy Pausch, of Carnegie Mellon University, was asked to give his "Last Lecture." Pausch, then 46, who had learned a year earlier that he was dying of pancreatic cancer, spoke to 400 people at Carnegie Mellon. A columnist from The Wall Street Journal *wrote a small story about the event, and the* Journal *posted a video of the lecture along with the story. Within 24 hours, news about the lecture and Pausch's message spread across the nation and the world, with the help of the Internet. Pausch then wrote a book about his life and the lecture, and his book,* The Last Lecture, *became a bestseller.*

Dying of Cancer, but Full of Life Lessons: Author Randy Pausch

by Vincent M. Mallozzi

Pittsburgh wide receiver Hines Ward arrived for this month's Steelers minicamp with two books tucked in his duffel bag: the team's playbook and a copy of *The Last Lecture*, co-written by Randy Pausch, who left his job as a computer science professor at Carnegie Mellon University last September [2007].

"Randy is an inspiration," Ward said by telephone last week. "He told me he's one of my biggest fans, and I told him that I'm one of his."

In September 2006, Pausch learned he had pancreatic cancer, a disease that is usually fatal within months of diagnosis. A year later, he used 76 minutes of borrowed time to talk to 400 spectators in Pittsburgh about the joys of living and reaching goals.

The lecture, which Pausch titled "Really Achieving Your Childhood Dreams," became an Internet phenomenon, with millions viewing it on YouTube. It was also the basis for the best-selling book, written with Jeffrey Zaslow, a columnist for *The Wall Street Journal*.

"I know the book is doing really well, but the only three copies that really mean anything to me are the ones that went to my children," Pausch, 47, said in a telephone interview last week from his home in Chesapeake, Va. "The rest is all gravy."

In the book, Pausch writes about his childhood fantasies. He grew up in Columbia, Md., wishing he could be Captain Kirk, experience the thrill of floating in zero gravity and play in the NFL.

A month after his last lecture, the Steelers made a little piece of Pausch's NFL dream come true, inviting him to a practice. Pausch showed up wearing Ward's No. 86 jersey and huddled with Ward, quarterback Ben Roethlisberger, safety Troy Polamalu and Coach Mike Tomlin.

"I promised them that if they got to the Super Bowl, I'd be around to see it," Pausch said with a chuckle. "Well, at least I kept my end of the bargain."

At practice, Pausch raced onto the field and began running pass routes, often diving for balls tossed by Ward.

"It was fantastic beyond my wildest dreams," Pausch said.

Under the tutelage of kicker Jeff Reed, Pausch made a field goal on his only attempt, a 20-yarder that created a buzz on the field.

"Randy was having so much fun, he was actually teaching us a lesson that day," Ward said. "He reminded us that we should never take anything for granted because nothing

(continued)

IMPACT
»» People

Dying of Cancer, but Full of Life Lessons: Author Randy Pausch (continued)

Danielle Hudak/The Pittsburgh Steelers

Professor Randy Pausch's book, *The Last Lecture*, became an instant bestseller when it was published in 2008. The book was based on a lecture Professor Pausch, dying from pancreatic cancer, was asked to give at Pittsburgh's Carnegie Mellon University in 2007. Video of the lecture, shared on YouTube, made Pausch an overnight celebrity, although he did not invite the attention. A month later, the Pittsburgh Steelers invited Pausch (in the center, flanked by Steelers Coach Mike Tomlin, left, and Hines Ward) to live out his lifelong dream of playing with the NFL. Pausch died on July 25, 2008.

is promised to us, and that we should enjoy every moment of our lives, on and off the football field."

Two weeks ago, Pausch thanked Ward by sending him an autographed copy of *The Last Lecture*. On May 2 [2008], at the start of a three-day minicamp, Ward called Pausch.

"He was on my mind, and I just wanted to see how he was doing," Ward said. "It's kind of difficult talking to a man you know is going to die, but with Randy, he's always so positive, he never seems to get down. He has a truly

amazing spirit. Here's a man who knows his time on earth is short, and yet he has written a book that has given me and so many others a greater appreciation for life. It takes a courageous human being to do something like that."

During their 15-minute conversation, Pausch gave Ward his version of the last pep talk.

"I told Hines that I wasn't so sure I'd be around for another Super Bowl," said Pausch, who has developed congestive heart failure and kidney failure in the last two months. "I told him to keep playing hard and to step up and be a mentor to the younger guys on the team. I told him that it's important to lead, and live, by example."

Ward said that for the rest of his career and beyond, he would hold on tight to a line from Pausch's book: "We cannot change the cards we are dealt, just how we play the hand."

Pausch said he was trying to play out his hand "with the dignity of an athlete at the end of a great career."

"There are times at the end of games when you look up at the scoreboard and do not like what you see, and this is one of those times," he added. "I'm hanging in there, trying to spend as much quality time with my wife and kids as possible, and though it's very frustrating to know I won't beat the cancer, there's a great satisfaction in knowing that I'm walking off the field with no regrets. There's nothing about my life that I would have changed."

- Alan Greenspan, the former chairman of the Federal Reserve, received an $8.5 million advance in 2007 for his memoir, *The Age of Turbulence*.

- Hillary Rodham Clinton received an $8 million advance for her memoir, *Living History*.

- Mystery writer Mary Higgins Clark received a $35 million advance from Simon & Schuster for six books. Simon & Schuster says that 22 million copies of Clark's books are in print in the United States.

Only the big publishing houses can afford such a bidding game. Some publishers have even developed computer models to suggest how high to bid for a book and still make a profit, but these high-priced properties are a very small part of book publishing, perhaps 1 percent. The majority of editors and writers rarely get involved in an argument over seven-figure advances. Many authors would be pleased to see five-figure advances in a contract.

Some critics believe that what has been called a *blockbuster complex* among publishing houses hurts authors who aren't included in the bidding. One Harper & Row editor told *The Wall Street Journal* that seven-figure advances "divert money away from authors who really need it and center attention on commercial books instead of less commercial books that may nonetheless be better. God help poetry or criticism."

Chain bookstores, such as Borders and Barnes & Noble, account for more than half of bookstore sales of trade books, and authors recognize that chain bookstore appearances boost sales and visibility. *CSI: New York* star Hill Harper and movie star Gabrielle Union appear together to sign his new book *Letters to a Young Sister: DeFINE Your Destiny* at Borders Books and Music in Chicago in June 2008.

Chain Bookstores and Internet Retailers Compete

The most significant changes in book marketing in the past 40 years have been the growth of bookstore chains and Internet retailers. The big chains, such as Borders and Barnes & Noble, account for more than half the bookstore sales of trade books. They have brought mass-marketing techniques to the book industry, offering book buyers an environment that is less like the traditional cozy atmosphere of a one-owner bookstore and more like a department store.

"The large chains are the power behind book publishing today," says Joan M. Ripley, a former president of the American Booksellers Association. "Blockbusters are going to be published anyway, but with a marginal book, like a volume of poetry, a chain's decision about whether to order it can sometimes determine whether the book is published."

Internet retailers, such as Amazon, are another big factor in book marketing. Internet retailers can buy in huge volume, and they buy books only from publishers that give them big discounts. Books that are published by smaller publishing houses, which usually cannot afford these large discounts, never reach the online buyer. For the blockbusters, issued by bigger houses, the Internet retailer is just one more outlet.

Like the resistance to book clubs when they first were introduced, the skepticism among book publishers about chain bookstores and Internet retailers has changed into an understanding that chain stores in shopping malls and Internet retailers have expanded the book market to people who didn't buy very many books before. But the competitive pricing that the Internet retailers bring emphasizes what can happen in an industry such as book publishing when a small number of companies control the distribution of an industry's products.

Small Presses Challenge Corporate Publishing

The nation's large publishing houses (those with 100 or more employees) publish 80 percent of the books sold each year, but some of the nation's publishers are small operations with fewer than 10 employees. These publishers are called *small*

I'VE GOT ALL THE WORDS I NEED FOR MY NOVEL, IT'S JUST A CASE OF PUTTING THEM IN THE RIGHT ORDER NOW!

Fran/Reprinted by permission of CartoonStock

presses, and they counterbalance the corporate world of large advances and multimedia subsidiary rights.

Small presses do not have the budgets of the large houses, but their size means they can specialize in specific topics, such as the environment or bicycling, or in specific types of writing that are unattractive to large publishers, such as poetry.

Small presses are, by definition, alternative. Many of them are clustered together in locations outside of the New York City orbit, such as Santa Fe, New Mexico, and Santa Barbara, California. The book titles they publish probably are not familiar: *Bicycle Technology: Technical Aspects of the Modern Bicycle* by Rob Van derPlas, published by Bicycle Books; *Nine-in-One, Grr! Grr!*, a Hmong folktale by Blia-Xiong and Cathy Spagnoli, published by Children's Book Press; *Warning! Dating May Be Hazardous to Your Health* by Claudette McShane, published by Mother Courage Press; or *48 Instant Letters You Can Send to Save the Earth* by Write for Action, published by Conari Press.

Still, some small presses and some small press books are quite successful. One example of a small press success

was *The Lemon Book* by Ralph Nader and Clarence Ditlow. This step-by-step guide to buying a car and what to do if you get a bad one grabbed the attention of the *Larry King Show*, *Good Morning America* and more than 50 other local TV and radio programs. The book sold 42,000 copies in its first year.

As *The Lemon Book* demonstrates, specialization and targeted marketing are the most important elements of small press success. However, because they have limited distribution capabilities, most small presses today struggle to survive.

Publishers Promote Audiobooks and Digital Alternatives

Always looking for more income from the content they own, book publishers are producing some books as audiobooks and electronic books.

AUDIOBOOKS. First introduced in the 1980s, *audiobooks* have been a growing sales category for book publishers. Book publishers produce classics and popular new titles on CDs for people who are more willing to listen to a book than to read it.

Some publishers think electronic books with links to databases for delivery of book content on a small screen will expand the market for books, but so far e-books have had a very limited market.

Audiobooks on CD are necessarily abridged copies of the originals because it takes too much space to record the entire book. One answer for longer books is MP3 technology, originally used on the Internet to share music. Digital formats such as MP3 mean consumers can download audiobooks, for a fee, from the Internet to be played in any portable device designed to play MP3 files.

ELECTRONIC BOOKS. The introduction of electronic books, or *e-books*, is the latest attempt by publishers to expand the market for their products. E-books are electronic versions of hardback or paperback books that can be downloaded and then read on a computer.

"As with digital music, multiple books—say, Shakespeare's collected works—can be stored on a memory card the size of a stick of gum, making them popular with travelers, students and professionals," says Reuters columnist Franklin Paul. According to software developer Adobe's Russell Brady, "Two audiences that will benefit best are young people who loathe the idea of a library . . . and aging people who want the convenience of large type on demand, or freedom from lugging heavy hardcover tomes.

Audiobooks Abridged versions of classic books and popular new titles on CDs.

E-books Electronic books.

"We think that in the long term, e-book technology has a great future. Market acceptance has not taken off quite as quickly as was predicted, but we are certainly continuing to invest in this area." Some publishers have expressed doubts that e-books will ever expand beyond a very small market, but independent companies continue to pursue the idea (see **Impact/Business**, "A Textbook Ending? College Students Lured to Lower Cost of E-Texts," page 35).

New Technologies Affect Production and Consumption

Technology is a major factor in most aspects of book publishing. Because books cost so much to publish, advances in technology can lower the cost of producing books, which benefits the industry.

Changes in Production

Technological advances in the last 20 years have led to six important changes in the way books are produced and promoted.

1. Because computers monitor inventories more closely, publishers can easily order new printings of books that are selling quickly so booksellers can keep the books in stock.

2. Book publishing is an on-screen industry. Publishers now receive most manuscripts from authors electronically via the Internet. Editors process the manuscripts on computers and then send the books into production online. This means books can be printed anywhere, often overseas.

3. Electronic graphics make books more interesting, and many book publishers are using CDs and DVDs to produce expanded versions of traditional books and to add materials that enhance a book's content and marketability.

4. Publishers are using Web sites to promote their books and to advertise blockbusters.

5. Large publishers are continuing to consolidate, and the number of small publishers is decreasing.

6. Many aspects of the publishing process, such as copyediting, photo research and even editing, are contracted to freelancers who work outside the publishing house. Because publishing can be done online, book projects can be managed from any location. This means that publishers have fewer in-house employees today and much of the work is contracted and sent overseas.

Changes in Consumption

In 2004, Google Inc. began to digitize millions of books to make them searchable online (see **Impact/Culture**, "Google Announces Massive Digital Book Project," page 46). This concept introduces a huge shift in the way books may be consumed in the future. Imagine a world in which every book ever written is available to search online. This is the vision of the Google Book Project, which contracted with several of the nation's libraries to scan the contents of the books the libraries hold so that eventually the books' contents will be available online. You could enter the word "romance," for instance, and call up a list of all the books in which the word had appeared. Or you could call up a famous phrase and trace its origin to the author who first used it.

This project, scheduled to take at least six years, is as controversial as it is ambitious. Authors and publishers have legal questions about copyright and royalties; booksellers wonder whether anyone will buy books if they're all available online; scholars wonder what will happen to the value of knowledge and information once it is searchable on such a wide scale. Still, Google says the company is committed to the project, which certainly will have wide-ranging consequences for the book publishing industry in the future. In 2008, Google paid $125 million to settle two copyright lawsuits brought by publishers and authors over the company's right to digitize books for online use. However, the settlement still "left unresolved the question of whether Google's unauthorized scanning of copyrighted books was permissible under copyright laws," according to *The New York Times*.

Book Publishing Is a Complex Business

Because book publishing has been in America's culture so long, the contrast between book publishing's simple beginnings and its complicated corporate life today is especially startling. This disparity may exist because Americans maintain a mistaken romantic idea about book publishing's early days, according to the authors of *The Culture and Commerce of Publishing*:

The myth is widespread that book publishing in the 19th and 20th centuries was a gentlemanly trade in which an editor catered to an author's every whim. . . . There once may have been more gentlemen in publishing than there are now, but there were surely sharp operators, hucksters and pirates galore. In publishing, as in many other spheres of social life, there is very little that is new.

IMPACT
»Culture

Google Announces Massive Digital Book Project

by Jon Van

Google Inc. will digitize up to 10 million books in university libraries at Northwestern University, the University of Chicago, University of Illinois campuses in Chicago and Urbana-Champaign and nine other Midwestern schools as part of its Book Search project.

The addition of the Midwestern libraries significantly expands a two-year effort to digitize library books so their contents may be searched online.

Adam Smith, a Google executive, said his company will pay the bulk of costs to digitize the printed works, while libraries will cover some of the lesser expenses of preparing books for scanning.

Material in the public domain will be available online through Google's book search;

copyrighted material will be digitized but not freely available. Searches will show the names of books and where they can be purchased, and authors of copyrighted material as well as a limited amount of content.

"It's the equivalent of picking up a book in a store and paging through it," Smith said.

Google is working on an arrangement under which searchers can download copyrighted material online after paying a fee to the publisher, Smith said.

Google's six-year agreement is with the Committee on Institutional Cooperation, a 12-university consortium formed 50 years ago to facilitate academic collaborations among large Midwestern research universities. Besides the Illinois universities, the

Review, Analyze, Investigate
REVIEWING CHAPTER 2

Publishers Nurture Ideas and Try to Make Money

✓ U.S. book publishers produce about 40,000 individual book titles every year.

✓ Publishers have always been torn between the goal of preserving the country's intellectual ideas and the need to make money.

✓ Many new owners of publishing houses are trying to limit uncertainty by publishing blockbusters and by spending money on promotional campaigns.

How American Book Publishing Grew

✓ Early publishers widened their audience by publishing political pamphlets, novels, poetry and humor.

✓ The International Copyright Law of 1891 expanded royalty protection to foreign writers, which also benefited American authors.

✓ The creation of publishing houses in the 19th and early 20th centuries centralized the process of producing books.

✓ The adoption of compulsory education throughout the United States was important for book publishing because schools buy textbooks and education creates more people who can read.

Cheaper Books Create a Mass Market

✓ Beginning in the 1920s, publishers dropped prices and introduced book clubs and paperbacks.

Google Inc. is digitizing the contents of many of the world's biggest libraries as part of the Google Search Project. Once the material is digitized, Google plans to make materials that is in the public domain available online. Copyrighted material will be digitized but not available free. At the London Book Fair, Google promotes its book project as a way to expand the audience for printed books.

group includes other Big Ten schools: Indiana, Iowa, Michigan, Michigan State, Minnesota, Ohio State, Penn State, Purdue and Wisconsin-Madison.

"This library digitization agreement is one of the largest cooperative actions of its kind in higher education," said Lawrence Dumas, Northwestern provost and CIC chairman.

Altogether the CIC libraries have more than 75 million volumes. Google will digitize up to 10 million from select and significant collections. These include Northwestern's Africana collection, the University of Chicago's South Asia holdings and a Chicago cultural collection at the University of Illinois at Chicago . . .

Scholars will be among the project's chief beneficiaries, said Paula Kaufman, librarian for the University of Illinois at Urbana-Champaign.

"In the print world," she said, "students and scholars are constrained by searching brief descriptions in card catalogs, tables of contents and indexes. Now we can search every word in every volume and make connections across works that would've taken weeks or years to make in the past."

Google Expands Book Project, by Jon Van, *Chicago Tribune*, June 7, 2007. Copyright © 2007 by Chicago Tribune Company. All rights reserved. Reprinted by permission.

✓ Early book clubs, such as Book-of-the-Month, expanded the market for books and widened the audience.

✓ The introduction of paperbacks that sold for as little as 25 cents meant the books could reach people who had never owned a book before.

Grove Press Tests Censorship

✓ Grove Press challenged book censorship by publishing *Lady Chatterley's Lover* in 1959 and *Tropic of Cancer* in 1961. Both books had been banned in the United States as obscene.

✓ The publication by Grove Press of *The Autobiography of Malcolm X* in 1965 was another challenge to censorship. The book became a bestseller.

Investors Buy Up Publishing Companies

✓ Before the 1960s, the book publishing industry was composed mainly of independent companies whose only business was books.

✓ Publishing company consolidation began in the 1960s, and this pattern of consolidation continues today.

Book Publishing at Work

✓ The process of publishing a book usually takes at least 18 months from the time an author is signed until the book is published.

✓ The six departments at a publishing house are acquisitions, production, design, manufacturing, marketing and fulfillment.

Authors and Agents: Where Books Begin

✓ Publishers acquire books in many ways. Some authors submit unsolicited manuscripts to a publishing house, hoping the publisher will be interested. However, many publishers refuse to read unsolicited manuscripts and accept only books that agents submit.

✓ Publishers pay authors a royalty for their work.

✓ Agents who represent authors collect fees from the authors they represent.

How Do Books Get Published?

✓ Book publishing requires an author, an acquisitions editor, a production editor, a designer, a manufacturing supervisor, a marketing department and fulfillment.

✓ Many publishing houses are small, with fewer than 20 employees.

Book Industry Has Five Major Markets

✓ Books can be grouped into five major categories: trade books, religious books, mass market paperbacks, textbooks, and university press books and book clubs.

✓ Textbooks account for about one-third of book publishing income.

Corporations Demand Higher Profits

✓ To reduce their risks, many publishers look for block-buster books (and best-selling authors) that they can sell through large-scale promotion campaigns.

✓ Publishers are especially interested in books with subsidiary- and international-rights potential.

Chain Bookstores and Internet Retailers Compete

✓ Chain bookstores and Internet retailers, such as Amazon, are big factors in book marketing. Chain bookstores and Internet retailers can buy in huge volume, and often they buy books only from publishers that give them big discounts.

✓ Internet retailing has expanded the book market, but has introduced competitive pricing.

Small Presses Challenge Corporate Publishing

✓ Small presses are, by definition, alternative.

✓ Many small presses exist outside the New York City orbit.

✓ Specialization and targeted marketing are important elements of small press success.

Publishers Promote Audiobooks and Digital Alternatives

✓ Audiobooks in MP3 format allow consumers to download and purchase book files on the Internet and listen to books on their computers or a specialized MP3 player.

✓ Electronic books (e-books) offer digital copies of thousands of titles instantly.

✓ Electronic graphics make today's books more interesting to read.

New Technologies Affect Production and Consumption

✓ Computers monitor inventories more closely.

✓ Publishers now receive and process manuscripts electronically via the Internet. Many aspects of the publishing process, such as copyediting and photo research, are contracted to freelancers who work outside the publishing house, including overseas.

✓ Electronic graphics make books more interesting to look at, and many book publishers even use Web sites to promote books and add available content.

✓ Large publishers are continuing to consolidate, and the number of small publishers is decreasing.

✓ The Google Book Project has contracted with several of the nation's libraries to scan the contents of books the libraries hold. Eventually Google plans to make the books' contents available online. The project has wide-ranging legal and economic consequences for the book publishing industry. In 2008, Google paid $125 million to settle copyright infringement claims, but the copyright issues inherent in the project still remain unresolved.

Book Publishing Is a Complex Business

✓ Book publishing, which had simple beginnings in America that still evoke mistaken romantic ideas, is a complicated corporate industry.

KEY TERMS

These terms are defined in the margins throughout this chapter and appear in alphabetical order with definitions in the Glossary, which begins on page 372.

Advance 37
Audiobooks 44
Blockbuster 40
E-books 44
Mass Market Books 40
Royalty 37
Subsidiary Rights 38

CRITICAL QUESTIONS

1. Why was passage of the International Copyright Law of 1891 so important to American authors?

2. List five ways the economics of book publishing changed from Benjamin Franklin's day to today.

3. Will new technologies like e-books replace print books? Why or why not?

4. Why are textbooks so important to the publishing industry?

5. Why is the Google Book Project so controversial?

WORKING THE WEB

This list includes both sites mentioned in the chapter and others to give you greater insight into book publishing.

Amazon
http://www.amazon.com

Since this pioneer Internet bookseller started in 1995, Amazon has expanded its e-commerce offerings to include a wide variety of products in multiple categories including Movies, Music & Games, Digital Downloads and even Grocery. Most recently, Amazon has released Kindle, a wireless, portable reading device with instant access to books at more than 50 percent savings from the print price, as well as blogs, newspapers and magazines. Amazon.com operates sites internationally, including the United Kingdom, France and Japan.

American Booksellers Association
http://www.bookweb.org

This national not-for-profit trade association for independent booksellers exists to protect and promote the interests of its members by providing "advocacy, education, opportunities for peer interaction, support services and new business models." Its IndieBound program (evolved from Book Sense, http://www.indiebound.org) is a national marketing program to raise consumer awareness of the value of independent bookstores.

American Booksellers Foundation for Free Expression
http://www.abffe.org

Founded by the American Booksellers Association in 1990, ABFFE is "The bookseller's voice in the fight against censorship." The Foundation opposes book banning and other restrictions on free speech, participates in legal cases about First Amendment rights and provides education on the importance of free expression to many entities including the public, the press and politicians.

Association of American Publishers
http://www.publishers.org

This organization deals with broad issues concerning publishers, as well as specific concerns in particular industry segments. Committees attend to such issues as intellectual property; new technology; First Amendment rights, censorship and libel; funding for education and libraries; postal rates and regulations; and international copyright enforcement.

Barnes & Noble
http://www.barnesandnoble.com

"The Internet's Largest Bookstore," Barnes & Noble.com uses mass-marketing techniques to sell books, DVDs, music and other merchandise. Web site features include online Book Clubs, B&N Review and B&N Studio, a video library with hundreds of webcasts where viewers can learn more about authors, musical artists and fellow book lovers.

Biblio
http://www.biblio.com

Biblio is an online marketplace for used, rare and out-of-print books. The booksellers are located around the world, and the list of links to specialists is very long (use the Book-

sellers tab and go to the "Specialist Bookstores" link). Users can search 50 million used and rare books, browse by subject or author, or browse collectible and rare books by featured category.

BookFinder
http://www.bookfinder.com

BookFinder.com is an e-commerce search engine for new, used, rare and out-of-print books and textbooks. It searches all the major online catalogs (such as Amazon and Barnes & Noble) and independent sources. Searches can be conducted in English, French, German or Italian. BookFinder's global network of book search engines includes JustBooks.de, JustBooks.co.uk and JustBooks.fr.

Google Book Search
http://books.google.com

This controversial project between Google and several libraries (including the University of Michigan, Harvard University, Stanford University, New York Public Library and Oxford University) has expanded to include partnerships with book publishers and authors. Google's plan "to digitize the world's books in order to make them easier for people to find and buy" has encountered much discussion and debate about copyright and authors' rights. Thoughts and opinions on the project can be viewed at http://books.google.com/googlebooks/newsviews/.

IndieBound
http://www.indiebound.org

Evolved from the ABA's Book Sense program, IndieBound "rallies passionate readers around a celebration of independent stores and independent thinking." Independently owned ABA member bookstores are automatically part of the program and are encouraged to use the logos, spirit lines, posters, buttons, T-shirts and more provided by the ABA. Other bookseller tools include The Indie Next List, which offers monthly picks; national, regional and specialty Indie Bestseller Lists; Bookseller DIY; and Independent Business Alliances.

Scholastic Corporation
http://www.scholastic.com

The world's largest publisher of children's books, Scholastic creates a variety of educational and entertainment materials and products for home and school use, and distributes them through various channels including school-based book clubs and book fairs, retail stores, television networks and Scholastic.com. Other business segments include Media, Licensing and Advertising; and International Operations. Research and Reports found on Scholastic.com include Kids and Families Reading Report, Adolescent Literacy: A National Crisis, and Research on Professional Development for teachers and administrators.

3

Newspapers: Expanding Delivery

Getty Images

In 2008, The New York Times Company moved to a new headquarters building in Manhattan.

What's Ahead?

In 1882, Harrison Gray Otis bought

a 25 percent share of the *Los Angeles Times* for $6,000. In 2000, the Chandler family (Otis' descendants) sold the Times Mirror Company, which included the *Los Angeles Times*, *Newsday*, *The Baltimore Sun* newspapers, the *Hartford Courant* and other media properties to the Chicago-based Tribune Company for $8.3 billion. Then in 2007, Chicago real estate tycoon Sam Zell paid $8.2 billion for the Tribune Company (including Times Mirror), less than the Tribune Company paid for Times Mirror alone seven years earlier. Then one year later, in December 2008, the

TimeFrame
1690 – Today

Mainstream Newspapers Adapt to Maintain Their Audience Share

1690 *Publick Occurrences,* America's first newspaper, is published.

1721. **James Franklin publishes *The New England Courant,* the first newspaper to appear without the Crown's "Published by Authority" sanction.**

Kean Collection/ Hulton Archive/ Getty Images

1734 John Peter Zenger is charged with sedition. While he is in jail, his wife, Anna Zenger, continues to publish *The New York Weekly Journal,* making her America's first woman publisher.

1808 *El Misisipi,* America's first Spanish-language newspaper, begins publication in Georgia.

1827 **John B. Russwurm and the Reverend Samuel Cornish (pictured) launch *Freedom's Journal,* the nation's first newspaper directed specifically at an African American audience.**

New York Historical Society

1828 Elias Boudinot launches the *Cherokee Phoenix.*

1831 In Boston, William Lloyd Garrison launches the abolitionist newspaper *The Liberator.*

1847 Frederick Douglass introduces the weekly *North Star,* considered America's most important African American pre–Civil War newspaper.

1848 Jane Grey Swisshelm publishes the first issue of the abolitionist newspaper the *Pittsburgh Saturday Visiter,* which also promoted women's rights.

1889 Ida B. Wells becomes part owner of the *Memphis Free Speech and Headlight* and begins her anti-lynching campaign.

1900 One third of the nation's newspapers follow the popular trend toward yellow journalism.

1950 **Newspaper readership begins to decline following the introduction of television.**

Fox Photos/Hulton Archive/ Getty Images

1982 **Gannett creates *USA Today,* using a splashy format and color throughout the paper.**

Cynthia Johnson/ Time & Life Pictures/ Getty Images

1990s Newspapers launch special sections to appeal to declining audiences—teens and women. Some newspapers launch Spanish-language editions.

Today **The newspaper business is consolidating as large newspaper companies buy up small newspapers and gather them in groups. To attract younger readers, newspapers have expanded their Internet editions and news-on-demand features.**

Bill Pugliano/Getty Images

Tribune Company filed for bankruptcy, citing the rapid decline in newspaper revenue. The acquisition of the *Los Angeles Times* by the Tribune Company and then by investor Sam Zell—two ownership changes in seven years, and then the bankruptcy filing—demonstrates the declining state of the newspaper business today.

American newspapers began in colonial America more than three centuries ago as one-page sheets that consisted primarily of announcements of ship arrivals and departures and old news from Europe. Today's large urban newspapers such as the *Los Angeles Times* rely on satellite-fed information, and these papers often run to 500 pages on Sunday. (*The New York Times* holds the record for the largest single-day's newspaper. On November 13, 1987, the *Times* published a 1,612-page edition that weighed 12 pounds.) In most cases, newspapers today also are just one part of large media companies rather than family-run operations.

First Mass Medium to Deliver News

Technological developments in the last century have changed the role of newspapers and the way news is delivered. From 1690 until the introduction of radio in 1920, newspapers were the only mass news medium available, attempting to deliver news and information as soon as it happened. Until 1920, newspapers were the only way for large numbers of people to get the same news simultaneously. There was no competition.

The invention of broadcasting in the early 20th century changed newspapers' exclusive access to news because broadcasting offered quicker access to information. Yet, despite increasing competition for its audience, newspapers continue to be a significant source of information and news.

The newspaper industry also historically has played an important role in defining the cultural concept of an independent press, based on the belief that the press must remain independent from government control to fulfill its responsibility to keep the public informed. Concepts about what the public should know, when they should know it and who should decide what the public needs to know developed in America during a time when newspapers were the main focus of these discussions.

Publishers Fight for an Independent Press

The issue of government control of newspapers surfaced early in the history of the colonies. At first, newspapers were the mouthpieces of the British government, and news was subject to British approval. The British government subsidized many colonial newspapers, and publishers actually printed "Published by Authority" on the first page of the paper to demonstrate government approval.

The first colonial newspaper angered the local authorities so much that the newspaper issued only one edition. This newspaper, *Publick Occurrences*, which was published in Boston on September 25, 1690, often is identified as America's first newspaper.

The first and only edition of *Publick Occurrences* was just two pages, each page the size of a sheet of today's binder paper (then called a half-sheet), and was printed on three sides. Publisher Benjamin Harris left the fourth side blank so people could jot down the latest news before they gave the paper to friends. Harris made the mistake of reporting in his first issue that the French king was "in much trouble" for sleeping with his son's wife. Harris' journalism was too candid for the governor and council of the Massachusetts Bay Colony, who stopped the publication four days after the newspaper appeared.

The nation's first consecutively issued (published more than once) newspaper was *The Boston News-Letter*, which appeared in 1704. It was one half-sheet printed on two sides. In the first issue, editor John Campbell reprinted the queen's latest speech, some maritime news and one advertisement telling people how to put an ad in his paper. Like many subsequent colonial publishers, Campbell reprinted several items from the London papers.

James Franklin's *New England Courant* Establishes an Independent Press Tradition

The next challenge to British control came when James Franklin started his own newspaper in Boston in 1721. His

Publick Occurrences was America's first newspaper, published in 1690. The newspaper was only two pages, each page the size of a sheet of today's binder paper.

United Kingdom National Archives

New England Courant was the first American newspaper to appear without the crown's "Published by Authority" sanction. *Thus, James Franklin began the tradition of an independent press in this country.*

Benjamin Franklin Introduces Competition

In 1729, Benjamin Franklin, James' younger brother, moved to Philadelphia and bought the *Pennsylvania Gazette* to compete with the only other newspaper in town, the *American Weekly Mercury* published by Andrew Bradford. The *Pennsylvania Gazette* became the most influential and most financially successful of all the colonial newspapers. In the same print shop that printed the *Gazette*, Franklin published *Poor Richard's Almanack* in 1732, an annual book that sold about 10,000 copies a year for the next 25 years. *Benjamin Frank-*

lin proved that a printer could make money without government sanctions or support.

Truth Versus Libel: The Zenger Trial

In New York, John Peter Zenger started the *New York Weekly Journal* in 1733. The *Journal* continually attacked Governor William Cosby for incompetence, and on November 17, 1734, Zenger was arrested and jailed, charged with printing false and seditious writing. (***Seditious language*** is language that authorities believe could incite rebellion against the government.) While Zenger was in jail, his wife, Anna, continued to publish the paper.

Zenger's trial began on August 4, 1735, nine months after his arrest. His defense attorney argued that *truth was a defense against libel*, and that if Zenger's words were true, they could not be libelous. (A ***libelous*** statement is a false statement that damages a person by questioning that person's character or reputation.)

The trial established a *landmark precedent for freedom of the press in America—the concept that truth is the best defense for libel.* If what someone publishes is true, the information cannot be considered libelous. (The issue of libel is explained in **Chapter 14**.)

Women's Early Role as Publishers

Colonial women were not encouraged to work outside the home at all. Therefore, women who published newspapers during the colonial period are especially notable because they are among the few examples of women who managed businesses early in the nation's history. Early colonial women printers, such as Anna Zenger, usually belonged to printing families that trained wives and daughters to work in the print shops. By the time the American Revolution began, at least 14 women had been printers in the colonies. One of these family-trained printers was the first woman publisher.

Elizabeth Timothy became editor of the weekly *South Carolina Gazette* in Charleston when her husband, Lewis, died unexpectedly and their son, Peter, was only 13. Elizabeth Timothy published her first edition on January 4, 1737, under her son's name. Her first editorial appealed to the community to continue to support the "poor afflicted widow and six small children." Mother and son ran the paper together until 1746, when Peter formally took over the business.

Birth of the Partisan Press

As dissatisfaction with British rule grew in the colonies, newspapers became political tools that fostered the debate that eventually led to the colonies' independence. By 1750, 14 weekly newspapers were being published in the colonies.

The Stamp Act

Opposition to the British Stamp Act in 1765 signaled the beginning of the revolutionary period. The Stamp Act taxed

Seditious Language Language that authorities believe could incite rebellion against the government.

Libelous A false statement that damages a person by questioning that person's character or reputation.

publishers a halfpenny for each issue that was a half-sheet or smaller and one penny for a full sheet. Each advertisement was taxed two shillings. All the colonial newspapers, even those loyal to the crown, fought the act.

Many newspapers threatened to stop publication, but only a few of them did. Most editors published newspapers that mocked the tax. William Bradford III issued the famous tombstone edition of the *Pennsylvania Journal* on October 31, 1765. The front page, bordered in black, showed a skull and crossbones where the official stamp should have been.

The Stamp Act Congress met in New York in October 1765 and adopted the now-familiar slogan, "No taxation without representation." Parliament, facing united opposition from all the colonial publishers, repealed the Stamp Act on March 18, 1766.

The Alien and Sedition Laws

During the early part of the country's history, journalists often used newspapers as a way to oppose the new government. The Alien and Sedition Laws, passed by Congress in 1798, were the federal government's first attempt to control its critics. Congress said that anyone who "shall write, print, or publish . . . false, scandalous and malicious writing or writings against the government of the United States, or either house of the Congress of the United States, or the President of the United States," could be fined up to $2,000 and jailed for two years.

Several journalists went to jail. A Boston publisher was jailed for libeling the Massachusetts legislature. A New York editor was fined $100 and jailed for four months. By 1800, the angry rhetoric had dissipated. The Alien and Sedition Laws expired after two years and were not renewed. However, *throughout American press history, the tradition of an independent press, established by James Franklin in 1721, continued to confront the government's desire to restrain criticism.*

Newspapers Take Advantage of Early Technology

Technological advances of the 19th century—such as cheaper newsprint, mechanized printing and the telegraph—meant newspapers could reach a wider audience faster than before. Confined to eastern cities and highly educated urban audiences during the 1700s, newspaper publishers in the 1800s sought new readers—from the frontier, from among the nation's growing number of immigrants and from within the shrinking Native American population. This expansion resulted in three new developments for American newspapers: frontier journalism, ethnic and cultural newspapers and the alternative press.

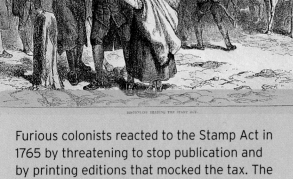

The Granger Collection

Furious colonists reacted to the Stamp Act in 1765 by threatening to stop publication and by printing editions that mocked the tax. The Stamp Act was repealed a year later.

Frontier Journalism

Gold, silver and adventure lured people to the West, and when the people arrived, they needed newspapers. The *Indiana Gazette*, the *Texas Gazette*, the *Oregon Spectator*, the *Weekly Arizonian* and Colorado's *Rocky Mountain News* met that need, aided by the telegraph, which moved news easily from coast to coast.

The wide-open land beckoned many journalists. The most celebrated journalist to chronicle the frontier was

Bettmann/CORBIS

On the frontier, journalists learned to improvise. This press operation, assembled to publish New Mexico's first newspaper, was set up under a juniper tree near Kingston, New Mexico.

Elias Boudinot (left) published the first Native American newspaper (right), the *Cherokee Phoenix*, from 1828 to 1832. The newspaper used the Cherokee language.

Samuel Clemens, who traveled to Nevada in 1861, prospecting for silver. Clemens didn't find any silver, but a year later the Virginia City *Territorial Enterprise*—the area's largest paper—hired him for $25 a week. Clemens first signed his name as Mark Twain on a humorous travel letter written for the *Enterprise*.

Ethnic and Native American Newspapers

English-language newspapers did not satisfy everyone's needs. In the first half of the 19th century, many newspapers sought to succeed by catering to ethnic and cultural interests. In the early 1800s, Spanish-speaking people in Georgia could read *El Misisipi*. Herman Ridder's German newspaper, *New Yorker Staats-Zeitung*, founded in 1845, was the most successful foreign-language newspaper in the United States. It formed the financial basis for today's Knight-Ridder chain, which was bought by the McClatchy Company in 2006.

People outside the mainstream of society, such as Spanish and German immigrants, used newspapers to create a sense of community and ethnic identity. In the 1800s, Native Americans who had been displaced by the settlers also felt a need to express their culture through a newspaper. As a non-mainstream group, they especially wanted to voice their complaints.

Alternative, or Dissident, Press Media that present alternative viewpoints that challenge the mainstream press.

On February 21, 1828, the nation's first Native American newspaper appeared. Elias Boudinot, a Native American who had been educated at a northern seminary, launched the *Cherokee Phoenix*. The Cherokee nation held exclusive control over the four-page paper, which was printed half in English and half in an 86-character alphabet that represented the Cherokee language. (Authorities shut down the press in 1832 because they felt Boudinot was arousing anti-government sentiment.)

Dissident Voices Create the Early Alternative Press

Two strong social movements—emancipation and women's suffrage—brought new voices to the American press. This **alternative press** movement signaled the beginning of a significant American journalistic tradition. Newspapers became an outlet for the voices of social protest, a tradition that continues today. (The alternative press also is called the **dissident press**.)

Six early advocates for domestic change who used the press to advance their causes—the abolition of slavery and suffrage for women—were John B. Russwurm, the Reverend Samuel Cornish, Frederick Douglass, William Lloyd Garrison, Jane Grey Swisshelm and Ida B. Wells.

In 1827, Russwurm and Cornish, who were African American, started *Freedom's Journal* in New York City with very little money. They launched their newspaper to respond to racist attacks in several local newspapers. *Freedom's Journal* lasted for two years and reached only a few readers, but it was the beginning of an African American press tradition that eventually created more than 2,700 newspapers, magazines and quarterly journals.

What has often been called the most important African American pre–Civil War newspaper was Frederick Douglass' weekly *North Star*. "Right is of no Sex—Truth is of no Color—God is the Father of us all, and we are all Brethren" read the masthead. Beginning in 1847, Douglass struggled to support the *North Star* by giving lectures. The newspaper eventually reached 3,000 subscribers in the United States and abroad with its emancipation message.

In 1831, William Lloyd Garrison began publishing *The Liberator*, a weekly abolitionist paper in Boston. As a white man fighting slavery and advocating women's rights, Garrison was attacked by a mob in 1835 but survived when the Boston mayor jailed him for his own protection. Garrison continued to publish *The Liberator* for 30 years.

Like Douglass and Garrison, Ida B. Wells and Jane Grey Swisshelm campaigned for civil rights. Swisshelm's

Frederick Douglass (left) established the weekly newspaper *North Star,* often called the most important African American pre-Civil War newspaper. William Lloyd Garrison (center), a Boston abolitionist, founded the New England Anti-Slavery Society and published *The Liberator* (right), another important abolitionist newspaper.

first byline appeared in 1844 in the *Spirit of Liberty,* published in Pittsburgh. Four years later she began her own abolitionist publication, the *Pittsburgh Saturday Visiter,* which also promoted women's rights. (For more information about Ida B. Wells, see **Impact/People,** "Ida B. Wells Uses Her Pen to Fight 19th-Century Racism," page 58.)

As a correspondent for Horace Greeley's *New York Tribune* in Washington, D.C., Swisshelm convinced Vice President Millard Fillmore to let her report from the Senate press gallery. The gallery had been open to male journalists for 55 years, and on May 21, 1850, Swisshelm became the first female journalist to sit in the gallery.

These pioneers—Russwurm, Cornish, Douglass, Garrison, Wells and Swisshelm—used newspapers to lobby for social change. These dissident newspapers offered a forum for protest and reform, which is an important cultural role for an independent press.

Newspapers Seek Mass Audiences and Big Profits

The voices of social protest reached a limited, committed audience, but most people could not afford to subscribe to a daily newspaper. Newspapers were sold by advance yearly subscription for $6 to $10 at a time when most skilled workers earned less than $750 a year. Then, in 1833, Benjamin Day demonstrated that he could profitably appeal to a mass audience by dropping the price of a newspaper to a penny and selling the paper on the street every day.

Benjamin Day's *New York Sun* published sensational news and feature stories for the working class. He was able to lower the price to a penny by filling the paper with advertising and by hiring newsboys to sell the paper on street corners. The first successful ***penny paper*** reported local gossip and sensationalized police news and carried a page and a half of advertising in the four-page paper.

Newsboys (and some newsgirls) bought 100 papers for 67 cents and tried to sell them all each day to make a profit. Even *The New York Times,* founded by Henry J. Raymond in 1851, was a penny paper when it began. The legacy of these early penny papers continues in today's gossip columns and crime reporting.

Newspapers Dominate the Early 20th Century

For the first 30 years of the 20th century—before radio and television—newspapers dominated the country. Newspapers were the nation's single source of daily dialogue about political, cultural and social issues. This was also the era of the greatest newspaper competition for readers.

Competition Breeds Sensationalism

In large cities such as New York, as many as 10 newspapers competed for readers at once, so the publishers

Penny Paper or Penny Press A newspaper produced by dropping the price of each copy to a penny and supporting the production cost through advertising.

IMPACT
»People

Ida B. Wells Uses Her Pen to Fight 19th-Century Racism

by Shirley Biagi

Ida B. Wells didn't start out to be a journalist, but the cause of emancipation drew her to the profession. Wells, who eventually became co-owner of the *Free Speech and Headlight* in Memphis, Tennessee, documented racism wherever she found it. She is known for her pioneering stand against the unjustified lynching of African Americans in the 1890s.

In 1878, both of Wells' parents and her infant sister died in a yellow fever epidemic, so 16-year-old Wells took responsibility for her six brothers and sisters, attended Rush College, and then moved the family to Memphis, where she became a teacher.

A Baptist minister who was editor of the Negro Press Association hired Wells to write for his paper. She wrote under the pseudonym Iola.

Ida B. Wells, part owner of the *Memphis Free Speech* and *Headlight*, wrote under the pseudonym Iola. Wells' struggle for social justice represents an early historical example of the role of the dissident press in American history.

In 1892, Wells wrote a story about three African American men who had been kidnapped from a Memphis jail and killed. "The city of Memphis has demonstrated that neither character nor standing avails the Negro, if he dares to protect himself against the white man or become his rival," she wrote. "We are outnumbered and without arms." While in New York, she read in the local paper that a mob had sacked the *Free Speech* office.

Wells decided not to return to Memphis. She worked in New York and lectured in Europe and then settled in Chicago, where she married a lawyer, Ferdinand Lee Barnett. Ida Wells-Barnett and her husband actively campaigned for African American rights in Chicago, and she continued to write until she died at age 69 in 1931.

---

looked for new ways to expand their audience. Two New York publishers—Joseph Pulitzer and William Randolph Hearst—revived and refined the **penny press** sensationalism that had begun in 1833 with Benjamin Day's *New York Sun*. Like Benjamin Day, Pulitzer and Hearst proved that newspapers could reap enormous fortunes for their owners. They also demonstrated that credible, serious reporting is not all that people want in a newspaper. Pulitzer and Hearst promoted giveaways, included gossip and fabricated stories.

An ambitious man who knew how to grab his readers' interest, Joseph Pulitzer published the first newspaper comics and sponsored journalist Nellie Bly on an around-

the-world balloon trip to try to beat the fictional record in the popular book, *Around the World in 80 Days*. Bly finished the trip in 72 days, 6 hours and 11 minutes, and the stunt brought Pulitzer the circulation he craved. In San Francisco, young William Randolph Hearst, the new editor of the *San Francisco Examiner*, sent a reporter to cover Bly's arrival.

In 1887, William Randolph Hearst convinced his father, who owned the *San Francisco Examiner*, to let him run the paper. Hearst tagged the *Examiner* "The Monarch of the Dailies," added a lovelorn column, and attacked several of his father's influential friends in the newspaper. He spent money wildly, buying talent from competing papers and staging showy promotional events.

Yellow Journalism Is Born: Hearst's Role in the Spanish-American War

In New York, Hearst bought the *New York Journal*, hired Pulitzer's entire Sunday staff and cut the *Journal*'s price to a penny, so Pulitzer dropped his price to match it. Hearst bought a color press and printed color comics. Then he stole Pulitzer's popular comic, "Hogan's Alley," which included a character named the Yellow Kid.

Hearst relished the battle, as the *Journal* screamed attention-grabbing crime headlines, such as "Thigh of the Body Found," and the paper offered $1,000 for information that would convict the murderer. Critics named this sensationalism *yellow journalism* after the Yellow Kid, an epithet still bestowed on highly emotional, exaggerated or inaccurate reporting that emphasizes crime, sex and violence. By 1900, about one-third of the metropolitan dailies were following the trend toward yellow journalism.

Beginning in 1898, the Spanish-American War provided the battlefield for Pulitzer and Hearst to act out their newspaper war. For three years, the two newspapers unrelentingly overplayed events in the Cuban struggle for independence from Spain, each trying to beat the other with irresponsible, exaggerated stories, many of them invented.

The overplayed events that resulted from the sensational competition between Pulitzer and Hearst showed that newspapers could have a significant effect on political attitudes. The Spanish-American War began a few months after the sinking of the U.S. battleship *Maine* in Havana harbor, which killed 266 crew members. The cause of the explosion that sank the ship was never determined, but Pulitzer's and Hearst's newspapers blamed the Spanish.

Hearst dubbed the event "the *Journal*'s War," but in fact Hearst and Pulitzer shared responsibility because both men had inflamed the public unnecessarily about events in Cuba. *The serious consequences of their yellow journalism vividly demonstrated the importance of press responsibility.*

Tabloid Journalism: Selling Sex and Violence

The journalistic legacy of Day, Pulitzer and Hearst surfaced again in the tabloid journalism of the 1920s, also called jazz journalism. In 1919, the publishers of the *New York Daily News* sponsored a beauty contest to inaugurate the nation's first tabloid. A *tabloid* is a small-format newspaper, usually 11 inches by 14 inches, featuring illustrations and sensational stories.

The battle for New York readers between Joseph Pulitzer (left) and William Randolph Hearst (right) provoked the Spanish-American War and spawned the term *yellow journalism*.

The *Daily News* merged pictures and screaming headlines with reports about crime, sex and violence to exceed anything that had appeared before. It ran full-page pictures with short, punchy text. Love affairs soon became big news and so did murders. In the ultimate example of tabloid journalism, a *Daily News* reporter strapped a camera to his ankle in 1928 and took a picture of Ruth Snyder, who had conspired to kill her husband, as she was electrocuted at Sing Sing prison.

Snyder's picture covered the front page, and the caption stated, "This is perhaps the most remarkable exclusive picture in the history of criminology." Photojournalism had taken a sensational turn. Today, yellow journalism's successors are the supermarket tabloids, such as the *National Enquirer*, which feature large photographs and stories about sex, violence and celebrities.

Yellow Journalism News that emphasizes crime, sex and violence; also called jazz journalism and tabloid journalism.

Tabloid A small-format newspaper that features large photographs and illustrations along with sensational stories.

This 1928 photo of Ruth Snyder's execution (left) exemplifies the screaming headlines and large photographs from early tabloids that still populate today's tabloid newspapers (right).

Unionization Encourages Professionalism

The first half of the 20th century brought the widespread unionization of newspaper employees, which standardized wages at many of the nation's largest newspapers. Labor unions were first established at newspapers in 1800, and the International Typographical Union went national in the mid-1850s.

Other unions formed to represent production workers at newspapers, but reporters didn't have a union until 1934, when *New York World-Telegram* reporter Heywood Broun called on his colleagues to organize. Broun became the Newspaper Guild's first president. Today, the Guild continues to cover employees at many of America's urban newspapers. Unions represent roughly one in five newspaper employees.

With the rise of unions, employee contracts, which once had been negotiated in private, became public agreements. In general, salaries for reporters at union newspapers rose, and this eventually led to a sense of professionalism, including codes of ethics.

Television Brings New Competition

The invention of television dramatically affected the newspaper industry. Newspaper publishers had learned how to

live with only one other 20th-century news industry—radio. In the 1920s, when radio first became popular, newspapers refused to carry advertising or time logs for the programs, but eventually newspapers conceded the space to radio.

In the 1950s, however, television posed a larger threat: TV offered moving images of the news, along with entertainment. The spread of television demonstrated how interrelated the media were. The newspaper industry gave up its position as the number one news medium and was forced to share the news audience with broadcasting. Eventually, television's influence changed both the look and the content of many newspapers.

Alternative Press Revives Voices of Protest

The social movements of the 1960s briefly revived one portion of the early newspaper industry—the alternative press. Like their 1800s predecessors in the abolitionist and emancipation movements, people who supported the revival of the alternative press in the 1960s believed the mainstream press was avoiding important issues, such as the anti–Vietnam War movement, the civil rights movement and the gay rights movement.

In 1964, as a way to pass along news about the antiwar movement, the *Los Angeles Free Press* became the first underground paper to publish regularly. The *Barb* in Berkeley, California, *Kaleidoscope* in Chicago and *Quick-*

silver Times in Washington, D.C., soon followed. In 1965, Jim Michaels launched the nation's first gay newspaper, the Los Angeles *Advocate*. What the 1960s underground press proved already had been proven in the 19th century: In America, causes need a voice, and if those voices are not represented in the mainstream press, publications emerge to support alternative views.

Newspapers Expand and Contract

Since the 1970s, the overall number of newspapers has declined. Many afternoon papers died when TV took over the evening news. Other afternoon papers changed to morning papers. Then, newspaper publishers realized television could provide the news headlines, but newspapers could offer the background that television news could not.

Newspaper publishers also began to play on the popularity of television personalities, and expanded their entertainment, business and sports news. Eventually, advertisers realized that newspapers gave people the broader news that TV couldn't deliver. Also, viewers couldn't clip coupons out of their television sets or retrieve copies of yesterday's TV ads, so advertisers began to use newspapers to complement television advertising campaigns. To try to match television's visual appeal, newspapers introduced advanced graphics and vivid color.

Today newspapers are facing declining readership, especially among young readers (see **Impact/Business**, "The Newspaper Death Watch," page 62), and many major newspapers have announced staff cuts in an attempt to stay as profitable as they have been in the past. To survive, the majority of today's small dailies are part of a chain, and most cities have only one newspaper.

Newspapers at Work

Many colonial publishers handled all the tasks of putting out a newspaper single-handedly, but today's typical newspaper operation is organized into two separate departments: the editorial side and the business side. The *editorial side* handles everything that you read in the paper—the news and feature stories, editorials, cartoons and photographs. The *business side* handles everything else—production, advertising, distribution and administration.

On the editorial side at a medium-size daily newspaper, different *editors*—a news editor, a sports editor, a features editor and a business editor, for example—handle different parts of the paper. The managing editor oversees these news departments. A copyeditor checks the reporters' stories before they are set in type, and a layout editor positions the stories. Editorial writers and cartoonists usually work for an

Bettmann/CORBIS

In the 1950s, newspaper readership began to decline with the introduction of television, as TV became America's primary source of news and entertainment. Television sets replaced radio receivers as the central piece of living room furniture; some TVs sported unusual shapes and styles.

editorial page editor. All these people report to the *editor-in-chief* or the *publisher* or both.

A *business manager* and his or her staff run the business side of the paper: getting the paper out to subscribers, selling advertising and making sure the paper gets printed every day. These people also ultimately report to the editor-in-chief or the publisher. Sometimes the publisher also owns the paper. If a corporation owns the paper, the publisher reports to its board of directors.

Almost all newspapers today run Web sites, and many newspapers have created New Media departments to introduce strong graphic and video elements to their Internet editions.

Syndicates

Newspapers also can add to their content without having to send their own reporters to stories by using **syndicates**, which are news agencies that sell articles for publication to a number of newspapers simultaneously. The first syndicated column was a fashion letter distributed in 1857.

Today, many newspapers syndicate their columns and features to try to add income. Syndicates mainly provide columnists such as Dear Abby, as well as comics and editorial

Syndicates News agencies that sell articles for publication to a number of newspapers simultaneously.

IMPACT
❯❯ Business

The Newspaper Death Watch

by Nat Ives

By now you know the story: The business of newspapers is in decline.

It's a terminal decline, if you believe experts such as Jeffrey Cole, director of the Center for the Digital Future at the University of Southern California at Annenberg. His research suggests traditional media in general must learn to shrink but newspapers in particular are a special case. "When an offline reader of a paper dies, he or she is not being replaced by a new reader," he said. "How much time do they [newspapers] have? We think they have 20 to 25 years. . . ."

"There is no solution, given the advances of digital marketing and the changes in digital reading, that is going to save the newspaper industry as it is," said Ken Doctor, an industry veteran now serving as a media analyst for OutSell, the research and advisory firm. "There's an acknowledgement that they've been resistant to make," he said. "The industry as it has been is not coming back. It's going to be a radically

The economics of the newspaper industry today are in transition because a large portion of the audience, including many sports fans, have abandoned the printed newspaper and instead get their news online.

different industry, especially for content creation and sales."

This process is not reversible, said Lauren Rich Fine, a former Merrill Lynch newspaper analyst now serving as a practitioner in resi-

---

cartoons. The price of the syndicated copy for each newspaper is based on the newspaper's circulation. A large newspaper pays more for syndicated copy than a small newspaper, but revenue from syndication is limited.

Newspapers Struggle to Retain Readers

In the 1980s, newspaper companies looking for new ways to make money rediscovered and expanded on some old ideas. Gannett introduced a new national newspaper, *USA Today*, in the 1980s with bold graphics and shorter stories, and more newspaper organizations joined the syndication busi-

ness. Many newspapers introduced Internet editions in the 1990s and today online publishing is an essential element of any newspaper business.

Newspapers depend primarily on advertising for support. Subscriptions and newsstand sales account for only a small percentage of newspaper income.

Today's newspapers are maintaining most of their readership but only because they've added Internet editions. (See **Illustration 3.1**.) Big-city newspapers lost readers as people moved to the suburbs, and suburban newspapers grew, as well as suburban editions of big-city papers.

But as people stopped reading the printed newspaper and migrated to the Internet, and as younger readers abandoned newspapers altogether (even online), newspaper rev-

dence at Kent State University's College of Communication and Information. "I wouldn't count on this industry becoming that profitable again," she said. "Anybody who thinks it's going back to the way it was is insane."

The newspaper industry, that is, must say goodbye to the double-digit profit margins that made it the darling of Wall Street, to its old unsurpassed authority, to its central place in American conversation and commerce.

There's already a great deal of innovating under way. Just last week, the eight biggest newspapers in Ohio began sharing articles with each other. *The New York Times* Web site introduced yet another ad unit to increase its digital revenue further. The young *Lakewood (Ohio) Observer* "newspaper" is publishing online every day—but going to print, where its ad revenue resides, only every two weeks. *The Wall Street Journal* is introducing a glossy magazine inside its newsprint pages. And one of the new-era owners, Brian Tierney in Philadelphia, has rooted out new business opportunities, such as selling sponsorship of the *Inquirer*'s TV-guide booklet to cable giant Comcast.

Pain to Come

"Whether it's that pain is a great motivator or what, I don't know," said John Kimball, senior VP and chief marketing officer at the Newspaper Association of America. "But the point is that there are a lot of things that newspapers are doing—not only to enhance the new product lines they have in the niche publications and those sorts of things, but also to find new ways to drive revenue into the core product in ways that you know we might not have seen four to five years ago."

But setting priorities will keep getting more painful, because most of these innovations just won't return newsroom budgets to their old sizes. Wringing sponsorship dollars from TV listings is smart, but that only works until TV listings finish following classifieds and stock tables into better digital venues.

Newspaper Web sites are growing fast, but there's no certainty that online advertising will ever match the rates achieved by newspaper ads in print. Even at The New York Times Co., whose NYTimes.com gets more unique visitors than any other paper's site, print revenue still made up 90 percent of last year's total. What's more, its online revenue growth slowed to 11.6 percent in the first quarter [of 2008] from 21.6 percent in the first quarter of 2007.

"To save a few jobs and to pop up a profit percentage point here or there, there are all kinds of innovations that are helpful," said Mr. Doctor, the analyst. "But they won't turn around the essential problem."

Nat Ives, "The Newspaper Death Watch," AdAge.com, April 28, 2008. Reprinted by permission.

---

enues have declined very quickly and some newspapers have even had to shut down. About 40 newspapers have closed in the U.S. in the last decade.

National Newspapers

In 1982, the Gannett newspaper chain (which owns more newspapers than any other chain) created *USA Today*, which it calls "The Nation's Newspaper." Gannett designed *USA Today* to compete with the country's two other major national newspapers, *The Wall Street Journal* and *The New York Times*. Dubbing it "McPaper" with only "McNuggets" of news, critics called *USA Today* the fast-food approach to news. It features expensive color graphics, a detailed national weather report, comprehensive sports coverage and news stories that rarely run longer than 600 words.

USA Today went after a different audience than the *Journal* and the *Times*—people who don't want to spend a lot of time reading but who want to know the headlines. Someone in an airport or someone who likes something to read on a coffee break, Gannett argued, may not need a paper the size of *The Wall Street Journal* or a large metropolitan daily. *USA Today* succeeded, and Gannett's innovations also have influenced many other newspapers, which have added graphics and color and have shortened the average length of stories.

USA Today, the *Journal* and the *Times* publish regional editions by satellite so that a local bank, for example, can

IMPACT
»» Audience

Illustration 3.1

Percentage of Population Who Say They Read a Newspaper Yesterday (includes online readers)

Adults age 18-35 are much less likely to read a daily newspaper—even online—than mature adults (age 45 and above).

Source: The Pew Research Center for the People and the Press, http://www.people-press.org/report/444/news-media.

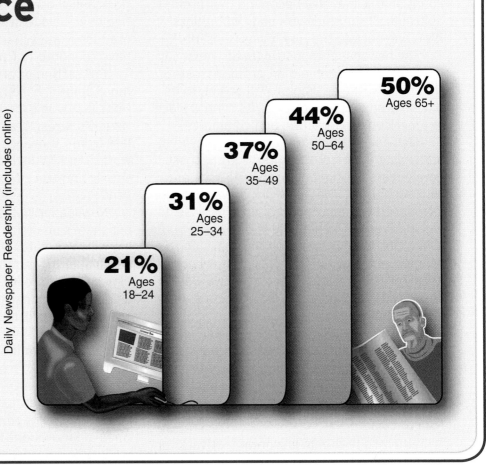

Daily Newspaper Readership (includes online)

21% Ages 18–24

31% Ages 25–34

37% Ages 35–49

44% Ages 50–64

50% Ages 65+

---

place an ad in a regional edition of a national newspaper. Each area's regional edition is distributed in a defined geographic area, so a local advertiser (such as the bank) pays a lower price than someone who advertises nationwide.

USA Today, the *Journal* and the *Times* are today's leaders in the competition to become the nation's leading national newspaper. Each paper has more than a million daily readers of its print edition, with an expanded audience online. Still, even the expanded online audience is not enough to consistently maintain profits.

Internet Editions

Newspaper publishing companies launched Internet editions in the late 1990s to try to capture new audiences for the information they gather. Newspapers arriving on-screen are an essential part of newspapers' reader-friendly strategy, but Internet editions don't generate as much revenue as paper editions because a paper edition can carry much more advertising than an online version. Papers editions

also generate revenue from newsstand sales and subscriptions but, of course, most Internet editions are available free.

Newspapers also are trying to generate some income from home and business Internet users. Information services, based on the huge archives of newspaper stories, also are becoming easier to access. Many larger newspapers offer the current week's news free online, but charge a fee to retrieve the full text of stories from their archives that are more than a week old.

Internet editions publish shorter highlights of the day's news, as well as special features that don't appear in the daily newspaper. Chat rooms offer subscribers the chance to discuss the news, for example, and other interactive features offer Internet links to more information edition and a list of archived stories on related topics plus updated photos and audio and video clips from breaking news events. This is just one way newspapers are trying to retain their audience and advertisers using a new delivery system.

Newspapers such as *The Kansas City Star* (left) and *The Miami Herald* (right) publish Internet editions to attract advertisers and boost their audience.

Technology Transforms Production

Since their colonial beginnings, newspapers have shown their ability to appeal to changing audiences, adapt to growing competition and continue to attract advertisers. The Newspaper Association of America and other newspaper analysts describe these recent advances:

- Reporters and photographers in the field send their stories from laptop computers using wireless technology. Photographers use video and digital cameras, transmitting their pictures to the newsroom electronically. News photography systems can reproduce still pictures for newspapers from video images and digital cameras.

- Newspapers are using the Internet to sell more of the information they gather. Once a story is in a digital format, the information can easily be sold to people who want that information, such as lawyers and researchers.

- Satellite publishing is bringing customized national newspapers in regional editions so advertisers can choose their audiences more selectively.

Today's technology also means that machines are doing work formerly done by people. For newspaper unions, this shift to technology has meant a consistent effort among newspaper owners to challenge union representation.

Before 1970, newspapers needed typographers to handset metal type, and labor unions represented most of these typographers. With the introduction of photocomposition, newspaper management slowly moved to eliminate the typographers' jobs. The unions fought the transition, and

Unionization of newspaper employees began in the 1800s. Unions continue to be a big factor at urban newspapers, but are less influential in mid-sized and small cities. Pressman Niel Nielsen examines a copy of the *San Francisco Chronicle* as it rolls off the press.

many newspaper workers went on strike—notably at the *New York Daily News* in 1990, at the *San Francisco Chronicle* and *San Francisco Examiner* in 1994 and at the *Detroit News* in 1996.

With the threat of technology eliminating even more jobs, newspaper unions are understandably worried. Membership in the Newspaper Guild (which covers reporters) has remained steady, but most of the other newspaper unions have lost members. Forecasts report that union influence at big-city newspapers will remain strong but that the effort by publishers to diffuse union influence at smaller newspapers will continue.

Consolidation Increases Chain Ownership

Because newspaper circulation is declining, large corporations have bought up many newspapers that once were family-owned. Instead of editors competing locally within a community, like Hearst battling Pulitzer, national chains now compete with one another. (See **Illustration 3.2.**)

Chain ownership doesn't necessarily mean that every newspaper in a chain speaks with the voice of the chain

IMPACT
»» Business

Illustration 3.2

Top 10 U.S. Newspaper Companies

Gannett, publisher of *USA Today*, is the nation's biggest newspaper company. Gannett owns more newspapers than any other chain.

Source: Advertising Age DataCenter 100 Leading Media Companies, September 29, 2008.

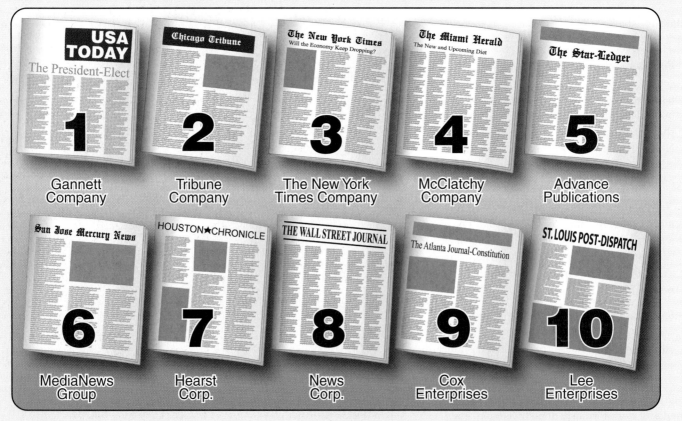

1. Gannett Company
2. Tribune Company
3. The New York Times Company
4. McClatchy Company
5. Advance Publications
6. MediaNews Group
7. Hearst Corp.
8. News Corp.
9. Cox Enterprises
10. Lee Enterprises

owner. Chains can supply money to improve a newspaper's printing plant and to add more reporters. But critics say the tendency to form chains consolidates and limits the traditional sources of information for readers. (See **Chapter 1** for more discussion of media consolidation.)

Today's Newspaper Audience Is a Moving Target

Although newspapers still hold power for advertisers, recent studies reveal that younger readers are deserting the medium. According to Grant Podelco, arts editor of the Syracuse (New York) *Herald-Journal*, "It dawned on us that if we don't start luring teenagers into the paper and start them reading us now, they may not subscribe in the future."

To stop the slide among young readers, many newspapers have added inserts directed to, and sometimes written by, teenagers. *The Wall Street Journal* introduced a high school classroom edition. At the *Chicago Tribune*, five teenage film reviewers appear in the newspaper every Friday with their choices, and a "Preps Plus" section covers high school sports. *The Dallas Morning News* runs a half-sheet called "The Mini Page," subtitled "Especially for Kids and Their Families," which carries puzzles, explanatory stories about current issues and a teacher's guide.

Female readers also are abandoning newspapers in unprecedented numbers. Karen Jurgensen, editorial page editor of *USA Today*, says that readership surveys show women today are less likely to read a daily newspaper than men. "Women across the board are more likely than men to feel that the paper doesn't speak to them," she says. To attract more female readers, *The Charlotte Observer* created a daycare beat, and some newspapers are attempting to devote more space to women's sports. Newspapers also are experimenting with a section targeted specifically for women. The *Chicago Tribune*, for example, launched a section called "WomaNews." Newspaper executives also blame television and the Internet for the declining audience, but others say people's reading habits reflect the changing uses of family time.

In some cities with large Latino populations, newspapers are expanding the market by publishing Spanish-language editions. In areas like Dallas–Fort Worth, where about a fifth of the population is Latino, newspaper companies see an ever-increasing audience with a desire for information.

Newspapers are competing to maintain their audience because audiences attract advertisers—and profits. People who don't read a printed copy of a newspaper may still

Jerry King/Reprinted by permission of CartoonStock

"Ever since I started reading the newspaper online, he's been bringing my computer to me."

want to read the news online. Some large newspapers have even introduced free newspapers, hoping the advertising revenue will support the free editions.

The challenge facing newspaper owners today is how to make money with something people can get free—either a free printed newspaper or a newspaper online. (See **Impact/Culture**, "A Future Filled with Vanishing Ink: With 50 Million Americans Going Online for News Each Day, the Web Has the Edge," page 68.) The average daily newspaper is about two-thirds advertising, and in some newspapers advertising runs as high as 70 percent. National advertisers (such as Procter & Gamble) buy much more television time than newspaper space, but small community businesses still need local newspapers to advertise their products and services.

The race is on to figure out a way to make a profit by bringing the news to an audience that is distracted by other free media and by the personal demands of their own lives. Newspapers also carry a tradition of bringing to the public information about controversies and conflicts that people sometimes would rather not acknowledge. "It's not always our job to give readers what they want," says Dean Baquet, former editor of the *Los Angeles Times*, now at *The New York Times*. The job of newspapers is to help readers understand the world, he told *The New Yorker*. "If we don't do that, who will?"

As the country's first mass medium for news, today's newspaper companies are no longer necessarily the first place people go for information. Today's newspapers are trying to rediscover how they can continue to fulfill their responsibility to keep the public informed and still stay profitable.

IMPACT
≫ Culture

A Future Filled with Vanishing Ink: With 50 Million Americans Going Online for News Each Day, the Web Has the Edge

by Tom Regan

... Let me give you a recent example of why I believe digital news is the news of the future. I still have a copy of *The New York Times* from Thursday, July 7, 2005. The front page showed Londoners celebrating the news that they had been awarded the 2012 summer Olympics Games. But this was old news by the time it hit the streets. On that morning, four young men staged a series of terrorist attacks in London that killed more than 50 people. I spent the entire day online reading news reports, looking at photos that passengers on underground cars had sent via cell phone cameras, glancing at blog postings from survivors and posting comments myself. That day, because of the Internet, I felt intensely connected to the event.

That was the day when I knew that the reign of print was over.

What about radio and TV? I like them, too. But again, those choices are dictated by what I want. Driving in the car or working in the yard, I reach for the radio. At the end of the day, when passive entertainment is all I want, I watch TV.

But while the reign of print as the most important news source may soon end, the role that newspapers play will continue to be important, albeit in an increasingly digital form. My stint at the ONA (Online News Association) taught me that people trust newspapers and that the first place people tend to look online for news is their newspaper's online edition. As people move to the Web,

Nicole Bengiveno/The New York Times/Redux Pictures

Printed newspapers are losing their audience as more people, especially young readers, get all their information online. The difference in generational reading habits today is clear among members of the Sims family of Old Greenwich, Conn., in their living room in 2008.

so are advertisers. Just last week, the Interactive Advertising Bureau released its 2005 report, which showed that online advertising grew by more than 30 percent over 2004.

I like news on the Web for another reason. In today's environment of huge media conglomerates, the Internet is, for now, the one place you can find a true diversity of news voices. A place where mainstream media is not the only choice for news and opinions.

The bottom line is that news organizations will continue to bring you the news in a variety of ways. Depending on the experience you're looking for, the choice is up to you.

Review, Analyze, Investigate
REVIEWING CHAPTER 3

First Mass Medium to Deliver News

✓ Between 1690 and 1920, newspapers were the only mass news medium available.

✓ Newspapers are historically important in defining the cultural concept of an independent press.

Publishers Fight for an Independent Press

✓ The issue of government control of newspapers surfaced early in colonial America, when the authorities stopped *Publick Occurrences* in 1690 after a single issue because the paper angered local officials.

✓ The tradition of an independent press in this country began when James Franklin published the first newspaper without the heading "Published by Authority."

✓ The John Peter Zenger case established an important legal precedent: If what a newspaper reports is true, the paper cannot successfully be sued for libel.

✓ As dissatisfaction grew over British rule, newspapers became essential political tools in the effort to spread revolutionary ideas, including opposition to the British Stamp Act and the Alien and Sedition Laws.

✓ Newspapers expanded their reach in the 1800s to include people on the frontier, the growing number of immigrants and the Native American population.

Newspapers Take Advantage of Early Technology

✓ The technological advances of the 19th century, such as cheaper newsprint, mechanized printing and the telegraph, meant that newspapers could reach a wider audience faster than ever before.

✓ New 19th-century technologies lowered production costs, which made newspaper publishing companies attractive investments.

✓ In the 1800s, newspapers sought new readers—Native Americans, immigrants and those on the nation's frontiers.

Dissident Voices Create the Early Alternative Press

✓ Emancipation and women's suffrage movements fostered the first alternative press movements.

✓ Six early advocates for domestic change were John B. Russwurm, The Rev. Samuel Cornish, Frederick Douglass, William Lloyd Garrison and Ida B. Wells.

Newspapers Seek Mass Audiences and Big Profits

✓ The penny press made newspapers affordable for virtually every American.

✓ The penny press made newspapers available to the masses.

✓ The legacy of the penny press continues today in gossip columns and crime reporting.

Newspapers Dominate the Early 20th Century

✓ Newspapers were the nation's single source of daily dialogue about politics, culture and social issues.

✓ Intense competition bred yellow journalism.

Unionization Encourages Professionalism

✓ Unions standardized wages at many of the nation's largest newspapers.

✓ Unions raised wages and created a sense of professionalism.

Television Brings New Competition

✓ The introduction of television contributed to a decline in newspaper readership that began in the 1950s.

✓ Newspapers were forced to share their audience with broadcasting.

Alternative Press Revives Voices of Protest

✓ The social causes of the 1960s briefly revived the alternative press.

✓ People who supported the alternative press believed the mainstream press was avoiding important issues such as the anti–Vietnam war movement, the civil rights movement and the gay rights movement.

Newspapers Expand and Contract

✓ Since the 1970s, the overall number of newspapers has declined.

✓ To try to match TV's visual appeal, newspapers introduced advanced graphics and vivid color.

✓ Today newspaper audiences are still declining, especially among young readers.

Newspapers at Work

✓ Newspaper operations are divided into two areas: business and editorial.

✓ Almost all newspapers today run Web sites.

Newspapers Struggle to Retain Readers

✓ Big-city newspapers are losing readers.

✓ Newspapers depend primarily on advertising for support.

✓ Most newspaper publishing companies have launched Internet editions to capture new audiences for the information they gather.

✓ The nation's three national newspapers are *USA Today*, *The New York Times* and *The Wall Street Journal*.

Technology Transforms Production

✓ Wireless technology has simplified field reporting.

✓ Newspapers are using the Internet to sell more of the information they gather.

✓ Satellite publishing means national newspapers can publish regional editions.

Consolidation Increases Chain Ownership

✓ Large corporations have bought up newspapers that once were family-owned.

✓ Instead of competing locally, national chains now compete with one another.

Today's Newspaper Audience Is a Moving Target

✓ The future financial success of newspapers depends on their ability to appeal to a shifting audience and meet growing competition.

✓ Newspapers still hold power for advertisers, but recent studies reveal that younger readers are deserting the medium faster than any other group. Readership among women also has declined.

✓ To stop the recent slide in readership, many newspapers have introduced features and special sections targeted toward teenagers and women. In cities with large Latino populations, newspapers have introduced Spanish-language editions. Some large newspapers are distributing free editions. Most newspapers publish Internet editions.

✓ To survive, newspapers must maintain their responsibility to keep the public informed and still stay profitable.

KEY TERMS

These terms are defined in the margins throughout this chapter and appear in alphabetical order with definitions in the Glossary, which begins on page 372.

Alternative, or Dissident, Press 56

Libelous 54

Penny Paper or Penny Press 57

Seditious Language 54

Syndicates 61

Tabloid 59

Yellow Journalism 59

CRITICAL QUESTIONS

1. Describe the circumstances surrounding the John Peter Zenger decision. Which important precedent did the case set for the American media? Why is this precedent so important?

2. Describe the contributions of two early colonial American women publishers.

3. Describe the impact on American society of the competition that developed between the Hearst and Pulitzer newspaper empires. Describe the style of news coverage that characterized that competition. Give an example of sensationalized reporting from your experience.

4. Discuss the growing importance of newspapers published in Spanish and other languages and of newspapers published on the Internet. Consider both the informational and the economic impacts of these changing audiences on local communities and the nation.

5. Describe some of the Internet services newspapers offer and discuss how they make newspapers more accessible to readers. Do you read a newspaper online? How often?

WORKING THE WEB

This list includes sites mentioned in the chapter and others to give you greater insight into newspaper publishing.

American Society of Newspaper Editors
http://www.asne.org

This professional organization for daily newspaper editors has committees and annual conventions that address such issues as ethics, diversity and the Freedom of Information Act. The ASNE also is concerned about improving journalism training and education. A current major focus is to press the new president to maximize transparency in his administration. Committees will also continue to press for passage of a federal shield law and improvements in freedom of information laws at all levels of government.

The Dallas Morning News
http://www.dallasnews.com

One of the major daily newspapers in Texas, *The Dallas Morning News* was a pioneer in creating an online version, DallasNews.com. *The Dallas Morning News* became the first major news organization to run an exclusive online story of convicted Oklahoma City bomber Timothy McVeigh before the printed version was distributed.

Honolulu Star-Bulletin
http://starbulletin.com

The oldest continuously published daily newspaper in Hawaii was bought from Gannett by a Canadian publisher in 2001. The *Star-Bulletin* has historical interest in economy, education and First Amendment rights. According to the newspaper, it has "earned journalistic awards in numbers out of proportion to its staff size."

Los Angeles Times
http://www.latimes.com

As one of California's major urban newspapers, the *Los Angeles Times* is known for the quality of its reporting and its coverage of entertainment-industry news. Since 1942, it has won 35 Pulitzer Prizes. On the Web site, viewers can personalize their news pages around the content that interests them.

The Miami Herald
http://www.miamiherald.com

South Florida's daily newspaper, owned by the McClatchy Company, has developed a reputation for its coverage of Caribbean and Latin American news due to Miami's large Latino population. The paper has published the International Edition for readers in the Caribbean and Latin America since 1946 and in Mexico since 2002. When the McClatchy Company bought Knight Ridder in 2006, the *Herald* was the largest paper acquired in the purchase.

The New York Times
http://www.nytimes.com

Long regarded as the nation's most credible and complete newspaper, the *Times* has won over 100 Pulitzer Prizes, more than any other news organization. The New York Times Company also owns the *International Herald Tribune*, *The Boston Globe*, WQXR-FM and more than 50 Web sites, including About.com.

Newspaper Association of America
http://www.naa.org

As the lobbying organization of the newspaper industry, NAA's goals are to improve newspapers' market shares, advocate their interests to the government, encourage a diverse workforce and provide business and technological guidance.

Seattle Post-Intelligencer
http://seattlepi.nwsource.com

The *Seattle Post-Intelligencer* is the oldest newspaper in Washington state and part of the Hearst Corporation. The online version of the paper, seattlepi.com, includes customizable content and blogs about news issues. Forums and features for parents are available on MomSeattle and DadSeattle. SPIseattle.com is an online-only magazine created and run by *Seattle P-I* interns, and readers create much of the content.

Topix
http://www.topix.net

A customizable news site founded in 2002 by developers of the Open Directory Project, Topix LLC is a privately held company with investment from Gannett, The McClatchy Company and Tribune Company. The Web site links news from 50,000 sources to 360,000 user-generated forums. In 2007, Topix opened its Web site to give all users the power to discuss, edit and share the news important to them.

The Washington Post
http://www.washingtonpost.com

The *Post* is the major daily newspaper of Washington, D.C., and the preeminent newspaper for national political news. The Washington Post Company also owns other media, including *Newsweek*, Cable One and six television stations.

4

Magazines: Targeting the Audience

AFP/Getty Images

In June 2008, an exhibit dedicated to the late actress Grace Kelly, Princess of Monaco, displayed an international array of the many magazine covers that featured the actress.

What's Ahead?

By the early 1950s, magazine

mogul Henry Luce's *Time* and *Fortune* were well established. He often traveled with his wife, Ambassador Clare Boothe Luce, and many of the people Henry Luce met overseas wanted to talk with him about sports instead of international politics.

"Luce knew nothing about sports," says *Los Angeles Times* sports columnist Jim Murray, who in the early 1950s was writing about sports for *Time* magazine. "But every place he'd go, all over the world, the conversation would veer to the World Cup or the British Open or whatever. He got

TimeFrame
1741 – Today

Magazines Grow as a Specialized Medium That Targets Readers

1741   **Benjamin Franklin and Andrew Bradford publish America's first magazines, *General Magazine* (Franklin) and *American Magazine* (Bradford).**

Herbert Orth/Time & Life Pictures/Getty Images

1821   *The Saturday Evening Post* becomes the first magazine to reach a wide public audience.

1830   Louis A. Godey hires Sarah Josepha Hale as the first woman editor of a general circulation women's magazine, *Godey's Lady's Book*.

1865   *The Nation,* featuring political commentary, appears in Boston.

1887   Cyrus Curtis begins publishing *The Ladies' Home Journal*.

1893   Samuel A. McClure founds *McClure's Magazine*, the nation's first major showcase for investigative magazine journalism, featuring muckrakers Ida Tarbell and Lincoln Steffens.

1910   W. E. B. Du Bois and the National Association for the Advancement of Colored People (NAACP) start *The Crisis*.

1923   **Henry Luce creates *Time*, the nation's first news magazine, and then *Fortune* and *Life*, and eventually *Sports Illustrated*.**

Reprinted through the courtesy of the Editors of TIME Magazine © 2008 Time Inc.

1925   Harold Ross introduces *The New Yorker*.

1945   **John Johnson launches *Ebony* and then *Jet*. Johnson's company eventually became the nation's most successful magazine publisher for African American readers.**

Steven L. Raymer/National Geographic/Getty Images

1985   Advance Publications buys *The New Yorker* for more than $185 million, beginning the era of magazine industry consolidation. Today Condé Nast, owned by Advance Publications, publishes *The New Yorker*.

1993   *Newsweek* launches an Internet edition of the magazine.

1997   **Dennis Publishing, which owns *Rolling Stone Magazine*, launches *Maxim*, the most successful magazine launch in the last decade.**

Jeff Fusco/Getty Images

1999   **Time Warner (publishers of *Time* magazine) merges with America Online to form the media giant AOL Time Warner (now Time Warner).**

HENNY RAY ABRAMS/AFP/Getty Images

2000   Oprah Winfrey launches the lifestyle magazine *O*.

2005   *Slate* magazine grows popular as an Internet magazine, one of the first magazine-type publications to be issued exclusively online.

Today   Magazines are very specialized, targeting narrow groups of readers for advertisers. Large media companies publish most magazines and some magazines are published only on the Internet.

fascinated and irritated, I guess, and finally said, 'Why this all consuming interest in games?' We said, 'Well, that's the way the world is, Henry.' He said, 'Well, maybe we ought to start a sports magazine.'" The result was *Sports Illustrated*, which today is ranked among the nation's most profitable magazine brands and is published by the media giant Time Warner.

Sports Illustrated was one of the earliest magazines to anticipate today's trend in magazines targeted to a specific audience. Today, successful magazines cater to their audiences with articles and advertising that reflect what each audience wants. What advertisers like most about magazines is that their readers are usually good targets for the products they see advertised around the articles.

You probably have seen a copy of *Sports Illustrated* recently, or perhaps you read *Glamour* or *Maxim*. These publications, ranked among the country's top magazines, give their readers information they can't find anywhere else, and their vast readership might surprise you.

Magazines Reflect Trends and Culture

Glamour, published by Condé Nast, reaches more than 2 million readers every month and is ranked among the nation's top 10 women's magazines. *Parenting*, the nation's most successful family magazine, caters primarily to new parents and parents with small children, and the magazine's readership is very attractive to advertisers. New parents need new products to take care of that new baby. Advertisers pay $200,000 a page to reach its readers.

Maxim, a flashy magazine aimed at young adult males, was one of the most successful magazine launches ever when it debuted in 1997. Published by the same company that produces *Rolling Stone*, *Maxim* has 2.5 million readers. In 2004, *Maxim* launched Maxim Radio on the satellite radio network Sirius (now Sirius XM Radio), to reach the same audience as the magazine, 21-to 34-year-old males, and in the same year expanded the brand to Latin America.

Glamour, *Parenting* and *Maxim* demonstrate a significant fact about the history of the magazine industry: *Magazines reflect the surrounding culture and the characteristics of the society.* As readers' needs and lifestyles change, so do magazines. The current trend toward specialty and Internet magazines is the latest chapter in this evolution.

Time & Life Pictures/Getty Images

From the beginning, women have been magazines' best audience. In 1948, actress Colleen Townsend sits in front of a display of popular magazines. Townsend is featured as a bride on the cover of *Woman* magazine, on the newsstand behind her.

Colonial Magazines Compete with Newspapers

In 1741, more than 50 years after the birth of the colonies' first newspaper, magazines entered the American media marketplace. Newspapers covered daily crises for local

Sarah Josepha Hale (above) edited *Godey's Lady's Book*.

The Granger Collection

readers, but magazines could reach beyond the parochial concerns of small communities to carry their cultural, political and social ideas to help foster a national identity.

The U.S. magazine industry began in 1741, in Philadelphia, when Benjamin Franklin and Andrew Bradford raced each other to become America's first magazine publisher. Franklin originated the idea of starting the first American magazine, but Bradford issued his *American Magazine* first, on February 13, 1741. Franklin's first issue of *General Magazine* came out three days later. Neither magazine lasted very long. Bradford published three issues and Franklin published six, but their efforts initiated a rich tradition.

Because they didn't carry advertising, early magazines were expensive and their circulations remained very small, limited to people who could afford them. Like colonial newspapers, early magazines primarily provided a means for political expression.

Magazines Travel Beyond Local Boundaries

Newspapers flooded the larger cities by the early 1800s, but they circulated only within each city's boundaries, so national news spread slowly. Colleges were limited to the wealthy, and books were expensive. Magazines became America's only national medium to travel beyond local boundaries, and subscribers depended on them for news, culture and entertainment.

The magazine that first reached a large public was *The Saturday Evening Post*, started in 1821. The early *Post*s cost a nickel each and were only four pages, with no illustrations. One-fourth of the magazine was advertising, and it was affordable.

Publishers Locate New Readers

Magazines like *The Saturday Evening Post* reached a wide readership with their general interest content, but many other audiences were available to 19th-century publishers, and they spent the century locating their readership. Four enduring subjects that expanded the magazine audience in the 1800s were women's issues, social crusades, literature and the arts, and politics.

Women's Issues

Because women were a sizable potential audience, magazines were more open to female contributors than were newspapers. A central figure in the history of women's magazines in America was Sarah Josepha Hale.

In 1830, Louis A. Godey was the first publisher to capitalize on a female audience. Women, most of whom had not attended school, sought out *Godey's Lady's Book* and its gifted editor, Sarah Josepha Hale, for advice on morals, manners, literature, fashion, diet and taste.

When her husband died in 1822, Hale sought work to support herself and her five children. As the editor of *Godey's* for 40 years beginning in 1837, she fervently supported higher education and property rights for women. By 1860, *Godey's* had 150,000 subscribers. Hale retired from the magazine when she was 89, a year before she died.

Bettmann/CORBIS

Pictured is a sample of 1875 fashions displayed in *Godey's*, one of the nation's first fashion magazines.

Social Crusades

Magazines also became important instruments for social change. The *Ladies' Home Journal* is credited with leading a crusade against dangerous medicines. Many of the ads in women's magazines in the 1800s were for patent medicines like Faber's Golden Female Pills ("successfully used by prominent ladies for female irregularities") and Ben-Yan, which promised to cure "all nervous debilities."

Ladies' Home Journal was the first magazine to refuse patent medicine ads. Founded in 1887 by Cyrus Curtis, the *Journal* launched several crusades. It offered columns about women's issues, published popular fiction and even printed sheet music.

Editor Edward Bok began his crusade against patent medicines in 1892, after he learned that many of them contained more than 40 percent alcohol. Next, Bok revealed that a medicine sold to soothe noisy babies contained morphine. Other magazines joined the fight against dangerous ads, and partly because of Bok's crusading investigations, Congress passed the Pure Food and Drug Act of 1906.

Fostering the Arts

In the mid-1800s, American magazines began to seek a literary audience by promoting the nation's writers. Two of today's most important literary magazines—*Harper's* and *The Atlantic*—began more than a century ago. *Harper's New Monthly Magazine*, known today as *Harper's*, first appeared in 1850.

The American literary showcase grew when *The Atlantic Monthly* appeared in 1857 in Boston. The magazine's purpose was "to inoculate the few who influence the many." That formula continues today, with *The Atlantic* and *Harper's* still publishing literary criticism and promoting political debate.

Political Commentary

With more time (usually a month between issues) and space than newspapers had to reflect on the country's problems, political magazines provided a forum for public arguments by scholars and critical observers. Three of the nation's progressive political magazines that began in the 19th and early 20th centuries have endured: *The Nation*, *The New Republic* and *The Crisis*.

The Crisis, founded by W. E. B. Du Bois in 1910 as the monthly magazine of the National Association for the Advancement of Colored People, continues to publish today.

The Nation, founded in 1865, is the oldest continuously published opinion journal in the United States, offering critical literary essays and arguments for progressive change. This weekly magazine has survived a succession of owners and financial hardship.

Another outspoken publication, which began challenging the establishment in the early 1900s, is *The New Republic*, founded in 1914. The weekly's circulation has rarely reached 60,000, but its readers enjoy the role it plays in regularly criticizing political leaders.

An important organization that needed a voice at the beginning of the century was the National Association for the Advancement of Colored People (NAACP). For 24 years, beginning in 1910, that voice was W. E. B. Du Bois, who founded and edited the organization's monthly magazine, *The Crisis*. Du Bois began *The Crisis* as the official monthly magazine of the NAACP. In *The Crisis*, he attacked discrimination against African American soldiers during World War I, exposed Ku Klux Klan activities, and argued for African American voting and housing rights. By 1919, circulation was more than 100,000. Today, *The Crisis* continues to publish monthly.

Postal Act Helps Magazines Grow

The Postal Act of 1879 encouraged the growth of magazines. Before the Act passed, newspapers traveled through the mail free while magazine publishers had to pay postage. With the Postal Act of 1879, Congress gave magazines second-class mailing privileges and a cheap mailing rate.

This meant quick, reasonably priced distribution for magazines, and today magazines still travel on a preferential postage rate.

Aided by lower mailing costs, the number of monthly magazines grew from 180 in 1860 to over 1,800 by 1900. However, because magazines travel through the mail, they are vulnerable to censorship (see **Chapter 14**).

McClure's Launches Investigative Journalism

Colorful, campaigning journalists began investigating big business just before the turn of the 20th century. They became known as ***muckrakers***. The strongest editor in the first 10 years of the 20th century was legendary magazine publisher Samuel S. McClure, who founded *McClure's Magazine* in 1893.

McClure and his magazine were very important to the Progressive era in American politics, which called for an end to the close relationship between government and big business. To reach a large readership, McClure priced his new monthly magazine at 15 cents an issue, while most other magazines sold for 25 or 35 cents. He hired writers such as Lincoln Steffens and Ida Tarbell to investigate wrongdoing.

Published since 1925, *The New Yorker* is one of the nation's most successful magazines and continues today to be the primary showcase for American writers and artists.

Muckrakers Investigative magazine journalists who targeted abuses by government and big business.

Ida Tarbell joined *McClure's* in 1894 as associate editor. Her series about President Lincoln boosted the magazine's circulation. Subsequently, Tarbell tackled a series about Standard Oil. (See **Impact/People**, "Muckraker Ida Tarbell Targets John D. Rockefeller," page 79.)

Tarbell peeled away the veneer of the country's biggest oil trust. Her 19-part series began running in *McClure's* in 1904. Eventually the series became a two-volume book, *History of the Standard Oil Company*, which established Tarbell's reputation as a muckraker. The muckrakers' targets were big business and corrupt government. President Theodore Roosevelt coined the term *muckraker* in 1906 when he compared reformers like Tarbell and Steffens to the "Man with the Muckrake" who busily dredged up the dirt in John Bunyan's book *Pilgrim's Progress*.

By 1910, many reforms sought by the muckrakers had been adopted, and this particular type of magazine journalism declined. The muckrakers often are cited as America's original investigative journalists.

The New Yorker and *Time* Succeed Differently

Magazines in the first half of the 20th century matured and adapted to absorb the invention of radio and then television. As with magazines today, magazine publishers had two basic choices:

1. Publishers could seek a *definable, targeted loyal audience,* or

2. Publishers could seek a *broad, general readership.*

3. Harold Ross, founding editor of *The New Yorker*, and Henry Luce, who started Time Inc., best exemplify these two different types of American publishers in the first half of the 20th century.

Harold Ross and *The New Yorker*

Harold Ross' *The New Yorker* magazine launched the wittiest group of writers that ever gathered around a table at New York's Algonquin Hotel. The "witcrackers," who met there regularly for lunch throughout the 1920s, included Heywood Broun, Robert Benchley, Dorothy Parker, Alexander Woollcott, James Thurber and Harpo Marx. Because they sat at a large round table in the dining room, the group came to be known as the Algonquin Round Table.

Harold Ross persuaded Raoul Fleischmann, whose family money came from the yeast company of the same name, to invest half a million dollars in *The New Yorker* before the magazine began making money in 1928, three years after its

IMPACT
» People

Muckraker Ida Tarbell Targets John D. Rockefeller

When John D. Rockefeller refused to talk with her, Ida Tarbell sat at the back of the room and watched him deliver a Sunday-school sermon. In her autobiography, *All in the Day's Work,* written when she was 80, Tarbell described some of her experiences as she investigated the Standard Oil Company:

"The impression of power deepened when Mr. Rockefeller took off his coat and hat, put on a skullcap and took a seat commanding the entire room, his back to the wall. It was the head which riveted attention. It was big, great breadth from back to front, high broad forehead, big bumps behind the ears, not a shiny head but with a wet look. The skin was as fresh as that of any healthy man about us. The thin sharp nose was like a thorn. There

In 1904, muckraker Ida Tarbell targeted oil magnate John D. Rockefeller, who called her "that misguided woman."

[LC-US262-53912/Library of Congress Prints and Photographs Division

were no lips; the mouth looked as if the teeth were all shut hard. Deep furrows ran down each side of the mouth from the nose. There were puffs under the little colorless eyes with creases running from them.

"Wonder over the head was almost at once diverted to wonder over the man's uneasiness. His eyes were never quiet but darted from face to face, even peering around the jog at the audience close to the wall. . . .

"My two hours' study of Mr. Rockefeller aroused a feeling I had not expected, which time has intensified. I was sorry for him. I know no companion so terrible as fear. Mr. Rockefeller, for all the conscious power written in face and voice and figure, was afraid, I told myself, afraid of his own kind."

---

launch. Ross published some of the country's great commentary, fiction and humor, sprinkled with cartoons that gave *The New Yorker* its charm. Ross edited the magazine until he died in 1951, and William Shawn succeeded him.

After one owner—the Fleischmann family—and only two editors in 60 years, *The New Yorker* was sold in 1985 to Advance Publications, the parent company of one of the nation's largest magazine groups, Condé Nast. *The New Yorker* continues today to be the primary showcase for contemporary American writers and artists.

Henry Luce's Empire: *Time*

Henry Luce is the singular giant of 20th-century magazine publishing. Unlike Harold Ross, who sought a sophisticated,

wealthy audience, Luce wanted to reach the largest possible readership. Luce's first creation was *Time* magazine, which he founded in 1923 with his Yale classmate Briton Hadden. Luce and Hadden paid themselves $30 a week and recruited their friends to write for the magazine.

The first issue of *Time* covered the week's events in 28 pages, minus six pages of advertising—half an hour's reading. "It was of course not for people who really wanted to be informed," wrote Luce's biographer W. A. Swanberg. "It was for people willing to spend a half-hour to avoid being entirely uninformed." The brash news magazine became the foundation of Luce's media empire, which eventually also launched *Fortune, Life, Sports Illustrated, Money* and *People Weekly.* Today, *Time* is only a small part of the giant company Time

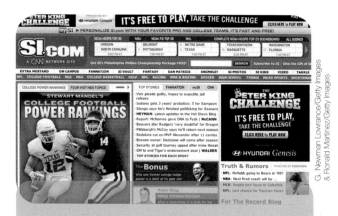

Originated by Henry Luce in the 1950s, *Sports Illustrated* was an immediate success. The SI.com Web site and *Sports Illustrated* are just two of the many media properties controlled today by media giant Time Warner.

Warner, which includes television stations, movie studios, book publishing companies, Home Box Office, CNN and America Online.

Luce's magazine fostered look-alikes called *Ebony*, an African American magazine introduced in the 1940s by John H. Johnson. The Johnson chain also launched *Jet* magazine. At the beginning of the 21st century, *Ebony* and *Jet* had a combined readership of three million people. Johnson groomed his daughter, Linda Johnson Rice, to assume management of the company, a job Rice assumed in 2005 when her father died.

Specialized Magazines Take Over

In the 1950s, television began to offer Americans some of the same type of general interest features that magazines provided. General interest magazines collapsed. Readers wanted specialized information they could not get from other sources. These new targeted magazines segmented the market, which meant each magazine attracted fewer readers.

Very few general interest magazines survive today. The trend, since television expanded the media marketplace,

Consumer Magazines All magazines sold by subscription or at newsstands, supermarkets and bookstores.

Trade, Technical and Professional Magazines Magazines dedicated to a particular business or profession.

Company Magazines Magazines produced by businesses for their employees, customers and stockholders.

is for magazines to find a specific audience interested in the information that magazines can deliver. This is called *targeting an audience*, which today magazines can do more effectively than any other medium.

Magazines Divide into Three Types

Today's magazines can be categorized into three types:

1. Consumer magazines
2. Trade, technical and professional magazines
3. Company magazines

You probably are most familiar with **consumer magazines**, which are popularly marketed: *Time*, *Glamour*, *Parenting* and *Maxim* are popular examples. In the magazine business, *consumer* magazines are not just those that give buying advice. This term refers to all magazines sold by subscription or at newsstands, supermarkets and bookstores. As a group, consumer magazines make the most money because they have the most readers and carry the most advertising.

People in a particular industry read **trade, technical and professional magazines** to learn more about their business. *Veterinary Practice Management*, for example, is a trade magazine, published as "a business guide for small animal practitioners." So are the *Columbia Journalism Review* (published by Columbia University) and *American Medical News* (published by the American Medical Association).

Media companies issue these magazines for their specific subscribers (*Veterinary Practice Management*, for example); universities or university-connected organizations, for their subscribers (*Columbia Journalism Review*, for example); or professional associations, for their members (*American Medical News*, for example). Most trade, technical and professional magazines carry advertising directed at the professions they serve.

Company magazines are produced by businesses for their employees, customers and stockholders. These magazines usually don't carry advertising. Their main purpose is to promote the company. Chevron, for instance, publishes a company magazine called *Chevron USA Odyssey*.

Magazines at Work

Magazine employees work in one of five divisions:

1. Editorial
2. Circulation sales
3. Advertising sales

4. Manufacturing and distribution

5. Administration

The *editorial* department handles everything regarding the content of the magazine, except the advertisements. This is the department for which magazine editors work, and they decide the subjects for each magazine issue, oversee the people who write the articles and schedule the articles for the magazine. Designers who determine the "look" of the magazine also are considered part of the editorial department.

The *circulation* department manages the subscription information. Workers in this department enter new subscriptions and handle address changes and cancellations, for example. The *advertising* department is responsible for finding companies that would like to advertise in the magazine. Advertising employees often help the companies design their ads to be consistent with the magazine format.

Manufacturing and *distribution* departments manage the production of the magazine and get it to readers. This often includes contracting with an outside company to print the magazine. Many magazine companies also contract with an outside distribution company rather than deliver the magazines themselves.

Administration, as in any media company, takes care of the organizational details—the paperwork of hiring, paying bills and managing the office, for example.

Because advertisers provide nearly half a magazine's income, tension often develops between a magazine's advertising staff and its editorial staff. The advertising staff may lobby the editor for favorable stories about potential advertisers, but the editor is responsible to the audience of the magazine. The advertising department might argue with the editor, for example, that a local restaurant will not want to advertise in a magazine that publishes an unfavorable review of the restaurant. If the restaurant is a big advertiser, the editor must decide how best to maintain the magazine's integrity.

The Audit Bureau of Circulations (**ABC**), an agency of print media market research, verifies and publishes circulation figures for member magazines. Advertisers use ABC figures to help them decide which magazines will reach their audience. Circulation figures (how many readers each magazine has) determine how much each magazine can charge for ads in the magazine.

Putting the magazine together and selling it (circulation, advertising, administration, manufacturing and distribution) cost more than organizing the articles and photographs that appear in the magazine (editorial). Often a managing editor coordinates all five departments.

Amanda Edwards/Getty Images

In 2005, Linda Johnson Rice succeeded her father, John H. Johnson, publisher and founder of Johnson Publications, after he died. Rice had worked with her father on the magazine since the 1980s. In 2006, CEO Rice delivered a speech at the 2nd Annual Ebony Oscar Celebration in Hollywood, which honors African Americans in film and television.

The magazine editor's job is to keep the content interesting so people will continue to read the magazine. (See **Impact/People**, "101 Secrets (and 9 Lives) of a Magazine Star," page 82.) Good magazine editors can create a distinctive, useful product by carefully choosing the best articles for the magazine's audience and ensuring the articles are well written.

Full-time magazine staffers write many of the articles, such as a food editor who creates recipes or a columnist who writes commentary. Nearly half the nation's magazines, however, use articles by *freelancers*. Freelancers do not receive a salary from the magazine; instead, they are paid individually for each of their articles published in the magazine. Many freelancers write for several magazines simultaneously. Some freelancers specialize—just writing travel articles, for example. Other freelancers work just as the tradition of their name implies: They have a pen for hire, and they can write about any subject a magazine editor wants.

ABC Audit Bureau of Circulations.

Freelancers Writers who are not on the staff of a magazine but who are paid for each individual article published.

IMPACT
»People

101 Secrets (and 9 Lives) of a Magazine Star

by David Carr

Walk by the magazine rack, turn on a television at dinnertime or sneak a peek at the gossip sites during work, and you will notice a lot of Angelina and a ton of Paris, and see far too much of Britney. But in all of those places, there is someone who is more ubiquitous, more oddly present, than all those women combined.

You would probably not pay her any mind if you saw her on a train–reading a magazine, of course–but the cultural footprint of Bonnie Fuller, a self-described geek from Canada, is everywhere you look. As the editor of a string of teenage, women's and celebrity magazines, Ms. Fuller has created a frothy world, and, like it or not, we all live in it.

When the current issue of *Glamour* promises "101 Racy Little Sex Ideas," you are seeing Ms. Fuller's twining of sex and numerology. Ditto for this week's *People*, which promises "91 Sexy and Single Guys."

Bonnie Fuller has had a very successful 20-year career as a magazine editor, creating the formula for today's celebrity and women's magazines such as *Us Weekly*, *Star* and *Cosmopolitan*.

The added single digit seems gratuitous, but admit it: you wonder what the 101st weapon in the erotic arsenal looks like and which guy came after the 90 other hotties. That pruri-

"Your magazine smells fabulous. May I kiss you?"

Magazines Compete for Readers in Crowded Markets

Today, trends in magazine publishing continue to reflect social and demographic changes, but magazines no longer play the cutting-edge social, political and cultural role they played in the past (see **Illustration 4.1**). Instead, most magazines are seeking a specific audience, and many more magazines are competing for the same readers.

Newsweek and *U.S. News & World Report* compete with *Time* in the newsweekly category to serve the reader who wants a weekly news roundup. *Fortune* is no longer alone; it has been joined by magazines like *BusinessWeek*,

ent need to know just a little more is pure Bonnie Fuller.

Celebrity magazines, which once seemed to be multiplying weekly, are full of Ms. Fuller's fundamental conceptual scoop: Stars, however stellar they may appear, are just like us—if you don't count the parts about unusually beautiful and impossibly wealthy. The sight of an A-lister having a Slurpee or taking out his garbage has become a huge get in the current media ecosystem.

And it doesn't stop with those tatty delights. Celebrities, even those famous for being infamous, have become muses for the most staid of publications. Britney Spears recently anchored the cover of *The Atlantic Monthly*. Yes, celebrities have always been with us, but not quite in the way they are now since Ms. Fuller rethought them as familiars, our fake friends whom we can slag or praise, depending on the moment.

By reinterpreting a magazine formula that first surfaced in Britain, Ms. Fuller, as the editor of *Us Weekly* and then *Star* magazine came up with a girly template rendered in bubbly pastels and embroidered with lots of over-narration about stars' foibles and mortality. The business results have been astonishing. During Ms. Fuller's 16-month tenure at *Us Weekly*, newsstand sales more than dou-

bled, to 600,000 copies. And *Star*'s overall circulation grew to 1.25 million from 1 million after the conversion to a glossy magazine. Ms. Fuller was named editor of the year, twice, by *Advertising Age*—once for *Cosmopolitan* and again for *Us Weekly*.

Ms. Fuller's fizzy reach extends to television, where *Entertainment Tonight* and *Access Hollywood* take to the latest inflection in the Brangelina story with seismic pronouncements. And, again, the mainstream has been sucked into the conversation, with morning shows and even CNN weighing in gravely when some celebribot tips over into dissolution.

And don't forget the Web, where celebrity ranks just behind porn, with all manner of breathless, by-the-second updates. Thus was born the perfectly confected TMZ, a celeb-chasing Web brand that Time Warner owns. It developed enough mojo to spawn its own television show.

So there you have it: Through nearly two decades of vision and relentlessness, Ms. Fuller created a way of objectifying the A and B list that turned celebrities into not only our "friends," but also American royals, unelected gods who walk among us.

Forbes and *Nation's Business* in the category of business magazines. Some new men's magazines, such as *Maxim*, have been launched successfully to appeal to a younger audience. However, the magazine audience has grown older and today read magazines like *Yachting* and *Better Homes and Gardens*. Still, women continue to be the single most lucrative audience for magazines.

Younger readers are less likely to read magazines than their parents. In 1990, for the first time, the number of magazines published in the United States stopped growing.

Family Circle and *Woman's Day* are called **point-of-purchase magazines** because they are sold mainly at the checkout stands in supermarkets and are one part of the women's market. *Vogue*, *Glamour* and *Cosmopolitan* cater to the fashion-conscious, and women's magazines have matured to include the working women's audience with *Savvy*, *Self* and *Working Woman*, for example. The market

is divided still further by magazines like *Essence*, aimed at professional African American women, and the specifically targeted *Today's Chicago Woman* for female executives who live in Chicago.

Segmenting the Audience

The newest segment of the magazine audience to be targeted by special-interest magazines is the young men's audience, represented by *Maxim* and its brother magazine *Stuff*. The tendency to specialize has not yet reached the level suggested by one magazine publisher, who joked that soon there

Point-of-Purchase Magazines Magazines that consumers buy directly, not by subscription. They are sold mainly at checkout stands in supermarkets.

IMPACT
»» Audience

Illustration 4.1

Top 10 U.S. Magazines by Category

Women's magazines are the top-selling magazine category, and men's magazines rank sixth among top-rated magazines.

Source: adage.com, DataCenter.

1 Women's
2 Home
3 Newsweeklies
4 Business & Finance
5 General Interest
6 Men's
7 Sports
8 Metropolitan/ Regional/State
9 Automotive
10 Boating & Yachting

Courtesy of Hispanic Business Inc.

To try to maintain profits, magazines are targeting specialized audiences, such as the Latino readership sought by the magazine *Hispanic Business.*

might be magazines called *Working Grandmother, Left-handed Tennis* and *Colonial Homes in Western Vermont.*

Magazine publishers are seeking readers with a targeted interest and then selling those readers to the advertisers who want to reach that specific audience—skiers, condominium owners, motorcyclists and toy collectors. Besides targeting a special audience, such as gourmets or computer hackers, magazines also can divide their audience further with regional and special editions that offer articles for specific geographic areas along with regional

advertising, or webzines, which are online magazines available on the Internet. The newsweeklies, such as *Time* and *Newsweek*, can insert advertising for a local bank or a local TV station next to national ads. This gives the local advertiser the prestige of a national magazine, at a lower cost.

Magazine Launches

Most new magazines are small-scale efforts produced on a computer and financed by loyal relatives or friends. Sex is a favorite category for new magazines, followed by lifestyle, sports, media personalities and home improvement. In 2000, television personality Oprah Winfrey launched a lifestyles magazine called *O*.

But only a few new magazines succeed. Today, only one in three new magazines will survive more than five years. The reason most magazines fail is that many new companies do not have the money to keep publishing long enough to be able to refine their editorial content, sell advertisers on the idea and gather subscribers—in other words, until the magazine can make a profit. (See **Impact/World**, "International Magazine Publishers See Future, but No Profit, in Shift to Internet," page 85.)

International Magazine Publishers See Future, but No Profit, in Shift to Internet

by Kevin J. O'Brien

In 1980, the aspiring global media baron Rupert Murdoch turned to the president of his U.S. newspaper operations, Donald Kummerfeld, and, as he was wont to do, made a bold prediction.

"Someday, Don," Murdoch said, according to Kummerfeld, "all news—and advertising—will be delivered digitally. There will really be no need for paper and ink."

International magazine publishing companies like Axel Springer (Germany) and Hachette (France) are struggling to take advantage of the vast potential magazine audience online.

More than a quarter of a century later, the world's largest publishing companies are struggling with the implications of Murdoch's future, as Internet-based news and information services steal their readers and advertising sales.

"We are on the cusp of a new era in media," said Kummerfeld, the former head of News America Publishing and now president and chief executive of the International Federation of the Periodical Press, based in London. "It is time for the industry to seize the possibilities." . . .

For most publishers at the conference, the Internet remains a greedy one-way vacuum, siphoning readers and advertising into an uncertain future.

After years of denying that online rivals posed a threat, some publishers said they were now following strategies to transform or defend their traditional print businesses.

The French publisher Hachette, a unit of Lagardère, began selling online subscriptions to 200 of its magazines in August [2006]. . . . Philippe Hautrive, the executive vice president for business operations at Hachette Distribution Services, said about 20,000 consumers had taken up the offer.

But Hachette is making sales, not profit. The economics of online publishing, though lower-cost because no paper or printing is used, are still daunting for companies like Hachette and Axel Springer of Germany, because most Internet-savvy readers expect online text to be free.

Hachette sells access to digital facsimiles of four magazines for just €9.90, or about $13 a month. Consumers download the magazines, which are enhanced with embedded audio and video, and read them off line. They can switch the four titles each month and there is no yearly commitment.

"There is no question that online sales are part of the future," Hautrive said, adding that Hachette planned to expand its online sales to 500 titles in France and, later this year, in Britain. "The only question is how big a part they will be."

(continued)

All magazines are vulnerable to changing economic and even technology trends. In 2005, *TV Guide* announced that it was discontinuing the magazine's role as a publisher of local TV schedules and, instead, re-launching the magazine in a new format exclusively devoted to celebrity news. Changing technology, and the expansion of TV channels, made it too hard for the magazine to keep up with TV programming, so the magazine chose to focus on the most popular part of the magazine—celebrity features.

The number of magazines people buy each year remains static, but revenues are increasing. Although magazines once were very inexpensive and advertising paid for most of the cost of production, publishers gradually have been charging more, and subscribers seem willing to pay more for the magazines they want.

Although circulation is down, advertising revenue at magazines is going up. Even though the audiences are smaller, magazines have increased the price they charge advertisers because magazine readers are a very good consumer audience. They're more likely to be interested in the specific products advertised in a magazine that's devoted to a subject they enjoy. (See **Illustration 4.2.**)

In 2000, Oprah Winfrey launched a lifestyle magazine called *O*, designed to capitalize on her popular TV show. The magazine is just one part of Winfrey's growing media empire. This 2008 photo shows Winfrey arriving in London at a charity dinner in honor of Nelson Mandela.

Dave Hogan/Getty Images

Readers Represent a Valuable Audience

The average magazine reader is a high school graduate, is married, owns a home and works full-time. This is a very attractive audience for advertisers. Advertisers also like magazines because people often refer to an ad weeks after they first see it. Many readers say they read a magazine as

IMPACT

>> **Audience**

Illustration 4.2

Top 10 U.S. Consumer Magazines

People magazine is America's top-selling magazine, while *Sports Illustrated* is ranked third and *Cosmopolitan* is ranked tenth.

Source: *Advertising Age Magazine 300,* October 6, 2008.

much for the ads as they do for the articles. This, of course, is also very appealing to advertisers. The Magazine Publishers Association reports that people keep a magazine issue an average of 17 weeks and that each issue has at least four adult readers on average. This magazine sharing is called *pass-along readership*.

Advertisers can target their audiences better in magazines than in most other media because magazines can divide their audiences for advertisers by geography, income, interests and even zip code. As an advertiser, this means you can advertise special offers for separate portions of the country or market expensive products in regional issues of the magazine that go to wealthy zip codes.

Companies Expand Ownership and Define Readership

In 1984, for the first time, the price paid for individual magazine companies and groups of magazines bought and sold in

Pass-Along Readership People who share a magazine with the original recipient.

IMPACT
»» Business

Illustration 4.3

Top 10 Web Sites Associated with Magazine Brands

Sports and fashion are popular topics for magazine-related content on the Internet.

Source: Media Industry Newsletter, provided exclusively to Magazine Publishers of America, www.magazine.org.

Top 10 Web Sites Associated with Magazine Brands

	Site	Media Magazine Parent
1	nymag.com	New York Magazine
2	mensvogue.com	Men's Vogue
3	4wheeloffroad.com	4Wheel & Off-Road
4	esquire.com	Esquire
5	harpersbazaar.com	Harper's Bazaar
6	style.com	Style.com
7	hallmark.com	Hallmark
8	SI.com	Sports Illustrated
9	archdigest.com	Architectural Digest
10	housebeautiful.com	House Beautiful

one year reached $1 billion. *U.S. News & World Report* sold for $100 million. *Billboard* sold for $40 million. Like other media industries, magazines are being gathered together under large umbrella organizations, and this trend continues today. A single magazine publishing company, such as Condé Nast, may publish 200 or more different magazines each month.

These companies tend to seek more refined audience targeting. As the audience becomes more segmented, magazine publishers envision a time when they will deliver to each reader exactly what he or she wants to read. This means an infinitely defined readership, so advertisers will be able to reach only the people they want.

"Our last cell phone call, and instead of getting us help, you renew your subscription to some car magazine?"

Jerry King/Reprinted by permission of CartoonStock

Internet Editions Offer New Publishing Outlets

The way magazines do business in the future will be affected by technology as well as by the shifting economics of the industry. The latest innovation in magazine publishing is Internet editions as a way to expand readership and give advertisers access to an online audience.

As early as 1993, *Newsweek* launched an Internet edition of its weekly magazine; in 1994, *BusinessWeek* began offering its magazine online, including a feature that gives readers access to Internet conferences with editors and newsmakers and forums where readers can post messages related to topics covered in each issue of the magazine. Many major consumer magazines today publish Internet editions (see **Illustration 4.3**).

The economics of online publishing also make it possible for someone using a personal computer, a scanner, a digital camera and desktop publishing software to publish a magazine just online, dedicated to a fairly small audience, with none of the expense of mail distribution. Some large magazine publishing companies have launched literary political online magazines, such as *Salon.com* and *Slate*, which have attracted a very loyal Internet readership. The economics of online publishing make it possible for someone to launch a new magazine with very little investment.

In 2005, *Slate* editor Michael Kinsley launched online **podcasts**, available by subscription on *Slate*'s Web site. Kinsley said *Slate* would offer "weekday podcasts of one or more of our articles read aloud (mostly by me, *Slate*'s resident radio guy). Think of this as books on tape—only without the books and without the tape." With podcasts, Kinsley said, readers would be able to "listen to some of your favorite *Slate* features while you're commuting or working out or sitting in a tedious meeting (make sure the boss can't see

your earbuds)." Podcasts are the latest way the Internet has helped magazines and newspapers expand their audiences beyond the printed page.

Why Magazines Survive

Magazines survive because they complement the other media and have their own special benefits. Wayne Warner, president of Judd's, Inc. (purchased in 2007 by RR Donnelley), which prints more than 77 American magazines as diverse as *The New Republic*, *Modern Plastics* and *Newsweek*, best describes the advantages of magazines as a medium: "With magazines, we can read *what* we want, *when* we want and *where* we want. And we can read them again and again at our pace, fold them, spindle them, mutilate them, tear out coupons, ads, or articles that interest us and, in short, do what we damn well please to them because they are 'our' magazines."

> **Podcast** An audio or video file made available on the Internet for anyone to download, often available by subscription.

Review, Analyze, Investigate
REVIEWING CHAPTER 4

Magazines Reflect Trends and Culture

✓ Magazines mirror the society.

✓ Today, magazines target specific audiences.

✓ Internet editions expand magazines' traditional reach.

Colonial Magazines Compete with Newspapers

✓ American magazines began in 1741 when Andrew Bradford published *American Magazine* and Benjamin Franklin published *General Magazine*.

✓ Like colonial newspapers, early magazines provided a means for political expression.

✓ *The Saturday Evening Post*, first published in 1821, was the nation's first general interest magazine.

✓ Early magazines were expensive and had small circulations.

Magazines Travel Beyond Local Boundaries

✓ The Postal Act of 1879 encouraged the growth of magazines because it ensured quick, reasonably priced distribution for magazines. Today's magazines still travel on a preferential postal rate.

✓ The *Saturday Evening Post* was the first national magazine with a large circulation.

Publishers Locate New Readers

✓ Magazines widened their audience in the 1800s by catering to women, tackling social crusades, becoming a literary showcase for American writers and encouraging political debate.

✓ Sarah Josepha Hale and Edward Bok were central figures in the development of early magazines in the United States.

✓ In 1910, W. E. B. DuBois launched *The Crisis*, published for an African American audience.

McClure's Launches Investigative Journalism

✓ *McClure's Magazine* pioneered investigative reporting in the United States early in the 20th century. *McClure's* published the articles of Ida Tarbell, who was critical of American industrialists.

✓ Early investigative magazine reporters were called muckrakers.

The New Yorker and *Time* Succeed Differently

✓ Magazines in the first half of the 20th century adapted to absorb the invention of radio and television. To adapt, some publishers sought a defined, targeted audience; others tried to attract the widest audience possible. *The New*

Yorker and *Time* magazines are media empires that began during the early 20th century.

Specialized Magazines Take Over

✓ Magazines in the second half of the 20th century survived by targeting readers' special interests.

✓ Specialization segments an audience for advertisers, making magazines the most specific buy an advertiser can make.

✓ Publishers can target their magazines by geography, income and interest group, as well as by zip code.

Magazines Divide into Three Types

✓ There are three types of magazines: consumer magazines; trade, technical and professional magazines; and company magazines.

✓ Consumer magazines make the most money because they have the most readers and carry the most advertising.

Magazines at Work

✓ Magazine employers work in one of five areas: editorial, circulation sales, advertising sales, manufacturing and distribution, and administration.

✓ The Audit Bureau of Circulations (ABC) monitors and verifies readership.

✓ Magazine prices are rising as subscribers are asked to pay as much as half the cost of producing each magazine.

Magazines Compete for Readers in Crowded Markets

✓ The audience for magazines is growing older, and young readers are less likely to read magazines.

✓ The number of magazines being published in the United States has stayed the same since 1990.

✓ Women continue to be the single most lucrative audience for magazines.

Readers Represent a Valuable Audience

✓ Each issue of a magazine, according to the Magazine Publishers Association, has at least four adult readers on average, and people keep an issue an average of 17 weeks.

✓ Magazines can target readers better than other media because they can divide their readers by geography, income and interests.

Companies Expand Ownership and Define Readership

✓ Magazines are consolidating into large groups just like other media.

✓ Magazine publishers envision a time when their readership will be even more specialized than today.

Internet Editions Offer New Publishing Outlets

✓ Many magazines have launched Internet sites to expand their readership.

✓ Today's Internet technology means people can start an online magazine without the production and mailing expense of a printed publication.

✓ Some magazines, such as *Salon.com* and *Slate*, are published only on the Internet.

Why Magazines Survive

✓ Magazines complement other media.

✓ Magazines are a very personal product.

KEY TERMS

These terms are defined in the margins throughout this chapter and appear in alphabetical order with definitions in the Glossary, which begins on page 372.

CRITICAL QUESTIONS

1. What important tradition in magazine journalism did Ida Tarbell and other muckrakers establish? Describe how Tarbell reported on the Standard Oil Company. Why is her reporting important?

2. Why do today's magazines target specialized audiences for readership? Give at least three specific examples of this phenomenon and the reasons for each.

3. Discuss the role that magazines like *Ebony* and *Jet*, targeted to a specific audience, play in the development of American society.

4. If you started a magazine, what kind would you launch? How would you fund it? Who would read and advertise in it? Would you print it or put it on the Internet or both? Using lessons from this chapter, how would you ensure its success?

5. What impact will developing media technologies have on magazines' future direction? Consider the audience for magazines, the way in which magazines are delivered to their readers, and the impact on advertisers and advertising.

WORKING THE WEB

This list includes both sites mentioned in the chapter and others to give you greater insight into the magazine industry.

AllYouCanRead.com
http://www.allyoucanread.com

The largest database of magazines and newspapers on the Internet, AllYouCanRead.com lists more than 22,000 media sources from all over the world. Listings are organized by topic and country of origin, and can also be searched by name or keyword. Registered users can personalize their news collections, and visitors can read their favorite sources online. Subscriptions to printed materials are also available.

American Society of Journalists and Authors
http://www.asja.org

The ASJA is a national organization for freelance writers where members can share information about writing rates, publishing contracts, editors and agents. It also provides a referral service where editors and others can search the membership list to hire experienced authors and journalists, as well as health insurance plans for members and a writers' emergency fund.

CondéNet—Web site for Condé Nast Publications
http://www.condenet.com

An Internet unit of Condé Nast publications, CondéNet is the leading creator and developer of upscale lifestyle brands online. It serves as a portal for prestigious online publications in fashion, men's lifestyle, food, travel and more. Users can link to style.com (the online home of *Vogue*), men.style.com (*Details* and *GQ*) and epicurious.com ("for people who love to eat"). Other magazine sites include *Glamour*, *Modern Bride*, *Golf Digest* and *Bon Appétit*. CondéNet is a founding member of the Online Publishers Association.

Folio: The Magazine for Magazine Management
http://www.foliomag.com

This online magazine for managers in all sectors of the magazine publishing industry reports industry trends and news. Information topics range from Audience Development to Sales and Marketing. The site also includes a Careers section, Industry Events and Webinars, and its own professional and social network, Folio: MediaPro.

Magazine Publishers of America (MPA) and the American Society of Magazine Editors (ASME)
http://www.magazine.org

As the "Definitive Resource for the Magazine Industry," Magazine Publishers of America represents more than 300 domestic and international publishing companies from AARP to Time Warner. Departments include Government and International Affairs, Consumer Marketing, and Professional Development. ASME supports the editorial division of the site and serves its members through awards, internship programs, forums and career development workshops.

Newsweek
http://www.newsweek.com

First published in 1933, Newsweek holds more National Magazine Awards (given by the ASME) than any other newsweekly. Its global network of correspondents, editors and reporters cover national and international affairs, business, science and technology, society, and arts and entertainment. Newsweek.com offers Web-only columns from the print magazine's top writers, as well as podcasts, mobile content and archives.

O, the Oprah Magazine
http://www.oprah.com/omagazine

The lifestyle magazine launched in 2000 by the popular talk-show host is now a minimal part of Oprah.com. The site itself is formatted as an online magazine, with featured daily content from the Oprah Winfrey Show, as well as articles in categories such as Spirit and Self, and Beauty and Style. Also included are links to Oprah's various projects, her book club, and Oprah and Friends Radio. Still included in the *O* Magazine section is The O List: "The must-haves that Oprah thinks are just great."

Salon
http://www.salon.com

This pioneer online magazine, headquartered in San Francisco with offices in New York City and Washington D.C., was founded in 1995. Because of the quality of its content, it has won many online journalism awards (such as the Webby). The company also sponsors Table Talk, an online discussion group, and The Well, a members-only online community.

Slate
http://www.slate.com

This online magazine of the Washington Post Company includes links to news stories in current issues of *The Washington Post* and *Newsweek*. Selected *Slate* stories can be heard on National Public Radio on "Day to Day." SlateV.com is an extensive webcast library of entertaining editorials from various interviewers as well as advice from "Dear Prudence." Users can also customize their news through "build your own Slate."

Sports Illustrated
http://sportsillustrated.cnn.com

Known for its use of color photos shot from dramatic perspectives and its talented sportswriters, *Sports Illustrated* is the preeminent weekly sports magazine owned by Time Warner. Its online counterpart, SI.com, offers scores, news, schedules, stats and more, all organized by sport. Users can personalize their views by favorite professional or college teams. Other features include On Campus ("college sports, college life"); SIKids; the notorious yearly swimsuit edition; and TAKKLE, the largest high school sports community online.

5

Recordings:
Demanding Choices

What's Ahead?

Douglas Mason/Getty Images

"Popular music is like a unicorn,"

writes R. Serge Denisoff in his book *Solid Gold*. "Everyone knows what it is supposed to look like, but no one has ever seen it." Half the music people buy each year is categorized as popular music—rock, rap/hip-hop, urban, country and pop—according to the Recording Industry Association of America. Other types of music—religious, classical, Big Band, jazz and children's recordings—make up the rest, but most of the

Jazz singer Esperanza Spalding performs at the JVC Jazz Festival in Newport, Rhode Island, in August 2008.

TimeFrame
1877 – Today

The Recording Industry Caters to a Young Audience

1877   Thomas Edison first demonstrates the phonograph.

1943   Ampex develops tape recorders, and Minnesota Mining and Manufacturing perfects plastic recording tape.

1947   **Peter Goldmark develops the long-playing record.**

Eric Schaal/Time Magazine/Time & Life Pictures/Getty Images

1956   Stereophonic sound arrives.

1958   **Motown, promoted as "Hitsville USA," introduces the Detroit Sound of African American artists, including the Supremes, popularizing rock 'n' roll. (Motown's original studio pictured.)**

Michael Ochs Archives/ Getty Images

1979   **Sony introduces the Walkman as a personal stereo (pictured next to a pack of cigarettes to show its relatively small size).**

Ted Thai/Time & Life Pictures/Getty Images

1985   The recording industry begins to consolidate into six major international corporations. Only one of these companies is based in the United States.

1999   MP3 technology makes it easy for consumers to download music files from the Internet.

2001   Napster, which used file-sharing software designed to download music on the Internet, shuts down after the Recording Industry Association of America sues for copyright infringement. Apple introduces the iPod portable music player.

2003   **Apple opens the online music store iTunes, offering music downloads for 99 cents per song.**

JOHN D MCHUGH/ AFP/Getty Images

2005   The U.S. Supreme Court says that the makers of file-sharing software can be sued for helping people violate recording industry copyright protections.

2007   A federal jury found online music consumer Jammie Thomas liable for copyright infringement and fined her $222,000—the first time a jury imposed a legal fine on someone for music piracy. In September 2008, the judge set aside the verdict and ordered a retrial.

Today   Four major companies dominate the recording industry. The industry earns more than half its revenue from popular music, and the industry is fighting copyright infringement and Internet file sharing to protect earnings. The iTunes online music store is the nation's dominant music retailer.

Jamie Rector/Getty Images

big profits and losses in the recording business result from the mercurial fury of popular music.

Like the radio and television industries, the recording industry is challenged by rapidly changing technology. The recording industry also is at the center of recent debates over the protection of artistic copyright. In 2003, the Recording Industry Association of America sued 261 people for downloading music from the Internet, saying CD shipments were down 15 percent from the year before.

Of all the media industries, the recording industry is the most vulnerable to piracy and has suffered the biggest losses as a result of Internet technology. But in 1877, when Thomas Edison first demonstrated his phonograph, who could foresee that the music business would become so complicated?

More than half the music people buy each year and most of the recording industry's profits come from sales of popular recording artists such as Brandi Carlile.

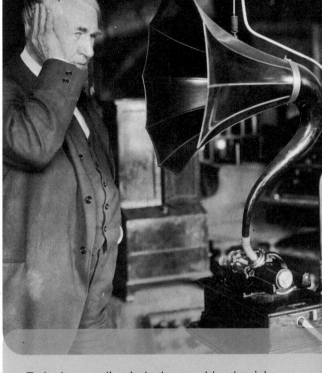

Today's recording industry would not exist without Thomas Edison's invention of the phonograph in 1877.

Edison Introduces His Amazing Talking Machine

Today's recording industry would not exist without Thomas Edison's invention, more than a century ago, of what he called a phonograph (which means "sound writer"). In 1877, *Scientific American* reported Thomas Edison's first demonstration of his phonograph. Edison's chief mechanic had constructed the machine from an Edison sketch that came with a note reading, "Build this." In 1887, Emile Berliner developed the gramophone, which replaced Edison's cylinder with flat discs.

Berliner and Eldrige Johnson formed the Victor Talking Machine Company (later to become RCA Victor) and sold recordings of opera star Enrico Caruso. Edison and Victor proposed competing technologies as the standard for the industry, and eventually the Victor disc won. Early players required large horns to amplify the sound. Later the horn was housed in a cabinet below the actual player, which made the machine a large piece of furniture.

In 1925, Joseph Maxfield perfected the equipment to eliminate the tinny sound of early recordings. The first jukeboxes were manufactured in 1927 and brought music into restaurants and nightclubs.

By the end of World War II, 78 *rpm* (revolutions *per minute*) records were standard. Each song was on a separate recording, and "albums" in today's sense did not exist. An album in the 1940s consisted of a bound set of 10 envelopes about the size of a photo album. Each record, with one song recorded on each side, fit in one envelope. (This is how today's collected recordings got the title "album," even though they no longer are assembled in this cumbersome way.) Each shellac hard disc recording ran three minutes. Peter Goldmark, working for Columbia Records (owned by CBS), changed that.

Peter Goldmark Perfects Long-Playing Records

In 1947, engineer Peter Goldmark was listening with friends to Brahms' Second Piano Concerto played by pianist Vladimir

Rpm Revolutions per minute.

Horowitz and led by the world-famous conductor Arturo Toscanini. The lengthy concerto had been recorded on six records, 12 sides.

Goldmark hated the interruptions in the concerto every time a record had to be turned over. He also winced at the eight sound defects he detected. After several refinements, Peter Goldmark created the long-playing (**LP**) record, which could play for 23 minutes, but LPs were larger than 78 rpm records.

William S. Paley Battles David Sarnoff for Record Format

William Paley, who owned CBS radio and also CBS records, realized he was taking a big risk by introducing LP records when most people didn't own a record player that could play the bigger 33-1/3 rpm discs. While the LP record was being developed, Paley decided to contact RCA executive David Sarnoff, since RCA made record players, to convince Sarnoff to form a partnership with CBS to manufacture LPs. Sarnoff refused.

Stubbornly, Sarnoff introduced his own 7-inch, 45 rpm records in 1948. Forty-fives had a quarter-size hole in the middle, played one song on a side and required a different record player, which RCA started to manufacture. Forty-fives

Time & Life Pictures/Getty Images

Improvements in recorded sound quality—hi-fi and stereo—contributed to the success of recording artists like Elvis Presley.

LP Long-playing record.

were a perfect size for jukeboxes, but record sales slowed as the public tried to figure out what was happening. Eventually Peter Goldmark and classical music conductor Arturo Toscanini convinced Sarnoff to manufacture LPs and to include the 33-1/3 speed on RCA record players to accommodate classical-length recordings.

CBS, in turn, agreed to use 45s for its popular songs. Later, players were developed that could play all three speeds (33-1/3, 45 and 78 rpm). A limited number of jazz artists were recorded, but most of the available recorded music was Big Band music from artists like Tommy Dorsey, Broadway show tunes and songs by popular singers like Frank Sinatra.

Hi-Fi and Stereo Rock In

In the 1950s, the introduction of rock 'n' roll redefined the concept of popular music. Contributing to the success of popular entertainers like Elvis Presley were the improvements in recorded sound quality that originated with the recording industry. First came *high fidelity*, developed by London Records, a subsidiary of Decca. Tape recorders grew out of German experiments during World War II.

Ampex Corporation built a high-quality tape recorder, and Minnesota Mining and Manufacturing (3M) perfected the plastic tape. The use of tape meant that recordings could be edited and refined, something that couldn't be done on discs.

Stereo arrived in 1956, and soon afterward came groups like Diana Ross and the Supremes with the Motown sound, which featured the music of African American blues and rock 'n' roll artists. At the same time, the FCC approved "multiplex" radio broadcasts so that monaural (one source of sound) and stereo (two sound sources) could be heard on the same stations. The development of condenser microphones also helped bring truer sound. (See **Impact/People**, "Berry Gordy, Jr., Motown Founder, Introduces the 'Detroit Sound,'" page 102.)

In the 1960s, miniaturization resulted from the transistor. Eventually the market was overwhelmed with tape players smaller than a deck of playing cards. Quadraphonic (four-track) and eight-track tapes seemed ready to become the standard in the 1970s, but cassette tapes proved more adaptable and less expensive.

In 1979, Sony introduced the Walkman as a personal stereo. (The company is Japanese, but the name Sony comes from the Latin *sonus* for sound and *sunny* for optimism.) Walkmans were an ironic throwback to the early radio crystal sets, which also required earphones.

Today's compact discs (CDs) deliver crystal-clear sound, transforming music into digital code on a 4.7-inch plastic and aluminum disc read by lasers. Discs last longer than records and cassettes ever did, making CDs a much more adaptable format.

Launched in the year 2000, CD players that included a *CD recorder* (also known as a CD writer or CD burner) and computers with **CD-RW** (Re-Writable) **drives** meant consumers could burn data such as music to a blank CD, allowing them to copy music, play it and then re-record on the same disc. Recordable discs gained widespread acceptance quickly after they were introduced, and these players and computer drives made it even harder for the recording industry to police unauthorized use of copyrighted material.

Music videos, the music channels MTV and VH1, and the availability of iPod music downloads also have expanded the audience and potential income for music artists. The Apple iPod portable music player, first introduced in 2001, allows users to store and play music downloads. Apple launched iTunes, its online music store, in 2003, charging 99 cents per song.

The Apple iPhone, launched in 2007, combined mobile phone technology with the capabilities of the iPod, expanding Apple's dominance in music retailing. Today, the iTunes online music store has become the dominant consumer source for contemporary music.

Recording Industry at Work

Recordings, like books, are supported primarily by direct purchases. But a recording company involves five separate levels of responsibility before the public hears a sound:

1. Artists and repertoire

2. Operations

3. Marketing and promotion

4. Distribution

5. Administration

Artists and repertoire (or A&R) functions like an editorial department in book publishing; it develops and coordinates talent. Employees of this division are the true talent scouts. They try to find new artists and also constantly search for new songs to record.

Operations manages the technical aspects of the recording, overseeing the sound technicians, musicians, even the people who copy the discs. This work centers on creating the master recording, from which all other recordings are made. Before stereophonic recording was developed in 1956, a recording session meant gathering all the musicians in one room, setting up a group of microphones and recording a song in one take. If the first take didn't work, the artists all had to stay together to do another, and then another.

It was common in the 1950s for a recording group to go through 50 takes before getting the right one. Today,

Michael Ochs Archives/Getty Images

In 1958, Berry Gordy introduced Motown, the "Detroit Sound" of African American artists such as Diana Ross and the Supremes, seen here performing in London in 1965.

artists on the same song—vocals, drums, bass, horns and guitars—can be recorded individually, and then the separate performances are mixed for the best sound. They don't have to be in the same room, or even in the same country because the sound can be mixed after each of the artists has recorded his or her portion.

The producer, who works within the operations group, can be on the staff of a recording company or a freelancer. Producers coordinate the artist with the music, the arrangement and the engineers.

Marketing and promotion decides the best way to sell the recording. These employees oversee the cover design

CD-RW Drives Computer drives that are used to read data and music encoded in digital form and can be used to record more than once.

The clear recorded sound of today's music artists, such as Rihanna, is a direct result of the development of sophisticated technology that began with CBS Records' introduction of LPs in the 1940s.

and the copy on the cover (jacket or sleeve). They also organize giveaways to retailers and to reviewers to find an audience for their product. Marketing and promotion might decide that the artist should tour or that the recording needs a music video to succeed. Recording companies often use promoters to help guarantee radio play for their artists. This has led to abuses such as payola (see **Chapter 6**).

Distribution gets the recording into the stores. There are two kinds of distributors: independents and branches. Independents contract separately with different companies to deliver their recordings. But independents, usually responsible for

discovering music that is outside of the mainstream, are disappearing as the big studios handle distribution through their own companies, called branches. Because branches are connected with the major companies, they typically can offer the music retailer better discounts.

Administration, as in all industries, handles the bills. *Accounting* tracks sales and royalties. *Legal departments* handle wrangles over contracts.

All these steps are important in the creation of a recording, but if no one hears the music, no one will buy it. This makes *marketing* and *promotion* particularly important. Live concerts have become the best way for artists to promote their music. Many recording artists say that music sales alone don't make them any money and that the only way to make a living is to perform before a live audience.

Concerts Bring in Important Revenue

Concerts have become high-profile showcases for technological innovation and provide an essential source of revenue for today's big bands. For example, the group Coldplay performed in 2008 at the three-day Pemberton Music Festival in Pemberton, British Columbia, along with Jay-Z, Tom Petty and the Heartbreakers, and 40 other music acts. A three-day pass for the festival cost $239.50.

The Pemberton concert staging for Coldplay is an example of the importance of today's complex digital engineering, which integrates new technologies to help showcase a band's music. Today someone who pays more than $200 for a concert ticket demands a spectacular experience.

"While the recording industry frets about the financial impact of music trading over the Internet, innovative bands . . . are embracing the latest technologies to create spectacular live concerts and phantasmagoric festival experiences that are more like computer-controlled theme parks than like the rock festivals of yesteryear," reports *The New York Times*.

Richard Goodstone, a partner at Superfly Productions, told *The New York Times*, "The real difference between your normal rock festival like Lollapalooza and Ozzfest is that there's a lot of music, but now we're trying to make it a complete experience in terms of the activities that really interact with the patrons out there, so it's not just a one-element kind of event." Digital technology has become an important element of selling a band to its fans, as well as selling the band's music. (See **Illustration 5.1**.)

To justify higher concert ticket prices, recording groups use complex digital sound and light engineering. Live concerts are one way recording groups such as Coldplay make income today. Recorded music sales are declining because many people are downloading free music from the Internet.

IMPACT
»Culture

Illustration 5.1

What Types of Music Do People Buy?

The recording industry's success rests on trends in popular music. For more than 50 years, rock music has maintained its lead as the most popular type of music.

Source: Recording Industry Association of America 2008.

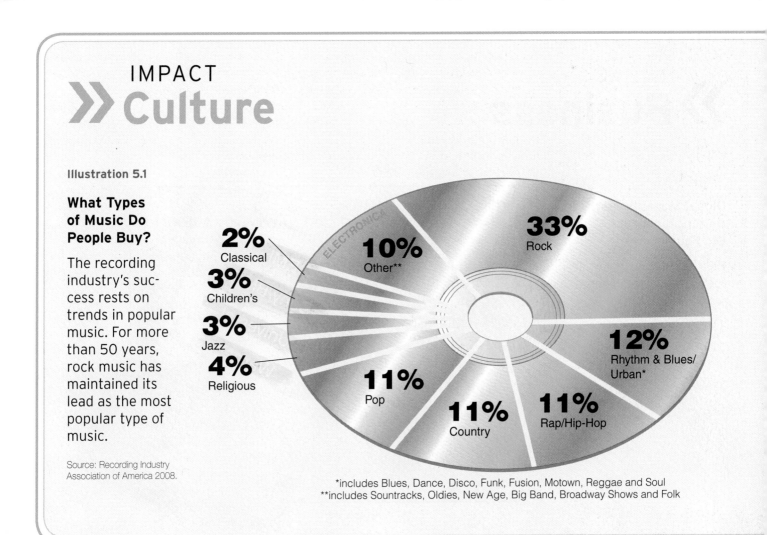

2% Classical
3% Children's
3% Jazz
4% Religious
10% Other**
33% Rock
11% Pop
11% Country
11% Rap/Hip-Hop
12% Rhythm & Blues/Urban*

*includes Blues, Dance, Disco, Funk, Fusion, Motown, Reggae and Soul
**includes Sountracks, Oldies, New Age, Big Band, Broadway Shows and Folk

Four Major Companies Dominate

About 5,000 companies in the United States produce music, but four companies dominate the global music business, together selling over two billion recordings each year. (See **Illustration 5.2**.) The main recording centers in the United States are Los Angeles, New York and Nashville, but most large cities have at least one recording studio to handle local productions.

The recording industry, primarily concentrated in large corporations, generally chooses to produce what has succeeded before. "Increasingly, the big record companies are concentrating their resources behind fewer acts," reports *The Wall Street Journal*, "believing that it is easier to succeed with a handful of blockbuster hits than with a slew of moderate sellers. One result is that fewer records are produced."

Most radio formats today depend on popular music, and these recordings depend on radio to succeed. The main measurement of what is popular is *Billboard*, the music indus-

try's leading trade magazine. *Billboard* began printing a list of the most popular vaudeville songs and the best-selling sheet music in 1913. In 1940, the magazine began publishing a list of the country's top-selling records.

Today, *Billboard* offers more than two dozen charts that measure, for example, airplay and album sales for popular artists such as Alison Krauss and Rihanna. Radio, governed by ratings and what the public demands, tends to play proven artists, so new artists are likely to get more radio attention if their recordings make one of the *Billboard* lists. This radio play, in turn, increases the artists' popularity and promotes their music.

Music Sales and Licensing Drive Industry Income

The industry also collects income from direct sales and from music licensing for radio, television and movies.

IMPACT
»Business

Illustration 5.2

Global Music Industry Dominated by the Big Four

Four corporations dominate the music business worldwide.

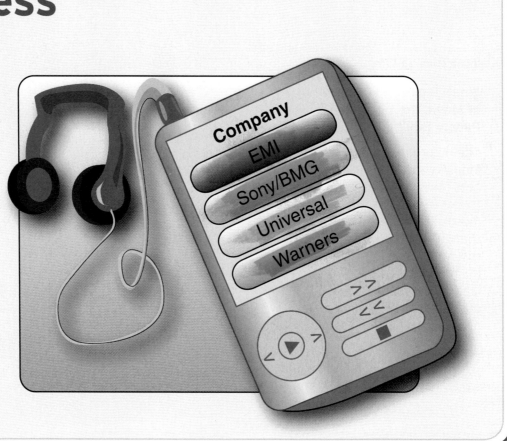

Company
EMI
Sony/BMG
Universal
Warners

Direct Sales

The promotional tour once was the only way a company sold recordings. But in the 1980s, music videos became a very visible form of promotion for an artist. This shift changed the industry's economics. Jennifer Lopez, for example, is attractive to music companies because she is a recording artist who can perform well in videos and also makes movies.

Music Licensing: ASCAP Versus BMI

For the first 30 years of commercial radio, one of the reasons broadcasters used live entertainment was to avoid paying royalties to the recording companies. Today, two licensing agencies handle the rights to play music for broadcast: the American Society of Composers, Authors and Publishers (ASCAP) and Broadcast Music, Inc. (BMI).

ASCAP American Society of Composers, Authors and Publishers.

BMI Broadcast Music, Inc.

ASCAP, founded in 1914, was the first licensing organization. As noted in **Chapter 6**, ASCAP sued radio stations in the 1920s that were playing recorded music. Eventually some radio stations agreed to pay ASCAP royalties through a blanket licensing agreement, which meant that each station that paid ASCAP's fee could play any music that ASCAP licensed.

Throughout the 1930s, many stations refused to pay ASCAP because they didn't have enough money. These stations agreed to explore the idea of forming a separate organization so they could license the music themselves.

In 1939, broadcasters came together to establish a fund to build their own music collection through **BMI**. ASCAP and BMI became competitors—ASCAP as a privately owned organization and BMI as an industry-approved cooperative. BMI used the same blanket licensing agreement, collecting payments from broadcasters and dividing royalties among its artists. ASCAP licensed the majority of older hits, but rhythm and blues and rock 'n' roll gravitated toward BMI.

Today, most broadcasters subscribe to both BMI and ASCAP. They also agree to play only licensed artists, which makes getting on the air more difficult for new talent. BMI and ASCAP, in turn, pay the authors, recording artists, producers, and sometimes even the recording companies—whoever owns the rights to use the music.

Recording industry income has received a boost from the higher prices that consumers pay for music. However, Internet piracy and file sharing on the Internet are the main reasons recording income is declining.

Industry Struggles to Protect Content Labeling

Three issues face today's recording industry: content labeling, overseas piracy and artists' copyright protection from file sharing on the Internet.

In 1985, the Parents Music Resource Center (PMRC) called for recording companies to label their recordings for explicit content. The new group was made up primarily of the wives of several national political leaders, notably Susan Baker, wife of then-Treasury Secretary James A. Baker III, and Tipper Gore, wife of then-Senator Al Gore.

Saying that recordings come under the umbrella of consumer protection, the PMRC approached the National Association of Broadcasters and the Federal Communications Commission with their complaints. "After equating rock music with the evils of 'broken homes' and 'abusive parents,' and labeling it a 'contributing factor' in teen pregnancy

Recording artist Alison Krauss with the band Union Station regularly make it to the Top 10 Country Music Artists List in *Billboard* magazine. This listing keeps their music on radio stations that feature country music. Krause and Union Station performed at Eric Clapton's Crossroads Guitar Festival in Bridgeview, Illinois, in 2007.

and suicide, they single[d] out Madonna, Michael Jackson, Mötley Crüe, Prince, Sheena Easton, Twisted Sister and Cyndi Lauper for their 'destructive influence' on children," reported Louis P. Sheinfeld, who teaches journalism law at New York University.

The result was that, beginning in January 1986, the ***Recording Industry Association of America*** (whose member companies account for 95 percent of U.S. recording sales) officially urged its members either to provide a warning label or to print lyrics on albums that have potentially offensive content. Like the movie industry when it adopted its own ratings system (see **Chapter 7**), the recording industry favored self-regulation rather than government intervention.

In 1990, the nation's two largest record retailers ordered all their outlets to stop stocking and selling sexually explicit recordings by the controversial rap group 2 Live Crew. A

"FOR MY NEXT SELECTION, I WILL DOWNLOAD A MUSIC FILE FROM THE INTERNET ."

RIAA (Recording Industry Association of America) Industry association that lobbies for the interests of the nation's major recording companies. Member companies account for 95 percent of all U.S. recording company sales.

IMPACT
»» People

Berry Gordy, Jr., Motown Founder, Introduces the "Detroit Sound"

by Erik Calonius

"Imagine a world without the Supremes, Smokey Robinson, Marvin Gaye, Stevie Wonder, Diana Ross, Michael Jackson, Lionel Richie, the Temptations and the Four Tops," someone once said, "and you've just imagined a world without Berry Gordy." Gordy, who worked on the Ford assembly line and sold cookware door-to-door, submitted in the end to his passion for songwriting and transforming no-names into stars.

As a songwriter, Gordy found early success with hits like "Lonely Teardrops," sung by Jackie Wilson. But Gordy soon realized he wanted more control. "To protect my songs, which are my loves, I had to find singers who could sing and record them like I heard them in my head." At 29, with an $800 loan from his family, Gordy founded Motown. He leased a two-story house at 2648 West Grand Boulevard in Detroit.

"Everything was makeshift," he says. "We used the bathroom as an echo chamber." Gordy borrowed from his assembly line

Berry Gordy, Jr., founder of Motown and Tamla Records, was an innovator who popularized Detroit's Mo(tor)town sound in the 1960s and 1970s.

experience in refining Motown acts. The kids learned harmony from the vocal coach, steps from the choreography coach and manners from the etiquette coach. Meanwhile, Motown's songwriters pounded out new tunes. When it was time to perform, the kids—Diana, Marvin, Stevie, Smokey and the rest—piled into the Motown Revue bus and headed out on the road, competing to see who could win the most applause.

By 1975, Motown had become the biggest black-owned business in America, with activities spanning several record labels, film and television. "I had no idea that Diana Ross would become an industry or that Michael Jackson would become an industry or that the Temptations would become an industry," Gordy says. "While I say I'm a songwriter and businessman, really, deep down, I think I'm a teacher, like my father."

Florida judge ruled that the group's album *As Nasty As They Wanna Be* was obscene, even though it carried a warning about explicit lyrics. The Luke Skywalker record label, which produced the album, said the controversy increased sales, but the ban meant that more than 1,000 stores nationwide refused to sell the music. Eventually, the decision was overturned, but sales of the album already had plummeted.

Overseas Piracy

Overseas pirates who copy prerecorded music that is then sold in the United States cost the recording industry a lot of money. The Recording Industry Association says pirates control 18 percent of album sales, and this represents a billion dollars a year in lost income.

Besides the lost revenue, counterfeit copies can easily fool consumers and usually are inferior quality, which doesn't truly represent the artist's music. This is a continuing battle for the music industry because many of the countries responsible for the counterfeit copying do not have agreements with the United States to force them to honor U.S. copyrights and prosecute the pirates.

File Sharing on the Internet

Portable MP3 players—electronic devices that allow users to download music to a computer chip–based player—were introduced in 1999. "They are the hottest new thing in portable audio players," Amy Hill, spokesperson for the Consumer Electronics Manufacturing Association, said in 1999. "Every teenager I know wants one of these things."

In 1999, a software-sharing program available at a Web site called *Napster.com* skyrocketed into popularity. With the program, computer users could download music over the Internet for free, called *file sharing*. Then, using MP3 technology (which provides high-quality sound and requires very little computer storage space), users could keep and use the music. The Recording Industry Association of America (RIAA) immediately sued Napster, claiming violation of copyright.

In April 2000, the heavy-metal rock group Metallica sued Napster for copyright infringement. Rapper Dr. Dre filed suit two weeks later. In July 2000, an appeals court ordered Napster to shut down the site, but Napster delayed. Napster finally shut down in 2001.

In 2003, Apple opened its iTunes Music Store, offering music downloads for 99 cents per song. Apple announced in April 2008 that the iTunes store had become the nation's largest music retailer. According to Apple, 50 million customers have bought more than 4 billion songs in the five years since the store opened.

Recording Industry Association Sues Downloaders

Even after Apple opened its Internet music store in 2003, people continued to download free music, aided by new free online music services such as *Kazaa* and *Grokster*. (See **Illustration 5.3**.) So in 2003, the RIAA sued 261 individual music downloaders across the United States, intensifying its efforts to stop music piracy. On average, each defendant had shared 1,000 songs each.

"A lot of people think they can get away with what they are doing because peer-to-peer file sharing allows them to hide behind made-up screen names," the president of the RIAA told *The New York Times*. "They are not anonymous. The law is very clear. What they are doing is stealing." Copy-

In 2007, a federal jury found Jammie Thomas (right) liable for copyright infringement and fined her $222,000–the first time a jury imposed a legal fine on someone for music piracy. Thomas appealed the decision. In September 2008, the judge set aside the verdict and ordered a retrial.

right laws allowed the industry to seek $750 to $150,000 for each violation.

The lawsuits included copies of screen shots of many users' entire online music-sharing accounts, showing the names of each song and how many times the user downloaded music. RIAA offered not to pursue the individual lawsuits for people who were willing to sign a notarized statement saying they would stop sharing music files and delete files they now had. A subsequent court ruling stopped the prosecution of people who downloaded free music, but the case headed to the U.S. Supreme Court.

U.S. Supreme Court Rules Against File Sharing

In June 2005, the U.S. Supreme Court announced a decision that eventually shut down many free music software providers. In *MGM Studios v. Grokster*, the court said the makers of Grokster, which allowed Internet users to browse freely and copy songs from each other, could be sued for their role in helping people violate recording industry copyright protections.

File Sharing Peer-to-peer swapping of copyrighted music over the Internet.

IMPACT

Audience

Illustration 5.3

Who Pays for Music?

Because many young listeners download shared music for free, people who are 25 and older account for **65** percent of the recording industry's annual income.

Source: Recording Industry Association of America 2008.

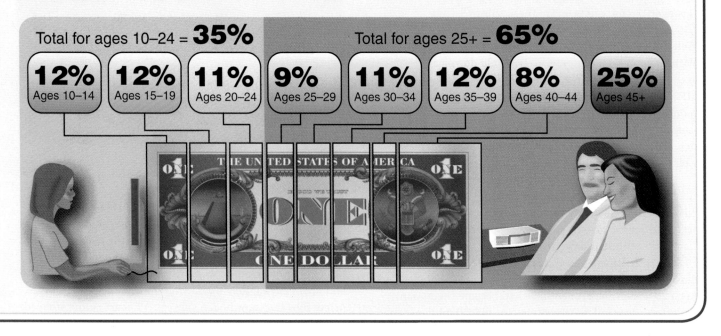

Total for ages 10–24 = **35%**   Total for ages 25+ = **65%**

| **12%** Ages 10–14 | **12%** Ages 15–19 | **11%** Ages 20–24 | **9%** Ages 25–29 | **11%** Ages 30–34 | **12%** Ages 35–39 | **8%** Ages 40–44 | **25%** Ages 45+ |

This Supreme Court decision gave the recording companies the legal ammunition they needed to shut down file-sharing services, and the services shut down.

Music Industry Wins, Then Drops Legal Action

In 2007, a federal jury ruled that a Minnesota woman, Jammie Thomas, was liable for copyright infringement because she had shared music online. The jury imposed a penalty against Thomas of $222,000—calculated at $9,250 in damages for each of the 24 songs involved in the trial. In September 2008, the judge set aside the original verdict and ordered a retrial.

The verdict represented the first time a federal jury had imposed a legal fine on someone for music piracy. Earlier in the summer, however, a judge dismissed record labels' claims that an Oklahoma woman had used an Internet address to share music.

According to evidence presented at the Thomas trial, the music downloads were linked to a Kazaa account user name that belonged to Thomas. Thomas denied she had a Kazaa account. Bringing the charges against Thomas were Capitol Records, the Universal Music Group, Sony BMG Entertainment and the Warner Music Group.

In late 2008, however, the RIAA announced that it was dropping the legal actions it had initiated against about 35,000 people for music downloading. Instead, the association said it planned to pursue agreements with Internet service providers where the RIAA would notify the provider when the RIAA learns that the provider's customers are making music available online to share with others. The provider would then, after notification, cancel the customers' account. The decision to drop the suits was seen as an admission by the RIAA that their initial legal strategy had failed to stop online file sharing.

Changing Technology Transforms Delivery

From the beginning, profits in the recording industry have been tied to technology. Ever since William S. Paley and David Sarnoff decided to produce LPs and 45s, the consumer has followed equipment manufacturers, looking for better, more convenient sound. The recent expansion of MP3 digital technology signaled a new era for music lovers, making good-quality music available on the Internet.

But recording companies worry that people's ability to download and copy digitized music on the Internet will financially ruin the industry. Once digitized, the music is available free to anyone and can be sent over the Internet around the world.

The challenge for music company executives is to develop a way to protect this new technology with an even newer technology that will make free copying impossible.

MP3 software and file-sharing services such as Kazaa and Grokster allowed any computer user with an Internet connection to download the latest music for free. Despite aggressive attempts by the RIAA to stop music file sharing, it is still a widespread practice with vast copyright and income implications for recording artists and recording companies. (See **Impact/Business**, "The True Cost of Free Music Downloading.'")

Aware of the potential damage to recording company income, officials of the RIAA have cracked down on Internet pirates and people who download copyrighted music on the Internet, but policing the Internet for music sharing is difficult and expensive. The economic implications

IMPACT
»Business

The True Cost of Free Music Downloading

by Mike Batt

Note: Mike Batt is one of Britain's most successful singer/songwriter/music producers. He owns the independent music label Dramatico.

Why do people illegally download music? Because they can. The [British] government recently announced that it has persuaded the internet service providers (ISPs) to sit down with the British Phonographic Industry (BPI) and thrash out measures to curb illegal downloads by creating a voluntary framework that might work within anticipated tighter legislation.

This has been welcomed by most musicians, industry organizations and fair-minded consumers. Reasonable people agree that musicians should be paid for their work. I declare an interest, as deputy chairman of the BPI, although I am writing this in my private capacity as a songwriter, performer and label owner.

But there has been negative comment. Last week I read an article by an otherwise sane and respected musician and journalist who said that downloading music free was like "downloading air," implying that because you can't see it, it should be free. He also said that it is "so cheap to get recorded music to the audience that artists no longer need a major label."

Hating major labels is about as useful as hating film companies and supermarkets. They exist. There will always be dominant players, but there are also about 800 independent record labels in the UK including my own, Dramatico, which has 14 staff and a network of about 50 freelancers around the world. Without the toil and passion of my employees my artists wouldn't be selling records. Without payment for the music

(continued)

IMPACT

» Business

The True Cost of Free Music Downloading (*continued*)

made by our artists we wouldn't be able to pay our staff. Then the staff would leave and so would the artists.

If you could download a loaf of bread free you would. But you can't, thank God, because otherwise bakers would cease to exist and there would be no bread to download. Then we'd all be dead, and good riddance to us, because we humans are greedy, thieving, conniving bastards, every last one of us. That's why there are laws to stop us. . . .

It's nothing new that the entertainment business is "dog eat dog." When I came up to London three times a week on the train from Winchester in 1968, a hopeful 18-year-old trying to sell my songs or get signed by, well, anyone really, there were four majors—EMI, Pye, Phillips and Decca. And there are four today—EMI, Universal, Warners and Sony/BMG. It was just as difficult to have a hit then as it is now. Just as hard to get noticed. The business was just as full of arrogant charlatans with kind, helpful faces.

Today it's a different mixture, though, with different challenges and opportunities. Bands and artists can display their wares on YouTube and MySpace, and record companies can audition artists without even leaving their offices.

But, because of this easier access, telling wheat from chaff is more difficult. Record companies have it easier and harder. It's easier to get the music to the online customer, but harder to protect it from theft. New business models are being sought and invented all the time. ISPs talking to record companies in order to limit online music theft through their broadband channels is good news for everyone except those who think all music should be free and musicians should go out of business.

Mike Batt, "The True Cost of Music Downloading," *London Times,* August 1, 2008. Reprinted by permission.

for the recording industry are substantial. In 2007, the RIAA estimated the industry had lost nearly $1 billion in revenue due to illegal music downloads. In 2008, the RIAA announced that music sales were down 11 percent worldwide from 2006 to 2007—their lowest level in over 20 years.

When Thomas Edison demonstrated his phonograph for the editors of *Scientific American* in 1877, the magazine reported that "Mr. Thomas Edison recently came into this office, placed a little machine on our desk, turned a crank, and the machine inquired as to our health, asked how we liked the phonograph, informed us that it was very well, and bid us a cordial good night. These remarks were not only perfectly audible to ourselves, but to a dozen or more persons gathered around."

None of the discoveries by Edison's successors has been a new invention, only a refinement. Berliner flattened the cylinder; Goldmark and Sarnoff slowed down the speed;

hi-fi, stereo and quadraphonic sound increased the fidelity; cassettes, compact discs, digital recorders and MP3 players refined the sound further; and file-sharing software allowed people to share copied music.

But the basic foundation for today's recording industry all began in 1877 with Thomas Edison. Reflecting on the movie version of Edison's life, Robert Metz describes the development of the phonograph: An Edison employee was tinkering with "a makeshift device consisting of a rotating piece of metal with a pointed piece of metal scratching its surface. The device was full of sound and fury—and signified a great deal. . . . And thus, supposedly through idle play, came the first permanent 'record' of ephemeral sound. By any measure, it was an invention of genius."

Review, Analyze, Investigate
REVIEWING CHAPTER 5

Edison Introduces His Amazing Talking Machine

✓ Thomas Edison first demonstrated his phonograph in 1877.

✓ Emile Berliner developed the gramophone in 1887.

✓ Berliner and Eldrige Johnson formed the Victor Talking Machine Company (later RCA Victor) to sell recordings.

✓ Joseph Maxfield perfected recording equipment to eliminate the tinny sound.

✓ The first standard records were 78 rpm.

Peter Goldmark Perfects Long-Playing Records

✓ Peter Goldmark, working for CBS' William S. Paley, developed the long-playing record (33 rpm).

✓ The first long-playing records played for 23 minutes and were larger than 78s.

William S. Paley Battles David Sarnoff for Record Format

✓ David Sarnoff's staff at RCA developed the 45 rpm record.

✓ Eventually record players that could play all different speeds—33-1/3 rpm, 45 rpm and 78 rpm—were sold.

Hi-Fi and Stereo Rock In

✓ Rock 'n' roll redefined the concept of popular music.

✓ Recording industry efforts to improve recorded sound quality contributed to the success of rock 'n' roll entertainers like Elvis Presley and Diana Ross.

✓ The introduction of the Walkman in the late '70s made music personal and portable.

✓ CD-RWs, compact discs that can record as well as play, meant consumers could create their own CDs.

✓ The Apple iPod portable music player, first introduced in 2001, allows users to store and play music downloads.

✓ Apple launched iTunes, its online music store, in 2003, charging 99 cents per song.

✓ The Apple iPhone, introduced in 2007, combines mobile phone technology with the capabilities of the iPod, expanding Apple's dominance in music retailing.

✓ Today, Apple's iTunes store has become the dominant consumer source for contemporary music.

Recording Industry at Work

✓ A recording company is divided into artists and repertoire, operations, marketing and promotion, distribution and administration.

✓ CD sales alone don't generate enough revenue to support most music groups.

Concerts Bring in Important Revenue

✓ Concerts require high-tech innovation.

✓ Concert ticket sales are an essential source of revenue for large bands.

Four Major Companies Dominate

✓ About 5,000 labels produce recordings in the United States, but four large corporations dominate the recording industry.

✓ Recording companies sell over two billion recordings a year.

✓ Radio depends on popular music to succeed.

Music Sales and Licensing Drive Industry Income

✓ The recording industry collects income from direct sales, music licensing and music videos, but recording income today is declining.

✓ Today two licensing agencies—ASCAP and BMI—handle the rights to play music for broadcast.

Industry Struggles to Protect Content Labeling

✓ Three issues facing today's recording industry are attempts to control music content through labeling, overseas piracy and copyright protection for music file sharing.

✓ The recording industry responded to threats of government regulation of music lyrics by adopting its own standards for music labeling.

✓ Music-sharing company Napster was sued in 1999 for copyright infringement by the Recording Industry Association of America and shut down in 2001.

✓ Consumers continued to use music-sharing sites such as Kazaa and Grokster, even though the downloaded songs were covered by copyright.

✓ MP3 digital technology, perfected in 1999, allows consumers to download and store good-quality music directly from the Internet.

Recording Industry Association Sues Downloaders

✓ In 2003, the Recording Industry Association of America sued 261 individual music downloaders, hoping to stop the flow of free music on the Internet, but people still continue to download.

✓ The lawsuits included specific names of people who had downloaded music.

U.S. Supreme Court Rules Against File Sharing

✓ In June 2005, the U.S. Supreme Court in *MGM Studios v. Grokster* said that the makers of Grokster, which allows Internet users to browse freely and copy songs from each other, could be sued for helping people violate recording industry copyright protections.

✓ *MGM Studios v. Grokster* gave the recording industry the legal standing they needed to try to stop illegal file sharing.

Music Industry Wins, Then Drops Legal Action

✓ In 2007, a federal jury imposed a penalty for file sharing of $222,000 against a woman named Jammie Thomas—calculated at $9,250 in damages for each of the 24 songs involved in the trial. In September 2008, the judge in the case ordered a retrial.

✓ The verdict against Thomas represented the first time a federal jury had imposed a legal fine on someone for music piracy.

✓ In late 2008, the RIAA dropped suits against 35,000 downloaders and said it would pursue downloaders through their Internet service providers.

Changing Technology Transforms Delivery

✓ Apple introduced the iPod portable music player in 2001.

✓ Apple's iTunes music store, launched in 2003, provides a legal way for people to download music.

✓ Recording company executives are looking for a new technology that will make file sharing impossible.

✓ In 2007, Apple introduced technology that allows users to share songs without copyright restrictions.

✓ The Apple iPhone, introduced in 2007, combines the functions of the Apple iPod and a mobile phone, making Apple the dominant music retailer.

KEY TERMS

These terms are defined in the margins throughout this chapter and appear in alphabetical order with definitions in the Glossary, which begins on page 372.

ASCAP 100
BMI 100
CD-RW Drives 97
File Sharing 103

LP 96
RIAA 101
Rpm 95

CRITICAL QUESTIONS

1. Describe the competition between William Paley's 33-1/3 records and David Sarnoff's 45s. How was that battle resolved? What does that battle tell you about the role that technology plays in the media industries?

2. Why are the recording industry and the radio industry so interdependent?

3. Give a brief history of Motown. Why was the company so important in the history of the music industry?

4. Discuss the response of the music recording industry to file sharing, and evaluate the extent to which it has been successful in protecting recording artists and recording companies. Do you believe file sharing will stop after the recent U.S. Supreme Court decision banning the practice? Explain.

5. How have recent technologies, such as the iPod and the iPhone, affected the music recording and performance industry in ways other than file sharing? Discuss.

WORKING THE WEB

This list includes both sites mentioned in the chapter and others to give you greater insight into the recording industry.

American Top 40 with Ryan Seacrest
http://www.at40.com

Along with America's longest running popular music weekend countdown, AT40 offers music news, artist pictures and podcasts, and user contests and blogs. AT40.com features a "Where to Listen" search that allows users to find local radio stations that play current music hits.

AOL Music
http://music.aol.com

The music division of America Online, AOL Music offers streaming radio, music downloads from a variety of genres, and entertainment news. Users can watch live performances on Sessions, and connect with other fans on Spinner and Popeater.

Apple.com/iTunes
http://www.apple.com/itunes

iTunes provides "music jukebox" software used to store music on a computer or a hand-held digital player such as an iPod. Apple's online music service opened in 2003, and its popularity has proven the feasibility of online music sales. In addition to music, the iTunes Store features audio books, TV shows, movies, iPod games and cell phone ringtones. The iPod is currently rivaled by Apple's own iPhone, which has all the iPod's capabilities plus Internet access, GPS mapping, cell phone service and more.

Billboard
http://billboard.biz and http://billboard.com

Billboard.biz is the official business Web site of Billboard magazine, the music industry's Bible. It includes breaking news about the music business, top-selling charts in all music categories and even a job bulletin board to lead readers to jobs in the music industry. The companion Web site, Billboard.com, offers samples from best-selling music albums and singles; news articles on artists, products and awards; interactive blogs, games and contests; and even a Billboard fashion store. Billboard.com is also available in Spanish at billboardenespanol.com.

Insound
http://www.insound.com

Developed in 1999 by "a bunch of indie rock kids" determined to improve the music mail-order business, Insound presents a wide variety of independent music. The Web site offers CDs, music downloads and vinyl records as well as T-shirts, posters and other merchandise. Favorite music lists created by staff, bands and guests are also available.

Napster
http://www.napster.com

One of the first music file-sharing services, Napster offers a subscription service, free legal on-demand music through freenapster.com, and a fast-growing mobile music platform. Originally (in 1999), the Web site simply provided an index to music files in other users' computers. Because much of the music was copyrighted, the music industry sued. After almost closing in 2002, Napster gained a new owner and was turned into a subscription service that pays royalties to the music companies.

Pandora: radio from the Music Genome Project
http://pandora.com

With the belief that each listener has an individual relationship with music, Pandora provides a customizable online listening experience. Users enter favorite artist or song names and Pandora's software analyzes melody, harmony, rhythm and more to identify and recommend similar music. Users can create unlimited listening "stations" customized to their preferences, or can browse new music by genre. Downloads are available for mobile and home systems.

Recording Industry Association of America
http://www.riaa.com

As the trade group representing U.S. music companies, the RIAA protects intellectual property rights and First Amendment rights globally, conducts consumer and technical research and monitors governmental regulations and policies. It also issues the awards for Gold and Platinum best-selling recordings.

Rhapsody.com
http://www.rhapsody.com

A music subscription service that began in 2001, Rhapsody offers jukebox software that allows users to play and manage digital music, import and burn CDs, transfer music to portable devices, play music on a home stereo and buy music. Rhapsody is the exclusive provider of music on the social network Facebook.

Universal Music Group
http://www.universalmusic.com

Owned by Vivendi, Universal Music Group has worldwide operations that cover recorded music and music publishing. UMG offers the world's largest digital music catalog and holds recording labels including Interscope Geffen A & M, Universal Motown and Nashville groups, and Universal Music Latino. Its Web site hosts videos in all music genres.

6

Radio:
Riding the Wave

Ethan Miller/Getty Images

Sirius (now called Sirius XM) displays its satellite radio products at the 2008 Consumer Electronics Show in Las Vegas.

What's Ahead?

Today, the nation's collective

memory and impressions about events that happened in the first half of the 20th century are directly tied to radio. Newspapers offered next-day reports and occasional extras, and magazines offered long-term analysis. But radio gave its listeners an immediate news record at a time when world events demanded attention. Radio also gave people entertainment: sports, big bands, Jack Benny,

TimeFrame
1889 – Today

Radio Technology and Format Programming Chase the Audience

1899   Guglielmo Marconi first uses his wireless radio to report the America's Cup Race.

1907   Lee de Forest introduces the Audion tube, which improves the clarity of radio signal reception. Reginald Aubrey Fessenden transmits the first voice and music broadcast.

Hulton Archive/Getty Images

1920   Station KDKA in Pittsburgh goes on the air, the nation's first commercial radio station.

1934   Congress establishes the Federal Communications Commission to regulate broadcasting.

R. Gates/Hulton Archive/Getty Images

1936   Edwin H. Armstrong licenses frequency modulation (FM).

1938   *Mercury Theater on the Air* broadcasts "War of the Worlds," demonstrating how quickly broadcast misinformation can cause a public panic.

1959   Gordon McLendon introduces format radio at station KABL in San Francisco.

1960   The Manhattan Grand Jury indicts disc jockey Alan Freed for payola.

1970   National Public Radio (NPR) goes on the air. By design, public radio was created as an alternative to commercial radio.

Layne Kennedy/CORBIS

1996   Congress passes the Telecommunications Act of 1996, which encourages unprecedented consolidation in the radio industry.

2001   Sirius Satellite Radio and XM begin offering digital satellite radio service.

2003   Congress questions the actions of Cox Communications, one of the nation's largest radio groups, for refusing to play the Dixie Chicks' music after the group's lead singer criticized President George W. Bush for the Iraq War.

Kevin Mazur/WireImage/Getty Images

2005   XM Radio announces it has four million subscribers and plans to have 10 million subscribers by 2010.

New York's Attorney General Eliot Spitzer charges that payola still is pervasive in the radio industry.

2007   Radio talk show host Don Imus is fired after he makes racially insensitive remarks on the air.

2008   Satellite radio companies XM and Sirius merge into a company called Sirius XM.

Today   The radio industry has consolidated primarily into large groups of stations that use standardized formats, but the industry also is splitting the audience into smaller pieces with the introduction of digital radio, satellite radio and Internet radio.

ISSOUF SANOGO/AFP/Getty Images

George Burns and Gracie Allen, Abbott and Costello, Bob Hope and the original radio character, the Shadow ("The weed of crime bears bitter fruit. Crime does not pay! The Shadow knows!").

Radio transformed national politics by transmitting the sounds of public debate, as well as the words, to the audience. Radio also expanded Americans' access to popular, as well as classical, culture. Opera played on the same dial as slapstick comedy; drama and music shared the airwaves with sports—all supported by advertising.

Radio Sounds Are Everywhere

The legacy of news and music remains on radio today, but the medium that once was the center of attention in everyone's front room has moved into the bedroom, the office, the car and the shower. Radio wakes you up and puts you to sleep. Radio goes with you when you run on the trail or sit on the beach. Internet radio even follows you to your desk at work. Consider these industry statistics about radio today:

- 99 percent of America's homes have radios.

- 95 percent of America's cars have radios, and radio reaches four out of five adults in their cars at least once each week.

- 40 percent of Americans listen to the radio sometime between 6 a.m. and midnight.

- 7 percent of America's bathrooms have radios.

- More than 3,000 stations are Webcasting on the Internet.

Although radio is more accessible today, what you hear is not the same as what your great-grandparents heard. Advertisers, who once sought radio as the only broadcast access to an audience, have many more places to put their ads. For audiences, radio has become an everyday accessory rather than a necessity. No one had envisioned radio's place in today's media mix when radio's pioneers began tinkering just before the turn of the 20th century. All these pioneers wanted to do was figure out a way to send sounds along a wire, not through the air.

Radio Takes a Technological Leap

Today we are so accustomed to sending and receiving messages instantaneously that it is hard to imagine a time when information took more than a week to travel from place to place. In the early 1800s, the pony express took ten and a half days to go from St. Joseph, Missouri, to San Francisco, California. Stagecoaches had to travel 44 hours to bring news from New York to Washington.

Technological advances brought rapid changes in how quickly information could move throughout the country. First came the invention of the telegraph and the telephone, which depended on electrical lines to deliver their messages, and then wireless telegraphy, which delivers radio signals through the air.

In 1835, *Samuel F. B. Morse* first demonstrated his electromagnetic telegraph system in America. In 1843, Congress gave him $30,000 to string four telegraph lines along the Baltimore & Ohio Railroad right-of-way from Baltimore to Washington. Morse sent the first official message—"What hath God wrought?"—from Baltimore to Washington, D.C., on May 24, 1844.

Telegraph lines followed the railroads, and for more than 30 years Americans depended on Morse's coded messages printed on tape, sent from one railroad station to another. On March 10, 1876, *Alexander Graham Bell* sent a message by his new invention, the telephone, to his associate Thomas A. Watson in an adjoining room of their Boston laboratory: "Mr. Watson, come here. I want you." Both Morse's telegraph and Bell's telephone used wires to carry messages.

Then in Germany in 1887, the physicist *Heinrich Hertz* began experimenting with radio waves, which became known as Hertzian waves—the first discovery in a series of refinements that led eventually to the development of radio broadcasting.

Broadcasting Is Born

Broadcasting was truly a revolutionary media development. Imagine a society in which the only way you can hear music or enjoy a comedy is at a live performance or by listening to tinny noises on a record machine. The only way you can hear a speech is to be in the audience. Movies show action but no sound.

Without the inventions of broadcasting's early pioneers such as Heinrich Hertz, you could still be living without the sounds of media that you have come to take for granted. Four pioneers besides Hertz are credited with advancing early radio broadcasting in America: Guglielmo Marconi, Reginald Aubrey Fessenden, Lee de Forest and David Sarnoff.

Wireless Breakthrough: Guglielmo Marconi

Twenty-year-old Guglielmo Marconi, the son of wealthy Italian parents, used the results of three discoveries by Morse, Bell and Hertz to expand his idea that messages should be able to travel across space without a wire. Marconi became obsessed, refusing food and working at home in his locked upstairs room, trying to make his invention work. Soon Marconi could ring a

In all parts of the world today, radio is an everyday accessory rather than the necessity it once was. A Tibetan girl listens to radio in her home in the small village of Lhasa, Tibet.

bell across the room or downstairs without using a wire. Eventually Marconi was able to broadcast over a distance of nine miles. "The calm of my life ended then," Marconi said later.

The *New York Herald* invited Marconi to the United States to report the America's Cup Race in October 1899. Marconi reported "by wireless!" American business people, intrigued by the military potential of Marconi's invention, invested $10 million to form American Marconi.

To experiment with the new discovery, amateur radio operators created radio clubs. Two experimenters, Reginald Aubrey Fessenden and Lee de Forest, advanced the Marconi discovery to create today's radio.

Experimental Broadcasts: Reginald Aubrey Fessenden

Reginald Aubrey Fessenden, a Canadian, began wireless experiments in the United States in 1900 when he set up his National Electric Signaling Company to attempt sending voices by radio waves. On Christmas Eve 1906, "ship wireless operators over a wide area of the Atlantic . . . were startled to hear a woman singing, then a violin playing, then a man reading passages from Luke. It was considered uncanny; wireless rooms were soon crowded with the curious," wrote broadcast historian Erik Barnouw.

The noises were coming from Fessenden's experimental station at Brant Rock, Massachusetts. Fessenden's 1906 experiment is considered the world's first voice and music broadcast.

Detecting Radio Waves: Lee de Forest

Lee de Forest called himself the father of radio because in 1907 he perfected a glass bulb called the *Audion* that could detect radio waves. "Unwittingly then," wrote de Forest, "had I discovered an invisible Empire of the Air." Besides being an inventor, de Forest was a good publicist. He began what he called "broadcasts" from New York and then from the Eiffel Tower.

In 1910, de Forest broadcast Enrico Caruso singing at the Metropolitan Opera House. Later his mother broadcast an appeal to give women the vote. Gradually, the Audion became the technical foundation of modern broadcasting.

Radio for the People: David Sarnoff

In 1912, 21-year-old wireless operator David Sarnoff relayed news from Nantucket Island, Massachusetts, that he had received a distress call from the *Titanic* on his Marconi Wireless. Four years later, when Sarnoff was working for the Marconi Company in New York, he wrote a visionary memo that predicted radio's future, although in 1916 his ideas were widely ignored.

"I have in mind a plan of development which would make radio a household utility. The idea is to bring music into the home by wireless," Sarnoff wrote. Eventually, as commercial manager and then president of RCA, Sarnoff watched his early vision for radio come true, and RCA became the nation's primary radio distributor.

Federal Government Regulates the Airwaves

The federal government decided to regulate broadcasting almost as soon as it was invented. This decision to regulate broadcasting separated the broadcast media, which are regulated by the federal government, from the print media, which are not regulated directly by any federal government agency.

As amateurs competed with the military for the airwaves, Congress passed the Radio Act of 1912 to license people who wanted to broadcast or receive messages. The federal government decided to license people to transmit signals because there only were a certain number of frequencies available to carry broadcast signals. Many amateurs, trying to send signals on the same frequency, were knocking each other off the air. The government intervened to try to keep the operators out of each other's way.

Then, during World War I, the federal government ordered all amateurs off the air and took control of all privately owned stations, and the military took over radio broadcasting. After the war, the federal government lifted the freeze, and the Navy argued that the military should maintain the monopoly over the airwaves that it had enjoyed during the war.

Government Approves Commercial Broadcasting

Faced with strong arguments by the amateurs that they should be able to return to the airwaves, Congress decided against a Navy monopoly. Instead, the government sanctioned a private monopoly formed by General Electric, Westinghouse, AT&T, Western Electric Company and United Fruit Company. General Electric bought out American Marconi and its patents, and in 1919, these five sympathetic interests pooled the patents they controlled to form Radio Corporation of America (RCA).

David Sarnoff became RCA's general manager in 1921. Because of this early monopoly, RCA dominated radio development for many years, but eventually smaller operations formed all over the country as radio fever spread from coast to coast.

Experimental Stations Multiply

A plaque in San Jose, California, celebrates the 1909 founding of the experimental station FN: "On this site in 1909, Charles D. Herrold founded a voice radio station which opened the door to electronic mass communication. He conceived the idea of 'broadcasting' to the public, and his station, the world's first, has now served Northern California for half a century." Today, that station is San Francisco's KCBS.

Various other stations claim they were among the earliest radio pioneers. Station 9XM broadcast music and weather reports from Madison, Wisconsin; 6ADZ broadcast concerts from Hollywood; 4XD sent phonograph music from a chicken coop in Charlotte, North Carolina; and 8MK in Detroit, operated by *Detroit News* publisher William E. Scripps, transmitted election returns.

These amateur radio operators broadcast messages to each other and their friends, but not to the general public; nevertheless, they are early examples of broadcast entrepreneurs. They were tinkerers, fascinated with an invention that could carry sounds through the air. One of these tinkers, Frank Conrad, is credited with creating the beginnings of the nation's first *commercial* radio station.

KDKA Launches Commercial Broadcasting

An ad in the September 29, 1920, *Pittsburgh Sun* changed broadcasting from an exclusive hobby to an easy-to-use medium available to everyone. The ad described a 20-minute

[LC-US262-91144]/Library of Congress Prints and Photographs Division

Using an early predecessor of today's iPod, a couple on Guglielmo Marconi's yacht, *Electra*, do the fox trot while sailing to Albany, New York, in 1922.

Bettmann/Corbis

The nation's first commercial radio station, KDKA in Pittsburgh, went on the air in 1920.

evening concert broadcast from the home of Frank Conrad, a "wireless enthusiast" who worked for Westinghouse.

Conrad often broadcast concerts from his garage on his station 8XK, but his boss at Westinghouse, Harry P. Davis, had an idea: Why not improve the broadcasts so more people would want to buy radios? Davis talked Conrad into setting up a more powerful transmitter at the Westinghouse plant by November 2, so Conrad could broadcast election returns.

On October 27, 1920, using the powers of the 1912 Radio Act, the U.S. Department of Commerce licensed station KDKA as the nation's first *commercial* radio station. The broadcast began at 8 p.m. on November 2, 1920, and continued past midnight, reporting that Warren G. Harding was the nation's next president. KDKA immediately began a daily one-hour evening schedule, broadcasting from 8:30 to 9:30 p.m.

Radio Audience Expands Quickly

The crude KDKA broadcasts proved that regular programming could attract a loyal audience. KDKA was just the beginning of what eventually became radio networks. The radio craze led almost immediately to a period of rapid expansion as entrepreneurs and advertisers began to grasp the potential of the new medium. Almost as quickly, government was compelled to step in to expand its regulation of radio broadcasting.

Radio's potential as a moneymaker for its owners fueled competition for the airwaves. Three important developments for radio's future were the

1. Blanket licensing agreement
2. Decision that radio would accept commercial sponsors
3. Radio Act of 1927

Blanket Licensing

At first, stations played phonograph records; then they invited artists to perform live in their studios. Some of the nation's best talent sought the publicity that radio could give them, but eventually the performers asked to be paid.

In 1923, the American Society of Composers, Authors and Publishers (**ASCAP**) sued several stations for payment. ASCAP claimed that if radio aired ASCAP-licensed music, people would buy less sheet music, so ASCAP members would be cheated out of royalties. Station owners argued that playing the songs on their stations would publicize the sheet music, which would mean ASCAP members would make more money.

Eventually the stations agreed to pay royalties to ASCAP through a **blanket licensing agreement**, which meant the stations paid ASCAP a fee ($250 a year at first). In exchange, the stations could use all ASCAP-licensed music on the air. (ASCAP licenses its music to stations the same way today.) Eventually another licensing organization, Broadcast Music, Inc., or BMI, also would collect broadcast royalties (see "Licensed Recordings Launch Disc Jockeys," page 119).

Commercial Sponsorship

Once station owners agreed to pay for their programs, they had to figure out where they would get the money. AT&T had the answer with an idea pioneered at its station WEAF in New York. WEAF started selling advertising time to sponsors. Its first sponsored program cost $100 for 10 minutes.

The success of commercial sponsorship as a way to support radio settled the issue of who would pay the cost of airing the programs. Advertisers paid for programs through their advertising; the American public paid for the programs indirectly by supporting the advertisers who supported radio.

ASCAP American Society of Composers, Authors and Publishers.

Blanket Licensing Agreement An arrangement whereby radio stations become authorized to use recorded music for broadcast by paying a fee.

FCC Federal Communications Commission.

Federal Radio Commission

As more stations began to crowd the air, their signals interfered with one another. With only so many good radio frequencies available, the provisions of the Radio Act of 1912 (see "Federal Government Regulates the Airwaves," page 114) began to seem inadequate. Congress passed the Radio Act of 1927, which formed the Federal Radio Commission under the jurisdiction of the Department of Commerce. The president appointed the commission's five members, with the Senate's approval.

The shortage of air space required that broadcasting in the United States operate under a type of government regulation unknown to newspaper and magazine publishers. The federal government licensed the stations for three years, and the commission required the stations to operate *"as a public convenience, interest or necessity requires."*

The commission, created to protect the stations by allocating frequencies, also became the license holder. The stations could operate only with the government's approval, and the stations needed commission approval to be sold or transferred. The Radio Act of 1927, including the concept that broadcasters must operate in the *"public convenience, interest or necessity,"* became the foundation for all broadcast regulation in the United States.

In 1934, Congress established the Federal Communications Commission (**FCC**) to regulate the expanding wireless medium, making the FCC a separate agency of government and no longer a part of the Department of Commerce. It is important to remember that the commission's original purpose was to allocate the broadcast spectrum so station broadcast signals would not interfere with one another. The FCC was not originally envisioned to oversee broadcast content.

The FCC began work on July 11, 1934, with seven commissioners appointed by the president, with Senate approval. This same basic structure and purpose govern the commission's actions today, but now there are only five commissioners. The establishment of the FCC in 1934 also set the precedent for the later regulation of television.

Radio Grows into a Powerful Force

Most radio stations mixed entertainment, culture and public service. Radio created a new kind of collective national experience. Radio in the 1930s and 1940s became a powerful cultural and political force and gave millions of people a new, inexpensive source of information and entertainment (see **Illustration 6.1**).

The commercialization of American broadcasting also gave advertisers access to this audience at home. Radio's massive group of listeners sat enraptured with sponsored programming of many types: comedy, music, serials, sports,

IMPACT

» Audience

Illustration 6.1

Where Do People Listen to the Radio?

Listeners tune into the radio more at work and in the car than they do at home. Advertisers, such as car dealers, use this demographic information to help target radio audiences with their messages.

Soource: Radio Advertising Bureau 2008.

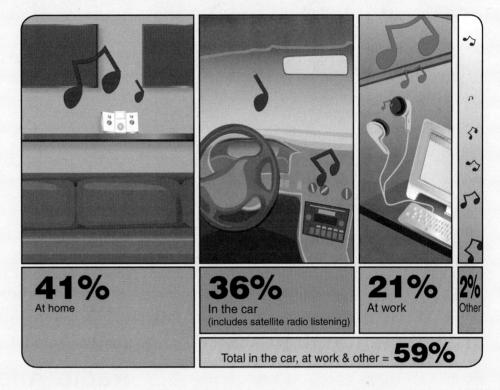

41%
At home

36%
In the car
(includes satellite radio listening)

21%
At work

2%
Other

Total in the car, at work & other = **59%**

---

drama and news. Eventually, all these types of programming migrated to television.

"War of the Worlds" Challenges Radio's Credibility

On Halloween Eve, October 30, 1938, the *Mercury Theater on the Air* broadcast a play based on the H. G. Wells story "War of the Worlds." The live 8 p.m. broadcast played opposite the very popular Edgar Bergen program on NBC, and rarely had even 4 percent of the audience. Very few people heard the announcement at the beginning of the program that the Mercury Theater was performing a version of the Wells story.

The program began with the announcer introducing some band music. A second voice then said, "Ladies and gen-

tlemen, we interrupt our program of dance music to bring you a special bulletin. At 20 minutes before 8 o'clock Central Time, Professor Farrell of Mount Jennings Observatory, Chicago, reports observing several explosions of incandescent gas occurring at regular intervals on the planet Mars."

More dance music followed and then more bulletins about a meteor, with the startling news that 1,500 people near Princeton, New Jersey, had died when the meteor hit the town. Then the announcer said it was not a meteor but a spaceship carrying Martians armed with death rays.

Two professors from the Princeton geology department actually set out to locate the "meteors." In Newark, more than 20 families rushed out of their homes, covering their faces with wet handkerchiefs to protect them from the "gas." After a burst of horrified calls, CBS began repeating the announcement that the program was just a play, but the damage had been done.

The episode demonstrated how easily alarming information could be innocently misinterpreted, especially because

The fear created by Orson Welles' "War of the Worlds" broadcast in 1938 demonstrated how easily alarming information could be misinterpreted on the radio. Orson Welles is shown here in 1938 on the air at CBS.

the listeners had no other source than radio to check the reliability of what they were hearing. Radio listeners truly were a captive audience.

Radio Networks Expand

The formation of radio networks as a source of programming and revenue is a crucial development in the history of American radio. A *network* is a collection of stations (radio or television) that offers programs, usually simultaneously, throughout the country, during designated times.

As the radio networks stretched across the country, they provided a dependable source of programming. Most stations found it easier to affiliate with a network and receive and distribute network programming than to develop local programs.

David Sarnoff Launches NBC

NBC grew out of the government's original agreement with RCA. RCA, GE and Westinghouse formed the National

Broadcasting Company in 1926. By January 1927, NBC, headed by David Sarnoff, had formed two networks: the Red network (fed from WEAF in New York) and the Blue network (originating from station WJZ in Newark).

Station engineers drew the planned hookups of the two networks with red and blue colored pencils, which is how the networks got their names. RCA faced criticism about its broad control over the airwaves because RCA continued to be the world's largest distributor of radios, which were made by Westinghouse and General Electric.

William S. Paley Starts CBS

Twenty-six-year-old William S. Paley, heir to a tobacco fortune, bought the financially struggling Columbia Phonograph Company in 1929. He changed the name to Columbia Broadcasting System, and put his CBS network on the air with 25 stations. Programming originated from WABC in New York. Paley became the nemesis of NBC, then controlled by David Sarnoff, and this early competition between Sarnoff and Paley shaped the development of American broadcasting.

Edward Noble Buys ABC

In 1941, the FCC ordered RCA to divest itself of one of its networks. In 1943, RCA sold NBC-Blue to Edward J. Noble (who had made his fortune as head of the company that produced LifeSavers candy). Noble paid $8 million for the network that became the American Broadcasting Company, giving the country a three-network radio system.

Radio Adapts to Television

Radio networks prospered from the 1940s to the 1980s, when NBC sold its radio network, and CBS and ABC devoted more attention to their television holdings. When television initially was launched in the 1940s, it seemed it would cause the death of radio. As soon as television proved itself, advertisers abandoned radio, said comedian Fred Allen, "like the bones at a barbecue."

The radio talent fled to television, too—original radio talents such as Bob Hope, Milton Berle and Jackie Gleason soon dropped their radio programs and devoted their talents to TV. Public affairs programs like *Meet the Press* made the move from radio to TV, as did Edward R. Murrow's radio news program, *Hear It Now*, which on television became *See It Now*.

Five developments in the 1940s, 1950s and 1960s transformed the medium of radio as well as guaranteed radio's survival alongside television:

1. FM radio frequency is accepted by the public.

2. Disc jockeys host music shows.

Network A collection of stations (radio or TV) that offers programs, usually simultaneously, throughout the country.

3. Radio formats streamline broadcasts.

4. People start buying clock and car radios.

5. The payola scandals focus on broadcast ethics.

Inventor Edwin H. Armstrong Pioneers FM

After working for more than a decade to eliminate static from radio broadcasts, engineer Edwin H. Armstrong applied to the FCC in 1936 to broadcast using his new technique, frequency modulation (FM). Because of the way FM signals travel through the air, FM offered truer transmission than AM with much less static. Armstrong faced difficult opposition from David Sarnoff at RCA, who had been an early Armstrong sponsor.

The FCC received 150 applications for FM licenses in 1939, but then froze licensing during World War II. After the war, Armstrong again faced Sarnoff, but this time Armstrong lost. RCA was using Armstrong's frequency modulation in its TV and FM sets but refused to pay Armstrong royalties, so Armstrong sued RCA.

RCA fought Armstrong for four years, saying that RCA had been among the early developers of FM and citing RCA's sponsorship of Armstrong's beginning experiments. In 1953, Armstrong became ill and suffered a stroke; then he committed suicide. RCA quickly settled the suit with Armstrong's widow for $1 million. Eventually FM became the spectrum of choice for music lovers, far surpassing the broadcast quality of AM.

Licensed Recordings Launch Disc Jockeys

Early radio station owners avoided playing records because they would have had to pay ASCAP royalties. The FCC also required stations that played records to remind their audiences every half-hour that the audience was listening to recorded music, not a live orchestra. This discouraged record spinning.

In 1935, newscaster Martin Block at New York's independent station WNEW began playing records in between his newscasts, and then he started a program called *Make Believe Ballroom*. He is generally considered America's first disc jockey. In 1940, the FCC ruled that once stations bought a record, they could play it on the air whenever they liked, without the half-hour announcements.

Edwin H. Armstrong's invention of FM made radio signals clearer. For nearly 20 years, Armstrong battled RCA's David Sarnoff for royalties. Disheartened by the legal battle, Armstrong committed suicide, but his widow eventually won the royalty payments.

David Sarnoff (left), who began his broadcast career as a wireless operator, eventually became president of Radio Corporation of America (RCA). William S. Paley (right), who launched CBS radio, often battled with Sarnoff. The continuing competition between Sarnoff and Paley shaped the development of American broadcasting.

Gordon McLendon introduced format radio in 1959, which meant stations could share standardized programs that they previously had to produce individually.

To counteract ASCAP's insistence on royalties, broadcasters formed a cooperative music licensing organization called Broadcast Music, Inc. Most rhythm and blues, country and rock 'n' roll artists eventually signed with **BMI**, which charged stations less for recording artists than ASCAP. This inexpensive source of music also created a new type of media personality—the disc jockey.

Clock and Car Radios Make Radio Portable

Clock and car radios helped ensure radio's survival by making it an everyday accessory. Transistor radios, first sold in 1948 for $40, were more reliable and cheaper than tube radios. Clock radios, introduced in the 1950s, woke people up and caused them to rely on radio for the first news of the day.

William Lear, who also designed the Lear jet, invented the car radio in 1928. Early car radios were enormous, with spotty reception, but the technology that was developed during World War II helped refine them.

BMI Broadcast Music, Inc., a cooperative music licensing organization.

Drive-Time Audiences People who listen to the radio in their cars during 6 to 9 a.m. and 4 to 7 p.m.

Payola The practice of accepting payment to play specific recordings on the air.

In 1946, 9 million cars had car radios. By 1963, the number was 50 million. A radio station owner coined the term **drive-time audiences** to describe people who listened in their cars on the way to work from 6 to 9 a.m. and on the way home from 4 to 7 p.m.

Gordon McLendon Introduces Format Radio

How would the stations know which mix of records to use and who would play them? The answer came from Gordon McLendon, the father of format radio. At KLIF in Dallas, McLendon combined music and news in a predictable rotation of 20-minute segments, and eventually KLIF grew very popular. Next he refined the music by creating the Top 40 format.

Top 40 played the top-selling hits continually, interrupted only by a disc jockey or a newscast. By 1959, McLendon launched the beautiful-music format at KABL in San Francisco. In 1964, he created a 24-hour news format for Chicago's WNUS, using three news vans with "telesigns" that showed news on the roofs in lights as the vans drove around town.

Formats meant stations could now share standardized programs that stations previously had to produce individually. Eventually, the idea of formatted programming spread, which made network programming and the networks themselves less important to individual stations.

Payola and Talk Show Scandals Highlight Broadcast Ethics

The rise of rock 'n' roll coincided with the development of transistor and portable radios, which meant radio played a central role in the rock revolution. "Rock and radio were made for each other. The relationship between record companies and radio stations became mutually beneficial. By providing the latest hits, record companies kept stations' operating costs low. The stations, in turn, provided the record companies with the equivalent of free advertising," wrote radio historian David MacFarland.

Eventually this relationship would prove too close. On February 8, 1960, Congress began hearings into charges that disc jockeys and program directors had accepted cash to play specific recordings on the air. The term **payola** was coined to describe this practice, combining *pay* and *Victrola* (the name of a popular record player).

In May 1960, the Manhattan grand jury charged eight men with commercial bribery for accepting more than $100,000 in payoffs for playing records. The most prominent among them was Alan Freed, who had worked in Cleveland (where he was credited with coining the term *rock 'n' roll*) and at New York's WABC.

In February 1962, Freed pleaded guilty to two counts of accepting payoffs, paid a $300 fine, and received six months

IMPACT
»Ethics

Off the Air: The Light Goes Out for Don Imus

by Bill Carter and Jacques Steinberg; Tina Kelley contributed reporting

In 2007, radio talk show host Don Imus (left) was fired by CBS after he described members of the Rutgers women's basketball team (right) as "nappy-headed hos." Imus later apologized to the team for the remark, but CBS had already fired him. A year later, Imus was hired by WABC-AM in New York.

CBS brought a weeklong confrontation over a racial and sexual insult by the radio host Don Imus to an end yesterday [April 12, 2007] when it canceled the "Imus in the Morning" program, effective immediately.

The move came a day after the cable television network MSNBC, a General Electric unit that has simulcast Mr. Imus' radio program for the last 10 years, removed the show from its morning lineup. The two moves, taken together, mean that Mr. Imus, who has been broadcasting the program for more than 30 years, no longer has a home on either national radio or television. . . .

Mr. Imus received the news at home in a telephone call. Many of his listeners learned of it during the afternoon radio show "Mike and the Mad Dog," which announced it on WFAN, the CBS-owned New York station that also carried Mr. Imus' program.

The CBS chief executive, Leslie Moonves, met yesterday afternoon with the Rev. Al Sharpton and the Rev. Jesse Jackson, leaders in what became a national movement to remove Mr. Imus from the air in the wake of his comments disparaging members of the Rutgers women's basketball team. On April 4, Mr. Imus referred on the air to the Rutgers athletes as "nappy-headed hos."

Both CBS and MSNBC had been under pressure from black leaders and women's groups, then advertisers began abandoning the Imus program and its networks this week, pulling out the financial underpinnings from the show. . . .

CBS and NBC originally announced a two-week suspension for Mr. Imus that was to begin on Monday, but the protests increased as the week went on. They gained momentum first from a news conference by the Rutgers team and then by the recounting of previous episodes when Mr. Imus and his supporting cast engaged in racially charged banter.

Executives at NBC said the discomfort of staff members and concerns about the network's reputation had influenced the decision to cut ties with Mr. Imus. But it was paying only a license fee to carry the show. CBS Radio and WFAN produced the show and contracted with Mr. Imus as its star.

CBS also manages Westwood One, the syndicator that has sold the Imus show to other stations around the country. Mr. Imus, 66, was among the most recognizable voices on radio, and commanded a salary estimated at $10 million a year.

Note: Don Imus' show returned to radio in June 2008, broadcasting on WABC-AM in New York.

Radio at Work

A Columbia University report, commissioned by NBC in 1954, defined radio's role after television. "Radio was the one medium that could accompany almost every type of activity. . . . Where radio once had been a leisure-time 'reward' after a day's work, television was now occupying that role. Radio had come to be viewed less as a treat than as a kind of 'companion' to some other activity." Like magazines, radio survived in part because the medium adapted to fill a different need for its audience.

Today, about 12,000 radio stations are on the air in the United States. They are about evenly divided between FM and AM. Network programming plays a much smaller role than when radio began because most stations play music and so don't need network programming to survive. National Public Radio is the only major public network. Many commercial stations today use *program services*, which provide satellite as well as formatted programming.

Most stations are part of a *group*, which means that a company owns more than one station in more than one broadcast market. Some stations are part of a combination AM/FM *(a combo)*, which means that a company owns both AM and FM stations in the same market. A few stations remain family-owned, single operations that run just like any other small business.

The management structure at a radio station usually includes a general manager, a program manager, account executives, the traffic department, production department, engineering department and administration.

The *general manager* runs the radio station. The *program manager* oversees what goes on the air, including the news programs, the station's format and any on-air people. Salespeople, who are called *account executives*, sell the advertising for programs.

The *traffic department* schedules the commercials, makes sure they run correctly and bills the clients. The *production department* helps with local programming, if there is any, and produces local commercials for the station. *Engineering* keeps the station on the air. *Administration* pays the bills, answers the phones and orders the paper clips. A small station requires five employees, or fewer, to handle all these jobs.

AP Photos

Disc jockey Alan Freed admitted in 1962 that he accepted payments for playing specific recordings on the air. In 1960, Congress amended the Federal Communications Act to prohibit the payment of cash or gifts in exchange for airplay (called *payola*).

probation. Then he was found guilty of income tax evasion. He died in 1965 while awaiting trial, at age 43. In September 1960, Congress amended the Federal Communications Act to prohibit the payment of cash or gifts in exchange for airplay; nevertheless, the issue of payola surfaced again in 2005 and resulted in stiff fines in 2007 (see "Competition Brings Back Payola," page 128).

Congress Creates National Public Radio

The Public Broadcasting Act of 1967 created the Corporation for Public Broadcasting and included funding for public radio and TV stations. National Public Radio launched a national program on FM in 1970, but many radios still didn't have an FM dial. Most public stations—owned by colleges and universities and staffed by volunteers—were staffed irregularly.

"I love it when you use your 'All Things Considered' voice."

Then NPR started the program *All Things Considered* for the evening drive-time and in 1979 launched *Morning Edition*, hosted by Bob Edwards until 2004. Today, *Morning Edition* and *All Things Considered* have a very loyal audience for their long interviews on topical issues and international reports. By design, public radio is an alternative to commercial radio. Today, NPR still receives some public funding, but it depends primarily on private donations to survive.

Portability and Immediacy Help Radio Survive

Instead of dying after the spread of television, radio managed to thrive by adapting to an audience that sought the portability and immediacy that radio offers. Nothing can beat radio for quick news bulletins or the latest hits. Radio also delivers a targeted audience much better than television, because the radio station you prefer defines you to an advertiser much better than the television station you watch.

The advertising potential for an intimate medium like radio is attracting entrepreneurs who have never owned a station and group owners who want to expand their holdings, given the FCC's deregulation. When you listen to the radio in your car or through earphones while you jog, for instance, radio is not competing with any other medium for your attention. Advertisers like this exclusive access to an audience. Three important issues for people in radio today are:

1. Deregulation

2. Ratings

3. Formats

Telecommunications Act of 1996 Overhauls Radio

The Telecommunications Act of 1996 was the first major overhaul of broadcast regulation since the Federal Communications Commission was established in 1934. Today the legacy of the Act is that commercial radio is regulated much less than it was in the 1970s. This is called a policy of ***deregulation***.

Before the 1996 Act passed, the FCC limited the number of radio stations that one company could own nationwide. The Telecommunications Act removed the limit on the number of radio stations a company can own, and in each local market the number of stations that one owner can hold depends on the size of the market. (For a complete discussion of the Telecommunications Act, see **Chapter 14**.)

The Telecommunications Act also allows ***cross-ownership***, which means that companies can own radio

FilmMagic/Getty Images

Popular singers like Los Lonely Boys make Spanish programming one of radio's most popular formats. Critics say that radio ratings do not accurately reflect the large number of non-English-speaking listeners.

and TV stations in the same market and broadcast and cable outlets in the same market. As soon as the Act passed in February 1996, radio station sales began to soar.

Today many radio companies own hundreds of stations each. Supporters of the changes say radio will become more competitive because these larger companies can give the stations better financial support than small, single owners. Opponents point out that consolidation in the radio industry will lead to less program variety for consumers and too much power for companies that own large numbers of radio stations nationwide.

Are Radio Ratings Accurate?

Radio station owners depend on ratings to set advertising rates, and the stations with the most listeners command the highest ad rates. A company called Arbitron gathers ratings

Deregulation Government action that removes government restrictions on the business operation of an industry.

Cross-Ownership The practice of one company owning radio and TV stations in the same broadcast market.

IMPACT
»»People

Vin Scully: A City Hangs on His Every Word
by Christine Daniels

LOS ANGELES–His voice belongs to then and now, an audio clip that carries us back to a bygone era even as it keeps us up-to-the-minute updated.

It has been there as long as big-league baseball has been in this city, actually pre-dating the Los Angeles Dodgers by several years, which was the biggest advantage the Dodgers had when they first arrived in 1958, certainly more important than any of the fading stars on the playing roster.

When Vin Scully settled in behind his microphone at the Coliseum 50 years ago, Los Angeles had the

Perhaps the finest sportscaster ever, Vin Scully has been the voice of the Dodgers on radio for more nearly 60 years.

narrator it needed and the Dodgers had the pitchman they required to break the ice, to melt any pockets of resistance that might have been scattered around the Southland.

But as the Dodgers crank up the celebratory machine to mark their 50th anniversary in Los Angeles, a different emotion surfaces when considering Scully's place with the Dodgers. Scully is 80. For the time being, anyway, every game, every inning Scully's calls carry with them an underlying, undeniable theme for listeners: Let us enjoy them while we can.

---

for the radio business. To find out what radio stations people are listening to, Arbitron requests that selected listeners complete and return diaries the company sends them.

Arbitron often is criticized because minorities, non–English-speaking listeners, and people ages 18 to 24 don't return the diaries in the same proportion as other people that Arbitron surveys. Arbitron acknowledges the problems and has tried filling out diaries for people over the phone and adding bilingual interviewers.

Still, questions persist, and radio stations are very dependent on ratings to set their rates for advertising.

Arbitron critics contend that its ratings hurt the different rock and urban formats, such as rap/hip-hop and Spanish language programming, while aiding the contemporary and news/talk/information formats, whose audiences are older and more responsive to the diaries. In November 2008,

the Nielson Media Company, which provides ratings for TV, announced that the company planned to launch a radio ratings service, in direct competition with Arbitron.

Radio Depends on Ready-Made Formats

Today's radio station owners, looking for an audience, can use one of several ready-made formats. By adjusting their formats, radio managers can test the markets until they find a formula that works to deliver their target audience to advertisers. (See **Illustration 6.2** on page 127.)

If you were a radio station manager today, and you wanted to program your station, you could choose from several popular formats:

Scully represents more than an era in Los Angeles sports history; he also represents an era in sports broadcasting when announcers were as indelibly linked to the teams they covered as the logo on the players' caps.

When Scully was hired by the Brooklyn Dodgers in 1950, his contemporaries included Mel Allen with the Yankees and Russ Hodges with the Giants. They were icons, with larger-than-life personas, as they served as the immediate conduits of information and news to fans hungry for details about their teams.

Over time, that part of the job description changed. More teams meant more job movement among announcers. New media, such as the Internet, meant more sources for information.

What has Scully meant to the Dodgers since 1958?

"Everything, with an exclamation point," former Dodgers owner Peter O'Malley said. When the Dodgers first arrived in Los Angeles, O'Malley said, Scully was "the face of the Dodgers. It wasn't the manager. It wasn't a player. It wasn't the owner. It wasn't where they played. It wasn't any of those things. He was the face and the voice of the Dodgers. And he made so many friends for us, then and now."

More than just defining L.A. baseball culture, Scully invented it. For a city perpetually on the move, Scully became essential listening for harried freeway drivers who, once grounded, continued the habit with portable transistor radios—and today with audio supplied via satellite and the Internet.

Al Michaels listened to Scully as a kid growing up in Brooklyn, then followed the Dodgers to Los Angeles in 1958 when his father had to relocate because of work.

"I never missed a beat," Michaels said. "I've listened to Vinny almost since Vinny started.

"When I think back, right now, I think about him in terms the way Chick Hearn was through all of those years. You could turn on the radio at any given moment and it's almost as if something very memorable would be said, or something tickled your fancy. Or was said in a way that you never heard before. And the enthusiasm level in both men is astonishing. To be able to do it over that period of time, and to still watch a game and broadcast a game with a sense of wonderment . . . to me that's the most astonishing thing about Vin Scully."

Excerpted from: Christine Daniels, "A City Hangs On His Every Word," *Los Angeles Times,* March 31, 2008. Reprinted by permission.

NEWS/TALK/INFORMATION/SPORTS. A station with this format devotes most of its airtime to different types of talk shows, which can include call-in features, where listeners question on-the-air guests. Its typical audience is 35 and older. It is difficult for a small radio station to survive on news alone, so most of these stations are in big cities because of the continuing source of news stories. The immediacy of the live news/talk format also can create problems for broadcasters (see **Impact/Ethics**, "Off the Air: The Light Goes Out for Don Imus," page 121).

The news/talk category also includes live sports broadcasts (see **Impact/People**, "Vin Scully: A City Hangs on His Every Word," page 124.), which are very popular because radio is a convenient way to follow the action in the car and at work.

ADULT CONTEMPORARY. This program format includes adult rock and light rock music by artists such as Kenny G and Anita Baker. It aims to reach 25- to 40-year-olds in all types of markets.

CONTEMPORARY HIT/TOP 40. Playing songs on *Billboard*'s current hits list, a Top 40 station closely follows trends among listeners, especially teenagers.

SPANISH. Spanish stations are the fastest-growing radio format, as radio owners target the nation's expanding Latino population. Spanish-language radio usually features news, music and talk. Most Spanish-language stations are AM stations that recently have been converted from less-profitable formats.

COUNTRY. The Grand Ole Opry first broadcast country music on WSM in Nashville in 1925, and this radio format

WireImage/Getty Images

Today's radio broadcasts are highly automated. Often the on-air talent also runs the equipment. Disc jockey Eddie Garcia of Sirius XM's "The Cit" broadcasts at a Toys for Tots Holiday fundraiser in 2007 in Los Angeles.

is aimed at 25- to 45-year-olds in urban as well as rural areas.

The most popular radio formats are country music and news/talk/information/sports programs.

News/talk radio is very popular in Los Angeles, but the most-listened-to radio station in the Los Angeles area is a Spanish-language station. The popularity of the station in an area with an expanding Spanish-language population shows how cultural changes in urban areas quickly can affect the economics of radio in that area. Stations can divide these traditional formats into even more subcategories: AOR is splitting into modern rock and oldies; some Spanish-language stations play only love songs.

The use of recorded program formats means that a station can specialize its programming simply by what it chooses to play. Many stations operate without any disc jockeys altogether or limit personality programming to morning and evening drive-time. The rest of the day and evening these stations rely on an engineer and an announcer to carry the programming. Today, networks, which once dominated radio programming, mainly provide national news to their affiliates.

Station managers can program their own stations, mixing local news, music and announcements. Stations also can get programming from syndicated and satellite program services. Syndicates provide pre-packaged program formats. Satellites make program distribution easier; satellite networks, such as Satellite Music Network, promise the broadcaster original, up-to-date programming without a large, local staff.

Audience Divides into Smaller Segments

The most significant trend in radio is the move toward more segmentation of the audience, similar to the division of audiences in the magazine industry. Identifying a specific audience segment and programming for it is called *narrowcasting*.

"With narrowcasting, advertising efficiency goes way up as overall costs go down. . . . We are approaching the unstated goal of all radio programmers: to create a station aimed so perfectly that the listener will no longer have to wait, ever, for the song that he wants to hear," says radio historian Eric Zorn.

Digital Audio Delivers Internet and Satellite Radio

A recent technology known as *digital audio broadcast* (DAB) eliminates all the static and hiss of current broadcast signals and means infinite program choices for consumers as all radio digital signals share the same delivery system. Today digital stations can send their digital signals over the Internet as well as over the air.

INTERNET RADIO. More than 3,000 stations now send their programming over the Internet. The Internet offers unlimited possibilities for radio to be distributed beyond the bounds of a local radio audience, and people in the United States can easily hear overseas stations such as the **BBC** (British Broadcasting Corporation). Even low-power stations such as IBDAA Radio 194, originating from Palestine, can be rebroadcast over the Internet.

Narrowcasting Segmenting the radio audience.

Digital Audio Broadcast A new form of audio transmission that eliminates all static and makes more program choices possible.

BBC British Broadcasting Corporation.

IMPACT
»»Business

Illustration 6.2

Which Radio Formats Are Most Popular?

The most popular radio formats are news/talk/information/sports and country music.

Source: Radio Advertising Bureau 2008.

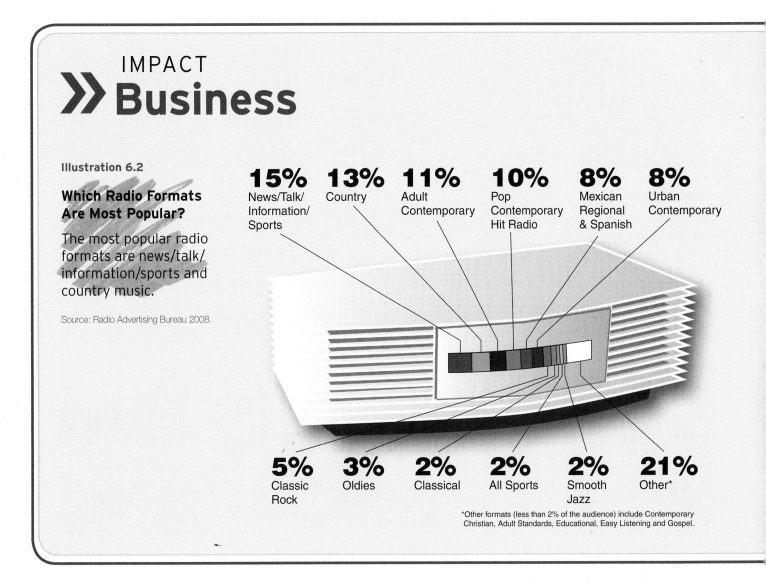

15% News/Talk/Information/Sports

13% Country

11% Adult Contemporary

10% Pop Contemporary Hit Radio

8% Mexican Regional & Spanish

8% Urban Contemporary

5% Classic Rock

3% Oldies

2% Classical

2% All Sports

2% Smooth Jazz

21% Other*

*Other formats (less than 2% of the audience) include Contemporary Christian, Adult Standards, Educational, Easy Listening and Gospel.

SATELLITE RADIO. Another recent technology in the radio business is **satellite radio**. Launched in 2001, satellite radio offers more than 100 channels of varied music and talk, with limited advertising on some stations and no advertising on others. For a subscription fee, two companies—Sirius Satellite Radio (based in New York) and XM (based in Washington)—offered the service (see **Illustration 6.3**). The companies charged $9.95 to $12.95 a month to hear uninterrupted programming, without commercial announcements

Satellite radio service requires special radios containing a miniature satellite radio receiver. In 2002, General Motors began offering satellite radios as a factory-installed option on some models. Ford and DaimlerChrysler began offering the service in 2003. Car buyers can pay the subscription fee with their automobile financing.

By 2005, XM boasted four million subscribers, and the company said it planned to have 10 million subscribers by

"Oh my gosh, this is terrific! I just tuned in satellite radio."

Satellite Radio Radio transmission by satellite, with limited or no advertising, available by subscription.

IMPACT
≫ Culture

Illustration 6.3

Satellite Radio

Two companies, Sirius and XM, began beaming digital radio signals from satellites in 2001. In 2008, Sirius and XM merged to become Sirius XM.

Here's how digital radio signals travel from the satellites to someone's car or home.

Source: *The New York Times,* Oct. 19, 2000, D-1. Copyright © The New York Times Co. Adapted with permission.

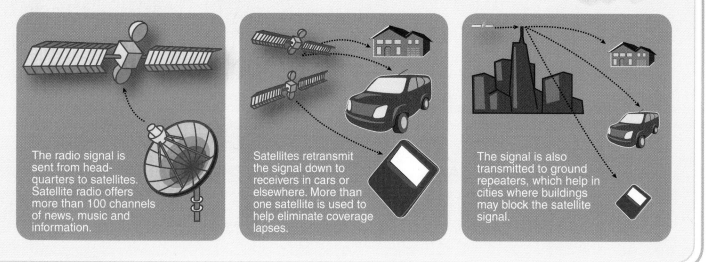

The radio signal is sent from head-quarters to satellites. Satellite radio offers more than 100 channels of news, music and information.

Satellites retransmit the signal down to receivers in cars or elsewhere. More than one satellite is used to help eliminate coverage lapses.

The signal is also transmitted to ground repeaters, which help in cities where buildings may block the satellite signal.

2010. In 2008, the Justice Department approved the merger of XM and Sirius. Today, the two program services combined have about 18 million subscribers.

Competition Brings Back Payola

As radio technology grows more complex and companies test new formats and different program delivery systems, the competition for your ear expands the choices that advertisers can make to reach you. However, as the competition among stations intensifies, some stations look for profits from a familiar but unethical source.

In 2005, New York's Attorney General Eliot Spitzer announced he was investigating the four major music companies to examine their practice of paying independent promoters to influence which songs the stations played on

the air. The practice often was criticized as a way for stations to get around laws prohibiting payola that date from the 1960s. (See "Payola and Talk Show Scandals Highlight Broadcast Ethics," page 120.) Some record labels paid individual stations as much as $100,000 to help promote their songs, Spitzer said. Other companies gave the stations luxury travel for station employees or gifts to use in station giveaways.

"To disguise a payoff to a radio programmer at KHTS in San Diego, Epic Records called a flat-screen television a 'contest giveaway,'" reported *The New York Times.* "Epic ... used the same gambit in delivering a laptop computer to the program director of WRHT in Greenville, N.C.—who also received PlayStation 2 games and an out-of-town trip with his girlfriend."

After payoffs like these at Sony were uncovered, Sony agreed to a $10 million settlement and fired the top promotion executive at its Epic label. Radio executives at some of the other corporations said they already had stopped paying independent promoters, but Spitzer said, "This is not a pretty picture; what we see is that payola is pervasive." In 2007, the stations agreed to pay an additional $12.5 million to the Federal Communications Commission to settle the complaints.

Digital Delivery Splits Radio Income

The more stations and digital radio services (such as satellite digital radio and Internet radio) that are available for customers, the harder every station and delivery service must compete for advertising. This means less revenue for each station because each station's potential audience becomes smaller.

Satellite and Internet radio delivery systems change the entire revenue equation for the radio industry as people pay subscription fees to hear radio on satellite without commercials and go to the Internet for access to new channels they couldn't hear before, offering listener-specific programming that isn't available on commercial radio in the United States.

Meanwhile, commercial radio is trying to stay afloat using the same commercial model that has served the industry for more than 80 years. In the 1950s, radio had to learn how to compete with television. Today the radio industry must learn how to compete with itself.

Gary Gershoff/WireImage for Sirius XM

Today satellite radio offers programs such as Chris "Mad Dog" Russo's live daily sports talk channel on Sirius XM. Satellite radio, paid for by subscription fees, is attracting listeners away from local over-the-air broadcast radio.

SIRIUS CONNECT — THE BEST — SIRIUS CONNECT

Review, Analyze, Investigate
REVIEWING CHAPTER 6

Radio Sounds Are Everywhere

✓ Radio transformed national politics and also expanded Americans' access to popular, as well as classical, culture.

✓ Radio is a commercial medium, supported almost entirely by advertising.

Radio Takes a Technological Leap

✓ Radio history began with Samuel F. B. Morse's invention of the telegraph, first demonstrated in 1835.

✓ Alexander Graham Bell invented the telephone, demonstrated in 1876, and Heinrich Hertz first described radio waves in 1887.

Broadcasting Is Born

✓ Guglielmo Marconi's promotion of wireless radio wave transmission began in 1897.

✓ Reginald Fessenden advanced wireless technology, but Lee de Forest called himself the father of radio because he invented the Audion tube to detect radio waves.

✓ David Sarnoff and William S. Paley made radio broadcasting a viable business in the United States.

Federal Government Regulates the Airwaves

✓ The federal government intervened to regulate broadcasting almost as soon as it was invented.

✓ Early regulation separated the broadcast media from the print media, which are not regulated directly by the federal government.

Radio Audience Expands Quickly

✓ Two important developments for commercial radio were blanket licensing and commercial sponsorship.

✓ Blanket licensing means that radio owners can use recorded music inexpensively.

✓ Commercial sponsorship established the practice of advertisers underwriting the cost of American broadcasting.

✓ The Radio Act of 1927 established the concept that the government would regulate broadcasting "as a public convenience, interest or necessity requires."

✓ The Radio Act of 1927 is the foundation for all broadcast regulation in the United States, including the establishment of the Federal Communications Commission (FCC) in 1934.

Radio Grows into a Powerful Force

✓ In the 1930s, radio programming expanded to include comedy, music, serials, drama and news.

✓ Radio also indirectly created a collective national experience that had not existed before.

✓ Commercials gave advertisers access to an audience at home.

"War of the Worlds" Challenges Radio's Credibility

✓ On Halloween Eve, October 30, 1938, *Mercury Theater on the Air* broadcast "War of the Worlds."

✓ The "War of the Worlds" broadcast demonstrated the vulnerability of a captive audience.

Radio Networks Expand

✓ Originally, the three radio networks (NBC, CBS and ABC) provided most radio programming. Today, most stations use a variety of sources to program themselves.

✓ David Sarnoff launched NBC radio in 1927, William S. Paley started CBS radio in 1929 and Edward Noble bought NBC-Blue, which became ABC, in 1941.

Radio Adapts to Television

✓ Edwin H. Armstrong is responsible for the invention of FM radio. Today, FM stations are three times as popular as AM stations.

✓ Clock and car radios expanded radio's audience, but the role of radio changed with the advent of TV, which meant radio had to compete with visual entertainment and TV news.

✓ Gordon McLendon launched format radio in 1959.

✓ In the 1960s, Congress uncovered the unethical practice of payola in the radio industry. Recording companies were paying station disc jockeys to play their songs on the air. These complaints resurfaced in 2005 when the New York attorney general filed payola charges against the four major music companies.

✓ In 2007, radio talk show host Don Imus was fired for making racially insensitive remarks on the air.

Radio at Work

✓ Radio is a portable medium that can accompany almost every activity.

✓ The management structure at a radio station includes a general manager, a program manager, account executives, the traffic and production departments, and administration.

Congress Creates National Public Radio

✓ The federal government began funding National Public Radio in 1967, and NPR began broadcasting national programming in 1970.

✓ Today, NPR programs such as *Morning Edition* and *All Things Considered* still attract a very loyal audience.

Portability and Immediacy Help Radio Survive

✓ As an advertising medium, radio delivers a targeted audience much better than TV.

✓ Radio is also portable—you can listen to it in your car or take it with you anywhere.

Telecommunications Act of 1996 Overhauls Radio

✓ The Telecommunications Act of 1996 was the first major overhaul of broadcast regulation since the FCC was established in 1934.

✓ The Act removed the limit on the number of stations one company can own, and in each local market the number of stations one owner can hold depends on the size of the market.

Are Radio Ratings Accurate?

✓ Arbitron is the primary ratings service for radio.

✓ Stations use ratings to set their rates for advertising.

✓ In November 2008, the Nielson Company launched a radio ratings service, in direct competition with Arbitron.

Radio Depends on Ready-Made Formats

✓ Formats systematize radio broadcasts.

✓ Stations use formats to target a specific type of radio listener and define the audience for advertisers.

✓ The most popular radio formats are news/talk/information/sports and country music.

Audience Divides into Smaller Segments

✓ The most significant trend in radio today is the move toward more segmentation of the audience, similar to the division of audiences in the magazine industry.

✓ Today, the radio industry's expanding delivery systems means stiffer competition.

Digital Audio Delivers Internet and Satellite Radio

✓ Digital audio broadcast, Internet radio and satellite digital radio mean more program choices for listeners.

Competition Brings Back Payola

✓ The payola scandals resurfaced in 2005 when New York's attorney general charged that the four major recording labels paid private promoters to get their songs on the air.

✓ Sony paid $10 million to settle the charges and in 2007 the radio stations paid the FCC an additional $12.5 million.

Digital Delivery Splits Radio Income

✓ Today radio listeners have more choices than ever.

✓ The addition of new sources for radio programming, such as satellite and Internet radio, are changing the economics of radio today.

KEY TERMS

These terms are defined in the margins throughout this chapter and appear in alphabetical order with definitions in the Glossary, which begins on page 372.

ASCAP 116

BBC 126

Blanket Licensing Agreement 116

BMI 120

Cross-Ownership 123

Deregulation 123

Digital Audio Broadcast 126

Drive-Time Audiences 120

FCC 116

Narrowcasting 126

Network 118

Payola 120

Satellite Radio 127

CRITICAL QUESTIONS

1. How did the Radio Act of 1912 set a precedent for American broadcasting?

2. How did the following developments in radio affect the industry? Why is each of them so important?
   a. Blanket licensing
   b. Commercial sponsorship
   c. Establishment of networks

3. Discuss the "War of the Worlds" broadcast and its effects upon its audience. How did it change people's perceptions of radio?

4. Briefly discuss the present-day state of format radio, including what formats are available, which are the most popular, which are the fastest growing, and which are disappearing.

5. Discuss the ethics issues involved in the payola scandals and the firing of talk show host Don Imus.

WORKING THE WEB

This list includes both sites mentioned in the chapter and others to give you greater insight into the radio industry.

The Broadcast Archive
http://www.oldradio.com

This is a site for radio historians, with an emphasis on radio technology. The site includes an archive of manuals and schematics, as well as historical narratives and biographies of people who worked in early broadcasting.

Canadian Broadcasting Corporation (CBC) Radio-Canada
http://www.cbc.ca/radio

The radio division of Canada's national public broadcasting system, the CBC was created in 1936 in response to concern about the growing U.S. influence in radio. Now encompassing television and new media services, the CBC has a mandate to provide a wide range of programming that informs, enlightens and entertains and that is predominantly and distinctively Canadian. The Web site provides live radio streams from CBC Radio One (news and talk) and Radio 2 (jazz, blues and classical music), as well as program schedules, podcasts and forums. It also has links to CBC Radio 3 (rock, pop, hip hop, electronica and alt-country music) and Sirius XM.

CBS Radio
http://www.cbsradio.com

As one of the largest U.S. major-market radio operators, CBS provides broadcast, digital and on-demand radio. In addition to operating 140 radio stations, it is home to 27 professional sports franchises.

Friday Morning Quarterback (FMQB)
http://www.fmqb.com

Recently celebrating 40 years of serving the music and radio industries with high-quality content, insightful articles and news, FMQB is the self-proclaimed "premier destination for music and radio industry professionals." The production division is renowned for its one-hour National Radio Series that feature major artists premiering new music. Web site features include breaking radio industry and music news, a voice talent vault, music available for airplay, ratings and job information, and industry links.

Inside Radio
http://www.insideradio.com

This radio industry publication features industry news, ratings and classifieds. Inside Radio also publishes Who Owns What (a weekly update on station ownership), Radio Journal (featuring FCC updates and technical news) and The Radio Book (a directory of radio stations in the U.S. and Canada).

National Public Radio
http://www.npr.org

NPR distributes and produces noncommercial news, talk and entertainment programs. Its more than 860 independently operated local stations mix national and local programming to fit the needs of their communities. Audio archives are available for a growing number of nationally produced shows.

Radio Advertising Bureau
http://www.rab.com

The goal of the RAB, the promotional arm of the commercial radio industry, is to increase the use of radio advertising and develop the skills of radio marketing representatives.

Radio Lovers
http://www.radiolovers.com

Radiolovers.com offers hundreds of vintage radio shows online for free. Its goal is to bring the world of Old Time Radio to a new generation of listeners. Users can browse by show genre or search by title. The site includes a disclaimer stating that the creators believe all show copyrights have expired or never existed and that they will remove any recording that is shown to violate a copyright.

Radio Time
http://radiotime.com

This electronic guide to radio allows users to find local programming by zip code; browse stations by location, genre and subcategories; listen to radio; and search by station, program or personality name. Also available by subscription is RedButton, software that records and pauses live radio.

Sirius XM
http://www.siriusxm.com

Sirius offers over 130 channels of satellite radio, including commercial-free music as well as sports, news and talk shows. Radios must be Sirius-ready. Programming top names include CNN, Martha Stewart and Howard Stern. Sirius also provides Internet radio and Backseat TV, the first live in-vechicle television network.

7

Movies:
Picturing the Future

What's Ahead?

Michael Buckner/Getty Images

Held in June 2008, The Maui Film Festival in Wailea, Maui, Hawaii—like hundreds of independent film festivals—showcases emerging moviemaking talent.

The movie industry has been

called "an industry based on dreams" because it has been such an imaginative, creative medium. It also would be easy to assume the movie industry is one of the biggest media businesses because the publicity surrounding movie celebrities captures a great deal of attention. So it often surprises people to learn that the movie industry makes less money each year than the newspaper, television or book businesses.

TimeFrame
1877 – Today

Movies Mature as a Popular Medium

1877   **Eadweard Muybridge catches motion on film when he uses 12 cameras to photograph a horse's movements for Leland Stanford in Palo Alto, California.**

Eadweard Muybridge/ CORBIS

1915   **Director D. W. Griffith introduces the concept of the movie spectacular with The Birth of a Nation.**

Hulton Archive/Getty Images

1916   Brothers Noble and George Johnson launch Lincoln Films, the first company to produce movies called "race films," serious narrative movies for African American audiences.

1919   Oscar Micheaux releases *Within Our Gates,* a response to D. W. Griffith's controversial, anti-black epic *The Birth of a Nation.*

1927   *The Jazz Singer,* the first feature-length motion picture with sound, opens in New York City.

1930   The Motion Picture Producers and Distributors Association adopts a production code to control movie content.

1947   The Hollywood Ten are called to testify before the House Un-American Activities Committee.

1948   The U.S. Supreme Court breaks up the large studios' control of Hollywood by deciding in the case of *United States v. Paramount*

Pictures, Inc., et al. that the studios are a monopoly. **(Pictured driving out of the MGM Studios parking lot is famous director Alfred Hitchcock.)**

Bettmann/CORBIS

1966   The Motion Picture Association of America introduces a voluntary content ratings system for the movies.

1994   **(Pictured left to right) David Geffen, Steven Spielberg and Jeffrey Katzenberg launch DreamWorks SKG, the first new independent movie studio created in the United States since United Artists.**

Kim Kulish/Sygma/ CORBIS

2001   To attempt to stop movie piracy, the Motion Picture Association of America challenges the availability of recordable DVD technology, but eventually DVD-Rs are allowed to be sold.

2005   DreamWorks is sold to Viacom, Inc., leaving the U.S. without a major independent movie studio.

Today   Movie theaters collect about one billion tickets a year, but more people see movies on video than in movie theaters. The market for American movies continues to grow overseas. Movie downloads are an expanding source of revenue. Movie distribution companies plan to send their movies by satellite to satellite dishes on top of theaters and directly to consumers' homes via subscription services.

Bertrand Rieger/ Hemis/CORBIS

Movies and movie stars need the public's attention because the size of the audience has a direct effect on whether or not movies succeed. Movies cost a lot to make, and most movies lose money. Investors, therefore, often favor "bankable" talent that brings fans to a movie, rather than new, untested talent. Even movies featuring established talent can fail; no one in the movie industry can accurately predict which movies will be hits.

Movies Mirror the Culture

Perhaps more than any other medium, movies mirror the society that creates them. Some movies offer an underlying political message. Other movies reflect changing social values. Still other movies are just good entertainment. And all movies need an audience to succeed. (See **Impact/World**, "Indian Movie Stars Take to the Stage, Giving 'Em the Old Bollywood Razzle-Dazzle," page 138.)

Like other media industries, the movie business has had to adapt to changing technology. Before the invention of television, movies were the nation's primary form of visual entertainment. The current use of special effects—something you seldom get from television—is one way the movie industry competes with television for your attention and dollars. But special effects don't fit every movie, and they are very expensive. Today, as always, the economics of moviemaking is very important.

Inventors Capture Motion on Film

Movies were invented at a time when American industry welcomed any new gadget, and inventors wildly sought patents on appliances and electrical devices. The motion picture camera and projector were two of the Industrial Revolution's new gadgets.

Early Inventors Nurture the Movie Industry

Movies were not the invention of one person. First, a device to photograph moving objects had to be invented, followed by a device to project those pictures. This process involved six people: Ètienne Jules Marey, Eadweard Muybridge, Thomas Edison, William K. L. Dickson, and Auguste and Louis Lumière.

Eadweard Muybridge/CORBIS

This dancing woman is one of the early images photographed by Eadweard Muybridge, who captured motion on film. Muybridge's experiments led to the development of the first motion picture camera.

Marey and Muybridge

Ètienne Jules Marey, a scientist working in Paris, sought to record an animal's movement by individual actions—one at a time—to compare one animal to another. He charted a horse's movements on graphs and published the information in a book, *Animal Mechanism*.

Unknown to Marey, photographer Eadweard Muybridge was hired by railroad millionaire and horse breeder Leland Stanford to settle a $25,000 bet. Stanford had bet that during a trot, all four of a horse's feet simultaneously leave the ground. In 1877, Muybridge and Stanford built a special track in Palo Alto, California, with 12 cameras precisely placed to take pictures of a horse as it moved around the track. The horse tripped a series of equidistant wires as it ran, which in turn tripped the cameras' shutters. Stanford won his $25,000—one photograph showed that all four of the horse's feet did leave the ground—and the photographic series provided an excellent study of motion.

Muybridge expanded to 24 cameras, photographed other animals and then took pictures of people moving. He traveled throughout Europe showing his photographs. Eventually, Muybridge and Marey met. In 1882, Marey perfected a photographic gun camera that could take 12 photographs on one plate—the first motion picture camera.

Thomas Edison

Thomas Edison bought some of Muybridge's pictures in 1888 and showed them to his assistant, William K. L. Dickson. Edison then met with Marey in Europe, where Marey had invented a projector that showed pictures on a continuous

IMPACT
»World

Indian Movie Stars Take to the Stage, Giving 'Em the Old Bollywood Razzle-Dazzle

by Jon Caramanica

UNIONDALE, N.Y.–Abhishek Bachchan was everywhere . . . at the Nassau Coliseum: walking through the sold-out stadium surrounded by bodyguards; soaring above the crowd on a platform, pointing out women and serenading them; rapping, in a red leather jacket, alongside the duo Vishal-Shekhar; running onstage to hug his wife, the actress Aishwarya Rai Bachchan, while she made pleas to the audience about sustainable development.

All that movement, and still he couldn't quite outrun the long shadow cast by his father, Amitabh, a veteran of more than 150 films. He worked half as hard as his son, but was the clear focal point of the Unforgettable

Tour, a four-hour song-and-dance-and-more extravaganza featuring several stars of Indian cinema.

There is no American equivalent to this spectacle, in which actors, joined by dozens of dancers, recreate musical numbers from popular movies. Here, all talents–acting, singing, dancing–are equal. Well, not always singing; in most Bollywood films, vocals are provided by playback singers while the stars on screen lip-sync. . . .

Though the musicians remained onstage for Amitabh Bachchan's first solo set, they were less consequential. His appearance was more an exercise in collective memory

---

strip of film, but the stripfilm moved unevenly across the projector lens, so the pictures jumped.

William K. L. Dickson

Back in America, Dickson perforated the edges of the film so that, as the film moved through the camera, sprockets inside the camera grabbed the perforations and locked the film in place, minimizing the jumps.

Dickson looped the strip over a lamp and a magnifying lens in a box 2 feet wide and 4 feet tall. The box stood on the floor with a peephole in the top so people could look inside. Edison named this device the kinetoscope. On April 11, 1894, America's first kinetoscope parlor opened in New York City. For 25 cents, people could see 10 different 90-second black-and-white films, including *Trapeze*, *Horse Shoeing*, *Wrestlers* and *Roosters*.

Auguste and Louis Lumière

In France, the Lumière brothers, Auguste and Louis, developed an improved camera and a projector that could show

film on a large screen. The first public Lumière showing was on December 28, 1895: 10 short subjects with such riveting titles as *Lunch Hour at the Lumière Factory*, which showed workers leaving the building, and *Arrival of a Train at a Station*. Admission was 1 franc and the Lumières collected 35 francs.

Edison Launches American Movies

Four months after the Lumière premiere in France, Edison organized the first American motion picture premiere with an improved camera developed by independent inventor Thomas Armat. Edison dubbed the new machine the Vitascope, and America's first public showing of the motion picture was on April 23, 1896, at Koster and Bial's theater in New York. Edison sat in a box seat, and Armat ran the projector from the balcony.

At first, movies were a sideshow. Penny arcade owners showed movies behind a black screen at the rear of the arcade for an extra nickel. But soon the movies were more

than a great performance. A star of strato-
spheric proportions, he was celebrated
with hagiographical videos and voice-overs.
("Even the way he stands makes an impact."
"They aped his hairstyle.") The younger Mr.
Bachchan performed one of his father's
best-known routines, from *Don*, while images
from that film flashed on a screen behind
him.

　　With a silver goatee and short dark hair,
the elder Mr. Bachchan cut an august figure.
But he, too, was not immune to the pulls
of legacy. Toward the end of the show, in
a segment that was part spoken-word performance, part "Inside the Actors Studio,"
he discussed his own parents with emotion.
First, he recited a few lines of "Agneepath," a
poem by his father, Harivansh Rai Bachchan,
which was, he said, "written to inspire the
Indians. . . ."

　　Then he spoke about his mother, who
died last year, and slipped into his character from the film *Deewaar*, who prays for his
mother's health. As Mr. Bachchan delivered
the lines, his voice grew deep, mean and
improbably raspy. And then, just as quickly

Indian film stars, including Amitabh Bachchan, performed
live in an unusual stage show in New York in 2008 to promote India's movies and movie stars to an American audience. Because filmmakers in India produce so many movies,
the country's film industry is called "Bollywood."

as he had begun, he snapped back to normal
and was greeted with the night's most sincere
standing ovation. On a night full of carefully
choreographed moments, this blatant blast of
acting also proved to be the truest.

Jon Caramanica, "Movie Stars Take to the Stage, Giving 'Em the Old Bollywood Razzle-Dazzle," *The New York Times*, August 18, 2008.

popular than the rest of the attractions, and the arcades
were renamed *nickel*odeons. In 1900, there were more than
600 nickelodeons in New York City, with more than 300,000
daily admissions. Each show lasted about 20 minutes. The
programs ran from noon until late evening, and many theaters blared music outside to bring in business.

　　By 1907, Edison had contracted with most of the
nation's movie producers, as well as the Lumière brothers
and the innovative French producer Georges Mèliés, to provide movies for the theaters. Licensed Edison theaters used
licensed Edison projectors and rented Edison's licensed movies, many of which Edison produced at his own studio. The
important exception to Edison's licensing plan was his rival,
the American Biograph and Mutoscope Company, commonly
called Biograph.

　　Biograph manufactured a better motion picture camera
than Edison's, and Edison was losing business. In 1908, Biograph signed an agreement with Edison, forming the Motion
Picture Patents Company (MPPC).

Filmmakers Turn Novelty into Art

All the early films were black-and-white silents. Sound
was not introduced to the movies until the 1920s, and color
experiments did not begin until the 1930s. Two innovative
filmmakers are credited with turning the novelty of movies
into art: Georges Mèliés and Edwin S. Porter.

Georges Mèliés

French filmmaker Georges Mèliés added fantasy to the movies. Before Mèliés, moviemakers photographed theatrical
scenes or events from everyday life. But Mèliés, who was a
magician and a caricaturist before he became a filmmaker,
used camera tricks to make people disappear and reappear
and to make characters grow and then shrink.

　　His 1902 film, *A Trip to the Moon*, was the first outer-
space movie adventure, complete with fantasy creatures.

Georges Mèliés created fanciful creatures for his 1902 movie, *A Trip to the Moon,* introducing fantasy to motion pictures.

When his films, which became known as *trick films*, were shown in the United States, American moviemakers stole his ideas.

Edwin S. Porter

Edison hired projectionist/electrician Edwin S. Porter in 1899, and in the next decade Porter became America's most important filmmaker. Until Porter, most American films were trick films or short documentary-style movies that showed newsworthy events (although some filmmakers used titillating subjects in movies such as *Pajama Girl* and *Corset Girl* to cater to men, who were the movies' biggest fans). In 1903, Porter produced *The Great Train Robbery*, an action movie with bandits attacking a speeding train.

Instead of using a single location like most other moviemakers, Porter shot 12 different scenes. He also introduced the use of dissolves between shots, instead of abrupt splices. Porter's film techniques—action and changing locations—foreshadowed the classic storytelling tradition of American movies.

Studio System and Independent Moviemakers Flourish

None of the players in the early movies received screen credit, but then fans began to write letters to Biograph star Florence Lawrence addressed to "The Biograph Girl." In 1909, Carl Laemmle formed an independent production company, stole Florence Lawrence from Biograph and gave her screen credit. She became America's first movie star.

Biograph was the first company to make movies using the studio system. The ***studio system*** meant that a studio hired a stable of stars and production people who were paid a regular salary. These people then signed contracts with that studio and could not work for any other studio without their employer's permission.

In 1910, Laemmle lured Mary Pickford away from Biograph by doubling her salary. He discovered, says film scholar Robert Sklar, "that stars sold pictures as nothing else could. As long as theaters changed their programs daily—and the practice persisted in neighborhood theaters and small towns until the early 1920s—building up audience recognition of star names was almost the only effective form of audience publicity."

The ***star system***, which promoted popular movie personalities to lure audiences, was nurtured by the independents. This helped broaden the movies' appeal beyond the working class. Movie houses began to open in the suburbs. In 1914, President Woodrow Wilson and his family watched a popular movie at the White House. From 1908 to 1914, movie attendance doubled.

In 1915, the first real titan of the silent movies, director D. W. Griffith, introduced the concept of spectacular entertainment. Most early movies were two reels long, 25 minutes. At first Griffith made two-reelers, but then he expanded his movies to four reels and longer, pioneering the feature-length film. In his best-known epic, *The Birth of a Nation* (1915), the Southern-born Griffith presented a dramatic view of the Civil War and Reconstruction, portraying racial stereotypes and touching on the subject of sexual intermingling of the races. The movie's cost—about $110,000—was five times more than that of any American film until that time.

In 1916, brothers Noble and George Johnson launched Lincoln Films, the first company to produce serious narrative movies for African American audiences, called "race films," paving the way for African American film stars Paul Robeson and Josephine Baker.

Moviemakers like the Johnson brothers and Oscar Micheaux proved that movies produced specifically for specialized audiences could succeed. From 1910 to 1950, filmmakers produced more than 500 movies directed at African American audiences. (See **Impact/Culture**, "Lighting Up a Black Screen: Early 'Race Films' Pioneered the Art of Breaking Stereotypes," page 141.)

With *The Birth of a Nation* and his subsequent epics, Griffith showed the potential that movies had as a mass medium for gathering large audiences. He also proved that people would pay more than a nickel or a dime to see a motion picture. The Johnson brothers and Oscar Micheaux demonstrated that films also could succeed with specialized

Studio System An early method of hiring a stable of salaried stars and production people under exclusive contracts to a specific studio.

Star System Promoting popular movie personalities to lure audiences.

audiences. Movies clearly had arrived as a popular, viable mass medium, moving from the crowded nickelodeon to respectability.

Movies Become Big Business

The movie business was changing quickly. Five important events in the 1920s transformed the movie industry:

1. The move to California

2. The adoption of block booking

3. The formation of United Artists

4. The industry's efforts at self-regulation

5. The introduction of sound

Studios Move to Hollywood

During the first decade of the 20th century, the major movie companies were based in New York, the theater capital. Film companies sometimes traveled to Florida or Cuba to chase the sunshine because it was easier to build sets outdoors to take advantage of the light, but this soon changed.

Michael Ochs Archives/Getty Images

JOSÉPHINE BAKER dans "ZOUZOU"

Josephine Baker was an early film star who appeared in "race films," movies produced for African American audiences.

IMPACT
»Culture

Lighting Up a Black Screen: Early "Race Films" Pioneered the Art of Breaking Stereotypes

by Teresa Moore

The halcyon age for African-Americans on the big screen was the period between 1910 and 1950 when blacks—and some whites—produced more than 500 "race movies," showcasing all-black casts in a variety of genres, including Westerns, mysteries, romances and melodramas. . . .

While most of the surviving films are grainy and crackly, with uneven casts and jagged storylines, they offer a wide range of black characters that subsequent films have yet to match. In the naturally sepia-toned world of race movies, African Americans could—and did—do just about anything.

Lena Horne shone as the *Bronze Venus*. Crooner Herb Jeffries was the *Bronze Buckaroo*. There were black millionaires and black detectives, black sweethearts and socialites.

(continued)

IMPACT
»Culture

Lighting Up a Black Screen: Early "Race Films" Pioneered the Art of Breaking Stereotypes (continued)

Black heroines who swooned—tender, wilting ladies who never swept a broom or donned a do-rag. Black heroes who could be gentle and genteel, tough and smart. Black villains of both genders, out to separate black damsels and grandees from their virtue or fortune.

Race movies were so called because they were made for black Southern audiences barred from white-owned theaters. The films were shown either in the black-owned movie palaces of the urban North and Midwest or in "midnight rambles"—special midnight-to-2 a.m. screenings in rented halls or segregated theaters of the South.

Under segregation, the moviemakers created an onscreen world that not only reflected the accomplishments of the rising black middle class but also transformed reality into a realm where race was no impediment to love, power or success. . . .

The leading directors and producers—Oscar Micheaux and the brother team of Noble and George Johnson—wanted to uplift African Americans. Besides presenting black images more appealing to black audiences, they also offered black perspectives on racial injustice.

"In some ways these filmmakers were more free because they were making the movies for themselves," said Michael Thompson, a professor of African American history at Stanford. In *Within Our Gates*, Micheaux's filmic response to D. W. Griffith's controversial, anti-black epic *The Birth of a Nation*, a white man tries to rape a young black woman—stopping only when he recognizes her as his illegitimate daughter. In this 1919 movie Micheaux, who handled controversial

Oscar Micheaux (center) was a pioneering African American filmmaker who produced "race movies," showing all-African American casts in a variety of roles. Micheaux's *Within Our Gates* was designed to counter the racism in D. W. Griffith's epic, "Birth of a Nation."

Science, Industry & Business Library, The New York Public Library, Astor, Lenox and Tilden Foundations

racial issues in most of his films, filmed a lynching scene so graphic it had to be cut before screening in some theaters. . . .

According to *Midnight Ramble*, Bestor Cram and Pearl Bowser's 1994 documentary on the black film industry, that industry developed alongside—and initially in reaction against—the white film industry. Virtually shut out of Hollywood, where a handful of black actors were usually cast as Indians and in various "ethnic" or "exotic" roles while whites in blackface cavorted onscreen, African Americans formed their own production companies, making hundreds of features and shorts.

Teresa Moore, "Lighting Up a Black Screen: Early 'Race Films' Pioneered the Art of Busting Stereotypes and Are Now Out on Video," *San Francisco Chronicle*, February 25, 1997, E-1. Reprinted with permission.

In 1903, Harry Chandler, who owned the *Los Angeles Times*, also owned a lot of Los Angeles real estate. He and his friends courted the movie business, offering cheap land, moderate weather and inexpensive labor. Soon the moviemakers moved to Hollywood.

(Left) Mary Pickford, D. W. Griffith, Charlie Chaplin and Douglas Fairbanks founded United Artists in 1919. (Right) In 1994, David Geffen, Jeffrey Katzenberg and Steven Spielberg launched DreamWorks SKG, the first new major independent movie studio created in the United States since United Artists in 1919. In 2005, DreamWorks was sold to the media conglomerate Viacom, leaving the United States without a major independent studio.

Distributors Insist on Block Booking

People who owned theater chains soon decided to make movies, and moviemakers discovered they could make more money if they owned theaters, so production companies built theaters to exhibit their own pictures. The connection between production, distribution and exhibition grew, led by Paramount's Adolph Zukor, who devised a system called ***block booking***.

Block booking meant a company, such as Paramount, would sign up one of its licensed theaters for as many as 104 pictures at a time. The movie package contained a few "name" pictures with stars, but the majority of the movies in the block were lightweight features with no stars. Because movie bills changed twice a week, the exhibitors were desperate for something to put on the screen. Often, without knowing which movies they were getting in the block, exhibitors accepted the packages and paid the distributors' prices.

United Artists Champions the Independents

In 1919, the nation's five biggest movie names—cowboy star William S. Hart, Mary Pickford, Charlie Chaplin, Douglas Fairbanks and D. W. Griffith—rebelled against the strict studio system of distribution and formed their own studio. Eventually Hart withdrew from the agreement, but the remaining partners formed a company called United Artists (UA). They eliminated block booking and became a distributor for independently produced pictures, including their own.

In its first six years, UA delivered many movies that today still are considered classics, including *The Mark of Zorro*, *The Three Musketeers*, *Robin Hood* and *The Gold Rush*. These movies succeeded even though UA worked outside the traditional studio system, proving that it was possible to distribute films to audiences without using a major studio.

Moviemakers Use Self-Regulation to Respond to Scandals

In the 1920s, the movie industry faced two new crises: scandals involving movie stars and criticism that movie content was growing too provocative. As a result, the moviemakers decided to regulate themselves.

The star scandals began when comedian Roscoe "Fatty" Arbuckle hosted a marathon party in San Francisco over Labor Day weekend in 1921. As the party was ending, model Virginia Rappe was rushed to the hospital with stomach pains. She died at the hospital, and Arbuckle was charged with murder. Eventually the cause of death was listed as peritonitis from a ruptured bladder, and the murder charge was reduced to manslaughter. After three trials, two of which resulted in hung juries, Arbuckle was acquitted.

Then director William Desmond Taylor was found murdered in his home. Mabel Normand, a friend of Arbuckle's, was identified as the last person who had seen Taylor alive. Normand eventually was cleared, but then it was revealed that "Taylor" was not the director's real name, and there were suggestions he was involved in the drug business. Hollywood's moguls and business people were shocked. The

Block Booking The practice of requiring theaters to take a package of movies instead of showing the movies individually.

Catholic Legion of Decency announced a movie boycott. Quick to protect themselves, Los Angeles business leaders met and decided that Hollywood should police itself.

Los Angeles Times owner Harry Chandler worked with movie leaders to bring in ex–Postmaster General and former Republican Party chairman Will Hays to respond to these and other scandals in the movie business. Hays' job was to lead a moral refurbishing of the industry. In March 1922, Hays became the first president of the Motion Picture Producers and Distributors Association (MPPDA), at a salary of $100,000 a year. A month later, even though Arbuckle had been acquitted, Hays suspended all of Fatty Arbuckle's films.

Besides overseeing the stars' personal behavior, Hays decided that his office also should oversee movie content. The MPPDA, referred to as the Hays Office, wrote a code of conduct to govern the industry. In 1930, the MPPDA adopted a production code, which began by stating three general principles:

1. No picture shall be produced which will lower the moral standards of those who see it. Hence the sympathy of the audience shall never be thrown to the side of crime, wrongdoing, evil or sin.

2. Correct standards of life, subject only to the requirements of drama and entertainment, shall be presented.

3. Laws, natural or human, shall not be ridiculed, nor shall sympathy be created for its violation.

The code then divided its rules into 12 categories of wrongdoing, including

- *Murder*: "The technique of murder must be presented in a way that will not inspire imitation."

- *Sex*: "Excessive and lustful kissing, lustful embraces, suggestive postures and gestures are not to be shown."

- *Obscenity*: "Obscenity in word, gesture, reference, song, joke, or by suggestion (even when likely to be understood only by part of the audience) is forbidden."

- *Costumes*: "Dancing costumes intended to permit undue exposure or indecent movements in the dance are forbidden."

An acceptable movie displayed a seal of approval in the titles at the beginning of the picture. Producers balked at the interference, but most of them, afraid of censorship from outside the industry, complied with the monitoring.

Although standards have relaxed, the practice of self-regulation of content still operates in the motion picture industry today.

New Technology Brings the Talkies

By the mid-1920s, silent movies were an established part of American entertainment, but technology soon pushed the industry into an even more vibrant era—the era of the talkies. MPPDA President Will Hays was the first person to appear on screen in the public premiere of talking pictures on August 6, 1926, in New York City. Warner Brothers and Western Electric had developed the movie sound experiment, which consisted of seven short subjects, called *The Vitaphone Preludes*.

The Warner brothers—Sam, Harry, Jack and Albert—were ambitious, upstart businessmen who beat their competitors to sound movies. On October 6, 1927, *The Jazz Singer*, starring Al Jolson, opened at the Warners' Theater in New York and was the first feature-length motion picture with sound. The movie was not an all-talkie, but instead contained two sections with synchronized sound.

The success of *The Jazz Singer* convinced Warners' competitors not to wait any longer to adopt sound. By July 1, 1930, 22 percent of theaters still showed silent films. By 1933, less than one percent of the movies shown in theaters were silents.

Big Five Studios Dominate

In the 1930s, the Big Five—Warner Bros., Metro-Goldwyn-Mayer, Paramount, RKO and 20th Century Fox—dominated the movie business. They collected more than two thirds of the nation's box office receipts. United Artists remained solely a distribution company for independent producers.

The Big Five all were vertically integrated: They produced movies, distributed them worldwide and owned theater chains, which guaranteed their pictures a showing. The studios maintained stables of stars, directors, producers, writers and technical staff. Film scholar Tino Balio calls the studios at this point in their history a "mature oligopoly"—a

"Why? You cross the road because it's in the script—that's why!"

group of companies with so much control over an industry that any change in one of the companies directly affected the future of the industry.

In the 1930s, Walt Disney became the only major successful Hollywood newcomer. He had released *Steamboat Willie* as "the first animated sound cartoon" in 1928. Disney was 26 years old, and he sold his car to finance the cartoon's sound track. After some more short-animated-feature successes, Disney announced in 1934 that his studio would produce its first feature-length animated film, *Snow White and the Seven Dwarfs*. The film eventually cost Disney $2.25 million, more than MGM usually spent on a good musical. *Snow White* premiered December 21, 1937, at the Cathay Circle Theater in Hollywood and became an instant hit.

Box office receipts sagged in the 1930s as the Depression settled into every aspect of America's economy. Facing bankruptcy, several theaters tried to buoy their profits by adding bingo games and cut-rate admissions. The one innovation that survived the 1930s was the double feature: two movies for the price of one.

Labor Unions Organize Movie Workers

The Depression introduced one more factor into motion picture budgets: labor unions. Before the 1930s, most aspects of the movie business were not governed by union agreements. But in 1937, the National Labor Relations Board held an election that designated the Screen Actors Guild to bargain for wages, working conditions and overtime.

The Screen Writers Guild was certified in 1938 and the Screen Directors Guild soon afterward. Unionization limited the studios' power over the people who worked for them, and by the late 1930s all the major studios had signed union agreements. Union agreements also introduced professionalism into the movie business. Then the Depression ended, and the studios once again prospered.

Movies Glitter During the Golden Age

With glamorous stars and exciting screenplays, supported by an eager pool of gifted directors, producers and technical talent, plus an insatiable audience, the movie industry reached its apex in the late 1930s and early 1940s. The most successful studio in Hollywood was MGM, which attracted the best writers, directors and actors. MGM capitalized on its star

Hollywood's most successful studio, MGM, boasted the biggest lineup of movie stars. In 1939, George Cukor (center) directed *The Women*, with an all-female cast of outstanding stars, including (left to right) Florence Nash, Phyllis Povah, Rosalind Russell, Joan Crawford, (Cukor), Norma Shearer, Paulette Goddard, Mary Boland and Joan Caulfield. A remake of the movie was released in 2008, with an all-star cast including Meg Ryan and Annette Bening.

lineup with movies such as *The Women*, *The Great Ziegfeld*, *The Wizard of Oz* and *Gone with the Wind*.

Not only did *Gone with the Wind*'s phenomenal success demonstrate the epic character that movies could provide, but the movie also was a technological breakthrough, with its magnificent use of color. The movie business was so rich that even MGM's dominance didn't scare away the competition.

Congress and the Courts Change Hollywood

Before television arrived throughout the country in 1948, two other events of the late 1940s helped reverse the prosperous movie bonanza that began in mid-1930:

1. The hearings of the House Un-American Activities Committee (HUAC)

2. The 1948 antitrust decision of the U.S. Supreme Court in *United States v. Paramount Pictures, Inc., et al.*

Dalton Trumbo/[LC-US262-119689]/Library of Congress Prints and Photographs Division.

The Hollywood Ten, targeted in 1947 by the House Un-American Activities Committee, eventually went to jail for refusing to answer questions before the committee about their political beliefs.

The House Un-American Activities Committee

In October 1947, America was entering the Cold War. This was an era in which many public officials, government employees and private citizens seemed preoccupied with the threat of Communism and people identified as "subversives." The House of Representatives Committee on Un-American Activities, chaired by J. Parnell Thomas, summoned 10 "unfriendly" witnesses from Hollywood to testify about their Communist connections. (Unfriendly witnesses were people whom the committee classified as having participated at some time in the past in "un-American activities." This usually meant that the witness had been a member of a left-wing organization in the decade before World War II.) These eight screenwriters and two directors came to be known as the Hollywood Ten.

The Ten's strategy was to appear before the committee as a group and to avoid answering the direct question, "Are you now or have you ever been a member of the Communist party?" Instead, the Ten tried to make statements that questioned the committee's authority to challenge their political

Blacklisting Studio owners' refusal to hire someone who was suspected of taking part in subversive activities.

Blind Booking The practice of renting films to exhibitors without letting them see the films first.

beliefs. In a rancorous series of hearings, the committee rejected the Ten's testimony; the witnesses found themselves facing trial for contempt. All of them were sentenced to jail and some were fined. By the end of November 1947, all the Hollywood Ten had lost their jobs. Many more movie people would follow.

In an article for the *Hollywood Review*, Hollywood Ten member Adrian Scott reported that 214 movie employees eventually were ***blacklisted***, which meant that many studio owners refused to hire people who were suspected of taking part in subversive activities. The movie people who were not hired because of their political beliefs included 106 writers, 36 actors and 11 directors. This effectively gutted Hollywood of some of its best talent.

United States v. Paramount Pictures, Inc., et al.

The U.S. Justice Department began an antitrust suit against the studios in 1938. In 1940, the studios came to an agreement with the government, while admitting no guilt. They agreed to

1. Limit block booking to five films.

2. Stop ***blind booking*** (the practice of renting films to exhibitors without letting them see the films first).

3. Stop requiring theaters to rent short films as a condition of acquiring features.

4. Stop buying theaters.

After this agreement, the Justice Department dropped its suit with the stipulation that the department could reinstitute the suit again at any time.

By 1944, the government still was unhappy with studio control over the theaters, so it reactivated the suit. In 1948, *United States v. Paramount Pictures, Inc., et al.* reached the Supreme Court. Associate Justice William O. Douglas argued that although the five major studios—Paramount, Warner Bros., MGM-Loew's, RKO and 20th Century Fox—owned only 17 percent of all theaters in the United States, these studios held a *monopoly* over first-run exhibition in the large cities. As a result of the Supreme Court decision, by 1954 the five major production firms had given up ownership or control of all their theaters. Production and exhibition were now split; vertical integration was crumbling.

When the movie companies abandoned the exhibition business, banks grew reluctant to finance film projects because the companies could not guarantee an audience— on paper. Soon the studios decided to leave the production business to the independents and became primarily distributors of other peoples' pictures. The result was the end of the studio system.

Movies Lose Their Audience to Television

In the 1950 Paramount movie *Sunset Boulevard*, aging silent screen star Norma Desmond (played by Gloria Swanson) romances an ambitious young screenwriter (played by William Holden) by promising him Hollywood connections.

"You're Norma Desmond. You used to be in silent pictures. You used to be big," says the screenwriter.

"I am big," says Desmond. "It's the pictures that got small."

Desmond could have been talking about the movie business itself, which got much smaller after 1948, when television began to offer home-delivered entertainment across the nation. The House hearings and the consent decrees in the Paramount case telegraphed change in the movie business, but television truly transformed Hollywood forever. In the 1950s, the number of television sets people owned grew by 400 percent, while the number of people who went to the movies fell by 45 percent.

Theaters tried to make up for the loss by raising their admission prices, but more than 4,000 theaters closed from 1946 to 1956. Attendance has leveled off or risen briefly a few times since the 1950s, but the trend of declining movie attendance continues today. The movie industry has tried several methods to counteract this downward trend.

Wide Screen and 3-D Movies

Stunned by television's popularity, the movie business tried technological gimmicks in the 1950s to lure its audience back. First came 3-D movies, using special effects to create the illusion of three-dimensional action. Rocks, for example, seemed to fly off the screen and into the audience. To see the 3-D movies, people wore special plastic glasses. The novelty was fun, but the 3-D movie plots were weak, and most people didn't come back to see a second 3-D movie.

Next came Cinerama, Cinemascope, VistaVision and Panavision—widescreen color movies with stereophonic sound. All of these techniques tried to give the audience a "you are there" feeling—something they couldn't get from television.

Changes in Censorship

On May 26, 1952, the Supreme Court announced in *Burstyn v. Wilson* that motion pictures were "a significant medium for the communication of ideas," designed "to entertain as well as to inform." The effect of this decision was to protect movies under the First Amendment, which meant fewer legal restrictions on what a movie could show.

In 1953, Otto Preminger challenged the movies' self-regulating agency, the Production Code Administration (PCA). United Artists agreed to release Preminger's movie *The Moon*

"I can also play a hippo."

LEO CULLUM/Reprinted by permission of CartoonStock

Is Blue, even though the PCA denied the movie a certificate of approval because it contained such risqué words as *virgin* and *mistress*. Then, in 1956, United Artists released Preminger's *Man with the Golden Arm*, a film about drug addiction, and the PCA restrictions were forever broken.

Buoyed by the *Burstyn* decision and the United Artists test, moviemakers tried sex and violence to attract audiences away from television. In the 1950s, Marilyn Monroe and Jane Russell offered generously proportioned examples of the new trend. Foreign films also became popular because some of them offered explicit dialogue and love scenes.

Spectaculars

One by one the studio moguls retired, and they were replaced by a new generation of moviemakers. This second generation "inherited a situation where fewer and fewer pictures were being made, and fewer still made money," says film historian Robert Sklar, "but those that captured the box office earned enormous sums. It was as if the rules of baseball had been changed so that the only hit that mattered was a home run."

Spectaculars like *The Sound of Music* (1965) and *The Godfather* (1971) and its sequels rewarded the rush for big money. But then a few majestic flops taught the studios that nothing demolishes a studio's profits like one big movie bomb.

Movie Ratings

In 1966, Jack Valenti, former presidential adviser to President Lyndon Johnson, became president of the Motion Picture Producers Association and renamed it the Motion Picture Association of America (MPAA). The MPAA protects the business interests of movie companies by lobbying Congress about issues that are important to the movie business, such as freedom from government censorship. One of Valenti's first acts was to respond to continuing public

Because of its appeal to children, *Star Wars* is the most enduring and successful movie project ever produced, with sequels and ancillary rights collecting unprecedented income for the movies' creator, George Lucas. In 2008, Lucasfilm released *Star Wars: The Clone Wars*, promoted by a parade of movie characters at the movie's premiere in Hollywood's Egyptian Theater.

criticism about shocking movie content. (Valenti ran the MPAA until his retirement in 2004.)

The MPAA began a rating system modeled on Great Britain's: G for general audiences, M (later changed to PG) for mature audiences, R for restricted (people under 17 admitted only with an adult), and X for no one under 18 admitted. The PG-13 rating—special parental guidance advised for children under 13—was added, and the X rating was changed to NC-17. Standards for the R rating have eased since the ratings system began, further blurring the effectiveness of the ratings system for the public.

Movies and Money Today

In today's system of moviemaking, each of the major studios (such as Disney, Viacom/Paramount and Sony Pictures Entertainment) usually makes fewer than 20 movies a year. The rest come from independent producers, with production, investment, distribution and exhibition each handled by different companies. Most of these independently produced movies are distributed by one of the large studios.

In an attempt to counteract the strong influence of the traditional movie studios, Steven Spielberg, Jeffrey Katzenberg and Geffen launched a company called DreamWorks SKG in 1994. DreamWorks was the first major independent

movie studio created in the United States since United Artists was formed in 1919 (see page 143). The company survived as an independent studio for 11 years, but in 2005 DreamWorks was sold to Viacom, leaving the United States without a major independent movie studio.

Today's movies are created by one group (the writers and producers), funded by another group (the investors), sold by a third group (the distributors) and shown by a fourth group (the exhibitors). No other mass media industry is so fragmented.

Today, the dream merchants aim at a mature audience. Movies are targeted at people of all ages, but especially children and people over 30. Today's moviemakers try to appeal to an over-30 audience, with movies such as *The Secret Life of Bees,* and films that appeal to children (who typically bring their parents with them to the show), such as *Star Wars: The Clone Wars.*

Losing Money: Ticket Sales Drop

In 1946, the movies' best year, American theaters collected more than four billion tickets. Today, as more people watch more movies on video and DVD, the number of theater admissions has dropped to about one billion. Exhibitors believe that if they raise their admission prices, they'll lose more patrons. This is why exhibitors charge so much for refreshments, which is where they make 10 to 20 percent of their income.

The movie studios claim they lose money on *most* of the pictures they underwrite. Producers claim that, by hiding beyond complicated financing schemes, the studios are able to keep exorbitant profits on the movies they distribute, which raises the cost of making movies for producers.

Movie finance is an important part of the movie business today because movies, like other media industries, are part of publicly owned corporations where stockholder loyalty comes first. Studios tend to choose safer projects and seek proven audience-pleasing ideas rather than take risks.

One way the movie industry collects predictable income is to make movies for television. Half the movies produced every year are made for television and are underwritten by the TV networks. Video sales also bring reliable revenues (see **Illustration 7.1**). Two other important factors for the future funding of the movie industry are the sale of ancillary rights and the advances of new technology.

Ancillary Rights Fund Projects

In 1950, a ticket to a movie cost about 50 cents. Today you can still see a movie for 50 cents if you rent a DVD for $3 or download a movie for $2.99 and invite five friends to join you at home to watch it. The explosion of video rentals and sales since the VCR was first marketed in 1976 has had a powerful effect on how the movie business operates today. The sale of movies on video and movie downloads are part of the

IMPACT
»Business

Illustration 7.1

How Does the Movie Industry Make Money?

Movie industry revenue comes from three major sources: programming produced for TV and in-flight movies, home video, and box office ticket sales (estimated for 2008).

Source: *Veronis Suhler Stevenson Communications Industry Forecast 2006–2010.*

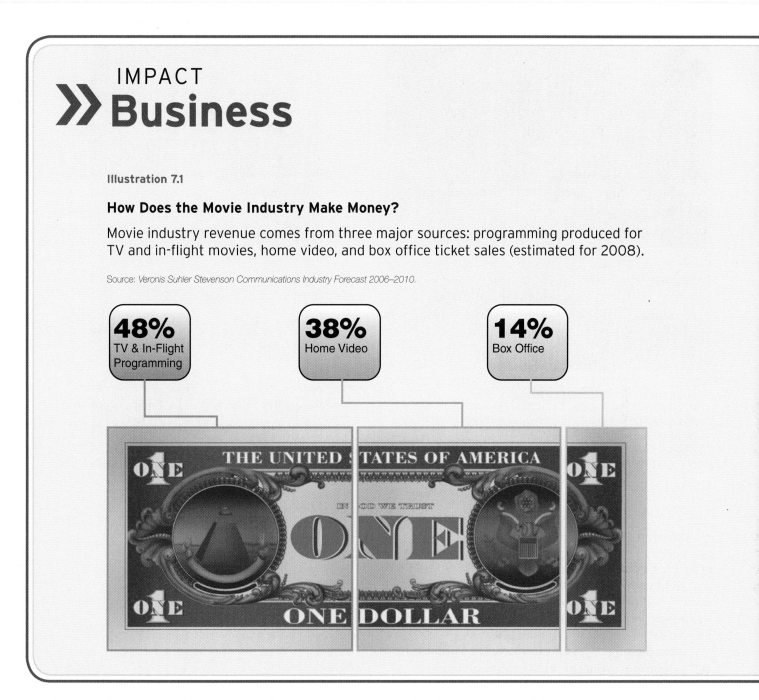

48%
TV & In-Flight Programming

38%
Home Video

14%
Box Office

---

ancillary rights market, which means marketing opportunities that are related to a movie, in addition to direct income from the movie itself.

The average cost to make a theatrical movie (as opposed to a made-for-television movie) is $107 million, and the studios claim only two out of 10 theatrical movies make money. "Some pictures make a lot of money," says movie analyst David V. Picker, "and a lot of pictures make no money."

Before a theatrical movie starts shooting, the investors want some assurances that they'll make their money back. Moviemakers use the sale of ancillary rights to try to guarantee investors a return on their investment. Ancillary rights include the following:

- Subscription television rights
- Network television rights
- Syndication rights (sales to independent TV stations)
- Airline rights for in-flight movies
- Military rights (to show films on military bases)
- College rights (to show films on college campuses)

Ancillary Rights Marketing opportunities related to a movie, in addition to direct income from the movie itself.

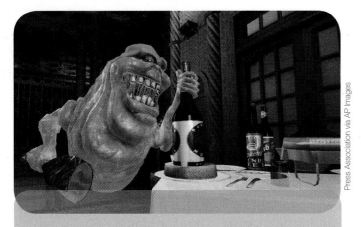

Because movies cost so much to produce, moviemakers generate income for a film by selling ancillary rights to create products that are related to the movie, such as the Ghostbusters videogame, based on the two 1980s movies of the same name.

- Song rights for soundtrack albums
- Book publishing rights (for original screenplays that can be rewritten and sold as books)
- DVD reproduction rights
- Product placement
- Video game rights
- Movie downloads

Movies are commercialized in the sense that they are tied to products, which are another way of advertising a movie. A movie that can be exploited as a package of ancillary rights, with commercial appeal, is much more attractive to investors than a movie with limited potential.

Often the only choice for a filmmaker who wants to make a film that doesn't have substantial ancillary-rights potential is to settle for a low budget. Once the film is made, the independent filmmaker must then find a way to distribute the movie. This severely limits the number of independent films that make it to the box office.

Movies at Work

Today the center of the movie industry is movie production. Most of the movies that are distributed by the major studios and exhibited at your local theater are produced by independent companies under agreements with individual studios. Although these production companies work independently, and each company is organized differently, jobs in movie production fall mainly into the following categories:

Movie studios today use the Internet to promote their movies. In 2008, Fox Searchlight used the Web to promote the hit movie *The Secret Life of Bees.*

1. Screenwriters
2. Producers
3. Directors
4. Actors
5. Production
6. Marketing and administration

The beginning for each movie is a story idea, and these ideas come from *screenwriters*. Screenwriters work independently, marketing their story ideas through agents, who promote their clients' scripts to the studios and to independent producers.

Typically, *producers* are the people who help gather the funding to create a movie project. Financing can come from banks or from individuals who want to invest in a specific movie. Sometimes producers or actors help finance the movies they make. Once the funding for the story is in place, a *director* organizes all the tasks necessary to turn the script into a movie. The director works with the producer to manage the movie's budget.

Obviously, *actors* are important to any movie project. Sometimes the producer and director approach particular stars for a project even before they seek funding, to attract

Independent filmmakers, who usually fund their movies without financial support from the major studios, must find a way to exhibit their movies. The Angelika Film Center in New York is one of the nation's largest theaters to exhibit independent films.

Movies are very expensive to make because so many people are involved. The average cost to make a movie today is $107 million. Actor Tom Hanks talked with the crew on the set of the movie *Angels and Demons* in June 2008, in Rome, Italy.

interest from the investors and also to help assure the investors that the movie will have some box office appeal.

Production includes all the people who actually create the movie—camera operators, set designers, film editors, script supervisors and costumers, for example. Once the movie is finished, the *marketing* people seek publicity for the project. They also design a plan to advertise and promote the movie to the public.

As in any media industry, people who work in *administration* help keep all the records necessary to pay salaries and track the employees' expenses, as well as keep track of the paperwork involved in organizing any business.

Digital Technology Drives the Business

New digital technologies affect three aspects of today's movie business:

1. Production
2. Distribution
3. Exhibition

Production

Smaller, portable cameras mean a camera operator can move more easily through a crowd. New types of film mean that filmmakers can shoot more scenes at night and in dark places with less artificial lighting. Directors electronically record scenes as they shoot them and immediately play back the scene to be sure they have the shot they want. Computer technology offers exciting special effects possibilities. Filmmakers also are experimenting with the holograph, which uses lasers to make a computer-generated three-dimensional image from a flat picture.

The ability to digitize color, using computers, also means the images in movies can be intensified, adjusted and even totally transformed after the movie is shot, in a way that was impossible even 10 years ago.

Distribution

Reproducing copies of films to send to theaters and guaranteeing their arrival is one of the costliest aspects of moviemaking. In the future, distribution companies plan to send their movies by satellite-to-satellite dishes on top of each theater and directly to consumers' homes. Live performances, such as a symphony concert or a major sports event, already are available by satellite at many local theaters, and eventually they will be sent directly to your home.

The theater industry is poised to replace the traditional film projector, invented more than 100 years ago, with digital projectors, which can show movies that are sent by satellite or recorded on optical discs. Digital movies are cheaper to distribute and can be shown on more screens, or

IMPACT
»»Ethics

Warner's Digital Watchdog Widens War on Pirates

by Laura M. Holson

Hollywood studios spend millions every year trying to get people to watch their movies. At Warner Brothers Entertainment, Darcy Antonellis is trying to get them to stop watching—illegally, that is.

Ms. Antonellis oversees the studio's growing worldwide antipiracy efforts as Hollywood's attention shifts from bootleg DVDs made in China to the problem of copyrighted television and movie clips showing up on sites like YouTube and MySpace.

While producers and celebrities garner most of the attention in Hollywood, technology executives like Ms. Antonellis are at the forefront of the industry as they try to protect the studio's control over its content.

With movies like the *Harry Potter* series and *Ocean's 11* franchise and television series like *Friends*, Warner has one of the largest libraries in Hollywood. As a result, it can exert more influence over its relationships with online partners, making it one of the most-watched studios both inside and outside the industry.

"People want to be more interactive and have a voice," said Ms. Antonellis. "We need to consider all the opportunities."

Piracy may seem like the biggest threat to Hollywood, but Ms. Antonellis suggested instead that changing consumer behavior will have a greater impact on the entertainment business.

Movie studios, like their peers in music and television, are in the midst of a signifi-

In 2008, Steve Jobs demonstrated Apple iTunes online movie rentals, which allows customers to download first-run movies for $2.99 each—a new method of distribution, designed to increase movie revenue through the sale of ancillary rights.

Tony Avelar/AFP/Getty Images

removed quickly from distribution, depending on audience demand. The Internet also allows independent moviemakers to produce movies inexpensively and transfer them to the Internet for downloading.

As computer video technology grew faster and more accessible, established movie studios and independent moviemakers devised a whole new distribution system, based on digital movie downloads delivered directly to consumers. In 2008, Apple iTunes launched online movie rentals, which allows customers to download first-run movies to their Macs, PCs, iPods and iPhones for $2.99 each—designed to increase movie revenue by creating another distribution network.

Subscription TV services, such as DirecTV and cable companies, also are stockpiling movies so they can set up a complete system of video-on-demand, available at home by subscription or pay-per-view. However, recordable DVDs (DVD-R) and online piracy pose new copyright hazards for the movie industry, which tries, but so far has failed, to stop their widespread use. (See **Impact/Ethics**, "Warner's Digital Watchdog Widens War on Pirates.")

cant and frightening shift as almost every form of media is becoming ubiquitous on the Internet. And through sites like YouTube, viewers have grown accustomed to seeing whatever they want to see, free.

"People thinking it is O.K. to take this stuff for free on a worldwide basis has a bigger impact than anything," said Ms. Antonellis.

Many entertainment companies are growing impatient watching companies like YouTube distribute clips of movies and television shows free. At the same time they are concerned that YouTube earns advertising revenue from Web sites that offer pirated movies for sale on the site. Even while negotiating with YouTube, NBC Universal and Fox announced their own joint video service, and Viacom filed a $1 billion lawsuit against Google, which owns YouTube.

Missteps made today could have grave consequences for the future, particularly when it comes to consumers' willingness to pay for movies and television shows online, she believes. To illustrate the point, she tells of her niece's fish, named Mortimer, who one

ROBERT ATANASOVSKI/AFP/Getty Images

Studios like Warner Brothers Entertainment are aggressively fighting movie piracy worldwide. In Macedonia, a bulldozer pours thousands of pirated CDs and DVDs into a sanitary landfill after the country vowed to stop the production and sale of counterfeit disks.

day leaped from his bowl, flopped on the table and gasped for air.

"Mortimer took the leap to freedom," she said. "He said, 'I'm free, but I'm dead,' " said Ms. Antonellis.

From "Warner's Digital Watchdog Widens War on Pirates," by Laura M. Holson, *The New York Times,* April 2, 2007. Copyright © 2007 New York Times. All rights reserved. Reprinted by permission.

Exhibition

Theaters are turning to the picture-palace environment that enchanted moviegoers in the 1930s. "The movie theater will have to become an arena; a palace to experience the full grandeur and potential of the theatrical motion picture," says futurist and electronic technology consultant Martin Polon.

In 1994, some of the nation's theater chains began offering "motion simulation" in a few of their theaters. Specially controlled seats moved in conjunction with a "ridefilm" to give the feeling of space travel or other adventures. Many of the nation's theme parks, such as Dollywood, already offer ridefilms to their patrons. "We're looking to marry the moviegoing experience to different kinds of technological experiences, thereby enhancing the attractiveness of the whole complex," said United Artists chairman Stewart Blair. Movie chains also have introduced stadium seating so that every moviegoer has a clear, unimpeded view of the movie.

Using a digital version of 1950s 3-D technology, New Line Cinema and DreamWorks are test screening 3-D technology to draw people into theaters. The new process is called RealD, using a single projector to merge two images—one for each eye—to give the movie its realistic effect.

However, before theaters can exhibit 3-D movies, they must buy new digital projection systems, which cost $75,000 per screen, but theaters can charge more for a RealD ticket. Several studios are planning to release RealD movies in 2009 and 2010, betting that the new technology will bring people out of their homes to see a movie and add to industry income.

International Markets Bring Concentrated Power

Today's movie industry is undergoing two major changes. One recent trend in the movie business is

The overseas market for American movies, such as *The Other Boleyn Girl* (*Die Schwester der Konigin*), accounts for one-third of the movie industry's profits.

JOHN MACDOUGALL/AFP/Getty Images

global ownership and global marketing. The second trend is the merging of the movie industry with the television industry.

Global Influence

Overseas companies own two of the major studios (Sony owns Sony Pictures Entertainment and Rupert Murdoch's News Corporation owns 20th Century Fox). Foreign ownership gives these companies easier access to overseas markets.

American motion pictures are one of America's strongest exports, and income from foreign sales accounts for more than one-third of the movie industry's profits. "If Hollywood has learned anything the past few years," says *Business Week*, "it's that the whole world is hungry for the latest it has to offer."

Concentrating Media Power

Today, people in the television business are buying pieces of the movie business and people in the movie business want to align themselves with television companies. In 1993, the Federal Communications Commission voted to allow the TV networks to produce and syndicate their own programs. This opened the door for TV networks to someday enter the movie business.

The result today is consolidated companies that finance movies, make movies and show those movies in their own theaters, on their own television stations and on video. By controlling all aspects of the business, a company can have a better chance to collect a profit on the movies it makes.

Sound familiar? The studios held this type of controlling interest in their movies before the courts dismantled the studio system with the 1948 consent decrees (see *"United States v. Paramount Pictures, Inc., et al.,"* page 146). Today's major studios are trying to become again what they once were: a mature oligopoly in the business of dreams.

Review, Analyze, Investigate
REVIEWING CHAPTER 7

Movies Mirror the Culture

✓ Before the invention of TV, movies were the nation's primary form of entertainment.

✓ Like other industries, the movie business has had to adapt to changing technology.

Inventors Capture Motion on Film

✓ Eadweard Muybridge and Thomas Edison contributed the most to the creation of movies in America. Muybridge demonstrated how to photograph motion, and Edison developed a projector, the kinetoscope.

✓ Edison also organized the Motion Picture Patents Company to control movie distribution.

Filmmakers Turn Novelty into Art

✓ William K. L. Dickson perfected the kinetoscope.

✓ French filmmaker Georges Mèliés envisioned movies as a medium of fantasy.

✓ Edwin S. Porter assembled scenes to tell a story.

Studio System and Independent Moviemakers Flourish

✓ Biograph became the first studio to make movies using what was called the studio system.

✓ The studio system put the studio's stars under exclusive contract, and the contract could not be broken without an employer's permission.

✓ The star system prompted popular movies to lure audiences.

✓ D. W. Griffith mastered the full-length movie. Griffith's best-known movie is a controversial view of the Civil War, *The Birth of a Nation.*

✓ From 1910 to 1950, filmmakers like Noble and George Johnson and Oscar Micheaux produced movies specifically directed at African American audiences, called "race films."

Movies Become Big Business

✓ The practice of block booking, led by Adolph Zukor, obligated movie houses to accept several movies at once, usually without previewing them first.

✓ The formation of United Artists by Mary Pickford, Charlie Chaplin, Douglas Fairbanks and D. W. Griffith was a rebellion against the big studios.

✓ UA distributed films for independent filmmakers.

✓ In the 1920s, the movie industry faced two crises: scandals involving movie stars and criticism that movie content was growing too explicit.

✓ The movie industry responded to the scandals and criticism about content by forming the Motion Picture Producers and Distributors Association under the direction of Will Hays.

Big Five Studios Dominate

✓ As the studio system developed, the five largest Hollywood studios were able to control production, distribution and exhibition.

✓ In 1930, the MPPDA adopted a production code, which created rules that governed movie content.

✓ Although standards have relaxed, the practice of self-regulation of content continues today.

Labor Unions Organize Movie Workers

✓ In the 1930s, labor unions challenged studio control and won some concessions.

✓ Union agreements limited the studios' power over their employees.

Movies Glitter During the Golden Age

✓ The movies' golden age was the 1930s and 1940s, supported by the studio system and an eager audience.

✓ The most successful Hollywood studio was MGM, which concentrated on blockbuster movies such as *The Wizard of Oz* and *Gone with the Wind*.

Congress and the Courts Change Hollywood

✓ Three factors caused Hollywood's crash in the 1950s: the House Un-American Activities Committee hearings, the U.S. Justice Department's antitrust action against the studios, and television.

✓ At least 214 movie employees eventually were blacklisted as a result of the hearings of the House Un-American Activities Committee (HUAC).

✓ In 1948, the U.S. Supreme Court decision in *United States v. Paramount Pictures* ended the studio system.

Movies Lose Their Audience to Television

✓ People abandoned the movies for television, and the trend of declining movie attendance continues today.

✓ Hollywood tried to lure audiences back to the movies in the 1950s with technological gimmicks, sultry starlets and spectaculars, but the rewards were temporary.

✓ Movie ratings were originally a response to criticism about immoral movie content, but the standards for these ratings have become blurred.

Movies and Money Today

✓ The median cost to make a movie today is $107 million, and only two out of ten theatrical movies make money.

✓ DreamWorks SKG, launched in 1994 by Steven Spielberg, Jeffrey Katzenberg and David Geffen, was the first major independent movie studio created in the United States since United Artists was formed in 1919. In 2005, DreamWorks was sold to Viacom, leaving the United States without a major independent movie studio.

✓ Today the number of moviegoers continues to decline, although DVD sales and rentals, as well as video game development, add to movie industry income.

✓ Most movies are funded in part by ancillary rights sales.

✓ Most movies are sold as packages, with all their potential media outlets underwriting the movie before it goes into production. This makes independent filmmaking difficult.

Movies at Work

✓ Movie production is the heart of the movie industry today.

✓ Screenwriters begin the moviemaking process; other jobs include producer, director, actor, technical production, marketing and administration.

Digital Technology Drives the Business

✓ The biggest technological changes in moviemaking today are the result of digital technology.

✓ Independent moviemakers can use computers to create movies inexpensively and distribute them on the Internet.

✓ Digital projectors allow theaters to receive movies by satellite, which will make movie distribution cheaper and faster.

✓ Recordable DVDs and Internet piracy pose serious copyright challenges for the movie industry, which is trying to stop their widespread use.

✓ In the future, distribution companies plan to send movies by satellite to satellite dishes on top of each theater and directly to consumers' homes.

✓ In 2008, Apple made first-run movie downloads available on its iTunes Web site for $2.99 each.

International Markets Bring Concentrated Power

✓ In 1993, the FCC voted to allow the TV networks to make and syndicate their own programs. This means that, in the future, the movie industry and the television industries may align themselves more closely. Eventually one company could control all aspects of moviemaking.

✓ Overseas sales of American movies account for more than one-third of movie industry income.

KEY TERMS

These terms are defined in the margins throughout this chapter and appear in alphabetical order with definitions in the Glossary, which begins on page 372.

Ancillary Rights 149
Blacklisting 146
Blind Booking 146

Block Booking 143
Star System 140
Studio System 140

CRITICAL QUESTIONS

1. Which audience age category is most attractive to today's moviemakers? Why?

2. What were race movies? Discuss the ways in which these films changed the perspective of African Americans in the films and for their audiences.

3. What was the effect of the practice of block booking on the movie industry? How and why did the practice end?

4. Why do you believe the Hollywood Ten became a target of the House Un-American Activities Committee? Could the same thing happen today? Why? Why not? Explain.

5. Describe the effects that digital technologies are having on moviemaking, distribution and exhibition.

WORKING THE WEB

This list includes both sites mentioned in the chapter and others to give you greater insight into the movie industry.

Academy of Motion Picture Arts and Sciences
http://www.oscars.org

This honorary association of over 6,500 motion picture professionals is the home of the Oscars. The organization's goals include advancing the arts and sciences of motion pictures, recognizing outstanding achievement and promoting technical research of methods and equipment. The Web site includes Academy publications, information on the Academy Film Archive and an Academy Awards database.

DEG Digital Entertainment Group
http://www.dvdinformation.com

DEG is a nonprofit trade consortium composed of electronics manufacturers, movie studios and music companies whose goal is to explore opportunities in other digital technologies and represent all aspects of the home entertainment industry. Members include Philips Consumer Electronics, Paramount Home Entertainment and Sony BMG Music Entertainment.

The Internet Movie Database (IMDB)
http://www.imdb.com

Owned by Amazon.com, IMDB says its mission is to provide "useful and up to date movie information freely available online across as many platforms as possible." What started as a hobby project by movie fans has grown into a database of over 15 million film and TV credits. Search capabilities include name, character, keyword and quote. The site also has movie and TV listings, trailers and interactive sections such as trivia, polls and message boards.

Lucasfilm
http://www.lucasfilm.com

This film and entertainment company founded by George Lucas in 1971 has produced such hits as *American Graffiti* and the *Star Wars* and *Indiana Jones* series. In addition to motion picture and television production, the company's businesses include Industrial Light & Magic (visual effects), Skywalker Sound and LucasArts (video games).

Motion Picture Association of America (MPAA) and Motion Picture Association (MPA)
http://www.mpaa.org

Advocates for the motion picture, home video and television industries, the MPAA and its international counterpart the MPA are responsible for the movie ratings and also work to protect copyrights and stem piracy of filmed works.

Netflix
http://www.netflix.com

The world's largest online movie rental source, Netflix provides subscribers access to more than 100,000 DVD titles and more than 10,000 instant downloads. DVDs are delivered free to subscriber households with a postage-paid return envelope, and there are no due dates or late fees.

Screenwriters Federation of America (SFA)
http://www.screenwritersfederation.org

Formerly the Screenwriters Guild of America, the SFA is an organization to promote the common interests of industry professionals. Its goals are to educate screenwriters about their craft and about the entertainment business, to create a network for screenwriters and to administer standards for marketing scripts. The Web site includes news excerpts and links to Indiwire.com, the independent film community's news, information and social networking site. Users can also search IMDb.com with one mouse click.

Sundance Institute
http://www.sundance.org

This nonprofit organization dedicates itself to discovering and developing independent movie makers. Founder Robert Redford began hosting labs in 1981 where emerging filmmakers could work with leading writers and directors to develop their original projects. The Institute is now an internationally recognized independent artist resource and the host of the annual Sundance Film Festival.

United Artists
http://www.unitedartists.com

Formed in November 2006 under a partnership between Tom Cruise, Paula Wagner and MGM, United Artists Entertainment LLC plans to revive the historic UA brand initially founded by movie greats Douglas Fairbanks, Charlie Chaplin, Mary Pickford and D. W. Griffith. The "new" independent studio will allow artists to "pursue their creative visions outside of the traditional studio system" and plans to release four films per year.

Warner Bros.
http://www.warnerbros.com

This company founded by the four Warner brothers began as a silent-film distributor in 1903 and became a successful producer of "talkies" and animated cartoons. The company, now a division of Time Warner Inc., also produces television shows, animation, DVDs and interactive entertainment.

8

Television: Changing Channels

Ray Tamarra/Getty Images

Late Show with David Letterman is a relatively recent successor to *The Tonight Show*, which first appeared on television in 1954. Late night entertainment shows are a staple of today's network TV programming.

What's Ahead?

" Nielsen has a mandate to follow the video wherever it goes. A lot of where video is going is outside the home."

Sara Erichson, Executive Vice President for Client Services, Nielsen Media Research

"Television is the pervasive

American pastime," writes media observer Jeff Greenfield. "Cutting through geographic, ethnic, class and cultural diversity, it is the single binding thread of this country, the one experience that touches young and old, rich and poor, learned and illiterate. A country too big for homogeneity, filled by people from all over the globe, without any set of core values, America never had a central unifying bond. Now we do. Now it is possible to answer the question, '*What does America do?*' We watch television."

TimeFrame
1884 – Today

Television Becomes the Nation's Major Medium for News and Entertainment

1884   Paul Nipkow patents the "electrical telescope" in Germany, which formed the basis for TV's development through the 1920s.

1907   The word *television* first appears in the June 1907 issue of *Scientific American*.

1939   **NBC debuts at the World's Fair in New York City with a broadcast that includes a blurry live image of President Franklin D. Roosevelt, the first U.S. president to appear on television.**

Bettmann/CORBIS

1947   NBC and CBS begin broadcasting television news on the *Camel News Caravan* (NBC) and *Television News with Douglas Edwards* (CBS).

1951   **CBS launches *I Love Lucy*, a situation comedy, which proved to be TV's most durable type of entertainment program.**

Bettmann/CORBIS

1962   *Telstar I* sends the first transatlantic satellite broadcast.

1963   Network television provides nonstop coverage of the assassination and funeral of President John F. Kennedy.

Public Television begins broadcasting as National Educational Television, featuring programs like *Mr. Roger's Neighborhood*.

Fotos International/Hulton Archive/Getty Images

1973   The television networks present live broadcasts of the Watergate Hearings.

1979   **Ted Turner starts Cable News Network. CNN's global reach gives the U.S. audience instant access to news about international events.**

Douglas Kirkland/CORBIS

1983   120 million people tune in for the final episode of *M*A*S*H*, the highest rated program ever.

1987   TV broadcasts the Iran-Contra hearings.

1993   More than 80 million people tune in for the final episode of *Cheers*.

2001   Television news offers nonstop, commercial-free coverage of the terrorist attacks at the World Trade Center, the Pentagon and in rural Pennsylvania.

2003   TV again becomes a focus of nationwide attention during the live news coverage of the Iraq War.

2006   Congress passes a law that requires TV broadcasters to switch totally to digital high-definition signals by February 17, 2009.

2008   More than 70 million people watch President-elect Barack Obama's election night victory on television on November 4, a record audience for a presidential election night.

Today   **Television programming is delivered on more than 500 different channels by over-the-air broadcast, cable and satellite. High-definition TV is the new standard.**

Najlah Feanny/CORBIS

Television is turned on in today's American households, on average, nearly eight hours a day, according to the A. C. Nielsen Company, which monitors television usage for advertisers. (See **Illustration 8.1**.) Even though you may not watch TV this much, the percentage of households in the United States who watch television a lot counterbalances the smaller amount of time you may spend with your television set.

Television Transforms Daily Life

It's not surprising that the effects of such a pervasive medium have attracted so much attention from parents, educators, social scientists, religious leaders, public officials and anyone else who wants to understand society's habits and values. TV has been blamed for everything from declines in literacy to rises in violent crime to the trivialization of national politics. Every once in a while it is praised, too, for giving viewers instant access to world events and uniting audiences in times of national crisis.

An industry with this much presence in American life is bound to affect the way we live. Someone who is watching television is not doing other things: playing basketball, visiting a museum, or looking through a telescope at the planets, for instance. Television can, however, bring you to a museum you might never visit or to a basketball game you cannot attend or to the surface of a planet you could only see through a telescope.

Television technology, adding pictures to the sounds of radio, truly transformed Americans' living and learning patterns. The word *television*, which once meant programs delivered by antennas through over-the-air signals, now means a *television screen*, where several different types of delivery systems bring viewers a diversity of programs.

The programs Americans watch today are delivered by antennas, cables and satellites, but they all appear on the

IMPACT
» Culture

Illustration 8.1

How Much Time Do People Spend Watching Television?

The time people spend watching TV has increased consistently every year since 1950. These statistics reflect total viewing per household, which means the total combined time that all people in the average household have the TV turned on.

Source: Nielsen Media Research, *The New York Times*, November 25, 2008.

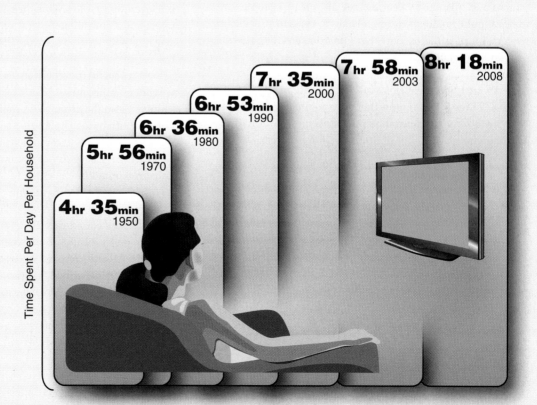

Time Spent Per Day Per Household

4hr 35min 1950

5hr 56min 1970

6hr 36min 1980

6hr 53min 1990

7hr 35min 2000

7hr 58min 2003

8hr 18min 2008

"Please stand by. We've run out of ideas."

Jonny Hawkins/Reprinted by permission of CartoonStock

same television screen, and as a viewer, you can't tell how the program arrived at your television set and probably don't care. What you do know is that television gives you access to all types of programs—drama, comedy, sports, news, game shows and talk shows. You can see all types of people—murderers, public officials, foreign leaders, reporters, soldiers, entertainers, athletes, detectives and doctors. The television screen is truly, as scholar Erik Barnouw observed, a "tube of plenty."

About 1,600 television stations operate in the United States. Three out of four of these are commercial stations, and the others are noncommercial stations. About half the commercial stations are affiliated with a network.

According to TV commentator Jeff Greenfield, "The most common misconception most people have about television concerns its product. To the viewer, the product is the programming. To the television executive, the product is the audience. Strictly speaking, television networks and stations do not make any money by producing a program that audiences want to watch. The money comes from selling advertisers the right to broadcast a message to that audience. The programs exist to capture the biggest possible audiences."

TV Delivers an Audience to Advertisers

To understand why we get the programming we do, it is important to remember that *commercial television exists primarily as an advertising medium.* Programming surrounds the advertising, but it is the advertising that is being delivered to the audience. Commercial television, from its inception, was created to deliver audiences to advertisers.

Because television can deliver a larger audience faster than other mass media, television can charge the highest rates of any medium for its advertising—which makes TV stations rich investments. A 30-second ad during a widely watched TV program like the Super Bowl (with an estimated audience of half the U.S. population) costs more than $2.5 million. Today, even the smallest television station is a multimillion-dollar operation. However, the television era began much more humbly, and with very little excitement, near the turn of the 20th century.

Visual Radio Becomes Television

The word *television* first appeared in the June 1907 issue of *Scientific American.* Before then, experiments in image transmission had been called visual wireless, visual radio and electric vision. Alexander Graham Bell's telephone and Samuel F. B. Morse's telegraph contributed to the idea of sending electrical impulses over long distances.

The first major technological discovery to suggest that pictures also could travel was the *Nipkow disk.* Twenty-four-year-old Paul Nipkow patented his "electrical telescope" in Germany in 1884. This disk, which formed the basis for television's development through the 1920s, was about the size of a phonograph record, perforated with a spiral of tiny holes.

Also crucial in television's (and radio's) development were Guglielmo Marconi and Lee de Forest. Marconi eliminated sound's dependence on wires and put sound on airwaves. De Forest contributed the Audion tube, which amplified radio waves so that people could hear the sound clearly.

In 1927, Secretary of Commerce Herbert Hoover appeared on a 2-inch screen by wire in an experimental AT&T broadcast. On September 11, 1928, General Electric broadcast the first dramatic production, "The Queen's Messenger"—the sound came over station WGY, Schenectady, and the picture came from experimental television station W2XAD. All the pictures were close-ups, and their quality could best be described as primitive.

Two researchers, one working for a company and one working alone, brought television into the electronic age. Then the same man who was responsible for radio's original popularity, RCA's David Sarnoff, became television's biggest promoter.

Vladimir Zworykin was working for Westinghouse when he developed an all-electronic system to transform a visual image into an electronic signal that traveled through the air. When the signal reached the television receiver, the signal was transformed again into a visual image for the viewer.

Philo T. Farnsworth, working alone in California, developed the cathode ray tube (which he called a dissector tube). Farnsworth's cathode ray tube used an electronic scanner to reproduce the electronic image much more clearly than Nipkow's earlier mechanical scanning device. In 1930, 24-year-old Farnsworth patented his electronic scanner.

NBC television's commercial debut was at the 1939 World's Fair in New York City at the Hall of Television. On April 30, 1939, President Franklin D. Roosevelt formally opened the fair and became the first president to appear on television. Sarnoff also spoke, and RCA displayed its 5-inch and 9-inch sets, priced from $199.50 to $600 (equivalent to $2950 to $8870 in today's dollars). NBC and CBS were the original TV networks. A *network* is a collection of radio or television stations that offers programs, usually simultaneously, throughout the country, during designated program times.

In 1943, ABC, the third major network, grew out of NBC's old Blue network. ABC labored from its earliest days to equal the other two networks but didn't have as many affiliates as NBC and CBS. The two leading networks already had secured the more powerful, well-established broadcast outlets for themselves. David Sarnoff and William Paley controlled the network game.

Television Outpaces Radio

By 1945, 10 television stations were on the air in the United States. According to media historian Eric Barnouw, "By the late 1940s, television began its conquest of America. In 1949, the year began with radio drawing 81 percent of all broadcast audiences. By the year's end, television was grabbing 41 percent of the broadcast market. When audiences began experiencing the heady thrill of actually seeing as well as hearing events as they occurred, the superiority of television was established beyond doubt."

Black-and-white television replaced radio so quickly as the nation's major advertising medium that it would be easy to believe television erupted suddenly in a surprise move to kill radio. But remember that the two major corporate executives who developed television—Sarnoff and Paley—also held the country's largest interest in radio. They used their profits from radio to develop television, foreseeing that television eventually would expand their audience and their income.

News with Pictures

Broadcast news, pioneered by radio, adapted awkwardly at first to the new broadcast medium—television. According to David Brinkley, a broadcast news pioneer who began at NBC, "When television came along in about 1947–1948, the

Bettmann/CORBIS

In 1939, NBC's David Sarnoff introduced television with a broadcast from RCA's Hall of Television at the New York World's Fair.

big time newsmen of that day—H. V. Kaltenborn, Lowell Thomas—did not want to do television. It was a lot of work, they weren't used to it, they were doing very well in radio, making lots of money. They didn't want to fool with it. So I was told to do it by the news manager. I was a young kid and, as I say, the older, more established people didn't want to do it. Somebody had to."

In 1947, CBS launched *Television News with Douglas Edwards* and NBC broadcast *Camel News Caravan* (sponsored by Camel cigarettes) with John Cameron Swayze (see **Chapter 12**). Eventually, David Brinkley joined Swayze for NBC's 15-minute national newscast. He recalled, "The first broadcasts were extremely primitive by today's standards. It was mainly just sitting at a desk and talking. We didn't have any pictures at first. Later we began to get a little simple news film, but it wasn't much.

"In the beginning, people would call after a program and say in tones of amazement that they had seen you. 'I'm out here in Bethesda, and the picture's wonderful.' They weren't interested in anything you said. They were just interested in the fact that you had been on their screen in their house."

Network A collection of radio or TV stations that offers programs, usually simultaneously, throughout the country, during designated program times.

The Andy Griffith Show, which ran from 1960 to 1968 on CBS, is an early example of one of TV's most durable types of prime-time programming—the situation comedy. Left to right: Andy Griffith (Andy Taylor), Jim Nabors (Gomer Pyle) and Don Knotts (Barney Fife).

At first, network TV news reached only the East Coast because there was no web of national hookups in place to deliver television across the country. By 1948, AT&T's coaxial cable linked Philadelphia with New York and Washington. The 1948 political conventions were held in Philadelphia and broadcast to the 13 Eastern states. When the 1952 conventions were broadcast, AT&T's national coaxial hookups joined 108 stations across the country.

CBS had developed a strong group of radio reporters during World War II, and by 1950 many of them had moved

Prime Time The TV time period from 7 to 11 p.m. when more people watch TV than at any other time.

Situation Comedy A TV program that establishes a fixed set of characters typically in a home or work situation. Also called a sitcom.

to the new medium. CBS News also made a practice, more than the other networks, of using the same reporters for radio and television. The major early news figure at CBS was Edward R. Murrow, who, along with David Brinkley at NBC, created the early standards for broadcast news. (See **Impact/People**, "Edward R. Murrow (1908–1965) Sets the Standard for Broadcast News," page 165.)

Public affairs programs like *See It Now* continued to grow along with network news, and in 1956 NBC teamed David Brinkley with Chet Huntley to cover the political conventions. The chemistry worked, and after the convention NBC put Huntley and Brinkley together to do the evening news, *The Huntley–Brinkley Report*. Brinkley often called himself "the other side of the hyphen."

Entertainment Programming

Early television entertainment also was the same as radio with pictures: It offered variety shows, situation comedies, drama, Westerns, detective stories, Hollywood movies, soap operas and quiz shows. The only type of show television offered that radio did not (besides movies, of course) was the talk show. (However, radio eventually created call-in programs, radio's version of the TV talk show.)

VARIETY SHOWS. The best radio stars jumped to the new medium. Three big variety show successes were Milton Berle's *Texaco Star Theater*, *The Admiral Broadway Revue* (later *Your Show of Shows*) with Imogene Coca and Sid Caesar, and Ed Sullivan's *Toast of the Town* (later *The Ed Sullivan Show*). These weekly shows featured comedy sketches and appearances by popular entertainers. *The Ed Sullivan Show*, for example, is where most Americans got their first glimpse of Elvis Presley and the Beatles. All of the shows were done live.

The time slot in which these programs were broadcast, 7 to 11 p.m., is known as **prime time**. Prime time simply means that more people watch television during this period than any other, so advertising during this period costs more. Berle's 8 p.m. program during prime time on Tuesday nights often gathered 85 percent of the audience. *Texaco Star Theater* became so popular that one laundromat installed a TV set and advertised, "Watch Berle while your clothes twirl."

SITUATION COMEDIES. Along with drama, the **situation comedy** (sitcom) proved to be one of TV's most durable types of programs. The situation comedy established a fixed set of characters in either a home or work situation. *I Love Lucy*, starring Lucille Ball and Desi Arnaz, originated from Los Angeles because the actors wanted to live on the West Coast. In 1951, Ball began a career as a weekly performer on CBS that lasted for 23 years.

In 1960, CBS launched *The Andy Griffith Show*, which followed the adventures of widower and Mayberry sheriff Andy Taylor who was raising his young son, Opie. Ron Howard played Opie and Don Knotts played Andy's nervous cousin, Barney Fife. *The Andy Griffith Show*, a spin-off of another sitcom, the *Danny Thomas Show*, ran for eight

IMPACT

»People

Edward R. Murrow (1908-1965) Sets the Standard for Broadcast News

by Theodore H. White

Note: Edward R. Murrow had established a reputation for excellence as a CBS radio news broadcaster when he migrated to television news in 1951. In this profile, veteran journalist Theodore H. White outlines Murrow's broadcast career and its impact on television audiences.

It is so difficult to recapture the real Ed Murrow from the haze that now shrouds the mythical Ed Murrow of history.

Where other men may baffle friends with the infinite complexity of their natures, Ed was baffling otherwise. He was so straightforward, he would completely baffle the writers who now unravel the neuroses of today's demigods of television. When Ed was angry, he bristled; when he gave friendship, it came without withholding.

He could walk with prime ministers and movie stars, GIs and generals, as natural in rumpled GI suntans as in his diplomatic homburg. But jaunty or somber, to those of us who knew him he was just plain old Ed. In his shabby office at CBS cluttered with awards, you could loosen your necktie, put your feet up and yarn away. The dark, overhanging eyebrows would arch as he punctured pretension with a jab, the mouth would twist quizzically as he questioned. And then there were his poker games, as Ed sat master of the table, a cigarette dangling always from his lips–he smoked 60 or 70 a day–and called the bets.

Then–I can hear him now–there was the voice. Ed's deep and rhythmic voice was compelling, not only for its range, halfway between bass and baritone, but for the words that rolled from it. He wrote for the ear–with a cadence of pauses and clipped, full sentences. His was an aural art but, in Ed, the art was natural–his inner ear composed a picture

In the 1950s, Edward R. Murrow (left) established a very high standard for TV news. The 2005 film *Good Night, and Good Luck* revived interest in Murrow, played by David Strathairn (right), as a central figure in the history of television news.

and, long before TV, the imagination of his listeners caught the sound and made with it their own picture.

We remember the voice. But there was so much more to Ed. He had not only a sense of the news but a sense of how the news fit into history. And this sense of the relation of news to history is what, in retrospect, made him the great pioneer of television journalism.

. . . He is very large now, for it was he who set the news system of television on its tracks, holding it, and his descendents, to the sense of history that give it still, in the schlock-storm of today, its sense of honor. Of Ed Murrow it may be said that he made all of us who clung to him, and cling to his memory still, feel larger than we really were.

From "When He Used the Power of TV, He Could Rouse Thunder," *TV Guide* 34, no. 3 (Jan. 18, 1986), pages 13–14. Reprinted by permission of the Julian Bach Literary Agency, Inc. © 1986 by Theodore H. White.

Kevin Winter/Getty Images

Talk show host Conan O'Brien appears on *The Tonight Show* with Jay Leno. In 2008, NBC announced that O'Brien would be Leno's successor. Late-night talk shows are a very enduring TV program format.

seasons, and is still shown today on TV Land. *Rules of Engagement, Two and a Half Men, The Office* and *The New Adventures of Old Christine* are examples of current situation comedy successes.

DRAMA. *The Loretta Young Show* offered noontime drama—broadcast live—every day in the 1950s. *The Hallmark Hall of Fame* established a tradition for high-quality dramatic, live presentations. For many years, TV dramas were limited to 1- or 2-hour programs. But in the 1970s, encouraged by the success of Alex Haley's *Roots*, which dramatized Haley's search for the story of his African ancestry, television began to broadcast as many as 14 hours of a single drama over several nights. Today, the series *CSI* is an example of a popular prime-time drama.

WESTERNS. TV went Western in 1954, when Jack Warner of Warner Brothers signed an agreement with ABC to provide the network with a program called *Cheyenne*. The outspoken Warner had openly criticized TV's effect on the movie business, but when ABC asked Warner to produce programs for them, Warner Brothers became the first movie company to realize that the studios could profit from television.

DETECTIVE STORIES. *Dragnet*, with Sergeant Friday, was an early TV experiment with detectives. The genre became a TV staple: *Dragnet*'s successors today are programs like *Law and Order*.

MOVIES. The movie industry initially resisted the competition from TV, but then realized there was money to be made in selling old movies to TV. In 1957, RKO sold 740 pre-1948 movies to television for $25 million. The other studios followed. Through various distribution agreements, movie reruns and movies produced specifically for television were added to television's program lineup.

SOAP OPERAS. Borrowed from radio serials, soap operas filled morning television programming. Today, game shows and reruns are more popular choices, but some soaps still survive. Soap operas have their own magazines, and some newspapers carry weekly summaries of plot development. Soap operas (*telenovelas*) also are an important feature of today's Spanish-language television.

TALK SHOWS. Sylvester "Pat" Weaver (actress Sigourney Weaver's father) created and produced television's single original contribution to programming: the talk show. Weaver's *Tonight Show* (originally *Jerry Lester's Broadway Open House*) first appeared in 1954. Through a succession of hosts from Lester to Steve Allen to Jack Paar to Johnny Carson to Jay Leno, (with Conan O'Brien scheduled to replace Leno in 2009) *The Tonight Show* has lasted longer than any other talk show on television. Modern-day imitators include David Letterman and Craig Ferguson.

QUIZ SHOWS. In the mid-1950s, all three TV networks introduced quiz shows, on which contestants competed with each other for big-money prizes.

Quiz Shows Bring Ethics Scandals

CBS's *$64,000 Question* premiered June 7, 1955, and was sponsored by Revlon. Contestants answered questions from a glass "isolation booth." Successful contestants returned in succeeding weeks to increase their winnings, and Revlon advertised its Living Lipstick. By September, the program was drawing 85 percent of the audience, and Revlon had substituted an ad for another product; its factory supply of Living Lipstick had completely sold out.

As the most popular quiz show on early television, *$64,000 Question* engendered imitation: *Treasure Hunt, Giant Step* and *Twenty-One*. Winnings grew beyond the $64,000 limit; Charles Van Doren won $129,000 on *Twenty-One*. In the fall of 1955, CBS replaced Murrow's *See It Now* with a quiz program.

Sponsors produced many network quiz shows like *$64,000 Question* for the networks, and these programs

Charles Van Doren (far left) won $129,000 on the quiz show *Twenty-One,* facing contestant Herb Stempel (far right). Contestants appeared in "isolation booths," allegedly to keep them from hearing quiz answers from the audience. The show's host was Jack Barry (center). Eventually, Van Doren admitted that the show's producers had fed him the answers and Stempel admitted he had thrown the show by giving an incorrect answer, at the producer's urging. Van Doren became a central figure in the 1950s quiz show ethics scandals.

Sports is among the most profitable types of TV programming today, especially live events. Venus Williams (right) teams with her sister Serena to play doubles at Wimbledon in 2008.

usually carried the sponsor's name. In the 1958–1959 quiz show scandals, Revlon was implicated when a congressional subcommittee investigated charges that the quiz shows were rigged to enhance the ratings. Charles Van Doren admitted before the congressional subcommittee that *Twenty-One*'s producer had fed him the answers. Staff members from other quiz shows confirmed Van Doren's testimony.

The quiz show scandals caused the networks to reexamine the relationship between advertisers and programs. Before the scandals, advertisers and their agencies produced one-quarter to one-third of network programming. As a result of the quiz show scandals, the networks turned to other sources, such as independent producers, for their programming.

By the late 1960s, advertisers provided less than 3 percent of network programming, and soon advertisers provided no network shows. The networks programmed themselves. They also used reruns of newly acquired studio movies to replace the quiz shows, but quiz shows resurfaced in 1983 with *Wheel of Fortune* and, fairly recently, *Who Wants to Be a Millionaire?*

Ratings Target the Audience

After the quiz show scandals, the major criticism of the networks was that they were motivated only by ratings. Ratings give sponsors information about the audience they're reaching with their advertising—what advertisers are getting for their money.

By the late 1950s, the A. C. Nielsen Company dominated the television ratings business. The national Nielsen ratings describe the audience to advertisers; based on the Nielsens, advertisers pay for the commercial time to reach the audiences they want.

Today, Nielsen provides two sets of numbers, known as rating and share. The ***rating*** is a percentage of the total number of households with television sets. If there are 95 million homes with TV sets, for example, the rating shows the percentage of those sets that were tuned in to a specific program. The ***share*** (an abbreviation for share-of-audience) compares the audience for one show with the audience for

Rating The percentage of the total number of households *with TV sets* tuned to a particular program.

Share The percentage of the audience *with TV sets turned on* that is watching a particular program.

IMPACT
» Audience

Illustration 8.2

Measuring the Audience: What TV Ratings Mean

Suppose that at 8 p.m. on Friday TVs are on in 50 million out of 95 million households and that 25 million TVs are tuned to Program A. Program A's *rating* is 26, meaning 26 percent of all TV households are tuned to Program A. Program A's *share* is 50, meaning that 50 percent of the total number of TV households watching TV are watching Program A.

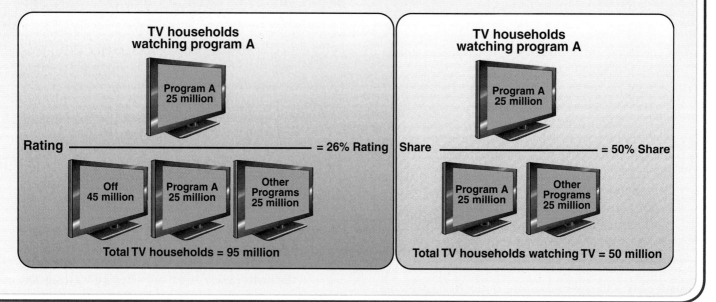

another. Share means the percentage of the audience with TV sets turned on that is watching each program.

If TV sets in 50 million homes were turned on at 8 p.m. on Friday night, and 25 million homes were tuned to program A, that program would have a rating of 26 (25 million divided by 95 million, expressed as a percentage) and a share of 50. (See **Illustration 8.2**.)

The most concentrated ratings periods for local stations are "sweeps" months—February, May and November. (Ratings are taken in July, too, but the numbers are not considered accurate because so many people are on vacation.) The

sweeps provide an estimate of the local TV audience, and advertisers use that information when they decide where to place their commercials.

Sweeps are the months when the ratings services gather their most important ratings, so the networks and local stations often use these important months to showcase their best programs. This is when you are most likely to see a special one-hour episode of a popular series, for example, or a lavishly produced made-for-TV movie.

Today's Nielsen ratings work essentially the same as they did in the 1950s, except that the Nielsens now deliver very specific information on *demographics*—age, occupation and income, for instance—and Nielsen can deliver daily ratings information to any client willing to pay for it. Advertisers use this ratings information to target their most likely consumers. Nike shoes might choose to create a new advertising campaign for the NBA playoffs, for instance, and Nielsen could tell Nike, from judging previous

Sweeps The months when TV ratings services gather their most important ratings—February, May and November.

Demographics Personal characteristics of the audience, such as age, occupation and income.

IMPACT
»Audience

Nielsen to Follow TV Viewers Out of the House and Into the Streets

by Louise Story

Who watches more television—the business traveler or the sports fan?

The Nielsen Company, the longtime arbiter of television viewing, may soon suggest an answer.

Beginning in September [2007], Nielsen will release national ratings for TV viewing away from home in places like bars, hotels, gyms and offices. For decades, Nielsen has rated television viewing based on what viewers in its panel watch while at home. The moment those viewers traveled or went to the gym, any television they watched was not recorded.

For some types of programs, the new ratings may provide a significant lift. Sports fans, for example, often watch games in restaurants or bars, and business executives often watch the news in airports, their offices or at hotels.

Networks like ESPN, CBS, and CNN have complained for years that out-of-home viewing was not counted and was costing them money—advertisers generally base their payments on Nielsen's numbers.

Networks and advertisers have criticized Nielsen for being slow to update its technologies. But Nielsen has been trying to respond. The ratings company started tracking delayed viewing on digital video recorders last year and will release ratings of commercials separate from its program ratings starting in May [2007].

In addition, Nielsen is working to replace the diaries, used in many local markets to

The Nielsen Company, which provides TV ratings to advertisers, has expanded its tracking service to count people who watch TV outside of the home, such as in bars, restaurants, airports, offices and retail stores.

record viewing, with automatic meters, since what people say they watch is not always the same as what they actually watch.

Nielsen has also announced ambitious plans to measure viewership everywhere it occurs, whether on televisions, computers, iPods, cell phones and other mobile devices. And it is working with large advertisers like Procter & Gamble to measure how many people watch programs and ads on television screens in retail stores.

Eventually, Nielsen plans to introduce ratings that roll viewing on all of these platforms into one comprehensive ranking.

"Nielsen has a mandate to follow the video wherever it goes," said Sara Erichson, executive vice president for client services at Nielsen Media Research North American, a

(continued)

IMPACT

>> **Audience**

Nielsen to Follow TV Viewers Out of the House and Into the Streets (continued)

unit of the Nielsen Company. "A lot of where video is going is outside the home. . . ."

Network executives said the new ratings were an important step in following television consumption wherever it occurs. As much as 20 percent to 30 percent of people watching major sports events may view them away from their houses, said David Poltrack, the chief research officer of the CBS Corporation. In January [2007], Nielsen started tracking TV viewing on college campuses for the first time, which jolted ratings of shows with lots of young fans. . . .

Networks have tried to measure TV viewing outside of the home on their own, and some networks have presented their findings to advertisers, hoping to persuade them to pay for those viewers.

But Nielsen will be the first neutral source to produce the ratings nationally on a regular basis, and advertisers might be more inclined to pay for out-of-home viewing when they can compare that viewing across all television programs.

"This is the first time there will be broad-based measuring of out-of-home viewing," said Taddy Hall, chief strategy officer at the Advertising Research Foundation, a nonprofit group in New York that studies advertising. "Think of it as a streetlamp on a dark street. This just expands the area on which there's some lighting."

From "Nielsen to Follow TV Viewers Out of the House and Into the Streets," by Louise Story, *The New York Times,* April 13, 2007. Copyright © 2007 by The New York Times Co. Reprinted by permission.

NBA championships, all about the people the company will reach with its ads.

Criticism about the ratings persists. The main flaw in the ratings today, critics contend, is the way the ratings are religiously followed and used by the broadcast community to determine programming.

Newton Minow Criticizes TV as a "Vast Wasteland"

The 1950s were a trial period for television, as the networks and advertisers tested audience interest in various types of programming. Captured by the miracle that television offered, at first audiences seemed insatiable; they watched almost anything that TV delivered. But in the

1960s, audiences became more discriminating and began to question how well the medium of television was serving the public.

Once television established itself throughout the country, TV needed a public conscience. That public conscience was Newton Minow. An unassuming soothsayer, Minow was named chairman of the Federal Communications Commission in 1961 by newly elected President John F. Kennedy. On May 9, 1961, speaking to the National Association of Broadcasters in his first public address since his appointment, Minow told broadcast executives what he believed were the broadcasters' responsibilities to the public. According to Minow, in his book *Equal Time*, he told the broadcasters:

> Your license lets you use the public's airwaves as trustees for 180 million Americans. The public is your beneficiary. If you want to stay on as trustees, you must deliver a decent return to the public—not only to your stockholders. . . .

Your industry possesses the most powerful voice in America. It has an inescapable duty to make that voice ring with intelligence and with leadership. In a few years this exciting industry has grown from a novelty to an instrument of overwhelming impact on the American people. It should be making ready for the kind of leadership that newspapers and magazines assumed years ago, to make our people aware of their world.

Ours has been called the jet age, the atomic age, the space age. It is also, I submit, the television age. And just as history will decide whether the leaders of today's world employed the atom to destroy the world or rebuild it for mankind's benefit, so will history decide whether today's broadcasters employed their powerful voice to enrich the people or debase them.

Minow then asked his audience of broadcast station owners and managers to watch their own programs. He said that they would find a "vast wasteland," a phrase that resurfaces today during any critical discussion of television.

Public Television Finds an Audience

The concept of educational television has been alive since the 1950s, when a few noncommercial stations succeeded in regularly presenting public service programs without advertisements, but the shows were low budget.

The educational network NET (National Educational Television) emerged in 1963 to provide some national programming (about 10 hours a week), sponsored mainly by foundations, with some federal support. Then in 1967, the Ford Foundation agreed to help pay for several hours of live evening programming.

Also in 1967, the Carnegie Commission on Educational Television released its report *Public Television: A Program for Action*, which included a proposal to create the Corporation for Public Broadcasting. CPB would collect money from many sources—including the enhanced federal funds the Carnegie report suggested—and disburse the money to the stations.

President Lyndon Johnson's administration and several foundations added money to CPB's budget. The Public Broadcasting Service was created to distribute programs. The extra money underwrote the creation of programs like *Sesame Street* and *The French Chef*. PBS also began to buy successful British television programs, which were broadcast on *Masterpiece Theater*. PBS programs actually started to show up in the ratings.

Today, the Corporation for Public Broadcasting, which oversees public television, still receives funding from the federal government. Local funding supplements

Frank Micelotta/Getty Images

PBS has provided many memorable programs like *Sesame Street*, yet PBS commonly attracts less than 3 percent of the national audience. In 1995, members of Congress called for the "privatization" of public television, which means it eventually would become self-sustaining. Muppets Kermit the Frog and Miss Piggy speak onstage at the TV Land Awards in Santa Monica.

this government underwriting, but within the past 10 years, public donations to public television have been declining. This decline in funding has led public broadcasters to seek underwriting from more corporate donors, but companies accustomed to advertising on commercial networks are reluctant to advertise on a network that commonly attracts less than 3 percent of the national audience.

For the first time, public television is beginning to pay attention to ratings. This attention to an audience of consumers means the pressure is building on public television executives to make each program profitable.

The FCC began liberalizing its rules for commercial announcements on public television in 1981. Now, corporate sponsors often make announcements, including graphics and video, at the beginning and the end of PBS-produced programs. The announcements often look the same as advertisements on commercial television. Critics of this commercialization of public television are calling for more government funding, but Congress seems unwilling to expand its underwriting. Today, public television is struggling to reinvent itself, and it still remains commercial television's stepchild.

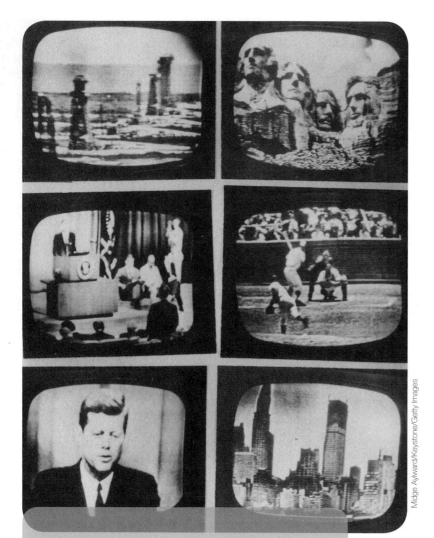

Midge Aylward/Keystone/Getty Images

On July 10, 1962, Telstar I sent the first transatlantic satellite broadcast, a single image. By 1972, Telstar was able to simultaneously transmit six images from America to Europe. Modern satellites make television delivery systems like DirecTV possible.

Satellites Make Transatlantic Television Possible

By 1965, all three networks were broadcasting in color. Television demonstrated its technological sophistication in December 1968 with its live broadcast from the *Apollo* spacecraft while the spacecraft circled the moon, and seven months later television showed Neil Armstrong stepping onto the moon.

On July 10, 1962, *Telstar I* sent the first transatlantic satellite broadcast. Before *Telstar*, copper cable linked the continents, film footage from overseas traveled only by plane, and in most homes a long-distance telephone call was a special event. Today, *Telstar*'s descendants orbit at a distance of more than 22,000 miles. A single modern communication satellite can carry 30,000 telephone calls and three television channels. Modern satellites make program services like CNN and satellite systems like DirecTV possible.

Television Changes National Politics

Just as radio matured first as an entertainment medium and then expanded to cover important news events, television first established itself with entertainment and then developed a serious news presence. Franklin D. Roosevelt had been the first president to understand and use radio, and John F. Kennedy became the country's first television president. Kennedy's predecessors had appeared on television, but he instinctively knew how to *use* television.

Observers claimed Kennedy's 1960 presidential victory was partly due to his success in the televised presidential debates with Richard Nixon. Kennedy also was the first president to hold live televised news conferences. In July 1962, he oversaw the launch of the first communications satellite, *Telstar I*. One year later news organizations used that same satellite technology to broadcast live coverage of the news events following President Kennedy's assassination on November 22, 1963.

Television received credit for uniting the nation during TV news coverage of the Kennedy assassination, but it also was blamed for dividing it. President Lyndon Johnson, beleaguered by an unpopular war in Vietnam, used television to make a national announcement in 1968 that he would not run for a second term.

Johnson's successor, President Richard Nixon, had always been uncomfortable with the press. The Nixon administration often attacked the press for presenting perspectives on world affairs that the Nixon administration did not like. Upset with the messages being presented, the Nixon administration battled the messenger, sparking a bitter public debate about the role of a free press (especially television) in a democratic society.

Ironically, television's next live marathon broadcast chronicled the ongoing investigation of the Nixon presidency—Watergate. The Watergate scandal began when burglars broke into the offices of the Democratic Party's national headquarters in the Watergate complex in Washington, D.C., on June 17, 1972. Some of the burglars had ties to President Nixon's reelection committee as well as to other questionable activities originating in the White House.

In the months following the break-in, the president and his assistants sought to squelch the resulting investigation. Although Nixon denied knowledge of the break-in and the cover-up, the U.S. Senate hearings about the scandal, televised live across the country, created a national sensation. (See also **Chapter 12**.) Eventually, faced with the prospect of impeachment, Nixon announced his resignation on television on August 8, 1974.

In 1987, television repeated its marathon coverage of an important national investigation with the Iran-Contra hearings, a congressional investigation of the Reagan administration's role in illegally providing weapons to Nicaraguan rebels, called contras.

TV News Images Bring Global Events into View

In 1997, TV became an international window on grief when the networks carried nonstop coverage of the events surrounding the death and funeral of Diana, Princess of Wales. On September 11, 2001, U.S. TV network news offered nonstop coverage of the terrorist events at New York's World Trade Center, the Pentagon and in rural Pennsylvania. Two years later, the TV networks brought viewers even closer to events when TV reporters and photographers sent live battlefield images and stories during the Iraq War.

Television at Work

A typical television station has eight departments:

1. Sales

2. Programming (which includes news as well as entertainment)

3. Production

4. Engineering

5. Traffic

6. Promotion

7. Public affairs

8. Administration

People in the *sales* department sell the commercial slots for the programs. Advertising is divided into *national* and *local*

David Silverman/Getty Images

Television news has matured from its early beginnings as a 15-minute newscast to CNN's 24-hour coverage today of news events around the world. On November 5, 2008, patrons at a bar in Tel Aviv watch a CNN broadcast announcing Barack Obama's presidential victory.

sales. Advertising agencies, usually based on the East Coast, buy national ads for the products they handle. Ford Motor Company, for instance, may buy time on a network for a TV ad that will run simultaneously all over the country.

But the local Ford dealers, who want you to shop at their showrooms, buy their ads directly from the local station. These ads are called local (or spot) ads. For these sales, salespeople (called account executives) at each station negotiate packages of ads based on their station's advertising rates. These rates are a direct reflection of that station's position in the ratings.

The *programming* department selects the shows that you will see and develops the station's schedule. Network-owned stations, located in big cities (KNBC in Los Angeles, for example), are called *O & Os*, which stands for owned and operated. *Affiliates* are stations that carry network programming but that the networks do not own. O & Os automatically carry network programming, but the networks

O & Os TV stations that are owned and operated by the networks.

Affiliates Stations that carry TV network programming but are not owned by the networks.

pay affiliates to carry their programming, for which the networks sell most of the ads and keep the money. An affiliate is allowed to insert into the network programming a specific number of local ads, for which the affiliate keeps the income.

Because affiliates can make money on network programming, and don't have to pay for it, many stations choose to affiliate themselves with a network. When they aren't running what the network provides, affiliates run their own programs and keep all the advertising money they collect from them.

Some of the nation's commercial TV stations operate as independents. Independent stations must buy and program all their own shows, but independents also keep all the money they make on advertising. Independents run some individually produced programs and old movies, but most of their programming consists of reruns such as *I Love Lucy* and *The Andy Griffith Show* that once ran on the networks. Independents buy these reruns from program services called **syndicators**.

Syndicators also sell independently produced programs such as *The Oprah Winfrey Show*. Independent programs are created and sold either by non-network stations or by independent producers. Stations pay for these first-run syndication programs individually; the price is based on the size of the station's market.

Local news usually makes up the largest percentage of a station's locally produced programming. In some large markets, such as Los Angeles, local news programming runs as long as two hours.

The *production* department manages the programs the station creates in-house. This department also produces local commercials for the station. The *engineering* department makes sure all the technical aspects of a broadcast operation are working: antennas, transmitters, cameras and any other broadcast equipment. The *traffic* department integrates the advertising with the programming, making sure that all the ads that are sold are aired when they're supposed to be. Traffic also handles billing for the ads.

The *promotion* department advertises the station—on the station itself, on billboards, on radio and in the local newspaper. These people also create contests to keep the station visible in the community. The *public affairs department* helps organize public events, such as a fun run to raise money for the local hospital. *Administration* handles the paperwork for the station—paychecks and expense accounts, for example.

Syndicators Services that sell programming to broadcast stations and cable.

Audiences Drive TV Programming

Today's most-watched television programs are situation comedies, sports and feature movies. More than 120 million people tuned in for the final episode of the situation comedy *M*A*S*H* in 1983, making it the highest-rated television program ever. In 1993, the final episode of the sitcom *Cheers* garnered an audience of 80 million, Super Bowls generally grab about half of the homes in the United States. In 2008, the surprise ratings leader was President-elect Barack Obama. More than 70 million people watched his election victory the night of November 4, 2008, a record number of viewers for a presidential election night.

Six developments promise to affect the television industry over the next decade: station ownership changes, the shrinking role of the networks, the accuracy of ratings, the growth of cable and satellite delivery, the profitability of sports programming and the growing audience for Spanish-language TV.

Station Ownership Changes and Mergers

The Telecommunications Act of 1996 (see **Chapter 14**) used a station's potential audience to measure ownership limits. The Act allowed one company to own TV stations that reach up to 35 percent of the nation's homes. Broadcasters also are no longer required, as they once were, to hold onto a station for three years before selling it. Today, stations may be sold as soon as they are purchased.

In 1999, the Federal Communications Commission adopted new regulations that allow media companies to own two TV stations in one market, as long as eight separately owned TV stations continue to operate in that market after the merger. The rules said the four top-rated stations in one market cannot be combined under the same ownership, but a station that is among the four top-rated stations can combine with one that is not in the top four.

In 2003, the FCC relaxed ownership rules even further, leaving few restrictions on network ownership. Like radio, fewer companies are putting together larger and larger groups of TV stations. Today, most local TV stations are not owned by local companies, as they once were. Television is *concentrating* ownership, but it is also *shifting* ownership, as stations are bought and sold at an unprecedented rate. This has introduced instability and change to an industry that until 1980 witnessed very few ownership turnovers.

The Networks' Shrinking Role

Advertisers always have provided the economic support for television, so in 1986 the networks were disturbed to see the

Illustration 8.3

Broadcast TV Networks' Share of the Prime-Time Audience (ABC, CBS, NBC and Fox)

The prime-time audience for the four major broadcast TV networks is declining because of increased competition from satellite and cable programming. Many consumers are also time-shifting—recording their favorite programs to watch whenever they choose. This practice of time-shifting is changing the concept of just what prime-time television means.

Source: *Veronis, Suhler Stevenson Communications Industry Forecast 2006–2010*; Bill Carter, "A Television Season That Lasts All Year," *The New York Times*, September 23, 2008.

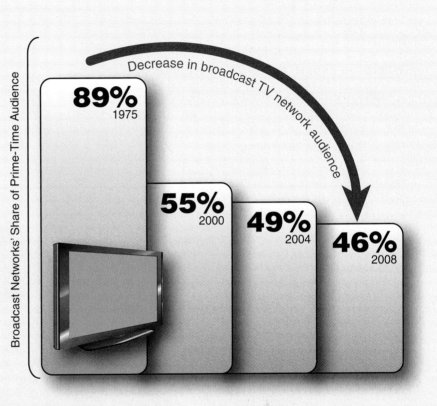

first decline in advertising revenues in 15 years. New and continuing developments—such as cable, satellite broadcast, VCRs and DVD players—turned the television set into a smorgasbord of choices. Audiences—and advertisers—began to desert the networks, and network ratings declined as a result.

Today, because there are so many new sources of information and entertainment for the audience, advertisers are looking for new ways to capture viewers. The network share of the *prime-time audience* has gone from 90 percent in 1978 to 46 percent today, reflecting the continued growth of syndicated programming and satellite and cable systems. (See **Illustration 8.3.**)

The networks' share of the audience for the evening news also is shrinking. The story is familiar, paralleling the decline in radio listening in the late 1940s when television first replaced radio and then television began competing with itself. Today more stations and more sources of programming mean the TV networks must expand their audi-

ence beyond the traditional prime-time evening time slot to stay profitable.

How Accurate Are TV Ratings?

People meters, first used in 1987 by the A. C. Nielsen Company to record television viewing, gather data through a 4-inch-by-10-inch box that sits on the television set in metered homes. People meters monitor the nation's Nielsen families (about 4,000 of them), and the results of these recorded viewing patterns (which Nielsen says reflect a cross section of American viewers), called ratings, establish the basis for television advertising rates. (See **Illustration 8.4.**)

Nielsen family members each punch an assigned button on top of the set when they begin to watch television. The system's central computer, linked to the home by telephone lines, correlates each viewer's number with information about that person stored in its memory.

Network ratings have plunged since people meters were introduced as a ratings system, and the networks have

IMPACT
»Audience

Illustration 8.4

Where Do People Watch TV at Home?

TV sets are spread throughout the house, which increases the likelihood that, at any given time, someone in the household has the TV set turned on. Most people still watch TV in the living room, but a majority of households also have a TV set in the master bedroom and one in five households has a TV set in the child's bedroom.

Source: Television Bureau of Advertising, tvb.org.

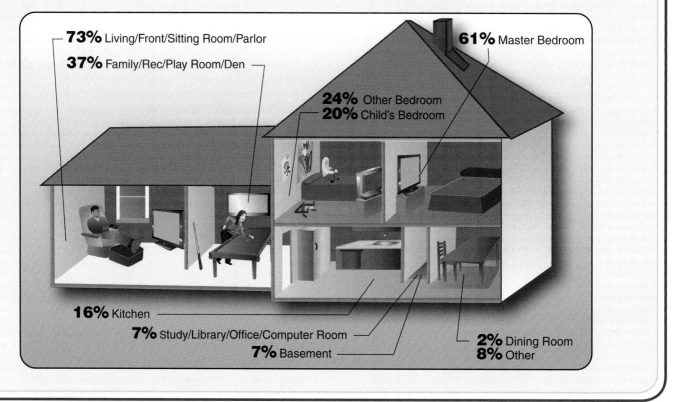

73% Living/Front/Sitting Room/Parlor
37% Family/Rec/Play Room/Den
61% Master Bedroom
24% Other Bedroom
20% Child's Bedroom
16% Kitchen
7% Study/Library/Office/Computer Room
7% Basement
2% Dining Room
8% Other

complained that the new measuring device underestimates specific audiences, especially African Americans and Latinos. Still, Nielsen is the only company in the United States offering TV audience measurement. (See **Impact/Audience**, "Nielsen to Follow TV Viewers Out of the House and Into the Streets," page 169.)

CATV Community antenna television or cable television.

Cable and Satellite Delivery

Today's cable giants, ESPN (Entertainment and Sports Programming Network) and CNN, are descendents of America's first cable TV system, which was established in Pennsylvania and Oregon to bring TV signals to rural areas that couldn't receive an over-the-air signal. Soon, this community antenna television (***CATV***) system spread to remote areas all over the country where TV reception was poor.

By 1970, there were 2,500 CATV systems in the United States, and commercial broadcasters were getting nervous

Cable channels began offering their own programming, separate from the networks, in 1972. Today, more than 500 program services, including American Movie Classics (AMC), are available by satellite. In 2008, AMC's program *Mad Men* received more Emmy nominations than any other television program in the history of the awards. *Mad Men*, a drama about the advertising business in New York City in the 1960s, stars (from left) Bryan Batt (Salvatore Romano), Jon Hamm (Don Draper) and Elisabeth Moss (Peggy Olson).

Cable channels like National Geographic, which offers programming such as *The Dog Whisperer*, give advertisers a very targeted audience. Cesar Millan works with his dogs Daddy (right) and Junior in 2008 at the taping of the 100th episode of his program.

about what they called *wired TV*. Cable operators were required by the FCC to carry all local broadcast programming, and programs often were duplicated on several channels. The FCC also limited the programs that cable could carry. One FCC ruling, for example, said that movies on cable had to be at least 10 years old.

Believing that cable should be able to offer its own programming, Home Box Office (then owned by Time Warner) started operating in Manhattan in 1972, offering a modest set of programs. Ted Turner's Turner Network Television (TNT) first relayed programs by satellite in 1976, and in 1979 Turner started Cable News Network (CNN). Today, more than 500 different program services, ranging from ESPN to the concert sounds of VH-1 to classic 1930s and 1940s movies on American Movie Classics (AMC), are available by satellite.

Cable television as an alternative to the traditional networks moved to the center of the national news agenda in 1991 when CNN offered 24-hour coverage of the Gulf War in Iraq. CNN's fast response to world events underlined the new global role that CNN and many other cable companies will play in future television developments.

In 1982, the FCC authorized direct broadcast satellite (**DBS**), making direct satellite-to-home satellite broadcasts possible. In 1994, a company called DirecTV began offering services directly to the home by satellite. For a monthly fee, DirecTV provides access to more than 500 *different worldwide* channels. The monthly fee is about the same as, or cheaper than, a monthly cable bill.

Today, the number of satellite subscribers is increasing, and the number of cable subscribers is declining. Cable and satellite program delivery systems now are collectively called *subscription television services*.

Cable and satellite programming, which divides viewers into smaller, targeted segments than the networks, also makes it easier for advertisers to target a specific audience. Programs like National Geographic's *The Dog Whisperer* starring Cesar Millan, for instance, bring dog lovers to any advertiser that wants to sell dog-related products.

DBS Direct broadcast satellites.

Subscription Television Services A term used to describe cable and satellite program delivery.

Alexander Tamargo/Getty Images

Spanish-language stations are beginning to draw more prime-time viewers in the 18-34 age group than the traditional broadcast networks—NBC, CBS, ABC and Fox. Actress Lorena Rojas (left) and actor Carlos Pitella perform a scene from an episode of the Telemundo soap opera *Pecados Ajenos* in October 2007 in Miami, Florida.

TV Changes Professional Sports

One of the most profitable types of television programming is sports. In 1964, CBS paid $28 million for television rights to the 1964–1965 National Football League (NFL) games. In 1990, the networks paid $3.6 billion to broadcast NFL football. Today the price is much higher.

Television fees fund most of the cost of organized sports. Today's televised sports have become spectacularly complex entertainment packages, turning athletes as well as sports commentators into media stars. The expansion of sports programming beyond the networks to cable channels such as ESPN means even more sports programming choices for viewers, and more money for American sports teams.

Spanish-Language Television Brings a New Audience

During the summer of 2005, Univision, the nation's largest Spanish-language station, drew more prime-time viewers

in the 18–34 age group than all the traditional broadcast networks—NBC, CBS, ABC and Fox. This was the first time Spanish-language TV had surpassed the networks, and the main draw was *telenovelas*, or Spanish soap operas.

This Spanish-language lead in prime time had been building for several years, as the nation's Latino population increased. According to *The New York Times*:

> Market researchers say that Latinos—no matter their age or dominant language—tend to tune in to Spanish-language television for two main staples: newscasts, because networks like Univision and Telemundo cover Latino issues and Latin America with more breadth and resources than English-language networks; and telenovelas, which function like a kind of cultural touchstone.

"Whether you're U.S.-born and you're introduced to it by a parent or grandparent or whether you're foreign-born and you grew up with it, it's the kind of thing that's inherent in the culture," multicultural marketing consultant Derene Allen told the *Times*. "It's as Mexican as eating tortillas and as Venezuelan or Colombian as eating arepas."

As traditional audiences shrink, and advertisers try to find new ways to sell their products, Spanish-language TV is emerging as one of the few promising markets for programming.

New Technology Changes TV's Focus

When technological developments move like a rocket, as they have in the past decade, program delivery becomes easier and less expensive. New technologies have brought more competition. Several new delivery systems have been developed to bring more choices to consumers than ever before—from the size of the screen to the clarity of the picture—and to change further the way people use television.

Digital Video Recorders

Digital video recorders (**DVR**s) download programming, using a set-top box that looks like a cable box and sits on or near the TV. DVRs use electronic storage to receive information from any program service (including the broadcast networks and satellite and cable programmers) to send viewers up-to-date information about what's on TV. DVRs transfer the information to an on-screen program guide, where viewers can decide what to watch and when, a practice called **time-shifting**.

One of the biggest features of a DVR is that it allows viewers to press the pause button during a show they're watching, leave the TV set on, and then start up the pro-

DVR Digital video recorders.

Time-Shifting Recording a television program on a DVR to watch at a more convenient time.

gram again when they return or to fast-forward through the recorded portion.

Because DVRs change viewers' control over which programming they watch (and, most importantly, which commercials, if any), all the major TV networks have invested in the companies that produce this technology, such as TiVo. The networks want to be able to influence what consumers can record and when, but total viewer control is one of DVRs' most attractive features for consumers.

High-Definition Television

A normal television picture scans 525 lines across the screen. *High-definition television (HDTV)* scans 1,125 lines. CBS first demonstrated HDTV in the United States in 1982. HDTV, which offers a wider, sharper digital picture and better sound, requires more spectrum space than conventional television signals. Digital TV also makes it easier for manufacturers to combine the functions of TV and the functions of a computer in the same TV set.

HDTV use is growing in the United States because the sets, which originally cost $10,000, are now priced at less than $400 for a starter model. HDTV is scheduled to become the industry standard in 2009.

Television Views the Future

Forecasts for the future of television parallel the forecasts for radio—a menu board of hundreds of programs and services available to viewers at the touch of a remote-control button. In the 1990s, regional telephone companies (called *telcos*) rushed to merge with cable TV companies to form giant telecommunications delivery systems.

"Cable TV companies and telephone companies are joining forces because each has something valuable that the other wants," reports the *Los Angeles Times*.

"Telephone companies have wired virtually every household in their service area and want to deliver the wide variety of program and information services controlled by the cable companies," says the *Times*. "The cable operators, on the other hand, want to use their cable TV wires to go into the phone business, delivering voice, data and video over . . . fiber-optic lines."

To try to maintain their audience dominance, the TV networks have invested heavily in satellite TV and Internet program services to develop the capability to deliver programs to screens as small as a cell phone, and these new financial powerhouses can spend large sums of money in research.

In one vision of the future, for example, your television could serve not only as a program service with unlimited

"Regular or high-definition?"

channels but also as an artificial reality machine, says *The Wall Street Journal*. This machine would use "remarkably crisp pictures and sound to 'deliver' a viewer to a pristine tropical beach, to a big football game or to a quiet mountaintop retreat. Japanese researchers envision golfers practicing their swings in front of three-dimensional simulations of courses."

In 2006, Congress passed a law that requires TV broadcasters to switch totally to digital signals in 2009. Only about 60 percent of U.S. households in 2006 were capable of receiving a digital TV signal, according to the Consumer Electronics Association. Broadcasters resisted the 2009 deadline because they are afraid they will lose part of their audience—people who don't have a digital TV—but the conversion is mandatory.

Once broadcasters have converted totally to digital signals, people with old TV sets will have to buy a converter box—an additional cost for consumers—to receive their local stations. For broadcasters and consumers, the cost of the conversion is estimated at $75 billion.

Digital technology has made television programs available on screens as big as 100″ and as small as 2″. New HDTV screens offer movie-quality pictures and CD-quality sound. Internet delivery offers programming that's mobile and can follow you wherever and whenever you want to view it.

The definition of what we call "television" is exploding. Lanny Smoot, an executive at Bell Communications Research, calls the future of television a *telepresence*. "This," he says, "is a wave that is not possible to stop."

> **High-Definition Television (HDTV)** A type of television that provides a picture with a clearer resolution than typical TV sets.
>
> **Telcos** An abbreviation for telephone companies.

Review, Analyze, Investigate
REVIEWING CHAPTER 8

Television Transforms Daily Life

✓ The word *television*, which once meant programs delivered by antennas through over-the-air signals, today means a *television screen*, where a variety of delivery systems brings viewers a diversity of programs.

✓ Many groups are concerned that, because of its pervasiveness, television influences the nation's values, habits and behavior.

✓ About 1,600 television stations operate in the United States. Three out of four of these are commercial stations and about half of U.S. stations are affiliated with a network.

TV Delivers an Audience to Advertisers

✓ More than any other media industry today, commercial television exists primarily as an advertising medium.

✓ A 30-second ad during the Super Bowl can cost more than $2.5 million.

Visual Radio Becomes *Television*

✓ Guglielmo Marconi put sound on airwaves. Lee de Forest invented the Audion tube. Vladimir Zworykin turned an electronic signal into a visual image. Philo T. Farnsworth added the electronic scanner.

✓ The rivalry between David Sarnoff (RCA) and William S. Paley (CBS) is central to the early history of television.

✓ The ABC network was formed when the Federal Communications Commission (FCC) ordered David Sarnoff to sell one of his two networks (Red and Blue). The Blue network became ABC.

Television Outpaces Radio

✓ The first television news broadcasts were primitive compared to today's broadcasts. Television news, like radio news, developed its own standard of excellence, led by news pioneers Edward R. Murrow and David Brinkley.

✓ Most television entertainment programming was derived from radio.

✓ The only type of program that didn't come from radio was the talk show, which appeared on television first and then moved to radio. The situation comedy proved to be one of television's most durable types of programming.

Quiz Shows Bring Ethics Scandals

✓ A congressional investigation revealed that several 1950s TV quiz shows were rigged to enhance their ratings.

✓ The 1950s quiz show scandals caused the networks to eliminate advertiser-produced programming.

✓ Charles Van Doren, who admitted he cheated, was a central figure in the quiz show scandals.

Ratings Target the Audience

✓ The Nielsen ratings determine the price that TV advertisers pay to air their commercials.

✓ TV audiences are measured as ratings and shares.

Newton Minow Criticizes TV as a "Vast Wasteland"

✓ In the 1960s, audiences grew more discriminating and began to question how well the medium of television was serving the public.

✓ An influential person who outlined TV's responsibility to its audience was then-FCC Chairman Newton Minow, who coined the phrase "vast wasteland" to describe television.

Public Television Finds an Audience

✓ National Educational Television (NET) is the predecessor of today's Corporation for Public Broadcasting.

✓ In 1981, the FCC loosened the rules for commercials on public television.

Satellites Make Transatlantic Television Possible

✓ In 1982, *Telstar I* sent the first transatlantic satellite broadcast.

✓ Modern satellites make CNN and DirecTV possible.

Television Changes National Politics

✓ In the 1960s, television drew criticism for the way it was perceived to influence politics and the dialogue about national issues.

✓ Television broadcast nonstop coverage of the Watergate hearings, President Nixon's resignation and investigations of the Iran-Contra scandal.

TV News Images Bring Global Events into View

✓ In 2001, U.S. TV network news offered nonstop coverage of the terrorist attacks at New York's World Trade Center, the Pentagon and in rural Pennsylvania.

✓ In 2003, the TV networks brought viewers even closer to events when TV reporters and photographers sent live battlefield images and stories to viewers during the Iraq War.

Television at Work

✓ A typical TV station has eight departments: sales, programming, production, engineering, traffic, promotion, public affairs and administration.

✓ Most TV stations are affiliated with a network.

Audiences Drive TV Programming

✓ The most-watched TV programs are situation comedies, sports and feature movies.

✓ Deregulation, with relaxed ownership rules, means that instability, mergers and change have become major characteristics of the television industry.

✓ Network ratings have plunged since people meters were introduced as a ratings system, and the TV networks also must compete with the huge variety of program options vying for consumers' attention.

✓ More than 200 program services now offer alternatives to network programming.

✓ Television licensing fees fund most of the cost of the nation's college and professional sports.

✓ Spanish-language networks draw increasing numbers of prime-time viewers.

New Technology Changes TV's Focus

✓ Several technological developments are changing the way programs are delivered to consumers, including digital video recorders, high definition television and the Internet.

✓ Digital television such as HDTV offers better pictures, clearer sound and a flatter screen than traditional TV.

✓ Digital TV makes it easier for manufacturers to combine the functions of TV and the functions of a computer in the same TV set.

Television Views the Future

✓ Cable, satellite and Internet program services have developed the capability to deliver programs to screens as small as a cell phone.

✓ In the future, TV could serve as a program service with unlimited channels and possibly even bring programming in a three-dimensional environment.

✓ In 2006, Congress passed a law that requires all TV broadcasts to switch totally to digital signals in 2009. The conversion is mandatory.

KEY TERMS

These terms are defined in the margins throughout this chapter and appear in alphabetical order with definitions in the Glossary, which begins on page 372.

CRITICAL QUESTIONS

1. Explain what media observer Jeff Greenfield means when he says, "To the television executive, the product [of television] is the audience." Give examples of why this is true.

2. How did the quiz show scandals of the 1950s affect the relationship between advertisers and the networks? Is the relationship between advertisers and the networks different or the same today? Explain.

3. Discuss Newton Minow's challenge to television in his speech before the National Association of Broadcasters in 1961. How did he describe television? In your opinion, is Minow right? Why or why not?

4. Discuss the economic challenges facing public broadcasting and the various sources of funding on which public broadcast stations, CPB and PBS rely. Summarize how public broadcasting has responded to the problems.

5. Explain the role of the Nielsen ratings in television, including such factors as ratings accuracy, advertiser dependence on ratings, the effect of ratings on programming, and the importance of ratings to commercial and public broadcasting networks.

WORKING THE WEB

This list includes both sites mentioned in the chapter and others to give you greater insight into the television industry.

Disney-ABC Television Group
http://www.disneyabctv.com

Home to Disney's international entertainment and news properties, the Disney-ABC Television Group includes the ABC Television Network (Daytime, Entertainment and News divisions), Disney Channels Worldwide, ABC Studios and Hyperion Books. The Group also manages the Radio Disney Network and the company's equity interest in Lifetime Entertainment Services and A&E Television Networks.

HDTV Network
http://www.HDTV.net

HDTV.net offers information about high-definition television, the newest TV technology. The site includes FAQs and links to retailers selling HDTVs. It also explains the differences between high definition television, digital television broadcasting (DTV) and digital cable transmission.

National Association of Broadcasters (NAB)
http://www.nab.org

The trade association for over-the-air radio and television broadcasters, the NAB provides networking opportunities, a career center and information about communication law. It also represents industry interests to government officials and provides research grants.

National Cable & Telecommunications Association
http://www.ncta.com

The principal trade association of the U.S. cable television industry, NTCA provides a unified voice for its members on all issues affecting cable and telecommunications. Its Web site includes information on other industry-related organizations, resources and services, as well legislative issues, filings and publications. Key issues for consumers include Internet regulation, TV parental controls and the digital television transition.

Nielsen Media Research
http://www.nielsenmedia.com

This research company provides the Nielsen ratings, which measure the popularity of various television programs. Its founder, Arthur C. Nielsen, was one of the fathers of modern marketing research. Its data play a large part in determining how much can be charged for ads. Useful features on the Web site include a TV History Timeline and a searchable glossary of media industry acronyms and terms.

Northwestern University Library: Broadcast, Cable and Satellite Resources on the Internet
http://www.library.northwestern.edu/media/resources/broadcast.html

This site offers a long list of links to useful media Web sites including the All in One Media Directory and the United States Information Agency.

Parental Media Guide
http://parentalguide.org

Sponsored by major entertainment industry associations such as the MPA, NAB and Entertainment Software Rating Board, this Web site provides a central resource for parents and caregivers seeking information on the voluntary parental guideline systems in place for television, movies, video games and recorded music.

Public Broadcasting (PBS)
http://www.pbs.org

This network of more than 350 noncommercial television stations reaches nearly 73 million viewers per week with content on air and online. PBS.org includes a program search, TV schedules and links to online featured topics such as History, Life & Culture and News & Views. PBS Kids Online (http://pbskids.org) provides educational entertainment for children as well as comprehensive sections for parents and teachers.

Television Bureau of Advertising (TVB)
http://www.tvb.org

This trade association for broadcast groups, advertising sales reps, syndicators, international broadcasters and individual television stations provides audience analyses and a business data bank. The Web site also offers advice for selling smarter, a job center and information on electronic business processes.

TV.com
http://www.tv.com

Powered by CNET, this fan-run site includes information about programs, episodes, actors, lines and trivia for TV shows from the 1940s to today. It has a wide variety of online forums sorted by show genre as well as news, celebrity photos, downloads and podcasts.

9

Digital Media: Widening the Web

Young gamers play video games at the Championship Gaming Series in Santa Monica in 2008.

What's Ahead?

Digital Communication Transforms Media

Digital Media Support Convergence

20th-Century Discoveries Made Internet Possible

Web Opens to Unlimited Access

What Happens to Old Media?

Transformation Takes 30 Years

Web Access Leaves Some People Behind

Internet Combines Commerce, Information and Entertainment

Mobile Media Chase the Audience

Government Attempts to Coordinate and Control the Net

Intellectual Property Rights Seek Protection

Internet Faces Four Challenges

New Technologies Mix with Old Ideas

"Today's world has become so

wired together, so flattened, that you can't avoid seeing just where you stand on the planet—just where the caravan is and just how far ahead or behind you are," says *New York Times* columnist Thomas L. Friedman. The main reason for today's flattened planet, of course, is the Internet. Within the last 30 years, the emergence of the Internet as a media delivery system has transformed the structure and the economics of the media business in the United States and throughout the world.

TimeFrame

1978 – Today

Digital Media Covers the Globe

1978
Nicholas Negroponte at the Massachusetts Institute of Technology first uses the term "convergence" to describe the intersection of the media industries.

1988
Less than one-half of 1 percent of U.S. households are online.

K Vreeland/ClassicStock/CORBIS

1989
Tim Berners-Lee develops programming languages that allow people to share all types of information online and the first browser, which allows people to view information online.

1994
Marc Andreessen and his colleagues at the University of Illinois introduce Mosaic, a browser that allows people to combine pictures and text in the same online document.

Congress names the new effort to coordinate all the different senders, channels and receivers in the United States The National Information Infrastructure (NII).

1995
Yahoo! is launched by David Filo (left) and Jerry Yang as a search engine company.

Ed Kashi/CORBIS

1996
Internet advertising reaches $200 million.

Congress passes the Communications Decency Act, an unsuccessful attempt to control Internet content.

1998
One in four U.S. households is online.

Congress passes the Digital Millennium Copyright Act, which makes it illegal to share copyrighted material on the Internet.

Larry Page (left) and Sergey Brin create Google as a company to create a better search engine for the Web.

Kim Kulish/CORBIS

1999
The Recording Industry Association sues Internet file-sharing company Napster for copyright infringement.

2000
The number of Internet businesses explodes.

2001
Napster shuts down.

The number of Internet start-ups begins to shrink and many existing companies close.

2003
The Recording Industry Association and the Motion Picture Association of America announce campaigns to aggressively fight online piracy.

2004
MySpace.com is launched as a personal Web site location directed primarily at teenagers and young adults. For the first time, bloggers cover a presidential election.

Erik Freeland/CORBIS

2005
File sharing company Grokster shuts down, settling a landmark intellectual property case.

After the success of Apple's online subscription music service, Apple announces online pay-per-view subscription access to first-run video.

2006
Internet advertising reaches $17 billion.

AOL announces a bulk e-mail service that charges bulk e-mailers a fee. Opponents call the fee a tax on free expression.

Google fights a U.S. Justice Department subpoena for records of its customers' online searches.

Google eventually agrees to a limited government request for information.

2007
Apple introduces the iPhone, making digital media more mobile than ever before.

2008
Google, the dominant search engine company, celebrates its 10th anniversary.

Today
73 percent of all Americans use the Internet. The Internet is causing an expansion of digital media development, as new and existing companies compete for consumers' attention in the huge online marketplace.

Mike Nelson/epa/CORBIS

Before the 1970s, media were defined by the systems that delivered them. Paper delivered the print media—newspapers, magazines and books. Antennas carried broadcast signals—radio and television. Movies required film, and music traveled on round discs. These traditional media each were specifically connected to their own method of delivery and organized into different types of companies—newspaper, magazine and book publishers; recording and movie studios; radio and TV stations.

Digital Communication Transforms Media

Today, the Internet delivers all types of media—print, broadcast, movies and recordings—using a single delivery system without barriers. You can receive all types of media just about anywhere you want, delivered by many different types of companies, carried on invisible electronic signals you can't see. The Internet has caused the emergence of new media products and new competition in the media business that were impossible to foresee when the Internet first emerged 30 years ago, designed by a group of scientists who were simply hoping to share information.

The Internet actually is a combination of thousands of computer networks sending and receiving data from all over the world—competing interests joined together by a common purpose, but no common owner. "No government or commercial entity owns the Net or directly profits from its operation," notes information designer Roger Fidler. "It has no president, chief executive officer or central headquarters."

In its global size and absence of central control, the Internet is completely different from traditional media. Originally developed to help researchers, scientists and educators communicate, the Internet has "evolved in a way no one planned or expected," says Fidler. "It is the relationships among people that have shaped the medium."

The term *digital media* describes all forms of communications media that combine text, pictures, sound and video using computer technology. Digital media read, write and store data electronically in numerical form—using numbers to code the data (text, pictures, sound and video). Because all digital media use the same numbered codes, digital media are *compatible*, which means they can function well with one another to exchange and integrate text, pictures, sound and video. This compatibility is the main reason digital media are growing so fast. Because of its rapid growth, digital communications has become the biggest factor in the development of all of today's mass media industries.

Rather than the one-way communication of traditional media, communication on today's compatible digital network means someone can receive and send information simultaneously, without barriers. Digital networks "free individuals from the shackles of corporate bureaucracy and geography and allow them to collaborate and exchange ideas with the

Jeff Haynes/AFP/Getty Images

The Internet today offers people wireless access to information just about wherever and whenever they want it, including this car wash in St. Charles, Illinois.

best colleague anywhere in the world," said futurist George Gilder. "Computer networks give every hacker the creative potential of a factory tycoon of the industrial [turn-of-the-century] era and the communications power of a TV magnate of the broadcasting era."

In an interconnected digital world, the speed and convenience of the network redefines the mass media industries and erases all previous notions of how mass communications should work. Today's media are constantly evolving. Digital media forms "do not arise spontaneously and independently from old media," says media scholar Roger Fidler. Digital media are related and connected to old media. Fidler says today's media are members of an interdependent system, with "similarities and relationships that exist among past, present and emerging forms."

Digital media are similar to traditional media, yet different in ways that make them distinct from their predecessors.

Digital Media All emerging communications media that combine text, graphics, sound and video using computer technology.

Compatible Media that can function well with one another to exchange and integrate text, pictures, sound and video.

Illustration 9.1

How the MIT Media Lab Described Convergence

The diagram on the left displays the alignment of the media in 1978, showing each media industry with a small amount of overlapping territory. In the diagram on the right, which shows Nicolas Negroponte's predictions for the year 2000, the three industries—broadcast and motion pictures, printing and publishing, and computers—completely overlap.

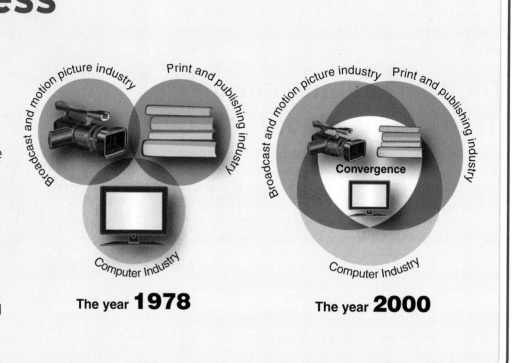

The year **1978**   The year **2000**

Because of the interdependence of all of today's mass media, this intense rate of change means all the media industries are transforming simultaneously.

Digital Media Support Convergence

In 1978, Nicholas Negroponte at the Massachusetts Institute of Technology was the first to identify a theory called *convergence*. This theory gave a name to the process by which the work of the various media industries in the late 1970s was beginning to intersect, and MIT was among the first places to foresee and identify this trend. (The concept of *convergence* is also discussed in **Chapter 1**.)

The media industries not only were combining economically, as media companies began to buy and sell each other, but the technology of the industries also was merging, according to MIT. This convergence meant that eventu-

Convergence The process by which the various media industries intersect.

ally the products the media companies produced began to resemble each other.

Negroponte also said that the combination of the traditional media industries with the computer industry would create a new type of communication.

To identify what was happening to the media industries, Negroponte created two models (see **Illustration 9.1**) to show the position of the media industries in 1978 and his projected vision for those industries in the year 2000. He listed three segments of the media business: (1) print and publishing, (2) broadcast and motion pictures and (3) the computer industry.

The first diagram in Negroponte's model displays the alignment of the media industries in 1978, which shows them with a small amount of integrated territory. In the second diagram, which shows Negroponte's predictions for the year 2000, the three segments of the media industries completely overlap. Negroponte's forecast was a very accurate prediction of exactly what happened, and it helped establish the framework for today's thinking about the Internet.

This early economic and technological convergence in the media industries is the most important reason for the development of today's digital media. At the end of the 20th

IMPACT

» Audience

'Omg My Mom Joined Facebook!!'

by Michelle Slatalla

. . . . Last week I joined Facebook, the social network for students that opened its doors last fall to anyone with an e-mail address. The decision not only doubled its active membership to 24 million (more than 50 percent of whom are not students), but it also made it possible for parents like me to peek at our children in their online lair.

At Facebook.com, I eyed the home page ("Everyone can join") with suspicion. I doubted Facebook's sincerity. . . .

Realizing that these were cynical, mocking thoughts cheered me—I felt edgier already—and gave me the courage to join.

After I got my Profile page, the first thing I did was to search for other members—my daughter and her friends—to ask them to be my friends.

Shockingly, quite a few of them—the friends, not the daughter—accepted my invitation and gave me access to their Profiles, including their interests, hobbies, school affiliations and in some cases, physical whereabouts.

Meanwhile, my Profile had News Feed to inform me of every development:

Michelle and Paige Ogden are now friends.
Michelle is out for a run.
Michelle and Jesse Bendit are now friends.

Social networking Web site Facebook has become a popular online meeting place for teenagers, but Michelle Slatalla found some resistance when she tried to join her daughter's Facebook community.

Leon Neal/AFP/Getty Images

Michelle is home. No word from my daughter, though . . .

I invited my friends—my actual friends—to join Facebook. Some did. I sent a "poke" to one to say hello. I wrote on another's "wall." I tagged a photo to make it appear on my friend Tina's Profile. In gratitude, she "poked" me.

Things were going really well, when suddenly something disturbing happened. An instant-message window appeared onscreen to deliver a verdict.

"wayyy creepy," it said. "why did you make one!"

Ah, there she was.

"What are you talking about?" I typed innocently.

"im only telling you for your own good," my daughter typed.

"Be my friend," I typed.

"You won't get away with this," she typed. "everyone in the whole world thinks its super creepy when adults have facebooks."

"Have facebooks? Is that what you think a Profile page is called?" I typed.

She disconnected.

Feeling as if I had achieved a minor victory in the name of parents of teenagers everywhere, I phoned Michael Wesch, an assistant professor of cultural anthropology

(continued)

'Omg My Mom Joined Facebook!!' *(continued)*

at Kansas State University whose research focuses on social networks, to offer him some real-life data to work with.

But although he didn't go so far as to say he disapproved of my parenting skills, Professor Wesch reminded me that what Facebook's younger users really are doing is exploring their identities, which they may not want to parade in front of their parents.

"Can't I explore my identity, too?" I asked. "Why does everything fun have to be for them?"

He pointed out that there are a number of other social networks—sober, grown-up places like Linkedin.com (for making business contacts) and Care2.com (for social activists) and Webbiographies.com (for amateur genealogists)—where I could cavort without offending my daughter.

"There is a really good social network for older people, too," Professor Wesch said. "It caters to the older generation with an automatic feed of news that relates to older generations and a number of features tailored to the way people in that generation would interact."

"What's it called?" I asked.

"I can't remember the name of it," he said.

"Exactly," I said. "I'm staying where it's fun. . . ."

In 1978, Nicholas Negroponte, of the Massachusetts Institute of Technology's Media Lab, popularized the concept of convergence. Today, Negroponte is promoting the concept of a $100 laptop, shown here at the World Economic Forum.

century, every media industry was equally well positioned to take advantage of new developments, and every media industry benefited from convergence.

20th-Century Discoveries Made Internet Possible

Several technological developments were necessary for people to be able to share text, graphics, audio and video online. These developments made the creation of the World Wide Web possible. The person most responsible for the World Wide Web is Tim Berners-Lee, a British native with an Oxford degree in physics. (See **Impact/People**, "Web Inventor Tim Berners-Lee Announces Worldwide Initiative to Expand the Internet's Benefits to Developing Nations," page 191.) Working in 1989, in Geneva, Switzerland, at the CERN physics laboratory, Berners-Lee created several new programming languages.

IMPACT
»People

Web Inventor Tim Berners-Lee Announces Worldwide Initiative to Expand the Internet's Benefits to Developing Nations

On September 14, 2008, Tim Berners-Lee, the person most responsible for inventing today's World Wide Web, announced the creation of the World Wide Web Foundation to promote and expand access to the Web's constructive benefits throughout the world.

"When you think about how the Web is today and dream about how it might be, you must, as always, consider both technology and people," says Berners-Lee. "Future technology should be smarter and more powerful, of course. But you cannot ethically turn your attention to developing it without also listening to those people who don't use the Web at all, or who could use it if only it were different in some way. The Web has been largely designed by the developed world for the developed world. But it must be much more inclusive in order to be of great value to us all."

Berners-Lee, 54, has continued to be involved in expansion of the Web since he introduced the concept to the

Diego Tuson/AFP/Getty Images

British computer scientist Tim Berners-Lee invented the World Wide Web and gave the Web its name. In 2008, Lee launched the World Wide Web Foundation to expand use of the Internet to developing countries.

world in the early 1990s. He currently serves as Director of the World Wide Web Consortium at the Massachusetts Institute of Technology (MIT) and also as Professor of Computer Science at the University of Southampton.

Berners-Lee announced that the new foundation will have three goals: 1) to advance a free and open Web; 2) to expand the Web's capability and robustness; and 3) to extend the Web's benefits to all people on the planet. "Our success will be measured by how well we foster the creativity of our children," he says. "Whether future scientists will have the tools to cure diseases. Whether people, in developed and developing economies alike, can distinguish reliable healthcare information from commercial chaff. Whether the next generation will build systems that support democracy, inform the electorate, and promote accountable debate."

One of these new computer-programming languages was **HTML** (hypertext markup language). Hypertext transfer protocol (**HTTP**) allowed people to create and send text, graphics and video information electronically and also to set up electronic connections (called **links**) from one source of information to another. These developments were very important in the Web's early days, and today, just a few years later, people can create their own Web pages without knowing the programming language that made the Web possible.

After he invented the language and mechanisms that would allow people to share all kinds of information electronically, Berners-Lee gave this invention its name—the World Wide Web. "The original goal was working together with others," says Berners-Lee. "The Web was supposed to be a creative tool, an expressive tool."

Berners-Lee also created the first **browser**, which allows people to search electronically among many documents to find what they want.

Marc Andreessen and his colleagues at the University of Illinois further defined the browser, and in 1994 they introduced software called Mosaic, which allowed people to put text and pictures in the same online document. Two of the successors to Mosaic are Mozilla Firefox and Internet Explorer, among the most widely used commercial browsers.

Another level of help for Web access is the **search engine**. This is a tool used to locate information in a computer database. Two familiar search engines are Google and Yahoo! These systems turn your typed request for information into digital bits that then go and search for what you want and return the information to you. Yahoo!, founded in 1995 as a search engine company, today makes money through subscriptions, advertising and classified ads and employs more than 8,000 people around the world. Google celebrated its tenth anniversary in 2008, with 20,000

employees. Google, launched by entrepreneurs Larry Page and Sergey Brin in 1998 with four computers and $100,000, is now worth $150 billion.

To encourage people to use their systems, both Berners-Lee and Andreessen placed their discoveries in the **public domain**, which meant that anyone with a computer and a modem could download them from the Internet and use them for free. *This culture of free information access, coupled with a creative, chaotic lack of direction, still permeates the Web today.*

The process of putting documents on the Web drew its terminology from print, the original mass medium. That's why placing something on the Web is called **publishing** and begins with a **home page**, the front door to the site—the place that welcomes the user and explains how the site works. However, even though Web sites are similar to published documents in the way they work, what is created on the Web has few of the legal limitations or protections placed on other published documents. (See **Chapter 14**.)

Web Opens to Unlimited Access

Once Tim Berners-Lee had created the tools for access so that all types of text and video images could become available on the Web, it was left to anyone who could use the tools to create whatever they wanted and make it available to anyone who wanted it.

"Nobody ever designed the Web," says Canadian sociologist Craig McKie, who maintains his own Web site. "There are no rules, no laws. The Web also exists without national boundaries." Any type of information—video, audio, graphics and text—can travel virtually instantly to and from anyone with a computer and access to the Internet anywhere in the world.

Universal access, limited only by the available technology, is what gives the Web the feeling and look of what has been called "anarchy"—a place without rules. The Web is a new medium, but its growth as a true *mass medium* for a majority of people seeking information and entertainment is limited only by digital technology and economics. The large media companies have huge amounts of money available to bankroll new technologies. These companies also have a shared interest in seeing their investments succeed. So convergence is continuing at a very rapid pace, which is the main reason new digital media products are being introduced so quickly.

As digital media products flood the marketplace, some succeed, and many do not. However, the potential reward if consumers adopt a digital media product is so large that all types of media companies are willing to take the risks associated with developing new products. For consumers,

HTML Hypertext markup language.

HTTP Hypertext transfer protocol.

Links Electronic connections from one source of information to another.

Browser Software that allows people to display and interact with information on Web pages.

Search Engine The tool used to locate information in a computer database.

Public Domain Publications, products and processes that are not protected by copyright and thus are available free to the public.

Publishing Placing items on the Web.

Home Page The first page of a Web site that welcomes the user.

this means a confusing array of product choices bombarding the marketplace as each company launches new products, such as *MySpace* and *Facebook* (see **Impact/Audience**, "'Omg My Mom Joined Facebook!!,'" page 189). Media and computer entrepreneurs try to capitalize on fast-moving developments to be the first to deliver new creative products that large numbers of people want to use.

There are many parallels between the development of the Internet and the early history of traditional media, such as movies. Like traditional media, today's emerging technologies are being used to try to create a new popular product the public craves that will result in new consumer uses.

In the early 1900s, when movies first were introduced as flickering images on a small screen, the moving images were something consumers hadn't seen before, but many people thought the silent movies were just a passing fad (see **Chapter 7**). The inventions Thomas Edison and his colleagues introduced at the time made the movies technologically possible, but the movies also needed creative minds like director D. W. Griffith and stars like Mary Pickford to create epic stories that people wanted to see. When new inventions brought sound to the movies, the success of the new medium was unstoppable.

This combination of technological development, creative expression and consumer demand was crucial for the movies' enduring prosperity. The same collision of economics, technology and creativity that drove the early days of the movie industry is behind today's race to develop digital media.

Harley Schwadron/Reprinted by permission of CartoonStock.

What Happens to Old Media?

How will the development of digital media affect older, traditional media? Some observers have predicted, for example, that print media are dead, yet book sales continue to be steady. The history of the evolution of media shows that the introduction of a new medium or a new delivery system does not mean the end of the old. The continuing overall growth and expansion of the media industries during the 20th century support this conclusion.

When television was introduced, for example, radio did not disappear. Instead, radio adapted to its new place in the media mix, delivering music, news and talk. Today, radio exists very comfortably alongside television. Movies, which also were threatened by the introduction of television, responded by delivering more spectacular and more explicit entertainment than people could see on television, and today movies still play an important role in the business of media.

"When newer forms of communication media emerge, the older forms usually do not die—they continue to evolve and adapt," says Roger Fidler. The different media compete for the public's attention and jockey for positions of dominance, but no medium disappears. Instead, each medium contributes to the development of its successors. Together, all media that now exist will contribute to media forms that are yet to be invented.

Transformation Takes 30 Years

Just how quickly consumers adopt new technologies is predictable, according to Paul Saffo, director of the Institute for the Future in Menlo Park, California. Saffo theorizes that for the past five centuries the pace of change has always been 30 years, or about three decades, from the introduction of a new technology to its complete adoption by the culture. (See **Impact/Culture**, "Paul Saffo Talks About Today's Media Revolution," page 194.)

Saffo calls his theory the ***30-year rule***, which he has divided into three stages, and each stage lasts about 10 years. In the first stage, he says, there is "lots of excitement, lots of puzzlement, not a lot of penetration." In the second stage, there is "lots of flux, penetration of the product into society is beginning." In the third stage, the reaction to the technology

30-Year Rule Developed by Paul Saffo, the theory that says it takes about 30 years for a new technology to be completely adopted within a culture.

IMPACT
» Culture

Paul Saffo Talks About Today's Media Revolution

Note: In these excerpts from an interview with futurist Paul Saffo, conducted by the San Francisco Chronicle in 2006, Saffo gave his perspective on the effect of technology on culture. Saffo has since left the Institute for the Future and now works as a private consultant.

Paul Saffo gets paid to look ahead at the trends, technologies and companies of Silicon Valley. But please don't call him a futurist.

In a wide-ranging interview, Saffo, who works with the Institute for the Future in Menlo Park, described himself as a "professional bystander" who uses the history of technology to forecast what may lie ahead.

Q: You've written that "Information Age" is "a profoundly wrongheaded description" of our times. What would be a better phrase?

Paul Saffo, former director of the Institute for the Future, developed the 30-year rule, which says that new technology takes about 30 years to be completely adopted within a culture.

A: It's not information. It's media. . . . It really is a media revolution and I think the closest parallel is what happened in the 1950s with the rise of television. The arrival of television established a mass media order that dominated the last 50 years. This is a personal media revolution. The distinction between the old order and the new order is very important.

Television delivered the world to our living room. In the old media, all we could do was press our noses against the glass and watch. This new world of personal media—the

is, "Oh, so what? Just a standard technology and everybody has it." By Saffo's standard, American society is beginning the third stage of acceptance of online technology because use of the Internet by consumers began in 1988, when less than one-half of 1 percent of the U.S. population was on the Internet. Today, 73 percent of the U.S. population is online. (See **Illustration 9.2** on page 196.)

Saffo's description of the third decade of acceptance coincides with the adaptability of today's media marketplace. New media is more familiar and people seem better able to incorporate combinations of new and existing media technology into their lives. The technological transformation is starting to stabilize.

E-mail Mail that is delivered electronically over the Internet.

Web Access Leaves Some People Behind

The initial sign of the expansion of the Internet to consumer and educational users in the first decade of change—the early 1990s—was the adoption by businesses and private users of electronic mail, or ***e-mail***, technology. With a computer, a modem and a telephone line, just about anyone could learn how to communicate electronically online.

"The driving force for achieving large subscriber gains is the incorporation of the Internet by consumers as part of their routine," according to Veronis Suhler Stevenson, a media research company. "The Internet has become a tool that allows users to economize on what has become their scarcest resource—time. Virtually all of the leading Internet applications allow users to accomplish tasks more quickly than they can through alternative means."

Web, the Internet and et cetera—not only delivers the world to your living rooms, but everywhere. And we get to answer back. And we're expected to answer back. . . .

Q: How does the speed of information and the way we obtain information impact our culture and politics?

A: As a global society we are performing a great experiment on ourselves. Half of the world population wants to race faster into the future. Go visit China and India. They're ready to go. And half of the world wants to drag us into the past. The problem is both sides have guns. I think there really is a reaction. A lot of people are saying enough is enough.

Q: Is information-sharing a force for peace or a force for conflict, or does it matter?

A: No. More information and more communications foster world peace and understanding. But connecting extremist nut cases together on the Web—whatever flavor extremism they are—is a really bad thing. More information may not be a good thing, either. As recently as the '70s, people were forced to see information that they didn't agree with in newspapers and the like. Now there is so much information you really can build your own walled garden that just has the stuff that reinforces your view.

Q: What else does technology force us to rethink?

A: Digital technology is the solvent leaching the glue out of all of our traditional institutions.

Q: Are we in control of technology or is technology in control of us?

A: So far, at least, the technology is not autonomous to be in charge. That will be the worry for people 20 to 40 years from now. It is people who are in control. The main lesson is that we invent our technologies and then we turn around and use our technologies to reinvent ourselves as individuals, communities and cultures. We're right in the middle of that now.

Take cyberspace as an example. We had this wonderful utopian vision of a new home for the mind. What we've reaped isn't cyberspace. It's cyberbia. It's this vast, bland wasteland of vulgar people and trivial ideas and pictures of half-naked starlets. But despite all the uncertainty, has there ever been a more fascinating moment to be alive?

Excerpted from "On the Record: Paul Saffo," *San Francisco Chronicle*, February 19, 2006, page J-1. Reprinted by permission.

E-mail at school, work or home still is the way most people first experience communicating in an electronic environment. Just as telephone answering machines in the 1970s changed voice communication by allowing people to send and receive messages on their own time schedule, e-mail allows people to communicate and receive information at their convenience.

E-mail is easy to use, and it is a text-based system, which means that people type in messages on a keyboard, a familiar tool. Familiarity and convenience are very important in the adoption of new technologies because people's fear of something they don't understand and misunderstandings about how new technologies work can keep them from changing their established habits.

About 27 percent of all Americans still do not go online— either because they can't afford it or they're afraid of it or they don't have access. This gap between people who have online access and those who do not is called the ***digital divide***.

According to the Pew Internet and American Life Project, one out of five American adults say they have never used the Internet or e-mail and do not live in an Internet-connected household (see **Illustration 9.2** on page 196).

Pew calls these people "truly disconnected adults"— people with less than a high school education, or who are over 65, or who live in a rural area. "Americans who are over the age of 65 or who have less education are the most likely to be completely disconnected from the Internet," says Susannah Fox, associate director of the Pew Internet Project. "If they needed to get information from a Web site or other online source, they probably could not easily do so."

Digital Divide The term used to describe the lack of access to digital technology among low-income, rural and minority groups.

Illustration 9.2

Who Uses the Internet?

Internet use in the United States is growing among most Americans, but people over 65 and people with less than a high school education are less likely to have online access. This division between people who have access to the Internet and people who don't is called the *digital divide*.

Source: Pew Internet & American Life Project, April 8–May 11, 2008 Tracking Survey.

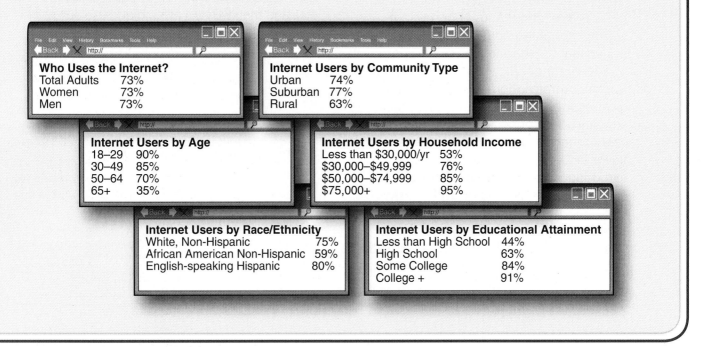

Who Uses the Internet?	
Total Adults	73%
Women	73%
Men	73%

Internet Users by Community Type	
Urban	74%
Suburban	77%
Rural	63%

Internet Users by Age	
18–29	90%
30–49	85%
50–64	70%
65+	35%

Internet Users by Household Income	
Less than $30,000/yr	53%
$30,000–$49,999	76%
$50,000–$74,999	85%
$75,000+	95%

Internet Users by Race/Ethnicity	
White, Non-Hispanic	75%
African American Non-Hispanic	59%
English-speaking Hispanic	80%

Internet Users by Educational Attainment	
Less than High School	44%
High School	63%
Some College	84%
College +	91%

Internet Combines Commerce, Information and Entertainment

What makes the Web as a mass medium different from traditional media is its capacity to combine commerce with access to information and entertainment. People not only can buy products on the Web; they can learn new things and enjoy themselves.

Most people pay an Internet service provider (**ISP**) such as America Online, Comcast or MSN to organize and deliver online information and entertainment. Today, this is the largest single source of Web income—the money people pay their ISP to stay connected to the Web. Besides the money people pay their ISP for online access, there are three potential sources of income on the Web: promoting commerce (connecting sellers with potential buyers), accepting advertising and providing online content.

Promoting Commerce

"Millions of Internet users are forsaking yard sales and the local dump for the prospect of selling their hand-me-downs and unwanted gear online," according to a 2005 report by the Pew Internet and American Life Project. "About one in six Internet-using adults have sold something online." This

ISP Internet service provider.

recent success of the Internet as a way for individuals to sell things is only one example of how people have begun to use the Internet's potential as a marketplace.

One of the most resilient commercial Internet operations is *Amazon.com*. Amazon.com began as a place where people could buy media products such as books, CDs and DVDs, but today consumers also can shop on Amazon.com for a variety of other items—clothes, cosmetics and sports equipment, for example—often at discount prices from individuals as well as large retailers, such as Target. Amazon.com has grown into an Internet department store.

Small retailers and even individual consumers also can use the Web to sell products directly, without setting up a store or spending a lot of money on expensive advertising. Another Internet commerce success story is *eBay*, a Web site that began about 25 years ago as a place where individual sellers offered products—mostly collectibles—in an online auction atmosphere.

Today, eBay is a vast marketplace where individuals sell collectibles, but eBay also promotes direct consumer-to-consumer sales for products as varied as automobiles, houses, even used jeans. Most individual sellers on the site do not have retail stores. Their only outlet is eBay, yet the Internet gives eBay sellers access to buyers all over the world.

Convenience, reliability and affordability sustain both these Web sites as successful commercial ventures—two examples of new businesses that could not survive without the Internet. "On the Internet, consumers looking for a particular product or service can shop over the entire country—the entire world—looking at photographs and comparing prices, features and terms, and then buy what they want with a credit card and arrange to have the purchase delivered to their home," says *Los Angeles Times* media critic David Shaw.

Accepting Advertising

When television was introduced to the public in the late 1940s, people assumed from the beginning that it would be a commercial medium—that is, advertisers who bought the commercials surrounding the programs would pay for the programming. This concept of using advertising to underwrite TV programs was a natural evolution from radio, where commercials also paid for the programming.

Advertisers follow the audience, so as consumers migrated to the Web, advertisers have tried to figure out how to follow them. Advertising is the second potential source of income on the Web. (See **Illustration 9.3**.)

Most commercial Web sites now carry some form of advertising. These appear as banners across the top of the Web site or run as borders alongside the site's pages. But just like traditional media, advertising can crowd out the original message and turn away consumers, and entrepreneurs continue to test the market to develop a Web site

advertising structure and design that eventually will help pay the bills.

Because the Web is such a targeted medium—the seller can know exactly who the buyer is—the Web holds better potential for monitoring consumers' buying habits than traditional methods of advertising. Ultimately, Web advertisers hope to "achieve the merchandiser's dream—targeting an audience far more precisely than it can with either newspapers or television by advertising a product only on sites that draw people likely to be interested in that product," says media critic David Shaw, with "nearly instantaneous electronic feedback on whether their ads are effective: How many people saw the ad? How many 'clicked' on it and went on to a more detailed presentation? How many bought the product right then, online?"

Internet "tracking" offers advertisers information about the audiences for their ads. Many sites give advertisers information about how many "hits" the sites receive—how many times people look at the site and how much time they spend. This information-gathering is so sophisticated that the data can even show an advertiser which specific user bought which specific products that were advertised on a specific site.

Companies also have developed "ad robots" that allow a business to, in effect, eavesdrop on chat room conversations while the user is online. If someone mentions a car problem online, for example, the robot recognizes the pattern of words in the discussion and sends the person an ad for car repair.

Always looking for new ways to target specific audiences, advertising agencies now offer services for ***search marketing***, which means placing client ads next to consumers' online search results so that when someone starts a search for SUVs, for example, the SUV car manufacturer's ad immediately appears on the screen next to the user's search results. Appearing within the SUV ad, of course, is a link to a Web site where the user can customize and order a car. By connecting consumers directly to advertisers, search marketers say, they can better trace and document the connection between Internet ads and their audiences, something many advertisers are demanding before they invest in the Internet audience.

Ad robots and search marketing are just two examples of the refined tools advertisers are developing so they can more accurately track and target the Internet consumer.

Paying for Online Content

The culture of the Web began with the idea that content on the Web would be free, so it has taken a long time for

Search Marketing Positioning Internet advertising prominently next to consumers' related online search results.

IMPACT
»Business

Illustration 9.3

How Much Do Businesses Spend Annually to Advertise on the Internet? (in billions)

Since 2000, advertisers have been racing to reach consumers by advertising products and services on the Internet.

Source: Internet Advertising Bureau, www.iab.net.

consumers to embrace the idea that they should pay for media content on the Web.

Slate, the online literary magazine, tried to start charging subscribers in 1997, but then decided against it. Editor Michael Kinsley said, "It would be better to establish a brand name with wide readership first." *Slate* celebrated its tenth anniversary in 2005, and still does not charge subscribers.

Some explicit Web sites charge for access, and some news and information sites, such as *The Wall Street Journal*, charge subscribers an annual fee for access to archived online content older than seven days—beyond what's available free on the main *Journal* news site. Other sites, such as the sports network *ESPN.com*, give away certain information and then charge for "premium" services. Internet game-makers, who offer video games on the Web, charge by the hour or use a tiered pricing structure—free, basic and premium.

In 2003, consumers showed they were willing to pay for music downloads when Apple founder Steve Jobs introduced iTunes, a music service for subscribers that allows people to download popular songs for a fee. Less than a year after its launch, iTunes celebrated its one-billionth music download.

Mobile Media Chase the Audience

Internet receivers have grown smaller and smaller, and the latest big target for expanding Internet media use is the cell phone. Much like radio broadcasters who followed radio listeners from their homes into their cars when car radios were invented, Web sites are chasing today's consumers right to their cell phones.

The nation's millions of cell phone users make mobile media consumers an inviting target. Consumers use cell phones to send text messages, take pictures, listen to music and download video. This makes cell phones and other mobile media attractive media markets. (See **Illustration 9.4** on page 200.)

Mobile media content has restrictions—content must be audible and/or clearly visible in the small viewing space a cell phone screen provides. News and sports bulletins, short video clips, podcasts, blogs and personalized Web pages—are perfectly suited for this media environment. "Advances in high-speed data networks, along with powerful new cell phones, are unlocking the promise of mobile television," reports the *San Francisco Chronicle*. Subscription video services charge customers a fee and offer stored content such as one-minute soap operas and animated cartoons.

In 2006, Rupert Murdoch's News Corporation created a mobile entertainment store devoted exclusively to developing cell phone content. All four of the major networks now offer most of their television entertainment programs and news video online, on demand, for computer and cell phone viewing.

Podcasts

Podcasting is the distribution of an audio or video file by online syndication, usually by subscription. With very little equipment, people can create and syndicate their own *podcasts*. Many news organizations, such as PBS and *The New York Times*, have added podcasts to their Web sites as a way to expand their offerings.

A podcast often enhances and expands discussion on a topic. There also are podcast networks that feature several shows on the same feed, similar to a radio station. Consumers can download podcasts and listen to them whenever and wherever they want, which also makes podcasts an ideal way to reach a mobile audience.

Blogs

By one estimate, there are 80,000 new blog sites launched daily, and there are 29 million blog sites tracked by the blog search engine *Technorati*. A *blog* (short for Web log) is an online discussion group where people can post comments about a topic in a running conversation with each other.

The text of the blog runs in reverse chronological order, with the most recent comments posted at the top of the blog so people can choose to read through the previous postings for background on the topic, or they can start reading what follows after they join the group. Typically blogs do not carry advertising and are created as a way to enhance other content on the Web.

Blogs also have become frequent sources of information for news organizations seeking public reaction to ongoing events. The 2004 presidential election was the first time bloggers actually were accredited as part of the presidential press corps, indicating the importance of the bloggers' role as commentators on topical issues.

Personalized Web Pages

While businesses and tech-savvy Internet users can easily create Web sites, new technology now allows neophytes to create personal Web sites, using prepackaged programs, in less than five minutes. MySpace and Facebook, currently the most successful personal Web site spaces, are aimed primarily at teens and young adults who want to join a social network.

Using click technology, users can create an *avatar*, an online personality complete with a "look" that personalizes the page, and create a short blog to post personal messages. Avatar images fit perfectly on a cell phone screen to accompany a teen's short diary-style postings about daily life. The ad-supported sites also offer custom features, such as music downloads and games. (See **Impact/Audience**, "At ESPN, Play-by-Play Goes Virtual," page 201.)

Until recently, MySpace also was a teen meeting place that few parents knew about. Then two events alerted parents to the vulnerability of people who post personal information on the Web. On February 23, 2006, police arrested a 16-year-old Denver boy who allegedly posted pictures on MySpace showing him holding handguns, which is illegal. Five days later, a man in Bakersfield, California, agreed to a plea bargain after he was arrested for seducing two girls, 13 and 14, that he'd met through MySpace. Still, MySpace and Facebook continue their growing popularity as teen meeting places.

Don Emmet/AFP/Getty Images

On June 29, 2007, a man celebrates as he leaves the Apple store in New York with two long-awaited iPhones, a product dedicated to an increasingly mobile consumer.

Podcast An audio or video file made available on the Internet for anyone to download, often available by subscription.

Blog Short for Web log. A running Internet discussion group, where items are posted in reverse chronological order. Blogs usually focus on a specific topic.

Avatar An icon or a representation of a user—a digital stand-in that people create to represent their online identity.

>> IMPACT
Audience

Illustration 9.4

How Do People Use Mobile Media?

Consumer use of mobile media is the fastest-growing area of media use. People most often use mobile devices, such as a cell phone or personal data assistant (PDA), to send text messages and take pictures, although an increasing number of consumers use mobile media to play games and listen to music.

Source: Pew Internet and American Life Project Survey, December 2007.

On a Typical Day . . .

- **31%** Send or Receive Text Messages
- **15%** Take a Picture
- **8%** Play a Game
- **8%** Send or Receive E-mail
- **7%** Access the Internet for News, Sports or Other Information
- **7%** Play Music
- **6%** Send or Receive Instant Messages
- **3%** Record a Video
- **3%** Get a Map or Directions to Another Location
- **3%** Watch a Video

Podcasts, blogs and personal Web sites are the latest ways the media business is working to expand its audience. It's important to remember that, in the history of the media business, advertisers always have followed the audience. To be successful, Internet providers know they must attract consumers to be able to capitalize on the advertising potential the audience brings with it.

Government Attempts to Coordinate and Control the Net

The federal government has attempted to coordinate and regulate the Internet in the same way government tradi-

tionally coordinated and regulated the broadcast media in its early days. However, the U.S. government has learned the hard way that it can exercise only limited control over the Internet, especially its content.

In 1994, in its first attempt to coordinate the growing presence of the Internet, the U.S. Congress named the effort to coordinate the nation's various senders, channels and receivers in the United States, the National Information Infrastructure (**NII**). This congressional intervention in the structure of the Internet was based on the history of radio and TV in the United States, which the government had regulated since the 1920s.

Three principles guided the creation of the nation's telecommunications structure, Congress said:

1. Private industry, not the government, would build the digital network.

2. Programmers and information providers would be guaranteed access to the digital network to promote a diversity of consumer choices.

NII National Information Infrastructure.

IMPACT
»Audience

At ESPN, Play-by-Play Goes Virtual

by Brooks Barnes

LOS ANGELES—ESPN, the cable powerhouse that calls itself "Worldwide Leader in Sports," is looking to extend its domain in virtual worlds by merging video game graphics with real-life sports anchors.

The network, which is owned by the Walt Disney Company, has spent the last year working on a new technology with Electronic Arts, the leading game publisher, that would allow ESPN commentators to interact live with realistic-looking, three-dimensional virtual players as they pontificate about coming matches during broadcasts.

"It's a way for us to remain relevant," said John Skipper, ESPN's executive vice president for content. "We want to make sure we remain connected to lots and lots of fans, and using the language that gamers understand is one way."

Boiled down, the complex technology, which will make its debut . . . on ESPN's popular "NFL Countdown" program, involves using an Electronic Arts' title—say Madden NFL 09—with specialized digital camera equipment in the studio. Presto: Both real and virtual people move around the ESPN set to demonstrate plays and possible situations.

And the sports behemoth has more ambitious plans down the road. Instead of using the technology, called EA Sports Virtual Playbook, to tell viewers what to look for before games, ESPN wants to use it in reverse to play the ultimate Monday morning quarterback.

Using real information from a game, ESPN anchors could reprogram an actual sequence to show, for example, what would have happened had Peyton Manning thrown right instead of left.

In 2008, ESPN began using interactive virtual players, which allows real and virtual people to move within the ESPN set to demonstrate plays and game possibilities. Football commentator Merril Hoge stands before a screen to demonstrate how the virtual football world works.

Much is made about how various forms of media—television, the Internet, radio—are all moving toward one another. And while television content has converged into video games, Virtual Playbook offers an example of convergence moving in the opposite direction. ESPN is bringing the look and feel of a video game to television for the sake of interactivity, flexibility and visual aid.

Television and movie executives have struggled for years to attract young consumers who play video games to more traditional forms of entertainment. At the same time, ESPN is on a mission to tap new areas of growth as it faces challenges in its core operations.

ESPN, three decades old, remains one of the media industry's biggest gold mines, with successful magazine and Internet

(continued)

IMPACT
»Audience

At ESPN, Play-by-Play Goes Virtual (continued)

operations to complement its suite of cable channels. Analysts estimate that ESPN represents about a quarter of Disney's annual operating income. . . .

"If ESPN wants to gain more exposure to the gamer audience, this seems like a smart way to go about it," said Michael Dowling,

the chief executive of Interpret, a new media consultancy based in Santa Monica, Calif. "It adds an element of coolness and realism that gamers really want."

"At ESPN, Play-by-Play Goes Virtual," by Brooks Barnes, *The New York Times,* September 5, 2008. Copyright © 2008 New York Times. All rights reserved. Reprinted by permission.

---

3. Steps would be taken to ensure universal service so that the digital network did not result in a society of information "haves" and "have-nots."

Then two years later, in its first attempt to control Internet content, Congress passed the Telecommunications Act of 1996. Included in that legislation was the Communications Decency Act (**CDA**), which outlined content that would be forbidden on the Internet. As soon as the act passed, civil liberties organizations challenged the law, and in 1997 the U.S. Supreme Court upheld the concept that the U.S. government could not control Internet content. (For more information about Congress and the U.S. Supreme Court's view of the Internet, see **Chapter 14**.)

Intellectual Property Rights Seek Protection

Money is the main reason the government wants to supervise the development of the Internet. Digitized bits, once they are widely available, can be easily stolen and reproduced for profit, which can means billions of dollars in lost revenue for the companies and individuals who produce

media content. Writers, moviemakers, singers and other creative people who provide the content for the media industries are especially concerned about their ideas being reproduced in several different formats, with no compensation for their property.

This issue, the protection of what are called ***intellectual property rights***, is a crucial part of the U.S. government's interest in the design of the Internet as a communications network. To protect online content, the various copyright holders have used court challenges to establish their legal ownership, but some groups still are trying to avoid detection by keeping their online activities hidden from government scrutiny.

With access to copyrighted digital content, someone could capture video from a Disney movie sent over the Internet and join sections of that video with comedy bits from an episode of *Saturday Night Live*, putting the two casts together in a newly digitized program, for example. Once this content is captured and stored, this content would be available to anyone who wants to use it.

The protection of content is one of the dilemmas created by digitized files that can be transmitted to anyone's storage system over an international network. The creative people who contribute this content, and the people who produce and own these programs, want laws and regulations structured to protect intellectual property rights.

Court Challenges

The issue of who owns copyrighted material that already exists, such as recordings and movies, is particularly tricky on a medium like the Internet with few controls and global access. In 1998, Congress passed the Digital Millennium

CDA Communications Decency Act.

Intellectual Property Rights Ownership of ideas and content published on the Web or in any other medium.

DMCA Digital Millennium Copyright Act.

Copyright Act (**DMCA**) to make it illegal to share copyrighted material on the Internet. (For more information about the DMCA, see **Chapter 14**.) Using this law and provisions of existing copyright law, industries with a big stake in content ownership have sued to stop people from sharing copyrighted content on the Internet.

The Recording Industry Association of America (**RIAA**) and the Motion Picture Association of America (**MPAA**) have been especially aggressive in seeking to prosecute people who take copyrighted content and make it available on the Web. In 1999, RIAA sued Napster, a company that provided a music-swapping service on the Internet. In 2001, after several appeals, the courts found that Napster was liable for "vicarious copyright infringement." Napster eventually shut down and then reopened as a subscription music service that pays royalties to companies that own rights to music available on the site.

MP3 technology allows users to convert songs on their CDs to MP3 files, which can be circulated freely on the Internet. The Web site MP3.com began as an underground movement in San Diego in 1999 among college students and spread fiercely. The major recording companies quickly began an all-out assault on MP3.com, suing for copyright infringement, and in November 2000, in a series of settlements, MP3.com agreed to pay more than $70 million in damages to the recording companies for the rights to license their music.

In 2001, the MPAA sued to stop publication of the code that allows a person to copy DVDs and place digital copies of the movies on the Internet. The court agreed with the MPAA, saying that even if people possess the code but don't use it, they are committing piracy. This was an important legal precedent for content sharing on the Web and has led to more corporate attempts to seek wider protections over copyrighted content.

In 2003, Apple launched iTunes, a service that charges a fee to download songs legally. iTunes was created to respond to the various court actions since 1999 designed to end illegal **file sharing**, which means downloading files placed on the Internet by another person, not necessarily the original copyright holder.

In 2005, the major remaining music-file-sharing network, Grokster, shut down after reaching a settlement with the movie and music industries about online piracy. Grokster replaced its popular Web site with a message that reads: "There are legal services for downloading music and movies. This service is not one of them." (For more information about file sharing, Grokster and iTunes, see **Chapter 14**.)

Creation of Darknets

To try to circumvent the law, groups called **darknets** have formed, given this name because they operate on the Internet outside of public view. Unlike Grokster, which allowed anyone to download digital files, darknet users gain access to these file-sharing communities only through established relationships. A darknet user must be invited to join, which gives the members greater privacy in which to operate, and the site's technology shields the user's identity.

Even though they hope to avoid public scrutiny for sharing copyrighted material, darknets still would face legal battles if copyright holders somehow gained access to the sites, identified any unauthorized file sharing and pursued their claims in court. Darknet supporters say the technology is designed primarily to protect political dissidents in repressive regimes so they can speak out without detection, but this doesn't answer the question about any illegal file sharing that darknets protect.

"Darknets are going to be with us," says J. D. Lasica, author of *Darknet: Hollywood's War Against the Digital Generation*. "Serious file traders have been gravitating toward them. There is just this culture of freedom that people feel they're entitled to, and they don't want anyone looking over their shoulders."

Internet Faces Four Challenges

Today, the Internet has evolved into a wireless delivery system, but the system faces at least four major challenges: free access, storage capacity, compatible delivery and consumer privacy.

Free Access

To protect their subscribers from too much unsolicited e-mail (called **spam**) or to weed out offensive e-mails, many Internet service providers use spam filters—technology that allows the ISP to block messages using software that tags suspicious messages, which the ISP filters before delivering, or stopping, them. Of the 135 billion e-mail messages sent every day in 2005, two-thirds of them were spam, according to Radicati Group, a technology research firm. However, many nonprofit organizations and political groups use bulk e-mail to solicit donations and support.

Like many other Internet service providers, AOL uses spam filters to block unwanted mail, but in 2006 AOL

RIAA Recording Industry Association of America.

MPAA Motion Picture Association of America.

File Sharing The peer-to-peer distribution of copyrighted material on the Internet without the copyright owner's permission.

Darknet A file-sharing service that restricts membership to keep its online activities private.

Spam Unsolicited bulk e-mail.

Data-compression technology reduces the electronic storage space necessary to store full-length movies such as *The Dark Knight*. This makes it possible for consumers to download first-run original movies for viewing online.

announced that it would start offering a service that would allow bulk e-mailers to send e-mail directly to users' mailbox without passing through AOL's spam filters. AOL said bulk e-mailers who paid the fee would receive a label alerting recipients that the messages were legitimate. Immediately, several interest groups—including the conservative activist group *RightMarch.com*, the liberal activist group *MoveOn.org* and the U.S. Humane Society—joined an alliance to fight the fee, calling it a tax on free expression and free access.

"We cannot pay for the service; we don't have the money," said Gilles Frydman of the Association of Cancer Online Resources. Frydman says some patients with rare forms of cancer could miss receiving important information. AOL's actions—and the response it provoked—demonstrate how commercial interests often compete with personal liberties in the online environment.

In another instance of commercial expediency, online search leader Google agreed in 2006 to censor online search results for its Chinese clients. According to Associated Press, Google was "adhering to the country's free-speech restrictions in return for better access in the Internet's fastest growing market." Google agreed to omit Web content that the government found objectionable.

Yahoo! and MSN previously had agreed to similar restrictions in China. Reporters Without Borders criticized the practice, saying, "When a search engine collaborates with the government like this, it makes it much easier for the Chinese government to control what is being said on the Internet."

Storage Capacity

The main technological advance that makes today's communications network possible is that electronic systems transform text, audio and video communication into the same type of digital information. However, no single consumer system exists to transfer all the text, audio and video information the Internet delivers from so many different sources. Digital systems theoretically should be compatible, but many places in the world and many media systems have not yet totally converted to the technology that efficient digital delivery requires.

For example, digital delivery requires a huge amount of electronic storage space. To try to eliminate the need for so much storage, researchers are developing a process called ***data compression***. A copy of a major movie, such as *The Dark Knight*, contains about 100 billion bytes of data. Compression squeezes the content down to about 4 billion bytes. But the time it takes to download a movie on a personal computer and the electronic storage space movies need still make it impractical for the average consumer.

As soon as researchers perfect data compression, it will mean that a movie program service, for example, will need much less storage space to keep movies available for use on demand. This helps make the movie affordable for a program service to deliver and usable for the customer, who won't need as much data space to view the movie.

Once the data is compressed, the company that delivers the service also must store the data. The next step in the process is a machine that grabs a movie the consumer has selected from a storage area and delivers it to the customer on request. This transfer machine is called a ***server*** because it must be able to serve thousands of programs to millions of subscribers, on demand, all at the same time.

Compatible Delivery

Today's communication system is a mixture of old and new technologies. The current delivery system is a combination of coaxial cable, copper wire, fiber optics and cellular technology. Before the new communications network will be complete, new technology must completely replace old technology throughout the system. Many broadcasters, for example, still send pictures and sounds over airwaves using the same tech-

Data Compression The process of squeezing digital content into a smaller electronic space.

Server The equipment that delivers programs from the program source to the program's subscribers.

nology they have used since the 1930s, when broadcasting was first introduced. This technology is called **analog**.

Analog technology encodes video and audio information as continuous signals. Then these signals are broadcast through the air on specific airwave frequencies to your TV set, which translates them into pictures and sounds. Analog technology is a very cumbersome way to move information from one place to another because the analog signal takes up a lot of space on the airwaves. However, because analog signals travel through the air by transmitters, consumers can receive them free using an antenna.

At least 10 million homes in the United States still receive only over-the-air broadcasts. They do not subscribe to cable or satellite. And although the federal government has mandated that TV stations in large cities digitize their signals by 2009, many smaller stations have not yet made the costly transition to digital.

Cable companies eliminated the need for antennas by using coaxial cable, buried underground or strung from telephone poles. Many coaxial cable systems still use analog technology. Cable operators capture programming, such as HBO, from satellite systems and put these together with analog broadcast signals from your local TV stations and then deliver all this programming to you, using a combination of coaxial cable, copper wire and optical fiber.

Optical fiber is composed of microscopic strands of glass that transmit messages in digitized "bits"—zeroes and ones. Each fiber optic strand can carry 250,000 times as much information as one copper wire. It can transmit the entire contents of the *Encyclopaedia Britannica* in one second. A fiber optics communication system is very efficient because fiber can carry digitized information easily and quickly from one place to another.

Satellite program services use digital signals to carry their programming. Programs that are delivered to a home satellite dish follow a wireless electronic journey from the program source through one of the many telecommunications satellites hovering around the globe. Satellite delivery, however, still requires a telephone line connection to deliver the programs and the menus for the programs to your home receiver.

Telephone companies have converted almost all their major communications delivery systems from coaxial cable and copper wire to fiber optics and cellular technology. However, the incompatibility between analog and digital technology means that all analog signals must be converted first to digital signals to be able to travel smoothly to everyone. Conversion is very expensive.

Digital technology is the most efficient method of delivery, but making the same system available throughout the nation using a standardized delivery system is very complicated, and each competing system wants to control the entire delivery system because control of the delivery system

means billions of dollars in revenue for whichever system consumers eventually adopt.

Personal Privacy

With all these media services and programs available, consumers must be able to use them without compromising their personal privacy. Telephone companies already have in place a fairly complex system that matches people with the phone calls they make and carries conversations on secure lines all over the world. To be effective, security for digital communications on the Internet must be at least as private as telephone communications.

Commercial operations, such as banks and retailers, have developed fairly secure systems for transferring transaction records on the Internet. Internet services such as PayPal offer buyers a way to protect their credit card information from being circulated to sellers by processing the transaction without sharing the consumers' credit card information with the seller.

To protect consumers' banking records, for example, banks use codes to secure the transactions from Internet hackers. Software companies have developed reliable systems to ensure that the personal records and content contained in interactive transactions are safe. An entirely new industry has evolved dedicated to the issue of Internet data security.

In 2006, however, questions erupted about government access to Internet communications. The U.S. Justice Department subpoenaed Google, Inc., asking the company to provide records of millions of its customers' Internet search requests. The government said it needed the records to prove that existing Internet spam filters were not preventing children from accessing online pornography and potentially offensive Web sites.

Yahoo!, MSN and Time Warner already had provided some of the search engine information the government wanted, but Google initially refused, setting the stage for another confrontation pitting the government against at least one Internet service provider. "If users believe that the text of their search queries into Google's search engine may become public knowledge, it only logically follows that they will be less likely to use the service," Google's lawyers argued.

In March 2006, in the first court hearing about the government's request, the government reduced its initial request to just a sampling of 5,000 search queries instead of its earlier request for a week's worth of searches, which would have totaled close to a billion items. The Justice Department also offered to pay Google's costs to provide the data, and eventually Google agreed to provide the 5,000-item search sampling.

Analog In mass communications, a type of technology used in broadcasting, whereby video or audio information is sent as continuous signals through the air on specific airwave frequencies.

The case shows how tempting and accessible digital data can be—for the government agencies and for attorneys. The judge in the Google case said he tried to balance privacy concerns with the government's request for information, but privacy advocates worry that relinquishing private data to companies like Google and Yahoo! erodes citizen confidentiality on the Internet.

"The mere fact that Google has stood up to the government is a positive thing," Aden J. Fine, an American Civil Liberties Union lawyer, told *The New York Times*. "The government cannot simply demand that third parties give information without providing a sufficient justification for why they need it."

Google made these arguments against U.S. government surveillance at the same time the company was being criticized for allowing the Chinese government to censor Google's search engine in China, just one example of the complexity of doing business in a worldwide environment.

New Technologies Mix with Old Ideas

The new communications network requires that everyone have access to digitized technology. Today, broadcasters and cable operators have access to the programming and the services, but many of these companies still use a mixture of old and new technologies. No one yet has created a storage system large enough to store and deliver every service consumers may want on demand.

"We met online."

DSL Digital Subscriber Line.

While businesses have been able to develop secure systems for online data transfer, some government officials have tried to get access to consumers' communications records without the consumers' knowledge, challenging the basic concept of consumer privacy. The rules that are developing to govern the new communications network will have a profound impact on individuals, businesses and the media industries.

For consumers, the Internet already affects many everyday activities—the way people shop, get their news, study, manage their money, even how they socialize with friends. For businesses, national and even global information already is instantly available to more companies simultaneously, making communication much easier, but bringing more intense competition.

For the media industries, the Internet places every element of the media business in transition. Today, owners and managers of the companies that make up the media industries are deciding daily how to invest in equipment, employees, and research and development to protect current income while trying to ensure their companies will be able to adapt to the Internet's new demands.

Since the definition of digital media is so broad, people who hope to get attention and financial support for new products throw around the term very easily. Some digital media inventions succeed, some are transitional products that will help develop new products and many already have failed. Until the digital media landscape is clearer, however, it is important to follow ongoing developments because no one can predict exactly where digital media are headed. Four ongoing technologies to watch are digital subscriber lines, virtual reality avatars, personalized channels and wikis.

Digital Subscriber Line

Today, nearly all the people with Internet access use a digital subscriber line (**DSL**). Available almost everywhere, DSL is more than 50 times faster than a dial-up modem. DSL is always on, which means subscribers don't have to dial their Internet service provider each time they want to use the Web. DSL also delivers audio and video signals much better than a standard telephone line.

Virtual Reality Avatars

In the 1960s, computer flight simulators began to be used to train military pilots. These simulators were predecessors of today's virtual reality (VR) systems. Virtual reality systems give the user the experience of being somewhere by creating a digital representation of reality and then placing a digital representative in that digital reality. In the Internet world, someone's digital representation is called an avatar. The name comes from Hindu mythology, describing a deity who took on human form.

An Internet avatar is simply an icon or a representation of a user—a digital stand-in—that people create to represent their online identity. A horse or a rabbit or a cartoon figure, for example, becomes their representative, their signature. Internet sites such as MySpace encourage users to create avatars—an online persona.

Personalized Channels

RSS technology (which stands for ***Really Simple Syndication***) allows people to select a personal set of Internet programs and services to be delivered to a single Web site location. The user can pull together free automatic feeds from several different Web sites in one place, which eliminates the need to visit each Web site individually. The technology uses an RSS aggregator, or news reader.

To use an RSS service, available from places like News-Gator and Bloglines, a user registers for the service and then chooses from a list of links that connect the user to the desired sites. The aggregator then gathers these links in one place, to be viewed whenever the user wants. RSS aggregators hope to make money from advertising on the RSS site that users see when they go to the site to view the information that's been compiled for them.

Wikis

The term ***wiki*** derives from a Hawaiian word that means fast. This technology allows many users to collaborate to create and update an Internet page. A wiki Web site allows registered users to add and edit content on a specific topic. The best-known wiki is *Wikipedia*, an online encyclopedia where registered contributors may post additions to any entry.

Wiki technology records the original material, plus the material that contributors add over time. Wikis have great potential to gather in one place contributions worldwide from all the specialists on one subject, for example, but there are not any safeguards that the material placed on the site is guaranteed accurate or reliable.

The future of digital media is bound only by the needs of consumers and the imaginations of media developers, as diverse as the people who are online today and going online tomorrow. The new media universe could become a purer reflection of the real universe than any medium yet created, with unprecedented potential, like all mass media, to both reflect and direct the culture.

"The Internet is still in its infancy, and its potential is enormous," writes media critic David Shaw. The Internet, says Shaw, could "revolutionize human communication even more dramatically than Johann Gutenberg's first printing press did more than 500 years ago."

RSS Really Simple Syndication. Allows a person to create a personal set of Internet programs and services to be delivered to a single Web site location.

Wiki Technology that allows many users to collaborate to create and update an Internet page.

Review, Analyze, Investigate
REVIEWING CHAPTER 9

Digital Communication Transforms Media

✓ The emergence of the Internet within the last 30 years has transformed the structure and economics of the U.S. media business.

✓ The Internet today offers people wireless access to information just about wherever and whenever they want it.

✓ The Internet delivers all types of media using a single delivery system.

✓ The Internet is a combination of thousands of computer networks sending and receiving data from all over the world.

✓ In its global size and absence of central control, the Internet is completely different from traditional media.

Digital Media Support Convergence

✓ Nicholas Negroponte at the Massachusetts Institute of Technology was the first person to identify the theory of convergence.

✓ The theory of convergence helped shape today's thinking about the Internet.

✓ Every media industry benefits from convergence.

20th-Century Discoveries Made Internet Possible

✓ The person most responsible for creating the World Wide Web is Tim Berners-Lee, who created the first browser and also gave the World Wide Web its name.

✓ Marc Andreessen at the University of Illinois created Mosaic, which allowed people to put text and pictures in the same online document.

✓ Both Andreessen and Berners-Lee placed their creations in the public domain, which meant that anyone with a computer and a modem could download them free.

✓ A culture of free information access, coupled with a creative, chaotic lack of direction, still permeates the Web today.

Web Opens to Unlimited Access

✓ Universal access, limited only by the available technology, is what gives the Web the feeling and look of what has been called "anarchy"—a place without rules.

✓ Today's media companies have a shared interest in seeing their investments in new technologies succeed.

What Happens to Old Media?

✓ The introduction of a new medium such as the Internet does not mean the end of the old.

✓ Older media forms continue to evolve and adapt to the new media environment.

Transformation Takes 30 Years

✓ Paul Saffo says the pace of change has consistently been about 30 years from the introduction of a new technology to its complete adoption by the culture.

✓ By Saffo's standard—the 30-year rule—American society is beginning to enter the third stage of acceptance, where the majority of the population has adapted to the new technology.

Web Access Leaves Some People Behind

✓ About 20 percent of Americans still do not go online—either because they can't afford it or they're afraid of it or they don't have access.

✓ The gap between people with online access and those who do not is called the *digital divide*.

Internet Combines Commerce, Information and Entertainment

✓ The largest single source of Web income is the money people pay their Internet service provider.

✓ Three other potential sources of income on the Web are promoting commerce, accepting advertising and providing online content.

✓ Most commercial Web sites now carry some form of advertising.

✓ Internet tracking tells advertisers about the audience's behavior.

Mobile Media Chase the Audience

✓ The latest big target for expanding Internet media use is the cell phone.

✓ Podcasts, blogs and personal Web pages are perfectly suited for the mobile media environment.

Government Attempts to Coordinate and Control the Net

✓ The federal government has attempted to coordinate and regulate the Internet, but the U.S. government has limited control over the Internet, especially its content.

✓ In 1994, the U.S. Congress named the effort to coordinate the nation's various senders, channels and receivers the National Information Infrastructure.

✓ In 1997, the U.S. Supreme Court upheld the concept that the U.S. government could not control Internet content.

Intellectual Property Rights Seek Protection

✓ Legal protections for digital content are called *intellectual property rights*.

✓ In 1998, Congress passed the Digital Millennium Copyright Act to make it illegal to share copyrighted material on the Internet.

✓ The Recording Industry Association of America and the Motion Picture Association of America have aggressively pursued copyright infringement.

✓ In 2003, Apple introduced iTunes, which allows people to download music legally.

✓ In 2005, the major remaining free music file-sharing network, Grokster, shut down after reaching a settlement with the movie and music industries about online piracy.

✓ To try to circumvent the law, groups called darknets have formed, operating on the Internet outside of public view.

Internet Faces Four Challenges

✓ Four major challenges facing the Internet are free access, storage capacity, compatible delivery and consumer privacy.

✓ In 2006, AOL announced a service that would allow bulk e-mailers to avoid its spam filters by paying a fee. Claiming the fee would shut them down, an alliance of interest groups formed to fight the fee, calling it a tax on free expression.

✓ In 2006, Google agreed to let the Chinese government censor its online search results for Chinese customers. Yahoo! and MSN previously had agreed to similar restrictions in China.

✓ Researchers are developing a process called data compression, which collapses the size of data files so they are easier to download.

✓ Today's communications system is a mixture of analog and digital technologies.

✓ At least 10 million homes in the United States still receive only over-the-air broadcasts. They do not subscribe to cable or satellite.

✓ In 2006, the U.S. Justice Department subpoenaed online search records from Google, Yahoo!, MSN and Time Warner. Eventually Google agreed only to give the government a small number of Web site addresses from customer searches, temporarily ending a legal battle over the government's right to have access to consumer Internet records.

New Technologies Mix with Old Ideas

✓ For the media industries, the Internet places every element of the media in transition.

✓ Four ongoing technologies that are affecting consumers' use of the Internet are digital subscriber lines, avatars, personalized channels driven by RSS and wikis.

KEY TERMS

These terms are defined in the margins throughout this chapter and appear in alphabetical order with definitions in the Glossary, which begins on page 372.

CRITICAL QUESTIONS

1. Explain the concept of the digital divide as outlined in this chapter. Why does the digital divide exist? List and explain three actions by government, corporations or individuals that would help eliminate the divide.

2. If only a few Web businesses have been commercially successful so far, why do experts predict that the Web has remarkable potential for revenue growth? Be specific.

3. Discuss Tim Berners-Lee's contributions to the development of the World Wide Web. What did he do, specifically? What was his basic philosophy for use of the Web? Do you agree? Why or why not?

4. Discuss some of the advantages of Internet file sharing. What is the core issue? How was it resolved? What is the future of file sharing?

5. Discuss the role of the U.S. government in regulating activity on the Internet, including issues relating to copyright, intellectual property, pornography and children's content. Discuss areas where the government has been both successful and unsuccessful in regulating the Internet.

WORKING THE WEB

This list includes both sites mentioned in the chapter and others to give you greater insight into the Internet.

Apple Computer, Inc.
http://www.apple.com

The main home page of Apple, this site's sections include Apple Store, iPod and iTunes, iPhone, Mac computers and software, Downloads and Support. Apple.com Worldwide allows users to shop internationally from Belgium to Portugal to Taiwan.

CNET
http://www.cnet.com

A CBS Interactive site, CNET provides electronic technology news and reviews and does comparison shopping for products. Its Tips & Tricks section includes more than 1,000 searchable tips with streaming video, online articles, forums and buying guides. Tips are designated by user level: all, beginner, intermediate and advanced.

Electronic Frontier Foundation
http://www.eff.org

This nonprofit organization was created in 1990 to protect digital rights. EFF tackles issues including Free Speech (online anonymity), Innovation (patents) and Transparency (e-voting rights). The site lists legal cases with descriptions, outcomes, related documents, press releases and other resources.

iVillage
http://www.ivillage.com

iVillage Inc., a division of NBC Universal, is the first and largest media company dedicated exclusively to connecting women at every stage of their lives. Content ranges from health, parenting, beauty and style to fitness, relationships, food and entertainment. Interactive features include social networking and message boards that allow women to connect with others and to seek advice and support.

Journal of Electronic Publishing

http://www.journalofelectronicpublishing.org

This forum for research and discussion of contemporary publishing practices is published by the Scholarly Publishing Office (SPO), a unit of the University of Michigan Library. When JEP began in 1995 it recognized the significant changes in print communication and the growing role of digital communication in transmitting published information. Journal articles present innovative ideas, best practices and leading-edge thinking about all aspects of publishing, authorship and readership.

MIT Media Lab Project

http://www.media.mit.edu

This innovative multidisciplinary research laboratory at the Massachusetts Institute of Technology explores human/computer interaction. Now in its third decade of operation, the Lab is focusing on "human adaptability" projects including initiatives to treat Alzheimer's disease and depression, sociable robots that can monitor the health of children or the elderly, and the development of prostheses that can mimic the capabilities of biological limbs.

MySpace

http://www.myspace.com

America's leading social networking site with more than 110 million active monthly unique users, MySpace is localized and translated in more than 20 international territories including Japan, Italy, France and Latin America. Users can create personal Web profiles, blogs and photo galleries in an interactive environment, and can download music and videos. Newest sections include MySpaceTV (where users can explore news, television shows, movies and MySpace original productions), online karaoke and games. MySpace is owned by Rupert Murdoch's News Corporation as a unit of Fox Interactive Media, Inc.

Online Publishers Association

http://www.online-publishers.org

A not-for-profit industry trade organization founded in 2001, the OPA represents online content providers to the advertising community, the press, the government and the public. Members, from *ABCNews* to *Washingtonpost.Newsweek Interactive*, agree to abide by standards of quality and credibility. It also publishes the biweekly OPA Intelligence Report, which summarizes important news and research for the online publishing industry.

Pew Internet & American Life Project

http://www.pewinternet.org

The Pew Internet Project explores the effect of the Internet on various aspects of life: children, families, communities, the work place, education, health care, and civic and political life. Information available on the site includes reports, presentations, data sets and current trends.

Whatis?com

http://whatis.techtarget.com

This self-education tool contains more than 4,500 individual information technology (IT) definitions, especially about the Internet and computers. Although the majority of its audience is IT professionals, even the layperson can search the site's encyclopedia for the most basic acronyms and terms. Users can find everything from a list of text messaging abbreviations to the definition of a zip drive.

10

Advertising: Motivating Customers

Hulton Archive/Getty Images

Advertising for hard liquor and cigarettes was very common in the 1950s, such as these neon advertisements in New York City's Times Square in 1955.

What's Ahead?

American consumers pay for most

of their media (newspapers, magazines, radio and television) by watching, listening to and reading advertisements. The American Marketing Association defines *advertising* as "any paid form of non-personal presentation and promotion of ideas, goods or services by an identified sponsor."

You pay directly for books, movies and recordings, although these media use advertising to sell their products. But the broadcast programs you want to hear and see, the articles you want to read, and the Internet sites you use every day are filled with advertisements placed by companies that want to sell you products.

Advertising Helps Pay for Media

Advertising is not a mass medium. Advertising carries the messages that come to you from the people who pay for the American mass media. Americans, however, were not the first consumers. In 1200 B.C., the Phoenicians painted messages on stones near the paths where people often walked. In the sixth century B.C., ships that came into port with products on board sent criers around town with signboards to announce their arrival.

In the 13th century A.D., the British began requiring trademarks to protect buyers and to identify faulty products. The first printed advertisement was prepared by printer William Caxton in England in 1478 to sell one of his books.

Advertising became part of the American experience even before the settlers arrived. "Never was there a more outrageous or more unscrupulous or more ill-informed advertising campaign than that by which the promoters for the American colonies brought settlers here," writes historian Daniel J. Boorstin.

"Brochures published in England in the 17th century, some even earlier, were full of hopeful overstatements, half-truths, and downright lies, along with some facts which nowadays surely would be the basis for a restraining order from the Federal Trade Commission. Gold and silver, fountains of youth, plenty of fish, venison without limit, all these were promised, and of course some of them were found."

Advertising in Newspapers

The nation's first newspaper advertisement appeared in *The Boston News-Letter*'s first issue in 1704 when the newspaper's editor included an ad for his own newspaper. The penny press of the 1800s counted on advertising to underwrite its costs. In 1833, the *New York Sun* candidly said in its first issue: "The object of this paper is to lay before the public, at a price within the means of everyone, all the news of the day and at the same time afford an advantageous medium for advertising."

Three years later, the *Philadelphia Public Ledger* reported that "advertising is our revenue, and in a paper involving so many expenses as a penny paper, and especially our own, the only source of revenue."

Because they were so dependent on advertisers, newspapers in the 1800s accepted any ads they could get. Eventually, customers complained, especially about the patent medicines that advertised cures for every imaginable disease and often delivered unwelcome hangovers. (Many of these medicines contained mostly alcohol.) Products like Anti-Corpulence pills claimed they would help someone lose 15 pounds a month. "They cause no sickness, contain no poison and never fail." Dr. T. Felix Couraud's Oriental Cream guaranteed it would "remove tan, pimples, freckles, moth patches, rash and skin diseases and every blemish on beauty."

The newspaper publishers' response to complaints was to develop an open advertising policy, which meant newspapers would accept advertising from anyone who paid for it. This allowed the publishers to continue accepting the ads and then criticize the ads on their editorial pages. The *Public Ledger*'s policy was: "Our advertising columns are open to the 'public, the whole public, and nothing but the public.' We admit any advertisement of any thing or any opinion, from any persons who will pay the price, excepting what is forbidden by the laws of the land, or what, in the opinion of all, is offensive to decency and morals."

But some editors did move their ads, which had been mingled with the copy, to a separate section. Advertising historian Stephen Fox says: "Advertising was considered an embarrassment . . . the wastrel relative, the unruly servant kept backstairs and never allowed into the front parlor. . . . A firm risked its credit rating by advertising; banks might take it as a confession of financial weakness.

"Everyone deplored advertising. Nobody—advertiser, agent or medium—took responsibility for it. The advertiser only served as an errand boy, passing the advertiser's message along to the publisher: the medium printed it, but surely would not question the right of free speech by making a judgment on the veracity of the advertiser."

FINALLY, I WANT TO STRESS ONCE AGAIN THAT THE SUPPOSED PRESSURE BY THE SPONSORS IS MERELY AN INVENTION OF THE MEDIA.

Advertising in Magazines

Until the 1880s, magazines remained wary of advertising, but Cyrus H. K. Curtis, who founded *Ladies' Home Journal* in 1887, promoted advertising as the way for magazines to succeed.

Once when he was asked what made him successful, he answered, "Advertising. That's what made me whatever I am. . . . I use up my days trying to find men who can write an effective advertisement." When Curtis hired Edward Bok as editor, Bok began a campaign against patent medicine ads and joined with *Collier's* and the American Medical Association to seek government restraints. Congress created the Federal Trade Commission (FTC) in 1914, and part of its job was to monitor deceptive advertising. The FTC continues today to be the major government watchdog over advertising (see "Federal Government Regulates Advertisers," page 225).

Advertising on Radio

WEAF in New York broadcast its first advertisement in 1922, selling apartments in New Jersey. B. F. Goodrich, Palmolive and Eveready commercials followed. In September 1928, the Lucky Strike Dance Orchestra premiered on NBC, and Lucky Strike sales went up 47 percent. More cigarette companies moved to radio, and Camel cigarettes sponsored weekly, then daily, programs.

Sir Walter Raleigh cigarettes sponsored the Sir Walter Raleigh Revue. In one hour, the sponsor squeezed in 70 references to the product. According to Stephen Fox in *The Mirror Makers: A History of American Advertising and Its Creators*, "The theme song ('rally round Sir Walter Raleigh') introduced the Raleigh Revue in the Raleigh Theater with the Raleigh Orchestra and the Raleigh Rovers; then would follow the adventures of Sir Walter in Virginia and at Queen Elizabeth's court, with ample mention of his cigarettes and smoking tobacco." In 1938, for the first time, radio collected more money from advertising than magazines did.

Advertising on Television

Television began as an advertising medium. Never questioning how television would be financed, the TV networks assumed they would attract commercial support. They were right. In 1949, television advertising totaled $12.3 million. In 1950, the total was $40.8 million. In 1951, advertisers spent $128 million on television. In 2007, television advertising revenue in the U.S. totaled nearly $40 billion.

In a practice adopted from radio, television programs usually carried ***direct sponsorship***. Many shows, such as *Camel News Caravan*, carried the sponsor's name in the

Scott Gries/Getty Images for MTV Networks

Television advertising revenue totaled nearly $40 billion in the U.S. in 2007. In 2008, Hank Close, president of U.S. ad sales for MTV, presents the fall programming lineup at a meeting of potential advertisers.

title and advertised just one product (Camel cigarettes). Advertising agencies became television's programmers. "Given one advertiser and a show title often bearing its name, viewers associated a favorite show with its sponsor and—because of a 'gratitude factor'—would buy the products," writes Fox.

Alfred Hitchcock became legendary for leading into his show's commercials with wry remarks about the sponsor: "Oh dear, I see the actors won't be ready for another 60 seconds. However, thanks to our sponsor's remarkable foresight, we have a message that will fill in here nicely." But Hitchcock's sarcasm was the exception, and the television industry today relies heavily on advertising support.

Advertising on the Internet

Advertisers flocked to major Internet sites when they first were established. They expected quick returns, as consumer use of the Internet skyrocketed. Advertisers primarily used banner advertising, which meant their advertising messages scrolled across a Web site or appeared in a box on the site.

Direct Sponsorship A program that carries an advertiser's name in the program title.

Internet sites also tried **pop-up** advertisements, which meant an ad popped up either behind a Web site screen when someone left the site or on top of the Web site home page when someone first visited. Advertisers quickly learned, however, that no matter how they packaged the message, advertising on an Internet site didn't necessarily bring increased sales for their products.

What advertisers call the **click-through rate** (the rate at which someone who sees an advertising message on an Internet site actually clicks through to learn more) is less than 1 percent. This is a very disappointing return, especially when Web site advertising can be expensive. By 2008, Internet ad spending reached $23 billion, and has been growing every year since. Advertisers today are still trying to figure out just what the magic formula is to reach consumers on the Internet, and they're willing to spend a lot of money to try to find out what works.

Ford, BMW, Coca-Cola and Absolut Vodka created "advertainments" on their Web sites—short movies (2 to 11 minutes) featuring lots of action and familiar movie stars. Many marketers are creating **viral marketing** to try to reach younger audiences. "Viral marketing" means creating an online message that is so entertaining or interesting that consumers pass it along through social networking sites, such as Facebook and MySpace and by e-mail links. The message becomes an online "virus" that promotes a product without the expense of a paid commercial. (See **Impact/ Culture**, "For Coors Light, a Night Out That Begins on MySpace," page 217.)

These new approaches are meant to make Internet advertisements seem less like advertisements—further blurring the line between information, entertainment and advertising.

Ads Share Three Characteristics

The word *advertise* originally meant to take note or to consider. By the 1700s, the word's meaning had changed. To advertise meant to persuade. "If we consider democracy not just a political system," says Daniel J. Boorstin, "but as a set of institutions which do aim to make everything available to everybody, it would not be an overstatement to describe advertising as the characteristic rhetoric of democracy."

Boorstin says that advertising in America shares three characteristics: repetition, style and ubiquity.

Repetition

In 1851, when Robert Bonner bought the *New York Ledger*, he wanted to advertise his newspaper in the competing *New York Herald*, owned by James Gordon Bennett. Bennett limited all his advertisers to the same type size, so Bonner paid for an entire page of the *Herald*, across which he repeated the message "Bring home the *New York Ledger* tonight." This is an early example of advertising's widespread practice of repeating a simple message for effect.

An Advertising Style

At first, advertising adopted a plain, direct style. Advertising pioneer Claude Hopkins, says Boorstin, claimed: "Brilliant writing has no place in advertising. A unique style takes attention from the subject. . . . One should be natural and simple . . . in fishing for buyers, as in fishing for bass, one should not reveal the hook." The plain-talk tradition is a foundation of what advertisers call modern advertising. But advertising today often adopts a style of hyperbole, making large claims for products. Boorstin calls this "tall-talk."

The tall-talk ad is in the P. T. Barnum tradition of advertising. Barnum was a carnival barker and later impresario who lured customers to his circus acts with fantastic claims. You may recognize this approach in some of the furniture and car ads on television, as an announcer screams at you that you have only a few days left until all the chairs or all the cars will be gone.

Both plain talk and tall-talk combine, Boorstin says, to create advertising's new myth. "This is the world of the neither true nor false—of the statement that 60 percent of the physicians who expressed a choice said that our brand of aspirin would be more effective in curing a simple headache than any other brand. . . . It is not untrue, and yet, in its connotation it is not exactly true."

Ubiquity

In America, advertising is everywhere. Advertisers are always looking for new places to catch consumers' attention. Ads appear on shopping carts, on video screens at sports stadiums, atop parking meters. Says Daniel Boorstin, "The ubiquity of advertising is, of course, just another effect of our uninhibited efforts to use all the media to get all sorts of information to everybody everywhere. Since the places to be filled are everywhere, the amount of advertising is not determined by the needs of advertising, but by the opportunities for advertising, which become unlimited."

In some cases, this ubiquity works to advertising's disadvantage. Many advertisers shy away from radio and

Pop-Up An advertisement on a Web site that appears on the screen either behind a Web page when someone leaves the site or on top of the Web site home page when someone first visits.

Click-Through Rate The rate at which someone who sees an ad on an Internet site clicks through to learn more.

Viral Marketing Creating an online message that is entertaining enough to get consumers to pass it on over the Internet like a virus.

IMPACT
≫Culture

For Coors Light, a Night Out That Begins on MySpace

by Stuart Elliott

Note: "Viral marketing" means creating an online message that is so entertaining or interesting that consumers pass it along through social networking sites, such as Facebook and MySpace and by e-mail links. The message becomes an online "virus," that promotes a product without the expense of a paid commercial. In 2008, Coors created a viral marketing campaign by placing a video of people completing the "perfect pour," a video created by Coors.

Beer has long been marketed as a sociable beverage, from a campaign for Budweiser that carried the theme "When gentlemen agree" to the Löwenbräu jingle that began, "Here's to good friends." Now, another beer brand, Coors Light, is extending its presence in the new media with efforts on the social networking Web sites Facebook and MySpace.

The initiatives are part of a campaign known as "Code Blue," centered on a "cold activated" feature introduced last year on Coors Light beer bottles: the mountains pictured on the labels turn from white to blue when the beer gets cold enough to drink.

For instance, consumers age 21 and older will be able to send friends "Code Blue" alerts on Facebook.com, inviting them to meet up for a beer—a Coors Light, natch. They can even use Facebook maps to direct their potential brew crew to a nearby bar. The Facebook feature, or application, is scheduled to start early next week.

The "Code Blue" campaign, a collaboration among Coors Light agencies, is indicative of the growing interest in the new media among marketers outside the realm of technology products and services. . . .

The social-networking aspects of the "Code Blue" campaign came after the maker of Coors Light—the Coors Brewing Company, part of the Molson Coors Brewing Company—took other steps to go beyond traditional

In 2008, Coors created a "perfect pour" viral marketing campaign to promote "Code Blue." Viral marketing means creating an online message that is so entertaining that consumers will voluntarily pass along the ad to their friends. The message becomes an online "virus," promoting a product without the expense of a paid commercial.

advertising like television commercials and print ads.

To help bring out a new "vented wide mouth" can for Coors Light, one of the brand's agencies, Avenue A/Razorfish, created a fanciful video clip of what looks like beer drinkers completing the "perfect pour" and uploaded it in two parts to YouTube. . . .

When it comes to the new media, "Everyone, particularly in offline businesses like ours, is still in a very experimental phase,"

(continued)

IMPACT
»Culture

For Coors Light, a Night Out That Begins on MySpace (continued)

Mr. England said. "We, along with our agencies, are trying to learn what works best and expand on those ideas."

For instance, "If you put a viral video out there," Mr. England said, like the "perfect pour" clips posted on YouTube, "how long should it be? How branded should it be?"

"We place bets in the office about this stuff," he added. . . .

"Facebook is so adept at bringing people together," said Tim Sproul, group creative director in the Portland, Ore., office of Avenue A/Razorfish, "and getting in touch with people quickly throughout the day."

"And if you have anything to pitch in a social environment, it makes sense to pitch beer," he added. "We feel like we're not intrusive in the online experience; we're relevant, by giving people a chance to connect."

"The goal in general to be online is increasing our relevance with our 25-year-old beer drinker," the target audience for Coors Light, Mr. Sproul said.

"It's new and it's uncharted waters," he added, "but we feel like we belong online; we have a place there and a story to tell."

Steve Jennings/WireImage/Getty Images

Advertisers use at least 15 different types of appeals to attract consumers. In 2008, Emporio Armani unveiled this poster featuring soccer star David Beckham in San Francisco's Union Square. Which one of the ad appeals listed by Jib Fowles does the Armani ad use?

TV because the ads are grouped so closely together. In 1986, in an attempt to attract more advertisers, TV began selling the "split-30" ad, which fits two 15-second ads into a 30-second spot. Even 10-second ads are available. Wherever these shorter commercials are sold, the station runs twice or three times as many ads for different products, crowding the commercial time even more. Too many ads that run together also means it becomes even harder for one ad to grab consumers' attention.

Ads Must Grab Your Attention

To sell the products, advertisers must catch your eye or your ear or your heart (preferably all three). A study by the Harvard Graduate School of Business Administration reported that the average American is exposed to 500 ads a day.

With so many ads competing for your attention, the advertiser must first get you to read, to listen or to watch one ad instead of another. "The immediate goal of advertising [is to] tug at our psychological shirt sleeves and slow us down long enough for a word or two about whatever is being sold," says humanities and human sciences professor Jib Fowles in *Mass Advertising as Social Forecast*. Research shows that there are at least 15 common ways ads appeal to consumers.

15 Ways Ads Appeal to Consumers

You make your buying decisions based on several sources of information besides advertising: friends, family and your own experience, for example. To influence your choices, the advertising message must appeal to you for some reason as you sift through the ads to make judgments and choose products. Fowles enumerated 15 appeals, which he calls an "inventory of human motives" that advertisers commonly use in their commercials:

1. **Need for sex.** Surprisingly, Fowles found that only 2 percent of the television ads he surveyed used this appeal. It may be too blatant, he concluded, and often detracts from the product.

2. **Need for affiliation.** The largest number of ads uses this approach: You are looking for friendship. Advertisers can also use this negatively, to make you worry that you'll lose friends if you don't use a certain product.

3. **Need to nurture.** Every time you see a puppy or a kitten or a child, the appeal is to your maternal or paternal instincts.

4. **Need for guidance.** A father or mother figure can appeal to your desire for someone to care for you, so you won't have to worry. Betty Crocker is a good example.

5. **Need to aggress.** We all have had a desire to get even, and some ads give you this satisfaction.

6. **Need to achieve.** The ability to accomplish something difficult and succeed identifies the product with winning. Sports figures as spokespersons project this image.

7. **Need to dominate.** The power we lack is what we can look for in a commercial: "Master the possibilities."

8. **Need for prominence.** We want to be admired and respected, to have high social status. Tasteful china and classic diamonds offer this potential.

9. **Need for attention.** We want people to notice us; we want to be looked at. Cosmetics are a natural for this approach.

10. **Need for autonomy.** Within a crowded environment, we want to be singled out, to be "a breed apart." This can also be used negatively: You may be too ordinary without a particular product.

11. **Need to escape.** Flight is very appealing; you can imagine adventures you cannot have. The idea of escape is pleasurable.

Critics of advertising claim advertising causes consumers to buy products they don't need. The advertising industry contends the ultimate test of any product is the marketplace because consumers will not continue to buy an unsatisfying product. In Los Angeles, morning commuters were greeted in 2007 with free pink-frosted donuts, accompanied by large balloons, at an event to promote the DVD release of *The Simpsons Movie*.

12. **Need to feel safe.** To be free from threats, to be secure is the appeal of many insurance and bank ads.

13. **Need for aesthetic sensations.** Beauty attracts us, and classic art or dance makes us feel creative, enhanced.

14. **Need to satisfy curiosity.** Facts support our belief that information is quantifiable, and numbers and diagrams make our choices seem scientific.

15. **Physiological needs.** Fowles defines sex (item no. 1) as a biological need, and so he classifies our need to sleep, eat and drink as physiological. Advertisements for juicy pizza are especially appealing late at night.

Advertisers Use Demographics

Advertisers target their messages to an audience according to the audience's needs. But an advertiser also seeks to determine the audience's characteristics. This analysis of observable audience characteristics is called **demographics**.

Demographics are composed of data about a target audience's gender, age, income level, marital status, geographic location and occupation. These data are observable because they are available to advertising agencies through census data and other sources. Advertising agencies use demographic audience analysis to help advertisers target their messages.

A motorcycle dealer certainly wouldn't want to advertise in a baby magazine, for example; a candy manufacturer probably wouldn't profit from advertising in a diet and exercise magazine. Advertising agencies try to match a client's product to a thoroughly defined audience so each advertising dollar is well spent.

Defining the audience is very important because the goal of advertising is to market a product to people who have the desire for the product and the ability to buy the product. Audience analysis tells an advertiser whether there are enough people who can be targeted for a product to make the advertising worthwhile.

Advertising Feeds Consumerism

According to Louis C. Kaufman, author of *Essentials of Advertising*, critics of advertising make three main arguments:

1. **Advertising adds to the cost of products.** Critics of advertising maintain that advertising, like everything that is part of manufacturing a product, is a cost. Ultimately, the consumer pays for the cost of advertising. But the industry argues that advertising helps make more goods and services available to the consumer and that the resulting competition keeps prices lower.

2. **Advertising causes people to buy products they do not need.** Says media scholar Michael Schudson, "Most blame advertising for the sale of specific consumer goods, notably luxury goods (designer jeans), frivolous goods (pet rocks), dangerous goods (cigarettes), shoddy goods (some toys for children), expensive goods that do not differ at all from cheap goods (non-generic over-the-counter drugs), marginally differentiated products that do not differ significantly from one another (laundry soaps),

and wasteful goods (various un-ecological throw-away convenience goods)."

The advertising industry contends the ultimate test of any product is the marketplace and that advertising may stimulate consumers to try a new product or a new brand, but consumers will not continue to buy an unsatisfying product.

3. **Advertising reduces competition and thereby fosters monopolies.** Critics point to the rising cost of advertising, especially television, which limits which companies can afford to launch a new product or a new campaign. The industry argues that advertising is still a very inexpensive way to let people know about new products.

"The cost of launching a nationwide advertising campaign may be formidable," writes Louis C. Kaufman, "but the cost of supporting larger, nationwide sales forces for mass-marketed goods would be greater still." Does advertising work? According to Schudson, "Apologists are wrong that advertising is simply information that makes the market work more efficiently—but so too are the critics of advertising who believe in its overwhelming power to deceive and to deflect human minds to its ends."

"Evaluating its impact," Kaufman says, "is more difficult than these simplicities of apology and critique will acknowledge."

Advertising at Work

Several worldwide advertising agencies are based in the United States, but most advertising agencies are small local and regional operations, earning less than $1 million a year. Advertising agencies buy time and space for the companies they represent. For this, they usually earn a commission (commonly 15 percent). Many agencies also produce television and radio commercials and print and Internet advertising for their clients.

Depending on the size of the agency, the company may be divided into as many as six departments:

1. Marketing research

2. Media selection

3. Creative activity

4. Account management

5. Administration

6. Public relations

Marketing research examines the product's potential, where it will be sold and who will buy the product. Agency researchers may survey the market themselves or contract with an outside market research company to evaluate potential buyers.

Demographics Data about consumers' characteristics, such as age, gender, income level, marital status, geographic location and occupation.

Media selection suggests the best combination of buys for a client—television, newspapers, magazines, billboards and/or Internet.

Creative activity thinks up the ads. The "creatives" write the copy for TV, radio, print and Internet. They design the graphic art, and often they produce the commercials. They also verify that the ad has run as many times as it was scheduled to run.

Account management is the liaison between the agency and the client. Account executives handle client complaints and suggestions and also manage the company team assigned to the account.

Administration pays the bills, including all the tabs for the account executives' lunches with clients. *Public relations* is an extra service that some agencies offer for companies that don't have a separate public relations office.

All these departments work together on an ad campaign. An ***advertising campaign*** is a planned advertising effort, coordinated for a specific time period. A campaign could last anywhere from a month to a year, and the objective is a coordinated strategy to sell a product or a service.

Typically, the company assigns the account executive a team of people from the different departments to handle the account. The account executive answers to the people who control the agency, usually a board of directors. The members of the campaign team coordinate all types of advertising—print and broadcast, for example—to make sure they share consistent content. After establishing a budget based on the client's needs, the campaign team creates a slogan, recommends a strategy for the best exposure for the client, approves the design of print and broadcast commercials and then places the ads with the media outlets. (See **Impact/Culture**, "U.S. Food Companies Promise to Limit Ads for Kids," page 222.)

Advertising agencies tend to be clustered in big cities such as New York, Los Angeles, San Francisco and Chicago. In part, this is by tradition. The agencies may want to be near their large clients in the cities. They also have access to a larger pool of talent and facilities such as recording studios, but today Internet technology enables greater flexibility for agency locations.

Media Depend on Advertising

The advertising business and the media industries are interdependent—that is, what happens in the advertising business directly affects the media industries. The advertising business is very dependent on the nation's economic health. If the national economy is expanding, the advertising business and the media industries prosper.

If the nation's economy falls into a recession, advertisers (see **Illustration 10.1** on page 224) typically reduce their ad

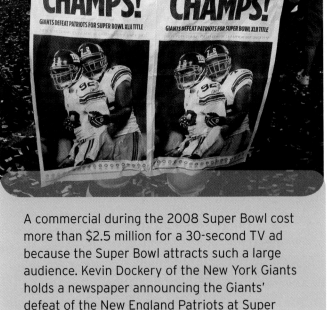

Donald Miralle/Getty Images

A commercial during the 2008 Super Bowl cost more than $2.5 million for a 30-second TV ad because the Super Bowl attracts such a large audience. Kevin Dockery of the New York Giants holds a newspaper announcing the Giants' defeat of the New England Patriots at Super Bowl XLII in Phoenix in 2008.

budgets, which eventually may lead to a decline in advertising revenue for the agencies and also for the media industries where the agencies place their ads. During a recession, advertisers also may change their advertising strategies—choosing radio over television because radio is much less expensive, for example.

The advertising industry today, therefore, must be very sensitive to economic trends. The success of an ad agency is best measured by the results an ad campaign brings. The agency must analyze the benefits of different types of advertising—broadcast, print, Internet—and recommend the most efficient combinations for their clients.

Advertising Campaign A planned advertising effort, coordinated for a specific time period.

IMPACT
»Culture

U.S. Food Companies Promise to Limit Ads for Kids

by Lilla Zuill and Julie Vorman

Some of America's largest food and drink companies, including McDonald's, Coca-Cola, PepsiCo and General Mills, promised on [July 18, 2007] to put stricter controls on advertising aimed at children under 12.

The voluntary steps varied among the 11 companies and were announced as the Federal Trade Commission held a forum to spotlight the need for more responsible food marketing to help address childhood obesity.

Mark Lennihan/AP Photo

In 2007, in response to an increase in childhood obesity, some of America's largest food and drink companies, including Hershey's, announced they planned to voluntarily place stricter controls on advertising aimed at children under 12.

McDonald's Corp. said 100 percent of its advertising primarily directed to children under 12 would further the goal of healthy dietary choices.

The Coca-Cola Company said it would not directly market any of its beverages to children under 12, although it said it had a number of drinks including water, juice, dairy and fortified beverages that would qualify for children.

PepsiCo Inc., which makes Frito-Lay snacks,

Commercials on Television

Even though the cost seems exorbitant, sponsors continue to line up to appear on network television. "Advertisers must use television on whatever terms they can get it, for television is the most potent merchandising vehicle ever devised," writes TV producer Bob Shanks in his book *The Cool Fire: How to Make It in Television*. Shanks is talking about national advertisers who buy network time—companies whose products can be advertised to the entire country at once.

Advertising minutes within every network prime-time hour are divided into 10-, 15- and 30-second ads. If an advertiser wants to reach the broad national market, television is an expensive choice because the average price for the TV time for a 30-second commercial is $100,000. The price tag for a 30-second commercial reaches $2.5 million for a widely watched program such as the Super Bowl.

National advertising on programs like CBS's *NCIS* is bought by national advertising agencies, which handle the country's biggest advertisers—Procter & Gamble and McDonald's, for example. These companies usually have in-house advertising and public relations departments, but most of the advertising strategy and production of commercials for these companies is handled by the agencies. National agencies buy advertising space based on a careful formula, calculated on a cost-per-thousand (*CPM*) basis—the cost of an ad per 1,000 people reached (M is the Roman numeral for 1,000).

Making a TV commercial for national broadcast is more expensive per minute than making a television program because each company wants its ads to be different from the rest. The price to create a TV commercial can run as much as $1 million a minute. That may be why, as one producer said, "the commercials are the best things on TV." Network

CPM Cost-per-thousand, the cost of an ad per 1,000 people reached. (M is the Roman numeral for 1,000.)

Quaker Foods breakfast cereals and drinks such as Pepsi and Gatorade, will advertise only two of its products to children—Baked Cheetos Cheese Flavored Snacks and Gatorade energy drinks—and said the ads will emphasize active lifestyles.

PepsiCo said it is taking the additional step of stopping advertising its products in elementary and middle schools.

General Mills Inc., whose products include Trix cereal and Progresso soups, said it will stop advertising foods containing more than 12 grams of sugar per serving to kids under 12. The company said it will also add nutrition highlights to its cereal packaging.

"We want to be part of the solution," said Chris Shea, a senior vice president of General Mills. "We believe that companies like ours can make a difference and can play an important role in providing lower calorie, higher nutrient products to parents and their children."

"I would like the media industries to come forward with their own set of voluntary commitments," said Rep. Edward Markey, a Massachusetts Democrat and chairman of the House telecommunications subcommittee. . . .

Among other companies, Campbell Soup Company said it would advertise certain soups, including its Less Sodium lines, to children as "sound food choices for them," as well as its Pepperidge Farm Goldfish Cheddar snack crackers.

Kraft Foods Inc. specified Post cereals, Kool-Aid beverages and Nabisco cookies and crackers among its brands with "child-directed ad campaigns," which it said would now be based on nutrition criteria.

Kellogg Company said its pledge covered ready-to-eat cereals, Pop-Tarts, snack lines and Eggo frozen breakfast products. Unilever Plc said its Skippy and Popsicle products were its current brands covered by the pledge.

Also taking pledges were candy and snack makers Hershey Co., Mars, Inc. and Cadbury Adams, which said it would no longer advertise Bubblicious to children under 12.

The food companies' pledges were posted on the Council of Better Business Bureau's Web site at http://www.cbbb.org/initiative/pledges.asp.

From "U.S. Food Companies Promise to Limit Ads for Kids," by Lilla Zuill and Julie Vorman, Reuters, July 18, 2007. Reprinted by permission.

television commercials certainly are the most visible type of advertising, but not everyone needs the reach of network television. The goal of well-placed advertising is to deliver the best results to the client for the lowest cost, and this may mean looking to other media.

Using the Internet, Print and Radio

Different types of media deliver different types of audiences. The Internet offers a large potential audience, but consumers also can quickly click past ads on the Web and block pop-up ads, so no one yet is quite sure how effective Web ads are.

Advertising agencies also buy less expensive time and space in local radio, newspapers and magazines to target a specific audience by demographics: age, education, gender and income. A radio station with a rock format delivers a different audience than an easy-listening station does. *The New York Times* delivers a different reader than the *Honolulu Advertiser*. *Sports Illustrated* targets a different group than *Ladies' Home Journal*. Language also can be a targeting

Advertisers must learn to adapt their messages for new audiences, such as Spanish-language consumers, as new technology including the Internet creates new outlets for advertising.

IMPACT
» Business

Illustration 10.1

Top 10 Advertisers in the U.S.

Auto manufacturers, such as Ford, Nissan and Chevrolet, have always spent a lot of money to advertise their products, but in 2007 telecommunications companies such as AT&T, Verizon and Sprint spent more to advertise their products than Ford (which ranked 4), Nissan (which ranked 8) and Chevrolet (which ranked 10).

Source: "100 Leading National Advertisers," *Advertising Age*, June 23, 2008, S-16.

1	AT&T	6	Toyota
2	Verizon	7	McDonald's
3	Sprint	8	Nissan
4	Ford	9	Target
5	Macy's	10	Chevrolet

factor. Some agencies use Spanish-language media to target Latino consumers, for example.

Media Compete Fiercely for Clients

The competition among different media for advertisers is fierce:

- A study commissioned by the American Newspaper Publishers Association reveals that only one in five prime-time adult viewers could remember the last ad they had seen on television.

- Print advertisers claim that because viewers can so easily change channels and skip the ads, TV commercials are an unreliable way to deliver an audience.

- *Time* advertises that more airline customers read its magazine than read *Newsweek*.

- *Newsweek* advertises that it delivers more people for the money than *Time*.

- "Radio is the medium working women don't have to make time for," boasts the Radio Advertising Bureau (RAB). Whereas working women spend 15 percent of their daily media time reading a newspaper, they spend half of their media time with radio, says the RAB.

- AT&T launches a talking Internet site to "express themselves better" to consumers.

Advertising agencies gather demographic information provided by Nielsen and Arbitron for broadcast and the Internet and by the Audit Bureau of Circulations for print; the audience is converted into numbers. Based on these numbers, agencies advise advertisers about ways to reach buyers for their products by advertising locally or through an advertising sales representative, for example.

Advertising Locally

Kaitlyn's Health and Fitness salon, a small downtown business, does not need to advertise on the *Late Show with David Letterman* or in *The New York Times*. Kaitlyn and other local businesses need to reach only their neighbors. Businesses larger than the fitness salon, such as a car dealer or a furniture store, may buy local television or radio time, but most of the local advertising dollar goes to newspapers.

A local advertising agency can design a campaign, produce the ad and place the ad just like the national agencies, but on a much smaller scale. Some small companies design and place their own ads directly with the local media. To attract customers, local media often help companies design their ads. Newspapers, for example, will help a small advertiser prepare an ad using ready-made art.

A radio or television station may include the services of an announcer or access to a studio in the price for a series of spot ads. Broadcast stations sometimes trade ads for services offered by the advertiser—dinner for two at the local restaurant in return for two spot ads, for example. Then the station gives the dinners away on one of its programs.

Advertising Sales Representatives

What if you manufacture sunglasses in Dubuque, Iowa, and you hire a local advertising agency to sell your product nationally? The agency tells you they've found a good market for your product on the West Coast. How is the agency going to find out the most efficient way to sell your sunglasses in Los Angeles?

In this situation, many advertising agencies would contact a *rep firm*—a company of advertising sales representatives who sell advertising time and space in their market to companies outside the area. The agency in Dubuque would first decide who were the most likely customers for your sunglasses. If the agency decided that L.A.-area males age 18 to 24 are the best potential customers, the agency would budget a certain amount of money for advertising in the Los Angeles area and then call the ad reps there.

The rep firm, in return, takes a percentage (usually 15 percent) of the advertising dollars for the ads they place. Ad reps are, in effect, brokers for the media in their markets. Each rep firm handles several clients. Some ad reps sell only broadcast advertising, and some specialize in print ads, but many rep firms sell all types of media.

In this case, each L.A. ad rep would enter the demographics ("demos") for your product into a computer. Based on ratings, readership and the price for the ads, each rep would come up with a CPM (cost per thousand people reached) for your product. The rep then would recommend

Harley Schwadron/Reprinted by permission of CartoonStock

the most efficient buy—how best to reach the people most likely to buy your sunglasses.

Each rep then presents an L.A. advertising plan for your product to the agency in Dubuque. Usually the buy is based on price: The medium with the lowest CPM gets the customer. But a rep who cannot match the lowest CPM might offer incentives for you to choose his or her plan. If you agree to provide 50 pairs of sunglasses, for example, the rep's radio station will give away the glasses as prizes during a local program, each time mentioning the name of your product. So even though the ad time you buy will cost a little more, you also will get promotional announcements every time the station gives away a pair of sunglasses. Other ad reps might offer different packages.

The agency in Dubuque then would decide which package is the most attractive and would present that proposal to you. This entire process can take as little as 24 hours for a simple buy such as the one for your sunglasses account, or as long as several weeks for a complicated campaign for a big advertiser.

Federal Government Regulates Advertisers

Government protection for consumers dates back to the beginning of the 20th century when Congress passed the Pure Food and Drug Act in 1906, mainly as a protection against patent medicine ads. The advertising industry itself

Rep Firm A company of advertising sales representatives who sell advertising time and space in their market to companies outside their area.

Spencer Platt/Getty Images

The Food and Drug Administration (FDA) oversees claims that appear on food labels or packaging, such as products sold in grocery stores. If the FDA finds a label is deceptive, the agency can require the advertiser to stop distributing products with that label.

has adopted advertising standards, and in some cases the media have established their own codes.

Government oversight is the main deterrent against deceptive advertising. This responsibility is shared by several government agencies: The Federal Trade Commission, the Food and Drug Administration and the Federal Communications Commission.

The Federal Trade Commission

The Federal Trade Commission (FTC), established in 1914, can "stop business practices that restrict competition or that deceive or otherwise injure consumers," according to *Essentials of Advertising*. If the FTC determines an ad is deceptive, the commission can order the advertiser to stop the campaign.

The commission also can require corrective advertising to counteract the deception. In 1993, for example, the FTC launched an investigation of the nation's weight-loss clinics, charging that they were using deceptive advertising.

The Food and Drug Administration

The Food and Drug Administration (FDA) oversees claims that appear on food labels or packaging. If the

FDA finds a label is deceptive, the agency can require the advertiser to stop distributing products with that label. Orange juice that is labeled "fresh," for example, cannot be juice that has been frozen first.

The Federal Communications Commission

The Federal Communications Commission (FCC) enforces rules that govern the broadcast media. The FCC's jurisdiction over the broadcast industry gives the commission indirect control over broadcast advertising. In the past, the FCC has ruled against demonstrations of products that were misleading and against commercials the FCC decided were tasteless.

TV Accepts Hard Liquor Ads

Although you regularly see advertisements on television for beer and wine, the TV networks traditionally did not advertise hard liquor. For three decades, the Distilled Spirits Council of the United States, operating under a voluntary Code of Good Practice, did not run television ads. In 1996, some liquor companies decided to challenge the voluntary ban by placing ads on local television.

Seagram's, the first company to challenge the ban, advertised Royal Crown whiskey on a local TV station in Texas. "We believe distilled spirits should have the same access to electronic media, just the same way beer and wine do," said Arthur Shapiro, executive vice president in charge of marketing and strategy for Seagram's in the United States.

The Federal Trade Commission and the Bureau of Alcohol, Tobacco and Firearms regulate the spirits industry, but neither agency has the authority to ban hard liquor ads on television. Because the TV networks can gain a great deal of income from advertising hard liquor, the TV networks now accept hard liquor ads.

Other government agencies, such as the Environmental Protection Agency and the Consumer Product Safety Agency, also can question the content of advertisements. Advertising agencies have formed the National Advertising Review Board (NARB) to hear complaints against advertisers. This effort at self-regulation among advertising agencies parallels those of some media industries, such as the movie industry's ratings code and the recording industry's record labeling for lyrics.

Advertising Business Must Deliver New Markets

The future of advertising will parallel changes in the media, in technology and in demographics. As more U.S. products seek international markets, advertising must be designed to reach those markets. American agencies today collect nearly half of the *world's* revenue from advertising. Three factors will affect the future of the advertising business: international markets, changing technology and shifting demographic patterns.

International advertising campaigns are becoming more common for global products, such as Coca-Cola and McDonald's, and this has meant the creation of international advertising markets. Cable News Network (CNN) sells advertising on CNN worldwide, so that any company in any nation with CNN's service can advertise its product to a worldwide audience. Overall, billings outside the United States are commanding an increasing share of U.S. agencies' business.

A second factor in the future of advertising is changing technology. As new media technologies create new outlets, the advertising community must adapt. Advertisers are trying to figure out how to reach consumers on the Internet. A tennis instructional video, for example, could include advertising for tennis products. One company is using lasers to create advertising in the evening sky. Several companies are trying to take advantage of the widespread use of cell phones by creating ads that are delivered directly to consumers' cell phones (See **Impact/Business**, "To Reach Mobile Users, Make Your Marketing Useful," page 228).

A third factor in the future of advertising is shifting demographic patterns. As the ethnicity of the nation evolves, marketing programs must adapt to reach new audiences. Future television ads may include dialogue in both English and Spanish. Some national ad campaigns already include multilingual versions of the same ad, targeted for different audiences.

The challenges for the advertising business are as great as the challenges for the media industries. The advertising industry will do what it has always done to adapt—follow the audience. The challenge for advertising will be to learn how to efficiently and effectively match the audience to the advertising messages the media deliver.

China Photos/Getty Images

International advertising campaigns are becoming more common for global products, like Coca-Cola. This has meant the creation of international advertising campaigns, such as these Coca-Cola bottles printed with images of Chinese sports stars for a Coke bottle design contest in Nanjing, China.

IMPACT
>> Business

To Reach Mobile Users, Make Your Marketing Useful

by Abbey Klaassen

When it comes to *mobile marketing*, advertisers have not only a challenge but a mandate to create something useful for consumers, according to a panel of experts *Advertising Age* gathered to talk about the opportunities—and potential pitfalls—of reaching consumers on their phones. Good mobile marketing, the consensus said, takes advantage of the channel's inherent traits and ties into other media.

Advertisers are designing mobile marketing campaigns to try to broaden their reach to include consumers on their cell phones, such as this man in Tokyo, Japan.

YOSHIKAZU TSUNO/AFP/Getty Images

Advertising Age: So let's get right to the point. Most people say they don't want ads on phones. Is that what mobile marketing is?

Maria Mandel: I think, in general, anytime you say to consumers, "Do you want to see an ad?" they're going to say no, regardless of whether it's a television ad or a mobile ad. And with mobile you get a much stronger response because the mobile device is such a personal device, with you 24/7. . . .

Ad Age: What is a good use of the medium?

Eric Bader: Smart marketers and brands are tailoring the experience to the mobility of the phone and the utility of the phone and are not making it an arduous experience to have a good time with a brand. They're offering something that consumers are going to get a benefit out of.

Cynthia McIntyre: I agree. This is an overused word, but it is about content; it's about the most relevant type of information. And just like the TV remote control . . . [consumers] can also zap you off the phone as well. . . .

Ms. Mandel: . . . Ultimately, a consumer is looking for one of three things. They're either looking for information that they're in need of—sort of the utility piece of mobile. Then there's entertainment, something that's going to engage, surprise and delight them. Or what we're seeing more and more of in mobile is that community piece, of how do you start getting conversations going, start building interaction between people using their mobile devices? It is ultimately where mobile started out, right? It's a communication tool.

Mobile Marketing An advertising campaign directed at cell phone users.

Abbey Klaassen, "To Reach Mobile Users, Make Your Marketing Useful," AdAge.com, September 8, 2008. Reprinted by permission.

Review, Analyze, Investigate
REVIEWING CHAPTER 10

Advertising Helps Pay for Media

✓ Advertising carries the messages that come to you from the sponsors who pay for the American media.

✓ As early as 1200 B.C., the Phoenicians painted messages on stones to advertise.

✓ In 600 B.C., ship captains sent criers around to announce that their ships were in port.

✓ In the 13th century A.D., the British began requiring trademarks to protect buyers.

✓ In 1704, newspapers were the first medium to use advertising. Magazines, radio, television and the Internet followed.

✓ Advertisers flocked to major Internet sites when they first were established. They expected quick returns as consumer use of the Internet skyrocketed. Advertisers quickly learned, however, that no matter how they packaged the message, advertising on an Internet site didn't necessarily bring increased sales.

✓ What advertisers call the *click-through rate* (the rate at which someone who sees an advertising message actually clicks through to learn more) is less than 1 percent.

✓ By 2008, Internet ad spending reached $23 billion.

✓ Viral marketing is a form of advertising that involves creating an online message that consumers pass on—an online "word of mouth."

✓ Advertisers today are still trying to figure out just what the magic formula is to reach consumers on the Internet. New approaches, such as mobile marketing, are meant to make advertisements seem less like advertisements—further blurring the line between information, entertainment and advertising.

Ads Share Three Characteristics

✓ Daniel Boorstin says that advertising in America shares three characteristics: repetition, an advertising style and ubiquity.

✓ The sheer number of ads sometimes works to advertisers' disadvantage because they can crowd each other so much that no individual ad stands out in consumers' minds.

Ads Must Grab Your Attention

✓ To influence consumers, an advertising message must appeal to you for some reason.

✓ Advertising can catch your attention, according to Jib Fowles, in 15 ways, including playing on your need to nurture, your need for attention and your need for escape.

Advertisers Use Demographics

✓ Advertisers target their messages according to an audience's characteristics.

✓ Demographics are composed of data about a target audience's gender, age, income level, marital status, geographic location and occupation.

Advertising Feeds Consumerism

✓ Advertising provokes three main criticisms: advertising adds to the cost of products; advertising causes people to buy products they do not need; advertising reduces competition and thereby fosters monopolies.

✓ Because the audience is increasingly fragmented, advertisers have used other tactics—from the Internet to viral marketing.

Advertising at Work

✓ Most advertising agencies are small, local operations.

✓ Depending on the size of the company, an advertising agency may be divided into as many as six departments: marketing research, media selection, creative activity, account management, administration and public relations.

Media Depend on Advertising

✓ The advertising business and the media industries are interdependent—what happens in the advertising business directly affects the media industries.

✓ The advertising business is very dependent on the nation's economic health.

Media Compete Fiercely for Clients

✓ Advertising is divided into national and local categories.

✓ Advertising sales representatives broker local accounts to out-of-town advertisers.

✓ The media compete with each other for the advertising dollar, and some media are better than others for particular products.

Federal Government Regulates Advertisers

✓ Government protection for consumers dates back to the beginning of the 20th century.

✓ Protection for consumers from misleading advertising comes from government regulation (the Federal Trade Commission, Food and Drug Administration and Federal Communications Commission, for example); from advertising industry self-regulatory groups (National Advertising Review Board, for example); and from codes established by the media industries.

TV Accepts Hard Liquor Ads

✓ In 1996, the distilled spirits industry challenged the industry-wide voluntary ban on hard liquor advertising on TV that had lasted for three decades. The liquor industry placed the ads on local TV stations, and some network executives have accepted the ads.

✓ Neither the Federal Trade Commission nor the Bureau of Alcohol, Tobacco and Firearms, which regulate the spirits industry, has the power to stop liquor ads from appearing on TV.

Advertising Business Must Deliver New Markets

✓ The future of advertising will parallel the development of international markets, the refinement and expansion of new media technologies (especially the Internet) and changing demographics.

✓ Today's advertising agencies use sophisticated technology to track demographics to help deliver the audience the advertiser wants.

✓ International advertising campaigns are becoming more common for global products, such as Coca-Cola and McDonald's, and this has meant the creation of international advertising campaigns.

✓ As the ethnicity of the nation evolves, marketing programs must adapt to reach new audiences.

KEY TERMS

These terms are defined in the margins throughout this chapter and appear in alphabetical order with definitions in the Glossary, which begins on page 372.

Advertising Campaign 221

Click-Through Rate 216

CPM 222

Demographics 220

Direct Sponsorship 215

Mobile Marketing 228

Pop-Up 216

Rep Firm 225

Viral Marketing 216

CRITICAL QUESTIONS

1. Why is advertising not a medium? What role does advertising play in the mass media?

2. What are the three main arguments given by advertising's critics and by its supporters?

3. What are the benefits to an advertiser of TV instead of print? Of radio instead of TV? Of the Internet instead of broadcast and print?

4. Discuss three of Jib Fowles' 15 psychological appeals for advertising in some detail, and present an example of an ad that demonstrates each of the three appeals you discuss.

5. Discuss government regulation and industry self-regulation of advertising. What government agencies are involved in advertising regulation? Do you think government regulation or industry self-regulation is more effective at protecting consumer interests? Explain.

WORKING THE WEB

This list includes both sites mentioned in the chapter and others to give you greater insight into the advertising business.

Adrants

http://www.adrants.com

Adrants provides marketing and advertising news "with an attitude" through its Web site and daily e-mail newsletter. No-holds-barred commentary on the state of the advertising and media industries includes emerging advertising trends, effects of demographic shifts on advertising strategies, and examination of paradigm shifts in the industry.

Advertising Age

http://www.adage.com

Adage.com is the Internet arm of *Advertising Age*, the weekly paper of advertising news. Other AdAge platforms include electronic newsletters, events and conferences, streaming video, audio webinars, podcasts and blogs. The news on the Web site is updated throughout the day.

Advertising Council

http://www.adcouncil.org

Leading producer of public service announcements, the non-profit Ad Council has sponsored such familiar campaigns as "Friends Don't Let Friends Drive Drunk" and Smokey Bear's "Only You Can Prevent Forest Fires." Its clients are both nonprofit and governmental organizations.

American Advertising Federation
http://www.aaf.org

A trade association with 130 corporate members, as well as clubs around the United States and over 200 college chapters, AAF is "The Unifying Voice for Advertising." It educates members about the latest trends, honors advertising excellence, promotes diversity in advertising and "applies the communication skills of its members to help solve community concerns."

American Association of Advertising Agencies
http://www2.aaaa.org

This management-oriented trade association provides research, media advice and information, and benefit programs such as liability insurance and retirement savings plans for its members. The Web site provides members with industry news, events (including webinars and speech transcripts), career development opportunities and advice, and links to publications and research.

American Marketing Association
http://www.marketingpower.com

The largest in North America, the AMA is a marketing association for individuals and organizations involved in the practice, teaching and study of marketing worldwide. AMA members are connected to a network of nearly 40,000 experienced marketers in academics, research and practice. Its Web site offers marketing data, articles, case studies, best practices and a job bank.

Association of Hispanic Advertising Agencies
http://www.ahaa.org

With the goal to "grow, strengthen and protect the Hispanic marketing advertising industry," the AHAA aims to raise awareness in the value of the Hispanic market to advertisers. Member agencies range from Acento (Los Angeles) to Zubi Advertising Services (Coral Gables, Fla.).

Clio Awards
http://www.clioawards.com

The most recognized global competition for advertising, the Clio Awards has celebrated excellence in a broad range of mediums for almost 50 years. Award categories include Interactive, Content & Contact, Billboard, Print, Radio and Television/Cinema/Digital. Students are awarded in limited categories, and Network, Agency, Production Company and Advertiser of the Year are also honored.

Federal Trade Commission
http://www.ftc.gov

As the U.S. government agency that protects consumers against fraud and misleading advertising and handles antitrust matters, the FTC's work is done by its Bureaus of Consumer Protection, Competition and Economics. It does not resolve individual disputes but rather looks for patterns of law violations. Mail order, telemarketing and used cars are among the businesses it regulates. Much of the information on the Web site is also available in Spanish.

MediaPost Communications
http://www.mediapost.com

An integrated publishing and content company, MediaPost is the leading advertising and media Internet portal providing news, events, directories and a social network to help members better plan and buy both traditional and online advertising. The site's media directory includes information on more than 35,000 publications, stations, networks, Web sites and more.

11
Public Relations: Promoting Ideas

What's Ahead?

Andrew H Walker/Getty Images

Menudo performs at the 2008 Arthur Ashe Kids' Day, a public relations event sponsored by the U.S. Tennis Association to promote children's tennis.

> "There needs to be credible, independent media, and the marketing industry should not be doing anything to undermine credible editorial quality."
>
> Mark Hass, CEO of Manning Selvage & Lee Public Relations Agency

You may think the cash rebate

programs that many of today's car manufacturers offer is a new idea, but in 1914, Henry Ford announced that if he sold 300,000 Model Ts that year, each customer would receive a rebate. When the company reached its goal, Ford returned $50 to each buyer. This was good business. It also was good public relations. Like Henry Ford, public relations people today work to create favorable images—for corporations, public officials, products, schools, hospitals and associations.

There are three ways to encourage people to do what you want them to do: power, patronage and persuasion. Power involves ruling by law, but it also can mean ruling by peer pressure—someone does something because his or her friends do. Patronage is a polite term for bribery—paying someone with favors or money to do what you want. The third method—persuasion—is the approach of public relations.

Persuasion is the act of using argument or reasoning to induce someone to do something. Like advertising, public relations is not a mass medium. Public relations is a media support industry. In the classic definition, **public relations** involves creating an understanding for, or goodwill toward, a company, a person or a product.

PR Helps Shape Public Opinion

One of the first political leaders to realize the importance of public relations was Augustus Caesar, who commissioned statues of himself in the first century to be erected throughout the Roman Empire to enhance his image. Many political leaders have ordered heroic images of themselves printed on coins and stamps. Today's public relations approach can be traced to the beginning of the 20th century. Journalists were an important reason for the eventual emergence of the public relations profession.

Before 1900, business believed that it could work alongside the press, or even ignore it. Many stories that appeared in the press promoted companies that bought advertising. Then the Industrial Revolution arrived, and some industrialists exploited workers and collected enormous profits. Ida Tarbell and Lincoln Steffens began to make businesspeople uncomfortable, writing stories for magazines like *McClure's* about the not so admirable characteristics of some companies.

According to *This Is PR: The Realities of Public Relations*: "No longer could the railroads butter up the press by giving free passes to reporters. No longer would the public buy whitewashed statements like that of coal industrialist George F. Baer, who in 1902 told labor to put their trust in 'the Christian men whom God in His infinite wisdom has given control of the property interests of the country.'"

Persuasion The act of using argument or reasoning to induce someone to do something.

Public Relations Creating understanding for, or goodwill toward, a company, a person or a product.

President Theodore Roosevelt fed public sentiment—public opinion—against the abuses of industry when he started his antitrust campaigns. According to *Effective Public Relations*, "With the growth of mass-circulation newspapers, Roosevelt's canny ability to dominate the front pages demonstrated a new-found power for those with causes to promote.

"He had a keen sense of news and knew how to stage a story so that it would get maximum attention. His skill forced those he fought to develop similar means. He fully exploited the news media as a new and powerful tool of presidential leadership, and he remade the laws and the presidency in the process." Roosevelt used his skills at swaying public opinion to gain support for his antitrust policies.

PR Pioneer Issues "Declaration of Principles"

The first publicity firm was called The Publicity Bureau and opened in Boston in 1900 to head off the growing public criticism of the railroad companies. The best-known early practitioner of public relations was Ivy Lee, who began his PR career by opening an office in New York with George F. Parker.

Lee and Parker represented coal magnate George F. Baer when coal workers went on strike. A former newspaper reporter, Lee issued a "Declaration of Principles" that he mailed to newspaper city editors. This declaration became a manifesto for early public relations companies to follow.

Reacting to criticism that The Publicity Bureau worked secretly to promote the railroads, Lee wrote in 1906 in *American Magazine*, "This [the firm of Lee & Parker] is not a secret press bureau. All our work is done in the open. We aim to supply news. . . . In brief, our plan is, frankly and openly, on behalf of business concerns and public institutions, to supply to the press and public of the United States prompt and accurate information concerning subjects which it is of value and interest to the public to know about."

Lee and Parker dissolved their firm in 1908, when Lee went to work as a publicity agent for the Pennsylvania Railroad. Eventually, John D. Rockefeller hired Lee to counteract the negative publicity that began with Tarbell's investigation of Standard Oil. (Lee worked for the Rockefellers until he died in 1934.)

The idea of in-house corporate public relations grew as Chicago Edison Company and American Telephone & Telegraph began promotional programs. The University of Pennsylvania and the University of Wisconsin opened publicity bureaus in 1904, and the YMCA of Washington, D.C., hired a full-time publicist to oversee fundraising in 1905—the first time someone hired a publicist to do fundraising.

Government Recruits PR Professionals

During World War I, the U.S. government set up the Committee on Public Information, organized by former newspaper reporter George Creel, blurring the line between propaganda and publicity. Creel recruited journalists, editors, artists and teachers to raise money for Liberty Bonds and to promote the nation's participation in the war. One of the people who worked for Creel was Edward L. Bernays. Both Bernays and Ivy Lee have been called the father of public relations.

In 1923, Bernays wrote the first book on public relations, *Crystallizing Public Opinion*, and taught the first course on the subject. Bernays was interested in mass psychology—how to influence the opinions of large groups of people. Procter & Gamble, General Motors and the American Tobacco Company were among his clients. "Public relations," Bernays wrote in 1955, "is the attempt, by information, persuasion and adjustment, to engineer public support for an activity, cause, movement or institution." In 1985, Bernays further defined public relations as "giving a client ethical advice, based on research of the public, that will win the social goals upon which the client depends for his livelihood."

To sell the New Deal in the 1930s, Franklin D. Roosevelt used every tactic he knew. Comfortable with the press and the public alike, and advised by PR expert Louis McHenry Howe, FDR "projected an image of self-confidence and happiness—just what the American public wanted to believe in. He talked to them on the radio. He smiled for the cameras. He was mentioned in popular songs. He even allowed himself to be one of the main characters in a Rodgers and Hart musical comedy (played by George M. Cohan, America's favorite Yankee Doodle Dandy)," according to *This is PR*.

To gain support for the nation's entry into World War II, the federal government mounted the largest public relations drive in its history, which centered around the Office of War Information, led by former newscaster Elmer Davis. After the war, the public relations business boomed along with the postwar economy.

Women Join PR Firms

Doris E. Fleischman was among the first women in public relations when she joined her husband, Edward L. Bernays, in his PR firm. Fleischman was an equal partner with Bernays in their public relations business. An early advocate of public relations as a profession for women, Fleischman wrote, in 1931, that "one finds women working side by side with men in forming the traditions and rules that will govern the profession of the future."

Bettmann/CORBIS

Edward L. Bernays wrote the first book on public relations, *Crystallizing Public Opinion*, and taught the first course on the subject.

Bettmann/CORBIS

Doris Fleischman, a public relations pioneer, began her career in the 1920s. Fleischman was an early advocate of public relations as a profession for women.

[LC-USZ62-90303] Library of Congress Prints and Photographs Division

In what was the largest public relations drive of its time, the Office of War Information promoted the role of the United States in World War II. Today, the federal government is the largest single employer of public relations people.

"Yes, but take away the rodent droppings and the occasional shard of glass, and you've still got a damn fine product."

Two other women who were public relations pioneers were Leone Baxter and Anne Williams Wheaton. Baxter formed Baxter and Whitaker in San Francisco with her husband, Clem Whitaker—the first public relations agency to specialize in political campaigns. In 1957, President Dwight Eisenhower appointed Anne Williams Wheaton as his associate press secretary.

Professionals Promote Ethics Codes

In the 1930s, the requirements for someone to work in public relations were loose, and many people who said they worked in public relations were press agents who often used tricks to get attention for their clients. Henry Rogers, co-founder of what was then the world's largest entertainment PR firm, Rogers & Cowan (based in Beverly Hills), admitted that in 1939 he created a "best-dressed" contest to promote little-known actress Rita Hayworth.

There had been no contest, but Rogers dubbed Hayworth the winner of this fictional event. *Look* magazine gave Hayworth a ten-page spread. "Press agents, and that's what we were, would dream up all sorts of phony stories," he said. "Journalists knew they were phony but printed them because they looked good in print."

During the 1950s, the question of ethics in public relations arose publicly when Byoir and Associates, hired by a railroad company to counteract the expansion of trucking, was charged with creating "front" organizations to speak out against the trucking industry. In court, Byoir's agency argued they were exercising free speech. In 1961, the U.S. Supreme Court upheld Byoir's right to represent a client even if the presentation was dishonest, but this left the ethical issue of honesty unresolved.

The Public Relations Society of America (PRSA) established its first code of ethics in 1954 and expanded that code in 1959 with a Declaration of Principles. That ethics code still exists today to guide the business of public relations. (Excerpts from the PRSA code are in **Chapter 15**.) PR professionals continue to argue among themselves about the differences between the profession's beginnings as press agentry (which often meant fabricating stories) and the concept of ethically representing a client's business, as Edward L. Bernays described (see **Impact/Ethics**, "Just So You Know, No One Paid for This Article," page 237).

Public relations grew throughout the 1960s and 1970s with the encouragement of television, the federal government and corporate America. In 1961, for example, the federal government had about 1,000 people working as writer-editors and public affairs specialists. Today, *the total number of people working in federal government public information jobs is nearly 4,000, making the federal government the nation's largest single employer of public information people.* (Public information is the name given to the job of government public relations.)

Public Relations at Work

Public relations is an industry of specialties. The most familiar public relations areas are financial public relations, product public relations and crisis public relations, but there are many other specialty areas.

Financial Public Relations

People in financial public relations provide information primarily to business reporters. "Business editors like a PR staff that can provide access to top management," wrote James K. Gentry in the *Washington Journalism Review*, "that knows its company well or can find needed information quickly, that demonstrates ethics and honesty and that knows and accepts the difference between news and fluff." Gentry then listed comments gathered from editors about what makes a bad PR operation:

- "Companies that think they can hide the truth from the public or believe it's none of the public's business."

- "I despise it when a PR person intercepts our calls to a news source but then isn't capable of answering our questions."

- "When they hire an outside PR firm to handle the job."

- "The 'no-comment' attitude. When they have little or no interest in going beyond the press release."

- "People who either get in the way of you doing your job, complain too much or are no help at all."

Product Public Relations

Product PR uses public relations techniques to sell products and services. Many companies have learned that seeking

IMPACT
»Ethics

Just So You Know, No One Paid for This Article

by Michael Bush

Mark Hass, CEO of the Publicis Groupe-owned public-relations agency Manning Selvage & Lee, had a rather alarming conversation last month with a "very senior" media planner from an agency outside of his parent holding company.

"I just don't understand what you guys [in the PR industry] do at the end of the day, because if I need a story for one of my clients, all I need to do is ask [a publisher or ad rep] and I get it," Mr. Hass recalled the agency executive saying to him.

A recent survey shows that that agency executive isn't alone. The sixth annual MS&L Marketing Management Survey, done in conjunction with *PRWeek,* found that 19 percent of the 252 chief marketing officers and marketing directors surveyed said their organizations had bought advertising in return for a news story. That represents one in five senior marketers and is up from 17 percent last year.

"I'm not saying it's a huge problem," Mr. Hass said. "But 19 percent of senior marketers saying they do it constitutes a problem."

That's particularly true in this age of transparency. "One type of coverage you buy and the other you achieve through persuasive argument, making it a credible source

Whole Foods CEO John Mackey used a pseudonym to post favorable comments about his company's financial results in chat rooms, raising ethical questions about corporate public relations in an online world.

of information and not something that has to be taken with a grain of salt," Mr. Hass said. "There needs to be credible, independent media, and the marketing industry should not be doing anything to undermine credible editorial quality."

The backlash that arises from any sort of underhanded scheming can and will spread like wildfire in the digital age. Just ask Wal-Mart and Whole Foods. Wal-Mart was called for running a pro-Wal-Mart fake blog, and Whole Foods CEO John Mackey was caught posting favorable comments, under a pseudonym, about his company and its financial results in chat rooms.

The study reveals that the online world is viewed as a place where marketers can ignore ethical guidelines, and it's that finding that Mr. Hass said he finds perturbing. . . .

"It's almost like there's a different standard for online activity, and that's a little worrisome because that's the growth area," Mr. Hass said. "That's something the industry needs to be attentive to, because the reputational damage that can occur if a marketer is dishonest online is huge."

"Just So You Know, No One Paid for this Article" by Michael Bush, AdAge.com, August 4, 2008. Reprinted by permission.

publicity for a product often is less expensive than advertising the product. Public relations "is booming partly because of price," reports *The Wall Street Journal*. A PR budget of $500,000 is considered huge, whereas an ad budget that size is considered tiny.

According to *The Wall Street Journal*, "At its best, PR can work better than advertising. Coleco Industries Inc. kicked off its Cabbage Patch Kids in 1983 with press parties thrown in children's museums, to which editors and their children were invited—and at which all received dolls to 'adopt.' 'Reporters who adopted dolls felt a part of the process,' a Coleco spokeswoman says. They had 'a personal interest in . . . continuing to publicize it.'" The initial publicity for the Cabbage Patch dolls snowballed, as Cartier's used the dolls to display jewelry in its windows and First Lady Nancy Reagan gave dolls to two Korean children who were in the United States for surgery. Richard Weiner, who handled the publicity, charged Coleco $500,000.

On a smaller budget, the Wieden & Kennedy agency in Seattle contracted Bigger Than Life, Inc., which makes large inflatables, to manufacture a 21-story pair of tennis shoes. The company attached the shoes to the Westin Copley Place

Odwalla, Inc., CEO Stephen Williamson drinks a bottle of spring water during a news conference at the company's headquarters. Odwalla's quick response to the discovery of *E. coli* bacteria in its fruit juice is cited as an example of good public relations.

AP/Wide World Photos

Crisis Communication A timely public relations response to a critical situation that could cause damage to a company's reputation.

Hotel during the Boston Marathon and to the Westin Hotel in downtown Cincinnati during the March of Dimes walk-a-thon. Pictures of the shoes appeared in *The New York Times*, in *The Cincinnati Enquirer* and in newspapers as far away as Japan. Wieden & Kennedy estimated that buying the same advertising would have cost $7 million. (See **Impact/Culture**, "Want Your Cause on Oprah? Try a Billboard," page 239.)

Crisis Public Relations

This aspect of public relations goes back as far as Edward Bernays responding to the charges against Standard Oil. The term *crisis public relations* (sometimes called **crisis communication**) describes the situation facing a company that faces a public relations emergency because of an unexpected event that could seriously hurt the company's reputation.

In October 1996, beverage maker Odwalla, Inc., faced a public relations crisis when *E. coli* bacteria was traced to unpasteurized apple juice that had been sold by the natural juice company. The bacteria eventually was held responsible for the death of a 16-month-old girl in Colorado and more than 50 cases of severe illness. Odwalla, the leading manufacturer of unpasteurized juices, had made its reputation on natural, unfiltered products. But as soon as Odwalla detected the bacteria, the company announced an immediate recall of 13 products in the seven western states and British Columbia.

Then the company worked with the Food and Drug Administration to scour the Odwalla processing facilities, which were found to be free of the bacteria. The company continued the investigation, including the processors who supplied fruit for the juice. At the same time, Odwalla Chief Executive Officer Stephen Williamson said the company was exploring all methods of processing the juice to kill the bacteria. Eventually, the company announced it would use a method of flash pasteurization, which the company said would keep more flavor than traditional pasteurization while maintaining public safety.

One month after the outbreak, Odwalla took out full-page ads in several newspapers, an "open letter" to its customers, thanking them for their support and offering sympathy for people diagnosed with *E. coli*–related illnesses after drinking Odwalla juices.

"I think Odwalla is making all the right moves," said Pam Smith, a retail stock analyst. Smith's advice for any company facing such a crisis was: "Be brutally honest, no matter what the results. And show your customers that you care about their safety." The Odwalla episode indicates how important specialization in crisis public relations can be within the public relations business. (For an example of a failure of crisis public relations, see **Impact/Business**, "Crisis Public Relations Fails in the 2007 Utah Mine Disaster," page 240.)

IMPACT
≫ Culture

Want Your Cause on Oprah? Try a Billboard

by Jeremy Mullman

How's this? Buy a single billboard, get your cause hyped during a full hour of *Oprah*.

A nonprofit Pennsylvania animal shelter managed exactly that in its continuing crusade against puppy mills. . . .

[In 2008], Main Line Animal Rescue bought a billboard four blocks from Ms. Winfrey's Chicago studio, hoping to draw the attention of one of the world's most influential celebrities (and animal lovers) and to wield that influence to educate her massive audience.

"OPRAH—please do a show on puppy mills; the dogs need you!" the billboard read.

Lo and behold, it worked. The show's producers quickly contacted the shelter and enlisted its help in a hidden-camera investigation of various puppy mills and pet stores, led by Lisa Ling, the show's investigative reporter.

Considering how hard armies of publicists typically slave to score even the slightest mention on the show, the animal shelter's low-cost, low-effort success was a coup. "Getting on Oprah is like winning the lottery," said Susan Harrow, author of *The Ultimate Guide to Getting Booked on Oprah*, who said she'd never heard of anyone getting on Ms. Winfrey's couch so easily. "The awareness it will raise for them is priceless."

Courtesy of Main Line rescue/www.mainline rescue.com/Billboard designed by Paul Hartacher

When the Main Line Animal Rescue of Pennsylvania wanted publicity for their campaign against puppy mills, the organization took out a billboard ad and placed it four blocks from Oprah Winfrey's TV studio in Chicago. The billboard got Winfrey's attention, and the show broadcast a story about the topic.

The program featured Ms. Ling's footage, an interview with Ms. Ling expanding on what she found, profiles of rescued puppies, and a tribute to Ms. Winfrey's late cocker spaniel, Sophie. . . .

"So I'm driving in to work, I see the billboard, 'Oprah, do this for the dogs because they need you.' It got my attention," Ms. Winfrey said on the air while interviewing the shelter's founder, Bill Smith.

Mr. Smith, for his part, said, "We were trying to come up with some ideas as far as who could reach more people than anyone else, and I thought of you, and I just thought that you would be able to spread the word and educate a lot of people."

Public Relations Adapts to the Internet

Because of its ability to deliver information quickly and directly, the Internet offers many benefits for public relations companies. Public relations people, in fact, often are very much involved in creating and modifying Web sites for their clients—creating a public face. News releases, product announcements and company profiles can be made available online, to be available on demand to the press, stockholders and anyone else who is interested.

IMPACT
»Business

Crisis Public Relations Fails in the 2007 Utah Mine Disaster

by Jon Harmon

As the Utah mine saga moves from catastrophe to, inevitably, a place beyond our collective front-page consciousness, the national media will leave Crandall Canyon families to mourn their losses. Reflecting on the news coverage of the tragedy, we are left to ponder the strange legacy of the chief executive of the mining company, Robert E. Murray, and his bizarre style of crisis communications.

The 67-year-old Murray was in Montana when he got word of the collapse at the mine owned by Murray Energy Corp. He hopped on a private jet and was at the scene within hours, taking command of the rescue operation, providing the media updates. All this was textbook PR in the best sense. The presence of the concerned chief executive on the scene of a disaster has been understood to be essential to successful crisis management

Public relations experts criticized Crandall Canyon coalmine co-owner Robert E. Murray for the way he handled the Utah Mine Disaster in 2007 as an example of poor crisis communications. Murray talked with reporters on August 16, 2007, when a rescue of the trapped miners was underway. After three rescuers were killed by a subsequent cave-in, Murray disappeared and sent a subordinate to deal with journalists.

The Internet also brings hazards. Disgruntled customers, pranksters and competitors can create their own sites to immediately challenge and even undermine a client's site. "In the pre-Internet days we used to say that a satisfied customer will tell one or two prospects but a dissatisfied customer will tell 10 or more," wrote G. A. Andy Marken, a public relations adviser, in *Public Relations Quarterly*. "With the Internet and the Web those same dissatisfied customers can tell millions of people . . . and they're doing it every day around the globe."

Cybersmears Negative information organized and presented on the Internet as continuing attacks against a corporation.

Marken says these attacks, which he calls ***cybersmears***, include anti-Disney, anti-McDonald's and anti–gun regulation sites, as well as chat rooms, discussion groups and online forums. To counter these negative messages, many businesses and organizations hire public relations firms to continuously monitor the Internet and alert their clients when negative information appears so the client can decide the best way to counter the information.

"It's a tedious task but any organization that isn't monitoring Internet traffic and Web activity could find itself in serious trouble," says Marken. "Companies and agencies spend hundreds and thousands of dollars on audio, video and print clipping services to analyze how their messages are being picked up, interpreted and used by the conventional media. They spend little or no time finding out what people are saying in real-time in cyberspace about them . . .

since Exxon's CEO infamously took far too long to travel to Valdez, Alaska, in 1989, to take stock of the oil spill that caused one of history's worst environmental disasters.

But after that, Murray broke so many rules of crisis communications he had news anchors, on-air, asking what they'd just witnessed. From his first briefings, Murray angrily denounced the media (seldom a winning strategy) and blamed union organizers for suggesting that the dangerous practice of "retreat mining" had led to the collapse. He blasted environmentalists for their crusade against global warming, calling it an affront to the coal industry and to the American economy.

Crisis communications experts universally panned Murray's rantings as "callous," "damaging" and "not helpful" to the families of the trapped miners.

Murray also insisted that an earthquake had caused the mine collapse, then doggedly held to that theory despite seismologists' conclusions that the tremors were caused by the collapse. In a crisis, there is always a temptation to provide answers before all the evidence is in and to hold on to beliefs even as contradicting facts mount.

In Utah, each passing day dimmed any reasonable hope that the six miners were still alive. After three rescuers were killed in a cave-in, Murray dropped out of sight, leaving a subordinate to conduct briefings. A representative for the miners' families said, "We feel Bob Murray has abandoned us."

Murray's failings will be an object lesson for corporate executives for years to come. Companies and their executives need to be prepared for a crisis. That does not mean one considers it acceptable or inevitable; indeed, an audit of vulnerabilities may uncover deficiencies that can be fixed. But responsible executives understand that things can and do go wrong.

Properly done, crisis communications is not spin or damage control. It is the calm and honest disposition of information at a time when information is incomplete and may be changing by the minute. The news media will demand immediate answers. Critics will criticize. And CEOs need training to resist the urge to argue or speculate in times of great stress. The sole focus should be the safety and welfare of any victims.

Note: Jon Harmon, a public relations consultant, spent 23 years at Ford Motor Co. and was responsible for media relations during the Ford-Firestone tire recall in 2000–2001.

"Crisis PR in the Mines," by Jon Harmon, *Los Angeles Times*, August 21, 2007. Reprinted by permission of the author.

What you don't hear can hurt you . . . and it could be fatal." By providing Internet monitoring, public relations people can play a big role in protecting their clients from negative publicity.

Public Relations Joins Ad Agencies

The estimated number of people in the country involved in public relations is 161,000, and more than 4,000 firms in the United States offer PR-related services. The largest public relations firms employ more than 1,000 people. Several major corporations have 100 to 400 public relations specialists, but most public relations firms have fewer than four employees.

Public relations people often deal with advertising agencies as part of their job, and because PR and advertising are so interrelated, several large public relations firms have joined several large advertising agencies. For example, J. Walter Thompson (advertising) joined Hill & Knowlton (public relations), and the London firm WPP Group PLC bought Young & Rubicam and now owns more than 250 public relations, advertising and marketing companies.

Combined agencies can offer both public relations and advertising services to their clients, and the trend toward advertising/public relations combinations continues today. The difference between public relations and advertising at the nation's largest agencies can be difficult to discern. Advertising is an aspect of marketing that aims to sell products. People in advertising usually *aren't* involved in a company's policy making. They implement the company's

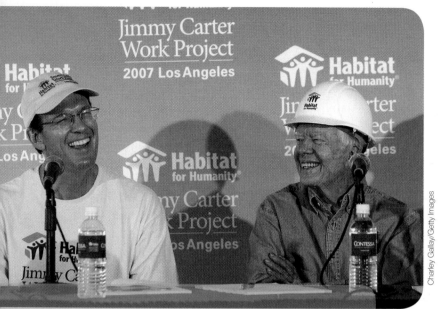

Charley Gallay/Getty Images

Public relations for nonprofit organizations, such as Habitat for Humanity, is growing especially fast as different charities compete for donations. In 2007, former U.S. President Jimmy Carter (on the right) and Habitat for Humanity CEO Jonathan Reckford talked with the press. Carter and his wife, Rosalynn, joined hundreds of volunteers to help with the Jimmy Carter Work Project, which built 100 houses in 2007.

policies after company executives decide how to sell a product, a corporate image or an idea.

Public relations people, in comparison, usually are involved in policy. A PR person often contributes to decisions about how a company will deal with the public, the press and its own employees.

Variety of Clients Use Public Relations

Public relations people work for several types of clients, including governments, educational institutions, nonprofit organizations, industry and business.

Government

The federal government is the nation's largest single employer of public information people. State and local governments also hire people to handle PR. Related to government are PR people who work for political candidates and for lobbying organizations. Media consultants also are involved in political PR. These people counsel candidates and officeholders about how they should present themselves to the public through the media.

Education

Universities, colleges and school districts often hire public relations people to promote these educational institutions and to handle press attention from the consequences of decisions that educators make.

Nonprofit Organizations

Nonprofit organizations include hospitals, churches, museums and charities. Public relations organizations help raise money for charities such as Habitat for Humanity, which builds and remodel homes for low-income communities. Public relations for nonprofit organizations is growing especially fast as different charities compete with each other for donations.

Industry

AT&T's early use of public relations strategies was one type of industry PR. Many industries are government-regulated, so this often means that the industry PR person works with government agencies on government-related issues that affect the industry, such as utility rate increases or energy conservation programs.

Business

This is the best-known area of public relations. Large companies keep an in-house staff of public relations people, and these companies also often hire outside PR firms to help on special projects. Product publicity is one of the fastest-growing aspects of business-related public relations.

Within many large businesses are people who handle corporate PR, sometimes called financial PR. They prepare annual reports and gather financial data on the company for use by the press. They also may be assigned directly to the executives of a corporation to help establish policy about the corporation's public image. Many companies also sponsor charity events to increase their visibility in the community.

Athletic Teams and Entertainment Organizations

A professional sports team needs someone to travel with them and handle the press requests that inevitably come at each stop. Sports information people also are responsible for the coaches,' the owner's and the team's relationship with the fans. College and university sports departments often hire public relations people to handle inquiries from the public and from the press. Organizations such as the U.S. Tennis Association also sponsor events, such as the Arthur Ashe Kids' Day at the U.S. Open.

As described earlier, in 1939 Henry Rogers learned how to use press agentry to gather publicity for actress Rita Hayworth. Today, entertainment public relations agencies promote movies and also handle TV personalities and well-known athletes who appear on the lecture circuit.

International

As the nation's consumer market broadens, more attention is being given to developing business in other countries. This means more opportunities in international PR. Hill & Knowlton and Burson-Marsteller, for example, are two big U.S. public relations firms that now also operate in Japan.

Public Relations Organizations Offer Many Services

Responsibilities of PR people include writing, editing, media relations and placement, special events, public speaking, production tasks, research, programming and counseling, training and management.

- **Writing.** Writing news releases, newsletters, correspondence, reports, speeches, booklet texts, radio and TV copy, film scripts, trade paper and magazine articles, institutional advertisements, product information and technical materials.

- **Editing.** Editing special publications, employee newsletters, shareholder reports and other communications for employees and for the public.

- **Media Relations and Placement.** Contacting news media, magazines, Sunday supplements, freelance writers and trade publications with the intent of getting them to publish or broadcast news and features about, or originated by, the organization. Responding to media requests for information or spokespersons.

- **Special Events.** Arranging and managing press conferences, convention exhibits, open houses, anniversary celebrations, fundraising events, special observances, contests and award programs.

- **Public Speaking.** Appearing before groups and arranging platforms for others before appropriate audiences by managing a speaker's bureau.

- **Production Tasks.** Creating art, photography and layout for brochures, booklets, reports, institutional advertisements and periodicals; recording and editing audio and Internet materials.

- **Research.** Gathering data to help an organization plan programs; monitoring the effectiveness of public relations programs. This is a fast-growing area of public relations

"Young people today need heroes—that's why I hired a P.R. firm."

that includes focus groups to test message concepts; research to target specific audiences; surveys of a company's reputation for use in improving the company's image; employee and public attitude surveys; and shareholder surveys to improve relations with investors.

- **Programming and Counseling.** Establishing a program for effective public relations within the company.

- **Training.** Working with executives and other people within the organization to prepare them to deal with the media.

- **Management.** Overseeing the costs of running the public relations program; paying the bills.

Publicity Means Free Media

Public relations work often means finding ways to attract the attention of the press. Seymour Topping, former managing editor of *The New York Times*, said, "PR people do influence the news, but really more in a functional manner rather than in terms of giving new editorial direction. We get hundreds of press releases every day in each of our departments. We screen them very carefully for legitimate news, and very often there are legitimate news stories. Quite a lot of our business stories originate from press releases. It's impossible for us to cover all of these organizations ourselves."

People in public relations provide ***publicity***, which creates events and presents information so the press and the public will pay attention. Publicity and advertising differ: An advertising message is *paid for*; publicity is *free*. Advertising

Publicity Uncontrolled free use of media by a public relations firm to create events and present information to capture press and public attention.

is a *controlled* use of media, because the person or company that places the ad governs the message and where it will appear. Publicity is considered an *uncontrolled* use of the media, because the public relations person provides information to the press but has no control over how the information will appear—the press presents the story.

"We know how the media work," says David Resnicow of the PR firm Ruder Finn & Rotman, "and we make judgments on that, providing access to events as it becomes necessary." It is precisely because people in the media and people in PR know how each other work that they argue about the role of public relations in the news.

The *Columbia Journalism Review* studied the relationship between corporate public relations and *The Wall Street Journal* by examining the stories in the *Journal* on a specific day and comparing the stories to press releases issued by PR people. Specific companies were mentioned in 111 articles. More than one-third of the news stories in the *Journal* that day, *CJR* reported in its analysis, were based solely on press releases. In 32 of the stories that were based on press releases, reporters paraphrased the releases almost verbatim; in the 21 remaining cases, only a small amount of additional reporting had been done.

The *Journal*'s executive director, Frederick Taylor, responded to *CJR*'s analysis by saying, "Ninety percent of daily coverage is started by a company making an announcement for the record. We're relaying this information to our readers."

Public Relations Grows Globally

Clever ways to attract attention are trademarks of today's successful public relations professional. Like advertising, the future of public relations is tied closely to the future of the media industries. The basic structure of the business will not change, but public relations practitioners find themselves facing the same challenges as people in the advertising business.

Growing international markets mean that many U.S. public relations firms have expanded overseas. Global communications mean that public relations agencies often work internationally on some projects, and the agencies have to adjust to the cultural differences that global exposure brings.

New technologies, especially the Internet, mean new ways to deliver public relations messages. Satellite technology has streamlined delivery of print, audio and video, giving PR agencies the same access to distributing information to news organizations that the news organizations possess themselves. As in the advertising industry, shifting demographic patterns mean growing potential markets for public relations services.

Review, Analyze, Investigate
REVIEWING CHAPTER 11

PR Helps Shape Public Opinion

✓ There are three ways to encourage someone to do what you want them to do: power, patronage and persuasion.

✓ Public relations people use persuasion to form public opinion about their clients.

✓ Modern public relations emerged at the beginning of the 20th century as a way for business to respond to the muckrakers and to Theodore Roosevelt's antitrust campaign.

PR Pioneer Issues "Declaration of Principles"

✓ President Roosevelt successfully used public relations to influence public opinion.

✓ The first U.S. publicity firm, called The Publicity Bureau, opened in Boston in 1900.

✓ The best-known practitioner of early public relations was Ivy Lee, who wrote a "Declaration of Principles" to respond to the secret publicity activities of The Publicity Bureau.

✓ The Chicago Edison Company and American Telephone & Telegraph were the first companies to begin in-house promotional programs.

Government Recruits PR Professionals

✓ Both Edward L. Bernays and Ivy Lee have been called the father of public relations.

✓ The Committee on Public Information, headed by George Creel, promoted the war effort during World War I.

✓ The Office of War Information, headed by newscaster Elmer Davis, promoted the country's efforts during World War II.

✓ Edward L. Bernays wrote the first book on public relations, *Crystallizing Public Opinion.*

✓ Franklin Roosevelt, assisted by public relations expert Louis McHenry Howe, successfully used public relations to promote the New Deal.

Women Join PR Firms

✓ Among the pioneering women who joined the public relations business were Doris E. Fleischman, Leone Baxter and Anne Williams Wheaton.

✓ Doris Fleischman and Edward L. Bernays were equal partners in the Bernayses' public relations firm.

✓ Doris Fleischman was an early advocate of public relations as a career for women.

Professionals Promote Ethics Codes

✓ The Public Relations Society established the profession's first code of ethics in 1954.

✓ Public relations expanded quickly in the 1960s and 1970s to accommodate television, the federal government and corporate America.

Public Relations at Work

✓ Three of the most common public relations specialties are financial public relations, product public relations and crisis public relations.

✓ Crisis public relations repaired the public image of Odwalla, Inc., but did not help in the 2007 Utah mine disaster.

Public Relations Adapts to the Internet

✓ Negative PR can spread very quickly on the Web, where anyone is free to post damaging comments about a company, organization or product.

✓ Companies and agencies must be continually vigilant to monitor how their messages are being used and interpreted on the Internet.

✓ Whole Foods CEO John Mackey was caught anonymously posting favorable messages about his company on the Internet, which negatively affected the company's public image when his actions were uncovered.

Public Relations Joins Ad Agencies

✓ Today, 161,000 people work in public relations nationwide. More than 4,000 firms offer PR-related services.

✓ Because PR and advertising are so interrelated, public relations people and advertising agencies often work together in the same company to offer advertising and marketing communications services.

Variety of Clients Use Public Relations

✓ Public relations people work in government, education, industry, business, nonprofit agencies, athletic teams, entertainment companies and international business.

✓ The federal government is the largest single employer of public relations people.

Public Relations Organizations Offer Many Services

✓ Responsibilities of PR people include writing, editing, media relations and placement, special events, public speaking, production tasks, research, programming and counseling, training and management.

Publicity Means Free Media

✓ The main difference between advertising and public relations is that advertising messages are controlled and public relations messages are uncontrolled.

✓ Public relations people create publicity, which is considered an uncontrolled use of media.

Public Relations Grows Globally

✓ New technologies, especially the Internet, mean new ways to deliver public relations messages.

✓ Electronic technology has streamlined print, audio and video delivery, giving PR the same access to information distribution as news organizations.

✓ Global communications mean many public relations agencies work internationally on some projects and must adjust to cultural differences that global exposure brings.

✓ Growing international markets mean that many U.S. public relations firms have expanded overseas.

✓ Shifting demographic patterns mean growing potential markets for public relations services.

KEY TERMS

These terms are defined in the margins throughout this chapter and appear in alphabetical order with definitions in the Glossary, which begins on page 372.

Crisis Communication 238

Cybersmears 240

Persuasion 234

Public Relations 234

Publicity 243

CRITICAL QUESTIONS

1. How did each of the following people contribute to the development of public relations?

   a. Ivy Lee and George F. Parker

   b. Edward L. Bernays

   c. Doris E. Fleischman

2. Explain in some detail how the Office of War Information contributed to positive public relations for World War II.

3. When is crisis public relations necessary for a company to diffuse a difficult situation? Give an example.

4. Describe the ways that advertising and public relations are different. Describe the ways they are similar.

5. Describe one or more example(s) of how negative information on the Internet can create problems for public relations practitioners.

WORKING THE WEB

This list includes both sites mentioned in the chapter and others to give you greater insight into the public relations industry.

All About Public Relations
http://www.aboutpublicrelations.net

This site provides information and links to PR jobs, careers and internships as well as desk references, agencies and PR basics. Subject links range from a How-to PR Toolkit to online public relations campaigns and strategies.

Chartered Institute of Public Relations
http://www.cipr.co.uk

The "eyes, ears and voice of the public relations industry," this professional organization for the British public relations industry provides training and events, a professional development program, PR news and research, and a PR jobs board. Its members sign an enforced code of conduct.

Center for Media and Democracy: PRWatch.org
http://www.prwatch.org

This nonprofit, nonpartisan organization investigates and exposes public relations spin and propaganda, and promotes media literacy and citizen journalism. The Center projects include *PR Watch*, a quarterly publication dedicated to investigative reporting on the PR industry; *Spin of the Day*, web-based daily reporting on PR propaganda and media spin; *SourceWatch*, an online "open content" encyclopedia of people, groups and issues that shape the public agenda; and *Congresspedia*, the "citizen's encyclopedia" of U.S. House and Senate members. Web site users can browse articles on topics including animal rights, health, race/ethnic relations, tobacco, war and peace, and much more.

Institute for Public Relations
http://www.instituteforpr.com

This independent nonprofit organization sponsors and disseminates scientific research about public relations and sponsors the Commission on Public Relations Measurement and Evaluation, which establishes standards and methods for PR research and issues best-practices white papers. The Commission on Global Public Relations Research was formed in 2005 to study the practice of PR across regions, countries and cultures. The Institute also offers several awards for excellence in PR practice and research, including one for a master's thesis.

Online Public Relations
http://www.online-pr.com

This straightforward Web site provides free online resources for public relations professionals. It is developed and maintained by James L. Horton, a PR executive and educator who specializes in using technology and the Internet to enhance client service. This list of media, reference and PR resources contains thousands of links to reliable sources categorized by subject and alphabetically indexed.

PR Newswire
http://prnewswire.com

This association provides electronic distribution, targeting, measurement, translation and broadcast services for government, association, labor and nonprofit customers world wide. PRNewswire provides search engine optimization, a professional community, user tracking, and multimedia and multicultural services to customers.

PRWeek
http://www.prweekus.com

A publication of Haymarket, producer of more than 100 international trade magazines, *PR Week* is the company's first weekly in the United States. The magazine provides timely news, reviews, profiles, techniques and groundbreaking research for PR professionals. As the companion Web site for the magazine, *PRWeek.com* offers a searchable archive of editorials, news, features, industry research and special reports.

PRWeb
http://www.prweb.com

Founded in 1997 to help small businesses use the Internet to communicate their news to the public, PRWeb pioneered the direct-to-consumer news release. Clients can create a free account, access the site's search engine optimization tools and upload a press release for online distribution. PRWeb has helped more than 40,000 organizations of all sizes maximize the online visibility of their news. The service is owned by Vocus, a leader in on-demand PR software.

Public Relations Society of America (PRSA)
http://www.prsa.org

The world's largest organization for public relations professionals, PRSA was established in 1947 and has nearly 32,000 members organized into more than 100 chapters. Representing for-profit and not-for-profit organizations from areas including business and industry, government, health and education, its primary objectives are to advance the standards of the profession by providing members with professional development opportunities, to strengthen the society by increasing members and enriching member services, and to establish global leadership in PR.

Public Relations Student Society of America (PRSSA)
http://www.prssa.org

An organization founded by the Public Relations Society of America for students, the PRSSA's goal is to make students aware of current theories and procedures of the profession, to appreciate ethical ideals and principles, and to understand what constitutes an appropriate professional attitude. It has 284 chapters on college campuses and offers a number of scholarships and travel opportunities.

12

News and Information: Getting Personal

The news media and interested tourists converge on Wall Street in front of the New York Stock Exchange on October 10, 2008. Stocks swung wildly during the day, signaling the beginning of the U.S.'s serious economic downturn.

What's Ahead?

Because the First Amendment

to the U.S. Constitution prescribes freedom of the press, it is important to understand the development of news reporting in this country. Today's news delivery is the result of a tug of war between audiences as they define the types of news they want and the news media who try to deliver it.

Publick Occurrences, the nation's first newspaper, published only one issue in 1690 before the authorities shut it down. The nation's first *consecutively issued* newspaper (published more than

Paul J. Richards/AFP/Getty Images

Today the public's appetite for news means there are more news outlets gathering more types of news than ever before. In June 2008, former White House Secretary Scott McClellan arrives to give testimony before the Judiciary Committee of the U.S. House of Representatives about reported attempts to cover up the involvement of White House officials in the leak of the covert identity of CIA officer Valerie Plame (see page 267).

once) was *The Boston News-Letter,* which appeared in 1704. In the first issue, editor John Campbell reprinted the queen's latest speech, some maritime news and one advertisement telling people how to put an ad in his paper.

From 1704 until the Civil War, newspapers spread throughout New England, the South and across the frontier. The invention of the telegraph, in 1844, meant news that once took weeks to reach publication could be transmitted in minutes.

Early News Organizations Cooperate to Gather News

In 1848, six newspapers in New York City decided to share the cost of gathering foreign news by telegraph from Boston. Henry J. Raymond, who owned *The New York Times,* drew up

Cooperative News Gathering Member news organizations that share the expense of getting the news.

the agreement among the papers to pay $100 for 3,000 words of telegraph news. Soon known as the New York Associated Press, this organization was the country's first ***cooperative news gathering*** association.

This cooperative meant the member organizations shared the cost of getting the news, returning any profits to the members. Today's Associated Press (AP) is the result of this early partnership, as newspapers joined together in a cooperative, with several members sharing the cost of gathering the news, domestic and foreign. United Press, founded in 1884 to compete with AP, devised a different way of sharing information. The United Press, which eventually became United Press International (UPI), was established not as a cooperative but as a privately owned, for-profit wire service. (Today wire services are called news services.)

Using satellites and computer terminals instead of the original telegraph machines, cooperative and for-profit news gathering by news services has become virtually instantaneous. Most American newspapers and broadcast news operations subscribe to at least one news service, such as AP. Many other news services send stories and broadcasts worldwide: Agence France-Presse (France), Reuters (Great Britain), the Russian Information Telegraph Agency (RITA), Agenzia-Nationale Stampa Associate (Italy), Deutsche Presse Agentur (Germany) and Xinhua (China).

The news services especially help small newspapers and broadcast stations that can't afford overseas correspondents. Large dailies with their own correspondents around the world still rely on news services when they can't get to a story quickly. AP today is still a cooperative, as it was when it began in New York. UPI had several owners and declined financially. Today, Associated Press serves as the nation's primary news service, constantly feeding stories to newspapers, broadcast outlets and Internet news services.

Some newspaper organizations in the United States—*The New York Times, The Washington Post* and *Chicago Tribune*—also run their own news services. Subscribers publish each other's news service stories. For many newspapers, news service stories provide information at a relatively low cost because the newspaper doesn't need as many staff reporters to cover the news.

Civil War Brings Accreditation and Photojournalism

In the 1860s, interest in the emotional issues of the Civil War sent many reporters to the battlefront. Hundreds of correspondents roamed freely among the soldiers, reporting for the North and the South. Two important results of Civil War reporting were the accreditation of reporters and the introduction of photographs to enhance written reports.

Government Accredits Journalists

The issue of government interests versus press freedom surfaced early in the Civil War. In 1861, Union General Winfield Scott forbade telegraph companies from transmitting military information because he was afraid some stories would help the South. At the Battle of Bull Run in 1861, *New York Times* editor Henry J. Raymond, reporting the war from the front, mistakenly telegraphed a story that said the North had won. When he followed up with the correct story, military censors blocked the news, arguing the information should be kept secret. Then General William T. Sherman ordered *New York Herald* correspondent Thomas E. Knox arrested and held as a spy for sending sensitive military information.

President Lincoln intervened to reach a compromise that would balance the needs of the press with the needs of the nation through a process called ***accreditation***. This meant that the federal government certified members of the press to cover the war. Accredited journalists were required to carry press passes issued by the military. The practice of accreditation continues today as the government's method of certifying war-reporting journalists. This concept of accreditation—that a journalist was someone who could be credentialed—served to add to a sense of professionalism among journalists.

Photojournalism Is Born

Also at the Battle of Bull Run was photographer Mathew Brady, who convinced President Lincoln that a complete photographic record of the war should be made. Until the Civil War, photography had been confined primarily to studio portraits because of the cumbersome equipment and slow chemical processing. Brady photographed the battles of Antietam and Fredericksburg and sent photographic teams to other battles.

Mathew Brady's photojournalism during the Civil War created a standard for future photojournalists to follow—using photo images to help capture a story.

Photojournalist Margaret Bourke-White photographed stories for *Fortune* and *Time* magazines, establishing a 20th-century standard for photojournalism.

Newspapers did not yet have a method to reproduce the photographs, but Brady's pictures were published in magazines, making Brady the nation's first news photographer. His 3,500 photographs demonstrated the practicality and effectiveness of using photographs to help report a news story, although newspaper photographs did not become widely used until the early 1900s.

The marriage of photographs and text to tell a better story than either text or photographs could tell alone formed the beginnings of today's concept of ***photojournalism***. It was photojournalism that made *Life* magazine, founded by *Time*'s Henry Luce, such a success and created stars out of gifted photographers like Margaret Bourke-White. The perfect image to accompany the words—the best photojournalism—has become an essential part of any good journalistic news story.

Accreditation The process by which the government certifies members of the press to cover government-related news events.

Photojournalism Using photographs to accompany text to capture a news story.

Before TV news existed, newsreels and news features such as *The March of Time* were very popular with movie audiences. Shown in movie theaters before the main feature, newsreels brought viewers closer to distant locations and newsworthy events.

March of Time/Time & Life Pictures/Getty Images

Tabloid News Takes Over

The beginning of the 20th century brought the expansion of newspapers—New York City once had more than 10 daily newspapers—and intensified competition. The introduction of the penny papers meant newspapers had to grab a bigger audience to survive. And, as described in **Chapter 3**, the race for readers ushered in yellow journalism—featuring stories about grisly crimes and illicit sex, often married to large, startling photographs. Substantial newspapers, covering important stories, were publishing in places all over the country, but today people still think first about tabloid journalism when they think about this period in newspaper history.

In the 1930s, people began to turn to radio for instant news headlines and information. Newspapers still flourished but, where they once had an exclusive corner on news, now they shared their audiences with radio. When World War II began, both radio and newspapers were in place to bring home news of the war.

Newsreels Bring Distant Events to American Moviegoers

Beginning at the turn of the 20th century and lasting until television took over news coverage, movie newsreels showed movie audiences distant locations and newsworthy events. Produced by companies including British Pathé (from 1900 until 1970) and by Fox Movietone News (between 1919 and 1960), newsreels were shown in movie theaters to audiences hungry for the pictures that radio couldn't provide. Newsreels and news features, such as *March of Time*, usually ran no longer than 10 minutes, with running commentary by a narrator, and were updated every week.

Because it took time to assemble the stories and develop the film, newsreel footage usually reached audiences a week or more after the events took place. Movietone News offered the most popular newsreel in the United States, produced by Fox, using more than 1,000 camera operators who roamed the globe to cover the news each day.

Besides serious news stories, the photographers captured Hollywood celebrities, scoured exotic travel locations and produced sports and feature stories. Another newsreel company, All-American News, produced newsreels directed at African American audiences and was often shown before feature movies in addition to, or instead of, Movietone newsreels.

Newsreels offered an important realistic glimpse at worldwide news and information events that audiences couldn't get anywhere else.

Radio Broadcasts the Sounds of World War II

The most honored print journalist during World War II was Ernie Pyle, who worked for the Scripps Howard news organization. His reporting, which focused on the men who were fighting the war rather than battles and casualty counts, reached deep into the emotions of people who were stateside waiting for word from the front. (See **Impact/People**, "Ernie Pyle: The War Correspondent Who Hated War," page 254.)

Radio is the news medium that began to shine during World War II because radio news broadcasts meant that, for the first time, people could hear the action as it was happening. Imagine the date is September 8, 1940. World War II has begun its second year in Europe. You don't have a television set. You are sitting at home in the United States, listening to your radio. CBS announces a special bulletin from journalist Edward R. Murrow, reporting the first bombing of London: 626 bombers have pounded the city, leaving more than 1,000 people dead and 2,000 people injured. You and your family listen intently in your living room as Murrow describes:

> men with white scarves around their necks instead of collars . . . dull-eyed, empty-faced women. . . . Most of them carried little cheap cardboard suitcases and sometimes bulging paper shopping bags. That was all they had left. . . .

A row of automobiles with stretchers racked on the roofs like skis, standing outside of bombed buildings. A man pinned under wreckage where a broken gas main sears his arms and face. . . .

. . . the courage of the people, the flash and roar of the guns rolling down streets . . . the stench of air-raid shelters in the poor districts.

This was radio news reporting at its best. For 26 years, from 1921 until the advent of television news in 1947, broadcast reporters like Murrow painted pictures with words. (For more information about Murrow's career in television, see **Chapter 8**.)

Radio reporters described Prohibition and its repeal, the stock market crash, the Depression, the election of Franklin D. Roosevelt, the New Deal, the bombings of London and Pearl Harbor, the Normandy invasion, Roosevelt's funeral and the signing of the armistice that ended World War II.

Most radio stations maintained their own radio news departments, until the advent of format radio. Today, very few radio stations maintain full-time news departments, and radio stations with news formats tend to be concentrated in the nation's big cities. Still, the heritage of colorful, exciting radio news formed the foundation for TV news, which began to blossom in the 1950s.

Jonathan Brown/Reprinted by permission of CartoonStock

Television News Enters Its Golden Age

The first network TV newscasts in the 1950s lasted only 15 minutes, but by the 1960s, TV network evening news had expanded to half an hour—the same amount of time the networks dedicate to national news today. Radio news stars like Edward R. Murrow moved from radio to television news, and eventually the TV networks created large news departments with bureaus and correspondents spread throughout the United States and overseas.

What has been called the Golden Age of Television News was the decade that began in 1961, with President John F. Kennedy's inauguration. The Kennedy family was very photogenic, and they invited press coverage. Kennedy's victory as president, in fact, had been credited to his on-camera presence during the Kennedy–Nixon debates in 1960. So it was fitting that Kennedy would be the first president to play Cold War brinkmanship on television, when TV news grew to become a part of politics, not just a chronicler of political events.

TV and the Cold War

President Kennedy asked all three networks to clear him time on Monday, October 22, 1962, at 7 p.m. Eastern time. The president had learned that missile sites were being built in Cuba with Russian help. Kennedy used television to deliver his ultimatum to dismantle the missile bases.

"Using the word 'nuclear' 11 times, Kennedy drew a panorama of devastation enveloping the whole hemisphere," according to media historian Eric Barnouw. "The moves that had made such things possible, said Kennedy, could not be accepted by the United States 'if our courage and our commitments are ever to be trusted again by either friend or foe.'"

Kennedy admonished Russian Premier Nikita Khrushchev and urged him to stop the ships the Soviet Union was sending to Cuba to help build the missile sites. Faced with such a visible challenge, the Soviet Union turned its ships around in the Atlantic and sent conciliatory messages in order to reach a settlement. The Cuban missile crisis had in fact been a carefully constructed live television drama, in which Kennedy performed well.

TV News as a Window on the World

In 1963, television news was forced into an unexpected role as it conveyed a sense of collective national grief following President Kennedy's assassination. For four days beginning at 1:30 p.m. Eastern time on Friday, November 22, 1963, the country witnessed the aftermath of the assassination of the president. Vice President Lyndon Johnson was sworn in as president on television.

IMPACT
≫ People

Ernie Pyle: The War Correspondent Who Hated War

Note: Ernie Pyle worked for Scripps Howard. Dan Thomasson, the editor of Scripps Howard News Service, wrote this reflection on Pyle's work to accompany a collection of Pyle's dispatches that was published in 1986.

The other day while going through some old files in our library, I came upon a yellowed and tattered dispatch.

It made me cry.

It was about the death of a Capt. Waskow during the Italian campaign of 1944. And it probably is the most powerful treatise on war and death and the human spirit I have ever read.

I took it out and had it treated and framed and I hung it in the office in a prominent position where now and then one of the younger reporters will come by and read it and try to hide the inevitable tear.

The man who wrote it, Ernest Taylor Pyle, is but a memory as distant as the war he covered so eloquently and ultimately died in.

But unlike so many who perished beside him, Pyle's contribution to what Studs Terkel calls "the last good war" remains with us in his work—thousands of words that will forever memorialize brave men and debunk the "glory" of war.

The column that says it best perhaps is the one drafted for the end of the fighting in Europe. It was found in his pocket by the foot soldiers who had risked their lives to retrieve his body on the Japanese island of Ie Shima in 1945:

"Dead men by mass production—in one country after another—month after month and year after year. Dead men in winter and dead men in summer.

"Dead men in such familiar promiscuity that they become monotonous.

War correspondent Ernie Pyle (1890-1945), the most honored journalist in the United States, died during the last days of World War II. Pyle (center) visits with a group of soldiers on April 1, 1945. He was killed by sniper fire on the Japanese island of Ie Shima on April 18, 1945.

"Dead men in such infinity that you come almost to hate them."

. . . When I was a kid starting out in this business, the trade magazines were full of job-seeking ads by those who claimed they could "write like Ernie Pyle." This was 10 years after his death and he was still everyone's model.

From "Why They Still Write Ernie Pyle Books," *Honolulu Advertiser,* June 20, 1986, page A-1. Reprinted by permission of Scripps Howard News Service.

J. R. Eyerman/Time Life Pictures/Getty Images

Television news provided a sense of collective national experience covering the events that followed the assassination of President Kennedy. CBS News Anchor Walter Cronkite reacted to the news on November 22, 1963, as he issued a live report that the president had died.

Graphic TV coverage of the Vietnam War shook American viewers as no previous war coverage had. It also gave them an appetite for live news coverage—instant information about events as they were happening. CBS Correspondent Morley Safer, shown in a on-screen capture of his live reporting from Cam Ne, Vietnam, in 1965, reported that U.S. Marines were indiscriminately setting small village huts on fire with Zippo lighters.

On Saturday, TV viewers watched the world's diplomats arrive for Kennedy's funeral. On Sunday, viewers watched the first murder ever broadcast live on television, as Jack Ruby killed assassination suspect Lee Harvey Oswald. Then, on Monday came the president's funeral.

As many as nine out of ten television sets were turned on during the marathon events surrounding the president's funeral. The networks canceled all commercials. "Some television employees had slept as little as six hours in three nights," wrote media historian Eric Barnouw. "They went on, almost welcoming the absorption in the task at hand." The network news broadcasts during the events surrounding the Kennedy assassination were called television's finest four days. Television had become the nation's "window on the world," wrote Barnouw. "The view it offered seemed to be *the* world. They trusted its validity and completeness."

Television News Changes the Nation's Identity

In the late 1960s and early 1970s, television played a defining role in two very important stories—the war in Vietnam and the Watergate hearings.

Vietnam Coverage Exposes Reality

The longest-running protest program in the nation's history began appearing on television news as anti–Vietnam War marchers showed up on camera daily in the late 1960s. During live coverage of the Chicago Democratic Convention in 1968, demonstrators faced police in a march toward the convention hall. Television covered the resulting violence, which caused injuries to hundreds of protesters and to 21 reporters and photographers.

"When the war in Vietnam began to escalate in 1965," wrote TV critic Jeff Greenfield, "it was the television networks, covering the war with few official restrictions, that brought to American homes pictures of the face of war that had never been shown before: not friendly troops welcomed by the populace, but troops setting fire to villages with cigarette lighters; troops cutting off the ears of dead combat foes; allies spending American tax money for personal gain."

Candid reporting from the war itself shook viewers as previous war reporting never had, but it also gave Americans

Gjon Mili/Time Life Pictures/Getty Images

At the Watergate Hearings in 1973, TV viewers took a look inside the Nixon presidency as North Carolina's Senator Sam Ervin questioned witnesses. Ervin is at the microphone, with Senator Howard Baker behind him. Nixon resigned in 1974.

an appetite for news and for live news coverage—instant information about events as they were happening.

Watergate Hearings Reveal Politics at Work

In 1973, live television news took another leap with the continuing broadcast of the U.S. Senate's Watergate hearings to investigate allegedly illegal activities of the Republican Committee to Re-elect the President (CREEP). A parade of government witnesses and political appointees fascinated viewers with descriptions of the inner workings of the Nixon presidency.

According to media scholars Christopher Sterling and John Kittross, "Running from May through August 1973, and chaired by North Carolina's crusty Sam Ervin, these hearings were a fascinating live exposition of the political process in America, and were 'must' television watching as a parade of witnesses told—or evaded telling—what they knew of the broad conspiracy to assure the reelection of Nixon and then to cover up the conspiracy itself." For more than a year the political drama continued to unfold on television's nightly news.

Embedded During the Iraq War, a term used to describe journalists who were allowed to cover the war on the frontlines, supervised by the U.S. military.

Ultimately, the Judiciary Committee of the House of Representatives began a televised debate on whether to impeach the president. For the first time in its history, the nation faced the prospect of seeing a president brought to trial live on national television. On August 8, 1974, President Nixon brought the crisis to an end by announcing his resignation—on television.

TV News Expands and Contracts

Because viewers were hungry for news, and wanted to *watch* it, local TV news operations expanded—some stations offering as much as two hours of local news plus the national news broadcasts. Throughout the 1970s and 1980s, networks and local news departments expanded. Then came broadcast deregulation in the 1980s. The networks were sold and consolidated, and local stations, many of which had been locally owned, became pieces of larger corporations.

In 1980, Ted Turner founded Cable News Network (CNN), which offered round-the-clock news on cable. CNN established overseas bureaus and the concept that all-news-all-the-time would grab an audience. Audiences responded, and CNN became an alternative to network news, often the first place audiences turned whenever there was a crucial international story that required constant updating.

In general, however, in the 1990s, the American public read fewer newspapers and watched less news on television. Network and local TV news audiences declined. News departments began to shrink. Soon, another medium replaced the public's seemingly insatiable need for instant news and information—the Internet.

Iraq War Produces "Embedded" Reporters

Since the Vietnam War, access to battlefield locations has been a battle between the press' aggressive need-to-know and the military's need-to-keep secret. (See **Chapter 14**, "Government Tries to Restrict Free Expression," page 296.) In 2003, military press relations took a new turn when the United States declared war on Iraq.

Before the battles began, the U.S. military announced a plan to *embed* more than 600 reporters with American troops. Embedding offered the reporters access to the frontlines, but also kept the reporters within the military's control. Still, it was a reversal of past Pentagon policy makers, who often had sought to keep the press far from military operations.

CNN and the major television networks offered nonstop coverage in the early days of the war, and people watched. "A lot of people have been surprised at the access and cooperation we've had in the field," said Tony Maddox, Senior Vice President Europe, Middle East and Africa for CNN International. "It's produced some remarkable images."

The Internet Transforms News Delivery

The immediacy of the Internet brought several changes to the news business. News became more personalized and the Internet began to replace broadcast news because it is more immediate.

Internet Personalizes the News

Today, the Internet is a nonstop news and information machine. Anyone with access to the Internet can choose the sources and subjects to investigate. America Online (AOL), with a significant number of online subscribers, compiles headlines from television and print news outlets—photos and stories from CBS, Associated Press and *The New York Times*—as well as updated headline stories from magazines like *Time* and *BusinessWeek*. For specialty information, and for more background, you can visit any corporate, association or nonprofit organization Web site without leaving your chair.

You can choose what to look for and also *when* you look. The Internet is available on your schedule—independent of any TV network or local broadcast time schedule. News rotates through CNN Headline News on television at 15-minute intervals, but you can log on to your computer and find just about anything you want to know—sports scores, the weather, international headlines—whenever you want to know it.

The Internet, unlike any other form of news and information delivery, is completely self-directed news and information—targeted to individual needs and not connected to a specific time of day or night. The Internet also is the place where people can get all the news in one location that they previously had to gather from several different sources. (See **Impact/Business**, "TV Networks Rewrite the Definition of a News Bureau, Create 'All-Platform Journalists,'" page 262.)

Internet Replaces Broadcast News

According to the most recent study from the Pew Research Center, Internet news is attracting large segments of the national audience. At the same time, many people are losing the news habit, according to the study. They pay attention to the news only when something important happens, and many watch broadcast news with the remote control nearby

Scott Peterson/Getty Images

In 2003, during the Iraq War, the Pentagon began embedding more than 600 reporters with American troops. Reporters prepared for Iraq duty by attending boot camp. Embedded photographer Shawn Baldwin of *The New York Times* (left) and Carol Rosenberg of *The Miami Herald* ride in the back of a U.S. Marine vehicle on May 1, 2004, on the edge of Fallujah, Iraq.

to skip uninteresting stories and move on to something they want to watch.

Today, one out of four Americans lists the Internet as a main source of news (compared to just 15 percent in 2000), and 44 percent say they receive news reports from the Internet at least once a week. At the same time, network evening television news viewership for the three major networks (ABC, CBS and NBC) has continued to drop (see **Illustration 12.1** on page 258). In general, the study also found that people who are interested in the news online tend to watch less network TV news.

Other important findings of the Pew study were

- As large numbers of younger Americans (people under age 30) turn to the Internet for news, people of all ages read the news online. Thirty-three percent of people under age 30 go online for news every day, but 27 percent of people in their 40s and 25 percent of people in their 50s get their news on the Internet, about the same proportion as people under 30. (See **Illustration 12.2** on page 259.)

- People who read online newspapers have a far less favorable view of network and local TV news programs than

IMPACT
» Audience

Illustration 12.1

Evening Television News Viewership 1980–2007

The number of people who watch traditional TV network news has been declining since 1980, but has fallen even faster since widespread use of the Internet began in the 1990s.

Source: *The State of the News Media 2008*, Project for Excellence in Journalism, journalism.org.

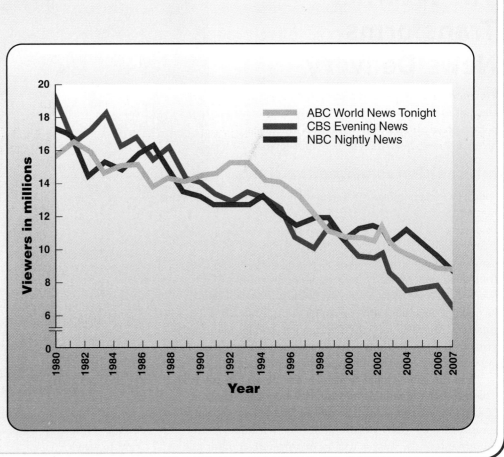

people who read the print version of the daily newspaper. (To learn how much local radio and TV newspeople earn, see **Illustration 12.3** on page 260.)

- More than half the TV audience say they turn to TV cable news, such as CNN, instead of the broadcast TV networks for breaking news, but the audience for cable news is not growing.

Information Access Creates a News Evolution

This evolution in people's news habits has taken nearly a century and required several technological innovations.

From print to radio to television to the Internet, as each new system of delivery emerged, the old systems still stayed in place. This means that today there's more news available from more news sources, delivered using more types of technology, than ever before.

People can select the information they want, when they want it, creating personal news. The news business is becoming even more competitive because consumers now have many sources—local, national and international plus the enormous resources available on the Internet—to research what they want and need to know.

Journalists at Work

"We sense the news business entering a new phase heading into 2007—a phase of more limited ambition," reported the Project for Excellence in Journalism (PEJ) in its 2007 annual

IMPACT
»» Audience

Illustration 12.2

Top Internet News Sites

The audience for news is migrating from newspapers and television to the Internet.

Source: *Key News Audiences Now Blend Online and Traditional Sources*, The Pew Research Center for the People and the Press, August 17, 2008.

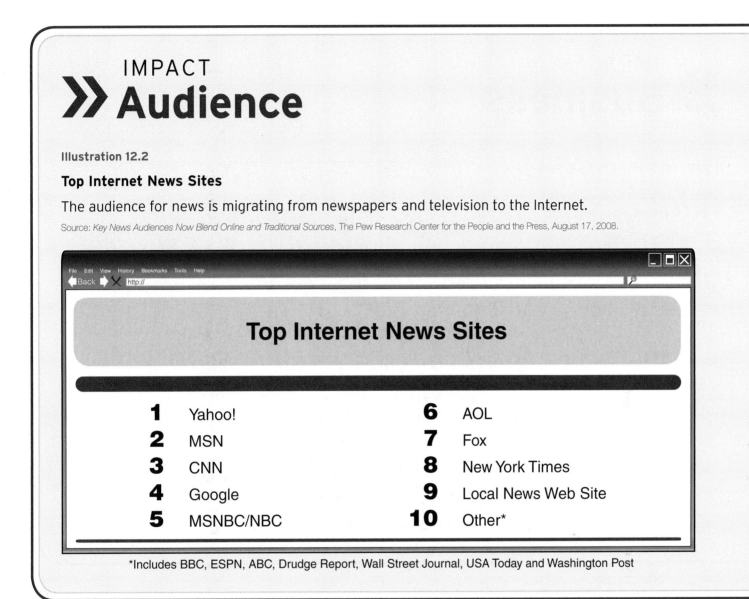

Top Internet News Sites

1	Yahoo!	**6**	AOL
2	MSN	**7**	Fox
3	CNN	**8**	New York Times
4	Google	**9**	Local News Web Site
5	MSNBC/NBC	**10**	Other*

*Includes BBC, ESPN, ABC, Drudge Report, Wall Street Journal, USA Today and Washington Post

report, *State of the News Media*. "Rather than try to manage decline, many news organizations have taken the next step of starting to redefine their appeal and their purpose based on diminished capacity. Increasingly outlets are looking for 'brand' or 'franchise' areas of coverage to build audience around."

The news business is at a critical juncture, the report says. The audience for news is shifting, and in many cases declining (especially print news sources, such as newspapers and magazines). With so many sources of news available, news organizations must each be satisfied with a smaller piece of the audience. In a practical sense, this means lower revenues for media that are losing their audience because advertising rates for those media are based on size—fewer readers, listeners or viewers means less money to hire people to write and report the news.

"The transformation facing journalism is epochal, as momentous as the invention of television or the telegraph, per-

haps on the order of the printing press itself," according to the PEJ report. "The effect is more than just audiences migrating to new delivery systems. Technology is redefining the role of the citizen—endowing the individual with more responsibility and command over how he or she consumes information—and that new role is only beginning to be understood.

"Our sense remains, too, that traditional journalism is not, as some suggest, becoming irrelevant. There is more evidence now that new technology companies have had either limited success in newsgathering (Yahoo, AOL), or have avoided it altogether (Google). Whoever owns them, old newsrooms now seem more likely than a few years ago to be the foundations for the newsrooms of the future.

"But practicing journalism has become far more difficult and demands new vision. Journalism is becoming a smaller part of people's information mix. The press is no longer gatekeeper over what the public knows."

IMPACT
Business

Illustration 12.3

How Much Do Local Radio and TV News People Earn?

This salary survey, conducted in 2005 and 2006 by the Radio-TV News Directors Association in conjunction with Ball State University, shows average salaries for local radio and TV news people in the United States.

Source: 2005 and 2006 RTNDA/Ball State University Salary Survey, as published by journalism.org.

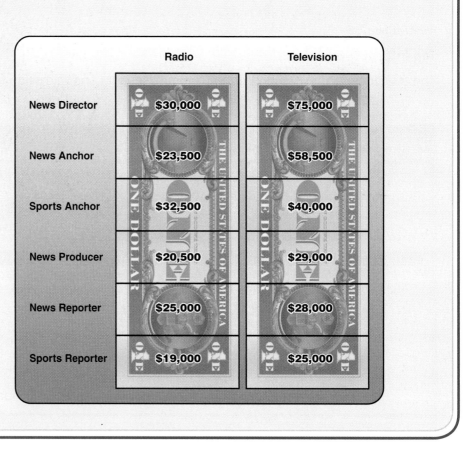

	Radio	Television
News Director	$30,000	$75,000
News Anchor	$23,500	$58,500
Sports Anchor	$32,500	$40,000
News Producer	$20,500	$29,000
News Reporter	$25,000	$28,000
Sports Reporter	$19,000	$25,000

The Project for Excellence describes seven major trends that will affect the future of the news media in the 21st century. (Excerpted from *The State of the News Media 2007: An Annual Report on American Journalism*, Project for Excellence in Journalism, www.journalism.org.)

1. **News organizations need to do more to think through the implications of this new era of shrinking ambitions.** There is already evidence that basic monitoring of local government has suffered. Regional concerns, as opposed to local, are likely to get less coverage. Matters with widespread impact but little audience appeal, always a challenge, seem more at risk of being unmonitored.

2. **The evidence is mounting that the news industry must become more aggressive about developing a new economic model.** The signs are clearer that advertising works differently online than in older media. Already the predictions of advertising growth on the Web are being scaled back. That has major implications. Among them, news organizations can broaden what they consider journalistic function to include activities such as online search and citizen media, and perhaps even liken their journalism to anchor stores at a mall, a major reason for coming but not the only one. Perhaps most important, the math suggests they almost certainly must find a way to get consumers to pay for digital content.

3. **The key question is whether the investment community sees the news business as a declining industry or an emerging one in transition.** If one believes that news will continue to be the primary public square where people gather—with the central newsrooms in a community delivering that audience across different platforms—then it seems reasonable that the economics in time will sort themselves out. In that scenario, people with things to sell still need to reach consumers, and the news will be a primary means of finding them. If news companies

do not assert their own vision here, including making a case and taking risks, their future will be defined by those less invested in and passionate about news.

4. **There are growing questions about whether the dominant ownership model of the last generation, the public corporation, is suited to the transition newsrooms must now make.** More executives are openly expressing doubt, too, whether public ownership's required focus on stock price and quarterly returns will allow media companies the time and freedom and risk taking they feel they need to make the transition to the new age. Public ownership tends to make companies play by the same rules. Private ownership has few leveling influences. And the new crop of potential private owners is unlike the press barons of the past, people trying to create their legacy in news. Most of them are people who made their fortunes in other enterprises.

5. **The Argument Culture is giving way to something new, the Answer Culture.** Critics used to bemoan what author Michael Crichton once called the "Crossfire Syndrome," the tendency of journalists to stage mock debates about issues on TV and in print. Such debates, critics lamented, tended to polarize, oversimplify and flatten issues to the point that Americans in the middle of the spectrum felt left out. A growing pattern has news outlets, programs and journalists offering up solutions, crusades, certainty and the impression of putting all the blur of information in clear order for people.

6. **Blogging is on the brink of a new phase that will probably include scandal, profitability for some, and a splintering into elites and non-elites over standards and ethics.** What gives blogging its authenticity and momentum—its open access—also makes it vulnerable to being used and manipulated. At the same time, some of the most popular bloggers are already becoming businesses or being assimilated by establishment media. All this is likely to cause blogging to lose some of its patina as citizen media.

7. **While journalists are becoming more serious about the Web, no clear models of how to do journalism online really exist yet, and some qualities are still only marginally explored.** What we found was that the root media no longer strictly define a site's character.

The field is still highly experimental, with an array of options, but it can be hard to discern what one site offers, in contrast to another. Sites have done more, for instance, to exploit immediacy, but they have done less to exploit the potential for depth.

Joseph Farris/Reprinted by permission of CartoonStock

"This is strictly off the record...."

"More people now feel they can get what traditional journalism offers from the Internet," concluded the report, "and that, too, is a challenge for the press. . . . There are reminders in the data of the continuing sense that journalism matters, and continuing doubts about whether it is being practiced in a way people want."

Are Journalists Biased?

It has not been shown in any comprehensive survey of news gathering that journalists with liberal or conservative values insert their personal ideology directly into their reporting or that the audience unquestioningly accepts one point of view. The belief in a causal relationship between the media and the audience's behavior is known as the ***magic bullet theory***. This belief was disproved long ago.

But the assumption that journalists' personal beliefs directly influence their professional performance is common. Although the reporting by some journalists and columnists certainly can be cited to support this idea, the majority of journalists, says media scholar Herbert J. Gans, view themselves as detached observers of events.

Magic Bullet Theory The assertion that media messages directly and measurably affect people's behavior.

IMPACT
»Business

TV Networks Rewrite the Definition of a News Bureau, Create "All-Platform Journalists"

by Brian Stelter

CNN announced [in August 2008] that it would assign journalists to 10 cities across the United States, a move that would double the number of domestic cities where the cable news network has outposts.

But in a reflection of the way television networks are reinventing the way they gather news, the journalists will not work from expensive bureaus—rather, they will borrow office space from local news organizations and use laptops to file articles for the Internet and TV. When news happens, they will use Internet connections and cell phone cameras to report live.

"We are harnessing technology that enables us to be anywhere and be live from anywhere," said Nancy Lane, the senior vice president for newsgathering for CNN/U.S., a unit of Time Warner. "It completely changes how we can report."

CNN may be putting itself in the vanguard of this newfangled approach, but it is hardly alone.

Last year ABC stationed seven "digital journalists" in far-flung cities, including New Delhi, Jakarta, Dubai and Nairobi, to act as one-person bureaus. Traditionally, the networks were able to maintain well-staffed bureaus in many major cities. The offices, camera crews, reporters and other resources they wielded were not only central to their newsgathering, but also symbolic of their journalistic dominance.

Today, as they confront new competition on the Web, television networks are increasingly embracing portable—and inexpensive—methods of production. Decades of budget cuts have forced the news divisions to reduce their global footprint, shutting bureaus and abandoning the old norm of four-person crews.

Journalists, like everyone else, have values, [and] the two that matter most in the newsroom are getting the story and getting it better and faster than their prime competitors—both among their colleagues and at rival news media. Personal political beliefs are left at home, not only because journalists are trained to be objective and detached, but also because their credibility and their paychecks depend on their remaining detached. . . .

The beliefs that actually make it into the news are professional values that are intrinsic to national jour-

nalism and that journalists learn on the job. However, the professional values that particularly antagonize conservatives (and liberals when they are in power) are neither liberal nor conservative but reformist, reflecting journalism's long adherence to good-government Progressivism.

Some press critics, in fact, argue that journalists most often present establishment viewpoints and are unlikely to challenge prevailing political and social values. In addition, the pressure to come up with instant analyses of news events may lead to conformity in reporting—an unwillingness to think independently.

Consensus journalism is the tendency among many journalists covering the same event to report similar conclusions about the event rather than to report conflicting

Consensus Journalism The tendency among many journalists covering the same event to report similar conclusions about the event.

NBC, ABC and CBS now pool most of their international resources in London and deploy reporters to other countries as needed.

But a new breed of reporter, sometimes called a "one-man band," has become the new norm. Though the style of reporting has existed for years, it is being adopted more widely as these reporters act as their own producer, cameraman and editor, and sometimes even transmit live video. . . .

ABC is considering assigning digital journalists to positions in the United States, he said. NBC has also trained some of its journalists to be one-man bands, even as it downsized some bureaus this year and created a system of hubs where offices in New York, Los Angeles and Atlanta oversee all news coverage of North and South America. . . .

At CNN, the new "**all-platform journalists**," as the network calls them, will frequently file for CNN.com and the network's other outlets. In Minneapolis, that person will work from a local TV affiliate that has a partnership with CNN. In other cities, the journalists may work at newspaper offices or other locations.

Michael Rosenblum, a consultant who has helped television networks like the BBC adopt the one-man band model, called it a "much more cost-effective way" to gather news.

Chip Somodevilla/Getty Images

News organizations like CNN and ABC News increasingly are using "all-platform journalists"—reporters who use laptops and shoot video to file articles for the Internet and TV simultaneously. Reporters covering presidential candidate John McCain file their stories sitting on the sidewalk outside of a McCain campaign stop on October 23, 2008 in Altamonte Springs, Fla.

At most networks, "they can't afford the bureaus, but they must have the news coverage," he said. "The easiest way to do it is to hand the journalist a camera, show them the 'on' and 'off' buttons, and tell them to go to work."

interpretations. The emergence of the Internet as a news source, however, means that people now have more places to look for news—even overseas—which means more viewpoints on stories are available. This puts more burden on the news consumer to seek out and verify the most reliable sources of information.

Reality Shows and Advertising Blur the Line

TV reality shows, such as *Survivor* and *The Biggest Loser*, blur the distinction between what is news and what is

re-created drama. These shows use interviews and reenactments in a documentary style that imitates live events. Reality shows, or docudramas, make it difficult for an audience to distinguish between packaged entertainment and spontaneous events.

"Infomercials"—programs that pretend to give viewers information but that are really advertisements for the sponsors' products—also are making it harder to discern what is reporting and what is advertising. The line between news and entertainment on television becomes even trickier

All-Platform Journalists Broadcast journalists who act as their own producer, cameraperson and editor, and sometimes even transmit live video.

Doug Mills/The New York Times

Getting the story faster and better than the competition is a major factor that influences journalistic values.

conducted by the Pew Research Center, "Ratings of large nationally influential newspapers such as *The New York Times* and the *Washington Post* . . . have dropped in recent years. . . . Local news outlets—local TV and papers that respondents are most familiar with—retain the highest favorability ratings among those who can rate them.

"Meanwhile, ratings of other political institutions have been falling at a comparable rate. The share giving a favorable rating to the Supreme Court stands at 66 percent today, down from 78 percent in 2001, while fewer (45 percent) give a favorable rating to Congress, down from 65 percent in 2001. As a result, news organizations continue to be seen more favorably by the American public than most governmental institutions, despite their declining ratings." (See **Illustration 12.4**.)

when advertisers produce programs that look like news but are really advertisements.

This merging of entertainment and news, as well as the entertaining graphics and the lighthearted presentation style of most local TV newscasts, makes it more difficult for viewers to separate fact from fiction, reality from reenactment and news from advertising. The result may be a decline in the audience's trust in the news media to deliver accurate information, and it makes it more important that so-called pseudo-news be properly labeled so it doesn't mislead the public.

How the Public Perceives the Press

Although people tend to follow the news only when something important happens, they do have strong opinions about the news media. According to the latest study

Journalists Embrace Specific News Values

News organizations often are criticized for presenting a consistently slanted view of the news. Often news values are shaped by the way news organizations are structured and the routines they follow. The press in America, it is generally agreed, doesn't tell people what to think but does tell people what and whom to think *about*. This is called *agenda-setting*. There are two types of agenda-setting: the flow of information from one news organization to another and the flow of information from news organizations to their audiences.

In the first type of agenda-setting, the stories that appear in the nation's widely circulated print media provide ideas to the other media. The print media, for example, often identify specific stories as important by giving them attention so that widely circulated print media can set the news agenda on some national issues.

To analyze the second type of agenda-setting—the picture of the world that journalists give to their audiences—is to examine the social and cultural values that journalists present to the public. The most significant recent study of news values was offered by Herbert J. Gans in his book *Deciding What's News*.

Agenda-Setting The belief that journalists don't tell you *what* to think but do tell you *what and whom to think about.*

Ethnocentrism The attitude that some cultural and social values are superior.

IMPACT
»Culture

Illustration 12.4

Public Favors News Media over Government Officials and Political Leaders

In a 2007 survey by the Pew Research Center for People and the Press, people said they had a more positive opinion of the military than of most of the news media institutions, but overall the news media ranked much higher than the U.S. Congress or either of the major national political parties.

Source: *Project for Excellence in Journalism, State of the News Media 2007.*

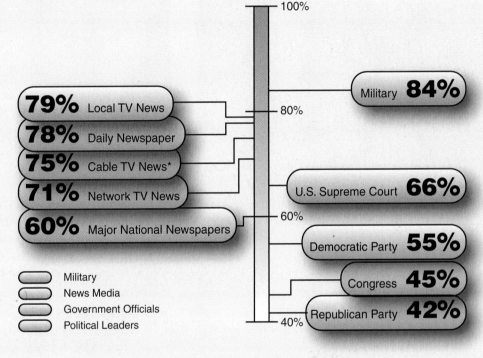

Percentage of people with favorable opinion of....

- 79% Local TV News
- 78% Daily Newspaper
- 75% Cable TV News*
- 71% Network TV News
- 60% Major National Newspapers

- Military
- News Media
- Government Officials
- Political Leaders

- Military 84%
- U.S. Supreme Court 66%
- Democratic Party 55%
- Congress 45%
- Republican Party 42%

Gans identified eight enduring values that emerged in his study of different types of news stories over a long period of time: ***ethnocentrism*** (the attitude that some cultural and social values are superior), altruistic democracy, responsible capitalism, small-town pastoralism, individualism, moderatism, order and leadership. These values, said Gans, often help define what is considered news. News in the United States conveys the ideas of

- *Ethnocentrism.* America is a nation to be valued above all others. "While the news contains many stories that are critical of domestic conditions, they are almost always treated as deviant cases, with the implication that American ideas, at least, remain viable," says Gans.

- *Altruistic democracy.* Politics should be based on public service and the public interest. The news media expect

all public officials to be scrupulously honest, efficient and public-spirited.

- *Responsible capitalism.* Open competition will create increased prosperity for everyone. Businesspeople should not seek unreasonable profits, and they should not exploit workers or customers.

- *Small-town pastoralism.* Small agricultural or market towns are favored over other settlements. Suburbs are usually overlooked as a place where news happens. Big cities are viewed as places with "urban" problems.

- *Individualism.* A heroic individual is someone who struggles against difficulties and powerful forces. Self-made people are admired.

- *Moderatism.* Moderation is valued; excesses and extremism are not.

In 2005, W. Mark Felt (photo on left) revealed that he was the famous confidential source known as Deep Throat. Felt's information formed the basis for many of the Watergate stories written in the 1970s by (above photo on right) Bob Woodward (right) and Carl Bernstein (left) for *The Washington Post*.

- *Order.* Importance is placed on political order. Says Gans, "The values in the news derive largely from reformers and reform movements, which are themselves elites. Still, the news is not simply a compliant support of elites, or the establishment, or the ruling class; rather, it views nation and society through its own set of values and with its own conception of the good social order."

- *Leadership.* Attention is focused on leaders. The president is seen as the nation's primary leader and protector of the national order.

These values exist throughout American society and come from historical assumptions based in our culture. As Gans suggests, this news ideology both supports and reflects elements of the social order in the United States.

Journalists Fight to Keep Sources Confidential

One enduring professional value of journalists is the protection of confidential sources. Despite outside pressure from courts over the last few decades, journalists have summarily refused to provide information they have agreed with sources to keep confidential.

To journalists, the ability to protect their sources is essential to being able to continue to report controversial stories. Confidential sources leak information for several reasons. They might want to get back at someone who has wronged them. They might believe that someone is misusing company or government funds. They might want to damage someone's reputation. All of these are reasons that sources talk to journalists confidentially.

Journalists realize that people who talk with them confidentially don't always have the purest motives, and news organizations typically require that any information from a confidential source that is used in a story has been verified by at least two sources. But it long has been a tenet of journalism that confidential sources stay confidential.

The most famous confidential source, nicknamed Deep Throat, played a major role in the stories Bob Woodward and Carl Bernstein wrote about the Watergate scandal for *The Washington Post* in the early 1970s. Eventually their reporting led to President Nixon's resignation in 1974.

Woodward and Bernstein agreed to keep Deep Throat's identity secret while he was alive. In 2005, a man named W. Mark Felt, who worked for the FBI during the Nixon years, revealed that he was in fact Deep Throat. Because Felt had revealed his identity, Woodward and Bernstein then acknowledged Felt's identity as Deep Throat. They had kept the biggest secret in journalism for more than 30 years.

Coincidentally, also in 2005, another case involving a president and someone who had leaked a story to journalists began to draw attention when Judith Miller of *The New York Times* and Matthew Cooper of *Time* magazine were ordered by a judge to reveal the source of a story about the Bush administration to a grand jury investigating the leak of an undercover CIA officer's identity.

"The investigation concerns whether a crime was committed when someone leaked the identity of CIA officer Valerie Plame, whose name was published by syndicated columnist Robert Novak on July 14, 2003," reported Associated Press. "The column appeared after Plame's husband, former Ambassador Joseph Wilson, wrote a newspaper opinion column criticizing President Bush's claim that Iraq had sought uranium in Niger, a claim the CIA had asked Wilson to check out. Wilson has said he believes his wife's name was leaked as payback for his outspokenness."

Eventually Cooper appeared before the grand jury and revealed his source, after he said the source released him from the agreement to keep the name confidential. Miller, however, went to jail on July 6, 2005, rather than reveal her source, even though the *Times* had not published the source's name in a story. She stayed in jail for almost four months until October 3, 2005, when she said she reached an agreement with her source that she could reveal his name as I. Lewis Libby, Vice President Dick Cheney's chief of staff. Libby eventually was indicted for lying to the grand jury, and he resigned.

After the actions of Cooper and Miller, the issue of journalists' protection of sources is no longer as clear-cut as it once was. Many states currently have **shield laws**, which protect journalists legally from revealing their sources in court, but there is no federal shield law, which would have been required to protect Miller and Cooper. After the Miller incident, a federal shield law was proposed in Congress, but Congress took no action on it. (For more information about shield laws, see **Chapter 14**.)

Credibility Attracts the Audience

Overall, the growing trust in Internet news sources and their growing popularity as information sources may be connected. If Internet news can maintain this believability standard, even more of the audience—which was leaving the broadcast networks even before online news began—may gravitate to the Internet.

This is a familiar pattern: In the nation's news history, newspaper audiences added radio and newsreels, then moved to television for news. Now news audiences have

Raymond Boyd/Michael Ochs Archives/Getty Images

In 2005, Matthew Cooper of *Time* magazine and Judith Miller of *The New York Times* were ordered by a judge to reveal the confidential source in the stories they published about CIA officer Valerie Plame, shown here. The U.S. government used the stories to support its decision to go to war in Iraq. Miller refused to reveal her source and spent four months in jail. Eventually I. Lewis Libby, Vice President Dick Cheney's chief of staff, gave Miller permission to reveal his involvement as the story's source, and Miller was released.

moved to the Internet. The Internet combines all the news outlets anyone could want in one place—news and information on the news consumer's own timetable. The Pew Center calls this trend a "digital tide," and it's a tide that may be impossible to stop.

Shield Laws Laws that protect journalists from being required to reveal confidential sources in a legal proceeding.

Review, Analyze, Investigate
REVIEWING CHAPTER 12

Early News Organizations Cooperate to Gather News

✓ The nation's first consecutively issued newspaper (published more than once) was the *Boston News-Letter*, which appeared in 1704.

✓ The invention of the telegraph in 1844 meant news that once took weeks to reach publication could be transmitted in minutes.

✓ In 1848, six newspapers in New York City formed the New York Associated Press, the first cooperative news gathering association.

✓ Today, most American newspapers and broadcast news operations subscribe to at least one news service, such as Associated Press (AP).

✓ Some U.S. newspaper organizations also run their own news services, which allow subscribers to publish each other's stories for a fee.

Civil War Brings Accreditation and Photojournalism

✓ In 1861, during the Civil War, President Lincoln introduced the practice of accreditation for journalists.

✓ During the Civil War, Mathew Brady introduced the concept of photojournalism—using images to help capture a story.

Tabloid News Takes Over

✓ The competition for newspaper readers spawned yellow journalism—stories about grisly crimes and illicit sex, often accompanied by large, startling photographs.

✓ In the 1930s, newspapers began to share the audience for news with radio.

Newsreels Bring Distant Events to American Moviegoers

✓ Produced by companies including British Pathé (from 1900 until 1970) and by Fox Movietone News (between 1919 and 1960), newsreels were shown in movie theaters to audiences hungry for the pictures that radio couldn't provide. Audiences also watched movie features such as *March of Time*.

✓ Newsreel footage usually took a week or more from the time it was shot to when audiences saw it.

Radio Broadcasts the Sounds of World War II

✓ In the 1930s, people began to turn to radio for instant news headlines and information.

✓ In the 1930s and 1940s, most radio stations maintained their own news departments until the advent of format radio.

✓ Journalist Ernie Pyle gave World War II the human touch because he wrote stories about the soldiers' lives, not troop movements.

✓ Very few radio stations today maintain full-time news departments, and radio stations with news formats tend to be concentrated in the nation's big cities.

Television News Enters Its Golden Age

✓ What has been called the Golden Age of Television News was the decade that began in 1961, with President John F. Kennedy's inauguration.

✓ In 1962, President Kennedy used live television to deliver his ultimatum to Soviet leader Nikita Khrushchev, urging him to stop sending ships to Cuba to help build missile sites in what was called the Cuban missile crisis. Faced with such an ultimatum, the Soviet Union turned its ships around.

✓ Television became a "window on the world" with its coverage of the events following the assassination of President Kennedy.

Television News Changes the Nation's Identity

✓ Coverage of the war in Vietnam gave Americans an appetite for live television news.

✓ The Watergate hearings showed viewers the inner workings of national politics.

TV News Expands and Contracts

✓ Ted Turner founded CNN in 1980, offering round-the-clock news on cable.

✓ The 1980s brought broadcast deregulation and consolidation of the TV networks.

✓ In the 1990s, in general, the American public read fewer newspapers and watched less news on television.

Iraq War Produces "Embedded" Reporters

✓ Before the War in Iraq began in 2003, the U.S. military announced a plan to "embed" more than 600 reporters with American troops. Embedding offered the reporters access to the frontlines but also kept the reporters within the military's control.

✓ In 2005, the Bush administration sought to influence coverage of the United States in Iraq by paying news outlets to publish stories written by American troops. Congress criticized the practice, saying the U.S. government should not attempt to manage the press.

The Internet Transforms News Delivery

✓ The Internet, unlike any other form of news and information delivery, is completely self-directed news and information—targeted to individual needs.

✓ The Pew Research Center studies reveal that network and local news viewership has dropped substantially. People, instead, are turning to the Internet for news.

✓ Internet news sites rank higher in believability than either print or broadcast outlets as sources of news.

Information Access Creates a News Evolution

✓ The immediacy of news on the Internet means people can personalize the news.

✓ The Internet began to replace broadcast news because of its immediacy.

Journalists at Work

✓ The Project for Excellence in Journalism describes seven major trends that will affect the future of the news media in the 21st century:

1. News organizations need to think through the implications of this new era of shrinking ambitions.

2. The news industry must become more aggressive about developing a new economic model.

3. The investment community is still deciding whether the news business as a declining industry or an emerging one in transition.

4. There are growing questions about whether the dominant ownership model of the last generation, the public corporation, is suited to the transition newsrooms must now make.

5. The Argument Culture is giving way to the Answer Culture.

6. A new phase of blogging will probably include scandal, profitability for some and a splintering into elites and non-elites over standards and ethics.

7. There are no clear models of how to do journalism online yet.

Are Journalists Biased?

✓ Contrary to the disproved magic bullet theory, most journalists see themselves as detached observers and reporters of events.

✓ Pressure to quickly analyze news events leads to consensus journalism, the tendency of journalists covering the same event to report similar conclusions about the event rather than conflicting interpretations.

Reality Shows and Advertising Blur the Line

✓ Reality TV shows and "infomercials" tend to blur the line between entertainment and news.

✓ The merging of entertainment and news makes it more difficult for viewers to separate facts from fiction.

How the Public Perceives the Press

✓ News organizations continue to rate higher with the public than most governmental institutions except the military.

✓ Favorable ratings for the news media are higher than ratings for Congress and the two major political parties.

Journalists Embrace Specific News Values

✓ Herbert J. Gans, in his book *Deciding What's News*, identified eight enduring news values: ethnocentrism, altruistic democracy, responsible capitalism, small-town pastoralism, individualism, moderatism, order and leadership.

✓ The press in America doesn't tell you what to think. It does tell you what and whom to think about. This is called agenda-setting.

✓ There are two types of agenda-setting: the flow of information from one news organization to another and the flow of information from news organizations to their audiences.

Journalists Fight to Keep Sources Confidential

✓ One enduring view among journalists is that they should protect their confidential sources.

✓ In 2005, breaking a silence of more than 30 years, W. Mark Felt revealed himself to be the central confidential source of Watergate, Deep Throat.

✓ Also in 2005, Judith Miller of *The New York Times* went to jail rather than reveal her confidential source to a grand jury investigating the leak of the name of a CIA operative, Valerie Plame, in the press.

Credibility Attracts the Audience

✓ The growing trust in Internet news sources may be related to the Internet's increasing popularity as a source of news.

✓ If Internet news can maintain its believability, more of the TV news audience may gravitate to the Internet.

KEY TERMS

These terms are defined in the margins throughout this chapter and appear in alphabetical order with definitions in the Glossary, which begins on page 372.

CRITICAL QUESTIONS

1. List two specific ways in which news coverage changed during the Civil War.

2. List and explain three ways the Internet has changed consumers' news habits.

3. Why do journalists embrace the belief that confidential sources should be protected? Do you agree with this principle? Why? Why not?

4. Discuss the decisions the Bush administration made that changed journalists' access and reporting on the Iraq War.

5. Discuss three important findings of the 2007 report of the Project for Excellence in Journalism.

WORKING THE WEB

This list includes both sites mentioned in the chapter and others to give you greater insight into news and information media.

Committee to Protect Journalists
http://www.cpj.org

This nonpartisan organization is dedicated to protecting freedom of the press around the world. It publishes stories about imprisoned and threatened journalists, organizes public protests and works through diplomatic channels to effect change. It also publishes Attacks on the Press, an annual survey of press freedom around the world. The Web site features links to news by country, special reports, and a multimedia section with video, audio and slideshows.

CyberJournalist.net
http://www.cyberjournalist.net

This news and resource site focuses on how the Internet, convergence and new technologies are changing the media. Included on the Web site are tips, news and commentary, examples of good online journalism and contributions from readers. Sections include Future of Media, Citizen Media and a job board. Cyberjournalist.net has been named a top 100 blog by CNET and has been recommended by dozens of publications including the *Columbia Journalism Review* and *USA Today*.

Fox Movietone News
http://www.sc.edu/library/newsfilm/index.html

A portion of the Fox Movietone News film is housed in the University of South Carolina's Newsfilm Library. A sample of video clips—from a 1924 city view of Baghdad to B.C. Forbes talking about the 1929 stock market crash—is available on the Web site.

Investigative Reporters and Editors, Inc.
http://www.ire.org

This organization, dedicated to improving the quality of investigative reporting, provides educational services to reporters and editors and works to maintain high professional standards. The Web site features news and publications, job and resource centers for members as well as a link to the National Institute for Computer-Assisted Reporting (NICAR), a program sponsored by IRE and the Missouri School of Journalism. Five IRE members were honored with Pulitzer Prizes in 2007 for a variety of topics, including local, national and investigative reporting.

The Online News Association (ONA)
http://www.journalist.org

An organization composed largely of professional online journalists, the ONA's membership includes news writers, producers, designers, editors, photographers and others who produce news for the Internet or other digital delivery systems. Member benefits include regional and national events, discounts on ONA activities, training opportunities, and online discussion and networking. ONA partners with the Annenberg School of Communication at the University of Southern California to honor online journalistic excellence with their annual Online Journalism Awards.

Pew Research Center for People and the Press
http://people-press.org/reports

This research project of the Pew Research Center studies attitudes toward the press, politics and public policy issues. The Web site includes Survey Reports by the Center on a variety of current issues. Findings of polls sponsored by media organizations also are available.

Project for Excellence in Journalism:
Understanding News in the Information Age
http://journalism.org

This research organization uses empirical methods to evaluate and study the performance of the press. Its goal is to help journalists and consumers develop a better understanding of what the press is delivering. Features of the site include Journalism Resources—with links to organizations, schools and career information—and the project's annual report on the State of the News Media.

Talking Points Memo (TPM)
http://www.talkingpointsmemo.com

The flagship blog of TPM Media, LLC, Talking Points Memo is a collection of comments on political events from a liberal perspective, gathered by writer Joshua Micah Marshall. TPMCafé hosts online discussions about various political topics as well as readers' blogs. TPMMuckraker is a news blog dedicated to chronicling, explaining and reporting on public corruption, political scandal and various abuses of the public trust. Streaming video accompanied by written commentary is available on TPMtv.

Unity: Journalists of Color, Inc.
http://www.unityjournalists.org

This strategic alliance advocates news coverage about people of color and challenges organizations at all levels to reflect the nation's diversity. It is comprised of four national associations: Asian American Journalists Association, National Association of Black J Hispanic Journalists Association. Its goals ticipation of the me cultures, increasing on people of color, and types and myths.

Vanderbilt University Televis
http://tvnews.vanderbilt.edu

"The world's most extensive and complete archive of television news" holds network evening news broadcasts from ABC, CBS and NBC from 1968 to the present, as well as a daily news program from CNN (beginning in 1995) and Fox News Reports (beginning in 2004). DVD duplications of entire broadcasts as well as compilation videotapes of individual news stories may be borrowed for a fee.

13

Society, Culture and Politics: Shaping the Issues

DOUG MILLS/AFP/Getty Images

President Barack Obama and First Lady Michelle Obama walk in the Inaugural Parade after President Obama was sworn in as the nation's 44th president on January 20, 2009.

What's Ahead?

Researchers at Southern Illinois

University School of Medicine have identified a new psychiatric condition they have dubbed "celebrity worship syndrome." This affliction is an unhealthy interest in the rich and famous. People who admire celebrities often want to be just like them, even though some celebrities set examples that aren't very positive. Celebrity worship is just one example of the effect of media on our lives.

Today, scholars understand that the media have different effects on different types of people with differing results, and generalizations about the media's effects are easy to make but difficult to prove. "We do not fully understand at present what the media system is doing to individual behavior, much less to American culture," according to media scholars William L. Rivers and Wilbur Schramm. "The media cannot simply be seen as stenciling images on a blank mind. That is too superficial a view of the communication process."

Early Media Studies Assess Impact

The concept that the media have different effects on different types of people is relatively new. Early media observers felt that an absolute one-to-one relationship existed between what people read, heard and saw and what people did with that information. They also believed that the effects were the same for everyone.

The magic bullet theory, discussed more in a following section and sometimes called the hypodermic needle theory, alleged that ideas from the media were in direct causal relation to behavior. The theory held that the media could inject ideas into someone the way liquids are injected through a needle. This early distrust of the media still pervades many people's thinking today, although the theory has been disproved.

Media research, like other social science research, is based on a continuum of thought, with each new study advancing slightly the knowledge from the studies that have come before. This is what has happened to the magic bullet theory. Eventually, the beliefs that audiences absorbed media messages uncritically and that all audiences reacted the same to each message were proven untrue. Research disclosed that analyzing media effects is a very complex task.

Some media research existed before television use became widespread in the mid-1950s, but TV prompted scholars to take an even closer look at media's effects. Two scholars made particularly provocative assertions about how the media influence people's lives. David M. Potter arrived at just the right moment—when the public and the scholarly community were anxiously trying to analyze media's effects on society. In his book *People of Plenty*, published in 1954, Potter first articulated an important idea: that American society is a consumer society driven primarily by advertising.

Potter, a historian, asserted that American advertising is rooted in American abundance. "Advertising is not badly needed in an economy of scarcity, because total demand is usually equal to or in excess of total supply, and every producer can normally sell as much as he produces. . . . It is when potential supply outstrips demand—that is, when abundance prevails—that advertising begins to fulfill a really essential economic function."

Potter then warned about the dangers of advertising. "Advertising has in its dynamics no motivation to seek the improvement of the individual or to impart qualities of social usefulness. . . . It has no social goals and no social responsibility for what it does with its influence." Potter's perspective was important in shaping the critical view of modern advertising. *People of Plenty* is still in print today.

Scholars Look for Patterns

Like Potter, Canadian Marshall McLuhan arrived at just the right moment. In the 1960s, McLuhan piqued the public's interest with his phrase "The medium is the message," which he later parodied in the title of his book *The Medium Is the Massage*. One of his conclusions was that the widespread use of television was a landmark in the history of the world, "retribalizing" society and creating a "global village" of people who use media to communicate.

McLuhan suggested that electronic media messages are inherently different from print messages—to watch information on TV is different from reading the same information in a newspaper. McLuhan never offered systematic proof for his ideas, and some people criticized him as a charlatan, but his concepts still are debated widely.

Scholars who analyze the media today look for patterns in media effects, predictable results and statistical evidence to document how the media affect us. Precisely because the media are ubiquitous, studies of their effects on American society are far from conclusive. In this chapter, you will learn about some

SIGNE
PHILADELPHIA DAILY NEWS
Philadelphia
USA

THE FOLLOWING SHOW CONTAINS GRATUITOUS AND DESENSITIZING VIOLENCE, GLORIFICATION OF WANTON SEX AND INSIDIOUS NIHILISM TOWARDS EVERYTHING.

COOL! LET'S WATCH!

CARTOONISTS & WRITERS SYNDICATE

Used by permission of Cartoonists & Writers Syndicate/cartoonweb.com

of the major studies that have examined the media's effects and some of the recent assertions about the role that the media play in our lives.

Media research today includes media effects research and media content analysis. **Media effects research** tries to analyze how people use the information they receive from the media—whether political advertising changes people's voting behavior, for example. **Media content analysis** examines what is presented by the media—how many children's programs portray violent behavior, for example. Sometimes these two types of analysis (effects research and content analysis) are combined in an attempt to evaluate what effect certain content has on an audience.

The Payne Fund Studies

The prestigious Payne Fund sponsored the first major study of media, conducted in 1929. It contained 12 separate reports on media effects. One of these studies concentrated on the effects of movies on children. In his interviews, researcher Herbert Blumer simply asked teenagers what they remembered about the movies they had seen as children. Using this unsystematic approach, he reported that the teenagers had been greatly influenced by the movies because they *said* they had been greatly influenced.

Blumer's conclusion and other conclusions of the Payne Fund Studies about the media's direct one-to-one effect on people were accepted without question, mainly because these were the first major studies of media effects, and the results were widely reported. This became known as the **magic bullet theory**, the belief that media messages directly and measurably affect people's behavior.

The Payne Fund studies also contributed ammunition for the Motion Picture Producers and Distributors Association Production Code, adopted in 1930, which regulated movie content.

The Cantril Study

The Martians who landed in New Jersey on the Mercury Theater "War of the Worlds" broadcast of October 30, 1939 (see **Chapter 6**, "'War of the Worlds' Challenges Radio's Credibility," page 117), sparked the next major study of media effects, conducted by Hadley Cantril at Princeton University. The results of the Cantril study contradicted the findings of the Payne Fund studies and disputed the magic bullet theory.

The Cantril researchers wanted to find out why certain people believed the Mercury Theater broadcast and others did not. After interviewing 135 people, Cantril concluded that high critical thinking ability was the key. Better-educated people were much more likely to decide the broadcast was a fake. This finding might seem to be self-evident today, but the importance of the Cantril study is that it differentiated among listeners: People with different personality characteristics interpreted the broadcast differently.

The Lasswell Model

In 1948, Harold D. Lasswell designed a model to describe the process of communication that is still used today. Lasswell said the communication process could be analyzed by answering the five questions shown in **Illustration 13.1**.

In other words, Lasswell said you could analyze the process of communication by determining who the sender is and what the sender says. Next, you must identify which channel—meaning the method—of communication the sender used. Then you must examine the audience and define the effect on that audience. Because Lasswell described the communication process so succinctly, most communications research that followed has attempted to answer his five questions.

How TV Affects Children's Behavior

The 1950s were a time of adjustment because of the addition of the new medium of television, which was seen first as a novelty and then as a necessity. Since 1960, four of the major studies of the effects of television have focused on children.

Television in the Lives of Children

Published in 1961, by Wilbur Schramm, Jack Lyle and Edwin Parker, *Television in the Lives of Our Children* was the first major study of the effects of television on children. Researchers interviewed 6,000 children and 1,500 parents, as well as teachers and school officials.

Schramm and his associates reported that children were exposed to television more than to any other mass medium. On average, 5-year-old children watched television two hours every weekday. TV viewing time reached three hours by the time these children were 8 years old. In a finding that often was subsequently cited, Schramm said that from the ages of 3 to 16, children spent more time in front of the television set than they spent in school.

Children used television for fantasy, diversion and instruction, Schramm said. Children who had troubled relationships with their parents and children who were classified as aggressive were more likely to turn to television for fantasy, but Schramm could find no serious problems related

Media Effects Research An attempt to analyze how people use the information they receive from the media.

Media Content Analysis An attempt to analyze how what the media present influences behavior.

Magic Bullet Theory The assertion that media messages directly and measurably affect people's behavior.

IMPACT
›› Audience

Illustration 13.1

Lasswell's Model

The Lasswell Model, used to analyze the communication process, asks five questions: Who? Says what? On which channel? To whom? With what effect?

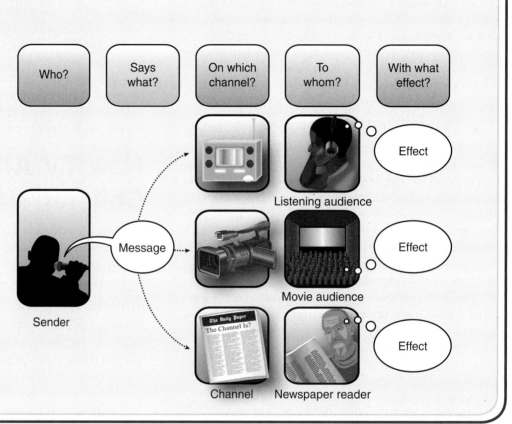

to television viewing. Schramm also found, in support of Cantril, that different children showed different effects.

Television and Social Behavior

Television and Social Behavior, a six-volume study of the effects of television, was funded by $1 million appropriated by Congress in 1969, after the violent decade of the 1960s. The U.S. Department of Health, Education and Welfare, which sponsored the study, appointed a distinguished panel of social scientists to undertake the research.

The study's major findings, published in 1971, concerned the effects of television violence on children. A content analysis of one week of prime-time programming, conducted by George Gerbner of the University of Pennsylvania, reported that eight out of 10 prime-time shows contained violence.

The conclusions of *Television and Social Behavior* did not make a direct connection between TV programming and violent behavior, however. The report said there was a "tentative" indication that television viewing caused aggressive behavior. According to the study, this connection between TV

violence and aggressive behavior affected only *some* children who were already classified as aggressive children and *only* in some environments.

Even though the report avoided a direct statement about violent behavior in children as a result of television viewing, the U.S. Surgeon General called for immediate action against violence on television. The television industry dismissed the results as inconclusive.

The Early Window

Several studies since 1971 have suggested that television violence causes aggression among children. In their 1988 book *The Early Window: Effects of Television on Children and Youth*, psychologists Robert M. Liebert and Joyce Sprafkin urged caution in drawing broad conclusions about the subject:

Studies using various methods have supported the proposition that TV violence can induce aggressive and/or antisocial behavior in children. Whether the effect will hold only for the most susceptible individuals (e.g., boys from disadvantaged homes) or whether it will hold for a wider range of youngsters obviously depends in part upon the measure being used. . . . The occurrence of serious violent or criminal acts results from several forces at once. Researchers have said that TV violence is *a* cause of aggressiveness, not that it is *the* cause of aggressiveness. There is no one, single cause of any social behavior.

Still, criticism of media violence persists. In 2005, protests erupted in Los Angeles over a billboard for rapper 50 Cent's new movie *Get Rich or Die Tryin,'* which showed 50 Cent with a microphone in one hand and a gun in the other. Protesters said the posters were placed near grammar schools where children could see them. Paramount, the studio that had produced the movie, removed the billboards.

"I understand people had picket signs protesting, saying my poster is violent because they see a gun," said 50 Cent. "They've seen a gun in tons of film advertising. If we walk into our local Blockbuster or place where we can rent a video, we'll see every kind of gun they manufacture on the cover of these films as a marketing tool. . . . I think Paramount made a business decision. I don't have a problem with it. At the end of the day, those kids are going to see the film. They insult the intelligence of the actual kids."

Television Advertising to Children

The effects of advertising on adults have been analyzed widely, but in 1979 the advertising of children's products became an object of serious government attention with the release of the 340-page report *Television Advertising to Children* by the Federal Trade Commission. The report, based on a two-year study, was designed to document the dangers of advertising sugar-based products to children, but embedded in the report was some provocative information about children's advertising.

Children are an especially vulnerable audience, said the FTC. The report concluded:

1. The average child sees 20,000 commercials a year, or about three hours of TV advertising a week.

2. Many children regard advertising as just another form of programming and do not distinguish between programs and ads.

3. Televised advertising for any product to children who do not understand the intent of the commercial is unfair and deceptive.

The report called for a ban on advertising to very young children, a ban on sugared products in advertising directed to children under age 12, and a requirement for counter-ads with dental and nutritional information to balance any ads for sugared products.

Jon Furniss/WireImage/Getty Images

Children are an especially vulnerable media audience because younger children, like the audience for SpongeBob SquarePants, pay more attention to television advertising than older children. SpongeBob attended the Nickelodeon Kids' Choice Awards in Britain in 2008.

This report and subsequent research about children's advertising suggest that younger children pay more attention to television advertising than older children. But by sixth grade, children adopt what has been called a "global distrust" of advertising.

Does Television Cause Violence?

Television and Behavior: Ten Years of Scientific Progress and Implications for the Eighties, published in 1982, by the National Institute of Mental Health, compiled information from 2,500 individual studies of television. According to the National Institute of Mental Health, three findings of these 2,500 studies, taken together, were that

1. A direct correlation exists between televised violence and aggressive behavior, yet there is no way to predict who will be affected and why.

Critics say television violence on TV shows like *CSI: Miami* may affect children's behavior negatively. In 1994, TV networks and cable and satellite programmers adopted a ratings code that warns viewers about violent content.

2. Heavy television viewers are more fearful, less trusting and more apprehensive than light viewers.

3. Children who watch what the report called "pro social" programs (programs that are socially constructive, such as *Sesame Street* and *SpongeBob*) are more likely to act responsibly.

Most of the latest studies of the media's role have continued to reinforce the concept that different people in different environments react to the media differently.

In 1994, cable operators and network broadcasters agreed to use an independent monitor to review programming for violent content. The agreement came after Congress held hearings on the subject in 1993, and threatened to introduce regulations to curb violence if the industry didn't police itself. The agreement also called for the development of violence ratings for TV programming and endorsed a "V" chip—V for "violence"—technology that would be built into a television set to allow parents to block programs rated as violent.

The monitoring is "qualitative" rather than "quantitative," according to the agreement. This means that the programs are examined for content, not just for incidents of violence. The Telecommunications Act of 1996 established a television ratings code for content. This agreement continues a tradition of media self-regulation. That is, the broadcast, recording and movie media industries have responded—often reluctantly—to congressional pressure by offering to

monitor themselves rather than invite the government to intrude on the content of their programs.

National Political Campaigns Depend on Mass Media

The media have transformed politics in ways that could never have been imagined when President Franklin D. Roosevelt introduced what were called Fireside Chats in 1933. Roosevelt was the first president to use the media effectively to stimulate public support.

The newest technology introduced during FDR's era—radio—gave him immediate access to a national audience. Roosevelt's media skill became an essential element in promoting his economic programs. Today, politics and the media seem irreversibly dependent on each other, one of the legacies of Roosevelt's presidency.

The Fireside Chats

In March 1933, just after he was inaugurated, FDR looked for a way to avoid a financial panic after he announced that he was closing the nation's banks. For a week, the country cooled off while Congress scrambled for a solution. On the Sunday night eight days after his inauguration, Roosevelt used radio to calm the nation's anxiety before the banks began to reopen on Monday. FDR went down to the basement of the White House to give his first Fireside Chat. There was a fireplace in the basement, but no fire was burning. The president could not find his script, so he borrowed a mimeographed copy from a reporter.

In his first address to the nation as president, FDR gave a banking lesson to his audience of 60 million people: "I want to talk for a few minutes with the people of the United States about banking. . . . First of all, let me state the simple fact that when you deposit money in a bank, the bank does not put the money into a safe deposit vault. It invests your money in many different forms." When he finished, he turned to people in the room and asked, "Was I all right?" America had its first media president, an elected leader talking directly to the people through the media.

Roosevelt's chats are cited as a legendary example of media politics, yet he gave only eight Fireside Chats in his first term of office. His other meetings with the press also enhanced his reputation for press access: In 13 years in office, he held more than 900 press conferences.

The People's Choice

The first major study of the influence of media on politics was *The People's Choice*, undertaken precisely because FDR

Ron P. Jaffe/© CBS/Courtesy: Everett Collection

seemed to be such a good media politician. This comprehensive examination of voter behavior in the 1940 presidential election was quite systematic.

Researchers Paul Lazarsfeld, Bernard Berelson and Hazel Gaudet followed 3,000 people in rural Erie County, Ohio, from May to November 1940, to determine what influenced the way these people voted for president. The researchers tracked how people's minds changed over the six-month period and then attempted to determine why. (It is important to remember this study was undertaken before television.) Radio became the prevailing medium for political advertising beginning in 1932, when the two parties spent more money for radio time than for any other item.) What effect, the researchers wanted to know, did the media have on people's choosing one candidate over another? The results were provocative.

Lazarsfeld and his colleagues found that only 8 percent of the voters in the study were actually *converted*. The majority of voters (53 percent) were *reinforced* in their beliefs by the media, and 14 percent were *activated* to vote. Mixed effects or no effects were shown by the remaining 25 percent of the people.

Lazarsfeld said opinion leaders, who got their information from the media, shared this information with their friends. The study concluded that instead of changing people's beliefs, the media primarily activate people to vote and reinforce already held opinions. *The People's Choice* also revealed that

- Family and friends had more effect on people's decisions than the media.

- The media had different effects on different people, reinforcing Cantril's findings.

- A major source of information about candidates was other people.

The finding that opinion leaders often provide and shape information for the general population was a bonus—the researchers hadn't set out specifically to learn this. This transmission of information and ideas from mass media to opinion leaders and then to friends and acquaintances is called the **two-step flow** of communication.

The Unseeing Eye

In 1976, a second study of the media and presidential elections, called *The Unseeing Eye: The Myth of Television Power in National Elections*, revealed findings that paralleled those of *The People's Choice*.

With a grant from the National Science Foundation, Thomas E. Patterson and Robert D. McClure supervised interviews with 2,707 people from early September to just before Election Day in the November 1972 race between George McGovern and Richard Nixon. The study did not discuss political media events, but it did analyze television campaign news and political advertising.

The researchers concluded that although political advertising influenced 16 percent of the people they interviewed, only 7 percent were manipulated by political ads. The researchers defined people who were influenced as those who decided to vote for a candidate based mostly on what they knew and only slightly on what the ads told them. The 7 percent of the people in the survey who were manipulated, according to Patterson and McClure, were people who cited political advertising as a major factor in their choices.

Patterson and McClure concluded that political advertising on TV has little effect on most people.

> By projecting their political biases . . . people see in candidates' commercials pretty much what they want to see. Ads sponsored by the candidate who shares their politics get a good response. They like what he has to say. And they like him. Ads sponsored by the opposing candidate are viewed negatively. They object to what he says. And they object to him.

It is important to remember, however, that in some elections a difference of a few percentage points can decide the outcome, and political advertising is designed to sway these swing voters. This is why political advertising continues to play such an important campaign role, attempting to reach the percentage of the population that remains vulnerable.

Election Campaigns on Television

So far, no convincing systematic evidence has been presented to show that the media change the voting behavior of *large* groups of people. Yet, since John F. Kennedy debated Richard Nixon during the 1960 presidential campaign, a deeply felt view has persisted among many people that the media—television in particular—have changed elections and electoral politics.

Kennedy's series of debates with Nixon in 1960 were the first televised debate of presidential candidates in American history. Kennedy's performance in the debates often is credited for his narrow victory in the election. In his book *Presidents and the Press*, media scholar Joseph C. Spear wrote:

> As the panel began asking questions, Nixon tended to go on the defensive, answering Kennedy point by point and ignoring his huge audience beyond the camera. Kennedy, by contrast, appeared rested, calm, informed, cocksure. Whatever the question, he aimed his answer at the millions of Americans viewing the program in their living rooms.

Two-Step Flow The transmission of information and ideas from mass media to opinion leaders and then to friends.

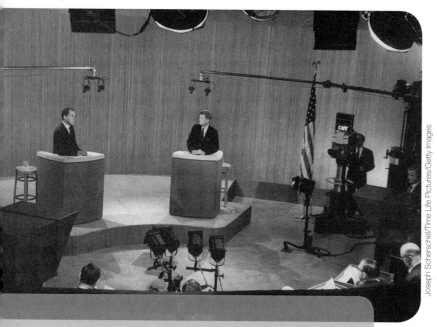

John F. Kennedy's series of debates with Richard Nixon in 1960 were the first televised debates of presidential candidates. Kennedy's performance in the debates often is credited for his narrow victory in the election. Shown is the fourth Kennedy-Nixon debate on October 1, 1960.

It was an unmitigated disaster for Nixon. In the second, third and fourth debates, he managed to recover somewhat from his initial poor performance, but it was too late. Surveys showed that an overwhelming percentage of the television audience had judged Kennedy the victor.

One legacy of Kennedy's television victory was that national political campaigns came to depend almost entirely on TV to promote presidential candidates, and televised presidential debates became a staple of every presidential election.

Television is a very efficient way to reach large numbers of people quickly, but campaigning for television also distances the candidates from direct public contact. Instead of meeting the public in person to promote and debate issues, candidates can isolate themselves from public scrutiny by using television ads to portray their views. (See **Impact/Culture**, "Under Obama, Web Is the Way," page 281.)

Cost of Political Advertising Skyrockets

Television advertising also is very expensive, and the cost of national campaigns in the past 20 years has skyrocketed. According to University of Southern California political scientist Herbert Alexander, presidential, gubernatorial and senatorial candidates devote 40 to 60 percent of their campaign budgets to advertising. Alexander is quick to point out that not all this money goes to television. In congressional elections, according to Alexander, "fewer than half the candidates use TV. Many of them are in districts like Los Angeles, where the media markets are much larger than the political jurisdictions."

Television advertising in such markets delivers a bigger audience than candidates need, so they use direct mail or print advertising. But a candidate running for Congress in Des Moines, Iowa, might use television because the entire district would be included in the local station's coverage, says Alexander. Historian James David Barber describes the public's role in politics:

> Particularly since television has brought national politics within arm's length of nearly every American, the great majority probably have at least some experience of the quadrennial passing parade. But millions vote their old memories and habits and interests, interpreting new perceptions that strike their senses to coincide with their prejudices and impulses.

> At the other end of the participation spectrum are those compulsive readers of *The New York Times* who delve into every twitch and turn of the contest. Floating in between are large numbers of Americans who pick up on the election's major events and personalities, following with mild but open interest the dominant developments.

> Insofar as the campaign makes a difference, it is this great central chunk of The People who swing the choice. They respond to what they see and hear. They are interested but not obsessed. They edit out the minor blips of change and wait for the campaign to gather force around a critical concern. They reach their conclusions on the basis of a widely shared common experience. It is through that middling throng of the population that the pulse of politics beats most powerfully, synchronizing to its insistent rhythm the varied vibrations of discrete events.

The rising cost of running for public office can exclude people without the means to raise huge sums of money. Since 1972, when national political campaigns first began to use widespread television advertising, presidential campaign expenditures have skyrocketed from less than $2 million in 1972 to $2.4 billion in 2008. (See **Illustration 13.2** on page 283.) Most of the money spent by the campaigns goes to pay for TV advertising.

If "the People who swing the choice," described by Barber, cannot easily participate in the political process,

IMPACT
» Culture

Under Obama, Web Is the Way

Unprecedented Online Outreach Expected

by Shailagh Murray and Matthew Mosk

CHICAGO—Armed with millions of e-mail addresses and a political operation that harnessed the Internet like no campaign before it, Barack Obama will enter the White House with the opportunity to create the first truly "wired" presidency.

Obama aides and allies are preparing a major expansion of the White House communications operation, enabling them to reach out directly to the supporters they have collected over 21 months without having to go through the mainstream media.

Just as John F. Kennedy mastered television as a medium for taking his message to the public, Obama is poised to transform the art of political communication once again, said Joe Trippi, a Democratic strategist who first helped integrate the Internet into campaigning four years ago.

"He's going to be the first president to be connected in this way, directly, with millions of Americans," Trippi said.

The nucleus of that effort is an e-mail database of more than 10 million supporters.

Justin Sullivan/Getty Images

Barack Obama's winning 2008 presidential campaign used many new technologies to communicate with voters. The new administration is expected to pursue many of these same technological solutions to help build a network of popular support for Obama's policies and programs.

The list is considered so valuable that the Obama camp briefly offered it as collateral during a cash-flow crunch late in the campaign, though it wound up never needing the loan, senior aides said. At least 3.1 million people on the list donated money to Obama.

Millions more made up the volunteer corps that organized his enormous rallies, registered millions of voters and held countless gatherings to plug the senator to friends and neighbors. On Election Day, they served as the backbone of Obama's get-out-the-vote operation, reaching voters by phone and at the front door, serving coffee at polling stations and baby-sitting so parents could stand in line at voting precincts.

After Obama declared victory, his campaign sent a text message announcing that his supporters hadn't heard the last from the president-elect. Obama conveyed a similar message to his staff in a campaign wide conference call Wednesday [November 5, 2008], signaling that his election was

(continued)

Under Obama, Web Is the Way (continued)

the beginning, and not the culmination, of a political movement.

Accordingly, the president-elect's transition Web site features a blog and a suggestion form, signaling the kinds of direct and instantaneous interaction that the Obama administration will encourage, perhaps with an eye toward turning its following into the biggest special-interest group in Washington.

Once Obama is sworn in, those backers may be summoned to push reluctant members of Congress to support legislation, to offer feedback on initiatives and to enlist in administration-supported causes in local communities. Obama would also be

positioned to ask his supporters to back his favored candidates with fundraising and turnout support in the 2010 midterm elections.

"There's this network of people now," said Martha Page, a neighborhood leader in Warren County, outside Cincinnati, where Obama managed to reduce a traditionally large Republican vote margin. Page received six calls Wednesday from volunteers looking for new assignments. "It's a sea change," she said.

From Shailagh Murray and Matthew Mosk, "Under Obama, Web Would Be the Way: Unprecedented Online Outreach Expected," *Washington Post,* November 10, 2008. Copyright © 2008 by the Washington Post Company. All rights reserved. Reprinted by permission.

eventually they may choose not to participate at all, eroding the number of people who run for office, vote in elections and work in political campaigns.

Today, the media are essential to American politics, changing the behavior of politicians as well as the electorate, raising important questions about governance and the conduct of elections.

"Is 'oblivious' the same as' undecided'?"

Voters Use the Internet

The 2004 presidential election marked the first election where the Internet began to play a role in national politics, as citizen blogs became an outlet for political debate and bloggers covered and commented on the presidential campaigns along with members of the established press corps.

According to *The New York Times*, "Democrats and Republicans are sharply increasing their use of e-mail, interactive Web sites, candidate and party blogs and text messaging to raise money, organize get-out-the-vote efforts and assemble crowds for rallies. The Internet, they say, appears to be far more efficient, and less costly, than the traditional tools of politics, notably door knocking and telephone banks."

The Pew Research Center reported that 75 million Americans used the Internet for political news during the 2004 presidential election. "The effect of the Internet on politics will be every bit as transformational as television was," Republican national chairman Ken Mehlman told the *Times*. "If you want to get your message out, the old way of paying someone to make a TV ad is insufficient: You need your message out through the Internet, through e-mail, through talk radio."

IMPACT

»» Audience

Illustration 13.2

TV Political Campaign Spending in Presidential Elections, 1972-2008

The amount of money presidential candidates spend on advertising has skyrocketed since 1972. Of the $2.4 billion collected by all the candidates in the 2008 presidential campaign, most of the money went to pay for TV advertising.

Source: Center for Responsive Politics, www.opensecrets.org.

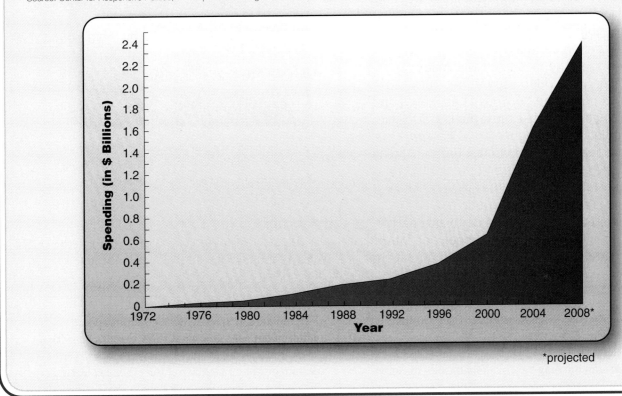

*projected

Political consultants also are experimenting with political podcasts that feature daily downloaded messages from candidates and viral marketing videos supporting the candidates (see **Chapter 10**). Supporters can pass along the video messages through e-mail to their friends—an online chain of free Internet political messaging that may prove more effective at reaching voters directly than traditional advertising.

However, even though Internet political marketing may reach large groups of people quickly and efficiently, there is the clear possibility that Internet political messages will change people's minds. One political consultant told the *Times*, "The holy grail that everybody is looking for right now is how can you use the Internet for persuasion." (See **Impact/Culture**, "Finding Political News Online, the Young Pass It On," page 284.)

Mass Media Reflect Cultural Values

Because media research is a continuing process, new ideas will emerge in the next decade from today's ideas and studies. Several provocative recent studies have extended previous boundaries of media research.

Silencing Opposing Viewpoints

Political scientist Elisabeth Noelle-Neumann has asserted that because journalists in all media tend to concentrate on the same major news stories, the audience is assailed on many sides by similar information. Together, the media

IMPACT
»Culture

Finding Political News Online, the Young Pass It On

by Brian Stelter

Senator Barack Obama's videotaped response to President Bush's final State of the Union address—almost five minutes of Mr. Obama's talking directly to the camera—elicited little attention from newspaper and television reporters in January.

But on the medium it was made for, the Internet, the video caught fire. Quickly after it was posted on YouTube, it appeared on the video-sharing site's most popular list and Google's most blogged list. It has been viewed more than 1.3 million times, been linked by more than 500 blogs and distributed widely on social networking sites like Facebook.

It is not news that young politically minded viewers are turning to alternative sources like YouTube, Facebook and late-night comedy shows like *The Daily Show*. But that

In 2008, young voters became avid users of the Internet and alternative sources of information such as *The Daily Show* with Jon Stewart.

is only the beginning of how they process information.

According to interviews and recent surveys, younger voters tend to be not just

present the consensus; journalists reflect the prevailing climate of opinion.

As this consensus spreads, people with divergent views, says Noelle-Neumann, may be less likely to voice disagreement with the prevailing point of view. Thus, because of a ***"spiral of silence,"*** the media gain more influence because opponents of the consensus tend to remain silent. The implication for future research will be to ask whether the media neutralize dissent and create a pattern of social and cultural conformity.

Losing a Sense of Place

In his book *No Sense of Place*, published in 1985, Joshua Meyrowitz provided new insight into television's possible effects on society. In the past, says Meyrowitz:

Spiral of Silence The belief that people with divergent views may be reluctant to challenge the consensus of opinion offered by the media.

Parents did not know what their children knew, and children did not know what their parents knew they knew. Similarly, a person of one sex could never be certain of what a member of the other sex knew. . . . Television undermines such behavioral distinctions because it encompasses children and adults, men and women and all other social groups in a single informational sphere or environment. Not only does it provide similar information to everyone but, even more significant, it provides it publicly and often simultaneously.

This sharing of information, says Meyrowitz, means that subjects that rarely were discussed between men and women, for instance, and between children and adults, have become part of the public dialogue.

A second result of television viewing is the blurred distinction between childhood and adulthood, says Meyrowitz. When print dominated the society as a medium, children's access to adult information was limited. The only way to learn about "adult" concepts was to read about them, so typi-

consumers of news and current events but conduits as well—sending out e-mailed links and videos to friends and their social networks. And in turn, they rely on friends and online connections for news to come to them. In essence, they are replacing the professional filter—reading *The Washington Post*, clicking on CNN.com—with a social one.

"There are lots of times where I'll read an interesting story online and send the U.R.L. to 10 friends," said Lauren Wolfe, 25, the president of College Democrats of America. "I'd rather read an e-mail from a friend with an attached story than search through a newspaper to find the story."

In one sense, this social filter is simply a technological version of the oldest tool in politics: word of mouth. Jane Buckingham, the founder of the Intelligence Group, a market research company, said the "social media generation" was comfortable being in constant communication with others, so recommendations from friends or text messages from a campaign—information that is shared, but not sought—were perceived as natural.

Ms. Buckingham recalled conducting a focus group where one of her subjects, a college student, said, "If the news is that important, it will find me."

A December [2007] survey by the Pew Research Center for the People and the Press looked broadly at how media were being consumed this campaign. In the most striking finding, half of respondents over the age of 50 and 39 percent of 30- to 49-year-olds reported watching local television news regularly for campaign news, while only 25 percent of people under 30 said they did.

Fully two-thirds of Web users under 30 say they use social networking sites, while fewer than 20 percent of older users do. MySpace and Facebook create a sense of connection to the candidates. . . .

Young people also identify online discussions with friends and videos as important sources of election information. The habits suggest that younger readers find themselves going straight to the source, bypassing the context and analysis that seasoned journalists provide.

cally a child was not exposed to adult ideas or problems, and taboo topics remained hidden from children.

In a video world, however, any topic that can be portrayed in pictures on television challenges the boundaries that print places around information.

This, says Meyrowitz, causes an early loss of the naïveté of childhood:

Television removes barriers that once divided people of different ages and reading abilities into different social situations. The widespread use of television is equivalent to a broad social decision to allow young children to be present at wars and funerals, courtships and seductions, criminal plots and cocktail parties. . . . Television thrusts children into a complex adult world, and it provides the impetus for children to ask the meanings of actions and words they would not yet have heard or read about without television.

Meyrowitz concedes that movies offered similar information to children before television, but he says that the pervasiveness of television today makes its effects more widespread.

Television is blurring social distinctions—between children and adults, and between men and women. Complicating the current study of media effects is the increase in the variety and number of available media sources.

Linking TV to School Performance

Many studies about children and television, such as the National Institute of Mental Health report, have concentrated on the effects of the portrayals of violence. But in 1981, a California study suggested a link between television viewing and poor school performance.

The California Assessment Program (CAP), which tests academic achievement, included a new question on the achievement test: "On a typical weekday, about how many hours do you watch TV?" The students were given a choice ranging from zero to six or more hours. An analysis of the answers to that question from more than 10,000 sixth graders was matched with the children's scores on the achievement test.

The results suggested a consistent relationship between viewing time and achievement. Students who said they watched a lot of television scored lower in reading, writing and mathematics than students who didn't watch any television. The average scores for students who said they viewed six or more hours of television a day were six to eight points lower than for those children who said they watched less than a half-hour of television a day.

Because the study didn't include information about the IQ score or income levels of these students, the results cannot be considered conclusive. The study simply may show that children who watch a lot of television aren't studying. But the results are particularly interesting because of the number of children who were included in the survey.

Further research could examine whether children are poor students because they watch a lot of television or whether children who watch a lot of television are poor students for other reasons.

Stereotyping

Journalists often use shorthand labels to characterize ethnic and other groups. In his 1922 book *Public Opinion*, political journalist Walter Lippmann first identified the tendency of journalists to generalize about other people based on fixed ideas.

When we speak of the mind of a group of people, of the French mind, the militarist mind, the bolshevik mind, we are liable to serious confusion unless we agree to separate the instinctive equipment from the stereotypes, the patterns, the formulae which play so decisive a part in building up the mental world to which the native character is adapted and responds. . . . Failure to make this distinction accounts for oceans of loose talk about collective minds, national souls and race psychology.

The image of women portrayed by the media has been the subject of significant contemporary studies by many media researchers. Observers of the stereotyping of women point to past and current media portrayals showing very few women in professional roles or as strong, major characters.

The media's overall portrayal of women in mass culture is slowly improving, but in her book *Loving with a Vengeance: Mass-Produced Fantasies for Women*, Tania Modleski says that the portrayal in popular fiction of women in submissive roles began in 1740, with the British novel *Pamela*, which was published in America by Benjamin Franklin in 1744. Modleski analyzed the historical content of gothic novels, Harlequin Romances and soap operas. Her study reveals:

In Harlequin Romances, the need of women to find meaning and pleasure in activities that are not wholly male-centered such as work or artistic creation is generally scoffed at.

Soap operas also undercut, though in subtler fashion, the idea that a woman might obtain satisfaction from these activities [work or artistic creation]. . . . Indeed, patriarchal myths and institutions are . . . wholeheartedly embraced, although the anxieties and tensions they give rise to may be said to provoke the need for the texts in the first place.

The implication in Modleski's research is that women who read romance novels will believe they should act like the women in the novels they read. A stereotype that has existed since 1740 still shows up in today's media.

Media Slow to Reflect Ethnic Diversity

Beginning in the year 2000, the U.S. census allowed Americans to use more than one racial category to describe themselves, and the categories have been changed to reflect America's changing face. In the past, people were forced to choose one category from among the following: Black, White, Asian or Pacific Islander, American Indian or Alaskan Native, or "Other—specify in writing."

In the 1990 census, about 10 million people checked "Other"—nearly all of Latino descent. The new range of choices for the year 2000 census was White, Black or African American, Asian, Hawaiian Native or Pacific Islander, American Indian or Alaska Native and Hispanic or Latino. People who identify with more than one group also were able to check more than one description—African American and Asian, for example. All government forms are required to use the new categories.

This new census method allows people to identify themselves to the government and shows the evolving social landscape of the U.S. population. Yet the American media have been very slow to acknowledge America's changing population patterns. In fact, critics charge that the media have responded reluctantly to reflect accurately America's growing multicultural mix.

Specific media outlets, such as African American and Latino newspapers and magazines, have been able to cater to specific audiences. But the mainstream media, especially daily newspapers and the TV networks, traditionally have represented the interests of the mainstream culture. Scores of media studies have documented stereotypical representation, and a lack of representation, of people of color in all areas of the culture, even though the potential audience for ethnic media is very large. (See **Impact/World**, "Spanish Players Defend Controversial Photo," page 287.)

Media scholar Carolyn Martindale, for example, in a content analysis of *The New York Times* from 1934 to 1994,

IMPACT
➤➤ World

Spanish Players Defend Controversial Photo
by Paul Logothetis

BEIJING, China—Players on Spain's Olympic basketball team defended a photo in an ad showing the players using their fingers to apparently make their eyes look more Chinese.

The photo, which has been running as a newspaper spread in Spain since Friday [August 8, 2008], shows all 15 players making the gesture on a basketball court adorned with a Chinese dragon. The photo was part of a publicity campaign for team sponsor Seur, a Spanish courier company, and is being used only in Spain.

"It was something like supposed to be funny or something but never offensive in any way," said Spain center Pau Gasol, who also plays for the Los Angeles Lakers. "I'm sorry if anybody thought or took it the wrong way and thought that it was offensive."

Point guard Jose Manuel Calderon said the team was responding to a request from the photographer.

"We felt it was something appropriate, and that it would be interpreted as an affectionate gesture," Calderon, who plays for NBA's Toronto Raptors, wrote on his *ElMundo.es* blog. "Without a doubt, some . . . press didn't see it that way."

International media criticized the photo. *London's Daily Telegraph* said Spain's "poor reputation for insensitivity toward racial issues has been further harmed" by the photo.

"This was clearly inappropriate, but we understand the Spanish team intended no offense and has apologized," Emmanuelle Moreau, a spokeswoman for the International Olympic Committee, said in an e-mail. "The matter rests there as far as the IOC is concerned."

AP Photo

The 2008 Spanish Olympic basketball team posed for a publicity photo, using their fingers apparently to make their eyes look more Chinese. Team members denied they meant any offense.

The OCA, an organization representing Asian-Pacific Americans, also found the photo disturbing. "It is unfortunate that this type of imagery would rear its head at a time that is supposed to be about world unity," George Wu, the group's deputy director, said in a statement.

The Spanish women's basketball team also posed for photo doing the same thing, and four members of Argentina's women's Olympic football team were shown making similar faces in a photograph published last week.

Gasol said it was "absurd" people were calling the gesture racist.

"We never intended anything like that," he said.

found that most nonwhite groups were visible "only in glimpses." According to Martindale, "The mainstream press in the U.S. has presented minorities as outside, rather than a part of, American Society."

After examining 374 episodes of 96 prime-time series on ABC, CBS, NBC, Fox, WB and UPN, the Center for Media and Public Affairs for the National Council of La Raza concluded that only 2 percent of prime-time characters during the 1994–1995 season were Latinos, and most of the roles played by those characters were minor. The study, *Don't Blink: Hispanics in Television Entertainment*, also revealed that although Latino characters were portrayed more positively than they had been in the past, they were most likely to be shown as poor or working class.

Based on a comprehensive analysis of the nation's newspapers, a 56-page *News Watch* report issued at a convention of the nation's African American, Asian, Latino and Native American journalists concluded that "the mainstream media's coverage of people of color is riddled with old stereotypes, offensive terminology, biased reporting and a myopic interpretation of American society." To counteract stereotyping, the Center for Integration and Improvement of Journalism at San Francisco State University (which sponsored the study) offered the following Tips for Journalists:

- Apply consistent guidelines when identifying people of race. Are the terms considered offensive? Ask individual sources how they wish to be identified.

- Only refer to people's ethnic or racial background when it is relevant.

- When deciding whether to mention someone's race, ask yourself: Is ethnic/racial identification needed? Is it important to the context of the story?

- Consult a supervisor if you are unsure of the offensiveness or relevance of a racial or ethnic term.

- Use sensitivity when describing rites and cultural events. Avoid inappropriate comparisons. For example, Kwanzaa is not "African American Christmas."

- Be specific when using ethnic or racial identification of individuals. Referring to someone as Filipino American is preferred to calling that person Asian. The latter term is better applied to a group.

The issue of accurate reflection by the media of a complex society invites analysis as traditional media outlets struggle to reflect the evolving face of an America that is growing more diverse every day.

Mass Media Face Gender Issues

In 1993, newspapers faced an editorial dilemma when cartoonist Lynn Johnston, who draws the very popular syndicated strip *For Better or For Worse*, decided to reveal that Lawrence, one of the teenagers in the comic strip, is gay. Most newspapers published the strip, but 19 newspapers canceled their contracts for the comic, which is carried by Universal Press Syndicate of Kansas City.

One newspaper editor who refused to carry the strip explained, "We are a conservative newspaper in a conservative town." Another editor said he "felt the sequence condoned homosexuality 'almost to the point of advocacy.'" Responding to criticism that, by revealing Lawrence's sexual preference, she was advocating homosexuality, Johnston said, "You know, that's like advocating left-handedness. Gayness is simply something that exists. My strip is a reality strip, real situations, real crises, real people." One newspaper executive at a paper that carried the strip wrote, "It seems to me that what we're talking about here isn't the rightness or wrongness of homosexuality. It is about tolerance."

More than 10 years later, in 2005, a cartoon drawn by veteran cartoonist Dan Piraro appeared in two different versions—the first showing a doctor outside a surgery room talking to a man, saying, "Your husband is in the recovery room. You could go back and see him if you like, but our government-sanctioned bigotry forbids it." Piraro's editor at King Features Syndicate, saying he had received

At the request of his editor, cartoonist Dan Piraro supplied two different captions in 2005 for the same cartoon, and newspapers could choose which caption they wanted to use. Some newspaper editors objected to the caption (left) that portrayed a same-sex couple.

IMPACT
»Culture

Study Says Stick to Skinny Models for Fat Profits

Ultra-Thin Bodies Make Women Like Brands More but Themselves Less

by Jack Neff

Thin is still in for advertising, new research suggests, unless you're trying to sell cookies or self-esteem.

Women who had just seen thin models were nearly four times more likely to turn down a snack pack of Oreo cookies offered as thanks for their participation in a recent study than women who hadn't.

Research by business professors at Villanova University and the College of New Jersey, inspired by Dove's "Campaign for Real Beauty," showed that ads featuring thin models made women feel worse about themselves but better about the brands featured.

Seeing thin models also made college-age women far more likely to turn down a snack pack of Oreo cookies offered as thanks for their participation in the study or to opt for a reduced-fat version. Women who had just seen thin models were nearly four times more likely to say no to Oreos than women who hadn't and 42 percent more likely to opt for reduced-fat cookies if they did indulge.

Women in a sample of 194 college students aged 18-24 expressed more negative feelings about their sexual attractiveness, weight and physical condition after seeing thin models than before. So-called high-self-monitoring women, or those most con-

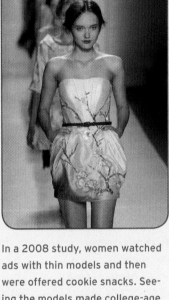

Scott Gries/Getty Images for IMG

In a 2008 study, women watched ads with thin models and then were offered cookie snacks. Seeing the models made college-age women four times more likely to refuse a snack pack of Oreo cookies. The research showed that ads featuring thin models made young women feel worse about themselves but better about the featured brand.

cerned about what others think of their appearance, were the most negatively affected by seeing the thin models in the study.

The professors are still preparing a written report on results from a second phase of the research, which found that despite the negative effect on their body image, women preferred ads showing thin models and said they were more likely to buy products featured in those ads than in ones showing "regular-size models," said Jeremy Kees, a business professor at Villanova. . . .

"The really interesting result we're seeing across multiple studies is that these thin models make women feel bad, but they like it," Mr. Kees said. "They have higher evaluation of the brands. With the more regular-size models, they don't feel bad. Their body image doesn't change. But in terms of evaluations of the brands, those are actually lower."

Mr. Kees acknowledged that the findings create something of a quandary for marketers, who might have a positive effect on young women's self-esteem by showing more typical women in ads, but suffer in the marketplace as a result.

From "Study Says Stick to Skinny Models for Fat Profits," by Jack Neff, AdAge.com, August 4, 2008. Reprinted by permission.

complaints about Piraro's liberal bias, asked Piraro to draw another version with the doctor talking to a man and saying, "She's going to be just fine—she's quite a fighter. The anesthesiologist has a black eye and I think she may have cracked my ribs."

Different papers chose which version to run, but some subscribers noticed the difference. "Not wishing to lose my voice entirely, I thought it was wise to send in a replacement caption for the same picture," Piraro said.

An understanding of the media portrayals of Americans' diverse lifestyles also received extra attention in 1997, when the television program *Ellen* portrayed two women exchanging a romantic kiss. Although promoted as the nation's first female television kiss, the first televised romantic lesbian relationship actually had been portrayed on *L.A. Law* in 1991.

Gender issues remained primarily a subject for the nation's lesbian and gay newspapers and magazines, although in 1996, *The New Yorker* ran a controversial cover that portrayed two men kissing on a Manhattan sidewalk. Bringing the issue to a mainstream audience, as the *Ellen* television program did when it was launched, presents a dilemma for the TV networks because, when notified beforehand about the content of the program, some local TV stations refused to show the episode. The reluctance of mainstream television to portray alternative relationships is as much a reflection of the networks trying to protect their economic interests as it is a reflection of the nation's social values.

By 2003, society's strong reactions to the portrayals of gay people on television seemed to have subsided when Bravo introduced its series *Queer Eye for the Straight Guy*. The title itself would have been shocking just a few years earlier, but audiences seemed ready for programming that featured gay men who advise a straight man about fashion, home decor, cuisine and culture. Television seems to be adapting to changing social standards, reflecting society's ability to begin to tolerate a more diverse set of characters on television.

How to Gauge Media Effects

Scholars once thought the effects of media were easy to measure, as a direct relationship between media messages and media effects. Contemporary scholars now know that the relationship between media and their audiences is complex.

Communications scholar Neil Postman poses some questions to ask about mass media's relationship to cultural, political and social issues:

- What are the main psychic effects of each [media] form?

- What is the main relation between information and reason?

- What redefinitions of important cultural meanings do new sources, speeds, contexts and forms of information require?

- How do different forms of information persuade?

- Is a newspaper's "public" different from television's "public"?

- How do different information forms dictate the type of content that is expressed?

These questions should be discussed, says Postman, because "no medium is excessively dangerous if its users understand what its dangers are. . . . This is an instance in which the asking of the questions is sufficient. To ask is to break the spell."

Review, Analyze, Investigate
REVIEWING CHAPTER 13

Early Media Studies Assess Impact

✓ Media scholars look for patterns in the effects of media rather than for anecdotal evidence.

✓ David Potter, in *People of Plenty*, described the United States as a consumer society driven by advertising.

Scholars Look for Patterns

✓ Canadian scholar Marshall McLuhan introduced the term *global village* to describe the way media bring people together through shared experience.

✓ The magic bullet theory, developed in the 1929 Payne Fund studies, asserted that media content had a direct causal relationship to behavior and that mass media affected everyone in the same way.

✓ Challenging the magic bullet theory, Hadley Cantril found that better-educated people listening to "War of the Worlds" were much more likely to detect that the radio broadcast was fiction. Today, scholars believe the media have different effects on different people.

✓ In 1948, political scientist Harold D. Lasswell described the process of communication as "Who? Says what? On which channel? To whom? With what effect?"

How TV Affects Children's Behavior

✓ In 1961, Wilbur Schramm and his associates revealed that children used TV for fantasy, diversion and instruction. Aggressive children were more likely to turn to TV for fantasy, said Schramm, but he could find no serious problems related to TV viewing.

✓ The 1971 report to Congress, *Television and Social Behavior*, made a faint causal connection between TV violence and children's violent behavior, but the report said that only some children were affected, and these children already had been classified as aggressive.

✓ Several recent studies have suggested that TV violence causes aggression among children. Researchers caution, however, that TV violence is not *the* cause of aggressiveness, but only *a* cause of aggressiveness.

✓ The Federal Trade Commission report, *Television Advertising to Children*, said that children see 20,000 commercials a year and that younger children are much more likely to pay attention to TV advertising than older ones.

Does Television Cause Violence?

✓ The summary study by the National Institute of Mental Health in 1982 asserted that a direct connection exists between televised violence and aggressive behavior, but there is no way to predict who will be affected and why.

✓ Most of the latest studies of the media's role have continued to reinforce the concept that different people in different environments react to the media differently.

National Political Campaigns Depend on Mass Media

✓ Media politics began in 1933 with President Franklin Roosevelt's Fireside Chats. John F. Kennedy broadened the tradition when he and Richard Nixon appeared in the nation's first televised debate of presidential candidates, in 1960.

✓ The first major study of politics and the media, *The People's Choice*, concluded that only 8 percent of the voters in the study were actually converted by media coverage of the 1940 campaign.

✓ The 1976 study, *The Unseeing Eye*, revealed that only 7 percent of the people in the study were manipulated by TV ads. The researchers concluded that political advertising has little effect on most people.

✓ Television is a very efficient way to reach large numbers of people quickly, but campaigning for television also distances the candidates from direct public contact.

Cost of Political Advertising Skyrockets

✓ The rising cost of national political campaigns is directly connected to the expense of television advertising.

✓ Opinion leaders shape political views, a transmission of ideas that is called the two-step flow of communication.

✓ TV political advertising affects only a small percentage of people, but just a few percentage points decide many elections.

Voters Use the Internet

✓ The 2004 presidential election was the first election where the Internet began to play a role in national politics. In that election, 75 million people used the Internet to obtain political news.

✓ Candidates use Web sites, e-mail, blogs, podcasts and social-networking sites such as MySpace and Facebook to reach the public. YouTube may be the Internet innovation that will have the most impact in future elections.

Mass Media Reflect Cultural Values

✓ Elisabeth Noelle-Neumann has asserted that, due to what she calls a "spiral of silence" supporting the consensus point of view, the media have more influence because opponents of the consensus tend to remain silent.

✓ Joshua Meyrowitz says that television viewing blurs the distinction between childhood and adulthood.

✓ A study by the California Assessment Program of children's TV viewing habits seems to support the idea that children who watch a lot of TV do not perform as well in schoolwork as children who watch less television.

✓ Walter Lippmann first identified the tendency of journalists to generalize about groups of people and create stereotypes.

✓ Scholar Tania Modleski says the media's inaccurate portrayals of women are not new but began in 1740 with the publication of *Pamela*, the first novel.

Media Slow to Reflect Ethnic Diversity

✓ The year 2000 census categories for racial designations more clearly reflect the multicultural nature of the U.S. population, yet the mass media have been slow to acknowledge America's changing population patterns.

✓ The mainstream media, especially daily newspapers and the TV networks, have traditionally represented the interests of the mainstream culture.

✓ A study of *The New York Times* from 1934 to 1994 found that most nonwhite groups were visible "only in glimpses."

✓ A study by the National Council of La Raza concluded that only 2 percent of prime-time characters during the

1994–1995 TV season were Latinos, and most of the roles played by those characters were minor.

✓ A 2005 study of ethnic media revealed that one-quarter of Americans regularly read or tune in to ethnic media.

Mass Media Face Gender Issues

✓ The lesbian character on the TV program *Ellen* and the gay character Lawrence in the cartoon strip *For Better or For Worse* focused attention on media portrayals of gender issues.

✓ By 2003, the strong reactions to the portrayals of gay people on television seemed to have subsided when Fox Television introduced its series *Queer Eye for the Straight Guy*.

✓ The experience of the cartoonist Dan Piraro in 2005 is a reminder that gender issues still are a sensitive subject for media. At the insistence of his editor, Piraro provided two captions for the same cartoon, one that reflected a male-female relationship and one that reflected a male-male relationship.

How to Gauge Media Effects

✓ The relationship between media and their audiences is complex.

✓ Communications scholar Neil Postman says that scholars should continue to analyze the media's effects so people will not just accept what they see without question.

KEY TERMS

These terms are defined in the margins throughout this chapter and appear in alphabetical order with definitions in the Glossary, which begins on page 372.

Magic Bullet Theory 275

Media Content
   Analysis 275

Media Effects
   Research 275

Spiral of Silence 284

Two-Step Flow 279

CRITICAL QUESTIONS

1. How did each of the following people contribute to media effects research?

   a. David M. Potter

   b. Marshall McLuhan

   c. Harold D. Lasswell

   d. George Gerbner

2. Describe three studies involving children and TV and discuss the results. Why are children often the subject of television effects research?

3. Discuss your understanding of the role of American media, especially television, in political campaigns.

Include reference to research about how political campaigns use media to try to influence voters.

4. Describe the nature and effects of the Internet on American politics.

5. How well and how fairly do you believe African Americans, Latinos and other ethnic groups are represented in American media? How well and fairly do you believe gender issues are portrayed in American mass media? If you were an executive at a major media company, how would you address these issues?

WORKING THE WEB

This list includes both sites mentioned in the chapter and others to give you greater insight into social, cultural and political issues research.

Benton Foundation
http://www.benton.org

This foundation's mission is "to articulate a public interest vision for the digital age and to demonstrate the value of communications for solving social problems." Its virtual library includes downloadable documents on issues ranging

from the "digital divide" to telecommunications regulation and legislation to television/community media. The foundation was established by William Benton, whom pollster George Gallup called a father of advertising consumer research. Benton was also publisher of the Encyclopedia Britannica and a U.S. senator.

Center on Media and Child Health (CMCH)
http://www.cmch.tv

Dedicated to "understanding and responding to the effects of media on the physical, mental and social health of children through research, production and education," this center is located at Children's Hospital Boston along with Harvard Medical School and Harvard School of Public Health. Hot Topics in the site's section for parents and teachers include violence in video games, educational television and literacy, and obesity. The CMCH Database of Research catalogs current research on the relationship of media exposure to health-risk behaviors.

Joan Shorenstein Center on the Press, Politics and Public Policy (Harvard University)

http://www.hks.harvard.edu/presspol/

Dedicated to "exploring and illuminating the intersection of press, politics and public policy in theory and in practice," this research center is based at the John F. Kennedy School of Government at Harvard University. Downloadable Research & Publications documents include books written by Center faculty, staff and associates, newsletters from the Center and a variety of reports, papers and case studies. The center offers some internships and scholarships for students.

Media Awareness Network (MNet)

http://www.media-awareness.ca

This Canadian nonprofit organization promotes Internet and media education by producing online programs and resources, partnering with Canadian and international organizations, and speaking to audiences in Canada and around the world. MNet's focus is on providing educational information and materials empowering young people to develop the critical thinking skills needed to be "functionally literate" in media messages. The Web site deals with issues including media violence, online hate and media stereotyping (of ethnic minorities, girls and women, boys and men, and gays and lesbians).

Media Effects Research Lab at Penn State University

http://www.psu.edu/dept/medialab/index.html

This research facility has conducted several experiments on hundreds of subjects testing the psychological effects of media content, form and technology. Research abstracts are available for viewing on a wide variety of subjects including Internet use and content credibility; cell phone usage and interaction with others; examinations of gender, racial and sexual minority stereotypes in the media; and fashion magazines' role in self-worth.

Media Research Hub (Social Science Research Council)

http://mediaresearchhub.ssrc.org

Part of the SSRC's Necessary Knowledge for a Democratic Public Sphere program, the Media Research Hub works to ensure that debates about media and communication technologies are shaped by "high-quality research and a rich understanding of the public interest." Its Resource Database is a community-maintained field mapping tool for work on the social dimensions of media, communications and technology. Research news, commentary and data are also available on the site. The program is run in partnership with the Center for International Media Action (CIMA) and the Donald McGannon Communication Research Center at Fordham University.

Moorland-Spingarn Research Center (MSRC) at Howard University

http://www.howard.edu/library/moorland-spingarn

One of the largest repositories for "documentation of the history and culture of people of African descent in Africa, the Americas and other parts of the world," this site includes a link to the archives of the center's electronic journal (HUArchivesNet). Links to the Library Division and the Manuscript Division go to brief descriptions and samples of the center's holdings.

National Journal

http://www.nationaljournal.com

National Journal Group publishes nonpartisan magazines, newsletters, books and directories "for people who have a professional interest in politics, policy and government." Web site users can access online content from *National Journal Magazine*, *The Hotline* (daily news service for political insiders), and *CongressDaily*.

University of Iowa Online Communication Studies Resources: Political Advertising

http://www.uiowa.edu/commstud/resources/pol_ads.html

This resource site provides links to articles and a long list of Web sites relating to political advertising. Examples are "The 30-Second Candidate," a feature-rich supplement to a PBS documentary; Ad Watch from Best Practices in Journalism; Dissect-an-Ad exercise from the Center for Media Literacy; The Living Room Candidate: Presidential Campaign Commercials 1952–2000; and links to several political media and consulting firms.

YouTube

http://www.youtube.com

Founded in 2005 and acquired by Google, Inc. just a year later, YouTube is the leader in online video. Users can watch anything from current events to quirky and unusual content, and can browse categories such as comedy, news and politics, pets and animals, and sports. Videos are further classified as "most discussed," "most viewed," and "top rated." YouTube partners with many content providers including CBS; BBC; Universal, Sony, and Warner Music Groups; NBA; The Sundance Channel and more.

14

Law and Regulation: Rewriting the Rules

Mario Tama/Getty Images

After several court challenges to reporters' ability to keep their sources confidential, journalists protested in front of the New York Times building in 2005, lobbying for a national shield law. Although many states have shield laws to protect journalists' sources, there is no federal shield law.

What's Ahead?

> " Providing a large number of journalists with a censored Internet connection when they were promised an open Internet is naturally going to draw a lot of critical stories in the media."
>
> Rob Faris, Harvard's Berkman Center for Internet and Society, commenting on the Chinese government's decision to censor journalists' Internet access during the 2008 Olympics

According to the precedent-setting

New York Times v. Sullivan case, which helped define press freedom in 1964, the U.S. media's role is to encourage "uninhibited, robust and wide-open" debate. Arguments among the public, the government and the media about the best way for the media to maintain this public trusteeship form the core of challenges and rebuttals to legal and regulatory limits on the media.

New York Times columnist Tom Wicker wrote, for example, "Even though absolute press freedom may sometimes have to accommodate itself to other high constitutional values, the repeal or modification of the First Amendment seems unlikely. . . . If the true freedom of the press is to decide for itself what to publish and when to publish it, the true responsibility of the press must be to assert and defend that freedom."

The media are businesses operating to make a profit, but these businesses enjoy a special trust under the U.S. Constitution. The legal and regulatory issues the media face are attempts by the government to balance this special trust with the interests of individuals and the interests of government.

U.S. Constitution Sets Free Press Precedent

All legal interpretations of the press' responsibilities attempt to determine exactly what the framers of the U.S. Constitution meant when they included the First Amendment in the Bill of Rights in 1791. The First Amendment established the concept that the press should operate freely:

> Congress shall make no law respecting an establishment of religion, or prohibiting the free exercise thereof; or abridging the freedom of speech, or of the press; or the right of the people peaceably to assemble, and to petition the Government for a redress of grievances.

In his book *Emergence of a Free Press*, Leonard W. Levy explains his interpretation of the First Amendment:

> By freedom of the press the Framers meant a right to engage in rasping, corrosive and offensive discussions on all topics of public interest. . . . The press had become the tribune of the people by sitting in judgment on the conduct of public officials. A free press meant the press as the Fourth Estate, [as] . . . an informal or extra-constitutional fourth branch that functioned as part of the intricate system of checks and balances that exposed public mismanagement and kept power fragmented, manageable and accountable.

While efforts to interpret the Framers' meaning continue, as do challenges and rebuttals to laws and regulations that have been passed, discussion of the restrictions and laws covering the press today can be divided into six categories: (1) federal government restrictions, (2) prior restraint, (3) censorship, (4) libel, (5) privacy and (6) the right of access.

Government Tries to Restrict Free Expression

At least four times in U.S. history before 1964, the federal government felt threatened enough by press freedom to attempt to restrict the press' access to information. These four notable attempts to restrict the way the media operate were the Alien and Sedition Laws of 1798, the Espionage Act of 1918, the Smith Act of 1940 and the Cold War congressional investigations of suspected communists in the late 1940s and early 1950s. All four challenges were attempts by the government to control free speech.

The Alien and Sedition Laws of 1798

Under the provisions of the Alien and Sedition Laws of 1798, 15 people were indicted, 11 people were tried and 10 were found guilty. The Alien and Sedition Laws set a fine of up to $2,000 and a sentence of up to two years in jail for anyone who was found guilty of speaking, writing or publishing "false, scandalous and malicious writing or writings" against the government, Congress or the president. The laws expired in 1801, and when Thomas Jefferson became president that year, he pardoned everyone who had been found guilty under the laws.

The Espionage Act of 1918

Although Henry Raymond challenged censorship of Civil War reporting (see **Chapter 12**), journalists and the general population during the Civil War accepted government control of information. But during World War I, Congress passed the Espionage Act of 1918. Not all Americans supported U.S. entry into the war, and to stop criticism, the Espionage Act made it a crime to say or write anything that could be viewed as helping the enemy. Under the act, 877 people were convicted. Many, but not all, of them were pardoned when the war ended.

The most notable person cited under the Espionage Act of 1918 was labor organizer and Socialist party presidential candidate Eugene V. Debs, who was sentenced to two concurrent 10-year terms for giving a public speech against the war. At his trial Debs said, "I have been accused of obstructing the war. I admit it. Gentlemen, I abhor war. I would oppose the war if I stood alone." Debs was released from prison by a presidential order in 1921.

The Smith Act of 1940

During World War II, Congress passed the Smith Act of 1940, which placed some restrictions on free speech. Only a few people were cited under it, but the press was required to submit stories for government censorship. President Roosevelt created an Office of Censorship, which worked out a voluntary Code of Wartime Practices with the press. The code spelled out what information the press would not report about the war, such as troop and ship movements. The military retained power to censor all overseas war reporting.

The Office of Censorship also issued guidelines for news broadcasts and commentaries, called the *Code of Wartime Practices for American Broadcasters*. (See **Impact/Culture**, "Excerpts from the 1943 Code of Wartime Practices for

American Broadcasters, " page 298) The government exercised special influence over broadcasters because it licensed broadcast outlets.

HUAC and the Permanent Subcommittee on Investigations

The fourth major move challenging the First Amendment protection of free speech came in the late 1940s and early 1950s, culminating with the actions of the House Un-American Activities Committee (**HUAC**) against the Hollywood Ten (see **Chapter 7**) and the Army-McCarthy hearings before the Permanent Subcommittee on Investigations presided over by Senator Joseph R. McCarthy.

These congressional committees set a tone of aggressive Communist-hunting. When television broadcasts of McCarthy's investigation of Communist influence in the army and other reports eventually exposed his excesses, McCarthy's colleagues censured him by a vote of 67 to 22. But while the hearings were being held, they established a restrictive atmosphere that challenged free expression.

Prior Restraint Rarely Used

Prior restraint means government censoring of information before the information is published or broadcast. The framers of the Constitution clearly opposed prior restraint by law. However, in 1931, the U.S. Supreme Court established the circumstances under which prior restraint could be justified.

Near v. Minnesota

J. M. Near published the weekly *Saturday Press*, which printed the names of people who were violating the nation's Prohibition laws. Minnesota authorities obtained a court order forbidding publication of *Saturday Press*, but the U.S. Supreme Court overturned the state's action. In *Near v. Minnesota* in 1931, the Court condemned prior restraint but acknowledged that the government could limit information about troop movements during war and could control obscenity. The court also said that "the security of community life may be protected against incitements to acts of violence and the overthrow of orderly government."

Saturday Press had not violated any of these prohibitions, so the court order was lifted. But future attempts to stop publication were based on the *Near v. Minnesota* decision, making it a landmark case.

In two important instances since *Near* (the Pentagon Papers and *United States v. The Progressive*), courts were asked to bar publication of information to protect national security. In two other situations (military offensives in Grenada and the Persian Gulf), the federal government took action to prevent journalists from reporting on the government's activities.

Bettmann/CORBIS

Senator Joseph McCarthy (at the easel) explained his theory of communism during the Army-McCarthy hearings in the 1950s. Army counsel Joseph N. Welch, who was defending people who had been declared subversive by McCarthy, is seated at the table. News reports and Edward R. Murrow's exposure of McCarthy's investigative excesses eventually triggered public criticism of McCarthy's tactics, and McCarthy's Senate colleagues censured him.

The Pentagon Papers

In June 1971, *The New York Times* published the first installment of what has become known as the Pentagon Papers, excerpts from what was properly titled *History of U.S. Decision-Making Process on Vietnam Policy*. The Pentagon Papers detailed decisions that were made about the Vietnam War during the Kennedy and Johnson administrations.

The documents were labeled top secret, but they were given to the *Times* by one of the report's authors, Daniel Ellsberg, an aide to the National Security Council. Ellsberg said he believed the papers had been improperly classified and that the public should have the information. After the first three installments were published in the *Times*, Justice Department attorneys received a restraining order against the *Times*, which stopped publication of the installments for two weeks while the *Times* appealed the case. While the case was being decided, *The Washington Post* began publishing

HUAC House Un-American Activities Committee.

Prior Restraint Government censorship of information before the information is published or broadcast.

IMPACT
»Culture

Excerpts from the 1943 Code of Wartime Practices for American Broadcasters

Note: During World War II, the Office of War Information tried to control what was broadcast from the United States. Following are some of the rules radio broadcasters were expected to follow.

News Broadcasts and Commentaries

It is requested that news in any of the following classifications be kept off the air unless made available for broadcast by appropriate authority or specifically cleared by the Office of Censorship.

(a) Weather—Weather forecasts other than those officially released by the Weather Bureau.

(b) Armed forces—Types and movements of United States Army, Navy, and Marine Corps units, within or without continental United States.

Programs

(a) Request programs—No telephoned or telegraphed requests for musical selections should be accepted. No requests for musical selections made by word-of-mouth at the origin of broadcast, whether studio or remote, should be honored.

(b) Quiz programs—Any program which permits the public accessibility to an open microphone is dangerous and should be carefully supervised. Because of the nature of quiz programs, in which the public is not only permitted access to the microphone but encouraged to speak into it, the danger of usurpation by the enemy is enhanced.

Foreign Language Broadcasts

(a) Personnel—The Office of Censorship, by direction of the president, is charged with the responsibility of removing from the

Under provisions of the 1943 Code of Wartime Practices for American Broadcasters, live radio shows by performers such as Frank Sinatra (left) and comedian Fred Allen were subject to on-air censorship.

air all those engaged in foreign language broadcasting who, in the judgment of appointed authorities in the Office of Censorship, endanger the war effort of the United Nations by their connections, direct or indirect, with the medium.

(b) Scripts—Station managements are requested to require all persons who broadcast in a foreign language to submit to the management in advance of broadcast complete scripts or transcriptions of such material.

From U.S. Government Office of Censorship, *Code of Wartime Practices for American Broadcasters*. Washington, D.C.: Government Printing Office, 1943, pages 1–8.

the papers, and the *Post* was stopped, but only until the U.S. Supreme Court decided the *Times* case.

In *New York Times Co. v. United States*, the court said the government did not prove that prior restraint was necessary. The *Times* and the *Post* then printed the papers, but the court action had delayed publication of the information for two weeks. This was the first time in the nation's history that the federal government had stopped a newspaper from publishing specific information. Legal fees cost the *Post* and the *Times* more than $270,000.

The *Progressive* Case

The next instance of prior restraint happened in 1979, when editors of *The Progressive* magazine announced that they planned to publish an article by Howard Morland about how to make a hydrogen bomb. The author said the article was based on information from public documents and interviews with government employees. The Department of Justice brought suit in Wisconsin, where the magazine was published, and received a restraining order to stop the information from being printed (*United States v. The Progressive*). *The Progressive* did not publish the article as planned.

Before the case could reach the U.S. Supreme Court, a Wisconsin newspaper published a letter from a man named Charles Hansen that contained much of the same information as the Morland article. Hansen sent eight copies of the letter to other newspapers, and the *Chicago Tribune* also published the letter, saying that none of the information was proprietary. Six months after the original restraining order, *The Progressive* published the article.

Government Manages War Coverage

The U.S. government historically has tried to control its image during wartime. Four recent examples of government press management are Grenada, the Gulf War, Afghanistan and Iraq.

Restricting Press Access in Grenada

In an incident in 1983 that never reached the courts but that was a type of prior restraint, the Reagan administration kept reporters away from the island of Grenada, where the administration had launched a military offensive. This caused a press blackout beginning at 11 p.m. on October 24, 1983. The administration didn't officially bar the press from covering the invasion, but the Pentagon refused to transport the press and then turned back press yachts and airplanes that attempted to enter the war zone. About a dozen print journalists and photographers were able to get in, but no television crews were allowed.

More than 400 journalists from 170 news organizations around the world who couldn't get to Grenada were left on

Barbados, waiting for the news to get to them. Charles Lachman of the *New York Post* flew to Barbados and then to St. Vincent. Then he and some other reporters paid $6,000 to charter a boat to Grenada. They arrived five days after the invasion and discovered that one of the casualties of the military's action had been a hospital.

Susan Wood/Getty Images

Daniel Ellsberg, author of the Pentagon Papers, after a court hearing in Los Angeles. Ellsberg gave the papers to *The New York Times*. In 1971, the federal government unsuccessfully tried to use prior restraint to stop the *Times* from publishing the documents.

News Blackouts and Press Pools During the Gulf War

In the 1990s, the Gulf War posed another tough battleground for the rights of reporters versus the rights of the military to restrict access. On Saturday, February 23, 1991, about three weeks into the Gulf War, the Defense Department announced the first total news blackout in U.S. military history.

For 24 hours, defense leaders were told to issue no statements about the actions of U.S. troops. Military officials said that instantaneous transmission of information from the battlefield meant that Iraq would be able to pick up live TV pictures. Press organizations protested the ban, but the military argued that modern communications technology necessitated the blackout.

Pentagon rules for war coverage, reached in cooperation with journalists, imposed stricter limits on reporting in the Persian Gulf than in any previous U.S. war. Reporters had to travel in small "pools," escorted by public affairs officers. Every story produced by the pool was subject to military censorship. This system, called ***pool reporting***, had been created in response to reporters' complaints about news blackouts during the Grenada incident.

> **Pool Reporting** An arrangement that places reporters in small, government-supervised groups to cover an event.

U.S. Commander in Iraq General David Petraeus answers questions during a press conference in September 2007. The military authorized embedded journalists to report on the wars in Iraq and Afghanistan, but critics say that embedding gives the military too much control over what journalists are allowed to see and report.

An unprecedented number of journalists—1,300 in Saudi Arabia alone—posed a challenge for military press officers. In a commentary protesting the restrictions, *The New Yorker* magazine said, "The rules, it is clear, enable the Pentagon to promote coverage of subjects and events that it wishes publicized and to prevent reporting that might cast it, or the war, in a bad light." Yet, in a *Los Angeles Times* poll of nearly 2,000 people two weeks after the fighting started, 79 percent approved of the Pentagon's restrictions and 57 percent favored even further limits.

When the war ended, many members of the U.S. press in the Middle East complained bitterly about their lack of access, but the military and the public seemed satisfied with the new rules for wartime coverage.

War in Afghanistan

During the war in Afghanistan, especially in the months immediately following the September 11, 2001, terrorist attacks in the United States, the military carefully controlled press access to information, citing security reasons. The military used press pools and also provided its own video footage of troop landings, produced by the military's combat film teams.

"In World War II, accredited journalists from leading news organizations were on the front lines to give the public an independent description of what was happening," says *The New York Times*. "In the new war on terrorism, journalists have had limited access to many of the United States forces that are carrying out the war. . . . The media's access

to American military operations is far more limited than in recent conflicts."

"Embedded" Reporters During Iraq War

Beginning in 2003, during the Iraq War, the U.S. government adopted a system called *embedding*, which meant that members of the press traveled with the military, but the press' movements were restricted and managed by their military units.

Embedding was a reaction to the press' limited access in Afghanistan, but many journalists said they still had limited access to the real action; however, the coverage left the impression with the public that the press was giving the whole story, when in fact the press had access to only a very limited view. (For more about embedded reporters, see **Chapter 12**.)

When should the government be able to prevent military information from reaching the public? When should the press have access? The Supreme Court has not yet specifically answered this question, and the U.S. press and news organizations remain vulnerable to military restrictions.

Librarians Resist the Patriot Act

In 2001, a few weeks after the terrorist attacks on the World Trade Center in New York City, Congress passed the Patriot Act, designed to give the U.S. government broad powers to track and detain people who were deemed a threat to the country for interrogation. Among the provisions of the Act was Section 215, which allows the Federal Bureau of Investigation to monitor public library records, including computer log-ins and the lists of books people check out of public libraries.

The U.S. government claims the Act says the government can obtain "business records," which could include public library records, although the Act does not specifically mention libraries. Librarians say they are ready to cooperate with an investigation if they are given a search warrant; however, they claim the Patriot Act allows officials to seize anything they wish without a search warrant, which librarians say inhibits the use of public libraries—a limit on free expression.

Some libraries have posted signs to warn patrons that federal authorities may review their records; others systematically shred patrons' sign-in sheets for using library computers. The American Library Association officially has gone on record opposing unwarranted government access to library records, as specified in Section 215. The American Civil Liberties Union sued in several different cities nationwide to keep library records private, and in 2004 a Los Angeles federal judge ruled that parts of the Patriot

Act were unconstitutional violations of the First and Fifth amendments to the U.S. Constitution.

In 2005, the Federal Bureau of Investigation (FBI) demanded library records from *Library Connection*, a nonprofit library group in Bridgeport, Connecticut, saying the agency needed the information as part of a terrorism investigation under the Patriot Act. The American Civil Liberties Union challenged the request in court, saying the request was unconstitutional. Eventually the FBI withdrew its request.

The Patriot Act expired in late 2005, and congressional opponents of some of the provisions of the Act, including Section 215, tried to block reauthorization of the Act. In March 2006 Congress reauthorized the Act for another four years, including Section 215. Opponents, including the American Library Association, vowed to renew their challenges to the most aggressive provisions of the Act, especially Section 215, to stop what opponents say is an intrusion into important American civil liberties.

In 2007, a federal judge in New York struck down provisions of the Patriot Act that had authorized the government to issue so-called National Security Letters (*NSLs*), compelling businesses (such as Internet service providers, telephone companies and public libraries) to release customer information without a judge's order or grand jury subpoena. U.S. District Judge Victor Marrero said using the Patriot Act, even as rewritten and reauthorized in 2006, to obtain customer information without court authorization "offends the fundamental constitutional principles of checks and balances and separation of powers." (See **Impact/World**, "Hundreds of Web Sites Censored at Beijing Olympics," page 302.)

What Is the Standard for Obscenity?

Different media industries historically have reacted differently to threats of *censorship*, the practice of suppressing material that is considered morally, politically or otherwise objectionable. Most threats of censorship concern matters of morality.

According to the American Library Association, the top three reasons critics try to challenge content are

1. The material is considered "sexually explicit."

2. The material contains "offensive language."

3. The material is "unsuited to an age group."

In the United States, censorship is almost always an issue after the fact. Once the material is printed or displayed, the courts can be asked to review the content for obscenity.

To try to avoid constant scrutiny, the motion picture and recording industries have accepted some form of self-

© Kurt Rogers/San Francisco Chronicle/CORBIS

U.S. librarians protested against language in the Patriot Act, passed a few weeks after the terrorist attacks on the World Trade Center in New York, which librarians claim allows federal authorities to seize public library records without a search warrant. A Santa Cruz, California, library posted a sign alerting patrons that, under the provisions of the Patriot Act, federal agents can review customers' reading habits.

regulation to avoid government intervention. The electronic media are governed by laws in the federal criminal code against broadcast obscenity, and the federal Cable Act of 1984 bars obscenity on cable TV.

Print media, including book publishers, have been the most vigorous defenders of the right to publish. The print media, of course, were the earliest media to be threatened with censorship, beginning with the philosopher Plato, who suggested in 387 B.C. that Homer's *Odyssey* be censored for immature readers.

Government efforts to block free expression happen on the local and federal levels.

Local Efforts

More than 2,000 years after Homer's *Odyssey* was threatened with censorship, Boston officials banned the sale of the April 1926 issue of H. L. Mencken's magazine *The American Mercury*. The local Watch and Ward Society had denounced a fictional story in the magazine as "salacious." The story featured the main character, "Hatrack," a prostitute whose clientele included members of various religious congregations who visited her after church.

NSL National Security Letter.

Censorship The practice of suppressing material that is considered morally, politically or otherwise objectionable.

IMPACT
»World

Hundreds of Web Sites Censored at Beijing Olympics

by David Sarno, Web Scout

"I think we will give the media complete freedom to report when they come to China." That was Wang Wei, secretary general of the Beijing Olympics organizing committee, after his country won its bid in 2001.

Cheering! Rousing Applause!

"I don't anticipate there will be any constraint," said Kevan Gosper, the head of the International Olympic Committee's press commission, in April. "They should have free access to the Internet."

Applause.

"My preoccupation and responsibility is to ensure that the Games competitions are reported openly to the world," Gosper said last Tuesday. "This didn't necessarily extend to free access and reporting on everything that relates to China."

Some confused clapping.

"I have also been advised that some of the IOC officials had negotiated with the Chinese that some sensitive sites would be blocked," Gosper said the next day.

Silence.

Yes, when reporters logged in at the Beijing Olympics' Main Press Center [in August

Although the Chinese government claimed it would give journalists "complete freedom" to report the 2008 Olympics, many reporters found that the government blocked access to dozens of humanitarian and media Web sites during the games.

2008] and found that dozens of humanitarian and media Web sites were digitally gagged—including, in some instances, the ones they worked for—they learned a civics lesson that a billion Chinese already knew: Silence is golden.

In Boston, surrounded by his supporters, Mencken sold a copy of the magazine at a prearranged time to a member of the Watch and Ward. The chief of the Boston Vice Squad arrested Mencken and marched him to jail, where he spent the night before going to court the next morning. "Mencken passed an un easy night," says Mencken's biographer Carl Bode, "knowing that he could be found guilty and perhaps even be imprisoned. . . . Returning to court he listened to Judge Parmenter's decision: 'I find that no offense has been committed and therefore dismiss the complaint.'"

Mencken spent $20,000 defending the *Mercury*, but according to Bode, "the net gain for both the *Mercury* and Mencken was great. The *Mercury* became the salient American magazine and Mencken the international symbol of freedom of speech."

Mencken was defending his magazine against local censorship. Until 1957, censorship in America remained a local issue because the U.S. Supreme Court had not considered a national censorship case.

U.S. Supreme Court Writes Obscenity Criteria

Today, censorship still is primarily a local issue, but two landmark Supreme Court cases—*Roth v. United States* and *Miller v. California*—established the major criteria for local censorship.

Despite a string of pyrite promises by both Chinese representatives and the IOC, Internet access at the Olympics was cratered with blacked-out sites, including Amnesty International, the L.A. Times Olympics Blog and Wikipedia. (Which left, what, MySpace and online backgammon?)

Rob Faris of Harvard's Berkman Center for Internet and Society called China's approach puzzling. "Providing a large number of journalists with a censored Internet connection when they were promised an open Internet is naturally going to draw a lot of critical stories in the media," he said.

And so it did. It seemed that every major U.S. newspaper and broadcast network had its own story on China's "Great Firewall," many stating how outrageous it was that Western media should have its information controlled by an oppressive regime.

"I'm just disappointed and frustrated," said one journalist interviewed on *NBC Nightly News*. Said another: "I can't rely on getting all the information I need."

But NBC missed the obvious irony: The censored Internet was giving Western journalists a taste of what the Chinese people live with—or without—every day.

The IOC, no doubt desperate to move past the scandal, released a statement saying, "The media should be seeing a noticeable difference in accessibility to websites that they need to report on the Olympic Games." Open Internet access, it continued, "has always been assured by [Beijing Organizing Committee] and the Chinese authorities, and the IOC is pleased to see these reassurances being upheld."

But both the IOC and the international media failed miserably to note that hundreds if not thousands of sites remained unavailable to both journalists and Beijing residents. And not just so-called sensitive sites relating to the Falun Gong movement, Tibet or Tiananmen Square. Huge personal and professional blogging platforms remained totally inaccessible. TypePad— home of many news blogs, including most of the Times'—is blocked, as is LiveJournal, one of the largest personal diary sites. MSN's Taiwan site was blocked, as were U.S. news portals like the *Philadelphia Inquirer* and the Huffington Post.

The IOC—backing far off of its original pledge of unfettered access, is now apparently content defining an open Internet as the set of Web pages journalists "need to report on the Olympic Games." Fine, but what happens in the likely event of a protest this month by any of the legion of Chinese dissent groups seeking to raise awareness of their human rights situation? If reporters "need" to seek information from the Falun Gong's Web site, or the sites of pro-Tibet groups, or blogs from Beijing residents who might know something, they better wear a helmet or risk slamming into a firewall.

From "Hundreds of Web Sites Still Censored at Beijing Olympics," by David Sarno, *Los Angeles Times,* August 5, 2008. Reprinted by permission of Los Angeles Times.

ROTH V. UNITED STATES. This decision in 1957 involved two separate cases. Samuel Roth was found guilty in New York of sending obscenity through the mail, and David S. Alberts was found guilty of selling obscene books in Beverly Hills. The case carries Roth's name because his name appeared first when the cases were combined for review. The U.S. Supreme Court upheld the guilty verdict and, according to legal scholar Ralph Holsinger, established several precedents:

- The First Amendment does not protect obscenity.

- Obscenity is defined as material "utterly without redeeming social importance."

- Sex and obscenity are not synonymous. Obscene material is material that appeals to "prurient [obsessively sexual] interest."

- A test of obscenity is "whether to the average person, applying contemporary community standards, the dominant theme of the material taken as a whole appeals to prurient interest." (This last description of obscenity has become known as the ***Roth test***.)

> **Roth Test** A standard court test for obscenity, named for one of the defendants in an obscenity case.

Magazines often have been the objects of censorship. Because there is no national standard for obscenity, local juries and government regulators in each community are free to decide what they consider offensive. What is acceptable in one community may be censored in another.

MILLER V. CALIFORNIA. In the late 1960s, a California court found Marvin Miller guilty of sending obscene, unsolicited advertising material through the mail. The case reached the U.S. Supreme Court in 1973. The decision described just which materials a state could censor and also set a three-part test for obscenity.

According to the Supreme Court, states may censor material that meets this three-part local test for obscenity. The local court, according to legal scholar Ralph Holsinger, must determine

1. Whether "the average person, applying contemporary community standards," would find that the work, taken as a whole, appeals to the prurient interest.

2. Whether the work depicts or describes, in a patently offensive way, sexual conduct specifically defined by the applicable state law.

3. Whether the work, taken as a whole, lacks serious *Lit*ary, *A*rtistic, *P*olitical or *S*cientific value—often called the **LAPS test**.

The *Roth* and *Miller* cases together established a standard for obscenity, leaving the decision in specific obscenity challenges to local courts. The result is that there are widely differing standards in different parts of the country because

local juries and government regulators are free to decide what they consider offensive in their communities. Books and magazines that are available to young readers in some states may be unavailable in other states.

School Boards as Censors

Many censorship cases begin at school and other local government boards, where parents' groups protest books, magazines and films that are available to students. For example:

- Norwood High School in Colorado banned Rudolfo Anaya's award-winning book, *Bless Me, Ultima*, because of what the school considered "offensive language."

- A school board in New York removed 11 books from school libraries, including the novels *Slaughterhouse-Five* by Kurt Vonnegut and *Black Boy* by Richard Wright, plus a work of popular anthropology, *The Naked Ape* by Desmond Morris.

- A school district in Little Rock, Arkansas, removed Harry Potter books from the school library because the school board claimed the tales of wizards and spells could harm schoolchildren.

- A school district in California required students to have parental permission to read *Ms.* magazine in the school library.

- A school board in Minnesota banned four books, including *Are You There, God? It's Me, Margaret* by Judy Blume, a writer well known for her young adult books.

- The state of Alabama ordered 45 textbooks pulled from the shelves after a federal judge said the books promoted "secular humanism."

The American Library Association (ALA) and the American Booksellers Foundation for Free Expression (ABFFE) fiercely oppose any attempt to censor or restrict access to information. Each year, the ALA and the ABFFE sponsor Banned Books Week to bring public attention to the issue of censorship. "Not every book is right for every person," said ALA President Carol Brey-Casiano during 2005 Banned Books Week, "but providing a wide range of reading choices is vital for learning, exploration and imagination. The abilities to read, speak, think and express ourselves freely are core American values."

One-third of all censorship incidents involve attempts to censor library books and school curricula. These cases usually are reversed when appealed, but while the specific issues are being decided, the books, magazines and films are unavailable, and censorship efforts have been increasing nationwide. The American Library Association, for example, says that for every book challenge reported, as many as four or five go unreported. (See **Impact/Culture**, "*And Tango Makes Three* Tops American Library Association's 2007 List of the 10 Most Challenged Books in the United States," page 306.)

LAPS Test A yardstick for local obscenity judgments, which evaluates an artistic work's literary, artistic, political or scientific value.

Jim Watson/AFP/Getty Images

The *Hazelwood* Case

In 1988, the U.S. Supreme Court for the first time gave public school officials considerable freedom to limit what appears in student publications. The case, *Hazelwood v. Kuhlmeier*, became known as the *Hazelwood* case because the issues originated at Hazelwood High School in Hazelwood, Missouri.

The high school paper, funded mostly from the school budget, was published as part of a journalism class. The principal at Hazelwood regularly reviewed the school paper before it was published, but in this case he deleted two articles the staff had written. One of the deleted articles covered the issue of student pregnancy and included interviews with three students who had become pregnant while attending school, using pseudonyms instead of the students' names.

The principal said he believed that the anonymity of the students was not sufficiently protected and that the girls' discussion of their use or nonuse of birth control was inappropriate for a school publication. By a vote of 5 to 3, the U.S. Supreme Court agreed.

"Even though the legal rights of children have gained broader recognition in recent years, it remains that children are not adults and that they have no explicit or implied right to behave with the full freedom granted to adults," wrote Jonathan Yardley, a *Washington Post* columnist. "Freedom entails the responsibility to exercise it with mature judgment, and this neither young children nor adolescents possess."

The same newspaper, however, carried an editorial that opposed the decision. "Even teenagers," the *Post* editorial said, "should be allowed to publish criticism, raise uncomfortable questions and spur debate on subjects such as pregnancy, AIDS and drug abuse that are too often a very real aspect of high school culture today."

At Hazelwood, the principal's action drew the attention of the *St. Louis Post-Dispatch*, which published the censored articles, bringing them a much wider audience than the students at Hazelwood High. Many states subsequently have adopted legislation to protect student newspapers from similar censorship. The decision is significant, however, because it may change the way local officials in some states monitor school publications.

Libel Law Outlines the Media's Public Responsibility

"Americans have increasingly begun to seek the refuge and vindication of litigation," writes legal scholar Rodney A. Smolla in his book *Suing the Press*. "Words published by the media no longer roll over us without penetrating; instead, they sink in through the skin and work inner damage, and a

OPEN YOUR MIND TO A BANNED BOOK

Banned BOOK

Banned BOOK THE ADVENTURES OF CAPTAIN UNDER PANTS

Banned BOOK MOTHER GOOSE

Banned BOOK JAMES AND THE GIANT PEACH

OPEN BOOKS FOR OPEN MINDS
BANNED BOOKS WEEK
CELEBRATE YOUR FREEDOM TO READ • www.ala.org/bbooks

Reprinted with permission of the Office for Intellectual Freedom of the American Library Association

The American Library Association and the American Booksellers Foundation for Free Expression fiercely oppose any attempt to censor or restrict access to information. Each year, the ALA and the ABFFE sponsor Banned Books Week to bring public attention to the issue of censorship.

consensus appears to be emerging that this psychic damage is serious and must be paid for." Four cases show why the media become targets of litigation:

1. In 1983, actress Carol Burnett sued the *National Enquirer* for $10 million for implying in an article that she was drinking too much and acting rude in a Washington, D.C., restaurant.

2. In late 1984, General William C. Westmoreland filed a $120 million suit against CBS, charging that he was defamed in a 1982 CBS documentary, *The Uncounted Enemy: A Vietnam Deception*.

3. In 1989, entertainer Wayne Newton was awarded $6 million in damages after he sued NBC-TV for a story that linked him to organized crime figures.

4. In 1999, parents of Scott Amedure sued Warner Bros., which owned the *Jenny Jones Show*, after a man named Jonathan Schmitz killed Amedure days after Amedure

IMPACT
>> **Culture**

And Tango Makes Three Tops American Library Association's 2007 List of the 10 Most Challenged Books in the United States

American Library Association

Note: With this press release, on September 9, 2008, the American Library Association (ALA) released its annual list of the most challenged books of 2007.

NEWS For Immediate Release
September 9, 2008

Book Banning Alive and Well in the U.S.

ALA calls on Americans to fight censorship, celebrate the freedom to read

CHICAGO—Are books like "The Adventures of Huckleberry Finn," or the Harry Potter series available at your public or school library? According to the American Library Association's (ALA) Office for Intellectual Freedom (OIF), due to book challenges, more than a book a day faces removal from public access in school and public libraries. Challenges are defined as formal, written complaints filed with a library or school requesting that materials be removed because of content or appropriateness.

In many cases, it is only through public intervention that books are saved from confiscation or from being kept under lock and key.

Each year, the OIF receives hundreds of reports on books and other materials that were "challenged" by people who asked that they be removed from school or library shelves. There were 420 known attempts to remove books in 2007, and more than 9,600 attempts since the ALA's OIF began to electronically compile and publish information on book challenges in 1990. Unfortunately, it is believed that for every challenge or banning

revealed during the videotaping of the show that he had a crush on another male guest on the program.

The first three cases involve the law of **libel**, which is one legal restraint on press freedom in the United States. (A libelous statement is one that unjustifiably exposes someone to ridicule or contempt.) The *Jenny Jones* case is not specifically a libel case, but it became part of a wrongful death suit that Amedure's family brought against Warner Bros., the most recent case of its kind to try to place some of the legal blame for a crime on the media organization that created an atmosphere for the eventual crime that occurred.

All four of these cases clearly indicate the media's legal vulnerability to charges of participating in and/or provoking irresponsible, damaging behavior. How can the country accommodate both the First Amendment concept of a free press and the right of the nation's citizens to keep their reputations from being unnecessarily damaged?

Sullivan Case Establishes a Libel Landmark

Modern interpretation of the free speech protections of the First Amendment began in 1964 with the landmark *New York Times v. Sullivan* case. With this case, the U.S. Supreme Court began a process that continues today to define how the press should operate in a free society. Many of today's arguments about the free press' role in a libel case derive from this decision.

The *Sullivan* case began in early 1960 in Alabama, where civil rights leader Dr. Martin Luther King, Jr., was arrested for perjury on his income tax form (a charge of which he was eventually acquitted). The Committee to

Libel A false statement that damages a person's character or reputation by exposing that person to public ridicule or contempt.

reported to OIF, there are four to five incidents not reported.

Most book challenges reported to OIF have been reported from schools (71 percent) and public libraries (24 percent). Parents lodged 61 percent of the book challenges, followed by library patrons at 15 percent and administrators at 9 percent.

The "10 Most Challenged Books of 2007" reflect a range of themes, and consist of the following titles:

1. *And Tango Makes Three* by Justin Richardson/Peter Parnell

2. *The Chocolate War* by Robert Cormier

3. *Olive's Ocean* by Kevin Henkes

4. *The Golden Compass* by Philip Pullman

5. *The Adventures of Huckleberry Finn* by Mark Twain

6. *The Color Purple* by Alice Walker

7. *TTYL* by Lauren Myracle

8. *I Know Why the Caged Bird Sings* by Maya Angelou

9. *It's Perfectly Normal* by Robie Harris

10. *The Perks of Being a Wallflower* by Stephen Chbosky

And Tango Makes Three was the book cited by the American Library Association in 2008 as the most frequently challenged book in 2007. The story of two male penguins who parent an egg from a mixed-sex penguin couple was challenged primarily because it deals with the issue of homosexuality.

Banned Books Week is sponsored by the American Booksellers Association, the American Booksellers Foundation for Free Expression, the ALA, the Association of American Publishers, the American Society of Journalists and Authors and the National Association of College Stores and is endorsed by the Library of Congress Center for the Book.

For more information on book challenges and censorship, please visit the ALA Office of Intellectual Freedom's Banned Books Web site at www.ala.org/bbooks.

From American Library Association.

Defend Martin Luther King bought a full-page ad in the March 29, 1960, *New York Times* that included statements about harassment of King by public officials and the police. The ad included a plea for money to support civil rights causes. Several notable people were listed in the ad as supporters, including singer Harry Belafonte, actor Sidney Poitier and former First Lady Eleanor Roosevelt.

L. B. Sullivan, who supervised the police and fire departments as commissioner of public affairs in Montgomery, Alabama, demanded a retraction from the *Times* regarding the statements about King's harassment, even though he had not been named in the ad. The *Times* refused, and Sullivan sued the *Times* for libel in Montgomery County, where 35 copies of the March 29, 1960, *Times* had been distributed for sale. The trial in Montgomery County lasted three days, beginning on November 1, 1960. The jury found the *Times* guilty and awarded Sullivan $500,000.

Eventually, the case reached the U.S. Supreme Court. In deciding the suit the Court said that although the *Times* might have been negligent because it did not spot some misstatements of fact that appeared in the ad, the *Times* did not deliberately lie—it did not act with what the court called *actual malice*.

To prove libel of a *public official*, the official must show that the defendant published information with *knowledge of its falsity* or out of *reckless disregard* for whether it was true or false, the court concluded. The *Sullivan* decision thus became the standard for subsequent libel suits: Public officials in a libel case must prove actual malice.

Redefining the *Sullivan* Decision

Three important cases further defined the *Sullivan* decision.

GERTZ V. ROBERT WELCH, INC. The 1974 decision in *Gertz v. Robert Welch* established the concept that the expression of opinions is a necessary part of public debate, and so opinions—an editorial or a restaurant review, for example—cannot be considered libelous. The *Gertz* case also expanded the definition of public *official* to public *figure*. Today, people involved in libel suits are classified as *public figures* or *private figures*. The criterion that distinguishes public and private figures is very important.

People who are defined as private citizens by a court must show only that the libelous information was false and that the journalist or news organization acted negligently in presenting the information. Public figures must show not only that the libelous information was false but also that the information was published with actual malice—that the journalist or the news organization knew that the information was untrue or that the journalist or news organization deliberately overlooked facts that would have proved the published information was untrue.

HERBERT V. LANDO. The 1979 decision in *Herbert v. Lando* established the concept that because a public figure suing for libel must prove actual malice, the public figure can use the *discovery process* (the process by which potential witnesses are questioned under oath before the trial to help define the issues to be resolved at the trial) to determine a reporter's state of mind in preparing the story. Because of this decision, today reporters are sometimes asked in a libel suit to identify their sources and to give up notes and tapes of the interviews they conducted to write their stories.

MASSON V. NEW YORKER MAGAZINE. In 1991, the U.S. Supreme Court reinstated a $10 million libel suit brought against *The New Yorker* magazine by psychoanalyst Jeffrey M. Masson. Masson charged that author Janet Malcolm libeled him in two articles in *The New Yorker* and in a book when she deliberately misquoted him. Malcolm contended that the quotations she used were tape-recorded or were written in her notes.

Malcolm wrote, for example, that Mr. Masson said, "I was like an intellectual gigolo." However, this exact phrase was not in the transcript of her tape-recorded interview. Masson contended that he never used the phrase. Issues in the case include whether quoted material must be verbatim and whether a journalist can change grammar and syntax. When the case was heard again in 1994, the court found that Malcolm had changed Masson's words but that the changes did not libel Masson. The *Masson* case is the most important recent example of a continuing interest in defining the limits of libel.

Qualified Privilege The freedom of the press to report what is discussed during legislative and court proceedings.

Charges and Defenses for Libel

To prove libel under today's law, someone must show that

- The statement was communicated to a third party.

- People who read or saw the statement would be able to identify the person, even if that person was not actually named.

- The statement injured the person's reputation or income or caused mental anguish.

- The journalist or the print or broadcast organization is at fault.

Members of the press and press organizations that are faced with a libel suit can use three defenses: (1) truth, (2) privilege and (3) fair comment.

TRUTH. The first and best defense against libel, of course, is that the information is true. True information, although sometimes damaging, cannot be considered libelous. Publishing true information, however, can still be an invasion of privacy, as explained later in this chapter. Furthermore, truth is a successful defense only if truth is proved to the satisfaction of a judge or jury.

PRIVILEGE. The press is free to report what is discussed during legislative and court proceedings, even though the information presented in the proceedings by witnesses and others may be untrue or damaging. This is called **qualified privilege**.

FAIR COMMENT. The courts also have carefully protected the press' freedom to present opinions. Because opinions cannot be proved true or false, the press is free to comment on public issues and to laud a play or pan a movie, for example.

Legal Outcomes Reflect Mixed Results

The outcomes of the four cases listed at the beginning of this discussion of Libel Law (on page 305) were

1. The jury in the Carol Burnett case originally awarded her $1.6 million, but the amount was reduced to $150,000 on appeal.

2. The William Westmoreland case was settled before it went to the jury. CBS issued a statement acknowledging that General Westmoreland had acted faithfully in performing his duties, but the combined legal costs for both parties were more than $18 million.

3. The jury awarded Wayne Newton $19.2 million in 1986. NBC appealed the case, and in 1990 the courts overturned the award, ruling there was not enough evidence to prove actual malice, but NBC's legal costs were in the millions of dollars.

4. In 1999, a Michigan jury returned a $25 million civil judgment against *The Jenny Jones Show* for negligence in the wrongful death of Scott Amedure. Warner Bros. appealed, and the award eventually was reversed. (*The Jenny Jones Show*, however, was canceled.)

Still, the *Jenny Jones* case (officially called *Graves v. Warner Bros.*—Patricia Graves is Scott Amedure's mother) showed that a jury believed the media shouldered some of the responsibility for the crime. And in the other three cases, the courts faulted members of the media for their reporting methods, even when members of the media and the media companies were not found legally responsible.

These four cases show that journalists and media organizations must always be diligent about their responsibilities, and there are serious financial and professional consequences for news organizations that forget to act responsibly and heed the law.

Most successful libel judgments eventually are reversed or reduced when they are appealed. In the year 2007, there were six libel, privacy or related cases based on editorial content, according to the Media Law Resource Center. One case ended in a mistrial. Of the five cases that went to trial, the media won four of the five cases.

Often the major cost of a libel suit for the media is not the actual award but the defense lawyers' fees. Large media organizations carry libel insurance, but a small newspaper, magazine, book publisher or broadcast station may not be able to afford the insurance or the legal costs.

"While most excessive trial awards are reduced in post-trial rulings or on appeal, the expense of litigating can be daunting. The danger is that excessive damage awards, and the cost of litigating and appealing them, may give editors and publishers pause when covering controversial people and topics," says Sandra S. Baron, executive director of the Libel Defense Resource Center.

Invasion of Privacy Defined Four Ways

The public seems to think invasion of privacy is one of the media's worst faults. However, libel suits are much more common in the United States than suits about invasion of privacy. Because there is no U.S. Supreme Court decision covering privacy like *The New York Times v. Sullivan* covers libel, each of the states has its own privacy protections for citizens and its own restrictions on how reporters can get the news and what can be published.

Privacy is an ethical issue as well as a legal one. (See **Chapter 15** for a discussion of the ethics of privacy.) Generally, the law says the media can be guilty of invasion of privacy in four ways:

1. By intruding on a person's physical or mental solitude.

2. By publishing or disclosing embarrassing personal facts.

3. By giving someone publicity that places the person in a false light.

4. By using someone's name or likeness for commercial benefit.

If they are successful, people who initiate privacy cases can be awarded monetary damages to compensate them for the wrongdoing. However, very few invasion of privacy cases succeed.

Physical or Mental Solitude

The courts in most states have recognized that a person has a right not to be pursued by the news media unnecessarily. A reporter can photograph or question someone on a public street or at a public event, but a person's home and office are private. For this reason, many photographers request that someone who is photographed in a private situation sign a release form, designating how the photograph can be used.

One particularly notable case establishing this right of privacy is *Galella v. Onassis*. Jacqueline Onassis, widow of President John F. Kennedy, charged that Ron Galella, a freelance photographer, was pursuing her unnecessarily. He had

Brad Elterman/Getty Images

Privacy is an ethical as well as a legal issue. In 1973, 10 years after her husband President John F. Kennedy was assassinated, a federal court established Jacqueline Kennedy Onassis' right to privacy in *Galella v. Onassis*. Galella, pictured on the right with the tape measure during Onassis' visit to Los Angeles in 1977, was under a restraining order to keep his distance from Onassis at the time.

"Do you ever have one of those days when everything seems unconstitutional?"

used a telephoto lens to photograph her on private property and he had pursued her children at private schools. Galella was ordered to stay 25 feet away from her and 30 feet away from her children.

Embarrassing Personal Facts

The personal facts the media use to report a story should be newsworthy, according to the courts. If a public official is caught traveling with her boyfriend on taxpayers' money while her husband stays at home, information about the boyfriend is essential to the story. If the public official is reported to have contracted AIDS from her contact with the boyfriend, the information probably is not relevant to the story and could be protected under this provision of privacy law.

In reality, however, public officials enjoy very little legal protection from reporting about their private lives. Information available from public records, such as court proceedings, is not considered private. If the public official's husband testifies in court about his wife's disease, this information could be reported.

Bartnicki v. Vopper

In an important case for the press, *Bartnicki v. Vopper*, the U.S. Supreme Court in 2001 reaffirmed the media's right to broadcast information and to comment on that information, no matter how the information was obtained.

The case resulted from a cell phone conversation between Pennsylvania teachers' union negotiator Gloria

Bartnicki and Anthony Kane, the union's president. The union was in the middle of negotiating a teachers' contract. During the conversation (which was intercepted and taped without Bartnicki's or Kane's knowledge), Kane is heard to say that if the school board didn't increase its offer, "We're going to have to go to their homes . . . to blow off their front porches."

A local activist gave the tape to radio station WILK-AM, and talk-show host Fred Vopper (who uses the on-air name Fred Williams) aired the tape. Bartnicki and Kane sued Vopper under the federal wiretap law, which provides civil damages and criminal prosecution for someone who disseminates information that is illegally intercepted. The case pitted the public's right to know versus the erosion of personal privacy by new technologies.

U.S. Supreme Court Justice John Paul Stevens wrote the opinion for the 6–3 majority that "a stranger's illegal conduct does not suffice to remove the First Amendment shield from speech about a matter of public concern." In this decision, the court again reaffirmed the press right to report information in the public interest.

False Light

A writer who portrays someone in a fictional version of actual events should be especially conscious of *false light* litigation. People who believe that what a writer or photographer *implies* about them is incorrect (even if the portrayal is flattering) can bring a false-light suit.

The best-known false-light suit is the first, *Time Inc. v. Hill*. In 1955, *Life* magazine published a story about a Broadway play, *The Desperate Hours*, that portrayed someone taking a hostage. The author of the play said he based it on several real-life incidents. One of these involved the Hill family, a husband and wife and their five children who had been taken hostage in their Philadelphia home by three escaped convicts. The Hills told police the convicts had treated them courteously, but the Hills were frightened by the events and eventually moved to Connecticut.

When *Life* decided to do the story about the play, the cast went to the Hills' old home, where *Life* photographed the actors in scenes from the play—one son being roughed up by the convicts and a daughter biting a convict's hand. None of these incidents had happened to the Hills, but *Life* published the photographs along with a review of the play.

The Hills sued Time Inc., which owned *Life* magazine, for false-light invasion of privacy and won $75,000, which eventually was reduced to $30,000. When the case went to the U.S. Supreme Court, the Court refused to uphold the decision, saying the Hills must prove *actual malice*. The Hills dropped the case, but the establishment of actual malice as a requirement in false-light cases was important.

False Light The charge that what was implied in a story about someone was incorrect.

In 1974, in *Cantrell v. Forest City Publishing Co.*, the U.S. Supreme Court held that a reporter for the Cleveland *Plain Dealer* had wrongly portrayed the widow of an Ohio man who was killed when a bridge collapsed. The story talked about the woman as if the reporter had interviewed her, although he had only interviewed her children. She was awarded $60,000 in her false-light suit, and the Supreme Court upheld the verdict.

"Eight justices held that a properly instructed jury had come to the correct conclusion in finding actual malice," writes legal scholar Ralph L. Holsinger. "There was enough evidence within the story to prove that the reporter's word portrait of Mrs. Cantrell was false. The story indicated that he had seen her and perhaps had talked with her. He had done neither." Only a few false-light cases have been successful, but the lesson for the press is that portraying events and people truthfully avoids the problem altogether.

Right of Publicity

This facet of privacy law is especially important in the advertising and public relations industries. A portable toilet seems a strange fixture to use to establish a point of law, but a case brought by former *Tonight Show* host Johnny Carson demonstrates how the right of publicity protects someone's name from being used to make money without that person's permission.

In *Carson v. Here's Johnny Portable Toilets*, Carson charged, in 1983, that a Michigan manufacturer of portable toilets misappropriated Carson's name to sell the toilets. The manufacturer named his new line Here's Johnny Portable Toilets and advertised them with the phrase "The World's Foremost Commodian." Carson said he did not want to be associated with the product and that he would be. Since he began hosting *The Tonight Show* in 1957, he said, he had been introduced by the phrase "Here's Johnny." The court agreed that "Here's Johnny" violated Carson's right of publicity.

The right of publicity can cover a person's picture on a poster or name in an advertisement. In some cases, this right is covered even after the person dies, so that the members of the immediate family of a well-known entertainer, for example, are the only people who can authorize the use of the entertainer's name or likeness.

Debate Continues over Fair Trial, Right of Access and Shield Laws

The answers to three other questions that bear on press freedoms and individual rights remain discretionary for the courts:

1. When does media coverage influence a jury so much that a defendant's right to a fair trial is jeopardized?

2. How much access should the media be granted during a trial?

3. Should journalists be required to reveal information they obtained in confidence while reporting a story if a court decides that information is necessary to the judicial process?

Fair Trial

The best-known decision affecting prejudicial press coverage of criminal cases is *Sheppard v. Maxwell*. In 1954, Dr. Samuel Sheppard of Cleveland was sentenced to life imprisonment for murdering his wife. His conviction followed reams of newspaper stories, many of which proclaimed his guilt before the jury had decided the case. The jurors, who went home each evening, were told by the judge not to read newspapers or pay attention to broadcast reports, but no one monitored what the jurors did.

Twelve years later, lawyer F. Lee Bailey took Sheppard's trial to the U.S. Supreme Court, where the conviction was overturned on the premise that Sheppard had been a victim of a biased jury. In writing the decision, Justice Tom C. Clark prescribed several remedies. He said that the reporters should have been limited to certain areas in the courtroom, that the news media should not have been allowed to interview the witnesses and that the court should have forbidden statements outside of the courtroom.

Courtroom Access

The outcome of the *Sheppard* case led to many courtroom experiments with restrictions on the press. The most widespread practices were restraining (gag) orders and closed proceedings. With a gag order, the judge limited what the press could report. Closed proceedings excluded the press from the courtroom. But since 1980, several court cases have overturned most of these limitations so that today the press is rarely excluded from courtroom proceedings, and the exclusion lasts only as long as it takes the news organization to appeal to a higher court for access.

The presence of cameras in the courtroom is a sticky issue between judges, who want to avoid the disruption that cameras present, and broadcast news people, who want to photograph what is going on. In selected cases, however, cameras have been allowed to record complete trials. In 1994, for example, Court TV broadcast the entire murder trial of O. J. Simpson. Allowing cameras in the courtroom is a state-by-state decision. (See **Illustration 14.1**.) Some states allow cameras during civil but not criminal trials. Other states try to completely limit access. The U.S. courts and the press are not yet completely comfortable partners.

IMPACT

»Audience

Illustration 14.1

Cameras in the Court-room: A State-by-State Guide

Most states allow at least some camera access to courtroom proceedings.

Source: Radio-Television News Directors Association and Foundation, 2008.

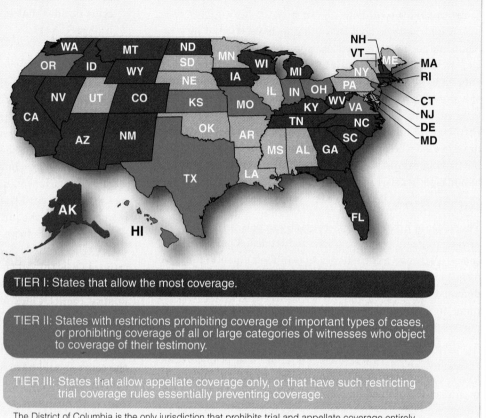

TIER I: States that allow the most coverage.

TIER II: States with restrictions prohibiting coverage of important types of cases, or prohibiting coverage of all or large categories of witnesses who object to coverage of their testimony.

TIER III: States that allow appellate coverage only, or that have such restricting trial coverage rules essentially preventing coverage.

The District of Columbia is the only jurisdiction that prohibits trial and appellate coverage entirely.

Shield Laws

Traditionally, U.S. courts have been reluctant to ask journalists to reveal information they gather from confidential sources as part of their reporting on stories. In 1972, in *Branzburg v. Hayes*, the U.S. Supreme Court ruled for the first time that journalists do not have a constitutional privilege to refuse to testify, but that there was "merit in leaving state legislatures free, within First Amendment limits, to fashion their own standards."

As of 2005, according to the Congressional Research Service, "31 states and the District of Columbia have recognized a journalists' privilege through enactment of press '***shield laws***,' which protect the relationship between reporters, their source, and sometimes, the information that may be communicated in that relationship." This means, for example, that reporters in California, Alaska and Colorado have state shield law protection, but reporters in Texas, South Dakota and Connecticut do not. There is no federal shield law that protects all U.S. journalists equally.

The role of shield laws in protecting journalists became particularly important in 2005, when *New York Times* reporter Judith Miller refused to testify before a federal grand jury that was investigating whether Bush administration officials leaked the identity of a Central Intelligence Agency operative, later identified as a woman named Valerie Plame. In the summer of 2005, Miller was called before a

Shield Laws Laws that protect journalists from revealing their sources and/or the information that is communicated between journalists and their sources in a journalistic relationship.

Washington, D.C., grand jury that was investigating the leak of Plame's name. Eventually Miller revealed to the grand jury that her source was I. Lewis Libby, Vice President Dick Cheney's chief of staff.

According to *The New York Times*, in an article published the day after Miller was released from prison, "At least four other reporters have testified in the investigation, which has repeatedly reached into the White House. They all testified wholly or partly about conversations with Mr. Libby, and one, Matthew Cooper of *Time* magazine, testified about a conversation with Karl Rove, the president's chief strategist. Only Ms. Miller, who never wrote an article about the CIA operative, was jailed in an effort to force her to testify."

After she had been in jail more than two months, her attorney contacted Libby, and Miller and Libby had a conversation in which, Miller said, Libby released her from their confidentiality agreement, which essentially was the same reason Matthew Cooper had given for his willingness to reveal Libby as his source.

Even though Miller said she had received Libby's permission to reveal his name, some lawyers and journalists expressed concern that Miller's actions had weakened journalists' lengthy legal history of protecting their sources.

"The inescapable conclusion that some could draw here is that after a certain period of time, when the reporter is fed up with being in prison, she will make a concession," University of Minnesota law professor Jane Kirtley told the *Times*. "I'm not saying that's what happened here. But that's the appearance. The danger is it will embolden others in more common garden-variety investigations to say to the judge: 'All you have to do is stick the reporter in jail, and we'll get what we want.'"

Eventually Libby, who had testified to a grand jury about the case, was found guilty of perjury and obstruction of justice, but President Bush commuted his sentence in 2007.

After the Miller case, some members of Congress introduced legislation to create a federal shield law to protect journalists on a national level, but Congress never seriously considered the issue. This leaves journalists still at the mercy of individual state shield laws.

FCC Regulates Broadcast and Cable

All the American media are expected to abide by the country's laws. Regulation of the media comes from government agencies that oversee aspects of the media business. The print industry is not regulated specifically by any government agency. The largest single area of regulation comes from the Federal Communications Commission (FCC), which oversees broadcasting. Other regulating agencies, such as

Mark Wilson/Getty Images

In 2005, *New York Times* reporter Judith Miller spent 85 days in jail because she refused to reveal a confidential source to a Washington, D.C., grand jury. Eventually she revealed the source's name as I. Lewis Libby (in center of photo, leaving a federal court hearing in 2007), Vice President Dick Cheney's chief of staff. Libby was found guilty of perjury and obstruction of justice, but in July 2007 President Bush commuted Libby's sentence.

the Federal Trade Commission, scrutinize specific areas that relate to the media, such as advertising.

Since 1927, the concept behind broadcast regulation has been that the airwaves belong to the public and that broadcasters are trustees operating in the public interest. The history of U.S. broadcast regulation can be traced to government's early attempt to organize the airwaves. The FCC, based in Washington, D.C., now has five commissioners who are appointed by the president and are approved by the Senate. Each commissioner serves a five-year term and the president appoints the chairperson.

Today FCC regulation touches almost every aspect of station operations. Most important, U.S. broadcast stations must be licensed by the FCC to operate. Because the print media are unregulated by any government agency, the government exercises more direct control over the broadcast media than over the print media. Like the print media, broadcasters must follow court rulings on issues such as libel, obscenity and the right of privacy. But broadcast stations also must follow the regulations that the FCC establishes.

Telecommunications Act of 1996 Changes the Marketplace

On February 8, 1996, President Clinton signed the Telecommunications Act of 1996, the most far-reaching reform in the way the U.S. government regulates mass media in more than 60 years. The Act affects all aspects of the media industries, especially broadcast, cable, telephone and computer networks. The Act is transforming the nation's media industries.

The last time the government intervened in a similar way to affect the development of the media business was in 1934, when Congress created the FCC to regulate broadcasting in the "public interest, convenience and necessity." The Telecommunications Act is merely an extension of the philosophy of deregulation—that free competition, with less government regulation, eventually will improve consumers' choices and encourage investment in new technologies. The theory is that free competition will lower costs for consumers and give them access to more types of media.

Critics, however, say the Act helps large media companies get bigger because only the large companies can afford to spend the money necessary to upgrade their equipment and delivery systems to take advantage of new markets. This philosophy of open competition, as established in the Telecommunications Act of 1996, will govern the media industries in the 21st century. The strategies of providing multiple services and targeting select users are two early examples.

Goal: To Sell Consumers "The Bundle"

"It's War!" declared *The Wall Street Journal* on September 16, 1996. The battlefield was telecommunications and the goal was *"The Bundle."* This term is being used in telecommunications to describe the combination of services the media industries can offer. Following passage of the 1996 Telecommunications Act, large companies began positioning themselves to deliver the combination of telecommunications services that they think consumers want.

"Thanks to a combination of deregulation and new technologies, war has broken out in the communications market," reported the *Journal.* "Everybody has joined the fray—long-distance telephone giants, the regional [local telephone] Bell companies and the cable-TV operators, the satellite outfits, the fledgling digital wireless phone firms and the Internet service providers. Even your old-fashioned power company."

"The Bundle" The combination of telecommunications services that the media industries can offer consumers.

RBOCs Regional Bell Operating Companies, or "Baby Bells."

"And they all want the same thing: to invade one another's markets and sell you one another's products and services. In short, they want to sell you The Bundle."

Your long-distance telephone company, such as AT&T or Sprint, would like to become your local telephone company, as well as your Internet services provider. This same long-distance company also would like to provide your TV programs, replacing the local cable system, adding these charges to your monthly telephone bill. Local telephone companies, the Regional Bell Operating Companies (*RBOCs*), sometimes called Baby Bells, want their slice of revenue, too, so in many areas of the country they are moving into the cable business.

Some cable companies offer telephone service. "The act so completely dismantles the existing regulatory structure that the telecommunications industry begins to look like a free-for-all," says Howard Anderson, founder and manager of Yankee Group, a Boston-based consulting firm. "Everyone is already trying to build multimedia networks to deliver everything from telephone and mobile services to Internet access and video-on-demand."

Targeting the "Power User"

This bundling of services would mean that you would pay one monthly bill for several types of media services to a single company, which, of course, would dramatically increase that company's portion of media revenue. "The goal for these companies is twofold," says Richard Siber, a wireless analyst for Andersen Consulting in Boston. "One is locking in a customer for life and providing one-stop shopping. And the other is revenue maximization, getting you to use their products more and more."

BusinessWeek magazine called this intense competition for customers a "Telescramble." The primary target is the so-called "power user," someone who uses a lot of media at home or in business. While the average consumer spends about $100 a month on media services, an upscale customer averages $300 a month, or $3,000 to $3,500 a year.

The Telecommunications Act of 1996 created this battlefield for consumers' attention with huge financial incentives for the winners. The economic future of every media company in the country is, in some way, being affected by this battle. That is why it is so important to understand this single piece of legislation, which is having such a dramatic effect on consumers and on the nation's media industries.

Deregulation Unleashes the Media

The major provisions of the Telecommunications Act affect telecommunications, broadcast and cable. The Communications Decency Act, which is part of the Telecommunications Act, attempted to regulate access to cable and television programming and monitor the content of computer networks, including the Internet.

Creates a Goal of Universal Service

The Telecommunications Act of 1996 established, for the first time in federal legislation, a goal of universal service—meaning that, as a matter of public policy, everyone in the United States should have access to affordable telecommunications services. "In a time when we increasingly use information as a commodity, telecommunications are becoming increasingly important for the delivery of that commodity," according to the Benton Foundation, a public interest group. The intent of the Act is to make telecommunications available to everyone.

The FCC, of course, defines which type of access is offered in the "universal service" package. Does "universal service" mean only a telephone, or should "universal service" include access to a modem to connect a computer to the Internet? The FCC decides what exactly constitutes "universal service" and whether access to a computer and a modem will be part of that service, in an effort to use telecommunications to improve the economies of rural areas and central cities, as well as the rest of the nation.

Deregulates Free Media

The Act continued a policy of deregulation of commercial radio and television ownership that began in the 1980s. Radio and over-the-air broadcast television are viewed as "free media."

Unlike cable stations and satellite companies, which require extra equipment and charge consumers for their services, over-the-air broadcasting is available to anyone with a radio or television—and 98 percent of U.S. households have a TV set. Over-the-air broadcasting therefore has the largest potential audience for free media.

Relaxes Ownership and Licensing Rules

Previously, broadcast companies were allowed to own only 12 television stations. The Act eliminated limits on television station ownership altogether and instead used a station's potential audience to measure ownership limits. The Act said existing television networks (such as NBC and ABC) could begin new networks, but they could not buy an existing network. NBC could not buy ABC, for example, but NBC could begin a second network of its own, such as NBC2.

Before the Act passed, radio broadcasters were allowed to own 20 AM or 20 FM radio stations nationwide. The Act removed the limit on the number of radio stations a company can own, and in each market, the number of stations that one owner can hold depends on the size of the market. In a large market with 45 or more commercial radio stations, for example, a broadcaster may own eight stations; in a market with 14 stations, a broadcaster may own up to five stations.

The Act also allows *cross-ownership*. This means that companies can own television and radio stations in the same broadcast market. Companies also can own broadcast and cable outlets in the same market.

In 1999, the FCC further relaxed TV station ownership rules by allowing one broadcast company to own two TV

Peter Mulhy 2004/Tampa Tribune

Newsroom employees of *The Tampa Tribune*, WFLA-TV and the Tampa Bay Online Web site, all owned by Media General, work closely together in Tampa, Florida. Media deregulation allows a company like Media General to expand and buy even more broadcast properties.

stations in the same market. A company can buy a second station in the same market, says the FCC, as long as eight other stations with different owners are still operating in the market after the deal. In 2002, the FCC began considering further relaxation of the ownership rules that, among other things, would allow broadcasters also to own newspapers.

Also, the FCC licenses every broadcast station in the country, television and radio. In the past, renewal was a very complicated, rigorous process. Television stations were required to renew their licenses every five years and radio every seven. The Telecommunications Act extended the renewal period for both radio and television to every eight years.

> **Cross-Ownership** The practice of one company owning TV and radio stations in the same broadcast market.

In 2003, the FCC removed even more restrictions on broadcast ownership, making it easier for media companies to expand the number of stations they own, and included the provision that allows a company to own TV stations that reach 35 percent of the U.S. population. Today, the 35 percent limit still applies.

Creates Local Phone Competition

Due to deregulation, cable, satellite and telephone companies today are competing to deliver telecommunications services to home customers.

To encourage competition for delivery of video services, the Telecommunications Act allowed local telephone companies to get into the video delivery business. The Act repealed the FCC's "telco-cable cross-ownership" restrictions (**telco** is an abbreviation for telephone company). Local telephone companies can deliver video services either by an agreement with a cable operator or by creating their own delivery system. In turn, the cable companies were allowed to enter the business offered in the past by local telephone companies. Large cable companies also may deliver new types of telephone services, such as carrying messages to and from wireless cell phones.

To add to competition in the local telephone business, the Act also allowed long-distance carriers to offer local telephone service to compete with the Regional Bell (local telephone) companies. Within two months of the Act's passage, the long-distance carrier AT&T filed to be allowed to offer local telephone service in all 50 states. "If we get this right," said former FCC Chairman Reed Hundt, "you'll be buying communications services like shoes. Different styles, different vendors."

Until the market for telecommunications stabilizes, however, the choices are confusing for consumers and frustrating for people in the media industries who are trying to position themselves for a new future that isn't yet completely defined.

Ends Cable Rate Regulation

The rates that cable companies can charge have been regulated since 1992. In an attempt to control spiraling cable charges to consumers, Congress passed the 1992 Cable Act to regulate rates. The cable companies, facing competition from the local telephone companies, argued that Congress should remove rate regulation to allow the cable companies to compete and to help raise cable income.

The Telecommunications Act removed most rate regulation for all cable companies. All that remains is regulation to monitor the "basic tier" of cable service, often called "basic cable."

abbreviation for telephone company.

Congress Attempts to Use Communications Decency Act

Along with the major provisions of the Telecommunications Act to increase competition, Congress added several provisions to control content. These provisions together, called the Communications Decency Act, attempted to define and control users' access to specific types of programs and content. However, many provisions of the Act subsequently were overruled by the Supreme Court as violations of the First Amendment.

Adds Program Blocking

The Telecommunications Act required cable owners to take steps within 30 days after the bill was signed to ensure that cable shows "primarily dedicated to sexually oriented programming or other programming that is indecent" did not accidentally become available to people who did not subscribe to the programs. This meant that every cable operator would have to provide a free "lock box" to every cable subscriber's home to block programs, whether or not the customer requested it.

On March 9, 1996, the day the program blocking provision of the Act was scheduled to go into effect, Playboy Enterprises successfully won a temporary restraining order, which prevented the application of the law. "Attorneys for Chicago-based Playboy argued that the provision violated constitutional protections of free speech and equal protection. Justice Department attorneys argued that the government has the right and duty to regulate the distribution of indecent material if it can be viewed or heard by children," reported *Bloomberg Business News*.

Addresses Indecent Material on the Internet

The Communications Decency Act made it a felony to send indecent material over computer networks. The Act also prohibited using a telecommunications device to

- Make or initiate any communication that is obscene, lewd, lascivious, filthy or indecent with intent to annoy, abuse, threaten or harass another person

- Make or make available obscene communication

- Make or make available an indecent communication to minors

- Transmit obscene material—including material concerning abortion—for any indecent or immoral use

The Act relied on a very broad definition of the term "indecent," and courts have generally ruled that such speech is protected under the First Amendment. Under the Act's provisions, violators could be charged with a felony and fined up to $250,000. More than 50 opponents of the Act's indecency provision, including the American Library Association and the American Civil Liberties Union, went to court in Philadelphia to challenge the law.

On June 12, 1996, a three-judge Philadelphia panel unanimously declared that the Internet indecency provision was unconstitutional, and the judges blocked enforcement of the law. The judges issued a restraining order, which meant that the Internet indecency provision could not be enforced and violations could not even be investigated.

The federal government had argued the Internet should be regulated like radio and television, but the judges said material on the Internet deserved the same protection as printed material. In presenting the court's opinion, Judge Stewart R. Dalzell made very strong arguments defending access to the Internet. "Just as the strength of the Internet is chaos," Judge Dalzell wrote, "so the strength of our liberty depends upon the chaos and cacophony of the unfettered speech the First Amendment protects."

In 1997, the U.S. Supreme Court struck down the indecency provision of the Communications Decency Act, making it much harder for Congress to limit Internet access in the future. What is interesting is that the courts are defining and protecting an electronic delivery system—the Internet—as if it were a print medium.

This effort is important because Congress and the president, through the FCC, historically have regulated the broadcast industries, but none of the regulations that apply to the broadcast media also apply to print. The content of the print media, by law and by practice, has historically remained unregulated because of the First Amendment's protection of free expression.

Child Online Protection Act Fails

In 1998, after the U.S. Supreme Court found the indecency provision of the Communications Decency Act unconstitutional, Congress passed the Child Online Protection Act (**COPA**), aimed at preventing minors from getting access to sexually explicit online material, even though the material is legal for adults. Congress based the legislation on the idea that the government has a responsibility to protect children from content that is legal for adults but could be considered harmful to minors.

Congress wanted to fine offenders $150,000 for each day they violated the law and face up to six months in prison. Among the law's provisions was the requirement that libraries and schools that receive federal funding must install filtering software on public computers. Janet LaRue of the Family Research Council, which supported the restrictions, told *Trial* magazine, "Public libraries with unrestricted Internet access are virtual peep shows open to kids and funded by taxpayers."

"And just what was that little window you clicked off when I came in?"

Several organizations, including the American Library Association and the American Civil Liberties Union (ACLU), immediately challenged the law in court on First Amendment grounds, saying the law was too restrictive. "Not one federal judge in the country has upheld these laws when applied to the Internet," ACLU attorney Chris Hansen told *Online Newsletter*. "Lawmakers should stop passing criminal laws for the Internet and focus instead on educating users to make their own choices about what content to view or avoid." In 2002, the U.S. Supreme Court agreed that Congress had no authority to limit Internet access.

Supreme Court Upholds Internet Filters for Public Libraries

One year later, however, the U.S. Supreme Court upheld another law that said that libraries that take federal funds must equip their computers with anti-pornography filters. The case was defended in court on behalf of 13-year-old Emalyn Rood, who logged onto the Internet in an Oregon library to research information on lesbianism, and Mark Brown, who found information about his mother's breast cancer on a Philadelphia library computer—information that might have been blocked by a commonly used Internet filter.

In a close 5–4 decision in *U.S. v. American Library Association*, the U.S. Supreme Court said the requirement for Internet filters is "a valid exercise of Congress' spending power." This decision means the U.S. government may now require Internet filters at libraries that receive federal funding. Librarians argued that Internet filters are a form of censorship that blocks valuable information from people who need it.

COPA Child Online Protection Act. A law aimed at preventing minors from getting access to sexually explicit online material.

Frank Micelotta/Getty Images

The Federal Communications Commission launched an indecency investigation of the CBS network after an incident during the 2004 Super Bowl when singer Justin Timberlake ripped off part of Janet Jackson's costume during their halftime performance. The FCC fined CBS $550,000 for the incident. CBS appealed the fine, and in 2008 a federal appeals court overturned the decision.

TV Industry Agrees to Ratings and the V-Chip

Under pressure from Congress, television executives agreed to devise a voluntary ratings system for television programs by January 1997. *Broadcasting and Cable* magazine called the imposition of the ratings system a "stunning defeat" for the television industry, which had long resisted all content regulation. Jack Valenti, then president of the Motion Picture Association of America, led the ratings task force (Valenti also helped establish the current system of movie ratings). In January 1997, the task force announced the new ratings system, which *applied to all programming except sports, news magazines and news shows.*

The new ratings divide programming into six categories, ranging from TVY (appropriate for all children but specifically designed for a very young audience, including children ages two to six) to TVMA (specifically designed to be viewed by adults and therefore may be unsuitable for children younger than 17).

Unlike movies (which are rated by an independent board), producers, networks, cable channels, syndicators and other people who originate the programs rate the TV shows. These ratings evaluate violence and sexual content, and the results are displayed on the screen at the beginning of each program and coded into each TV program. The codes are read by a "V-chip," a microchip device required to be included with all new television sets. The V-chip allows parents to program the TV set to eliminate shows the parents find objectionable, although follow-up studies have shown that few parents use this option.

Six months after this rating system was adopted, the TV networks added a more specific rating for violent or sexual content. Most of the broadcast networks agreed to use specific program content ratings.

Government Monitors Broadcast Indecency

In early 2004, responding to congressional pressure for more government control over the airwaves, the Federal Communications Commission proposed a $775,000 fine against Clear Channel Communications for a Florida radio broadcast of various episodes of "Bubba the Love Sponge." The FCC fined Clear Channel the maximum amount then allowed—$27,500 for each time the episode ran (a total of $715,000) plus $40,000 for record-keeping violations at the station. Clear Channel said the programs were meant to entertain, not to offend its listeners.

Then-FCC Chairman Michael Powell also urged Congress to increase the maximum fine for indecency to $275,000 per incident, saying the maximum fine of $27,500 per episode wasn't large enough to discourage objectionable programming. Just a few days later, singers Janet Jackson and Justin Timberlake, performing on CBS-TV during halftime at the Super Bowl, caused another controversy when Timberlake reached over to Jackson and ripped off part of her costume, exposing her breast to an American audience estimated at 90 million people and a much bigger worldwide audience.

Jackson and Timberlake apologized for the incident, but FCC Chairman Powell launched an investigation, saying, "I am outraged at what I saw. . . . Like millions of Americans, my family and I gathered around the television for a celebration. Instead, that celebration was tainted by a classless, crass and deplorable stunt. Our nation's children, parents and citizens deserve better."

FCC rules say that radio and over-the-air TV stations may not air obscene material at any time. The rules also bar stations from broadcasting indecent material—references to sex or excretions—between 6 a.m. and 10 p.m., when the FCC says children are more likely to be listening or watching. Cable and satellite programming is not covered by the restrictions. The FCC fined CBS $550,000 for the Janet Jackson incident.

CBS appealed the Jackson fine in 2007 before Philadelphia's 3rd U.S. Circuit Court of Appeals, saying the network had taken precautions beforehand to avoid any incidents, including a five-second audio delay. In 2008 a federal appeals court overturned the decision, saying that "the FCC cannot impose liability on CBS for the acts of Janet Jackson and Justin Timberlake, independent contractors hired for the limited purposes of the Halftime Show."

In February 2004, Clear Channel Communications suspended radio personality Howard Stern from six of its stations—the only Clear Channel stations that carried the Howard Stern show—citing sexually explicit content aired on Stern's call-in program. Clear Channel said it would restore Stern's program when the show conformed to acceptable broadcast standards. The program continued to air on rival network Infinity Broadcasting, which syndicated the show, but by April 2004, Clear Channel had completely dropped Stern's show. In 2005, Stern left network radio and moved to satellite radio, where his program is available by subscription.

In March 2006, under a new FCC chairman, Kevin J. Martin, the FCC raised indecency fines to $32,500 per incident and proposed a $3.6 million fine against dozens of CBS stations and affiliates for a December 2004 CBS crime drama *Without a Trace*, citing the graphic depiction of "teenage boys and girls participating in a sex orgy." CBS strongly disagreed with the FCC's findings, saying the program "featured an important and socially relevant storyline warning parents to exercise greater supervision of their teenage children."

The $3.6 million fine was the largest the FCC ever had levied and was packaged with several other broadcast indecency fines announced at the same time, responding to what the FCC said were 300,000 complaints about 50 TV shows the agency received between 2002 and 2005. The fines continue to be reversed on appeal, however.

These controversies highlight the difficulties that arise when a federal government agency attempts to monitor free

AP Photo

Clear Channel Communications suspended and then dropped radio personality Howard Stern from six of its stations in 2004, citing sexually explicit content aired on Stern's program, another example of sensitivity among some broadcast stations to recent government criticism about controversial program content. In 2005, Stern moved his program to satellite radio, where the FCC does not have regulatory power over his subscription program.

expression when no clear national standards of broadcast obscenity have been established. The definition of broadcast indecency often is based on politics and public pressure at the FCC, which shifts emphasis from one presidential administration to another. The main issues are, How much power should a government entity have to decide what's obscene and/or indecent and then to enforce those restrictions? And what, if any, effect will these decisions have on broadcast programming in a media environment with so many alternative, unregulated outlets available to consumers? While the courts review the constitutionality of the indecency regulations, the FCC has not levied a new indecency fine since 2006. (See **Impact/Audience**, "YouTube Users' Privacy Prevails in Viacom Case," page 320.)

IMPACT
»» Audience

YouTube Users' Privacy Prevails in Viacom Case

Party on, YouTubers. No Need to Worry about Your Privacy

by Jessica Guynn

JULY 16, 2008—Google Inc. has reached a deal with Viacom Inc. to protect the privacy of tens of millions of YouTube viewers. A judge had ordered Google, YouTube's corporate parent, to hand over user data as part of the $1 billion copyright infringement case brought by Viacom.

According to the agreement, YouTube will mask the identities of individual viewers when it provides viewership records to Viacom. Among the things YouTube will cloak: user IDs and Internet protocol addresses (the unique numbers for each Web-connected device).

YouTube is handing over the database to Viacom under a court order that was widely criticized by privacy advocates and irate bloggers. U.S. District Court Judge Louis Stanton in New York dismissed such concerns.

Viacom has said that, under the court's confidentiality order, the data will be released only to its outside attorneys and consultants and can be used only in this lawsuit, not to pursue individuals. But Viacom remains interested in finding out whether YouTube employees had viewed its shows on the site. That issue has not been resolved.

Viacom, which owns movie studio Paramount and cable networks including MTV and Comedy Central, requested the information as part of its lawsuit. It is seeking to show that YouTube has built its success by letting people post Viacom shows.

Viacom, which owns movie studio Paramount and cable networks including MTV and Comedy Central, requested YouTube records as part of its $1 billion copyright lawsuit against YouTube, claiming the Web site allows people to post Viacom shows on the YouTube Web site. In 2008, a judge ordered Google (which owns YouTube) to turn over the necessary data, but the identities of individual viewers were masked.

Chris Hondros/Getty Images

"YouTube Users' Privacy Prevails in Viacom Case," by Jessica Guynn, *Los Angeles Times*, July 16, 2008. Reprinted by permission of Los Angeles Times.

Intellectual Property Rights Affirmed

The right of ownership for creative ideas in the United States is legally governed by what are called **intellectual property rights**. Three recent developments—the Digital Millennium Copyright Act, the U.S. Supreme Court decision in the *New York Times Co. v. Tasini* case and the *MGM v. Grokster* case—have begun to define the issues of electronic copyright in the digital era. Additionally, independent progressive organizations have been working to give copyright holders greater flexibility in handling their intellectual property.

Digital Millennium Copyright Act

Passed in 1998, the Digital Millennium Copyright Act (**DMCA**) is comprehensive legislation that begins to address the copyright issues provoked by the Internet. The law makes several changes in U.S. copyright law to bring it in compliance with two World Intellectual Property Organization (**WIPO**) treaties about digitally transmitted copyrighted and stored material. The WIPO is responsible for promoting the protection of intellectual property throughout the world.

The DMCA is designed to prevent illegal copying of material that is published and distributed on the Internet. The DMCA makes it illegal to circumvent technology that protects or controls access to copyrighted materials, such as the recordings shared on the Internet. The DMCA also makes it illegal to manufacture materials that will help people gain access to copyrighted materials. Congress allowed a two-year period before the Act was implemented so that Congress could study its ramifications. The DMCA became effective on October 28, 2000.

Supporters of the DMCA—which includes most of the media industries that hold the copyright on creative works, such as movies, books and recordings—say the DMCA is an important law that must be enforced to protect intellectual property. Opponents say the law goes too far by limiting technological development.

In March 2007, media conglomerate Viacom, whose media properties include MTV, Comedy Central and Nickelodeon, sued Google and YouTube, saying the companies deliberately gathered a library of copyrighted video clips without permission. Earlier in 2007 Viacom asked YouTube to remove 100,000 clips that it said infringed on Viacom copyrights.

Google said the so-called "safe harbor" provisions of the DMCA covered the company. Generally these provisions say that Web site owners are not liable for copyrighted material that others upload to their site if the Web site owners promptly remove the material when the copyright owner asks them to do so.

According to *The New York Times*, Google argued that the DMCA "balances the rights of copyright holders and the need to protect the Internet as an important new form of communication. By seeking to make carriers and hosting providers liable for Internet communications, Viacom's complaint threatens the way hundreds of millions of people legitimately exchange information, news, entertainment, and political and artistic expression." However, Google announced four months later that it was developing video recognition technology that could detect and remove copyrighted material from its site before it was posted.

New York Times Co. v. Tasini

In 2001, a U.S. Supreme Court decision in *New York Times Co. v. Tasini* affirmed that freelance writers separately own the electronic rights to material they have written, even though a publisher has first published their writing in printed form. In 1993, freelance writer Jonathan Tasini, president of the National Writers' Union, discovered that an article he had written for *The New York Times* was available on a database for Mead Data Center Corporation, which was paying royalties for the material to the *Times*. Tasini hadn't been paid for this use, so Tasini sued *The New York Times* and several other publishing companies (including Newsday Inc., the Atlantic Monthly Company and Time Inc.).

The suit claimed the publishers had violated copyright law by using writers' work on electronic databases without their permission and that this limited the rights of freelance authors to have their articles published and receive compensation for their work. Several writers' organizations, including the Authors' Guild, joined Tasini in the suit. The *Times* claimed the digital versions of written works were simply "revisions" of paper copies, which meant the rights belonged to the publisher so the writers deserved no further compensation.

On June 25, 2001, by a vote of 7–2, the U.S. Supreme Court agreed with Tasini. Writing the majority opinion, Judges Breyer and Stevens said that upholding the freelance authors' copyright would encourage the development of new technologies and the creation of new artistic work. The court said the *Times* must delete thousands of articles from its database for which it had not obtained the rights. "Once again, the legal system has come down in favor of the individual creator's rights in the digital age," Tasini told *Publishers Weekly*. "Everywhere you look, the law supports creators."

This case is very important—not only for freelancers, but also for anyone who creates intellectual property in the future. The court established the legal concept that the right to reproduce creative material electronically is very separate from the right to reproduce creative material in print and that writers and other creative artists should be compensated separately for electronic rights to their work.

Metro-Goldwyn-Mayer Studios Inc. et al. v. Grokster Ltd. et al.

In 2005, the U.S. Supreme Court ruled in a unanimous decision that a software company can be held liable for copyright infringement if someone uses the company's software to illegally download songs and movies, known as file sharing. The decision effectively shut down the Internet sites *Grokster* and *StreamCast*, also named in the suit. The companies provided free software that allowed users to download Internet content for free.

The *Grokster* case is another example of the strong legal tradition in the U.S. of guaranteeing intellectual copyright protection for creative content.

Intellectual Property Rights The legal right of ownership of ideas and content published in any medium.

DMCA Digital Millennium Copyright Act.

WIPO World Intellectual Property Organization.

Courts and Regulators Govern Advertising and PR

Advertising and public relations are governed by legal constraints and by regulation. *New York Times v. Sullivan* (see page 306) was a crucial case for advertisers as well as for journalists. Since that decision, two other important court cases have defined the advertising and public relations businesses—the *Central Hudson* case for advertising (which is defined as "commercial speech" under the law) and the *Texas Gulf Sulphur* case for public relations.

Central Hudson Case

In 1980, in *Central Hudson Gas & Electric Corp. v. Public Service Commission*, the U.S. Supreme Court issued the most definitive opinion yet on commercial speech. During the energy crisis atmosphere of the 1970s, the New York Public Utilities Commission had banned all advertising by public utilities that promoted the use of electricity. Central Hudson Gas & Electric wanted the ban lifted, so the company sued the commission.

The commission said the ban promoted energy conservation; the Supreme Court disagreed, and the decision in the case forms the basis for commercial speech protection today. "If the commercial speech does not mislead, and it concerns lawful activity," explains legal scholar Ralph Holsinger, "the government's power to regulate it is limited. . . . The state cannot impose regulations that only indirectly advance its interests. Nor can it regulate commercial speech that poses no danger to a state interest." The decision prescribed standards that commercial speech must meet to be protected by the First Amendment.

The main provisions of the standards are that (1) the advertisement must be for a lawful product and (2) the advertisement must not be misleading. This has become known as the ***Hudson test***. To be protected, then, an advertisement must promote a legal product and must not lie. This would seem to have settled the issue, but controversy continues.

Should alcohol advertising be banned? What about advertisements for condoms or birth control pills? Courts in different states have disagreed on these questions, and no Supreme Court decision on these specific issues exists, leaving many complex questions undecided. The Hudson test remains the primary criteria for determining what is protected commercial speech.

Texas Gulf Sulphur Case

The most important civil suit involving the issue of public relations occurred in the 1960s in *Securities and Exchange Commission v. Texas Gulf Sulphur Company*. Texas Gulf Sulphur (TGS) discovered ore deposits in Canada in late 1963 but did not announce the discovery publicly. TGS quietly purchased hundreds of acres surrounding the ore deposits, and TGS officers began to accumulate more shares of the company's stock. Meanwhile, the company issued a press release that said that the rumors about a discovery were "unreliable." When TGS announced that it had made a "major strike," which boosted the price of the company's stock, the Securities and Exchange Commission took the company to court.

The U.S. Court of Appeals ruled that TGS officers had violated the disclosure laws of the Securities and Exchange Commission. The court also ruled that TGS had issued "a false and misleading press release." Company officers and their friends were punished for withholding the information. According to *The Practice of Public Relations*, "the case proved conclusively that a company's failure to make known material information (information likely to be considered important by reasonable investors in determining whether to buy, sell or hold securities) may be in violation of the antifraud provision of the Securities and Exchange Acts."

The *Texas Gulf Sulfur* case remains today as a landmark in the history of public relations law. The decision in the case means public relations people can be held legally responsible for information that they do not disclose about their companies. This case says that public relations people at publicly held corporations (businesses with stockholders) are responsible not only to their companies but also to the public.

Government Regulates Advertisers

The main regulatory agency for advertising and public relations issues is the Federal Trade Commission (FTC), although other agencies such as the Securities and Exchange Commission and the Food and Drug Administration sometimes intervene to question advertising practices.

In 1914, the Federal Trade Commission assumed the power to oversee deceptive interstate advertising practices under the Federal Trade Commission Act. Today, the FTC's policy covering deceptive advertising says, "The Commission will find an act or practice deceptive if there is a misrepresentation, omission or other practice that misleads the consumer acting reasonably in the circumstances, to the consumer's detriment."

The commission acts when it receives a complaint the staff feels is worth investigating. The staff can request a *letter of compliance* from the advertiser, with the adver-

Hudson Test A legal test that establishes a standard for commercial speech protection.

tiser promising to change the alleged deception without admitting guilt. Next, the advertiser can argue the case before an administrative law judge, who can write a consent agreement to outline what the advertiser must do to comply with the law. A cease-and-desist order can be issued against the advertiser, although this is rare. The FTC can fine an advertiser who doesn't comply with an FTC order.

The Federal Trade Commission's five members serve seven-year terms. They are appointed by the president and confirmed by the U.S. Senate, and no more than three of the members can be from one political party. Because the FTC's members are presidential appointees, the commission's actions often reflect the political climate under which they operate. In the 1970s, the FTC became a very active consumer advocacy agency. This was challenged in the 1980s, when presidential policy favored easing regulations on business practices. Under President Clinton in the 1990s, the FTC moved aggressively to cite companies for wrongdoing. For example, in 1997, the FTC conducted hearings to determine whether the government should impose safeguards on information access on the Internet to protect consumers'

privacy. The George W. Bush administration has been less aggressive in monitoring advertising claims.

Law Must Balance Rights and Responsibilities

Legal and regulatory issues governing advertising and public relations, then, are stitched with the same conflicting values that govern all aspects of media. The courts, the FCC, the FTC and other government agencies that monitor the media industries are the major arbiters of ongoing constitutional clashes.

Important legal decisions make lasting and influential statements about the role of law in protecting the constitutional guarantee of free expression in a country with constantly shifting public values. Through the courts and regulation, the government also must balance the business needs of the media industries with the government's role as a public interest representative.

Review, Analyze, Investigate
REVIEWING CHAPTER 14

U.S. Constitution Sets Free Press Precedent

✓ The U.S. media's role is to encourage "uninhibited, robust and wide-open" debate.

✓ The legal and regulatory issues that media face are attempts to balance the media's rights and responsibilities.

Government Tries to Restrict Free Expression

✓ Before 1964, the First Amendment faced only four notable government challenges: the Alien and Sedition Laws of 1798, the Espionage Act of 1918, the Smith Act of 1940 and the Cold War congressional investigations of suspected communists in the late 1940s and early 1950s.

✓ All of these challenges created a restrictive atmosphere in an attempt to limit free expression.

Prior Restraint Rarely Used

✓ American courts rarely have invoked prior restraint. The two most recent cases involved the publication of the Pentagon Papers by *The New York Times* and the publication of directions to build a hydrogen bomb in *The Progressive* magazine. In both cases, the information eventually was printed, but the intervention of the government delayed publication.

Government Manages War Coverage

✓ Attempts by the Reagan administration to limit reporters' access to Grenada during the U.S. invasion in October 1983 were a subtle form of prior restraint.

✓ Pentagon rules for 1991 war coverage, reached in cooperation with journalists, imposed stricter restrictions on reporting in the Gulf War than in any previous U.S. war. In contrast, when the U.S. government delivered humanitarian aid to Somalia in 1992, the military encouraged press coverage.

✓ In 2001, the U.S. government controlled release of information to the American public about the war in Afghanistan even more than in the Gulf War.

✓ During the early months of the war in Afghanistan, the military used press pools and also provided its own video footage of troop landings, produced by the military's combat film teams.

✓ During the Iraq War in 2003, the U.S. government used a system called embedding, which meant that members of the press traveled with the military, but the press' movements were restricted and managed by their military units.

Librarians Resist the Patriot Act

✓ Among the provisions of the Patriot Act is Section 215, which allows the Federal Bureau of Investigation to monitor library records, including computer log-ins and the lists of books people check out of public libraries.

✓ The American Library Association and the American Civil Liberties Union challenged Section 215 in court.

✓ In 2007, a federal district court agreed that some provisions of the Patriot Act go against constitutional principles of checks and balances and separation of powers.

What Is the Standard for Obscenity?

✓ *Roth v. United States* defined obscenity as material that is "utterly without redeeming social importance."

✓ *Miller v. California* established a three-part local test for obscenity: whether "the average person, applying contemporary community standards," would find that the work, taken as a whole, appeals to the prurient interest; whether the work depicts or describes, in a patently offensive way, sexual conduct specifically defined by the applicable state law; and whether the work, taken as a whole, lacks serious literary, artistic, political or scientific value (often called the LAPS test).

✓ In the 1988 *Hazelwood* case, the U.S. Supreme Court gave public school officials considerable freedom to limit what appears in student publications.

Libel Law Outlines the Media's Public Responsibility

✓ In 1964, the *New York Times v. Sullivan* case set a precedent, establishing that to be successful in a libel suit, a public official must prove actual malice.

✓ The press can use three defenses against a libel suit: truth, privilege and fair comment.

✓ The median amount awarded in a libel suit, in 2004, was $3.4 million, although most successful libel judgments eventually are reduced when they are appealed.

✓ *Gertz v. Robert Welch* established the concept that the expression of opinions is a necessary part of public debate.

✓ Because of the *Herbert v. Lando* decision, today reporters can be asked in a libel suit to identify their sources and to surrender their notes.

✓ The *Masson v. New Yorker Magazine* case addressed the journalist's responsibility for direct quotations.

Invasion of Privacy Defined Four Ways

✓ Invasion-of-privacy lawsuits are much less common than libel suits.

✓ There is no U.S. Supreme Court decision that governs invasion of privacy, so each state has its own interpretation of the issue.

✓ Generally, the media can be guilty of invading someone's privacy by intruding on a person's physical or mental solitude, publishing or disclosing embarrassing personal facts, giving someone publicity that places the person in a false light or using someone's name or likeness for commercial benefit.

✓ In an important case for the press, *Bartnicki v. Vopper*, in 2001, the U.S. Supreme Court reaffirmed the media's right to broadcast information and to comment on that information, no matter how the information was obtained.

Debate Continues over Fair Trial, Right of Access and Shield Laws

✓ *Sheppard v. Maxwell* established the legal precedent for limiting press access to courtrooms and juries.

✓ In 2005, *New York Times* reporter Judith Miller spent 85 days in jail because she refused to reveal a confidential source to a Washington, D.C., grand jury. Eventually she revealed her source's name and was released after her conversation with the source (I. Lewis Libby, Vice President Dick Cheney's chief of staff) in which, Miller said, he released her from their confidentiality agreement. Libby was convicted of perjury and obstruction of justice, but President Bush commuted his sentence in 2007.

✓ Individual state shield laws protect journalists from being compelled to reveal their sources, but no federal shield law guarantees these rights to every journalist nationwide.

FCC Regulates Broadcast and Cable

✓ Unlike print, the broadcast media are regulated by a federal agency, the Federal Communications Commission.

✓ Since 1972, the concept behind broadcast regulation has been based on the belief that broadcasters are trustees operating in the public interest.

Telecommunications Act of 1996 Changes the Marketplace

✓ The Telecommunications Act of 1996 is the most far-reaching reform in the way the U.S. government regulates mass media in more than 60 years.

✓ Following passage of the Telecommunications Act, large companies began positioning themselves to deliver the combination of telecommunications services they think consumers want.

✓ The major provisions of the Telecommunications Act of 1996 affect telecommunications, broadcast, satellite and cable.

Deregulation Unleashes the Media

✓ The FCC under President Clinton moved to a policy of deregulation of station ownership and regulation of broadcast programming.

✓ In 2003, the FCC adopted regulations that allow one company to control 35 percent of the broadcast audience. Those regulations are still in place today.

Congress Attempts to Use Communications Decency Act

✓ The Communications Decency Act, which was part of the Telecommunications Act, attempted to regulate access to cable and TV programming and monitoring of computer networks, including the Internet.

✓ In 1997, the U.S. Supreme Court blocked enforcement of the Internet indecency provisions of the Communications Decency Act.

✓ In 1998, Congress passed the Child Online Protection Act, aimed at preventing minors from getting access to sexually explicit material, even though the material is legal for adults. Several organizations, including the American Library Association and the American Civil Liberties Union, immediately challenged the law in court on First Amendment grounds. In 2002, the U.S. Supreme Court agreed that Congress has no authority to restrict Internet access.

✓ In 2003, the U.S. Supreme Court ruled that the federal government may withhold funding from schools and libraries that refuse to install Internet filters for pornography on their computers.

TV Industry Agrees to Ratings and the V-Chip

✓ Under pressure from Congress, television executives devised a voluntary system of ratings for TV programming.

✓ The new programming codes can be read by a V-chip, which allows parents to program a TV set to eliminate objectionable programs.

Government Monitors Broadcast Indecency

✓ In 2004, the FCC increased fines for broadcast programs the FCC determines are indecent.

✓ The Howard Stern show was fined repeatedly for explicit broadcast content. Stern moved to satellite radio in 2005, where his program is not subject to FCC regulations.

Intellectual Property Rights Affirmed

✓ The right of ownership of creative ideas in the United States is legally governed by what are called intellectual property rights. Three recent developments—the Digital Millennium Copyright Act, the U.S. Supreme Court decision in *New York Times Co. v. Tasini*, and the U.S. Supreme Court decision in *Metro-Goldwyn Mayer Studios Inc. et al. v. Grokster Ltd. et al.*—have begun to define the issues of electronic copyright in the digital era.

✓ All three cases affirm the strong legal tradition in the United States of guaranteeing intellectual copyright for creative content.

Courts and Regulators Govern Advertising and PR

✓ The Hudson test for advertising means that to be protected by the First Amendment, an advertisement must promote a legal product and must not lie.

✓ The *Texas Gulf Sulphur* case established the concept that a publicly held company is responsible for any information it withholds from the public.

✓ The main government agency regulating advertising is the Federal Trade Commission. This agency adopted aggressive policies of protecting consumers' rights in the 1990s but today is less aggressive about policing advertisers.

Law Must Balance Rights and Responsibilities

✓ The courts, the FCC and the FTC arbitrate the media's rights and responsibilities.

✓ Government must balance the media's business needs with the government's role to protect the interests of the public.

KEY TERMS

These terms are defined in the margins throughout this chapter and appear in alphabetical order with definitions in the Glossary, which begins on page 372.

"The Bundle" 314

Censorship 301

COPA 317

Cross-Ownership 315

DMCA 321

False Light 310

HUAC 297

Hudson Test 322

Intellectual Property Rights 321

LAPS Test 304

Libel 306

NSL 301

Pool Reporting 299

Prior Restraint 297

Qualified Privilege 308

RBOCs 314

Roth Test 303

Shield Laws 312

Telco 316

WIPO 321

CRITICAL QUESTIONS

1. Cite five major events/legal decisions in the evolution of the interpretation of the First Amendment in America from its beginnings to today.

2. Why is *New York Times v. Sullivan* such a precedent-setting case for the American media?

3. List and describe the four elements necessary to prove libel.

4. Why are the courts generally so reluctant to use prior restraint to stop publication? List two cases in which the courts did invoke prior restraint.

5. Discuss the controversy between the U.S. government and American librarians over the Patriot Act, which Congress passed in 2001. What are the provisions of the Act that affect libraries? What have been the responses of librarians? How would you balance the need of the government to gather information and the need of citizens to have access to books and information through libraries without government scrutiny?

WORKING THE WEB

This list includes both sites mentioned in the chapter and others to give you greater insight into media law and regulation.

American Booksellers Foundation for Free Expression (ABFFE)

http://www.abffe.org

The self-described "bookseller's voice in the fight against censorship," this foundation participates in legal cases about First Amendment rights and provides education about the importance of free expression. Archived articles from the ABFFE Update and the downloadable Banned Books Week Handbook are available on the Web site.

American Library Association (ALA)

http://www.ala.org

This association's mission is to provide leadership for the development, promotion and improvement of library and information services and the profession of librarianship in order to enhance learning and ensure access to information for all. However, the ALA is open to any interested person or organization. Among the professional tools available on the Web site of this 130-year-old organization are articles, guidelines and other resources about such issues as censorship, copyright, diversity and equal access. ALA also sponsors a number of electronic discussion lists for participation by members and others with shared interests.

Federal Communications Commission (FCC)

http://www.fcc.gov

This U.S. government agency, established by the Communications Act of 1934, regulates interstate and international communications by radio, television, wire, satellite and cable. Its jurisdiction covers the 50 states, the District of Columbia and U.S. possessions. The site holds FCC news headlines—daily and archived—as well as links to media rules and regulations, strategic goals of the commission, bureaus and offices, advisory committees, and even a kids' zone. The Consumer and Governmental Affairs Bureau section allows consumers to file or research individual informal complaints relating to FCC regulations.

FindLaw

http://www.findlaw.com

FindLaw provides legal information for the public on a host of topics, including intellectual property, copyright and the Internet as well as civil rights, education law, employees' rights and criminal law. Users can find and share legal information on FindLaw Q&A.

Freedom of Information Center (University of Missouri School of Journalism, Columbia)

http://www.nfoic.org/foi-center/

Founded in 1958, the Center provides information to the general public and the media through a collection of more than 1 million articles and documents about access to government information at local, state and federal levels. The Web site features links to state and international FOI laws, a media law guide, and an index to research files that have been compiled since the Center's inception.

Index on Censorship

http://www.indexoncensorship.org

This Web site of a periodical founded in 1972 by a group of writers, journalists and artists describes itself as "one of the world's leading repositories of original, challenging, controversial and intelligent writing on free expression issues." Users can explore censorship issues from around the world as well as news, sponsored events, projects and awards. Index Arts is a specialist arm designed to promote and support freedom of artistic expression.

Media Center at New York Law School

http://www.nyls.edu/centers/centers_and_institutes/media_center

The Media Center sponsors pedagogy, scholarship and projects relating to evolving communication and information technologies and the laws that regulate them. Its goals are to promote scholarship, to preserve democratic values through effective media policy and to train lawyers to understand the law of media and the role of media in the law. The Center's Library holds comprehensive indexes of U.S. laws and cases, as well as articles and papers on various media law issues.

Media Law Resource Center (MLRC)

http://www.medialaw.org

This nonprofit information clearinghouse is a membership organization for media companies (publishers, broadcasters and web content providers), insurers, and professional and public interest organizations. Available to the general public on the Web site is Libel FAQs, a basic introduction to libel, privacy and related law in the media, in addition to selected articles and reports from MLRC.

Silha Center for the Study of Media Ethics and Law (University of Minnesota)

http://silha.umn.edu/

The Silha Center examines the theoretical and practical applications of freedom and fairness in journalism. Major projects include media accountability, points of convergence of media ethics and law, and libel and privacy. The Web site includes articles from the quarterly Silha Center Bulletin and links to law-related and media-ethics-related Web sites as well as legislative testimony and briefs on a number of issues.

Student Press Law Center (SPLC)
http://www.splc.org

This advocate for student free-press rights provides information, advice and legal assistance to students and educators. News Flashes link to current and archived articles about high school and college journalism controversies. Articles from the SPLC Report since 1996 are also archived. The Resource Center includes information about obtaining legal help, browsing through the online law library and testing your knowledge of student press law (30-minute quiz) and the First Amendment (10-minute quiz).

15

Ethics:
Placing Responsibility

Chris Hondros/Getty Images

Members of the press attempt to interview an employee of Lehman Brothers Holdings in New York City as he carries a box out of a company headquarters meeting and hails a cab on Sunday, September 14, 2008. The next day, the 158-year-old company declared bankruptcy.

What's Ahead?

"Most of us would rather publish

a story than not," explains journalist Anthony Brandt in an *Esquire* magazine article about ethics. "We're in the business of reporting, after all; most of us believe the public should know what's going on, has a right to know, has, indeed, a responsibility to know, and that this right, this responsibility, transcends the right to privacy, excuses our own pushiness, our arrogance, and therefore ought to protect us from lawsuits even when we are wrong.

329

"But most reporters also know there are times when publishing can harm or ruin people's lives. Members of the press sometimes print gossip as truth, disregard the impact they have on people's lives, and are ready to believe the worst about people because the worst sells. . . . We in the media have much to answer for."

Ethics Define Responsibilities

Discussions about how journalists answer for what they do center on *ethics*. The word derives from the Greek word *ethos*, meaning the guiding spirit or traditions that govern a culture. Part of America's culture is the unique protection offered to journalists by the First Amendment of the U.S. Constitution, so any discussion of ethics and the American media acknowledges the cultural belief that the First Amendment privilege carries with it special obligations. Among these obligations are professional ***ethics***, the rules or standards governing the conduct of the members of a profession.

Journalists are no more likely to exploit their positions than people in other professions, but when journalists make the wrong ethical choices, the consequences can be very damaging and very public. "It may well be that if journalism loses touch with ethical values, it will then cease to be of use to society, and cease to have any real reason for being," writes media ethics scholar John Hulteng. "But that, for the sake of all of us, must never be allowed to happen."

Journalists sometimes make poor ethical judgments because they work quickly and their actions can be haphazard, because the lust to be first with a story can override the desire to be right, because they sometimes don't know

"Please pay attention, as the ethics have changed."

Ethics The rules or standards that govern someone's conduct

enough to question the truthfulness of what they're told, because they may win attention and professional success quickly by ignoring ethical standards, and because journalists sometimes are insensitive to the consequences of their stories for the people they cover.

The media face four different types of ethical issues:

1. Truthfulness
2. Fairness
3. Privacy
4. Responsibility

Consider these actual situations:

1. **Truthfulness.** A public relations agency hired by the U.S. government paid a commentator to promote a new federal government education initiative. The contract also required the commentator to gain access for government officials to other journalists to convince the journalists about the new law's merits. By not disclosing the payment, did the commentator mislead his readers, or was he simply doing the job he was paid to do? Were the opinions he promoted truly his positions on the issues or did he take the positions because he'd been paid to publicly promote a specific agenda?

2. **Fairness.** A journalist, married to a public official and on leave from her job as a program host at a TV network, reportedly used her personal influence to stop an author's TV appearance because she was reportedly afraid the author's book contained negative information about her that would damage her husband's political career. Is the journalist irresponsibly using her personal influence or is she just trying to protect her family?

3. **Privacy.** A reporter verified that a well-known public figure was dying of AIDS, although the public figure would not admit his illness. The story was published. Did the reporter infringe on the person's privacy, or did the readers deserve to know the extent of this serious public health hazard?

4. **Responsibility.** A photojournalist in Los Angeles rammed his minivan into a celebrity's Mercedes, hoping to get unflattering pictures of the star as she reacted to the accident. If a news event is staged—provoked by a reporter—is it a true event? Should movie stars just accept these stalking tactics as part of the price of being a celebrity, or should the press be expected to cover what happens rather than provoking an event to occur?

Truth versus falsehood is the issue for the journalist who accepted payment to write stories in example 1. Fairness versus bias is the question for the journalist who used her personal influence with the TV network in example 2. Personal privacy versus invasion of privacy is the debate facing the reporter who published the AIDS information in example 3. Responsibility versus irresponsibility is the issue for the photojournalist who staged the accident in example 4.

Some ethical debates are easier to resolve than others. These four incidents and several other examples described in this chapter demonstrate the amazing range of situations covered by media ethics and the different ways media organizations use to get their jobs done.

Truthfulness Affects Credibility

Truthfulness in reporting means more than accuracy and telling the truth to get a story. Truthfulness also means not misrepresenting the people or the underlying motives of a story to readers and viewers, as well as not reporting disinformation. Another aspect of truthfulness is the belief that government officials should not use the media for their own ends by "planting" stories that aren't true.

Hidden Motives or Sponsors

The journalist described in example 1 (on page 330) is syndicated columnist Armstrong Williams, who received $250,000 from a public relations firm to promote President Bush's No Child Left Behind Act to African Americans. In 2005, *USA Today* revealed the arrangement, saying the PR contract said Williams would "utilize his long-term working relationships with *America's Black Forum* [an African American news program] to encourage the producers to periodically address the No Child Left Behind Act."

When Williams' payment arrangement became public, Williams attributed the lapse to the fact that he was not trained as a journalist. He apologized for "blurring his roles as an independent conservative commentator and a paid promoter."

Misrepresentation

The most recent celebrated case of misrepresentation happened in 2006 when author James Frey admitted that his personal memoir, *A Million Little Pieces*, contained many fabrications. In the book, selected by Oprah Winfrey in September 2005 for her book club, Frey detailed his battle with drug addiction and his ultimate recovery. The book quickly became a best seller.

In January 2006, *The Smoking Gun* posted information on its Web site that disputed the truthfulness of many of the incidents Frey described. Frey's publisher, Doubleday, initially defended the book, but then Winfrey invited Frey to appear on her show, where Frey admitted he'd falsified many parts of *A Million Little Pieces*, including descriptions of time he spent in police custody and in jail.

He also admitted to Winfrey that the first pages of his just-published sequel, *My Friend Leonard*, were a fabrication, since *Leonard* started with Frey's 87th day in jail, which never occurred. Frey told Winfrey the invented stories "portrayed me in ways that made me tougher and more daring and more aggressive than in reality I was, or I am." He then publicly apologized to his readers.

Doubleday said they would include a detailed list of Frey's fabrications, compiled by the author, to accompany all future copies of *A Million Little Pieces*. *The New York Times Book Review* continued to categorize the book on its best-seller list as nonfiction, but the editors added a note saying, "Both author and publisher acknowledge that this memoir contains numerous fabrications."

In 2006, author James Frey admitted to Oprah Winfrey that his memoir, *A Million Little Pieces*, contained many fabrications. Frey's book had been chosen as an Oprah Book Club selection, and he previously had promoted the book on her show.

Ulf Andersen/Getty Images

A month after Frey admitted his mistakes on television, Riverhead Books, which published *Leonard* and had signed Frey to write two more books, cancelled the contract, and his agent dropped him. Sales of *A Million Little Pieces* dropped quickly after the Oprah confrontation; however, *The New York Times* reported in March 2006 that Frey's royalties for 2005 totaled more than $5 million.

Another recent case of serious journalistic misrepresentation involved Jayson Blair, a reporter for *The New York Times*. On May 1, 2003, the *Times* published a front page story, "*Times* Reporter Who Resigned Leaves Long Trail of Deception," which began: "A staff reporter for *The New York Times* committed frequent acts of journalistic fraud while covering significant news events in recent months, an investigation by *Times* journalists has found. The widespread fabrication and plagiarism represent a profound betrayal of trust and a low point in the 152-year

Jennifer Szymaszek/AP Photo

In May 2003, *The New York Times* admitted in a front page story that *Times* reporter Jayson Blair had fabricated comments, concocted scenes, stolen material from other newspapers and news services and selected details from photos to create an impression he had been in certain places and interviewed people when he hadn't.

history of the newspaper." The *Times* said that as a reporter for the *Times*, 27-year-old Blair had

- Written stories purported to be filed in Maryland, Texas and other states, when often he was still in New York
- Fabricated comments
- Concocted scenes
- Stolen material from other newspapers and wire services
- Selected details from photographs to create the impression he had been somewhere or seen someone, when he hadn't

The *Times* then published an exhaustive, unprecedented eight-page accounting of 73 significant falsehoods in Blair's stories the *Times* had published, detailing every traceable error, based on an internal investigation by its own reporters. In one story, for example, Blair had reported details from inside the National Naval Medical Center in Bethesda, Maryland, but the hospital said Blair had never visited the hospital. In another story about a stricter National Collegiate Athletic Association standard for class attendance, Blair quoted someone who said he never talked to Blair and used quotes from another newspaper as his own.

When discussing Blair's case, Alex S. Jones, a former *Times* reporter and co-author of *The Trust: The Private and Powerful Family Behind The New York Times*, told the *Times*: "To the best of my knowledge, there has never been anything like this at *The New York Times*. . . . There has never been a systematic effort to lie and cheat as a reporter at *The New*

York Times comparable to what Jayson Blair seems to have done."

Less than two months later, the *Times*' two top editors, who were responsible for hiring and supervising Blair, resigned.

In another well-known case of fabrication, Janet Cooke was a reporter for the *Washington Post* in 1980 when she wrote "Jimmy's World," a story about an 8-year-old heroin addict. After she was awarded the Pulitzer Prize for the story in April 1981, reporters began to check up on her background, and the *Post* learned she had lied on her résumé. The editors then questioned her for several hours about the story. Cooke admitted "Jimmy" was a composite of several children she had interviewed. She was allowed to resign.

" 'Jimmy's World' was in essence a fabrication," she wrote in her resignation letter. "I never encountered or interviewed an 8-year-old heroin addict. The September 19, 1980, article in the *Washington Post* was a serious misrepresentation which I deeply regret. I apologize to my newspaper, my profession, the Pulitzer board and all seekers of truth."

Misrepresenting the facts or expressing opinions because someone has paid you to do so causes readers to question the information or opinions in other nonfiction books, newspaper stories and columns. Which are actual people and which are not? Is the story fiction or fact? It also seriously affects the credibility of the company that publishes the books, stories or columns and indirectly affects the credibility of all authors, all journalists and all columnists.

Disinformation

In October 1986, the press learned that two months earlier the Reagan administration had launched a ***disinformation*** campaign to scare Libyan leader Moammar Qadhafi. Selected U.S. government sources planted stories with reporters that U.S. forces were preparing to strike Libya.

The first report about the bogus preparations appeared in the August 25, 1986, issue of *The Wall Street Journal*, which first used the word *disinformation* to describe the practice of government officials intentionally planting false information with reporters.

On the basis of this story and a statement by White House spokesman Larry Speakes that the article was "authoritative," other newspapers, including the *Washington Post*, carried the story. This example brings up the ethical question of the government's responsibility to tell the truth and not to use the news media for its own ends. State Department spokesman and former television reporter Bernard Kalb resigned when he learned about the disinformation campaign, saying, "Faith in the word of America is the pulse beat of our democracy."

Disinformation was at the center of the 2007 trial of presidential adviser I. Lewis Libby, in which Libby was found guilty of perjury and obstruction of justice for leaking

Disinformation The intentional planting of false information by government sources.

**"Ok honesty is the best policy.
Let's call that option A."**

Ken James/CORBIS

The New York Times reported in 2005 that Maria Shriver used her connections at her former employer, NBC, to keep the author of a book about her husband, Governor Arnold Schwarzenegger, which she reportedly thought contained negative information about her, from appearing on the show.

the name of CIA operative Valerie Plame to journalists and then denying before a Washington, D.C., grand jury that he had done so. (See **Chapter 14.**) President Bush commuted Libby's sentence. Former *New York Times* Executive Editor Max Frankel said the case showed "the shameless ease with which top-secret information is bartered in Washington for political advantage."

Fairness Means Evenhandedness

Fairness implies impartiality—that the journalist has nothing personal to gain from a report, that there are no hidden benefits to the reporter or to the source from the story being presented or not being presented. Criticism of the press for unfairness results from debates over

- Close ties that may develop between reporters and the stories they cover—called *insider friendships*

- Reporters who accept personal or financial benefits from sources, sponsors or advertisers—called *conflicts of interest*

- Reporters who pay their sources for stories—called *checkbook journalism*

Insider Friendships

The TV reporter in Example 2 (on page 330) is Maria Shriver, wife of California governor Arnold Schwarzenegger. In 2005, halfway through her husband's first term as governor, Shriver had resigned from NBC's *Today* and was serving as an unpaid adviser to her husband. According to *The New York Times*, a producer at NBC's *Today* told St. Martin's Press, which published a book by Laurence Leamer about Schwarzenegger, that Shriver first would have to approve the author's appearance on the program.

In an e-mail, the producer asked the publisher to "ask Maria to call me so I can just make sure she is OK with us doing the Leamer book." Leamer contacted Shriver and, according to Leamer, Shriver said, "There must be something negative about me in the book." Shriver then asked him to send her the galleys, which he didn't do because he believed it would be unethical. *Today* did not schedule Leamer for the program.

"The blurring of politics and celebrity, governance and journalism, has made it difficult to discern exactly which agendas are at work here," wrote *New York Times* columnist David Carr. "You might expect Ms. Shriver, a long-time, well-respected member of the NBC family, to get a heads-up about Mr. Leamer's appearance, but giving the wife of a governor the right to approve a guest on its network, whether out of personal loyalty or the desire to maintain access, would be a remarkably bad move for a major news organization."

In the Shriver example, NBC let its insider contacts affect its news coverage. How can the public trust a news organization that allows an insider friendship to affect what the network reports? Insider friendships remove the very important element of a news organization's independence from the people and events it covers.

In April 2006, federal investigators charged Jared Paul Stern, a contributor to *The New York Post*'s celebrity column Page Six, with trying to extort money from wealthy businessman Ronald W. Burkle, who accused Stern of demanding money in exchange for keeping negative information about Burkle out of the *Post*'s Page Six gossip column.

Stern denied the charges, but *The New York Times* reported that private investigators recorded several conversations between Burkle and Stern, which included a discussion about "protection" against negative coverage in exchange for $100,000 plus a $10,000 monthly stipend. When the payment didn't arrive as scheduled, according to New York's *Daily News*, Stern also reportedly sent e-mails asking where the money was.

The criminal charges against Stern, if true, added an unusual twist to the issue of insider friendships because they involved a request for direct payment to Stern. "Taking money in exchange for treatment is . . . what is different here," reported *The New York Times*. "But given the murky world in which gossip is reported, the prospect of a cash for coverage deal is not an unimaginable one."

Conflicts of Interest

Reporters with conflicts of interest are divided between at least two loyalties, and the ethical question is, how will the stories the reporters write and the integrity of the organizations for which they work be affected?

One type of conflict of interest happens when reporters accept free meals and passes to entertainment events (freebies) and free trips (junkets). In one survey of newspapers, nearly half said they accepted free tickets to athletic events, and nearly two-thirds accepted free tickets to artistic events.

Walt Disney World, for example, invited journalists from all over the world to attend an anniversary celebration in Orlando, Florida, and more than 10,000 journalists and their guests accepted the invitation. Most of the press guests let Disney pay for the hotel, transportation and meals. *Variety* called the event "one of the biggest junkets in showbiz history," at an estimated cost of $8 million to Disney, the airlines, hotels and tourism agencies. In an editorial about the junket, *The New York Times* said, "Accepting junkets and boondoggles does not necessarily mean that a reporter is being bought—but it inescapably creates the appearance of being bought."

Accepting a free trip can create an appearance of conflict of interest—even if the reporters don't write favorably about the places they visit—but financial reporters are especially vulnerable to direct conflicts of interest. Financial reporters often have access to proprietary information about stocks and investments, and stories about these investments may cause fluctuation in specific stock prices—up and down—that offer a chance for the reporters to make a quick profit.

In 2005, former CBS MarketWatch columnist Thom Calandra agreed to pay more than $540,000 to settle federal regulators' charges that he used his investment newsletter in 2003 to promote small, penny stocks he owned. When the stocks rose as a result of his newsletter's recommendation, he then sold the stocks at a profit. In one transaction, Calandra wrote in his newsletter that a company called Pacific Minerals was "at the beginning of its meteoric rise,"

In April 2006 federal investigators charged *New York Post* contributor Jared Paul Stern with attempting to extort money from a wealthy businessman.

Walt Disney World invited more than 10,000 journalists and their guests to attend the theme park's 15th anniversary, and the journalists then reported on the park. This is an example of conflict of interest.

Media critics said CBS paid singer Michael Jackson for an interview on the program *60 Minutes* as part of a package deal for a 2004 entertainment special. CBS denied it paid for the interview.

People magazine paid $400,000 for exclusive use of photos that showed Angelina Jolie's pregnancy with boyfriend Brad Pitt, an example of checkbook journalism.

and then sold thousands of shares within a few days, according to *The New York Times*.

CBS MarketWatch said that company rules required that commentators who recommended investments, such as Calandra, disclose when they personally traded stocks they discussed in their columns. By 2005, Calandra, one of the original founders of CBS MarketWatch, had resigned as a commentator and was working as a research consultant for an investment company.

Checkbook Journalism

In 2006, *People* magazine paid actress Angelina Jolie $400,000 for the exclusive use of photos that confirmed she was pregnant with Brad Pitt's child. Jolie donated the fee to her favorite charity, but the incident caused alarm about the practice of movie stars charging the media to photograph them, a common practice in Europe. The issue of a news organization paying someone for an interview is called *checkbook journalism*.

In 2004, CBS paid singer Michael Jackson $1 million for an entertainment special and an interview on *60 Minutes* during a time when Jackson was under investigation for child molestation. CBS had contracted with Jackson for the special, but when prosecutors filed the charges against Jackson, CBS told Jackson the network would not broadcast the special unless Jackson addressed the charges against him. Jackson asked for the payment, which CBS paid.

CBS denied they paid for the interview, saying the payment was all part of the package deal for the special. "In essence they paid him . . . but they didn't pay him out of the *60 Minutes* budget; they paid him from the entertainment budget, and CBS just shifts around the money internally. That

way *60 Minutes* can say *60 Minutes* didn't pay for the interview," an associate of Jackson's told *The New York Times*.

Besides ethical questions about whether journalists, movie stars and even criminals should profit financially from manufactured publicity, there are other hazards in any type of checkbook journalism. One danger is that a paid interviewee will sensationalize the information to bring a higher price, so the interviewee's truthfulness cannot always be trusted. A second hazard is that such interviews often become the exclusive property of the highest bidder, shutting out smaller news organizations and independent journalists from the information. A third possibility is that the person who is paid by the news organization to comment could possibly carry a hidden agenda.

Privacy Involves Respect

Reporting on illnesses and on rape is the most visible example of a complex ethical dilemma of privacy: How does the press balance the goal of truthfulness and fact-finding with

Checkbook Journalism The practice of a news organization paying for an interview or a photograph.

the need for personal privacy? Is the private grief that such a report may cause worth the public good that can result from publishing the information?

Reporting an Illness

Because some people with AIDS are homosexual, announcing that a person is ill with AIDS can reflect on the person's private sexual behavior. One argument in favor of the press reporting the nature of the illness in these cases is that covering up the information means the public won't understand the widespread extent of the public health problem that AIDS represents.

"Covering up the truth, by doctors or journalists, stigmatizes other sufferers—the less widely the disease is acknowledged, the less easily they can be accepted. And it shields communities and industries from understanding the full, devastating effect of AIDS," argued *Newsweek* in a story called "AIDS and the Right to Know." The counterargument is that a person's illness and death are strictly private matters and that publishing the information is a violation of that person's privacy.

Roy Cohn became a public figure in the 1950s during the McCarthy hearings, as counsel for the Senate committee investigating communist activity. As a lawyer in the 1980s, he defended many organized crime figures, and he lived a high-profile existence in New York City. A week before Cohn died, columnists Jack Anderson and Dale Van Atta published a story saying that Cohn was being treated with azidothymidine (AZT), then used exclusively for AIDS patients.

Journalist William Safire criticized Anderson and Van Atta in *The New York Times*, saying, "Doctors with some sense of ethics and journalists

David Peterson, 1990, The Des Moines Register and Tribune Company. Reprinted with permission.

In 1990, *The Des Moines Register* published the name of rape victim Nancy Ziegenmeyer in a story about her rape, with Ziegenmeyer's cooperation. Publication of the victim's name sparked an ethical debate among news organizations about whether it is an invasion of privacy to use the victim's name in a rape story. While other adult crime victims' names routinely are used in stories, the names of rape victims commonly are not.

with some regard for a core of human privacy are shamed by [this] investigative excess." After Cohn's death, *Harper's* magazine published copies of the hospital records on which Van Atta had based his column, which showed that Cohn had been a victim of AIDS.

Entertainer Liberace also withheld information about his illness before he died in 1987. Liberace's illness first was revealed in the *Las Vegas Sun* about two weeks before he died. *Sun* publisher Brian Greenspun appeared on ABC's *Nightline* to defend publishing the information before the entertainer's death. Because only the *Sun* had access to the documentation, other members of the media who wrote about Liberace's illness attributed the information to the *Sun*. After Liberace died, the county coroner confirmed that Liberace suffered from a disease caused by AIDS.

A third example of a story about someone dying of AIDS represents one journalist's answer to the debate. *Honolulu Star-Bulletin* managing editor Bill Cox announced in a column published September 1, 1986, that he was going on disability leave because he had AIDS. "As a journalist," he wrote, "I have spent my career trying to shed light in dark corners. AIDS is surely one of our darkest corners. It can use some light." (For more information about privacy law and the media, see **Chapter 14**.)

Reporting on Rape

Privacy is an important issue in reporting on rape cases. Common newsroom practice forbids the naming of rape victims in stories. In 1989, editor Geneva Overholser of *The Des Moines Register* startled the press community when she wrote an editorial arguing that newspapers contribute to the public's misunderstanding of the crime by withholding not only the woman's name, but an explicit description of what happened.

In 1990, the *Register* published a five-part series about the rape of Nancy Ziegenmeyer, with Ziegenmeyer's full cooperation. Ziegenmeyer had contacted the *Register* after Overholser's column appeared, volunteering to tell her story. The Ziegenmeyer series has provoked wide-ranging debate among editors about this aspect of privacy. Is there more benefit to society by printing the victim's name, with the victim's permission, than by withholding it? Should the press explicitly describe sexual crimes, or is that merely sensationalism, preying on the public's salacious curiosity?

The Cohn, Liberace and Ziegenmeyer cases demonstrate how complex privacy issues in today's society have become. When is it in the public interest to divulge personal information about individuals? Who should decide?

Responsibility Brings Trust

The events journalists choose to report and the way they use the information they gather reflect on the profession's sense of public responsibility. Most reporters realize that they often change the character of an event by covering that event. The mere presence of the media magnifies the importance of what happens. (See **Impact/Culture**, "Virginia Tech Massacre: New-Media Culture Challenges Limits of Journalism Ethics," page 338.)

The media can be exploited by people in trouble or by people who covet the notoriety that media coverage brings. The media can exploit an event for its shock value to try to attract an audience, without adequately verifying the information in the story. The following examples demonstrate how some members of the media act—and the people they cover react—to aggressive tactics.

A Staged Accident

In 2006, a freelance photojournalist deliberately rammed into movie star Lindsay Lohan's Mercedes on a crowded street in Los Angeles. This is example 4 (on page 330). As soon as Lohan's car was hit, three other photographers showed up to take pictures of her reaction. Police arrested one photographer and charged him with assault.

Soon after the accident, Lohan joined with movie stars Cameron Diaz and Justin Timberlake, asking the Los Angeles police to open an investigation into what the stars describe as "a new breed of photojournalist willing to flout the law, drive recklessly and even slam into celebrities' cars."

Less than a year later, Los Angeles prosecutors charged Lohan with reckless driving, two counts each of driving under the influence, driving with a blood-alcohol level above .08 percent and being under the influence of cocaine. Police said they found cocaine on Lohan during two drunken-driving arrests in May and July 2007. Reporters published the arrest story, along with the mug shot released by the police department following Lohan's arrest.

The staged accident demonstrates the important responsibility that all members of the media share for what some of them do. The credibility of any news organization rests on the way the reporters get the story as much as on the story that's reported. Portraying inaccurate or staged information, even in just one story, ultimately causes readers and viewers to doubt the believability of all stories.

Sometimes reporters' rush to get a story or bad judgment causes serious mistakes to be aired or printed. During the 2004 presidential election campaign, two incidents proved that even large news organizations aren't immune to serious journalistic lapses.

Fabricated Documents

On September 8, 2004, CBS News Correspondent Dan Rather presented documents on the CBS program *60 Minutes* that purported to show there were gaps in President Bush's Vietnam-era Texas Air National Guard service. Almost immediately after the broadcast, questions arose about whether the documents CBS used were authentic, but for several days CBS and Rather stood by the report.

Splash News

When a freelance photographer rammed her car in Los Angeles to provoke a unfavorable reaction, Lindsay Lohan joined several other movie stars in asking for an investigation of aggressive and invasive media stalking. The photographer was arrested for the incident. Less than a year later, in a separate incident, Lohan was charged with reckless driving and driving under the influence.

The documents were supposed to have come from the files of Bush's squadron commander, but then the man who gave the files to CBS admitted that he lied about where the documents came from. A week later, Rather, who also anchored the *CBS Evening News* at the time, apologized during the evening newscast. "I want to say personally and directly I'm sorry," he said. "This was an error made in good faith." CBS appointed a fact-finding panel, which launched a three-month investigation into why Rather's *60 Minutes* producers did not substantiate the information before airing the story.

In January 2005, the panel issued its report, which found, among other things, that the program's primary producer, Mary Mapes, did not scrutinize the background of the person who had provided the documents and that the segment's producers did not report that four experts who looked at the documents could not guarantee their authenticity. CBS fired Mapes and asked three other producers who had been involved in the report to resign.

Rather, who said he previously had considered stepping down as *CBS Evening News* anchor, was replaced, but Rather stayed on as a correspondent. CBS then instituted

IMPACT
»Culture

Virginia Tech Massacre: New-Media Culture Challenges Limits of Journalism Ethics

by Joe Garofoli

The Virginia Tech shooting is the first major U.S. news story in which traditional media and new-media technologies became visibly interdependent. Yet how that combination of old and new enabled the world to see the final ramblings of mass murderer Cho Seung-Hui raises an uncomfortable question: When everybody can publish in the world of new media, what will the world see next?

As new-media expert Jeff Jarvis wrote on his *BuzzMachine.com* blog Thursday, "There is no control point anymore. When anyone and everyone—witnesses, criminals, victims, commentators, officials and journalists—can publish and broadcast as events happen, there is no longer any guarantee that news and society itself can be filtered, packaged, edited, sanitized, polished, secured."

NBC News anchor Brian Williams called the photos, videos and text Cho mailed directly to his network a "multimedia manifesto." The network released only heavily

The Virginia Tech shooting is the first major U.S. news story in which traditional media and online media became interdependent.

edited parts of Cho's submission, enough so it could convey "the mind-set of the troubled gunman," Williams said.

Now, some media analysts are wondering what the next multimedia manifesto will

new procedures that required independent review for investigative stories and appointed a new vice president for Standards and Practices, Linda Mason. "Standards are not an end in themselves," Mason told *The New York Times*. "Standards are a way we can achieve fairness and accuracy."

Phony Web Story

In October 2004, less than a month after the CBS incident, Fox News was forced to apologize to visitors to the Fox News Web site after Fox's Chief Political Correspondent Carl Cameron posted a story that quoted presidential candidate John Kerry saying, "Didn't my nails and cuticles look great? What a good debate!" after his October televised debate with President Bush. "Women should like me! I do manicures," the story also quoted Kerry as saying.

Fox quickly retracted the article, and Paul Schur, a network spokesman, said, "This was a stupid mistake and a lapse in judgment, and Carl regrets it." Schur said Cameron had been reprimanded, but Schur did not explain how such an irresponsible story managed to escape review before it appeared on the Fox site.

All news organizations must accept responsibility for a lack of editorial review and oversight of stories that should have been stopped before they reach the public. In the CBS case, producers hurried to get the story on the air before checking it thoroughly. At Fox News, an errant reporter called the credibility of the entire news organization into question, but the news organization itself ultimately is at fault for its lack of safeguards. Responsible news organizations encourage ethical behavior as well as constantly

contain. Will somebody upload a live hostage situation?

And given the "let-the-masses-decide" ethos of this new-media landscape, some want NBC to release everything Cho sent. . . .

The Virginia Tech story offered the most vivid example yet of how traditional news sources, like cable news networks, and new-media sources, like the social networking site Facebook, are jointly creating a mosaic of news coverage. Yet the Cho video showed how that marriage of technology could be outpacing ethical standards.

"It is future shock," said Micah Sifry, executive editor of the Personal Democracy Forum, a New York think-tank that explores the intersections of technology and politics.

"The technology has developed so fast that the culture hasn't caught up with all of it.

"On one hand, you have the advocates, who want NBC to release all of [Cho's manifesto]. On the other, you have people who are saying, 'Wait a minute.' This is a very challenging moment."

As Sifry wrote [April 19, 2007] on his blog, www.personaldemocracy.com, "The father in me doesn't want my kids finding this on the Web. . . . the openness advocate in me agrees that we don't make horrors go away by hiding them. I'm conflicted about this."

"Conflicted is the right word," said Dave Winer, a pioneering blogger and influential figure in new media. He would like to see NBC release all of Cho's material. "Yes, I realize that it's unfortunate right now that this guy gets to control the discussion. . . ."

But Winer and Sifry don't think the answer to these ethical dilemmas is to restrict the freedom of people to publish. "What works best is an open-networked system," Sifry said, "It's the difference between trusting a few people to make decisions for everyone and trusting many people. . . ."

Traditional outlets acknowledge that current technology enables offensive material to circulate, no matter what they do.

"In the end, it's going to get out there," said Jay Wallace, executive producer for news at Fox News Channel. "Even if every newspaper and cable news channel doesn't put it out there, somebody will."

"The lesson for this week is that the news is everywhere. The news is on Facebook," said Jennifer Sizemore, editor in chief of MSNBC.com. Like other news outlets, MSNBC turned to social networking sites like MySpace and Facebook to find students to interview about the Virginia Tech slayings.

"I don't view them as the competition," said Sizemore. "I see them as enlarging the conversation."

From "Virginia Tech Massacre: New-media Culture Challenges Limits of Journalism Ethics," by Joe Garofoli, *San Francisco Chronicle*, April 20, 2007. Reprinted by permission.

remind reporters about their special responsibility to the public and to their profession.

Five Philosophical Principles Govern Media Ethics

Scholars can prescribe only general guidelines for moral decisions because each situation presents its own special dilemmas. First it is important to understand the basic principles that underlie these philosophical discussions. In their book *Media Ethics*, Clifford G. Christians, Kim B. Rotzoll and Mark Fackler identify five major philosophical principles underlying today's ethical decisions: (1) Aristotle's golden mean, (2) Kant's categorical imperative, (3) Mill's principle of utility, (4) Rawls' veil of ignorance and (5) the Judeo-Christian view of persons as ends in themselves.

1. *Aristotle's golden mean.* "Moral virtue is appropriate location between two extremes." This is a philosophy of moderation and compromise, often called the *golden mean*. The journalistic concept of fairness reflects this idea.

2. *Kant's categorical imperative.* "Act on that maxim which you will to become a universal law." Eighteenth-century philosopher Immanuel Kant developed this idea, an extension of Aristotle's golden mean. Kant's test—that you make decisions based on principles that you want to be universally applied—is called the *categorical imperative*.

This means you would act by asking yourself the question, "What if everyone acted this way?"

3. *Mill's principle of utility.* "Seek the greatest happiness for the greatest number." In the 19th century, John Stuart Mill taught that the best decision is one with the biggest overall benefit for the most human beings.

4. *Rawls' veil of ignorance.* "Justice emerges when negotiating without social differentiations." John Rawls' 20th-century theory supports an egalitarian society that asks everyone to work from a sense of liberty and basic respect for everyone, regardless of social position.

5. *Judeo-Christian view of persons as ends in themselves.* "Love your neighbor as yourself." Under this long-standing ethic of religious heritage, people should care for one another—friends as well as enemies—equally and without favor. Trust in people and they will trust in you.

In American society, none of these five philosophies operates independently. Ethical choices in many journalistic situations are not exquisitely simple. What is predictable about journalistic ethics is their unpredictability. Therefore, journalists generally adopt a philosophy of "situational" ethics: Because each circumstance is different, individual journalists must decide the best action to take in each situation.

Should the press adopt Rawls' idea of social equality and cover each person equally, or should public officials receive more scrutiny than others because they maintain a public trust? Is it a loving act in the Judeo-Christian tradition to allow bereaved parents the private sorrow of their child's death by drowning, or is the journalist contributing to society's greater good by warning others about the dangers of leaving a child unattended? Questions like these leave the press in a continually bubbling cauldron of ethical quandaries.

Media's Ethical Decisions Carry Consequences

Ethical dilemmas might seem easier to solve with a rulebook nearby, and several professional media organizations have tried to codify ethical judgments to ensure the outcomes in difficult situations. Codes of ethics can be very general ("Truth is our ultimate goal"—Society of Professional Journalists); some are very specific ("We will no longer accept any complimentary tickets, dinners, junkets, gifts or favors of any kind"—*The San Bernardino* [California] *Sun*); and some are very personal ("I will try to tell people what they ought to know and avoid telling them what they want to hear, except when the two coincide, which isn't often"—former CBS commentator Andy Rooney).

Some ethical decisions carry legal consequences—for example, when a journalist reports embarrassing facts and invades someone's privacy. First Amendment protections shield the media from government enforcement of specific codes of conduct, except when ethical mistakes also are judged by the courts to be legal mistakes. In most cases, however, a reporter or a news organization that makes an ethical mistake will not face a lawsuit.

The consequences of bad ethical judgments usually involve damage to the newsmakers who are involved and to the individual journalist, damage to the reputation of the news organization where the journalist works and damage to the profession in general. (See **Impact/Ethics**, "Amid Cheating Allegations, Columbia Journalism Class Picks Up Pens," page 341.)

Professional Associations Proscribe Behavior

Professional codes of ethics set a leadership tone for a profession, an organization or an individual. Several groups have attempted to write rules governing how the media should operate.

Television stations that belonged to the National Association of Broadcasters (**NAB**), for example, once subscribed to a code of conduct the NAB developed. This code covered news reporting and entertainment programming. One provision of the NAB code said, "Violence, physical or psychological, may only be projected in responsibly handled contexts, not used exploitatively. Programs involving violence should present the consequences of it to its victims and perpetrators." Members displayed the NAB Seal of Approval before broadcasts to exhibit their compliance with the code.

In 1976, a decision by a U.S. federal judge in Los Angeles abolished the broadcast codes, claiming the provisions violated the First Amendment. Today, codes of ethics for both print and broadcast are voluntary, with no absolute penalties for people who violate the rules. These codes are meant as guidelines. Many media organizations, such as CBS News, maintain their own detailed standards and hire people to oversee ethical conduct. Other organizations use guidelines from professional groups as a basis to develop their own philosophies. Advertising and public relations organizations also have issued ethics codes.

NAB National Association of Broadcasters, the lobbying organization that represents broadcasters' interests.

IMPACT
»Ethics

Amid Cheating Allegations, Columbia Journalism Class Picks Up Pens

by Karen W. Arenson

As Columbia University continues to grapple with allegations of cheating on a final exam in a journalism ethics course, students have been assigned to write an essay on an issue that parallels the one faced by their own professors.

The topic: What should a newspaper's executive editor do after receiving "a tip from a credible source that one or more unspecified articles in recent editions of the newspaper contain fabricated material"?

The assignment was given on Friday, a day after a Web site, *RadarOnline.com*, posted an account, attributed to an unidentified source, that said the Columbia Graduate School of Journalism suspected some students of cheating on the exam, an open-book, take-home test that students could gain access to via computer any time during a 30-hour period. Both the exam and the course are graded as pass, fail or honors.

The test had to be completed in 90 minutes. According to a student who attended a class meeting on Friday, at least one student who had taken the exam reportedly offered to tell at least one other student who had not yet taken it what the essay questions were, which would give the second student extra time to prepare before the clock started ticking.

A student who was approached reportedly notified a teaching assistant, but did not identify the student who made the offer.

The more than 200 students in the required course, Critical Issues in Journalism, were notified by e-mail before Thanksgiving that they were required to attend the

At Columbia University in 2006, students in the journalism school were charged with cheating on an open-book, take-home test.

extra class meeting, where they heard briefly from teachers and school officials, and then offered their own views.

The meeting was not open to reporters, but students, professors and other participants discussed it afterward. The lead professor in the course was Samuel G. Freedman, who also contributes columns about education and religion to *The New York Times*.

Barbara Fasciani, a spokeswoman for the school, said the matter would be referred to the school's disciplinary committee, which would determine how to proceed.

"It is not our style to have a witch hunt," Ms. Fasciani said. "At the same time, the school has to see what it can do."

The essay, of up to 500 words, is due on Thursday.

Three widely used codes of ethics are the guidelines adopted by the Society of Professional Journalists, the Radio-Television News Directors Association and the Public Relations Society of America.

Society of Professional Journalists Outlines Conduct

This code lists specific canons for journalists. The code's major points follow.

SEEK TRUTH AND REPORT IT. Test the accuracy of information from all sources and exercise care to avoid inadvertent error. Deliberate distortion is never permissible.

- Identify sources whenever feasible. The public is entitled to as much information as possible on sources' reliability.

- Make certain that headlines, news teases and promotional material, photos, video, audio, graphics, sound bites and quotations do not misrepresent. They should not oversimplify or highlight incidents out of context.

- Never distort the content of news photos or video. Image enhancement for technical clarity is always permissible. Label montages and photo illustrations.

- Avoid misleading reenactments or staged news events.

- Never plagiarize.

- Avoid stereotyping by race, gender, age, religion, ethnicity, geography, sexual orientation, disability, physical appearance or social status.

- Distinguish between advocacy and news reporting. Analysis and commentary should be labeled and not misrepresent fact or context.

- Distinguish news from advertising and shun hybrids that blur the lines between the two.

- Recognize a special obligation to ensure that the public's business is conducted in the open and that government records are open to inspection.

MINIMIZE HARM. Show compassion for those who may be affected adversely by news coverage. Use special sensitivity when dealing with children and inexperienced sources or subjects.

- Be sensitive when seeking or using interviews or photographs of those affected by tragedy or grief.

- Recognize that gathering and reporting information may cause harm or discomfort. Pursuit of the news is not a license for arrogance.

- Show good taste. Avoid pandering to lurid curiosity.

- Balance a criminal suspect's fair trial rights with the public's right to be informed.

ACT INDEPENDENTLY. Avoid conflicts of interest, real or perceived.

- Remain free of associations and activities that may compromise integrity or damage credibility.

- Refuse gifts, favors, fees, free travel and special treatment, and shun secondary employment, political involvement, public office and service in community organizations if they compromise journalistic integrity.

BE ACCOUNTABLE. Clarify and explain news coverage and invite dialogue with the public over journalistic conduct.

- Encourage the public to voice grievances against the news media.

- Admit mistakes and correct them promptly.

- Expose unethical practices of journalists and the news media.

- Abide by the same high standards to which they hold others.

Radio-Television News Directors Association Code Covers Electronic News

The RTNDA Code of Ethics and Professional Conduct, last updated in September 2000, offers general principles for electronic news reporters ("Professional electronic journalists should recognize that their first obligation is to the public"), as well as specific guidelines ("Professional electronic journalists should not manipulate images or sounds in any way that is misleading"). Following is the RTNDA ethics code, reprinted in its entirety.

PREAMBLE

Professional electronic journalists should operate as trustees of the public, seek the truth, report it fairly and with integrity and independence, and stand accountable for their actions.

PUBLIC TRUST: Professional electronic journalists should recognize that their first obligation is to the public. Professional electronic journalists should:

- Understand that any commitment other than service to the public undermines trust and credibility.

- Recognize that service in the public interest creates an obligation to reflect the diversity of the community and guard against oversimplification of issues or events.

- Provide a full range of information to enable the public to make enlightened decisions.

- Fight to ensure that the public's business is conducted in public.

TRUTH: Professional electronic journalists should pursue truth aggressively and present the news accurately, in context, and as completely as possible.

Professional electronic journalists should:

- Continuously seek the truth.
- Resist distortions that obscure the importance of events.
- Clearly disclose the origin of information and label all material provided by outsiders.

Professional electronic journalists should not:

- Report anything known to be false.
- Manipulate images or sounds in any way that is misleading.
- Plagiarize.
- Present images or sounds that are reenacted without informing the public.

FAIRNESS: Professional electronic journalists should present the news fairly and impartially, placing primary value on significance and relevance.

Professional electronic journalists should:

- Treat all subjects of news coverage with respect and dignity, showing particular compassion to victims of crime or tragedy.
- Exercise special care when children are involved in a story and give children greater privacy protection than adults.
- Seek to understand the diversity of their community and inform the public without bias or stereotype.
- Present a diversity of expressions, opinions, and ideas in context.
- Present analytical reporting based on professional perspective, not personal bias.
- Respect the right to a fair trial.

INTEGRITY: Professional electronic journalists should present the news with integrity and decency, avoiding real or perceived conflicts of interest, and respect the dignity and intelligence of the audience as well as the subjects of news.

Professional electronic journalists should:

- Identify sources whenever possible. Confidential sources should be used only when it is clearly in the public interest to gather or convey important information or when a person providing information might be harmed. Journalists should keep all commitments to protect a confidential source.
- Clearly label opinion and commentary.
- Guard against extended coverage of events or individuals that fails to significantly advance a story, place the event in context, or add to the public knowledge.
- Refrain from contacting participants in violent situations while the situation is in progress.
- Use technological tools with skill and thoughtfulness, avoiding techniques that skew facts, distort reality, or sensationalize events.
- Use surreptitious newsgathering techniques, including hidden cameras or microphones, only if there is no other way to obtain stories of significant public importance and only if the technique is explained to the audience.
- Disseminate the private transmissions of other news organizations only with permission.

Professional electronic journalists should not:

- Pay news sources who have a vested interest in a story.
- Accept gifts, favors, or compensation from those who might seek to influence coverage.
- Engage in activities that may compromise their integrity or independence.

INDEPENDENCE: Professional electronic journalists should defend the independence of all journalists from those seeking influence or control over news content.

Professional electronic journalists should:

- Gather and report news without fear or favor, and vigorously resist undue influence from any outside forces, including advertisers, sources, story subjects, powerful individuals, and special interest groups.
- Resist those who would seek to buy or politically influence news content or who would seek to intimidate those who gather and disseminate the news.
- Determine news content solely through editorial judgment and not as the result of outside influence.
- Resist any self-interest or peer pressure that might erode journalistic duty and service to the public.
- Recognize that sponsorship of the news will not be used in any way to determine, restrict, or manipulate content.
- Refuse to allow the interests of ownership or management to influence news judgment and content inappropriately.
- Defend the rights of the free press for all journalists, recognizing that any professional or government licensing of journalists is a violation of that freedom.

ACCOUNTABILITY: Professional electronic journalists should recognize that they are accountable for their actions to the public, the profession, and themselves.

Professional electronic journalists should:

- Actively encourage adherence to these standards by all journalists and their employers.
- Respond to public concerns. Investigate complaints and correct errors promptly and with as much prominence as the original report.
- Explain journalistic processes to the public, especially when practices spark questions or controversy.
- Recognize that professional electronic journalists are duty-bound to conduct themselves ethically.
- Refrain from ordering or encouraging courses of action that would force employees to commit an unethical act.
- Carefully listen to employees who raise ethical objections and create environments in which such objections and discussions are encouraged.
- Seek support for and provide opportunities to train employees in ethical decision-making.

Public Relations Society of America Sets Standards

The Code of Professional Standards, first adopted in 1950 by the Public Relations Society of America, has been revised several times since then. Here are some excerpts:

- A member shall deal fairly with clients or employers, past, present, or potential, with fellow practitioners and with the general public.

- A member shall adhere to truth and accuracy and to generally accepted standards of good taste.

- A member shall not intentionally communicate false or misleading information, and is obligated to use care to avoid communication of false or misleading information.

- A member shall be prepared to identify publicly the name of the client or employer on whose behalf any public communication is made.

- A member shall not guarantee the achievement of specified results beyond the member's direct control.

Media Respond to Criticism

Prescriptive codes of ethics are helpful in describing what journalists should do, and informal guidelines can supplement professional codes. Many journalists use good judgment, but what happens when they don't? People with serious complaints against broadcasters sometimes appeal to the Federal Communications Commission, but what about complaints that must be handled more quickly? The press has offered three solutions: news councils, readers' representatives and correction boxes.

News Councils

News councils originated in Great Britain. They are composed of people who formerly worked or currently work in the news business, as well as some laypeople. The council reviews complaints from the public, and when the members determine that a mistake has been made, the council reports its findings to the offending news organization.

In 1973, the Twentieth-Century Fund established a National News Council in the United States, which eventually was funded through contributions from various news organizations. The council was composed of 18 members from the press and the public. The council was disbanded in 1984, largely because some major news organizations stopped giving money to support the idea, but also because several news managers opposed the council, arguing that the profession should police itself.

Today, only two news councils exist in the United States, the Minnesota News Council and the Honolulu Community Media Council. The Minnesota council is the older. Since 1970, the council's 24 members, half of them journalists and half of them public members such as lawyers and teachers, have reviewed complaints about the state's media. Half of the complaints have been ruled in favor of the journalists. The council has no enforcement power, only the power of public scrutiny. Media ethics scholar John Hulteng writes:

> It would seem that—as with the [ethics] codes—the great impact of the press councils is likely to be on the responsible editors, publishers and broadcasters who for the most part were already attempting to behave ethically. . . . An additional value of the councils may be the mutual understanding that grows out of the exchange across the council table between the members of the public and the managers of the media. These values should not be dismissed as insignificant, of course. But neither should too much be expected of them.

Readers' Representatives

The *readers' representative* (also called an ombudsperson or public reporter) is a go-between at a newspaper who responds to complaints from the public and regularly publishes answers to criticism in the newspaper.

About two dozen newspapers throughout the country, including *The Washington Post*, *The Kansas City Star* and the Louisville *Courier-Journal*, have tried the idea, but most newspapers still funnel complaints directly to the editor.

Correction Boxes

The *correction box* is a device that often is handled by a readers' representative but also has been adopted by many papers without a readers' representative. The box is published in the same place, usually a prominent one, in the newspaper every day.

As a permanent feature of the newspaper, the correction box leads readers to notice when the newspaper retracts or modifies a statement. It is used to counter criticism that corrections sometimes receive less attention from readers than the original stories.

Professional Ethics Preserve Media Credibility

News councils, readers' representatives and correction boxes help newspapers handle criticism and avert possible legal problems that some stories foster, but these solutions address only a small percentage of issues and only for print journalism. In newsrooms every day, reporters face the same ethical decisions all people face in their daily lives—whether to be honest, how to be fair, how to be sensitive and how to be responsible.

The difference is that, unlike personal ethical dilemmas that other people can debate privately, reporters and editors publish and broadcast the results of their ethical judgments, and those judgments become public knowledge—in newspapers, magazines and books and on radio, television and the Internet. So potentially, the media's ethical decisions can broadly affect society.

A profession that accepts ethical behavior as a standard helps guarantee a future for that profession. The major commodity the press in America has to offer is information,

and when the presentation of that information is weakened by untruth, bias, intrusiveness or irresponsibility, the press gains few advocates and acquires more enemies. Writes John Hulteng:

> The primary objective of the press and those who work with it is to bring readers, listeners and viewers as honest, accurate and complete an account of the day's events as possible. . . . The need to be informed is so great that the Constitution provides the press with a First Amendment standing that is unique among business enterprises. But as with most grants of power, there is an accompanying responsibility, not constitutionally mandated but nonetheless well understood: that the power of the press must be used responsibly and compassionately.

Review, Analyze, Investigate
REVIEWING CHAPTER 15

Ethics Define Responsibilities

✓ The word *ethics* derives from the Greek word *ethos*, which means the guiding spirit or traditions that govern a culture.

✓ When journalists make the wrong ethical choices, the consequences are very public.

✓ Journalists' ethical dilemmas can be discussed using four categories: truthfulness, fairness, privacy and responsibility.

Truthfulness Affects Credibility

✓ Truthfulness means more than telling the truth to get a story. Truthfulness also means not misrepresenting the people or the situations in the story for readers or viewers.

✓ Syndicated columnist Armstrong Williams received $250,000 from a public relations firm to promote President Bush's No Child Left Behind Act to African Americans. In 2005, after *USA Today* revealed the arrangement, Williams attributed the lapse to the fact that he was not trained as a journalist.

✓ Truthfulness means that government agencies should not knowingly provide disinformation to the press.

✓ The term disinformation was the issue at the 2007 trial of presidential advisor I. Lewis Libby.

✓ Truthfulness means that published photographs should be accurate portrayals of events and should not intentionally distort reality.

✓ In 2006, author James Frey admitted he had fabricated many incidents in his memoir *A Million Little Pieces*.

✓ An example of a journalistic misrepresentation is Jayson Blair, a reporter for *The New York Times*, who admitted in May 2003 that he had fabricated comments, concocted scenes, stolen material from other newspapers and news services and selected details from photos to create an impression he had been in certain places and interviewed people when he hadn't.

Fairness Means Evenhandedness

✓ Fairness implies impartiality—that the journalist has nothing personal to gain from a report and that there are no hidden benefits to the reporter or to the source from the story being presented.

✓ Financial reporters are especially vulnerable to ethical lapses because they often have access to proprietary information that offers a chance to make a quick profit.

✓ Criticism of the press for unfairness results from debates over insider friendships, conflicts of interest and checkbook journalism.

✓ In the example involving Maria Shriver and Governor Arnold Schwarzenegger, NBC let its insider contacts affect its news coverage, which is called insider friendships.

Privacy Involves Respect

✓ Two important invasion-of-privacy issues are the publication of names of AIDS victims and the publication of the names of rape victims.

✓ Reporters must decide whether the public interest will be served.

✓ Media coverage of the Virginia Tech shooting demonstrated the difficulty of controlling the release of troubling images in an era where new-media technologies make control impossible.

Responsibility Brings Trust

✓ Responsibility means that reporters and editors must be careful about the way they use the information they gather.

✓ During the 2004 presidential campaign, CBS's *60 Minutes'* undocumented report of President Bush's Air National Guard service and Fox News' phony report about presidential candidate Senator John Kerry are two examples of news organizations that forgot their responsibilities to the public.

✓ Staged events, such as the car that rammed into Lindsay Lohan, offer especially perilous ethical situations.

Five Philosophical Principles Govern Media Ethics

✓ Five philosophical principles underlying the practical application of ethical decisions are (1) Aristotle's golden mean, (2) Immanuel Kant's categorical imperative, (3) John Stuart Mill's principle of utility, (4) John Rawls' veil of ignorance and (5) the Judeo-Christian view of persons as ends in themselves.

✓ Journalists adopt a philosophy of "situational ethics."

Media's Ethical Decisions Carry Consequences

✓ Some ethical decisions carry legal consequences, such as when a journalist reports embarrassing facts and invades someone's privacy.

✓ In most cases, a reporter or a news organization that makes an ethical mistake will not face a lawsuit.

Professional Associations Proscribe Behavior

✓ Several media professions have adopted ethics codes to guide their conduct.

✓ Three of these ethics codes are the guidelines adopted by the Society of Professional Journalists, the Radio-Television News Directors Association and the Public Relations Society of America.

Media Respond to Criticism

✓ The three responses of the U.S. press to criticism have been to create news councils, to employ readers' representatives and to publish correction boxes.

✓ The National Press Council, created to hear consumer complaints about the press, was created in 1973 but disbanded in 1984. Today only two news councils still exist in the United States—the Minnesota News Council and the Honolulu Community Media Council.

Professional Ethics Preserve Media Credibility

✓ The media's ethical decisions can broadly affect society.

✓ The major commodity the American press has to offer is credibility, and when the presentation of that information is weakened by untruth, bias, intrusiveness or irresponsibility, the press gains few advocates and acquires more enemies.

KEY TERMS

These terms are defined in the margins throughout this chapter and appear in alphabetical order with definitions in the Glossary, which begins on page 372.

Checkbook Journalism 335

Disinformation 332

Ethics 330

NAB 340

CRITICAL QUESTIONS

1. When you read about high-profile media ethics cases like the ones in this chapter, do you ever think about the possibility that what you're reading, hearing or seeing in the mass media may not be true, or at least not what you understand it to be? How does this affect the way you obtain or use information?

2. How does "checkbook journalism" affect the quality of reporting?

3. Pick any of the ethical situations specified in this chapter and describe how each of the following philosophical principles would define your decision.

   a. Aristotle's golden mean

   b. Kant's categorical imperative

   c. Mill's principle of utility

   d. Rawls' veil of ignorance

4. What is your opinion about the question in the Ziegenmeyer case of releasing the name of a victim of rape with the victim's consent? How would you balance the protection of victims with the public's interest in the non-anonymous comments of the victim? Should rape victims be more deserving of anonymity than victims of other crimes? Explain.

5. What effect do you believe ethics codes, such as those described in this chapter, have on the professionals for whom they have been adopted?

WORKING THE WEB

This list includes both sites mentioned in the chapter and others to give you greater insight into media ethics.

Columbia Journalism Review (CJR)

http://www.cjr.org

The mission of this publication from Columbia University Graduate School of Journalism is "to encourage and stimulate excellence in journalism in the service of a free society." The Web site's search capabilities allow users to access all past posts from *CJRDaily.org* and Campaign Desk (political journalism coverage), as well as 17 years of back issues (http://backissues.cjrarchives.org). Its Resources include "Who Owns What," a guide to what the major media companies own; "Language Corner," a guide to writing in English; and CJR study guides for journalism students. The site promises fresh media analysis and criticism every day as well as specials and interactive features about the performance and problems of the press.

EthicNet, European Ethics Codes

http://ethicnet.uta.fi/

This databank holds links to English translations of journalism codes of ethics from most European countries (maintained by the Department of Journalism and Mass Communication, University of Tampere, Finland). There are also links to press councils' Web sites, Ethics on the World Wide Web from California State University at Fullerton, and the Asian Journalism Network (http://ethicnet.uta.fi/links).

Fairness & Accuracy in Reporting (FAIR)

http://www.fair.org/index.php

This national media watch group offers "well-documented criticism of media bias and censorship." An anticensorship organization, FAIR is a progressive group that believes structural reform is needed to promote strong nonprofit sources of information. FAIR's critique of the current state of the media is explained in its overview, "What's Wrong with the News?" Viewers can browse archived articles on issues from Abortion to Youth.

Freedom Forum

http://www.freedomforum.org

This nonpartisan foundation is dedicated to "free press, free speech and free spirit for all people." The Freedom Forum is the main funder of the Newseum, an interactive museum of news in Washington, D.C. (http://www.newseum.org); the First Amendment Center, which features current news and commentary as well as a First Amendment glossary and lesson plans (http://www.firstamendmentcenter.org); and the Diversity Institute, based at the John Seigenthaler Center at Vanderbilt University in Nashville, Tennessee, dedicated to developing and retaining a diverse workforce in U.S. newsrooms (http://freedomforumdiversity.org).

Indiana University Index of Journalism Ethics Cases

http://journalism.indiana.edu/resources/ethics/

This set of cases was created to help teachers, researchers, professional journalists and consumers of news explore ethical issues of journalism. The issues include sensitive news topics, covering politics, invading privacy and being first.

Minnesota News Council

http://news-council.org

Based on the British Press Council (now the Press Complaints Commission), the News Council is a group half composed of journalists and half of laypeople that hears complaints against news organizations. The Web site contains past articles from the Council's *Newsworthy* magazine, a monthly electronic newsletter—*Newsworthy Online*—and a long list of links to various ethics resources, including other news councils, ethics codes, media law and alternative dispute resolution resources, and sites about media history, media literacy and media consolidation.

Poynter Online

http://www.poynter.org

This Web site of the St. Petersburg, Florida, center for journalists, future journalists and journalism teachers features news and tips for students about reporting and writing, ethics and diversity, journalism education and more. The training section includes information on seminars and webinars, career coaching and Poynter publications. Users can connect with an online community of groups based on various journalism topics.

Public Relations Society of America (PRSA)

http://www.prsa.org

This organization for public relations professionals has over 100 chapters nationwide. The Web site features sections on advocacy, conferences, diversity, resources and professional development, and includes the PRSA Member Code of Ethics and other ethics resources. The Public Relations Student Society of America (http://www.prssa.org) offers news and events, conferences, scholarships, career information and an online community.

Radio-Television News Directors Association and Foundation (RTNDA and RTNDF)

http://www.rtnda.org

RTNDA is a professional organization that serves the electronic news profession. Its membership consists of more than 3,000 news directors, associates, educators and students. The association's educational arm, RTNDF, was created to help members uphold ethical journalism standards in the newsroom. Ethics information—including the association's Code of Ethics and Professional Conduct, details on the Journalism Ethics Project, and coverage guidelines—is available in the Web site's Best Practices section.

Society of Professional Journalists (SPJ)

http://www.spj.org

The nation's most broad-based journalism organization, SPJ is dedicated to "encouraging the free practice of journalism and stimulating high standards of ethical behavior." Features include freedom of information; ethics (including the SPJ Code of Ethics); a diversity toolbox, SPJ blogs and discussion boards and access to daily Press Notes and other publications including the current issue of *Quill*.

16

Global Media: Discovering New Markets

© KERIM OKTEN/epa/CORBIS

Fans and news photographers mob Los Angeles Lakers star Kobe Bryant at the men's basketball final of the Beijing Olympics in August 2008. Today's market for American mass media celebrities is global.

What's Ahead?

In the United States, many students

assume that mass media in most countries throughout the world operate like the U.S. media, but media industries in different countries are as varied as the countries they serve. Can you identify the countries in the following media situations?

1. People in this country have access to more wireless Internet *hot spots* than anywhere else in the world. (A hot spot is a public area like a restaurant or hotel where a wireless Internet router allows people with laptops and hand-held Internet devices to use the Internet without a wired connection.)

2. In this country, a weekly TV game show features people eating overly spicy foods. The champion is dubbed Super Spiciness King.

3. In this nation, the president of the country decided in 2007 not to renew the broadcast license for the nation's oldest broadcast station, a persistent critic of his administration. The station was forced to go off the air.

4. This country's TV License Police can knock on the door of people's homes, fine people approximately $250 and threaten them with jail if they don't pay the annual TV license fee.

Television owners in Britain pay an annual license fee that supports the British Broadcasting Corporation. The BBC has expanded its audience in the United States with its popular program BBC America daily newscast. (left to right) Garth Ancier, president of BBC Worldwide America; Rome Hartman, BBC News executive producer; Matt Frei, news anchor.

Hot Spot A public area like a restaurant or hotel where people with laptops and hand-held Internet devices can connect to the Internet without a wire.

BBC British Broadcasting Corporation, the government-funded British broadcast network.

World Media Systems Vary

The country in the world with the largest number of wireless locations is the United States, according to JiWire, a leading hot spot directory. (See **Illustration 16.1**.) In the U.S., the city with the most wireless locations (hot spots) is New York City with 1,077, more than twice the number that is available in Los Angeles (487).

The TV game show with the spicy cast (example 2) is very popular in Japan, where *TV Champion* is one of several shows in which contestants vie for modest prizes and national attention by showing *gaman*, or endurance.

The station that was forced off the air is Venezuela's RCTV, shut down by President Hugo Chavez in May 2007. To replace the station, entrepreneurs that are friendly to the president have launched government-sponsored stations. "Media vehicles should not be engaged in politics," said one of the president's supporters, who launched a station friendly to the president called TeleCaribe. (See **Impact/People**, "Venezuelan President Hugo Chavez's Move Against Critic Highlights Shift in Media Support," page 362.)

The British are responsible for paying a yearly TV license fee (example 4). The fee is due at the post office each year, so the collectors who fine people who haven't paid the fee are actually members of the post office. The government collects more than $2 billion a year from the fees, which allows the British Broadcasting Corporation (**BBC**) to operate two TV stations without advertising.

These examples help demonstrate the complexity of defining today's international media marketplace, which clearly is a marketplace in rapid transition. This chapter examines various aspects of global media, including political theories and the media; world media systems; news and information flow; and global media markets.

Five Political Theories Help Describe How World Media Operate

No institution as sizable and influential as the mass media can escape involvement with government and politics. The media are not only channels for the transmission of political information and debate but also significant players with a direct stake in government's regulatory and economic policies, as well as government's attitude toward free speech and dissent.

Remember that *the way a country's political system is organized affects the way the media within that country operate.* Media systems can be divided broadly into those systems that allow dissent and those that do not.

IMPACT
» Audience

Illustration 16.1

Top 10 Countries with Free and Pay Wireless Locations

There are many more free and wireless locations (hot spots) in the United States than in China or Russia. The United States, which is the country ranked first, with the most wireless Internet hot spots, has more than ten times as many wireless locations as Italy, which is ranked tenth.

Source: JiWire.com, January 5, 2009.

1	United States, 66,729 wireless locations	6	South Korea, 12,818
2	United Kingdom, 27,696	7	Japan, 11,327
3	France, 23,785	8	Russian Federation, 10,614
4	Germany, 14,559	9	Switzerland, 5,355
5	China, 13,712	10	Italy, 4,806

To categorize the political organization of media systems, scholars often begin with the 1956 book *Four Theories of the Press*, by Fred S. Siebert, Theodore Peterson and Wilbur Schramm. These four theories, which originally were used to describe the political systems under which media operated in different countries, were (1) the Soviet theory, (2) the authoritarian theory, (3) the libertarian theory and (4) the social responsibility theory. Scholars recently added a fifth description, the more modern (5) developmental theory, to update the original categories used to help describe the world's mass media systems.

The Soviet Theory

Historically in the Soviet Union (which dissolved in 1991 into several independent nations and states), the government owned and operated the mass media. All media employees were government employees, expected to serve the government's interests.

Top media executives also served as leaders in the Communist Party. Even when the press controls loosened in the 1980s, the mass media were part of the government's policy. Government control came *before* the media published or broadcast; people who controlled the media could exercise

prior restraint. They could review copy and look at programs before they appeared.

This description of the Soviet press system was conceived before the events of the 1990s challenged the basic assumptions of Soviet government. Many Eastern bloc countries, such as Romania, Slovakia and the Czech Republic, which once operated under Soviet influence, based their media systems on the Communist model. Today, the media systems in these countries are in transition.

The Authoritarian Theory

Media that operate under the authoritarian theory can be either publicly or privately owned. This concept of the press developed in Europe after Gutenberg. Until the 1850s, presses in Europe were privately owned, and the aristocracy (which governed the countries) wanted some sort of control over what was printed about them. The aristocracy had the financial and political power necessary to make the rules about what would be printed.

The first idea was to license everyone who owned a printing press so the license could be revoked if someone published something unfavorable about the government. The British crown licensed the first colonial newspapers

A variety of magazines await readers at a Vietnam newsstand in Ho Chi Minh City on June 5, 2008. The political theory that best describes the way the media in Vietnam operate is the most recent, the developmental theory.

in America. Licensing wasn't very successful in the United States, however, because many people who owned presses didn't apply for licenses.

The next authoritarian attempt to control the press was to review material after it was published. A printer who was discovered publishing material that strongly challenged the government could be heavily fined or even put to death. Today, many governments still maintain this type of rigid control over the media. Most monarchies, for example, operate in an authoritarian tradition, which tolerates very little dissent. Media systems that serve at the government's pleasure and with the government's approval are common.

The Libertarian Theory

The concept of a libertarian press evolved from the idea that people who are given all the information on an issue will be able to discern what is true and what is false and will make good choices. This is an idea embraced by the writers of the U.S. Constitution and by other democratic governments.

This theory assumes, of course, that the media's main goal are to convey the truth and that the media will not cave in to outside pressures, such as from advertisers or corporate owners. This theory also assumes that people with opposing viewpoints will be heard—that the media will present all points of view, in what is commonly called the free marketplace of ideas.

The First Amendment to the U.S. Constitution concisely advocates the idea of freedom of the press. Theoretically, America today operates under the libertarian theory, although this ideal has been challenged often by changes in the media industries since the Constitution was adopted.

The Social Responsibility Theory

This theory accepts the concept of a libertarian press but prescribes what the media should do. Someone who believes in the social responsibility theory believes that members of the press will do their jobs well only if periodically reminded about their duties. The theory grew out of the 1947 Hutchins Commission Report on the Free and Responsible Press. The commission listed five goals for the press, including the need for truthful and complete reporting of all sides of an issue.

The commission concluded that the American press' privileged position in the Constitution means that the press must always work to be responsible to society.

If the media fail to meet their responsibilities to society, the social responsibility theory holds that the government should encourage the media to comply. In this way, the libertarian and the social responsibility theories differ. The libertarian theory assumes the media will work well without government interference; the social responsibility theory advocates government oversight for media that don't act in society's best interest.

The Developmental Theory

A fifth description for media systems that has been added to describe today's mass media is the Developmental or Third World theory. Under this system, named for the developing

"I just feel fortunate to live in a world with so much disinformation at my fingertips."

nations where it is most often found, the media *can* be privately owned, but usually are owned by the government.

The media are used to promote the country's social and economic goals and to direct a sense of national purpose. For example, a developmental media system might be used to promote birth control or to encourage children to attend school. The media become an outlet for some types of government propaganda, then, but in the name of economic and social progress for the country.

Although the theory that best describes the American media is the libertarian theory, throughout their history the American media have struggled with both authoritarian and social responsibility debates: Should the press be free to print secret government documents, for example? What responsibility do the networks have to provide worthwhile programming to their audiences? The media, the government and the public continually modify and adjust their interpretations of just how the media should operate.

It has been more than five decades since scholars began using the four theories of the press to define the world's media systems. With today's transitional period in global history, even the recent addition of the developmental theory still leaves many media systems beyond convenient categorization.

Media systems vary throughout the world. The print media form the basis for press development in North America, Australia, Western Europe and Eastern Europe, where two thirds of the world's newspapers are published. Many developing countries matured after broadcast media were introduced in the 1920s, and newsprint in these countries often is scarce or government-controlled, making radio their dominant communications medium. Radio receivers are inexpensive, and many people can share one radio.

Television, which relies on expensive equipment, is widely used in prosperous nations and in developing countries' urban areas. Yet many countries still have only one television service, usually run by the government. In many developing countries all broadcasting—television and radio—is owned and controlled by the government.

What follows is a description of today's media systems by geographic region: Western Europe and Canada; Eastern Europe; the Middle East and North Africa; Africa; Asia and the Pacific; and Latin America and the Caribbean.

Western Europe and Canada Are Similar to the United States

Western European and Canadian media prosper under guarantees of freedom of expression similar to the First Amendment, but each nation has modified the idea to

Kaveh Kazemi/Getty Images

Women browse through children's books at the Tehran International Book Fair in 2008. In Iran, female authors dominate the best-seller list.

reflect differing values. For example, in Great Britain the media are prohibited from commenting on a trial until the trial is finished, and in 2003, Britain banned all tobacco advertising in newspapers, on billboards and on the Internet.

France and Greece, unlike the United States, give more libel protection to public figures than to private citizens. Scandinavian journalists enjoy the widest press freedoms of all of Western Europe, including almost unlimited access to public documents. Of the Western nations, Canada is the most recent country to issue an official decree supporting the philosophy of press freedom. In 1982, Canada adopted the Canadian Charter of Rights and Freedoms. Before 1982, Canada did not have its own constitution, and instead operated under the 1867 British North America Act, sharing the British free press philosophy.

Print Media

Johannes Gutenberg's invention of movable type rooted the print media in Western Europe. Today, Western European and Canadian media companies produce many fine newspapers. *The Globe and Mail* of Toronto, *The Times* of London, *Frankfurter Allgemeine* of Germany, *Le Monde* of France and Milan's *Corriere della Sera* enjoy healthy circulations.

Whereas Canadian journalists have adopted the U.S. values of fairness and balance as a journalistic ethic, Western European newspapers tend to be much more partisan than the U.S. or Canadian press, and newspapers (and journalists) are expected to reflect strong points of view.

© Shirley Biagi 2007. Used with permission.

In Western Europe—where the print media, including newspapers, are more popular than broadcast—people watch half as much television as people in the United States.

Audio and Video Media

As in the United States, the print media in Western Europe are losing audiences to broadcast and cable. Government originally controlled most of Western Europe's broadcast stations. A board of governors, appointed by the queen, supervises the British Broadcasting Corporation, for example.

To finance the government-run broadcast media, countries tax the sale of radios and TVs or charge users an annual fee. Broadcasting in Western Europe is slowly evolving to private ownership and commercial sponsorship.

Western Europeans watch about half as much television as people in the United States—an average of three hours a day per household in Europe, compared with seven hours a day per household in the United States. One reason for the difference in viewing time may be that many Western European TV stations don't go on the air until late afternoon. In the majority of countries, commercials are shown back to back at the beginning or the end of a program.

Europe gets much of its programming from the United States. Of the 125,000 hours of TV broadcast in Western Europe each year, less than half of the programming hours are produced in Europe. Most of the programming comes from the United States, with a few shows imported from Australia and Japan. U.S. imports are attractive because buying U.S. programs is cheaper than producing programming themselves.

The European Union (EU) constitutes a single, unified European market. The policy adopted by the EU is "Television Without Frontiers," which promotes an open marketplace for television programs among countries in the EU and between EU countries and the United States.

Some members of the EU (especially France) have proposed quotas to limit imported TV programs, charging that the U.S. imports are an example of "cultural imperialism." Countries that favor quotas fear that the importation of U.S. programs imposes a concentration of U.S. values on their viewers.

The United States opposes such quotas, of course, because Western European commercial broadcasting offers a seemingly insatiable market for recycled U.S. programs.

Eastern Europe Is Transforming

The democratization of Eastern Europe is transforming the media in these countries at an unprecedented pace. Some examples:

- In the six months after the Berlin Wall opened in 1990, circulation of East Germany's national newspapers *Neues Deutschland* and *Junge Welt* dropped 55 percent as the East German population, hungry for news from the West, embraced the flashy West German mass circulation daily *Bild*.

- In Poland, Eastern Europe's first private television station, Echo, went on the air in February 1990, with a total cash investment of $15,000. The station broadcast programs from the windowless janitor's room of a student dormitory.

- In 2003, U.S. venture capitalist Esther Dyson announced a new technology, developed with a Russian company, that allows anyone with an Internet connection and a printer to receive exact images of participating newspapers from throughout the world. NewspaperDirect, based in New York, will sell the service throughout the world.

Everette E. Dennis, then executive director of the Gannett Center for Media Studies, and Jon Vanden Heuvel described the Eastern European challenges in a report issued after a Gannett-sponsored fact-finding trip: "Mass communication in the several countries of the region was reinventing itself. While grassroots newspapers and magazines struggled for survival, new press laws were being debated and enacted; elements of a market economy were coming into view; the media system itself and its role in the state and society were being redefined, as was the very nature of journalism and the job description of the journalist, who was no longer a propagandist for the state." Eastern Europe is in transition, defining a new balance between the desire for free expression and the indigenous remnants of a government-controlled system.

In many of these countries, the media played a central role in upsetting the established power structure. Often one of the first targets of the revolutionary movements was a nation's broadcast facilities. For example, in Romania in 1989, opposition leaders of the National Salvation Committee and sympathetic employees barricaded themselves in a Bucharest TV station, rallying the audience to action. "Romania was governed from a hectic studio littered with empty bottles, cracked coffee mugs and half-eaten sandwiches, and run by people who had not slept in days," the Associated Press reported.

Audio and Video Media

Television in the Eastern bloc countries developed under Communist direction because the Communist governments were in power before TV use was widespread. Radio broadcasting also was tightly controlled, although foreign broadcasts directed across Eastern European borders, such as Voice of America and Radio Free Europe, usually evaded jamming attempts by Radio Moscow.

Print Media

Print media were strictly controlled under Communism, with high-ranking party officials forming the core of media management. Because paper supplies were limited, newspapers rarely exceeded 12 pages. Revolutionary leader Vladimir Lenin, who said a newspaper should be a "collective propagandist," a "collective agitator" and a "collective organizer," founded *Pravda*, the Soviet Union's oldest newspaper, in 1912. The Eastern European nations developed their press policies following the Soviet model.

In the late 1980s, Soviet President Mikhail Gorbachev relaxed media controls as part of his policy of *glasnost*. In 1988, the first paid commercials (for Pepsi-Cola, Sony and Visa credit cards) appeared on Soviet TV, and in 1989, the Soviet daily newspaper *Izvestia* published its first Western ads (including ads for perfume and wines from the French firm Pechiney and for Dresdner, a German bank).

In 1990, the Supreme Soviet, the legislative body, outlawed media censorship and gave every citizen the right to publish a newspaper. Within five months, more than 100 newspapers began publication. Then, showing how quickly government positions can change, in early 1991, Gorbachev asked the Supreme Soviet to suspend these press freedoms, but they refused. Less than a year later, Gorbachev's successor, President Boris Yeltsin, again began to relax government control of the press. In 1996, facing bankruptcy, *Pravda* ceased publication. Today, Russian officials, such as Prime Minister Vladimir Putin, maintain a tight reign on the press. (See **Impact/People**, "Magomed Yevloyev, Owner of Russian Opposition Web Site, Is Killed," page 356.)

As the Eastern European governments change and realign themselves, the adjustments facing Eastern European media are unprecedented. According to Everette E. Dennis and Jon Vanden Heuvel: "Once the revolution came, among the first acts of new government was to take (they would say liberate) electronic media and open up the print press. Permitting free and eventually independent media was a vital beginning for democracy in several countries and a clear break with the past. The freeing up of the media system, speedily in some countries and incrementally in others, was the lifting of an ideological veil without saying just what would replace it."

Middle Eastern and North African Media Work Under Government Controls

Press history in the Middle East and North Africa begins with the newspaper *Al-Iraq*, first published in 1817, although the first daily newspaper didn't begin publishing until 1873. With one exception, development of the press throughout this region follows the same pattern as in most developing countries: More newspapers and magazines are published in regions with high literacy rates than in regions with low literacy rates.

The exception is Egypt, where less than half the people are literate. Yet Cairo is the Arab world's publishing center. *Al Ahram* and *Al Akhbar* are Egypt's leading dailies.

Print Media

The Middle Eastern press is controlled tightly by government restrictions, through ownership and licensing, and it is not uncommon for opposition newspapers to disappear and for journalists to be jailed or to leave the country following political upheaval.

According to global media scholar Christine Ogan, "Following the revolution in Iran, all opposition and some moderate newspapers were closed, and according to the National Union of Iranian Journalists (now an illegal organization), more than 75 percent of all journalists left the country, were jailed, or no longer work in journalism." The Palestinian press was subject to censorship by the Israeli government, and all Palestinian newspapers and magazines once required permission from the Israeli government to be published.

Audio and Video Media

The foreign-language press is especially strong in the Middle East because of the large number of immigrants in the area, and foreign radio is very popular. Governments within each country control radio and television almost completely, and television stations in smaller countries (Sudan and Yemen, for example) broadcast for only a few hours a day beginning in mid-afternoon.

In the larger Arab states (Jordan, Lebanon, Saudi Arabia and Egypt), TV stations typically broadcast from

IMPACT
≫ People

Magomed Yevloyev, Owner of Russian Opposition Web Site, Is Killed
by Reuters

NAZRAN, Russia (Reuters)—The owner of an opposition Internet news site in Russia's troubled Ingushetia region was shot dead on Sunday after being detained by police, prompting his colleagues to call for a protest rally.

Magomed Yevloyev is one of the most high-profile journalists killed in Russia since investigative reporter Anna Politkovskaya was shot dead outside her Moscow apartment in 2006, provoking condemnation of Russia's record on media freedom.

Yevloyev, owner of the www.Ingushetiya .ru Web site, was a vocal critic of the region's Kremlin-backed administration, which critics accuse of crushing dissent and free speech.

A lawyer for the site—which survived repeated official attempts to close it down—said police met Yevloyev at the steps of the

Former world chess champion and Kremlin critic Garry Kasparov speaks during a rally in Moscow on August 30, 2008, held in memory of murdered investigative journalist Anna Politkovskaya, pictured in a photograph behind Kasparov. The next day, Magomed Yevloyev, who owned an opposition Internet Web site in Russia's Ingushetia region, was shot dead after being detained by police.

early morning until midnight. Radio signals beamed from Europe have become one of the region's alternative, affordable sources of news. According to the *Los Angeles Times*, "Because of tight censorship, newspapers and television stations in the Arab world frequently reflect the biases or outright propaganda of their governments. But radio broadcasts from outside the region travel easily across borders and long distances, and many Arabs regard those stations as the most reliable sources of unbiased news." The BBC (based in London) and Radio Monte Carlo Middle East (based in Paris) are the main across-the-border program sources.

Also, because of careful government control of television programming, another alternative medium has emerged—videos and DVDs. Says global media scholar Christine Ogan, "Saudi Arabia and some of the Gulf countries have the highest VCR penetration levels in the world. . . . And since only Egypt, Turkey, Lebanon and Israel [of the Gulf

countries] have copyright laws, pirated films from Europe, the United States, India and Egypt circulate widely in most countries. . . . The widespread availability of content that cannot be viewed on television or at the cinema (Saudi Arabia even forbids the construction of cinemas) has reduced the popularity of broadcast programming."

In the Middle East, as in other developing regions, the government-owned media are perceived as instruments of each country's social and political programs. The rapid spread of technological developments, such as videos, DVDs, the TV network Al Jazeera and its new Arab competitor Al-Arabiya, demonstrate new challenges to the insulated Middle Eastern media cocoon.

Founded in 1996, Al Jazeera today is the Middle East's most-watched network, and has made its reputation through comparatively independent news reporting and coverage. In 2006, Al Jazeera launched an English-language channel.

aircraft after he flew in to Ingushetia's airport, put him in a Volga saloon car and drove him away.

"As they drove he was shot in the temple . . . They threw him out of the car near the hospital," lawyer Kaloi Akhilgov told Reuters by telephone.

"He was discovered there and they quickly put him on the operating table, which is where he died."

Akhilgov said Yevloyev, who was in his thirties, was detained after flying from Moscow on the same flight as the Kremlin-backed local leader Murat Zyazikov. A spokesman for Zyazikov could not be reached for comment.

A posting on Yevloyev's site called on "all those who are not indifferent" to his killing to gather for a demonstration in Ingushetia's biggest town, Nazran, where Zyazikov's opponents have clashed with riot police in recent years.

"A preliminary investigation is being carried out into the incident as a result of which M. Yevloyev was killed," said Vladimir Markin, a spokesman for the investigations unit of the Prosecutor General's Office in Moscow.

Markin said police had tried to bring Yevloyev in for questioning but that an incident occurred in which he received a gunshot wound that led to his death.

Interfax news agency quoted an unnamed law enforcement source as saying Yevloyev was shot by accident.

Media freedom groups say Russia is one of the world's most dangerous countries for journalists.

Ingushetia is a poor, mainly Muslim, region in Russia's North Caucasus region and borders Chechnya, scene of a separatist rebellion that has now been largely quelled.

Ingushetia's leader, Zyazikov, has been struggling to contain a low-level insurgency by Islamist militants. Opponents accuse Zyazikov of persecuting opposition activists.

Zyazikov, a former security service officer in the local KGB, has criticized the reporting by Ingushetiya.ru and brought a court case earlier this year trying to close down the site.

Akhilgov, the lawyer for Yevloyev's Internet site, told Reuters he doubted the shooting was an accident.

"It was in no way a mistake," he said. "It will be very interesting to see what the consequences of this are for Ingushetia: there will be demonstrations in Nazran and in Moscow over this tragedy."

African Media Find a New Voice

Most of the new nations of Africa were born after 1960, a remarkable year in U.S. media history that witnessed the Kennedy-Nixon debates and the maturing of U.S. television as a news medium. African history is a record of colonialism, primarily by the British, French, Dutch and Portuguese, and the early print media were created to serve the colonists, not the native population.

Print Media

The first English-language newspaper in sub-Saharan Africa, the *Capetown Gazette and African Advertiser*, appeared in 1800; a year later, the first black newspaper, the *Royal Gazette and Sierra Leone Advertiser*, appeared in Sierra Leone.

French settlement in Africa is reflected in the pages of *Fraternié-Matin*, the only major daily in French Africa. A Portuguese settler founded *Noticias*, published in Mozambique. In Kenya, three tabloid newspapers enjoy wide circulations with relative independence: the English-language *Daily Nation* and *The Standard* and the Swahili daily *Taifa Leo*.

According to media scholar L. John Martin, Africans have never had an information press. Theirs has always been an opinion press. Advocacy journalism comes naturally to them. To the extent that they feel a need for hard news, that need is satisfied by the minimal coverage of the mass media, especially of radio. Soft news—human-interest news or what media scholar Wilbur Schramm has called immediate-reward news—is equally well transmitted through the folk media, such as the "bush telegraph," or drum; the "grapevine," or word-of-mouth and gossip; town criers and drummers; and traditional dances, plays and song.

The Middle Eastern TV network Al Jazeera, launched in 1996, continues to be a focus of global attention by broadcasting messages from terrorist Osama Bin Laden. An English-language version of Al Jazeera launched on November 15, 2006. The headquarters of the satellite channel is in Doha, Qatar.

the region. Because of violent demonstrations supporting the opposition African National Congress, President P. W. Botha declared a state of emergency in the country in 1985. In 1988, the government suspended the *New Nation* and four other alternative publications. The suspensions and regulations that prevented journalists from covering unrest show the power of government to limit reporting on dissent.

Audio and Video Media

Radio is a much more important medium in Africa than print or television. One reason for radio's dominance over print is that literacy rates are lower in Africa than in many other regions of the world. Radio is also very accessible and the cheapest way for people to follow the news. Some governments charge license fees for radio sets, which are supposed to be registered, but many go unregistered. Most stations accept advertising, but the majority of funding for radio comes from government subsidies.

Only a small percentage of the African public own a TV set, and Internet access is rare. (See **Impact/Culture**, "Africa, Offline: Waiting for the Web," page 359.) Television in the region is concentrated in the urban areas, and TV broadcasts last only a few hours each evening. Says L. John Martin, "TV remains a medium of wealthy countries."

Media Explode in Asia and the Pacific

The development of media in this region centers primarily in four countries: Japan, with its prosperous mix of public and private ownership; Australia, where media barons contributed their entrepreneurial fervor; India, which has seen phenomenal media growth; and the People's

Martin points out that African culture is very diverse, with an estimated 800 to 2,000 language dialects, making it impossible to create a mass circulation newspaper that can appeal to a wide readership. The widest circulating publication in the region is a magazine called *Drum*, published in South Africa but also distributed throughout Africa.

Today, most newspapers in South Africa, for example, are owned and edited by whites, who publish newspapers in English and in Afrikaans, a language that evolved from South Africa's 17th-century Dutch settlers. South Africa's first Afrikaans newspaper, *Di Patriot*, began in 1875. South Africa's highest circulation newspaper is the *Star*, which belongs to the Argus Group, South Africa's largest newspaper publisher.

The Argus Group also publishes the *Sowetan*, a handsome newspaper based in Johannesburg, with color graphics, an appealing design and a healthy circulation of about 120,000. Many of the Argus Group's editors spent time in jail for speaking out against apartheid. As South Africa's largest newspaper publisher, the Argus Group owns a total of nine major papers, six of them dailies, in several African countries.

From 1985 to 1990, the South African government demonstrated its distaste for dissident speech when it instituted strict limits on domestic and international news coverage in

"Watching people argue about the world situation night after night makes me feel I'm doing something about it."

IMPACT
»Culture

Africa, Offline: Waiting for the Web

by Ron Nixon

Attempts to bring affordable high-speed Internet service to the masses have made little headway on the [African] continent. Less than 4 percent of Africa's population is connected to the Web; most subscribers are in North African countries and the republic of South Africa.

A lack of infrastructure is the biggest problem. In many countries, communications networks were destroyed during years of civil conflict, and continuing political instability deters governments or companies from investing in new systems. E-mail messages and phone calls sent from some African countries have to be routed through Britain, or even the United States, increasing expenses and delivery times. About 75 percent of African Internet traffic is routed this way and costs African countries billions of extra dollars each year that they would not incur if their infrastructure was up to speed.

"Most African governments haven't paid much attention to their infrastructure," said Vincent Oria, an associate professor of computer science at the New Jersey Institute of Technology and a native of the Ivory Coast. "In places where hunger, AIDS and poverty are rampant, they didn't see it as critical until now."

Africa's only connection to the network of computers and fiber optic cables that are

Less than 4 percent of Africa's population is connected to the Web. A customer in a Kigali, Rwanda, coffee shop uses one of the country's limited number of wireless connections.

the Internet's backbone is a $600 million undersea cable running from Portugal down the west coast of Africa. Built in 2002, the cable was supposed to provide cheaper and faster Web access, but so far that has not happened.

Prices remain high because the national telecommunications linked to the cable maintain a monopoly over access, squeezing out potential competitors. And plans for a fiber optic cable along the East African coast have stalled over similar access issues. Most countries in Eastern Africa, like Rwanda, depend on slower satellite technology for Internet service.

The result is that Africa remains the least connected region in the world, and the digital gap between it and the developed world is widening rapidly. "Unless you can offer Internet access that is the same as the rest of the world, Africa can't be part of the global economy or academic environment," said Lawrence H. Landweber, professor emeritus of computer science at the University of Wisconsin in Madison, who was also part of an early effort to bring the Web to Africa in the mid-1990s. "The benefits of the Internet age will bypass the continent."

Aijaz Rahi/AP Photo

Dubbed Bollywood, India's flourishing film industry is centered in a place called Film City, near Mumbai, where 16 film studios turn out 800 films a year, second in output only to Hollywood.

"The government cannot veto any program or demand that any program be aired. It leaves the NHK free to set the level of license fees and to do its own fee collecting (which may be why it rates as the richest of the world's fee-supported broadcasting organizations)."

Private ownership is an important element in the Japanese media, and newspaper publishers own many broadcasting operations. NHK owns many more radio properties than private broadcasters do; NHK shares television ownership about equally with private investors. However, Japan has very few cable systems, which will hinder access to global communications networks.

Australia

In Australia, acquisitions by media magnates such as Rupert Murdoch skyrocketed in the 1980s. The Murdoch empire controls an astounding 60 percent of Australia's newspaper circulation, which includes the *Daily Telegraph Mirror* in Sydney and *The Herald-Sun* in Melbourne. Murdoch, although somewhat burdened with debt because of his acquisitions binge in the 1980s, emerged in the 1990s as Australia's uncontested print media baron.

Australian Broadcasting Corporation (**ABC**), modeled after the BBC, dominates broadcasting in Australia. Three nationwide commercial networks operate in the country, but all three were suffering financial difficulty in the 1990s, a legacy "of the heydays of the 1980s, when aspiring buyers, backed by eager bank lenders, paid heady prices for broadcast and print assets," reported *The Wall Street Journal*.

India

Entrepreneurship is an important element in the print media of India, which gained independence from Britain in 1947. Forty years following independence, in 1987, Indian print media had multiplied 1,000 times—from 200 publications in 1947 to nearly 25,000 publications in 1987.

Broadcasting in India follows its British colonial beginnings, with radio operating under the name All India Radio (AIR) and TV as Doordarshan ("distance view"). Doordarshan uses satellite service to reach remote locations, bringing network TV to four out of five people in the country. As in most developing countries, the network regularly broadcasts programs aimed at improving public life and about subjects such as family planning, health and hygiene.

The most prosperous industry in India today is filmmaking. The film industry, which produces 800 films a year (second in output only to Hollywood), is centered around a place called Film City near Mumbai, where 16 film studios employ thousands of people who work at dozens of sprawling sets. The industry is known as "Bollywood," a cross between Bombay, the former name of Mumbai, and Hollywood.

Republic of China, with its sustained government-controlled media monopoly.

Japan

Japan boasts more newspaper readers than any other nation in the world. Japan's three national daily newspapers—*Asahi Shimbun, Yomiuri Shimbun* and *Mainichi Shimbun*—are based in Tokyo. These three papers, each of them more than 100 years old, account for almost half the nation's newspaper circulation. Broadcast media in Japan developed as a public corporation called the Japanese Broadcasting Corporation (NHK). During World War II, NHK became a propaganda arm of the government, but after the Japanese surrender, the United States established the direction for Japanese broadcasting.

Japan created a licensing board similar to the Federal Communications Commission, but an operating board similar to that of Great Britain's BBC. Japan also decided to allow private broadcast ownership. As a result of this, Japan today has a mixed system of privately owned and publicly held broadcast media. NHK continues to prosper and, according to broadcast scholar Sydney W. Head, "NHK enjoys more autonomy than any other major public broadcasting corporation. In a rather literal sense, the general public 'owns' it by virtue of paying receiver fees.

ABC Australian Broadcasting Corporation.

People's Republic of China

Social responsibility is a very important element of media development in the People's Republic of China, where a media monopoly gives government the power to influence change. At the center of Chinese media are the two party information sources, the newspaper *People's Daily* and Xinhua, the Chinese news agency. These two sources set the tone for the print media throughout China, where self-censorship maintains the government's direction.

Broadcasting in China, as in India, offers important potential for social change in a vast land of rural villages. China's three-tier system for radio includes a central national station; 100 regional, provincial and municipal networks; and grassroots stations that send local announcements and bulletins by wire to loudspeakers in outdoor markets and other public gathering places.

A television set is a prized possession in China, where the Chinese have bought some U.S. programs and accepted some U.S. commercials, but generally produce the programming themselves. The 1989 demonstrations in Tiananmen Square cooled official enthusiasm for relationships with the West, and Chinese media today sometimes use information and entertainment programming from the West to show the dangers of Western influence, proving the power and the reach of a government media monopoly. In the new market economy in China, there are 10 times as many newspapers and magazines today as there were in 1978.

With the increased competition for readers, some of the print media are beginning to look like Western tabloids, running some sensationalist stories. This sensationalism has angered Communist Party officials, who are trying to maintain control on what is published. In 1996, the president of the popular newspaper *Beijing Youth Daily* was disciplined after the paper ran a story about a poisoning case involving a state-run business.

"The leadership of the news media must be tightly held in the hands of those who are loyal to Marxism, the party and the people," said President Jiang Zemin. With the inevitable influx of Western media during the 2008 Beijing Olympics, the Chinese government originally pledged to open up media outlets completely, but still restricted journalists' access to many Western news outlets (See **Chapter 14**, "Hundreds of Web Sites Censored at Beijing Olympics," page 302.)

Quinn Rooney/Getty Images

A television set is a prized possession in China, where Chinese broadcasters have bought some U.S. programs and accepted some U.S. commercials, but generally produce the programming themselves. Residents crowded around a television on a Beijing street to watching the opening ceremony of the 2008 Summer Olympics in Beijing.

Government, Large Corporations and Family Dynasties Control Latin American and Caribbean Media

In Latin America, where hectic political change is the norm, media have been as volatile as the region. Media are part of the same power structure that controls politics, business and industry. In some Latin American countries, such as Brazil, a family dynasty dominates the media.

For example, Televisa, based in Mexico, owns more than 258 affiliated TV stations, 31 pay TV channels, and 158 different publications. Organization Editorial Mexicana owns 70 newspapers, 24 radio stations and 43 Internet sites.

Print Media

In Santiago, Chile, the newspaper *El Mercurio* was founded in 1827. Today El Mercurio newspapers total 9 and the

IMPACT
»» People

Venezuelan President Hugo Chávez's Move Against Critic Highlights Shift in Media Support

by Simon Romero

Arturo Sarmiento speaks upper crust English polished at Sandhurst, Britain's aristocratic military school. He made fortunes trading oil and importing whiskey. Now Mr. Sarmiento, just 35 and a staunch supporter of President Hugo Chávez, owns an expanding television network here [in Caracas, Venezuela].

As tempers flare around Mr. Chávez's decision not to renew the license of RCTV, the nation's oldest broadcaster and a vocal critic, effectively shutting it down on Sunday [May 27, 2007], a new media elite is emerging. It is made up of ideological devotees to Mr. Chávez, senior government officials and tycoons like Mr. Sarmiento.

That is a marked contrast with the state of the news media when Mr. Chávez's rule began in 1999. Then, the industry was largely privately owned by moneyed interests hostile to Mr. Chávez. His supporters say that old guard—as partisan as newspapers in the early

United States—sought to derail his actions during much of his presidency.

Mr. Chávez has dueled with opponents in the news media while fortifying news organizations loyal to him. For instance, newspapers favorable to the government have received nearly 12 times more government advertising, said Andrés Cañizález, a researcher at Andrés Bello University, citing a study of four leading dailies.

"Previous administrations in Venezuela also used advertising as a way to consolidate media support," Mr. Cañizález said. "The difference now is that the government has made growing its own media operations and combating its opponents in the media central elements of its political strategy."

In what may point to a rare example of widespread disagreement with the popular president, recent polls show that most Venezuelans oppose Mr. Chávez's decision not to renew RCTV's license.

El Mercurio company also owns 32 radio stations. *O Estado de São Paulo* in Brazil, owned by the Mesquita family, has represented editorial independence in the region for more than 100 years and often is mentioned as one of the country's best newspapers. Argentina's *La Prensa* refuses government subsidies and has survived great conflicts with people like dictator Juan Perón, who shut down the newspaper from 1951 to 1955.

Home delivery for newspapers and magazines is uncommon in Latin America; the centers of print media merchandising are street-corner kiosks, where vendors offer a variety of publications. *Manchete*, published in Brazil, is one of the most widely circulated national magazines, similar in size and content to *Life* magazine.

Audio and Video Media

Broadcasting operates in a mix of government and private control, with government often owning a few key stations and regulating stations that are privately owned, but the pattern is varied.

Cuba's broadcast media are controlled totally by the government, for example. In Costa Rica and Ecuador, almost all the broadcast media are privately owned. In Brazil, private owners hold most of the radio stations and television networks, including TV Globo Network, which claims to be the world's fourth largest network (after the United States' original three TV networks).

JON BARRETO/AFP/Getty Images

Venezuelan President Hugo Chavez has recently silenced his media critics by shutting down his opponents' privately owned media outlets and launching new government-sponsored stations. Protestors demonstrated outside RCTV, the nation's oldest broadcaster, which has been critical of Mr. Chavez. Chavez announced in May 2007 that he was shutting down the station. (The sign reads "No to silence, journalists united for freedom of expression.")

Thousands of people marched through downtown here on Saturday to RCTV's headquarters to show support for the network, following a protest by opposing groups

late Friday in front of Globovisión, another dissident network, that left its building and neighboring buildings painted with pro-Chávez slogans.

The president accuses RCTV and other private broadcasters of supporting what amounted to a 48-hour coup. In RCTV's case, the government says the network colluded with the coup's conspirators by conducting a news blackout after Mr. Chávez's removal and broadcasting cartoons when he returned to office two days later.

As Mr. Chávez's political power has grown, with loyalists controlling the Supreme Court, the national assembly and most state governments, RCTV has remained critical of Mr. Chávez. Two other nationwide broadcasters, Televen and Venevisión, have curtailed critical coverage. Globovisión, the cable news channel that drew the anger of pro-Chávez groups on Friday, remains critical of Mr. Chávez but is viewed by a relatively small part of the population.

Mr. Chávez's partisans often say critical coverage of the government illustrates elitist and racist sentiments, while dissidents say the news media are their only outlet for expression, since other institutions are controlled by Mr. Chávez.

"Venezuelan President Hugo Chávez's Move Against Critic Highlights Shift in Media," by Simon Romero, *The New York Times,* May 27, 2007. Copyright © 2007 by the New York Times. All rights reserved. Reprinted by permission.

Reporters Risk Their Lives to Report World Events

Latin American media as well as journalists in many developing countries often are targets for political and terrorist threats, and a journalist's life can be very hazardous.

According to *Global Journalism: Survey of International Communication*, "Threats to journalists come not only from governments but from terrorist groups, drug lords and quasi-government hit squads as well. Numerous news organizations have been bombed, ransacked and destroyed by opponents. Dozens of Latin American journalists have been murdered for their beliefs or for writing articles that contain those beliefs."

Journalists face danger in this region because the media often represent potential opposition to the political power of a country's leadership. Perhaps more than in any other part of the world, the Latin American media are woven into the fiber of the region's revolutionary history.

Yet journalists in many developing countries face unbelievable dangers just for reporting the news. According to Reporters Without Borders, which tracks deaths and injuries suffered by journalists throughout the world, 417 journalists and media assistants were killed in 2007 while they were on the job. (See **Impact/Culture**, "Reporters Without Borders Monitors Press Attacks," page 365.)

Critics Cite Western Communications Bias

Countries in Latin America and in many other developing nations have criticized what they believe is a Western bias to the flow of information throughout the world. These countries charge that this practice imposes cultural imperialism, centered in Western ideology. In fact, most of the major international news services are based in the West.

The Associated Press, Reuters (Great Britain), Agence France-Presse (France), Deutsche Presse-Agentur (Germany) and Agencia Efe (Spain) supply news to the print and broadcast media. Visnews, based in Great Britain, the U.S.–based Cable News Network and World International Network (WIN) offer international video services. Sky TV in Europe and Star TV in Asia deliver programs by satellite.

Despite Western dominance of global news organizations, many regions of the world support information services within their own countries and even within their regions. Middle East News Agency (MENA), based in Egypt, serves all the countries of the Middle East, while News Agency of Nigeria (NAN) limits services to Nigeria, for example.

Within the past 50 years, news services outside the Western orbit have been created—Russian Information Agency (RIA); Asian-Pacific News Network in Japan; Caribbean News Agency (CANA); Pan-African News Agency (PANA); Non-Aligned News Agency (NANA), linking the nonaligned nations with the national news agencies, based in Yugoslavia; and Inter Press Service (IPS), based in Rome as an "information bridge" between Europe and Latin America.

Even with the creation of these added sources of information, Western news services dominate. Critics of the present system of news and information flow have labeled this issue the New World Information and Communications Order (**NWICO**), saying that the current system is *ethnocentric*, or promoting the superiority of one ethnic group (in this case, the Western world) over another.

NWICO New World Information and Communications Order. The concept that media can include all areas of the world, not just the West.

Ethnocentric Promoting the superiority of one ethnic group over another.

According to Robert G. Picard in *Global Journalism: Survey of International Communication*:

Developing world media and newly independent governments have been highly critical of this situation, arguing that coverage from the major services contains ethnocentric occidental values that affect its content and presentation. Coverage from these media most often include political, economic, Judeo-Christian religious and other social values that are not universal. . . . In addition, developing world media and governments have argued that Western ethnocentrism creates an unequal flow of information by providing a large stream of information about events in the developed world but only a very small flow from the developing world.

UNESCO's 1978 Declaration Promotes Self-Reliance

The United Nations organization UNESCO adopted a declaration in 1978 supporting the principles of self-reliant communications and self-determination for countries as they establish their own communications policies. Critics of the statement, especially journalists, felt that some aspects of the declaration supported government control of the flow of information out of a country, because some news services are official government mouthpieces.

MacBride Report Provokes Controversy

Four years later, UNESCO, which had appointed a 16-member commission headed by Irish statesman Sean MacBride, received the commission's recommendations at the general conference of UNESCO in Belgrade, Yugoslavia. These recommendations became known as the MacBride Report.

The report listed 82 ways to help achieve the New World Information and Communications Order, but after the report was issued neither critics of the current status of communications nor those who opposed the report's recommendations were satisfied.

According to Sydney Head, "The West objected to the report's skepticism about a free market in communication, including its opposition to advertising, for example; many NWICO supporters objected to its downplaying of government controls (for example, its advocacy of self-imposed rather than government codes of ethics for journalists)." The Belgrade conference passed a general resolution supporting NWICO, but in 1983, citing opposition to some of the principles outlined in the MacBride Report, the Reagan administration withdrew its $50 million in financial support for UNESCO, seriously crippling the organization because the United States had been its largest contributor.

UNESCO has since turned to other issues. NWICO still remains a theoretical idea that scholars of global media continue to debate because of its implications for the international media community.

IMPACT
»Culture

Reporters Without Borders Monitors Press Attacks

For 2007, Reporters Without Borders, which monitors violent attacks against journalists abroad, reported the following statistics:

- Journalists killed: 87

- Media assistants killed: 20

- Journalists imprisoned: 138

- Media assistants imprisoned: 138

- Cyberdissidents (online journalists) imprisoned: 72

Source: Reporters Without Borders, http://www.rsf.org.

ERIC FEFERBERG/AFP/Getty Images

Each year, many journalists are injured and killed while reporting on world events. Based in France, but covering dangers throughout the world, Reporters Without Borders posted pictures at a recent rally showing incidents of violence against journalists.

Global Media Markets Widen Rapidly

Today's media markets are increasingly global. U.S. media companies are looking for markets overseas at the same time that overseas media companies are purchasing pieces of media industries in the United States and other countries. MTV, for example, is available 24 hours a day in St. Petersburg, Russia. Here are some more examples:

- U.S.-based Yahoo Inc. paid $1 billion to buy a 40 percent interest in China's biggest online commerce firm, *alibaba .com*. China is now the world's second largest Internet market.

- The U.S. TV network ABC and the British Broadcasting Corporation have formed a newsgathering partnership to share television and radio news coverage worldwide. This service will compete with CNN to deliver news by satellite.

- Rupert Murdoch expanded his Hong Kong–based satellite TV network, British Sky Network, into India. Murdoch said he planned to offer more than just TV coverage in India. "Our plan is not just to beam signals into India but also to take part in Indian films, make television programs and broadcast them."

- Jun Murai, who has been called the father of Japan's Internet, created a nonprofit network to connect all of Japan's universities to the Internet, without government approval. Ultimately, he says, he "wants to connect all the computers in this world."

- U.S./British advertising and public relations partnerships are on the rise. The British firm Shandwick is the largest agency in the United Kingdom. More than half of Shandwick's business comes from the United States.

All these companies have positioned themselves to manage the emerging global media marketplace. This media marketplace includes news and information services, print,

Evaristo Sa/AFP/Getty Images

Digital technology has blurred the territorial boundaries between countries. Today cellular telephone signals are available in many areas of the world, including Brasilia, Brazil, where native peoples met with the Brazilian President in 2008 to lobby for protection of the country's indigenous preserves.

programming, films and recordings, as well as products and the advertising to sell those products.

Fueling the move to global marketing is the decision by the European countries to eliminate all trade barriers among countries. A further sign of the times is the shrinking proportion of worldwide advertising expenditures accounted for by the United States, which has long been the world's advertising colossus. In recent years, advertising spending by companies *outside* the United States has overtaken the amount spent by companies *in* the United States.

Media Companies Chase International Consumers

International communication on the Internet is just the beginning of an easy, affordable and accessible transfer of information and entertainment back and forth between other countries and the United States. Media companies in the United States also are looking longingly at the large populations in other countries that are just beginning to acquire the tools of communication, making millions of people instantly available for all types of products.

IHT International Herald Tribune, the world's largest English-language newspaper.

The number of TV sets in the world has jumped to more than 1 billion—a 50 percent increase in the past five years. According to the *Los Angeles Times*: "TV sets are more common in Japanese homes than flush toilets. Virtually every Mexican household has a TV, but only half have phones. Thai consumers will buy a TV before an electric fan or even a refrigerator. . . . Vans roam Bogotá streets with miniature satellite dishes on the roof and a megaphone blaring promises of hookups for $150. In New Delhi, 'dish wallahs' nail satellite receivers to crowded apartment buildings."

The *International Herald Tribune* Seeks a Worldwide Audience

One of the largest global media presences is the *International Herald Tribune* (**IHT**), based in Paris and published in English. Called "The World's Daily Newspaper," the *International Herald Tribune* was founded in 1887 by American entrepreneur J. Gordon Bennett, Jr., and today is the world's largest English-language newspaper. (See **Impact/Business**, "*International Herald Tribune* Timeline 1887–Today," page 367.) Known for its independence, the newspaper was co-owned by the *Washington Post* and *The New York Times* until 2003, when *The New York Times* became the paper's sole owner.

The *IHT* is the first truly global newspaper, published at 35 sites around the world and covering world news every day. With a global outlook and available by subscription in an electronic edition, the *IHT* counts most of the world's opinion leaders and decision makers among its subscribers. The New York Times Company owns the *IHT*.

The paper has a circulation of 241,000 and an international readership in 180 countries throughout Europe, Asia, the Middle East, Russia, Africa and the Americas. Its biggest regular audience is American tourists traveling abroad.

Internet Expands Media's Global Reach

When communication stays within borders, it is easier for governments to control information. The Internet is a whole new story, making it possible for information and entertainment to travel effortlessly across borders.

Governments that are used to controlling information, especially in developing countries, have tried to stop the information flow by pricing Internet access out of the reach of the average consumer, charging as much as $200 a month for Internet access. Also, many countries simply don't have reliable telecommunications technology in place—telephone, broadband, cellular or satellite connections—to handle Internet access.

This often means that in poorer countries, only the wealthy have access to the international flow of information

IMPACT
≫ Business

International Herald Tribune Timeline 1887-Today

1887 On October 4, American entrepreneur J. Gordon Bennett Jr. publishes the first issue of the *New York Herald*'s European edition in Paris.

1928 *The Herald* becomes the first newspaper distributed by airplane, flying copies to London from Paris in time for breakfast.

1940 The occupation of Paris interrupts publishing.

1944 Publishing resumes.

1959 The *New York Herald Tribune* and its European edition are sold to John Hay Whitney, then the U.S. ambassador to Britain.

1966 The New York paper closes. The Whitney family keeps the Paris paper going through partnerships. In December the *Washington Post* becomes a joint owner.

1967 In May *The New York Times* becomes a joint owner and the newspaper becomes the *International Herald Tribune*, emphasizing its global perspective.

1974 The *IHT* pioneers the electronic transmission of facsimile pages across countries with the opening of a printing site near London. A second site was opened in Zurich in 1977.

1980 The *IHT* begins sending page images via satellite from Paris to Hong Kong, making it the first daily newspaper to be electronically sent across continents, making it simultaneously available to readers on opposite sides of the world.

1991 The *Washington Post* and *The New York Times* become sole and equal shareholders of the newspaper.

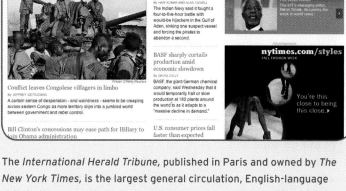

Courtesy of International Herald Tribune

The *International Herald Tribune*, published in Paris and owned by *The New York Times*, is the largest general circulation, English-language daily in the world. Its Web site, iht.com, receives seven million visitors a month.

2001 IHT.TV, a fast-paced 30-minute business program, launches.

2003 *The New York Times* acquires full ownership of the *International Herald Tribune*.

2005 The 25th anniversary of the *International Herald Tribune* publishing activities in Asia is marked by the opening of *IHT*'s Hong Kong newroom, allowing *IHT* to be published in both Paris and Hong Kong.

The *IHT* expands its digital portfolio, allowing users to access IHT.COM by mobile phone.

2006 The *IHT* becomes the first international daily newspaper to be printed in Russia, ensuring early morning distribution with the *Moscow Times*.

2008 IHT & Reuters join forces to launch Business with Reuters and Business Asia with Reuters. Seven million users visit IHT.com each month.

Source: from New York Times Company: International Herald Tribune Timeline, http://www.ihtinfo.com/ pages/ab_nphistory.html.

the Internet offers. As technology grows more affordable, however, it will be difficult for even developing countries to stop information from seeping across their borders.

The Internet is as close as a laptop and an Internet connection and is becoming an indispensable tool for business and economic growth. More than any other factor, the economic uses of the Internet guarantee its future as a global communications medium.

Ideas Transcend Borders

Along with the transfer of information in the new global communications future, however, comes the transfer of ideas. Says the *Los Angeles Times*:

> Historically, the empowered elite have always sought to suppress the wider distribution of ideas, wealth, rights and, most of all, knowledge. This is as true today as it was 536 years ago, when the German printer Gutenberg invented movable type to print the Bible. For two centuries afterward, government tightly controlled what people could read through the widespread use of "prior restraint." . . .
>
> Just as censorship of the printed word could not continue with the emergence of democracy in 17th century Britain and 18th century America, so today suppression of the electronic media is thwarted by technology and rapidly growing economies around the world.

Governments that are accustomed to controlling the information that crosses their borders face unprecedented access within their borders to global information sources. According to media theorist Ithiel de Sola Pool, "International communications is often considered a mixed blessing by rulers. Usually they want technical progress. They want computers. They want satellites. They want efficient telephones. They want television. But at the same time they do not want the ideas that come with them."

Many governments that control the media, especially broadcast media and the Internet, are expected to continue to control the messages as long as they can supervise access to newsprint and satellites, but this is becoming increasingly difficult. In 1994, the Chinese government passed regulations to ban satellite dishes and prohibit people from watching foreign broadcasts. Factories that own dishes were required to broadcast only approved programs, but many Chinese simply refused to abide by the edict.

Videos can travel in a suitcase across borders, and video signals can travel unseen to pirated satellite dishes, assembled without government knowledge. The airwaves are truly "borderless." Reports the *Los Angeles Times*, "Asked once what had caused the stunning collapse of communism in Eastern Europe, Polish leader Lech Walesa pointed to a nearby TV set. 'It all came from there.' "

As more and more national media boundaries open up throughout the world, news, information and entertainment will be able to move instantly from each home country to become part of the global media dialogue. Today the media industries operate in a media marketplace without boundaries, a global marketplace that is truly "transnational." According to *The Economist*,

> Optimists declare that the world is headed unstoppably for an electronic Renaissance. How arrogant; how naive. The essence of a technology of freedom is that it endows its users with the freedom to fail. But pessimists are equally wrong to think that failure is inevitable. Nothing is inevitable about this technology except its advance. . . . As the universe behind the screen expands, it will be the people in front who shape the soul of the new machine.

Review, Analyze, Investigate
REVIEWING CHAPTER 16

World Media Systems Vary

✓ Media industries in different countries are as varied as the countries they serve.

✓ The U.S. isn't necessarily always the leader in adopting innovative technologies.

Five Political Theories Help Describe
How World Media Operate

✓ The original four theories on the press (the Soviet theory, the authoritarian theory, the libertarian theory and the social responsibility theory) plus the developmental theory still leave many press systems beyond specific categorization.

✓ The global media theory that best describes the American media is the libertarian theory, although American media also have struggled with authoritarian and social responsibility debates.

Western Europe and Canada Are
Similar to the United States

✓ Until the 1850s, presses in Europe were privately owned.

✓ The print media form the basis for press development in North America, Australia, Western Europe and Eastern Europe.

✓ Today Western European and Canadian media prosper under guarantees of freedom of expression similar to the First Amendment of the U.S. Constitution, although each nation has modified the idea to reflect differing values.

✓ In 1982, Canada adopted the Canadian Charter of Rights and Freedom, becoming the most recent Western country to issue an official decree supporting the philosophy of press freedom.

✓ Scandinavian journalists enjoy the widest press freedoms of all of Western Europe, including almost unlimited access to public documents.

✓ Western European newspapers tend to be much more partisan than either U.S. or Canadian newspapers.

✓ Western Europeans watch about half as much TV as people in the United States.

✓ Many TV stations in Europe don't go on the air until late afternoon.

✓ Most Western European programming comes from the United States.

✓ U.S. programs are attractive to European broadcasters because buying U.S. programs is cheaper than producing their own.

✓ Some members of the European community have proposed quotas on the importation of U.S. programs.

Eastern Europe Is Transforming

✓ Many Eastern European nations developed their press policies following the Soviet model.

✓ Eastern Europe, which is in transition, is defining a new balance between the desire for free expression and the remnants of government control.

✓ In many Eastern European countries, the media play a central role in upsetting the established power structure.

✓ Television in the Eastern bloc countries developed under Communist direction because the Communist governments were in power before TV use was widespread; radio broadcasting also was tightly controlled.

✓ *Pravda*, the Soviet Union's oldest newspaper, was founded in 1912.

✓ Media freedom groups say Russia is one of the world's most dangerous countries for journalists.

Middle Eastern and North African Media Work Under Government Controls

✓ Press history in the Middle East and North Africa begins with the newspaper *Al-Iraq*, first published in 1817, although the first daily newspaper didn't begin publishing until 1873.

✓ In the Middle East and North Africa, more newspapers and magazines are published in regions with high literacy rates than in regions with low literacy rates; the one exception is Cairo, Egypt, which is the Arab world's publishing center.

✓ Radio often is the dominant medium in developing countries; television is in widespread use in prosperous nations and in urban areas of developing countries. Yet most countries still have only one TV service, usually run by the government.

✓ Radio Monte Carlo and the BBC offer alternative radio programming across Middle Eastern borders. VCRs and DVDs also are very popular.

✓ The Middle Eastern press is tightly controlled by government restrictions, through ownership and licensing.

✓ Al Jazeera is the Middle East's most-watched network, which has made its controversial reputation through comparatively independent news reporting and coverage.

✓ In the Middle East, as in other developing regions, the media are perceived as instruments of each country's social and political agendas.

African Media Find a New Voice

✓ The first English-language newspaper in sub-Saharan Africa appeared in Capetown, South Africa, in 1800; a year later, the first black newspaper appeared in Sierra Leone.

✓ African culture is very diverse, making it impossible to create a mass circulation newspaper that can appeal to a wide readership.

✓ In Africa, radio is a much more important medium than print because it is an inexpensive way for people to follow the news.

✓ Suspension of five publications in South Africa throughout the state of emergency during 1985–1990 demonstrates the power of government to limit reporting on dissent.

✓ People in Africa have limited access to the Internet.

Media Explode in Asia and the Pacific

✓ Japan's three major newspapers are each more than 100 years old.

✓ The three major Japanese national dailies account for almost half the nation's newspaper circulation.

✓ Japan today has a mixed system of privately owned and publicly held broadcast media.

✓ Entrepreneurs, including Rupert Murdoch, control large segments of Australia's media.

✓ The Australian Broadcasting Corporation dominates broadcasting in Australia.

✓ Since India's independence in 1947, the number of publications has increased 1,000 times.

✓ Broadcasting in India follows its British colonial beginnings.

✓ The most successful media business in India is filmmaking, an industry nicknamed Bollywood. The industry is based in Film City, a settlement near Mumbai.

✓ Chinese media operate under a government monopoly, supported by a belief in the media's social responsibility.

Government, Large Corporations and Family Dynasties Control Latin American and Caribbean Media

✓ Media in Latin America are part of the power structure, and media often are owned by family dynasties.

✓ In Santiago, Chile, the Edwards family has owned *El Mercurio* since 1880.

✓ Dictator Juan Perón shut down Argentina's independent newspaper *La Prensa* from 1951 to 1955.

Reporters Risk Their Lives to Report World Events

✓ Journalists in Latin America and many other developing countries face danger because the media represent a challenge to political power.

✓ In 2007, 117 journalists and media assistants were killed on the job.

Critics Cite Western Communications Bias

✓ Many developing nations criticize the news media for their Western slant.

✓ Despite Western dominance of global news organizations, many regions of the world have their own news services.

✓ The New World Information and Communications Order, supported by UNESCO, advocated parity for the media in all countries.

Global Media Markets Widen Rapidly

✓ U.S. media companies are looking for markets overseas at the same time that overseas media companies are purchasing pieces of media industries in the United States and other countries.

✓ Fueling the move to global marketing is the decision by the European countries to eliminate all trade barriers.

✓ Founded in 1883 by American entrepreneur J. Gordon Bennett, Jr., the *International Herald Tribune* is the world's largest circulation, general interest English-language daily.

Internet Expands Media's Global Reach

✓ Governments that are used to controlling information, especially in developing countries, have tried to stop the information flow by pricing Internet access out of the reach of the average consumer.

✓ Many countries simply don't have reliable telecommunications technology in place—telephone, broadband, cellular or satellite connections—to handle Internet access.

✓ More than any other factor, the economic uses of the Internet guarantee its future as a global communications medium.

✓ Today China is the world's second-largest Internet market.

Ideas Transcend Borders

✓ Along with the transfer of information in the new global communications future comes the transfer of ideas.

✓ Governments that are accustomed to controlling the information that crosses their borders face unprecedented access within their borders to global information sources.

✓ Today the media industries operate in a marketplace that is "transnational."

KEY TERMS

These terms are defined in the margins throughout this chapter and appear in alphabetical order with definitions in the Glossary, which begins on page 372.

ABC 360

BBC 350

Ethnocentric 364

Hot Spot 350

IHT 366

NWICO 364

CRITICAL QUESTIONS

1. In what ways might a nation's media system be shaped by its government's political philosophy? Cite some specific examples.

2. Compare the evolution of mass media in the various regions of the world. Give specific examples.

3. Discuss the role of radio in developed and less-developed countries. Cite specific examples.

4. Explain how the *International Herald Tribune* became one of the largest global media presences. What will the *IHT* have to do to stay competitive in the growing global media market?

5. Discuss the global consequences of international access to the Internet, including the impact of the Internet on government control of information and ways that developing countries attempt to deal with the loss of control.

WORKING THE WEB

This list includes both sites mentioned in the chapter and others to give you greater insight into global media.

BBC News
http://www.bbc.co.uk

The British Broadcasting Company's Web site with a UK and an international version is customizable with content choices including news, sports, weather, radio, TV, entertainment, history and blogs. The international version, which offers news and audio in 32 languages, has links to BBC TV and radio channels around the world. Its Country Profiles (located in the News section) provide background on every nation in the world. Learning English pages include help with news English and business English. A complete A–Z directory of BBC sites is also available.

Foreign Policy Magazine
http://www.foreignpolicy.com

A bimonthly magazine about global politics and economics, *Foreign Policy*'s mission is to explain "how the process of globalization is reshaping nations, institutions, cultures, and, more fundamentally, our daily lives." Articles from current issues are available for free as well as Special Reports, which combine *Foreign Policy* articles and links to other sources, and Breaking Global News, stories from international and regional news hubs updated every minute.

Global Media Journal (GMJ)
http://lass.calumet.purdue.edu/cca/gmj/index.htm

A journal published by Purdue University Calumet since 2002, *GMJ* aims to publish works that assess global media concentration, global media and consumer culture, media regulations, alternative media and other timely issues. *GMJ* has established African, American, Arabic, Australian, Canadian, Chinese, Indian, Pakistan, Persian, Polish, Spanish, Mediterranean and Turkish editions, and plans to continue to add new editions around the globe.

Global Media Monitor (GMM)
http://lass.calumet.purdue.edu/cca/gmm

Serving as a "clearinghouse for numerous issues related to global communication and mass media studies," the *GMM* Web site was founded by editor Yahya R. Kamalipour of Purdue University Calumet while working on his e-journal *Global Media Journal*. The Web site houses numerous reference links to a variety of mass media subjects including international news and programs, news agencies, organizations, scholars and experts.

International Center for Journalists
http://www.icfj.org

This nonprofit professional organization promotes quality journalism around the world, and believes that "independent, vigorous media are crucial in improving the human condition." It offers programs, seminars and fellowships for journalists in the United States and abroad, as well as online resources, instructor-led and distance courses in English, Arabic and Persian. The chairman of its board is James Hoge, Jr., the editor of *Foreign Affairs*. It sponsors the International Journalists' Network (http://www.IJNet.org), Knight International Journalism Fellowships and Medios y Libertad en las Américas for Latin American journalists.

International Herald Tribune
http://www.iht.com

The "global edition of the New York Times," the *International Herald Tribune* is the world's daily newspaper for global readers with articles from its own correspondents and *New York Times* reporters. Its sections are those of any local paper (Business, Tech/Media, Travel, Style, Culture, Health, Sports and Opinion), but the content is international (including a currency converter in the Business Market Tools section). The Web site includes four regional versions: Europe, the Americas, Asia-Pacific and Africa and Middle East.

International Women's Media Foundation (IWMF)
http://www.iwmf.org

This organization raises awareness about, creates opportunities for and builds networks of female journalists around the world. "No press is truly free unless women share an equal voice" is its motto. Online resources include links to online training, tips and guides, statistics and studies, links to Web sites of interest to women in the media, and publications and newsletter articles. The IWMF's U.S. Leadership Institute provides critical career building skills and networking opportunities. Prior projects in the Former Soviet Republics and Africa have successfully coached women in newsroom leadership and management skills.

Internews
http://www.internews.org

An international media development organization based in California, Internews has offices in 23 countries in Africa, Asia, Europe, the Middle East and North America. Its goal is to foster independent media and access to information for people worldwide. Current Internews activities include providing training for media professionals in journalism, production and management; supporting media infrastructure; and adopting and implementing fair media laws and policies.

Funders of projects have included the Bill and Melinda Gates Foundation, the National Science Foundation, UNICEF, the World Bank, and many others. A long list of related organizations is available on the Web site.

Reporters Without Borders
http://www.rsf.org

An international organization that works for freedom of the press around the world, Reporters Without Borders defends journalists who are threatened, imprisoned or persecuted; works to improve the safety of journalists in war zones; and opposes censorship. The Web site provides news and online petitions in five languages about attacks on press freedom and journalists in Africa, the Americas, Asia, Europe and the former USSR, the Middle East and Northern Africa, within the United Nations and on the Internet. Its *Handbook for Bloggers and Cyber-Dissidents* can be downloaded.

Worldpress.org
http://www.worldpress.org

Worldpress.org is a digest of world news from the world's newspapers. The site contains originally written material and articles reprinted from the press outside the United States. Besides the latest news stories, resources include world headlines (updated every 15 minutes), a directory of world newspapers, World Press and other RSS news feeds, country maps and profiles (from the CIA World Factbook), the texts of documents in the news and links to think tanks and nongovernmental organizations. The homepage also has a link to world cartoons, a currency converter and World-timeserver.com. The site's most recent feature is World Blogs.

Glossary

ABC Audit Bureau of Circulations or Australian Broadcasting Corporation.

Accreditation The process by which the government certifies members of the press to cover government-related news events.

Advance An amount the publisher pays the author before the book is published.

Advertising Campaign A planned advertising effort, coordinated for a specific time period.

Affiliates Stations that carry TV network programming but are not owned by the networks.

Agenda-Setting The belief that journalists don't tell you *what* to think but do tell you *what and whom to think about.*

All-Platform Journalists Broadcast journalists who act as their own producer, cameraperson and editor, and sometimes even transmit live video.

Alternative, or Dissident, Press Media that present alternative viewpoints that challenge the mainstream press.

Analog In mass communications, a type of technology used in broadcasting, whereby video or audio information is sent as continuous signals through the air on specific airwave frequencies.

Ancillary Rights Marketing opportunities related to a movie, in addition to direct income from the movie itself.

ASCAP American Society of Composers, Authors and Publishers.

Audiobooks Abridged versions of classic books and popular new titles on CDs.

Avatar An icon or a representation of a user—a digital stand-in—that people create to represent their online identity.

BBC British Broadcasting Corporation, the government-funded British broadcast network.

Blacklisting Studio owners' refusal to hire someone who was suspected of taking part in subversive activities.

Blanket Licensing Agreement An arrangement whereby radio stations become authorized to use recorded music for broadcast by paying a fee.

Blind Booking The practice of renting films to exhibitors without letting them see the films first.

Block Booking The practice of requiring theaters to take a package of movies instead of showing the movies individually.

Blockbuster A book that achieves enormous financial success.

Blog Short for Web log. A running Internet discussion group, where items are posted in reverse chronological order. Blogs usually focus on a specific topic.

BMI Broadcast Music, Inc., a cooperative music licensing organization.

Browser Software that allows people to display and interact with information on Web pages.

Bundle A collection of programs and/or media services offered together for a set fee.

CATV Community antenna television or cable television.

CDA Communications Decency Act.

CD-RW Drives Computer drives that are used to read data and music encoded in digital form and can be used to record more than once.

Censorship The practice of suppressing material that is considered morally, politically or otherwise objectionable.

Checkbook Journalism The practice of a news organization paying for an interview or a photograph.

Click-Through Rate The rate at which someone who sees an ad on an Internet site clicks through to learn more.

Company Magazines Magazines produced by businesses for their employees, customers and stockholders.

Compatible Media that can function well with one another to exchange and integrate text, pictures, sound and video.

Concentration of Ownership The current trend of large companies buying smaller companies so that fewer companies own more types of media businesses.

Conglomerates Companies that own media companies as well as businesses that are unrelated to the media business.

Consensus Journalism The tendency among many journalists covering the same event to report similar conclusions about the event.

Consumer Magazines All magazines sold by subscription or at newsstands, supermarkets and bookstores.

Convergence The melding of the communications, computer and electronics industries. Also used to describe the economic alignment of the various media companies with each other to take advantage of technological advancements.

Cooperative News Gathering Member news organizations that share the expense of getting the news.

COPA Child Online Protection Act. A law aimed at preventing minors from getting access to sexually explicit online material.

CPM Cost-per-thousand, the cost of an ad per 1,000 people reached. (M is the Roman numeral for 1,000.)

Crisis Communication A timely public relations response to a critical situation that could cause damage to a company's reputation.

Cross-Ownership The practice of one company owning radio and TV stations in the same broadcast market.

Cybersmears Negative information organized and presented on the Internet as continuing attacks against a corporation.

Darknet A file-sharing service that restricts membership to keep its online activities private.

Data Compression The process of squeezing digital content into a smaller electronic space.

DBS Direct broadcast satellites.

Demographics Data about consumers' characteristics, such as age, gender, income level, marital status, geographic location and occupation.

Deregulation Government action that removes government restrictions on the business operation of an industry.

Digital Audio Broadcast A new form of audio transmission that eliminates all static and makes more program choices possible.

Digital Communication Data in a form that can be transmitted and received electronically.

Digital Divide The term used to describe the lack of access to digital technology among low-income, rural and minority groups.

Digital Media All emerging communications media that combine text, graphics, sound and video using computer technology.

Direct Sponsorship A program that carries an advertiser's name in the program title.

Disinformation The intentional planting of false information by government sources.

DMCA Digital Millennium Copyright Act.

Drive-Time Audiences People who listen to the radio in their cars during 6 to 9 a.m. and 4 to 7 p.m.

DSL Digital Subscriber Line.

DVR Digital video recorders.

E-books Electronic books.

E-mail Mail that is delivered electronically over the Internet.

Embedded During the Iraq War, a term used to describe journalists who were allowed to cover the war on the frontlines, supervised by the U.S. military.

Ethics The rules or standards that govern someone's conduct.

Ethnocentric Promoting the superiority of one ethnic group over another.

False Light The charge that what was implied in a story about someone was incorrect.

FCC Federal Communications Commission.

Feedback A response sent back to the sender from the person who receives the communication.

File Sharing The peer-to-peer distribution of copyrighted material on the Internet without the copyright owner's permission.

Freelancers Writers who are not on the staff of a magazine but who are paid for each individual article published.

High-Definition Television (HDTV) A type of television that provides a picture with a clearer resolution than typical TV sets.

Home Page The first page of a Web site that welcomes the user.

Hot Spot A public area like a restaurant or hotel where people with laptops and hand-held Internet devices can connect to the Internet without a wire.

HTML Hypertext markup language.

HTTP Hypertext transfer protocol.

HUAC House Un-American Activities Committee.

Hudson Test A legal test that establishes a standard for commercial speech protection.

IHT *International Herald Tribune*, the world's largest English-language newspaper.

Intellectual Property Rights Ownership of ideas and content published on the Web or in any other medium.

Interactive A message system that allows senders and receivers to communicate simultaneously.

Internet An international web of computer networks.

ISP Internet service provider.

LAPS Test A yardstick for local obscenity judgments, that evaluates an artistic work's literary, artistic, political or scientific value.

Libel A false statement that damages a person's character or reputation by exposing that person to public ridicule or contempt.

Links Electronic connections from one source of information to another.

LP Long-playing record.

Magic Bullet Theory The assertion that media messages directly and measurably affect people's behavior.

Mass Communication Communication from one person or group of persons through a transmitting device (a medium) to large audiences or markets.

Mass Market Books Books distributed through "mass" channels—newsstands, chain stores, drugstores and supermarkets.

Mass Media Industries Eight types of media businesses: books, newspapers, magazines, recordings, radio, movies, television and the Internet.

Media Plural of the word *medium*.

Media Content Analysis An attempt to analyze how what the media present influences behavior.

Media Effects Research An attempt to analyze how people use the information they receive from the media.

Medium The means by which a message reaches the audience. The singular form of the word *media*.

Message Pluralism The availability to an audience of a variety of information and entertainment sources.

Mobile Marketing An advertising campaign directed at cell phone users.

MPAA Motion Picture Association of America.

Muckrakers Investigative magazine journalists who targeted abuses by government and big business.

NAB National Association of Broadcasters, the lobbying organization that represents broadcasters' interests.

Narrowcasting Segmenting the radio audience.

Network A collection of radio or TV stations that offers programs, usually simultaneously, throughout the country, during designated program times.

NII National Information Infrastructure.

Noise Distortion (such as static) that interferes with clear communication.

NSL National Security Letter.

NWICO New World Information and Communications Order. The concept that media can include all areas of the world, not just the West.

O & Os TV stations that are *o*wned and *o*perated by the networks.

Pass-Along Readership People who share a magazine with the original recipient.

Payola The practice of accepting payment to play specific recordings on the air.

Penny Paper or Penny Press A newspaper produced by dropping the price of each copy to a penny and supporting the production cost through advertising.

Persuasion The act of using argument or reasoning to induce someone to do something.

Phonetic Writing The use of symbols to represent sounds.

Photojournalism Using photographs to accompany text to capture a news story.

Pictograph A symbol of an object that is used to convey an idea.

Podcast An audio or video file made available on the Internet for anyone to download, often available by subscription.

Point-of-Purchase Magazines Magazines that consumers buy directly, not by subscription. They are sold mainly at checkout stands in supermarkets.

Pool Reporting An arrangement that places reporters in small, government-supervised groups to cover an event.

Pop-Up An advertisement on a Web site that appears on the screen either behind a Web page when someone leaves the site or on top of the Web site home page when someone first visits.

Prime Time The TV time period from 7 to 11 p.m. when more people watch TV than at any other time.

Prior Restraint Government censorship of information before the information is published or broadcast.

Public Domain Publications, products and processes that are not protected by copyright and thus are available free to the public.

Public Relations Creating understanding for, or goodwill toward, a company, a person or a product.

Publicity Uncontrolled free use of media by a public relations firm to create events and present information to capture press and public attention.

Publishing Placing items on the Web.

Qualified Privilege The freedom of the press to report what is discussed during legislative and court proceedings.

Rating The percentage of the total number of households *with TV sets* that is watching a particular program.

RBOCs Regional Bell Operating Companies, or "Baby Bells."

Rep Firm A company of advertising sales representatives who sell advertising time and space in their market to companies outside their area.

RIAA Recording Industry Association of America.

Roth Test A standard court test for obscenity, named for one of the defendants in an obscenity case.

Royalty An amount the publisher pays an author, based on an established percentage of the book's price; royalties run anywhere from 6 to 15 percent.

RPM Revolutions per minute.

RSS Really Simple Syndication. Allows a person to create a personal set of Internet programs and services to be delivered to a single Web site location.

Satellite Radio Radio transmission by satellite, with limited or no advertising, available by subscription.

Search Engine The tool used to locate information in a computer database.

Search Marketing Positioning Internet advertising prominently next to consumers' related online search results.

Seditious Language Language that authorities believe could incite rebellion against the government.

Selective Perception The concept that each person processes messages differently.

Server The equipment that delivers programs from the program source to the program's subscribers.

Share The percentage of the audience *with TV sets turned on* that is watching a particular program.

Shield Laws Laws that protect journalists from being required to reveal confidential sources in a legal proceeding.

Situation Comedy A TV program that establishes a fixed set of characters typically in a home or work situation. Also called a sitcom.

Spam Unsolicited bulk email.

Spiral of Silence The belief that people with divergent views may be reluctant to challenge the consensus of opinion offered by the media.

Star System Promoting popular movie personalities to lure audiences.

Studio System An early method of hiring a stable of salaried stars and production people under exclusive contracts to a specific studio.

Subscription Television Services A term used to describe cable and satellite program delivery.

Subsidiary Rights The rights to market a book for other uses—to make a movie or to print a character from the book on T-shirts, for example.

Sweeps The months when TV ratings services gather their most important ratings—February, May and November.

Syndicates News agencies that sell articles for publication to a number of newspapers simultaneously.

Syndicators Services that sell programming to broadcast stations and cable.

Tabloid A small-format newspaper that features large photographs and illustrations along with sensational stories.

Telco An abbreviation for telephone company.

30-Year Rule Developed by Paul Saffo, the theory that says it takes about 30 years for a new technology to be completely adopted within a culture.

Time-Shifting Recording a television program on a DVR to watch at a more convenient time.

Trade, Technical and Professional Magazines Magazines dedicated to a particular business or profession.

Two-Step Flow The transmission of information and ideas from mass media to opinion leaders and then to friends.

Vertical Integration An attempt by one company to simultaneously control several related aspects of the media business.

Viral Marketing Creating an online message that is entertaining enough to get consumers to pass it on over the Internet like a virus.

Wi-Fi An abbreviation for *Wireless Fi*delity.

Wiki Technology that allows many users to collaborate to create and update an Internet page.

WIPO World Intellectual Property Organization.

Yellow Journalism News that emphasizes crime, sex and violence; also called jazz journalism and tabloid journalism.

Media Information Resource Guide

This directory is designed to familiarize you with some of the publications that will help you find background and current information about the media. Also included is a list of associations that can provide information about specific media businesses.

The study of media covers many areas of scholarship besides journalism and mass communication. Historians, psychologists, economists, political scientists and sociologists, for example, often contribute ideas to media studies.

This directory therefore includes a variety of information sources from academic and industry publications as well as from popular periodicals.

Media Research Sources You Should Know

The Wall Street Journal is the best daily source of information about the business of the media. You can find articles specifically about the media every day plus regular reports on earnings, acquisitions and leaders in the media industries. *The Wall Street Journal* archive online will help you find the articles you need.

The *Los Angeles Times* daily section "Calendar" follows the media business very closely, especially television and movies, because the majority of these companies are based in Los Angeles. The print edition is available online in its entirety.

The New York Times and *The Washington Post* also carry media information and both archives are indexed online.

Advertising Age publishes special issues throughout the year focusing on newspapers, magazines and broadcasting. *Advertising Age* has an online index but charges a fee or requires user registration for some articles.

Columbia Journalism Review and *American Journalism Review* regularly critique developments in the print and broadcast industries. *Columbia Journalism Review* is published by New York's Columbia University Graduate School of Journalism. The Philip Merrill College of Journalism at the University of Maryland publishes *American Journalism Review*.

Communication Abstracts, Communication Research, Journal of Communication and *Journalism Quarterly* offer scholarly articles and article summaries about media issues. Journals that cover specific media topics include *Journalism History, Journal of Advertising Research, Newspaper Research Journal* and *Public Relations Review*.

Advertising Age publishes regular estimates of actual advertising receipts as each year progresses. Universal McCann in New York publishes annual projections of advertising revenue in a publication called *Insider's Report*.

Included are ongoing tables on total advertising revenue for each year, as well as a breakdown of national and local advertising.

The Veronis, Suhler Stevenson Communications Industry Forecast, published annually in July, follows all the media industries. The *Forecast* offers historical media tables, tracking past performance, as well as projections for future media industry growth. VSS MediaResearchNet is the online version of the *Forecast*.

Broadcasting & Cable Yearbook is an annual compilation of material about the broadcast industry. Also listed are syndicators, brokers, advertising agencies and associations.

Editor & Publisher International Yearbook, published annually, lists all U.S. and Canadian, as well as many foreign, newspapers. Advertising trends and newspaper rankings by circulation size are profiled in tables, and information is available on industry services and organizations. A separate volume, "Who's Where," is a directory of names, phone numbers and job functions of major players in the newspaper business.

Encyclopedia of American Journalism (edited by Stephen Vaughn, 2007) documents the distinctions between print media, radio, television and the Internet and their roles in the formation of a variety of phenomena in American society, including peace and protest, civil and consumer rights, environmentalism and globalization.

Ulrich's Periodicals Directory lists journals, magazines and newspapers alphabetically and by subject. Its online counterpart, Ulrichsweb.com, is continually updated with new information and includes an archive of changes.

Standard Directory of Advertising Agencies shows advertising agencies alphabetically, along with the accounts they manage.

Questia is an online library of books, journals and magazine and newspaper articles. The communication section features categories such as media studies on film, TV, Internet and print media; journalism history and ethics; and advertising and public relations.

ASCAP (The American Society of Composers, Authors and Publishers) lists a number of reference books, periodicals, directories and professional organizations pertaining to the recording industry in its online resource guide.

Radio Yearbook (published by BIA Financial Network) is a complete directory of commercial radio stations, owners, personnel and service providers.

Hollywood Creative Directory, produced by *The Hollywood Reporter*, is a comprehensive list that includes names, numbers and Web site listings of producers and executives in film and television, production companies, studios and networks.

Digital Media Wire publishes daily newsletters and directories about the business of digital media, including *Digital Entertainment & Media Directory*.

Sources to Help Uncover American Media History

The Journalist's Bookshelf by Roland E. Wolseley and Isabel Wolseley (R. J. Berg, 1986) is a comprehensive listing of resources about American print journalism.

The classic early history of American magazines is Frank Luther Mott's *History of American Magazines* (D. Appleton, 1930). *Pages from the Past: History and Memory in American Magazines* by Carolyn Kitch (The University of North Carolina Press, 2008) examines the role of magazines in creating collective memory and identity for Americans.

Christopher H. Sterling and John M. Kittross provide an overview of radio and television history in *Stay Tuned: A Concise History of American Broadcasting*, 2nd ed. (Wadsworth, 1990). The classic television history is Eric Barnouw's *Tube of Plenty* (Oxford University Press, 1975). *The Columbia History of American Television* by Gary Edgerton (Columbia University Press, 2007) follows the technological developments and cultural relevance of TV from its pre-history to the present. *Listening In: Radio and American Imagination* by Susan J. Douglas (University of Minnesota Press, 2004) and *Radio Reader: Essays in the Cultural History of Radio* by Michele Hilmes (Routledge, 2001) discuss the cultural impact of radio in the 20th century.

A History of Films by John L. Fell (Holt, Rinehart & Winston, 1979) and *Movie-Made America* by Robert Sklar (New York: Random House, 1994) provide a good introduction to the history of movies. Works examining the cultural, social and economic impacts on American society include *American Film: A History* by Jon Lewis (W.W. Norton, 2007); *Movie-Made America: A Cultural History of American Movies* by Robert Sklar, revised edition (Vintage, 1994); and *Movies and American Society* edited by Steven J. Ross (Wiley-Blackwell, 2002).

Halliwell's Film, Video and DVD Guide (Harper Collins, 2007) by Leslie Halliwell and John L. Walker, updated annually, is a great encyclopedic source for movie information. Another good movie information resource is *The Film Encyclopedia* (Collins, 2008), currently in its sixth edition, by Ephraim Katz.

Sterling and Kittross' *Stay Tuned* (Wadsworth, 1990) provides some information about the recording industry. *This Business of Music* by M. William Krasilovsky, Sidney Shemel, John M. Gross and Jonathan Feinstein (Billboard Publications, 2007) explains how the recording industry works.

John P. Dessauer's *Book Publishing: What It Is, What It Does* (R. R. Bowker, 1981) succinctly explains the history of the book publishing business. Another historical perspective and overview is available in *Books: The Culture & Commerce of Publishing* by Lewis A. Coser et al. (Basic Books, 1982). *The Book Publishing Industry* by Albert N. Greco, second edition (Lawrence Erlbaum, 2004) discusses marketing, production, and changing technology. *Book Business: Publishing Past, Present and Future* by Jason Epstein (W.W. Norton & Company, 2002) assesses the past and present book business.

Three histories of American advertising are *The Making of Modern Advertising* by Daniel Pope (Basic Books, 1983), *The Mirror Makers: A History of American Advertising and Its Creators* by Stephen Fox (University of Illinois Press, 1997), and *Advertising the American Dream* by Roland Marchand (Berkeley: University of California Press, 1986).

In 1923, Edward L. Bernays wrote the first book specifically about public relations, *The Engineering of Consent* (Norman: University of Oklahoma Press, reprinted in 1955). For an understanding of today's public relations business, you can read *This Is PR: The Realities of Public Relations* by Doug Newsom, Judy VanSlyke Turk, and Dean Kruckeberg (Wadsworth, 2006).

A Social History of the Media: From Gutenberg to the Internet by Peter Burke and Asa Briggs, second edition (Polity, 2005) and *Convergence Culture: Where Old and New Media Collide* by Henry Jenkins (NYU Press, 2008) discuss the emergence and evolution of communications media, their social impact and the relationship between the media producer and consumer.

To learn more about newsreels and to view the actual films, visit the University of South Carolina Web site, www.sc.edu/library/newsfilm. Other major newsreel collections exist at the National Archives and Records Administration Web site at www.archives.gov and at the Library of Congress, www.loc.gov/library/libarch-digital.html. British Pathé newsreels are located at www.britishpathe.com.

The most comprehensive academic journals specifically devoted to media history are *American Journalism*, published by the American Journalism Historians Association, and *Journalism History*, published by the E.W. Scripps School of Journalism at Ohio University, with support from the History Division of the Association for Education in Journalism and Mass Communication.

For information about historical events and people in the media who often are omitted from other histories, you can refer to *Up from the Footnote: A History of Women Journalists* by Marion Marzolf (Hastings House, 1977); *Great Women of the Press* by Madelon Golden Schilpp and Sharon M. Murphy (Southern Illinois University Press, 1983); *Taking Their Place: A Documentary History of Women and Journalism* by Maurine Hoffman Beasley and Sheila Jean Gibbons, 2nd Edition (Strata Publishing, 2002); *Journalistas: 100 Years of the Best Writing and Reporting by Women Journalists*, edited by Eleanor Mills (Seal Press, 2005); *Black Journalists: the NABJ Story*, by Wayne Dawkins, updated edition (August Press, 1997); *Ladies' Pages: African American Women's Magazines and the Culture that Made Them* by Noliwe M. Rooks (Rutgers University Press, 2004); *Minorities and Media: Diversity and the End of Mass Communication* by Clint C. Wilson and Felix Gutiérrez (Sage Publications, 1985); *Gender, Race and Class in Media* by Gail Dines and Jean M. Humez (Sage Publications, 2002); and *Facing Difference: Race, Gender and Mass Media* by Shirley Biagi and Marilyn Kern-Foxworth (Pine Forge Press, 1997).

Web Sites Where You Can Find Current Media News

Thousands of Web sites on the Internet offer useful material. What follows is an alphabetical list of the specific sites that also are listed at the end of each chapter. If you can't reach the Web site at the address listed, search using the site's name, listed in **bold type**.

To find a group of Web sites on a specific media topic, check **Working the Web** at the end of each chapter.

Academy of Motion Picture Arts and Sciences
http://www.oscars.org

Adrants
http://www.adrants.com

Advertising Age
http://www.adage.com

Advertising Council
http://www.adcouncil.org

All About Public Relations
http://www.aboutpublicrelations.net

AllYouCanRead.com
http://www.allyoucanread.com

Amazon.com
http://www.amazon.com

American Advertising Federation
http://www.aaf.org

American Association of Advertising Agencies
http://www2.aaaa.org

American Booksellers Association
http://www.bookweb.org

American Booksellers Foundation for Free Expression (ABFFE)
http://www.abffe.org

American Library Association (ALA)
http://www.ala.org

American Marketing Association
http://www.marketingpower.com

American Society of Journalists and Authors
http://www.asja.org

American Society of Newspaper Editors
http://www.asne.org

American Top 40 with Ryan Seacrest
http://www.at40.com

AOL Music
http://music.aol.com

Apple Computer, Inc.
http://www.apple.com

Apple.com/iTunes
http://www.apple.com/itunes

Association of American Publishers
http://www.publishers.org

Association of Hispanic Advertising Agencies
http://www.ahaa.org

Barnes & Noble
http://www.barnesandnoble.com

BBC News
http://www.bbc.co.uk

Benton Foundation
http://www.benton.org

Biblio
http://www.biblio.com

Billboard
http://billboard.biz and http://billboard.com

BookFinder
http://www.bookfinder.com

The Broadcast Archive
http://www.oldradio.com

Canadian Broadcasting Corporation (CBC) Radio-Canada
http://www.cbc.ca/radio

CBS Corporation
http://www.cbscorporation.com

CBS Radio
http://www.cbsradio.com

Center for Media and Democracy: PRWatch.org
http://www.prwatch.org

Center on Media and Child Health
http://www.cmch.tv

Chartered Institute of Public Relations (association of European public relations professionals)
http://www.cipr.co.uk

Clio Awards
http://www.clioawards.com

CNET
http://www.cnet.com

Columbia Journalism Review (CJR)
http://www.cjr.org

Committee to Protect Journalists
http://www.cpj.org

CondéNet
http://www.condenet.com

Cyberjournalist.net
http://www.cyberjournalist.net

The Dallas Morning News
http://www.dallasnews.com

DEG Digital Entertainment Group
http://www.dvdinformation.com

Disney-ABC Television Group
http://www.disneyabctv.com

Electronic Frontier Foundation
http://www.eff.org

EthnicNet, European Ethics Codes
http://ethicnet.uta.fi/

Fairness & Accuracy in Reporting (FAIR)
http://www.fair.org/index.php

Federal Communications Commission (FCC)
http://www.fcc.gov

Federal Trade Commission
http://www.ftc.gov

FindLaw
http://www.findlaw.com

Folio: The Magazine for Magazine Management
http://www.foliomag.com

Foreign Policy Magazine
http://www.foreignpolicy.com

Fox Movietone News
http://www.sc.edu/library/newsfilm/index.html

Freedom Forum
http://www.freedomforum.org

Freedom of Information Center (University of Missouri School of Journalism, Columbia)
http://www.nfoic.org/foi-center

Friday Morning Quarterback (FMQB)
http://www.fmqb.com

Gannett Company, Inc. (owners of USA Today)
http://www.gannett.com

General Electric (major owner of NBC Universal)
http://www.ge.com

Global Media Journal
http://lass.calumet.purdue.edu/cca/gmj/index.htm

Global Media Monitor
http://lass.calument.purdue.edu/cca/gmm

Google Book Search
http://books.google.com

HDTV Network
http://www.HDTV.net

Honolulu Star-Bulletin
http://www.starbulletin.com

Index on Censorship
http://www.indexoncensorship.org

Indiana University Index of Journalism Ethics Cases
http://journalism.indiana.edu/resources/ethics/

IndieBound
http://www.indiebound.org

Inside Radio
http://www.insideradio.com

Insound
http://www.insound.com

Institute for Public Relations (public relations research)
http://www.instituteforpr.com

International Center for Journalists
http://www.icfj.org

International Herald Tribune
http://www.iht.com

International Women's Media Foundation
http://www.iwmf.org

The Internet Movie Database (IMDb)
http://www.imdb.com

Internews
http://www.internews.org

Investigative Reporters and Editors
http://www.ire.org

iVillage
http://www.ivillage.com

Joan Shorenstein Center on the Press, Politics and Public Policy (Harvard University)
http://www.hks.harvard.edu/presspol/

Journal of Electronic Publishing
http://www.journalofelectronicpublishing.org

Los Angeles Times
http://www.latimes.com

Lucas Film
http://www.lucasfilm.com

Magazine Publishers of American (MPA) and the American Society of Magazine Editors (ASME)
http://www.magazine.org

Media Awareness Network (MNet)
http://www.media-awareness.ca

Media Center at New York Law School
http://www.nyls.edu/pages/107.asp

Media Effects Research Lab at Penn State University
http://www.psu.edu/dept/medialab/index.html

Media Law Resource Center (MLRC)
http://www.medialaw.org

Media Research Hub (Social Science Research Council)
http://mediaresearchhub.ssrc.org

MediaPost Communications
http://www.mediapost.com

The Miami Herald
http://www.miamiherald.com

Minnesota News Council
http://news-council.org

MIT Media Lab Project
http://www.media.mit.edu

Moorland-Spingarn Research Center (MSRC) at Howard University
http://www.howard.edu/library/moorland-spingarn

Motion Picture Association of America (MPAA) and Motion Picture Association (MPA)
http://www.mpaa.org

MySpace
http://www.myspace.com

Napster
http://www.napster.com

National Association of Broadcasters
http://www.nab.org

National Cable & Telecommunications Association
http://www.ncta.com

National Journal
http://www.nationaljournal.com

National Public Radio
http://www.npr.org

NBC Universal
http://www.nbcuni.com

Netflix
http://www.netflix.com

The New York Times
http://www.nytimes.com

News Corporation
http://www.newscorp.com

Newspaper Association of America
http://www.naa.org

Newsweek
http://www.newsweek.com

Nielsen Media Research
http://www.nielsenmedia.com

Northwestern University Library: Broadcast, Cable and Satellite Resources on the Internet
http://www.library.northwestern.edu/media/resources/broadcast.html

O, the Oprah Magazine
http://www.oprah.com/omagazine

The Online News Association (ONA)
http://www.journalist.org

Online Public Relations
http://www.online-pr.com

Online Publishers Association
http://www.online-publishers.org

Pandora: Music from the Music Genome Project
http://pandora.com

Parental Media Guide
http://parentalguide.org

Pew Internet and American Life Project
http://www.pewinternet.org

Pew Research Center for People and the Press
http://people-press.org/reports

Poynter Online
http://www.poynter.org

PR Newswire
http://prnewswire.com

PR Week
http://www.prweekus.com

Press Release News Wire
http://www.prweb.com

Project for Excellence in Journalism: Understanding News in the Information Age
http://journalism.org

Public Broadcasting (PBS)
http://www.pbs.org

Public Relations Society of America (PRSA)
http://www.prsa.org

Public Relations Student Society of America (PRSSA)
http://www.prssa.org

Radio Advertising Bureau
http://www.rab.com

Radio Lovers
http://www.radiolovers.com

Radio Time
http://radiotime.com

Radio-Television News Directors Association and Foundation (RTNDA and RTNDF)
http://www.rtnda.org

Recording Industry Association of America
http://www.riaa.com

Reporters Without Borders
http://www.rsf.org

Rhapsody.com
http://www.rhapsody.com

Salon Magazine
http://www.salon.com

Scholastic Corporation
http://www.scholastic.com

Screenwriters Federation of America (SFA)
http://www.screenwritersfederation.org

Seattle Post-Intelligencer
http://seattlepi.nwsource.com

Silha Center for the Study of Media Ethics and Law (University of Minnesota)
http://silha.umn.edu

Sirius Satellite Radio
http://www.sirius.com

Slate Magazine
http://www.slate.com

Society of Professional Journalists (SPJ)
http://www.spj.org

Sony Corporation of America
http://www.sony.com

Sports Illustrated
http://sportsillustrated.cnn.com

Student Press Law Center (SPLC)
http://www.splc.org

Sundance Institute
http://www.sundance.org

Talking Points Memo (TPM)
http://www.talkingpointsmemo.com

Television Bureau of Advertising (TVB)
http://www.tvb.org

Time Warner
http://www.timewarner.com

Topix
http://www.topix.net

Tribune Company
http://www.tribune.com

TV.com
http://www.tv.com

United Artists
http://www.unitedartists.com

Unity: Journalists of Color
http://www.unityjournalists.org

Universal Music Group
http://www.universalmusic.com

University of Iowa Online Communication Studies Resources: Political Advertising
http://www.uiowa.edu/commstud/resources/pol_ads.html

U.S. Census Bureau 2007 Statistical Abstract: Information and Communications
http://www.census.gov/compendia/statab/cats/information_communications.html

Vanderbilt University Television News Archive
http://tvnews.vanderbilt.edu

Viacom (owners of MTV, BET and Paramount Pictures)
http://www.viacom.com

Vivendi
http://www.vivendi.com

Walt Disney Company (owners of ABC)
http://corporate.disney.go.com

Warner Bros.
http://www.warnerbros.com

The Washington Post
http://www.washingtonpost.com

Whatis?com
http://whatis.techtarget.com

Worldpress.org
http://www.worldpress.org

YouTube
http://www.youtube.com

More Media Research Sources You Can Use

Many magazines publish information about the mass media industries and support industries. The following is a listing of the major magazines in each subject area. Many of these magazines have companion Web sites.

ADVERTISING

Advertising Age

Adweek and *Adweek: National Marketing Edition*

Journal of Advertising

Journal of Advertising Research

BROADCASTING

Broadcasting & Cable

Emmy, published by the Academy of Television Arts and Sciences

Federal Communications Law Journal

Journal of Broadcasting and Electronic Media, published by Broadcast Education Association

RTNDA Communicator, published by the Radio-Television News Directors Association

TV Guide

MAGAZINE AND BOOK PUBLISHING

Bookwoman, published by the Women's National Book Association

Folio, the magazine for magazine management

Publishers Weekly, the journal of the book industry

MOVIES

Film Comment, published by the Film Society of Lincoln Center

Hollywood Reporter

Variety

Video Age

NEWSPAPERS

Editor & Publisher

Journalism & Communication Monographs, published by the Association for Education in Journalism and Mass Communication

Newspaper Research Journal, published by the Association for Education in Journalism and Mass Communication

Presstime, published by the Newspaper Association of America

Quill, published by the Society of Professional Journalists

PUBLIC RELATIONS

Public Relations Journal

PR Week

RECORDINGS

Billboard

Cash Box

Down Beat

Music Index, a separate index that covers articles on the music industry

Rolling Stone

DIGITAL MEDIA AND THE WEB

AI Magazine

Communications Daily

Computer Gaming World

MacWorld

PC Magazine

PC World

Technical Communication

Information Today

Wired

Global Media

ADVERTISING
International Journal of Advertising, England

BROADCASTING
Broadcast, London

Cable and Satellite Europe, London

MOVIES
Cineaction, Canada

Empire, London

Film Ireland

Film Ink, Australia

RECORDINGS
Musical America International Directory of the Performing Arts

OTHER
OPMA Overseas Media Guide, England

MEDIA-RELATED TOPICS
Censorship News, published by the National Coalition Against Censorship

Communication Research

Entertainment Law Reporter, covers motion pictures, radio, TV and music

News Media and the Law, published by Reporters Committee for Freedom of the Press

Nieman Reports, published by the Nieman Foundation for Journalism at Harvard University

Chapter References

Chapter 1 Mass Media and Everyday Life

Associated Press (2007, April 18). Clear Channel accepts $19.4 billion offer. Money.aol.com.

Austen, I. (2007, May 16). Thomson adds Reuters in $17 billion bid to be giant. *The New York Times,* C1.

Bagdikian, B. (1980, Spring). Conglomeration, concentration, and the media. *Journal of Communication,* 60.

Bagdikian, B. (1983). *The media monopoly.* Boston: Beacon Press.

Bee News Services (2006, December 15). Perpetually plugged in. *The Sacramento Bee,* A1.

Carr, D. (2007, January 15). 24-hour newspaper people. *The New York Times,* C1.

Cerf, V. G. (2001, September). The invisible Internet. *Communications of the ACM,* 34.

Compaine, B. (1979). *Who owns the media?* White Plains, N.Y.: Knowledge Industry Publications.

DeWitt, P. E. (1993, April 12). Electronic superhighway. *Time,* 53.

Geller, A. (2000, November 6). High tech wearables take to the catwalk. *San Francisco Chronicle,* D15.

Gilder, G. (1994, February 28). Life after television, updated. *Forbes,* 17.

Graham, J. (2005, May 20). Google gets personal. *USA Today,* 6B.

Greene, J. (2003, April 28). The year of living wirelessly. BusinessWeek.com.

Higgins, J., & McClellan, S. (2001, October 8). Media executives' new boast. *Broadcasting & Cable,* 6.

Jenkins, H. (2000, March). Digital land grab. *Technology Review,* 103.

Kharif, O. (2005, June 21). Nearly everything gets unplugged. BusinessWeek.com.

Kim, R. (2005, May 28). Sales of cell phones totally off the hook. *San Francisco Chronicle,* C1.

King, T. R. (1994, August 23). News Corp.'s Twentieth Century Fox forms unit to make "mainstream" films. *The Wall Street Journal,* B5.

Kirkpatrick, D. D. (2003, April 14). Murdoch's first step: Make the sports fan pay. *The New York Times,* C1.

Knight-Ridder Newspapers (1994, January 12). Launching the info revolution. *The Sacramento Bee,* G1.

Landler, M. (1997, September 20). Westinghouse to acquire 98 radio stations. *The New York Times,* Y23.

Levy, S. (1997/1998, December 29–January 5). A blow to the empire. *Newsweek,* 58–60.

Liebling, A. J. (1961). *The press.* New York: Ballantine.

Lipman, J. (1986, March 9). Ad agencies feverishly ride a merger wave. *The Wall Street Journal,* 6.

Markoff, J. (2004, December 4). Internet eats up user's day. *The Sacramento Bee,* D1.

McClain, D. L. (2005, August 8). It's a gadget, gadget, gadget world. *The New York Times,* C5.

Plato (1961). *Collected works.* Princeton, N.J.: Phaedrus.

Raine, G. (2005, September 27). Net ad revenues grow steadily. *San Francisco Chronicle,* D1.

Robinson, M. J., & Olszewski, R. (1980, Spring). Books in the marketplace of ideas. *Journal of Communication,* 82.

Rose, L. (2007, February 7). The best-paid talking heads. Forbes.com.

Scott, A. O. (2008, November 23). The screening of America. *The New York Times Magazine,* 21.

Siebert, F., Peterson, T., & Schramm, W. (1963). *The four theories of the press.* Urbana: University of Illinois Press.

Siebert, T. (2007, February). World wide web: Hearing is believing. Mediapost.com.

Siklos, R. (2005, August 1). Behind Murdoch rift, a media dynasty unhappy in its own way. *The New York Times,* C1.

Siklos, R. (2007, May 13). Tilting at a digital future. *The New York Times,* 3-1.

Siklos, R., & Holson, L. (2005, August 8). NBC Universal aims to be prettiest feather in G.E.'s cap. *The New York Times,* C1.

Smith, A. (1980). *Goodbye Gutenberg.* New York: Oxford University Press.

Soto, M. (2000, May 4). Microsoft executive Nathan Myhrvold resigns. *The Seattle Times.*

Story, L. (2007, January 15). Anywhere the eye can see, it's now likely to see an ad. *The New York Times,* A1.

Sutel, S. (2003, October 9). Vivendi deal gives NBC media clout. *San Francisco Chronicle,* B1.

Sutel, S. (2005, September 20). *New York Times* to cut 4 percent of work force. Associated Press, AOL Business News.

Thomas, S. G. (1999, November 15). Getting to know you.com. *U.S. News & World Report,* 102–104.

Ziegler, B. (1994, May 18). Building the highway: New obstacles, new solutions. *The Wall Street Journal,* B1.

Chapter 2 Books: Rearranging the Page

Austen, I. (2007, May 12). Thomson agrees to sell educational group. Nytimes.com.

Bohlen, C. (2001, November 8). "We regret we are unable to open unsolicited mail." *The New York Times,* E4.

Boss, S. (2007, May 13). The great mystery: Making a best-seller. *The New York Times,* 3-1.

Carvajal, D. (1999, December 14). Two book club giants are said to be poised to join forces. *The New York Times,* C1.

Coser, L. A., Kadushin, C., & Powell, W. F. (1982). *Books: The culture and commerce of publishing.* New York: Basic Books.

Crawford, W. (2001, August). MP3 audiobooks: A new library medium? *American Libraries,* 64.

Davis, K. C. (1984). *Two-bit culture: The paperbacking of America.* Boston: Houghton Mifflin.

Dessauer, J. P. (1974). *Book publishing: What it is, what it does.* New York: R. R. Bowker.

Donadio, R. (2008, February 3). Waiting for it. *The New York Times Book Review,* 31.

Donadio, R. (2008, April 27). You're an author? Me too! *The New York Times Book Review,* 27.

Goldberg, B. (2001, April). Censorship watch. *American Libraries,* 25.

Goldstein, B. (2003, January 20). Some best-seller old reliables have string of unreliable sales. *The New York Times,* C1.

Hansell, S. (2003, July 23). Amazon says rise in sales helped cut loss by half. *The New York Times,* C4.

Hart, J. D. (1950). *The popular book.* Berkeley: University of California Press.

Helft, M. (2008, October 29). Google settles suit over book-scanning. Nytimes.com.

Hoffman, J. (2007, April 15). Comparative literature. *The New York Times Book Review,* 27.

Itale, H. (2005, June 5). Booksellers seeing changes in customers. Associated Press, AOL Business News.

Jesdanun, A. (2005, May 21). Publishers fret over college book policies. Associated Press as published in the *San Mateo County Times,* Business-3.

Kelly, K. (2006, May 14). What will happen to books? *The New York Times Magazine,* 43–71.

Kennedy, R. (2005, June 5). Cash up front. *The New York Times Book Review,* 14.

Kirby, C. (2002, December 18). Russian company acquitted in Adobe eBook copyright case. *San Francisco Chronicle,* B1.

Landro, L. (1986, February 3). Publishers' thirst for blockbusters sparks big advances and big risks. *The Wall Street Journal,* 21.

Lara, A. (2003). For superstar authors, the publicity machine runs nonstop. *San Francisco Chronicle.*

Maryles, D. (2001, September 10). Roberts scores with mass turnover. *Publishers Weekly,* 19.

Newman, A. A. (2006, March 2). Authors find their voice, and audience, in podcasts. *The New York Times,* B7.

Paul, F. (2003, September 15). Digital books down but not out. Reuters on AOL.

Randolph, E. (2008, June 18). Reading into the future. Nytimes.com.

Raugust, K. (2001, October 29). Where the action is. *Publishers Weekly,* 24.

Read, M. (2007, February 7). Instead of turning pages, students may be turning on their MP3 players. *San Francisco Chronicle,* C3.

Rich, M. (2007, June 1). Sales barely up, book trade yearns for next blockbuster. *The New York Times,* C3.

Rich, M. (2008, July 27). Literacy debate: Online, r u really reading? *The New York Times,* A1.

Ross, M. (2000, March 8). Simon & Schuster to release story by Stephen King on the Web only. *The Wall Street Journal,* B8.

Rothstein, E. (2007, April 9). Sampling, if not digesting, the digital library. *The New York Times,* B3.

Streitfield, D. (2005, July 17). Publisher loses ruling on e-books. *Los Angeles Times.*

Trachtenberg, J. A. (2007, March 22). Borders' business plan gets a rewrite. Wsj.com.

Veronis, Suhler & Associates (2006, July). *Communications industry forecast: 2006–2010.* New York.

White, E. B. (1976). *Letters of E. B. White.* New York: Harper & Row.

Wyatt, E. (2005, June 2). Expo week arrives, and books are back. *The New York Times,* B1.

Zeitchik, S. (2001, April 23). ABA reaches settlement with B & N, Borders. *Publishers Weekly,* 9.

Chapter 3 Newspapers: Expanding Delivery

Associated Press (2002, April 17). Dawn of a new sun in New York. *San Francisco Chronicle,* A2.

Auletta, K. (2005, October 10). Fault line. *The New Yorker,* 51.

Avriel, E. (2007, July 2). *NY Times* publisher: Our goal is to manage the transition from print to Internet. Haaretz.com.

Carr, D. (2007, April 3). A new owner who is hedging his bets. *The New York Times,* C1.

Dawley, H. (2007, February 8). The endangered newspaper that is not. Medialife.com.

De La Merced, M. (2009, December 8). Tribune files for bankruptcy. Nytimes.com.

Dertouzos, J., & Quinn, T. (1985, September). Bargaining responses to the technology revolution: The case of the newspaper industry. *Labor management cooperation brief.* Washington, D.C.: U.S. Department of Labor.

Holson, L. M., & Waxman, S. (2007, April 3). Zell and Tribune make a deal. *The New York Times,* C1.

Jurgenson, K. (1993, Spring). Diversity: A report from the battlefield. *Newspaper Research Journal,* 92.

Kessler, K. (1984). *The dissident press.* Beverly Hills, Calif.: Sage Publications.

Marzolf, M. (1977). *Up from the footnote.* New York: Hastings House.

McDonald, M. (2001, May 7). A different paper chase. *U.S. News & World Report,* 35.

O'Brien, T. L. (2005, June 26). The newspaper of the future. *The New York Times,* 3-1.

Perez-Pena, R. (2007, May 1). Newspaper circulation in steep slide across nation. *The New York Times,* C10.

Perez-Pena, R. (2008, April 7). Tough guy in a mean business. *The New York Times,* C1.

Reid, C. (2001, July 16). NWU, authors sue NYT again. *Publishers Weekly,* 73.

Romero, S. (2003, August 4). Dallas-Fort Worth papers fight it out in Spanish. *The New York Times,* C6.

Rose, A. (2001, October 30). Can newspapers hold on to post-attack readers? *The Wall Street Journal,* B4.

Rutherford, L. (1963). *John Peter Zenger.* Gloucester, Mass.: Peter Smith.

Schilpp, M. G., & Murphy, S. M. (1983). *Great women of the press.* Carbondale: Southern Illinois University Press.

Seelye, K. Q. (2005, March 14). Can papers end the free ride? *The New York Times,* C1.

Seelye, K. Q. (2005, September 19). Even a darling of the newspaper industry is starting to sweat a bit. *The New York Times,* C1.

Seelye, K. Q. (2005, September 21). Times company announces 500 job cuts. *The New York Times,* C5.

Seelye, K. Q. (2005, November 8). Newspaper daily circulation down 2.6%. *The New York Times,* C1.

Seelye, K. Q. (2007, February 1). Newspaper readers of a different kind. *The New York Times,* C5.

Seelye, K. Q., & Sorkin, A. R. (2007, April 2). Tribune accepts real estate magnate's bid. Nytimes.com.

Siklos, R. (2007, May 3). *Wall Street Journal* weighs life under Murdoch. *The New York Times,* A1.

Siklos, R., & Seelye, K. Q. (2007, April 4). Bidders for Tribune plan moves. *The New York Times,* C1.

Smith, A. (1980). *Goodbye Gutenberg.* New York: Oxford University Press.

Sorkin, A. R. (2007, May 2). First the bid, now the jockeying. *The New York Times,* C1.

Swanberg, W. A. (1971). *Citizen Hearst.* New York: Bantam Books.

Tedeschi, B. (2005, October 17). All the news that you can use. And more. *The New York Times,* C6.

Thomas, L., Jr. (2007, April 20). Times Co., Gannett and Tribune Co. report declines. *The New York Times,* C2.

Wells, I. B. (1970). *The crusade for justice: The autobiography of Ida B. Wells.* Chicago: University of Chicago Press.

Wenner, K. S. (2000, December). Slimming down. *American Journalism Review,* 38.

Wurman, R. S. (1989). *Information anxiety.* New York: Doubleday.

Zezima, K. (2005, August 8). Abolitionist's family celebrates a legacy of nonconformity. *The New York Times,* A10.

Chapter 4 Magazines: Targeting the Audience

Biagi, S. (1987). *NewsTalk I.* Belmont, Calif.: Wadsworth.

Carr, D. (2003, August 4). A magazine's radical plan: Making a profit. *The New York Times,* B1.

Carr, D. (2003, August 4). Gossip goes glossy and loses its stigma. *The New York Times,* B1.

Elliot, S. (2005, August 22). The cover models may not be fatter, but the issues are. *The New York Times,* C7.

Farzad, Roben (2005, August 16). To market a magazine, fill it with celebrity gossip. *The New York Times,* C4.

Fost, D. (2003, August 8). Bay Area still a magazine mecca. *San Francisco Chronicle.*

Holson, E. (2007, May 25). OMG! Cute boys, kissing lips and lots of pics as magazines find a niche. *The New York Times,* C1.

Kobak, J. B. (1985, April). 1984: A billion-dollar year for acquisitions. *Folio,* 14, 82–95.

Kuczynski, A. (2001, September 10). Variety of brash magazines upset the old stereotypes. *The New York Times.*

Lee, F. R. (2005, August 10). He created a mirror for black America. *The New York Times,* B1.

Mechanic, M. (2001, March 19). Doing the bare minimum media: Magazines are rethinking the Internet. *Newsweek,* 62F.

O'Brien, K. J. (2007, March 18). Magazine publishers see future, but no profit in shift to Internet. Iht.com.

Paneth, D. (1983). *Encyclopedia of American journalism.* New York: Facts on File.

Perez-Pena, R. (2008, July 20). Undercover publisher. *The New York Times,* BU1.

Rose, M. (2000, November 6). Problems for magazines come into view. *The Wall Street Journal,* B18.

Schilpp, M. G., & Murphy, S. M. (1983). *Great women of the press.* Carbondale: Southern Illinois University Press.

Seelye, K. Q. (2007, January 19). Time Inc. cutting almost 300 magazine jobs to focus more on Web sites. Nytimes.com.

Seelye, K. Q. (2007, February 23). New Republic to cut back publication schedule. Nytimes.com.

Seelye, K. Q. (2007, March 27). *Life* magazine, its pages dwindling, will cease publication. Nytimes.com.

Seelye, K. Q., & Siklos, R. (2007, January 15). As Time Inc. cuts jobs, one writer on Britney may have to do. Nytimes.com.

Swanberg, W. A. (1972). *Luce and his empire.* New York: Scribner's.

Tarbell, I. (1939). *All in the day's work.* New York: MacMillan.

Wyatt, E. (2005, June 2). 80 years of *The New Yorker* to be offered in disc form. *The New York Times,* B3.

Chapter 5 Recordings: Demanding Choices

Associated Press (2008, July 26). Merger of Sirius and XM approved by F.C.C. Nytimes.com.

Barnard, B. (2000, December). Bertelsmann. *Europe,* 4.

Boucher, G. (2002, September 12). Labels, retailers face the music—cheaper CDs. *San Francisco Chronicle,* D9.

Chmielewski, D. C. (2004, October 27). iPod's rock and roll-out. Mercurynews.com.

Denisoff, R. S. (1975). *Solid gold.* New Brunswick, N.J.: Transaction Books.

Deutsch, C. H. (2002, October 1). Suit settled over pricing of recordings at big chains. *The New York Times,* C1.

Evangelista, B. (2000, November 15). Legal deal has MP3 singing. *San Francisco Chronicle,* C1.

Evangelista, B. (2003, April 25). Apple kicks off online music store. *San Francisco Chronicle,* B1.

Evangelista, B. (2003, April 30). New tactic by record industry. *San Francisco Chronicle,* B1.

Evangelista, B. (2003, September 3). RIAA decries drop in CD sales. *San Francisco Chronicle,* B1.

Evangelista, B. (2003, October 10). Napster back from the dead. *San Francisco Chronicle,* B3.

Frost, L. (2007, January 26). Music industry pauses over ad-funded downloads. Money.aol.com.

Gomes, L. (2001, February 13). Napster suffers a rout in appeals court. *The Wall Street Journal,* A3.

Gomes, L. (2001, March 5). Judge starts process of silencing Napster. *The Wall Street Journal,* B6.

Holloway, L. (2003, June 26). Recording industry to sue Internet music swappers. *The New York Times,* C4.

Kopytoff, V. (2003, September 4). Music lawsuits snare 18 in Bay Area. *San Francisco Chronicle,* A1.

Lee, E. (2007, March 22). Music industry threatens student downloaders at UC. Sfgate.com.

Leeds, J. (2005, November 8). Grokster calls it quits on sharing music files. *The New York Times,* C1.

Leeds, J. (2007, February 13). Grammy sweep by Dixie Chicks is seen as a vindication. *The New York Times,* B1.

Leeds, J. (2007, February 19). Music labels offer teasers to download. *The New York Times,* C1.

Leeds, J. (2007, April 3). EMI to sell music online in Apple deal. *The New York Times,* C1.

Leeds, J. (2007, May 28). Plunge in CD sales shakes up big labels. *The New York Times,* B1.

Leeds, J. (2007, October 5). Labels win suit against song sharer. Nytimes.com.

Leland, J. (2005, February 13). Balding rockers and big money. *The New York Times,* WK7.

Leonard, D. (2001, September 3). Mr. Messier is ready for his closeup: A maverick Frenchman auditions for the part of an American media mogul. *Fortune,* 136+.

Levine, R. (2007, March 12). Who owns the live music of days gone by? *The New York Times,* C1.

Levine. R. (2008, June 9). For some music, it has to be Wal-Mart and nowhere else. *The New York Times,* C1.

McBride, S. & Smith, E. (2008, December 19). Music industry to abandon mass suits. Wsj.com.

Mathews, A. W. (2001, January 29). Radio firms sue to block measure on music royalties. *The Wall Street Journal,* B8.

Metz, R. (1975). *CBS: Reflections in a bloodshot eye.* Chicago: Playboy Press.

Oppelaar, J. (2000, August 28). DVD case has ripple effect on music biz. *Variety,* 6.

Pareles, J. (2003, July 20). What albums join together, everyone tears asunder. *The New York Times,* WK3.

Pareles, J. (2005, August 23). Swaggering past 60, unrepentant. *The New York Times,* B1.

Pogue, D. (2005, August 7). Britney to rent, lease or buy. *The New York Times,* 2-1.

Rendon, J. (2003, July 20). From a store with 300,000 titles, a big music lesson. *The New York Times,* BU5.

Sabbagh, D. (2008, June 18). Music sales fall to their lowest level in over 20 years. Timesonline.com.

Sachs, T., & Nunziato, S. (2007, April 5). Spinning into oblivion. Nytimes.com.

Sanneh, K. (2007, February 27). Rappers find that a small label can have its uses. *The New York Times,* B1.

Sanneh, K. (2007, April 25). Don't blame hip-hop. Nytimes.com.

Schiesel, S. (2003, August 7). A musical theme park for 60,000. *The New York Times,* E1.

Smart, J. R. (1977). *A wonderful invention: A brief history of the phonograph from tinfoil to the LP.* Washington, D.C.: Library of Congress.

Smith, E. (2004, October 11). Concert industry blames creeping prices for slow summer. *The Wall Street Journal,* B1.

Starrett, B. (2001, August). The end of CDR? *EMedia Magazine,* 34.

Surowiecki, J. (2001, August 20 & 27). Video kills the video star. *The New Yorker,* 59.

Tan, C. Y. (2001, August). The Internet is changing the music industry. *Communications of the ACM,* 62.

Tedeschi, B. (2003, July 23). Buy.com chief is introducing a music site. *The New York Times,* C4.

Trachtenberg, J. A. (1994, August 2). Music industry fears bandits on the information highway. *The Wall Street Journal,* B21.

Veiga, A. (2003, May 2). Students settle music suit. *San Francisco Chronicle,* B1.

Veiga, A. (2003, October 9). New version of Napster service debuts. AOL Business News.

Chapter 6 Radio: Riding the Wave

Associated Press (2007, April 14). $12.5 million "payola" fine. *San Francisco Chronicle,* C2.

Barnouw, E. (1978). *Tube of plenty.* New York: Oxford University Press.

Billboard (2003, July 26). Beyond the Dixie Chicks, A8.

Bittner, J. (1982). *Broadcast law and regulation.* Englewood Cliffs, N.J.: Prentice Hall.

Carter, B., & Steinberg, J. (2007, April 13). Off the air: The light goes out for Don Imus, *The New York Times,* C1.

Carvajal, D. (2007, June 3). FM radio waves are stopped at the border. Iht.com.

Dow Jones/Associated Press (2007, February 13). Auction is set for Air America. *The New York Times,* C7.

Dow Jones Newswire (2005, May 16). XM satellite radio surpasses 4 million subscribers; nears target. AOL Business News.

Evangelista, B. (2001, November 19). Space-age sound. *San Francisco Chronicle,* E1.

Evangelista, B. (2002, October 11). FCC clears way for CD-quality FM sound. *San Francisco Chronicle,* A1.

Feder, B. J. (2002, October 11). FCC approves a digital radio technology. *The New York Times,* B1.

Fleishman, G. (2005, July 28). Revolution on the radio. *The New York Times,* C11.

Fornatale, P., & Mills, J. E. (1980). *Radio in the television age.* New York: Overlook Press.

Goodman, F. (2003, February 16). Country radio: Nowhere in New York. *The New York Times,* 2-1.

Herbert, B. (2007, April 16). Signs of infection. *The New York Times,* A23.

Labaton, S. (2007, March 7). FCC chief questioning radio deal. *The New York Times,* C1.

Leeds, J. (2005, July 28). Payola or no, edge still to the big. *The New York Times,* B1.

Leeds, J. (2007, March 6). Broadcasters agree to fine over payoffs. *The New York Times,* C1.

Leeds, J. (2007, April 16). Amid turbulence at CBS Radio, an old hand is back. *The New York Times,* C4.

Leeds, J., & Story, L. (2005, July 26). Radio payoffs are described as Sony settles. *The New York Times,* A1.

Levine, R. (2007, March 19). A fee per song can ruin us, Internet radio companies say. *The New York Times,* C4.

MacFarland, D. R. (1979). *The development of the top 40 radio format.* New York: Arno Press.

Manly, L. (2005, July 31). Spin control: How payola went corporate. *The New York Times,* 4-1.

Mindlin, A. (2007, May 7). Counting radio listeners stirs controversy. *The New York Times,* C4.

Muto, S. (2001, February 5). The Internet offers a radio station life after death. *The Wall Street Journal,* B5.

Norris, F. (2007, February 23). Satellite radio: Good music, bad investment. *The New York Times,* C1.

Nugent, B. (2001, September 15). Radio active: Top 40 rules the airwaves, but there's an Internet station for every earthly genre of music. *Time,* 30+.

Pickler, N. (2001, September 26). First satellite radio service begins. *San Francisco Chronicle,* B3.

Settel, L. (1960). *A pictorial history of radio.* New York: Citadel Press.

Shenon P. (2008, March 25). Justice dept. approves XM merger with Sirius. *The New York Times,* C1.

Siklos, R. (2007, February 14). Is radio still radio if there's video? *The New York Times,* C1.

Sperber, A. M. (1986). *Murrow: His life and times.* New York: Freundlich.

Strauss, N. (2001, September 19). After the horror, radio stations pull some songs. *The New York Times.*

Sutel, S. (2006, October 13). Air America files for Chapter 11. Associated Press on aol.com.

Sutel, S. (2007, March 20). Online broadcast ruling is opposed. *The Sacramento Bee,* D3.

Sweetland, P. (2002, January 11). Radio station ponders change, and Ole Opry's fans worry. *The New York Times,* B1.

Swett, C. (2000, October 12). New heights for car radio. *The Sacramento Bee,* D1.

Taub, E. A. (2000, October 19). Drive-time radio on 100 channels. *The New York Times,* D1.

Veronis, Suhler & Associates (2006, July). *Communications industry forecast: 2006–2010.* New York.

Chapter 7 Movies: Picturing the Future

Ault, S. (2001, July 9). Movies via Net still to come. *Broadcasting & Cable,* 30.

Balio, T. (1976). *The American film industry.* Madison: University of Wisconsin Press.

Barnes, B. (2008, May 9). To reduce costs, Warner Brothers closing 2 film divisions. *The New York Times,* C2.

Barnes, B. (2008, July 27). A director's cut. *The New York Times,* BU1.

Carr, D. (2005, August 8). In Hollywood, all players but no power. *The New York Times,* C1.

Carr, D. (2007, February 27). Old-line Hollywood takes back the night. *The New York Times,* B1.

Carr, D. (2008, February 26). In Los Angeles, Oscar statues become a popular export. Nytimes.com.

Cheshire, G. (2000, October 8). A moment from the past recovers its sound. *The New York Times,* AR28.

Chinnock, C. (1999, August 9). Lights! Camera! Action! It's the dawn of digital cinema. *Electronic Design,* 32F.

Dargis, M. (2007, March 18). The revolution will be downloaded (if you're patient). *The New York Times,* C1.

Denby, D. (2007, January 8). Big pictures. *The New Yorker,* 54.

Ellis, J. C. (1985). *A history of American film,* 2nd ed. Englewood Cliffs, N.J.: Prentice Hall.

Evangelista, B. (2003, April 28). Heading off film piracy. *San Francisco Chronicle,* E1.

Evangelista, B. (2003, September 8). Movielink service polishes its act. *San Francisco Chronicle,* C1.

Fabrikant, G., & Waxman, S. (2005, December 9). Viacom's Paramount to buy DreamWorks for $1.6 billion. Nytimes.com.

Gentile, G. (2003, May 20). Disney to test options for movie viewing. *San Francisco Chronicle,* B3.

Germain, D. (2005, June 20). Hollywood slow despite $47 million *Batman* debut. Associated Press on AOL Entertainment News.

Goldberg, B. (2001, September). DMCA nets a criminal prosecution and prompts a protest. *American Libraries,* 18.

Graser, M. (2001, July 23). Casting a wider 'Net. *Variety,* 27.

Gross, D. (2005, July 10). Detroit is so Hollywood and vice versa. *The New York Times,* WK14.

Grove, C. (2000, June 19). Digital dilemma. *Variety,* 43.

Grover, R. (2003, July 14). Hollywood heist: Will tinseltown let techies steal the show? *BusinessWeek,* 74.

Guthman, E. (2003, January 20). Sundance grows up. *San Francisco Chronicle,* D1.

Halbfinger, D. M. (2005, September 26). Going deep for digital. *The New York Times,* C1.

Halbfinger. D. M. (2008, March 13). With theaters barely digital, studios push 3-D. *The New York Times,* B1.

Helft, M. (2007, January 16). The shifting business of renting movies, by the disc or the click. *The New York Times,* C1.

Holson, L. M. (2005, December 19). Before you buy a ticket, why not buy the DVD? *The New York Times,* C1.

Holson, L. M. (2005, July 22). Film studios said to agree on digital standards. *The New York Times,* C9.

Holson, L. M. (2005, November 6). Can Hollywood evade the death eaters? *The New York Times,* 3-1.

Holson, L. M. (2007, February 5). The director lines up a shot. *The New York Times,* C1.

Kehr, D. (2004, September 18). What's in a name? Winds of change at studios. *The New York Times,* A17.

King, T. (1994, August 18). Theater chain has plans to jolt movie viewers. *The Wall Street Journal,* B1.

LaSalle, M. (2005, July 13). Blame the economy, the product, the theaters—we're just not going to movies the way we used to. Sfgate.com.

Leeds, J. (2007, March 1). A comeback in 3-D, but without those flimsy glasses. *The New York Times,* B9.

Lohr, S. (2003, June 19). Where cineastes, software and schools converge. *The New York Times,* E7.

Lyman, R. (2003, January 23). Old-style Sundance vs. starry premieres. *The New York Times,* B1.

Motion Picture Association of America (1954). *Motion picture production code.*

Peers, M. (2001, January 29). Video on demand arrives—sort of. *The Wall Street Journal,* B1.

Scott, A. O. (2007, March 18). The shape of cinema, transformed at the click of a mouse. *The New York Times,* 2-1.

Seelye, K. Q. (2007, February 19). Old media partying with Oscar online. *The New York Times,* C1.

Siklos, R. (2007, March 4). Mission improbable: Tom Cruise as mogul. *The New York Times,* 3-1.

Sklar, R. (1975). *Movie-made America.* New York: Random House.

Smith, G. (2001, May). Fear of a digital planet. *Film Comment,* 2.

Squire, J. E. (ed.). (1983). *The movie business book.* New York: Simon & Schuster.

Stross, R. E. (2000, October 2). Chill, Hollywood, chill. *U.S. News & World Report,* 46.

Taub, E. A. (2003, July 21). DVDs meant for buying but not for keeping. *The New York Times,* C1.

Thompson, N. (2003, June 26). Netflix's patent may reshape DVD rental market. *The New York Times,* C4.

Trumbo, D. (1962). *Additional dialogue: Letters of Dalton Trumbo,* 1942–1962. New York: M. Evans.

Veronis, Suhler & Associates (2006, July). *Communications industry forecast: 2006–2010.* New York.

Waxman, S. (2005, October 8). Study finds young men attending fewer films. *The New York Times,* A17.

Waxman, S. (2005, December 12). DreamWorks deal played like a drama. *The New York Times,* C1.

Waxman, S. (2007, April 26). Hollywood's shortage of female power. *The New York Times,* B1.

Chapter 8 Television: Changing Channels

Barnes, B., & Jordan, M. (2005, May 2). Big four TV networks get a wake-up call—in Spanish. Wsj.com.

Barnouw, E. (1975). *Tube of plenty.* New York: Oxford University Press.

Bauder, D. (2007, May 9). 2.7 million TV viewers missing this spring. *San Francisco Chronicle,* A2.

Biagi, S. (1987). *NewsTalk II.* Belmont, Calif.: Wadsworth.

Brown, L. (1971). *Television: The business behind the box.* New York: Harcourt Brace Jovanovich.

Carter, B. (2001, September 7). Many ABC programs to be in high-definition TV format. *The New York Times,* C6.

Carter, B. (2003, May 23). Fox mulls how to exploit the mojo of "American Idol." *The New York Times,* C1.

Carter, B. (2007, March 22). After "Sopranos," a need for a hit. *The New York Times,* C1.

Chen, K., & Peers, M. (1999, August 6). FCC relaxes its rules on TV station ownership. *The Wall Street Journal,* A3.

Colker, D. (2003, April 17). Living on television's cutting edge. *Los Angeles Times.*

Coyle, J. (2007, March 12). TV counting on viewer-created content. *San Francisco Chronicle,* C3.

Dvorak, P. (2005, April 21). Advanced TV will be a test of Sony revival. Wsj.com.

Elliott, S. (2007, May 16). Gauging viewer tastes: A new dose of escapism. *The New York Times,* C6.

Elliott, S. (2007, June 13). What was old is new as TV revisits branding. *The New York Times,* C5.

Evangelista, B. (2002, September 23). Thin screens, hefty prices. *San Francisco Chronicle,* E1.

Futterman, M. (2008, August 13). NBC's race for ratings gold continues. *The Wall Street Journal,* B1.

Gill, J. (2000, Winter). Managing the capture of individuals viewing within a peoplemeter service. *International Journal of Market Research,* 431.

Grant, P. (2005, September 22). The war for your remote: Satellite gains on cable. Wsj.com.

Greenfield, J. (1977). *Television: The first fifty years.* New York: Abrams.

Hansell, S. (2005, August 1). Logging on to tune in TV. *The New York Times,* C1.

Jordan, M. (2004, October 11). Nielsen's search for Hispanics is a delicate job. *The Wall Street Journal,* B1.

Kantor, J. (2005, October 30). The extra-large, ultra-small medium: What happens when television becomes a matter of extremes. *The New York Times,* 2-1.

Kopytoff, V. (2004, October 25). One-stop way to read news, blogs online. *San Francisco Chronicle,* C1.

Labaton, S. (2005, October 21). Digital TV bills gets Senate panel's OK. *San Francisco Chronicle,* C6.

Manly, L., & Hernandez, R. (2005, August 8). Nielsen, long a gauge of popularity, fights to preserve its own. *The New York Times,* C1.

McClellan, S. (2001, August 20). Does TV need a nip? *Broadcasting & Cable,* 12.

McGrath, C. (2008, February 17). Is PBS still necessary? *The New York Times,* AR1.

Meyerson, B. (2007, April 2). Cell phones now feature TV shows—for a price. *San Francisco Chronicle,* C3.

Minow, N. (1964). *Equal time: The private broadcaster and the public interest.* New York: Atheneum.

Navarro, M. (2005, November 6). The prime time of the telenovela. *The New York Times,* 2-1.

Pasztor, A. (2001, July 31). DirecTV takes aim at illicit consumers. *The Wall Street Journal,* A3.

Radio Advertising Bureau (2001, November 26). Competitive media update: High-definition television.

Ramstad, E. (2000, October 6). FCC spurs rethinking of digital-TV strategy. *The Wall Street Journal,* B6.

Schiesel, S. (2001, October 30). Now, the difficult gamble: Approval in Washington. *The New York Times,* C1.

Schiesel, S. (2003, July 31). Cable or satellite? Stay tuned. *The New York Times,* E1.

Severo, R. (2003, June 13). David Brinkley, 82, newsman model, dies. *The New York Times,* A26.

Sorkin, A. R. (2001, October 30). Trying to stack the deck so even a loss is a win. *The New York Times,* C1.

Sorkin, A. R. (2003, April 10). Murdoch adds to his empire by agreeing to buy DirecTV. *The New York Times,* C1.

Srinivasan, K. (2001, June 13). FCC chief tells cable industry not to misuse dominance. *San Francisco Chronicle,* C3.

Stanley, A. (2007, April 8). This thing of ours: It's over. *The New York Times,* 2-1.

Steinberg, J. (2007, June 7). Converters signal a new era for TVs. *The New York Times,* C3.

Stelter, B. (2008, March 10). Serving up television without the TV set. *The New York Times,* C1.

Stelter, B. (2008, April 14). At CBS, bad news doesn't end at 7. *The New York Times,* C1.

Stelter, B. (2008, May 12). In the age of TiVo and web video, what is prime time? *The New York Times,* C1.

Stelter, B. (2008, August 8). For Olympic viewers, a long wait. NYtimes.com.

Sterling, C., & Kittross, J. (1990). *Stay tuned: A concise history of American broadcasting,* 2nd ed. Belmont, Calif.: Wadsworth.

Story, L. (2007, January 29). At last, television ratings go to college. *The New York Times,* C1.

Story, L. (2007, June 1). Agencies and networks ponder Nielsen ad ratings. *The New York Times,* C6.

Sutel, S. (2005, January 24). Likely toned-down Super Bowl ads hidden in secrecy. Associated Press on AOL News.

Tarquinio, J. A. (2003, July 20). Poised to ride the next wave in digital media equipment. *The New York Times,* BU3.

Taub, E. A. (2003, March 31). HDTV's acceptance picks up pace as prices drop and networks sign on. *The New York Times,* C1.

Taub, E. A. (2007, January 11). On display, the video frontier. *The New York Times,* C11.

Tedeschi, B. (2005, October 3). New video search sites offer glimpse of future TV. *The New York Times,* C4.

Wallenstein, A. (2005, November 8). NBC, CBS to offer shows on demand for 99 cents. Reuters on AOL Business News.

Chapter 9 Digital Media: Widening the Web

Arango, T. (2008, March 26). Social site's new friends are athletes. *The New York Times,* C1.

Barbaro, M. (2005, November 30). Sales climb at retailers on Internet. *The New York Times,* C1.

Bridis, T. (2004, March 10). Internet providers sue hundreds over spam. Associated Press on AOL Business News.

Cohen, N. (2007, March 12). After false claim, Wikipedia to check degrees. *The New York Times,* C6.

Cookson, C. (2001, August 2). IBM joins push to construct next generation Internet. *Financial Times,* 1.

Duryee, T., Davis, C., & Ball, E. (2007, June 30). Answering iPhone's call. *The Seattle Times,* A1.

Eisenberg, A. (2003, September 11). Beyond voice recognition, to a computer that reads lips. *The New York Times,* E8.

Evangelista, B. (2005, February 28). Podcasting gives voice to amateurs. *San Francisco Chronicle,* E1.

Evangelista, B. (2005, April 18). You are what's on your playlist. *San Francisco Chronicle,* E1.

Fidler, R. (1997). *Mediamorphosis.* Thousand Oaks, Calif.: Pine Forge Press.

Fitzgerald, M. (2001, June 25). Papers' e-content with profit. *Editor & Publisher,* 36.

Fitzgerald, T. (2005, July 7). Music to your cell phone. *The New York Times,* C9.

Flynn, L. J. (2007, February 6). After long dispute, two Apples work it out. *The New York Times,* C1.

Gaither, C. (2001, November 9). Microsoft explores a new territory: Fun. *The New York Times,* C1.

Gaither, C., & James, M. (2005, May 22). Internet lures advertisers from TV. *The Sacramento Bee*, D1.

Glassman, M. (2003, July 31). Fortifying the in box as spammers lay siege. *The New York Times*, E8.

Gnatek, T. (2005, October 5). Darknets: Virtual parties with a select group of invitees. *The New York Times*, E2.

Graham, J. (2005, October 10). Mystery of what Google will do next deepens. *USAtoday.com* on AOL News.

Hansel, S. (2003, May 25). How to unclog the information artery. *The New York Times*, 3-1.

Helft, M. (2007, February 8). Numbers are out on how rich the YouTube deal was. *The New York Times*, C2.

Hildebrand, A. (2001, November 4). A computer screen for your eyes only. *The New York Times*, C2.

Holson, L. M. (2005, October 17). Now playing on a tiny screen. *The New York Times*, C1.

Jesdanun, A. (2005, August 30). The Internet is still a work in progress as it turns 35. Associated Press on AOL News.

Kirby, C. (2003, September 4). Many more worms will wriggle into our future. *San Francisco Chronicle*, B1.

Kopytoff, V. (2004, September 17). Digital divide of kids narrows. *San Francisco Chronicle*, C1.

Liptak, A., & Stone, B. (2008, February 19). Web site that posts leaked material ordered shut. Nytimes.com.

Lohr, S. (2005, November 6). Just googling it is striking fear into companies. Nytimes.com.

Lohr, S. (2007, March 25). Slow down, brave multitasker, and don't read this in traffic. *The New York Times*, A1.

Lohr, S. (2008, March 13). Video road hogs stir fear of Internet traffic jam. *The New York Times*, A1.

Maher, B. (2001, February). 50+ Web surfers. *Target Marketing*, 104.

Mandel, M. J., & Hof, R. D. (2001, March 26). Rethinking the Internet. *BusinessWeek*, 117–122.

Mann, C. C. (2001, March). Electronic paper turns the page. *Technology Review*, 44.

Mann, C. C. (2001, September). Taming the Web. *Technology Review*, 44.

Markoff, J. (2005, November 14). Control the Internet? A futile pursuit, some say. *The New York Times*, C6.

Markoff, J., & Holson, L. M. (2005, October 13). With New iPod, Apple aims to be a video star. *The New York Times*, C1.

Mintz, J. (2007, January 18). MySpace hit with online predator suit. Associated Press on AOL Money & Finance News.

Pew Internet & American Life Project (2005, October 5). Two-thirds of American adults go online and one-third do not. Pew Internet & American Life Project Press Release.

Pimentel, B. (2003, September 9). Dell says some tech firms doomed. *San Francisco Chronicle*, B1.

Ratliff, E. (2005, October 10). The zombie hunters: On the trail of cyberextortionists. *The New Yorker*, 44.

Richtel, M. (2003, July 6). The lure of data: Is it addictive? *The New York Times*, 3-1.

Richtel, M., & Tedeschi, B. (2007, June 17). Some buyers grow Web-weary, and online sales lose steam. *The New York Times*, A1.

Simpson, G. R. (2001, March 21). The battle over Web privacy. *The New York Times*, B1.

Steele, L. (2007, February 8). Internet2: The faster Web. KiplingerForecasts.com.

Story, L. (2007, June 17). Yes, the screen is tiny, but the plans are big. *The New York Times*, 3-1.

Stross, R. (2008, July 27). First it was song downloads. Now it's organic chemistry. *The New York Times*, BU4.

Sutel, S. (2001, November 2). Top TV networks sue over recorder. *San Francisco Chronicle*, B9.

Swartz, J. (2005, August 22). Anti-porn spam laws to shield kids backfire. *USAtoday.com* on AOL News.

Szep, J. (2008, July 7). Technology reshapes America's classrooms. Nytimes.com.

Tedeschi, B. (2007, February 26). New hot properties: YouTube celebrities. *The New York Times*, C1.

Wilson, M. (2005, September 1). Loved ones turn to Web for searches in flood zone. *The New York Times*, A16.

Wright, A. (2008, June 17). The web time forgot. *The New York Times*, D1.

Wright, R. (1997, May 19). The man who invented the Web. *Time*, 68.

Wyatt, E. (2005, November 4). Want *War and Peace* online? How about 20 pages at a time? Nytimes.com.

Yang, D. J. (2001, April 9). New tolls on the info highway. *U.S. News & World Report*, 44.

Yi, M. (2003, July 13). Battle of wits over spam. *The New York Times*, I11.

Chapter 10 Advertising: Motivating Consumers

Atwan, R. (1979). Newspapers and the foundations of modern advertising. In *The commercial connection*, ed. J. W. Wright. New York: Doubleday.

Auletta, K. (2005, March 21). Annals of communication: The new pitch. Newyorker.com.

Barboza, D. (2003, April 3). If you pitch it, they will eat. *The New York Times*, 3-1.

Beatty, S. G. (1996, June 11). Seagram flouts ban on TV ads pitching liquor. *The Wall Street Journal*, B1.

Boorstin, D. J. (1986). The rhetoric of democracy. In *American mass media: Industries and issues*, 3rd ed., ed. R. Atwan, B. Orton, & W. Vesterman. New York: Random House.

Cardwell, A. (2001, February 1). The new ad game: Online games are more than just a good time; they're the hottest new ad space on the Web. *Ziff Davis Smart Business for the New Economy*, 53.

Deutsch, C. H. (2005, August 8). A fresh approach to marketing for Procter's fresh approach to laundry. *The New York Times*, C7.

Elliott, S. (2002, March 31). Advertising's big four: It's their world now. *The New York Times,* 3-1.

Elliott, S. (2005, July 26). I can't believe it's not a TV ad! *The New York Times,* C4.

Elliott, S. (2005, August 17). For everyday products, ads using the everyday woman. *The New York Times,* C1.

Elliott, S. (2005, August 24). *Housewives* is a big hit on Madison Ave., too. *The New York Times,* C9.

Elliott, S. (2005, September 21). It's a game. No, it's an ad. No, it's advergame. *The New York Times,* C5.

Elliott, S. (2005, November 3). Liquor ads move to satellite radio. *The New York Times,* C6.

Elliott, S. (2007, February 6). Thanks to the Web, the scorekeeping on the Super Bowl has just begun. *The New York Times,* C22.

Elliott, S. (2008, January 31). In a switch, this year's Super Bowl ads will be gentle and sweet. *The New York Times,* C11.

Elliott, S. (2008, February 6). An ad with talking pandas, maybe, but not with Chinese accents. *The New York Times,* C4.

Feder, B. (2007, January 29). Billboards that know you by name. *The New York Times,* C4.

Flint, J., Branch, S., & O'Connell, V. (2001, December 14). Breaking longtime taboo, NBC network plans to accept liquor ads. *The Wall Street Journal,* B1.

Fowles, J. (1985). Advertising's fifteen basic appeals. In *American mass media: Industries and issues,* 3rd ed., ed. R. Atwan, B. Orton, & W. Vesterman. New York: Random House.

Fox, S. (1984). *The mirror makers: A history of American advertising and its creators.* New York: Morrow.

Holson, L. M. (2007, May 7). Hollywood loves the tiny screen. Advertisers don't. *The New York Times,* C1.

Ives, N. (2003, June 16). Online profiling, separating the car buff from the travel seeker, is a new tool to lure advertisers. *The New York Times,* C10.

Ives, N. (2005, January 27). Fake commercial spots spread quickly on the Internet. Nytimes.com.

Jones, E. R. (1979). *Those were the good old days.* New York: Simon & Schuster.

Kaufman, L. (1987). *Essentials of advertising,* 2nd ed. New York: Harcourt Brace Jovanovich.

Kiley, D. (2005, March 7). A green flag for booze. *BusinessWeek,* 95.

Leeds, J. (2007, February 7). Super Bowl day: TV viewers get game plan, too. *The New York Times,* A1.

Maly, L. (2005, October 2). When the ad turns into the story line. *The New York Times,* 3-1.

Price, J. (1986). Now a few words about commercials. In *American mass media: Industries and issues,* 3rd ed., ed. R. Atwan, B. Orton, & W. Vesterman. New York: Random House.

Rosencrance, L. (2000, July 24). FTC warns sites to comply with children's privacy law. *Computerworld,* 10.

Schudson, M. (1984). *Advertising: The uneasy persuasion.* New York: Basic Books.

Story, L. (2007, April 28). Overture to an untapped market. *The New York Times,* B1.

Story, L. (2008, March 10). To aim ads, web is keeping closer eye on what you click. *The New York Times,* A1.

Sylvers, E. (2003, June 3). Breaking away, with a sponsor. *The New York Times,* W1.

Sylvers, E. (2007, February 14). The ad-free cellphone may soon be extinct. *The New York Times,* C5.

Tedeschi, B. (2003, August 4). If you liked the Web page, try the ad. *The New York Times,* C1.

Whitaker, L. (2001, July 21). Converting Web surfers to buyers: Online promotion. *Time,* 46+.

Chapter 11 Public Relations: Promoting Ideas

Ambrosio, J. (1980, March/April). It's in the *Journal,* but this is reporting? *Columbia Journalism Review, 18,* 35.

Barringer, F. (2005, July 18). Public relations campaign for research office at EPA may include ghostwritten articles. Nytimes.com.

Bernays, E. L. (1955). *The engineering of consent.* Norman: University of Oklahoma Press.

Blyskal, B., & Blyskal, M. (1985). *PR: How the public relations industry writes the news.* New York: Morrow.

Blyskal, B., & Blyskal, M. (1985, December). Making the best of bad news. *Washington Journalism Review,* 52.

Bumiller, E. (2003, February 9). War public relations machine is put on full throttle. *The New York Times,* A1.

Bumiller, E. (2003, April 20). Even critics of war say the White House spun it with skill. *The New York Times,* B14.

Cutlip, S., Center, A., & Broom, A. (1985). *Effective public relations,* 6th ed. Englewood Cliffs, N.J.: Prentice Hall.

D'Innocenzio, A., & Kabel, M. (2005, October 28). Wal-Mart works on its image. Associated Press on AOL Business News.

Fleischman, D. E. (1931, February). Public relations—A new field for women. *Independent woman.* As quoted in S. Henry, *In her own name: Public relations pioneer Doris Fleischman Bernays.* Paper presented to the Committee on the Status of Women Research Session, Association for Education in Journalism and Mass Communication, Portland, Ore., July 1988.

Foster, L. G. (1983, March). The role of public relations in the Tylenol crisis. *Public Relations Journal,* 13.

Gentry, J. K. (1986, July). The best and worst corporate PR. *Washington Journalism Review,* 38–40.

Glover, M. (1996, March 6). Juice maker in PR mode: Odwalla's ads explain status. *The Sacramento Bee,* B6.

Goldsborough, R. (2001, June). Dealing with Internet smears. *Campaigns & Elections,* 50B6.

Graham, J. (2007, March 9). Apple buffs marketing savvy to a high shine. *USA Today,* 1B.

Kaufman, J. (2008, June 30). Need press? Repeat: 'green,' 'sex,' 'cancer,' 'secret,' 'fat.' Nytimes.com.

Lee, C. (2005, March 15). Administration rejects ruling on PR videos. Washingtonpost.com.

Lustig, T. (1986, March). Great Caesar's ghost. *Public Relations Journal,* 17–19.

Marken, A. (1998, Spring). The Internet and the Web: The two-way public relations highway. *Public Relations Quarterly,* 31–34.

McDonough, S. (2005, May 26). Paid promotions sneaking into broadcasts. *San Francisco Chronicle,* C6.

Morse, S. (1906, September). An awakening on Wall Street. *American Magazine,* 460.

Newsom, D., & Scott, A. (1986). *This is PR: The realities of public relations,* 3rd ed. Belmont, Calif.: Wadsworth.

Nocera, J. (2007, March 3). A double shot of nostalgia for Starbucks. *The New York Times,* B1.

O'Brien, T. (2005, February 13). Spinning frenzy: PR's bad press. *The New York Times,* 3-1.

Pear, R. (2005, October 1). Buying of news by Bush's aides is ruled illegal. *The New York Times,* A1.

Pizzi, P. (2001, July 23). Grappling with "cybersmear." *New Jersey Law Journal,* S12.

Randall, C. (1985, November). The father of public relations: Edward Bernays, 93, is still saucy. *United,* 50.

Sarkar, P. (2005, October 26). Wal-Mart's worldview. *San Francisco Chronicle,* C1.

Seitel, F. P. (1984). *The practice of public relations,* 2nd ed. Columbus, Ohio: Charles E. Merrill.

Chapter 12 News and Information: Getting Personal

Abate, T. (2003, February 14). Technology creates a new form of activism. *San Francisco Chronicle,* A17.

Amanpour, C. (2000). Address to the Radio-Television News Directors Association.

Associated Press (2007, March 12). CIA leak trial prompts scrutiny of news reporting practices. Iht.com.

Balz, D., & Smith, R. J. (2005, June 1). Conflicted and mum for decades. *Washington Post,* A1.

Bennett, S. (2003, July 1). How the Iraq War was seen overseas. *World and I,* 62.

Benson, H. (2003, February 12). National day of poetry against the war today. *San Francisco Chronicle,* A19.

Carr, D. (2007, February 5). Skipping merrily along as others take the heat. *The New York Times,* C1.

Carter, B. (2002, February 21). Networks' new life. *The New York Times,* A1.

Carter, B. (2003, April 14). Nightly news feels pinch of 24-hour news. *The New York Times,* C1.

Carter, B. (2007, April 20). NBC News defends its use of material sent by killer. *The New York Times,* A17.

Carvajal, D. (2007, March 7). 1,000 journalists killed in ten years while reporting. *The New York Times,* A3.

Charles, D. (2005, September 7). Federal government seeks to block photos of dead. Reuters on AOL News.

Chepesiuk, R. (2000, June). Preserving history on film at the newsfilm library. *American Libraries,* 88.

Clifton, D. (2005, June 30). Jailing reporters, silencing the whistleblowers. Plaindealer.com.

Cohen, N. (2008, March 10). Journalism in the hands of the neighborhood. *The New York Times,* C3.

Cowell, A. (2007, June 13). Blair compares news media to "feral beast" in angry parting shot. *The New York Times,* A5.

Fisher, M. (2001, October). Meeting the challenge: How the media responded to September 11. *American Journalism Review,* 18.

Flint, J. (1999, November 11). *Washington Post,* NBC form alliance to share editorial, Internet resources. *The Wall Street Journal,* B14.

Gans, H. (1985, December). Are U.S. journalists dangerously liberal? *Columbia Journalism Review,* 32–33.

Gans, H. (1986). *The messages behind the news.* In *Readings in mass communication,* 6th ed., ed. M. Emery & T. Smythe. Dubuque, Iowa: Wm. C. Brown.

Garwood, P. (2005, January 21). Deadline passes with no word on reporter's fate. Associated Press on AOL News.

Gerth, J., & Shane, S. (2005, December 1). U.S. is said to pay to plant articles in Iraq papers. *The New York Times,* A1.

Goodman, T. (2005, September 7). In the madness of hurricane and its aftermath, TV is the unblinking eye that brings clarity. *San Francisco Chronicle,* E1.

Gordon, M. (2001, October 31). Military is putting heavier limits on reporters' access. *The New York Times,* B3.

Green, J. (2004, November). Karl Rove in a corner. TheAtlantic.com.

Johnston, D. C. (2005, July 11). Most editors say they'd publish articles based on leaks. Nytimes.com.

Just, M., & Rosenstiel, T. (2005, March 26). All the news that's fed. *The New York Times,* A27.

King, N., Jr., & Cloud, D. S. (2001, December). This is all that we hoped for. *The New York Times,* B1.

Kuttab, D. (2003, April 6). The Arab TV wars. *The New York Times Magazine,* 45.

Lewis, N. A., & Shane, S. (2007, January 31). Ex-reporter for *Times* testifies for prosecutor who jailed her. *The New York Times,* A1.

Lippmann, W. (1965). *Public opinion.* New York: Free Press.

Liptak, A. (2005, February 16). Jailing of reporters in CIA leak case is upheld by judges. *The New York Times,* A1.

Liptak, A. (2005, June 30). Judge gives reporters one week to testify or face jail. *The New York Times,* A12.

Liptak, A. (2005, July 1). Time Inc. to yield files on sources, relenting to U.S. *The New York Times,* A1.

Liptak, A. (2005, July 11). For Time Inc. reporter, a frenzied decision to testify. Nytimes.com.

Lipton, E. (2007, March 7). Members of a sympathetic jury describe emotional but inevitable conclusion. *The New York Times,* A17.

McDermott, T. (2007, March 17). Blogs can top the presses. Latimes.com.

McFadden, R. D. (2005, July 9). Newspaper withholding two articles after jailing. Nytimes.com.

O'Connor, J. D. (2005, July). "I'm the guy they called Deep Throat." *Vanity Fair,* 86.

Perez-Pena, R. (2007, April 21). Media outlets ease off video of killer, but not because of complaints, they say. *The New York Times,* A13.

Pew Research Center (2005, June 26). Public more critical of press, but goodwill persists.

Pincus, W., & VandeHei, J. (2005, July 21). Plame's identity marked as secret. *Washington Post,* A1.

Polgreen, L. (2008, April 8). *Times* reporter is released on bail in Zimbabwe. Nytimes.com.

Project for Excellence in Journalism (2007). The state of the news media 2007: An annual report on American journalism. Journalism.org.

Project for Excellence in Journalism (2008). The state of the news media 2008: An annual report on American journalism. Stateofthenewsmedia.org/2008.

Purdum, T. S. (2005, June 3). Three decades later, "Woodstein" takes a victory lap. *The New York Times,* A14.

Purdum, T. S., & Rutenberg, J. (2005, June 2). In the prelude to publication, intrigue worthy of Deep Throat. *The New York Times,* A1.

Quinn, P. (2006, January 7). American journalist kidnapped in Iraq. Associated Press on AOL News.

Rainey, J. (2007, March 13). Media's focus narrowing, report warns. Latimes.com.

Regan, J. (2003, October 3). Newsreels of years gone by. *The Christian Science Monitor,* 25.

Rich, Frank (2005, July 24). Eight days in July. Nytimes.com.

Robins, W. (2001, January 22). Cooperation, not competition: Newspaper of 2001 must be built around information services. *Editor & Publisher,* 32.

Rosenberg, J. (2001, September 24). A SLAPP fight over sources. *Editor & Publisher,* 4.

Rutenberg, J. (2003, April 20). Spectacular success or incomplete picture? Views of TV's war coverage are split. *The New York Times,* B15.

Rutten, T. (2003, April 5). A 24/7 war pulls viewers to cable news. *Los Angeles Times,* C1.

Salamon, J. (2003, April 6). New tools for reporters make war images instant but coverage no simpler. *The New York Times,* B13.

Schmitt, E. (2005, December 2). Senate summons Pentagon to explain effort to plant reports in Iraqi news media. *The New York Times,* A10.

Schmitt, E. (2005, December 13). Military admits planting news in Iraq. *The New York Times,* A11.

Schwartz, J. (2003, March 31). War puts radio giant on the defensive. *The New York Times,* C1.

Seelye, K. Q. (2005, March 14). Fewer sources go nameless in the press, survey shows. *The New York Times,* C6.

Seelye, K. Q. (2005, August 1). Newsrooms seek ways to shield identities. *The New York Times,* C1.

Seelye, K. Q. (2005, August 15). Editors ponder how to present a broad picture of Iraq. *The New York Times,* C2.

Seelye, K. Q. (2005, October 4). Freed reporter says she upheld principles, A23. *The New York Times.*

Seelye, K. Q. (2005, November 10). *Times* reporter agrees to leave the paper. *The New York Times,* A21.

Seelye, K. Q. (2007, April 16). Best-informed also view fake news, study says. *The New York Times,* C5.

Shane, S. (2007, March 8). Debate over possible pardon erupts after verdict on Libby. *The New York Times,* A1.

Shanker, T., & Schmitt, E. (2004, December 13). Military debates how to win war of words. *San Francisco Chronicle,* P1.

Steinberg, J. (2005, June 30). Writer in sources case laments threat to jail 2. *The New York Times,* A12.

Steinberg, J. (2005, July 7). Response from journalists is not unanimous. *The New York Times,* A17.

Steinberg, J. (2008, June 8). For new journalists, all bets, but not mikes, are off. *The New York Times,* WK3.

Stelter, B. (2008, August 12). TV networks rewrite the definition of a news bureau. Nytimes.com.

Stepp, C. S. (2001, March). Signs of progress. *American Journalism Review,* special insert.

Stolberg, S. G. (2007, March 7). Libby, ex-Cheney aide, guilty of lying in CIA leak case. *The New York Times,* A1.

Swett, C. (2007, January 25). Internet grows as news source. *The Sacramento Bee,* D2.

Turegano, P. (2001, October 2). Too much red, white and blue on TV news for objectivity? *The San Diego Union-Tribune,* E1.

Weaver, D. H., & Wilhoit, G. C. (1996). *The American journalist in the 1990s.* Mahwah, N.J.: Lawrence Erlbaum.

Wheeler, R. E. (1993, February-March). News for all Americans. *American Visions,* 40.

Wilson, Joseph C. (2003, July 6). What I didn't find in Africa. Nytimes.com.

Woodward, B. (2005, June 2). How Mark Felt became "Deep Throat." *Washington Post,* A1.

Worth, R. F. (2005, September 20). Reporter working for *Times* abducted and slain in Iraq. Nytimes.com.

Yost, P. (2005, July 6). Judge orders *New York Times* reporter jailed. Associated Press on AOL News.

Chapter 13 Society, Culture and Politics: Shaping the Issues

Alexander, H. E. (1983). *Financing the 1980 election.* Lexington, Mass.: D. C. Heath.

Alexander, H. E., & Haggerty, B. (1987). *Financing the 1984 election.* Lexington, Mass.: D. C. Heath.

Barber, J. D. (1986). *The pulse of politics: Electing presidents in the media age.* New York: Norton.

Bauder, D. (2001, February 3). Critics fault TV coverage of election. *San Francisco Chronicle,* A3.

Carter, B. (2007, April 10). Don Imus suspended from radio show over racial remarks. *The New York Times,* C1.

Cieply, M. (2007, April 13). Report says the young readily buy violent games and movies. *The New York Times,* C3.

Fairfield, H., & Palmer, G. (2008, July 6). Cashing in on Obama and McCain. *The New York Times,* BU1.

Fetler, M. (1985). Television viewing and school achievement. *Mass Communication Review Yearbook,* vol. 5. Beverly Hills, Calif.: Sage.

Graham-Silverman, A. (2001, April). Campaign ad rates: Going up, up and away? *Campaigns & Elections,* 10.

Healy, P., & Zeleny, J. (2007, July 24). Novel debate format, but same old candidates. Nytimes.com.

Hua, V. (2005, June 6). Audience for ethnic media huge. *San Francisco Chronicle,* A7.

Kollars, D. (1991, November 9). Callers flood AIDS hotlines; Johnson cheered on *Arsenio. The Sacramento Bee,* A22.

Krueger, A. B. (2005, August 18). Fair? Balanced? A study finds it does not matter. *The New York Times,* C2.

Liebert, R. M., & Sprafkin, J. (1988). *The early window,* 3rd ed. New York: Pergamon Press.

Lippmann, W. (1965). *Public opinion.* New York: Free Press.

Martindale, C. (1995, August). *Only in glimpses: Portrayal of America's largest minority groups by The New York Times* 1934–1994. Paper presented at the Association for Education in Journalism and Mass Communication Annual Convention, Washington, D.C.

Meyrowitz, J. (1985). *No sense of place.* New York: Oxford University Press.

Mindlin, A. (2007, January 15). Boys and girls use social sites differently. *The New York Times,* C3.

Modleski, T. (1982). *Loving with a vengeance: Mass-produced fantasies for women.* New York: Methuen.

Nauman, A. (1993, April 11). Comics page gets serious. *The Sacramento Bee,* B1.

Patterson, T., & McClure, R. (1976). *The unseeing eye: The myth of television power in national elections.* New York: Putnam.

Pickler, N. (2007, July 24). Democrats face off in YouTube debate. Associated Press on AOL.

Postman, N. (1985). *Amusing ourselves to death.* New York: Viking Penguin.

Potter, D. M. (1954). *People of plenty.* Chicago: University of Chicago Press.

Reuters (2005, October 28). Rapper 50 Cent says billboard flap helps his movie. Reuters on AOL News.

Reyes, L. I., & Rampell, E. (2007, February 23). Movies' multicultural milestone year. *San Francisco Chronicle,* B11.

Rivers, W. L., & Schramm, W. (1986). The impact of mass communications. In *American mass media: Industries and issues,* 3rd ed., ed. R. Atwan, B. Orton, & W. Vesterman. New York: Random House.

Smith, L. (1994, June 24). Calls to L.A. domestic abuse lines jump 80 percent. *Los Angeles Times,* A1.

Spear, J. (1984). *Presidents and the press.* Cambridge, Mass.: M.I.T. Press.

Stanley, A. (2008, June 8). No debate: It's great TV. *The New York Times,* MT1.

Stein, M. L. (1994, August 6). Racial stereotyping and the media. *Editor & Publisher,* 6.

Steinberg, J. (2007, April 11). Imus struggling to retain sway as a franchise. *The New York Times,* A1.

Stelter, B. (2008, March 27). Finding political news online, young viewers pass it along. *The New York Times,* A1.

Tam, P. W. (2001, July 31). Crusading reporters help U.S. ethnic press thrive in tough times. *The Wall Street Journal,* A1.

Waxman, S. (2003, December 31). Michael Jackson's $1 million interview deal. *The New York Times,* A1.

Wright, J. W. (1979). *The commercial connection.* New York: Dell (Synopsis of FTC staff report on television advertising to children).

Zeller, T. (2007, January 29). In politics, the camera never blinks (or nods). *The New York Times,* C4.

Chapter 14 Law and Regulation: Rewriting the Rules

American Library Association (2007, September 6). Federal judge declares NSL gag order unconstitutional. Ala.org.

Ardito, S. C. (2001, November). The case of Dmitry Sklyarov: This is the first criminal lawsuit under the Digital Millennium Copyright Act. *Information Today,* 24.

Associated Press (2003, August 18). Patriot Act comes under fire. *Medford Mail-Tribune,* 1A.

Associated Press (2005, January 28). Bush won't appeal media ownership rules. AOL Business News.

Associated Press (2005, June 3). Cameron Diaz sues the *National Enquirer.* AOL Entertainment News.

Associated Press (2005, December 30). Justice Department opens inquiry into leak of domestic spying. Nytimes.com.

Associated Press (2006, June 8). Fines to rise for indecency in broadcasts. *The New York Times,* C7.

Associated Press (2007, September 6). Judge strikes down part of Patriot Act. Nytimes.com.

Associated Press (2007, December 18). F.C.C. relaxes media ownership rule. Nytimes.com.

Baker, P. (2007, March 7). For an opaque White House, a reflection of new scrutiny. Washingtonpost.com.

Bee News Services (1999, May 8). $25 million judgment in *Jenny Jones* case. *The Sacramento Bee,* A1.

Benton Foundation (1996). *The Telecommunications Act of 1996 and the changing communications landscape.* Washington, D.C.: Author.

Blyskal, J., & Blyskal, M. (1985). *PR: How the public relations industry writes the news.* New York: Morrow.

Bode, C. (1969). *Mencken.* Carbondale: Southern Illinois University Press.

Braestrup, P. (1985). *Battle lines: Report of the Twentieth Century Fund Task Force on the Military and the Media.* New York: Priority Press.

Climan, L. (2001, September). Writers battle media companies. *Dollars & Sense,* 6.

Coile, Z. (2007, February 17). House Dems back federal shield law. *San Francisco Chronicle,* A5.

Congressional Research Service (2005, March 8). Journalists' privilege to withhold information in judicial and other proceedings: State shield statutes. Library of Congress.

Cowan, A. L. (2005, September 1). At stake in the court, the use of the Patriot Act to get library records. *The New York Times,* A18.

Cowan, A. L. (2005, September 2). Libraries wary as U.S. demands records. *The New York Times,* A21.

Cowan, A. L. (2005, September 10). Plaintiffs win round in Patriot Act lawsuit. Nytimes.com.

Crawford, K. (2005, June 27). Hollywood wins Internet piracy battle. Money.cnn.com.

Davis, J. (2001, April 9). Decision: A defining moment in libel law. *Editor & Publisher,* 9.

Deutsch, L. (2004, January 26). Judge rules part of Patriot Act unconstitutional. *Associated Press.*

Dow Jones & Co., (2006, January 19). Google records subpoenaed in porn probe. Dow Jones & Co. on AOL Money & Finance.

Dunbar, J. (2007, September 11). FCC chair promotes post-digital TV rule. Aol.com.

Egelko, B. (2003, March 10). Librarians try to alter Patriot Act. *San Francisco Chronicle,* A1.

Elliott, S. (2004, February 3). The Super Bowl of stupidity? *The New York Times.*

Evangelista, B. (2005, April 20). House passes piracy measure. *San Francisco Chronicle,* C1.

Farhi, P., & Ahrens, F. (2007, April 24). Law curbing TV violence pushed. *The Sacramento Bee,* A1.

Fitzgerald, M. (2001, May 28). Supremely good ruling. *Editor & Publisher,* 10.

Fitzgerald, M. (2001, July 2). "Tasini" reality test. *Editor & Publisher,* 11.

Gerhardt-Powals, J. (2000, November 27). The Digital Millennium Copyright Act: A compromise in progress. *New Jersey Law Journal,* 28.

Godwin, M. (2001, October). Standards issues. *Reason,* 56.

Greenhouse, L. (2004, December 11). Justices agree to hear case on sharing of music files. *The New York Times,* B1.

Greenhouse, L. (2007, March 18). Free-speech case divides Bush and religious right. *The New York Times,* YT18.

Hakim, D. (2008, June 10). Web providers to block sites with child sex. *The New York Times,* A1.

Hellwege, J. (2001, June). Civil liberties, library groups challenge the latest law restricting Web access. *Trial,* 93.

Hill, G. C. (1996, September). It's war! The battle for the telecommunications dollar is turning into a free-for-all. *The Wall Street Journal,* B1.

Holland, J. J. (2005, December 16). Senate blocks extension of Patriot Act. Associated Press on AOL News.

Holsinger, R. (1991). *Media law,* 2nd ed. New York: McGraw-Hill.

Hulse, C. (2005, June 16). House blocks provision for Patriot Act inquiries. *The New York Times,* A17.

Kitigaki, P. (2003, September 22). Librarians step up. *The Sacramento Bee,* A1.

Klein, K. E. (2001, September). The legalities of reporting the news. *The Quill,* 26.

Klinenberg, E. (2007, February 28). Saving radio in the satellite era. *The New York Times,* A19.

Labaton, S. (2003, May 11). Give-and-take FCC aims to redraw media map. *The New York Times,* A1.

Labaton, S. (2003, June 5). Senators move to restore FCC limits on the media. *The New York Times,* C1.

Labaton, S. (2003, July 23). Republicans are adding weight to reversal of FCC media rule. *The New York Times,* A1.

Labaton, S. (2007, June 5). Decency ruling thwarts FCC on vulgarities. *The New York Times,* A1.

Lessig, L. (2007, March 18). Make way for copyright chaos. *The New York Times,* WK12.

Levin, M. (2005, January 27). Lawsuits take aim at ads for alcohol. Latimes.com.

Levine, R. (2007, March 12). Old concerts on new media lead to lawsuits. Iht.com.

Levy, L. (1985). *Emergence of a free press.* New York: Oxford University Press.

Lewis, P. (1996, June 13). Judges turn back law intended to regulate Internet decency. *The New York Times,* A1.

Lichtblau, E. (2005, August 26). FBI demands library records. *San Francisco Chronicle,* A5.

Lichtblau, E. (2005, November 19). Extension of Patriot Act faces threat of filibuster. *The New York Times,* A23.

Lichtblau, E. (2006, January 17). Groups file lawsuits over eavesdropping. Nytimes.com.

Lichtblau, E. (2007, September 9). FBI data mining reached beyond initial targets. *The New York Times,* A1.

Lichtblau, E., & Shenon, P. (2008, May 10). From places unexpected, support for the press. *The New York Times,* A11.

Liptak, A. (2007, December 31). In the fight over piracy, a rare stand for privacy. Nytimes.com.

McGrath, P., & Stadtman, N. (1985, February 4). What the jury—and *Time* magazine—said. *Newsweek,* 58.

McMasters, P. K. (2006, January 1). Prying by the press exposes spying on Americans. First Amendment Center.

Media Law Resource Center (2005, February 25). Media won seven of 12 trials in 2004, study of media law trials shows. Medialaw.org.

Media Law Resource Center (2007, September 11). Annual study of media trials analyzes fourteen trials in 2006: Nine wins, five losses. Medialaw.org.

Milliot, J. (2000, November 6). Decision supports Web copyrights. *Publishers Weekly,* 56.

Mills, M. (1996, July 10). Burning the midnight oil on new phone rules. *Washington Post,* F6.

National Coalition Against Censorship (1985). *Books on trial: A survey of recent cases.* New York.

Peek, T. (1999, January). Taming the Internet in three acts. *Information Today,* 28.

Pike, G. H. (2001, October). Understanding and surviving *Tasini. Information Today,* 18.

Pope, K. (1996, December 19). ABC network loses libel suit over *20/20. The Wall Street Journal,* B1.

Radio-Television News Directors Association (2007, September 7). Cameras in the court: A state-by-state guide. Rtnda.org.

Reid, C. (2001, October 15). Writers 2, publishers 0. *Publishers Weekly,* 12.

Reuters (2007, September 11). "Wardrobe malfunction" goes to court. Nytimes.com.

Richtel, M. (2008, February 14). H.P. agrees to settle journalist spy case. *The New York Times,* C5.

Risen, J., & Lichtblau, E. (2005, December 16). Bush lets U.S. spy on callers without courts. Nytimes.com.

Rosenstiel, T. (1991, February 20). The media take a pounding. *Los Angeles Times,* A1.

Rousseau, C. (2003, April 23). *Harry Potter* back in schools. *San Francisco Chronicle,* A2.

Salant, J. (2004, January 27). FCC proposes fining Clear Channel $755,000. *Associated Press.*

Seitel, F. P. (1984). *The practice of public relations,* 2nd ed. Columbus, Ohio: Charles E. Merrill.

Shane, S. (2007, July 3). Bush commutes Libby sentence, saying 30 months "is excessive." *The New York Times,* A1.

Shields, T. (2000, December 11). Supreme consideration: Free speech vs. privacy. *Editor & Publisher,* 7.

Shrieves, L., & Owens, D. (2004, February 3). Jackson gives TV sex war wider exposure. *The Sacramento Bee,* A-1.

Smith, R. J. (2007, March 7). Cheney's suspected role in security breach drove Fitzgerald. Washingtonpost.com.

Smolla, R. (1986). *Suing the press.* New York: Oxford University Press.

Sniffen, M. J. (2005, December 16). Patriot Act's sunset provisions are limited. Associated Press on AOL News.

Steinberg, J. (2003, May 26). Easier rules may not mean more newspaper-TV deals. *The New York Times,* C1.

Stern, C. (1996, February 12). The V-chip First Amendment infringement vs. empowerment tool. *Broadcasting & Cable,* 8.

Stone, B., & Helft, M. (2007, February 19). New weapon in Web war over piracy. *The New York Times,* C1.

Sullivan, J. (2000, August 18). Movie industry wins a round in DVD copyright case. *The New York Times.*

Swett, C. (2008, January 2). F.C.C. auction may reshape telecom field. Sacbee.com.

Taub, E. (2005, December 19). With Stern on board, satellite radio is approaching a secure orbit. *The New York Times,* C1.

Trigoboff, D. (2001, May 28). Suits, laws and audiotape. *Broadcasting & Cable,* 12.

Ungar, S. (1975). *The papers and the papers: An account of the legal and political battle over the Pentagon papers.* New York: Dutton.

Van Natta, D., Liptak, A., & Levy, C. J. (2005, October 16). The Miller case: A notebook, a cause, a jail cell and a deal. *The New York Times,* A1.

Varian, H. R. (2007, May 31). Copyrights that no one knows about don't help anyone. *The New York Times,* C3.

Wicker, T. (1978). *On press.* New York: Viking.

Chapter 15 Ethics: Placing Responsibility

Alter, J., & McKillop, P. (1986, August). AIDS and the right to know. *Newsweek,* 46.

Associated Press (2007, March 12). *New York Times* says former reporter's link to source included a $2,000 payment. Iht.com.

Atta, D. (1986, November). Faint light, dark print. *Harper's,* 57.

Barnes, B. (2008, November 21). Story behind the cover story: Angelina Jolie and her image. *The New York Times,* A1.

Barry, D. (2003, May 1). *Times* reporter who resigned leaves long trail of deception. *The New York Times,* A1.

Barstow, D., & Stein, R. (2005, March 13). Government video reports blur media ethics. *The New York Times,* A5.

Brandt, A. (1984, October). Truth and consequences. *Esquire,* 27.

Calame, B. (2007, March 25). Money, a source and new questions about a story. *The New York Times,* WK12.

Carr, D. (2005, June 6). Is Shriver still working for *Today? The New York Times,* C1.

Christians, C., Rotzoll, K., & Fackler, M. (1987). *Media ethics,* 2nd ed. New York: Longman.

Frankel, M. (2007, March 25). The Washington back channel. Nytimes.com.

Freeman, S. (2005, April 9). Newspaper panel to investigate Mitch Albom. Associated Press on AOL Sports News.

Friedman, J. (2007, March 10). Blogging for bucks stirs uproar over ethics. *Los Angeles Times* as published in *The Sacramento Bee.*

Goldstein, T. (1985). *The news at any cost.* New York: Simon & Schuster.

Goodman, T. (2007, April 19). Has NBC ushered in a new era for multimedia? *San Francisco Chronicle,* A14.

Halbfinger, D. M., & Weiner, A. H. (2005, June 9). As paparazzi push ever harder, stars seek a way to push back. *The New York Times,* A1.

Harwood, R. (1994, March 12). What is this thing called "news"? *Washington Post,* A12.

Hulteng, J. (1985). *The messenger's motives: Ethical problems of the news media.* Englewood Cliffs, N.J.: Prentice Hall.

Hulteng, J. (1986, Winter). Get it while it's hot. *feed/back,* 16.

Ives, N. (2005, April 11). Meeting a deadline, repenting at leisure. Nytimes.com.

Jensen, E. (1993, March 23). NBC-sponsored inquiry calls GM crash on news program a lapse in judgment. *The Wall Street Journal,* B10.

Kelly, K. J. (2006, January 13). *People*'s baby scoop: Mag wrote sizeable check for Angelina's pet charity. Nypost.com.

Kirkpatrick, D. D. (2005, January 8). Payola for education policies. *San Francisco Chronicle,* A1.

Kirkpatrick, D. D. (2007, January 29). Feeding frenzy for a big story, even if it's false. *The New York Times,* A1.

Kornblut, A. E., & Barstow, D. (2005, April 15). Debate rekindles over government-produced "news." Nytimes.com.

Macropoulos, A. (2007, April 2). A misfired memo shows close tabs on reporter. *The New York Times,* C4.

Mnookin, S. (2003, May 26). The *Times* bomb. *Newsweek,* 41.

New York Times (2007, September 15). Lohan is charged with misdemeanors. Nytimes.com.

Prendergast, A. (1987, January/February). Mickey Mouse journalism. *Washington Journalism Review,* 9, 32.

Public Relations Society of America Member Code of Ethics, 2000.

Radio-Television News Directors Association Code of Ethics and Professional Conduct, 2000.

Rich, Frank (2005, February 20). The White House stages its "Daily Show." Nytimes.com.

Rubenstein, S., Lee, H. K., & King, J. (2007, April 19). The video: Should it have been shown? *San Francisco Chronicle,* A14.

Scott, J. (2003, June 6). A formidable run undone by scandal and discontent. *The New York Times,* A1.

Society of Professional Journalists Code of Ethics, September 1996.

Stein, M. L. (1986, May 31). Survey on freebies. *Editor & Publisher,* 11.

Steinberg, J. (2003, June 6). *Times'* top editors resign after furor on writer's fraud. *The New York Times,* A1.

Wallace, M. (1996, December 18). The press needs a national monitor. *The Wall Street Journal,* A1.

Chapter 16 Global Media: Discovering New Markets

Andrews, E. L. (2007, April 7). Piracy move on China seen as near. *The New York Times,* B1.

Associated Press (1991, August 27). Media chiefs fired; allegedly backed coup. *The Sacramento Bee,* A11.

Associated Press (2005, July 5). Yahoo bets a billion in China. *The Sacramento Bee,* D1.

Austen, I. (2007, March 16). Canada: Blackout on early vote results upheld. *The New York Times,* A6.

Barboza, D. (2005, July 4). Hollywood movie studios see the Chinese film market as their next rising star. Nytimes.com.

Chen, A. C., & Chaudhary, A. G. (1991). Asia and the Pacific. In *Global journalism: Survey of international communication,* 2nd ed. New York: Longman.

Chivers, C. J. (2007, August 29). Russia arrests ten in killing of Putin critic. Nytimes.com.

Conde, C. H. (2003, May 11). Filipino journalists find death threats are part of job. *The New York Times,* A10.

Cowell, A. (2003, July 31). Independent for 81 years, the BBC is facing a challenge. *The New York Times,* A3.

Damsell, K., & McFarland, J. (2000, August 1). The Hollinger selloff. *The Globe and Mail,* B1.

DeGiorgio, E. (2000, April). The African Internet revolution. *African Business,* 30.

Dennis, E., & Vanden Heuvel, J. (1990, October). Emerging voices: East European media in transition. *Gannett Center for Media Studies,* 2.

Fathi, N. (2005, June 29). Women writing novels emerge as stars in Iran. *The New York Times,* B1.

Fine, J. (2001, October 1). Arabian knight woos west. *Variety,* 34.

French, H. W. (2007, December 7). As Chinese media grow, foreign news is left out. *The New York Times,* A4.

Fuchs, D. (1999, October). The Americanization of the Spanish press. *The Quill,* 8. (2003, June 21).

Fuller, T. (2007, April 5). Thailand blocks users' access to YouTube. *The New York Times,* C12.

Gerth, J. (2005, December 11). Military's information war is vast and often secretive. *The New York Times,* A1.

Green, P. S. (2003, July 30). Prague is fighting to remain in the picture. *The New York Times,* W1.

Hays, L., & Rutherford, A. (1991, January 1). Gorbachev bids to crack down on Soviet press. *The Wall Street Journal,* A8.

Head, S. W. (1985). *World broadcasting systems.* Belmont, Calif.: Wadsworth.

Heingartner, D. (2003, June 5). Roaming the globe, laptops alight on wireless hot spots. *The New York Times,* E4.

Helliker, K. (1993, September 27). Drop that remote! In Britain, watching TV can be a crime. *The Wall Street Journal,* A1.

Hindley, A. (1999, April 23). Breaking the taboos. *Middle East Economic Digest,* 6.

Hindley, A. (2000, February 11). Internet usage, the boom in access. *Middle East Economic Digest,* 27.

Hoo, S. (2004, December 9). Going global: Major foreign expansion is part of China's strategy. *The Sacramento Bee,* D1.

Ivry, S. (2007, April 16). Now on YouTube: The latest news from Al Jazeera, in English. *The New York Times,* C5.

Jensen, E. (1993, March 26). ABC and BBC to pool their radio-TV news coverage. *The Wall Street Journal,* B1.

Jervis, R., & Sabah, Z. (2005, December 9). Probe into Iraq war news coverage widens. USAtoday.com.

JiWire WiFi HotStats (2007, September). Jiwire.com.

Kahn, J. (2003, January 5). Made in China, bought in China. *The New York Times,* 3-1.

Kim, R. (2007, March 29). Foreign nations take tech title. Sfgate.com.

Kramer, A. E. (2007, March 22). Editor of Russian edition of Forbes guilty of defamation. *The New York Times,* C4.

Lippman, J. (1992, October 20). Tuning in the global village. *Los Angeles Times,* H2.

Lowndes, F. S. (1991). The world's media systems: An overview. In *Global journalism: Survey of international communication,* 2nd ed. New York: Longman.

MacFarquhar, N. (2006, January 15). In tiny Arab state, Web takes on ruling elite. Nytimes.com.

Markoff, J. (2007, January 29). At Davos, the squabble resumes on how to wire the Third World. *The New York Times,* C1.

Marshall, T. (1990, July 31). East Germans dazzled by western press. *Los Angeles Times,* H8.

Martin, L. J. (1991). Africa. In *Global journalism: Survey of international communication,* 2nd ed. New York: Longman.

McDowall, A. (2001, April 20). Uncorking the bottlenecks. *Middle East Economic Digest,* 45.

Melymuka, K. (2001, July 2). Africa 1.0. *Computerworld,* 35.

Mista, N. (2003, September 15). India's film city is gobbling tribal land. *San Francisco Chronicle,* D1.

Ogan, C. (1991). Middle East and North Africa. In *Global journalism: Survey of international communication,* 2nd ed. New York: Longman.

Paraschos, M. (1991). Europe. In *Global journalism: Survey of international communication,* 2nd ed. New York: Longman.

Picard, R. G. (1991). Global communications controversies. In *Global journalism: Survey of international communication,* 2nd ed. New York: Longman.

Pintak, L. (2007, April 27). Reporting a revolution: The changing Arab media landscape. Arabmediasociety.com.

Reporters Without Borders (2006, December 31). Press freedom day by day. Rsf.org.

Romero, S. (2007, May 27). Chavez's move against critic highlights shift in media. Nytimes.com.

Rosenblum, M. (1989, December 1). TV takes the center stage in Romanian revolution. *The Sacramento Bee,* A11.

Saltz, R. (2007, April 21). Using Bollywood ideas to portray today's India. *The New York Times,* A19.

Salwen, M. B., Garrison, B., & Buckman, R. (1991). Latin America and the Caribbean. In *Global journalism: Survey of international communication,* 2nd ed. New York: Longman.

Scholastic, Inc. (2000, October 2). The Internet index. *New York Times Upfront,* 24.

Siebert, F., Peterson, T., & Schramm, W. (1963). *Four theories of the press.* Urbana: University of Illinois Press.

Smith, C. (2000, October 4). Tough new rules don't faze Chinese Internet start-ups. *The New York Times,* C2.

Strobel, W. P. (2005, April 18). Arab satellite channel al Jazeera goes global. Mercurynews.com.

Strupp, J. (2000, March 13). More windows on the world. *Editor & Publisher,* 26.

Timmons, H. (2008, May 20). Newspapers on upswing in developing markets. *The New York Times,* C6.

Tunstall, J. (2008). *The media were American.* New York: Oxford University Press.

Wallace, C. (1988, January 7). Radio: Town crier of the Arab world. *Los Angeles Times,* 1.

Weiner, T. (2001, November 20). Four foreign journalists, ambushed, are believed killed by Taliban. *The New York Times,* B1.

Index

Note: References with *italicized* page numbers indicate boxes, figures, photos and tables.